LABORATORY MANUAL AND WORKBOOK FOR BIOLOGICAL ANTHROPOLOGY: ENGAGING WITH HUMAN EVOLUTION

SECOND EDITION

LABORATORY MANUAL AND WORKBOOK FOR BIOLOGICAL ANTHROPOLOGY: ENGAGING WITH HUMAN EVOLUTION

SECOND EDITION

K. ELIZABETH SOLURI CABRILLO COLLEGE
SABRINA C. AGARWAL UNIVERSITY OF CALIFORNIA, BERKELEY

W. W. NORTON & COMPANY
NEW YORK • LONDON

To all of our students for inspiring us to reach for new heights in our teaching.

W. W. Norton & Company has been independent since its founding in 1923, when William Warder Norton and Mary D. Herter Norton first published lectures delivered at the People's Institute, the adult education division of New York City's Cooper Union. The firm soon expanded its program beyond the Institute, publishing books by celebrated academics from America and abroad. By midcentury, the two major pillars of Norton's publishing program— trade books and college texts—were firmly established. In the 1950s, the Norton family transferred control of the company to its employees, and today—with a staff of five hundred and hundreds of trade, college, and professional titles published each year—W. W. Norton & Company stands as the largest and oldest publishing house owned wholly by its employees.

Editor: Jake Schindel
Developmental Editor: Sunny Hwang
Project Editor: Taylere Peterson
Associate Editor: Rachel Goodman
Managing Editor, College: Marian Johnson
Managing Editor, College Digital Media: Kim Yi
Associate Director of Production, College: Benjamin Reynolds
Media Editor: Miryam Chandler
Media Project Editor: Rachel Mayer
Media Associate Editor: Ariel Eaton
Digital Production: Michael Hicks
Marketing Manager, Anthropology: Kandace Starbird
Designer: Jillian Burr
Photo Editor: Travis Carr
Director of College Permissions: Megan Schindel
Permissions Specialist: Elizabeth Trammell
Composition: Achorn International, Inc.
Illustrations: Imagineering Art
Manufacturing: Transcontinental—Beauceville, QC

Permission to use copyrighted material is included alongside the appropriate images and in the backmatter.

ISBN: 978-0-393-68068-3 (pbk.)

W. W. Norton & Company, Inc., 500 Fifth Avenue, New York, NY 10110

wwnorton.com

W. W. Norton & Company Ltd., 15 Carlisle Street, London W1D 3BS

2 3 4 5 6 7 8 9 0

CONTENTS

K. Elizabeth Soluri (Cabrillo College) is faculty in the Anthropology Department at Cabrillo College. She received her B.A. from New York University and her M.A. and Ph.D. from the University of California, Berkeley. She has conducted anthropological field and laboratory research across the United States, including work in Valley Forge National Historical Park, Hawaii, and the central California coast. Elizabeth is especially interested in pedagogy and issues of student learning, and her ongoing research focuses on redesigning, implementing, and evaluating effective teaching methods for undergraduate anthropology courses, particularly biological anthropology. Elizabeth has taught anthropology courses at several 2-year and 4-year institutions throughout the San Francisco Bay area.

Sabrina C. Agarwal (University of California, Berkeley) is professor of anthropology at the University of California, Berkeley. She received her B.A. and M.Sc. from the University of Toronto and her Ph.D. from the same institution, working in both the Department of Anthropology and the Samuel Lunenfeld Research Institute of Mount Sinai Hospital, Toronto. Her research interests are focused broadly on age-, sex-, and gender-related changes in bone quantity and quality, particularly the application of biocultural and life course approaches to the study of bone maintenance and fragility and its application to dialogues of social identity and developmental plasticity in bioarchaeology. Sabrina has authored numerous related scholarly articles and edited volumes, and she is the co-editor-in-chief for *Bioarchaeology International*. She is interested in the philosophies of teaching, and she is actively involved in the pedagogical training of current and future college instructors.

FOR INSTRUCTORS
Active, Engaging, Flexible

The introductory laboratory in biological anthropology can be an inspiring place. It is exciting to see students interact with materials and concepts that may be entirely novel and unfamiliar to them. Of course, it is a challenging place, too, a place with many students who enrolled without foreseeing the scientific content and detail of the course. This was the case when we taught introductory biological anthropology at the University of California, Berkeley, and decided to redesign the laboratory portion of the course in 2005. In doing so, we had three overarching goals: (1) we wanted to emphasize active student engagement as a way to strengthen learning and long-term retention of course content, (2) we wanted to help students from diverse backgrounds and with varying degrees of experience in anthropology learn the key information about human biology and evolution, and (3) we wanted a lab manual that would be simple for instructors to implement in their classes, whether it is used in pieces or as a whole.

We decided to attack this task both with creativity and with a research and empirical approach emphasizing constant reassessment and improvement. We began simply by creating weekly lab exercises that corresponded to the topics covered in the course and were based on principles of learning from current pedagogy and cognition literature. Then, we spent the next several years trying these lab assignments in classrooms, tweaking them, and testing them again. We also collected empirical data about student engagement, initial learning, and long-term retention of knowledge from the lab component of the course. The data formed the basis for one author's (Soluri) doctoral dissertation, which explicitly examined effective pedagogical methods in biological anthropology instruction. With proof of concept at the initial implementation at U.C. Berkeley, the exercises, questions, and text were then expanded, tested, and refined in additional classroom environments, including community college courses in the San Francisco Bay area. We wanted to make sure our approach would work with as broad an audience as possible.

As a result, we believe this manual has developed into something unique among biological anthropology laboratory manuals.

1. The manual addresses a wide range of topics relevant to introductory biological anthropology courses, including genetics and evolutionary theory, skeletal biology and forensic anthropology, primatology, and paleoanthropology. We provide a balanced approach to the topics that gives students a well-rounded foundation in the discipline. We also present concepts, such as modern human variation, that are central to biological anthropology but are often not emphasized in laboratory texts. In doing this, we help students build the most comprehensive biological anthropology skill set possible. Each of the lab exercises has been designed with real students in mind, and their effectiveness has been tested and fine-tuned over many semesters in real classrooms at various institutions.

2. The authors' concern with employing effective pedagogy has resulted in a distinctive text that explicitly emphasizes a student-centered learning experience. The manual applies active-learning pedagogy, which emphasizes the importance of students' hands-on involvement in learning. It is ideal for laboratory contexts where the goal is to foster the development of key skills as well as content knowledge.

3. The text is exceptional in its further emphasis on cooperative pedagogy, which highlights the importance of student teamwork to complete learning tasks. This approach helps students develop the critical thinking and communication skills that will aid them in the biological anthropology classroom and beyond. We have designed the manual's exercises and discussions with cooperative pedagogy in mind, and we encourage instructors to have students work in groups when completing the Lab Exercises and Critical Thinking Questions.

4. We have given additional attention to designing a text that is appropriate for a variety of learning environments and types of learners. Therefore, the exercise format is varied throughout the text, offering a range of activities that target particular learning styles. This variation helps each student to connect with the material, regardless of learning background. It also allows instructors to choose particular activities suitable for the unique student makeup of each class.

5. Although the units and labs are arranged in the order in which the topics are often covered in classrooms, we have designed them to be modular. Units and labs can be taught in any order that suits the instructor's needs.

6. In addition to its topical breadth, the manual is unusual because of the varied professional experience of its authors. Dr. Soluri's research has focused on the pedagogical aspects of teaching biological anthropology, and she has experience teaching biological anthropology lecture and laboratory courses at large 4-year institutions and community colleges in the United States. Dr. Agarwal's research has focused on bioarchaeology and skeletal analysis, and she has experience teaching biological anthropology lecture and laboratory courses at large and small 4-year institutions in the United States and Canada. Together, their collective research and teaching experience results in a well-rounded text that is appropriate for a wide range of college and university classrooms.

Changes in the Second Edition

The newest edition of *Laboratory Manual and Workbook for Biological Anthropology: Engaging with Human Evolution* includes the latest scientific discoveries and fossil finds from a dynamic discipline. It also highlights the research process and people behind these discoveries to help students better understand the value of the skills they are developing and to imagine themselves as the scientists of the future. The Second Edition maintains the same core pedagogical structure and modular flexibility found in the First Edition, while adding new content and additional questions and exercises for even more instructional options. The key updates include:

- **New content on ethics in the discipline.** The Second Edition pays particular attention to the discipline's primary ethical guidelines in Lab 1. The application of these principles is reinforced through specific scenarios and real-life examples in this and other labs throughout the book.

- **New content to reflect recent discoveries.** The Second Edition updates existing content with the latest research in the discipline. New text and lab questions feature recently identified living primate species, such as *Pongo tapanuliensis*, newly discovered fossil primates, such as *Nyanzapithecus alesi*, and hominin species, such as *Australopithecus deyiremeda* and *Homo naledi*.

- **Expansion of illustrations and figures.** This edition builds on the excellent art program of the First Edition with even more illustrations in both the chapter text and the lab exercises, where students are guided with drawn instructions as they complete steps in complex multi-part exercises. The image collection has been expanded to include new angles and specimens for students to study. Special attention has also been paid to the use of ethically sourced images throughout the Second Edition.

- **Revision for greater clarity, based on extensive student and instructor feedback.** As in the First Edition, complicated concepts are broken into smaller parts and reinforced with relevant figures and tables. In some labs, content has been reorganized to improve readability and learning flow. The wording of questions and exercises has also been streamlined to ensure students comprehend what is being asked.

- **Even more emphasis on the scientific method and research processes.** In addition to the specific attention paid in Lab 1, the scientific method is now more explicitly reinforced throughout the book as students complete exercises where they apply stages of the method to particular biological anthropology research topics covered in later labs.

- **Biological Anthropology in Practice features.** In each of the four units of this edition, a contemporary biological anthropology researcher is featured to show students the people and research processes behind the content they are learning.

- **New Lab Exercises.** The Second Edition adds new and expanded lab exercises. Particular attention was paid to improving student engagement with challenging content, reinforcing stages of the scientific method, and supporting the new content added to the chapter text. These lab exercises include:

  - Ethics Case Study (Lab 1)

  - Extract Your Own DNA (Lab 2)

  - Protein Synthesis (Lab 2)

  - Using the Scientific Method to Investigate Mendelian Traits in Humans (Lab 3)

  - Sex-Linked Traits (Lab 3)

  - Overlapping Forces of Evolution (Lab 4)

  - Surface Anatomy of the Skeleton (Lab 6)

- Sexing [now including traits from the humerus, femur, and scapula] (Lab 7)

- Fragmentary Remains [in Forensic Anthropology and Bioarchaeology] (Lab 7)

- Clinal Distributions (Lab 8)

- Overlap of Multiple Traits (Lab 8)

- Body Mass Index (Lab 8)

- Tooth Types (Lab 12)

- Tooth Shape as Adaptation (Lab 12)

- Locomotion and Locomotor Adaptations [now including intermembral index] (Lab 12)

- The Bipedal Gait (Lab 14)

- The Evolution of Bipedalism: Postural Feeding (Lab 14)

- Australopith Dentition (Lab 15)

- *Australopithecus sediba* (Lab 15)

- *Homo erectus* Variation (Lab 16)

- **More instructional flexibility in Lab Exercises.** In exercises where students are asked to identify or list traits, the wording has been adjusted to allow instructors to require a greater number of traits if desired. Additional space has also been provided for students to submit longer trait lists.

- **Updates to Image Libraries.** The images provided at the end of labs, for teaching contexts with limited cast material, have been redesigned. They are organized with clearer titles and visual cues to better facilitate students' identification of the appropriate images for each exercise. They are also updated to include the highest quality and most current images available, and when possible multiple views of the same material are provided.

- **Expansion and updating of Critical Thinking Questions.** As in the earlier edition, the Critical Thinking Questions in the Second Edition ask students to think more deeply about what they have learned and to apply their knowledge and skills in new ways. The Critical Thinking Questions throughout the book have been updated to include current issues in the discipline and in students' lives, such as forensic anthropology at the U.S.-Mexico border. In labs with charts for primate or fossil species, Critical Thinking Questions have been

added to help students compare and synthesize the information captured in their charts.

Organization and Pedagogy

Four flexible units. Our text covers a range of biological anthropology topics in 16 chapters, or labs. The labs are equally distributed into four units, or parts. Part One (Labs 1–4) focuses on genetics and evolutionary theory. It places biological anthropology in the context of anthropology and of science more generally, and it provides information about what evolution is and how it works. Part Two (Labs 5–8) focuses on modern humans. It introduces the major bones of the human skeleton and teaches some of the skills and methods used by forensic anthropologists. This unit also examines issues of modern human variation and adaptation. Part Three (Labs 9–12) focuses on primatology. It reviews issues of biological classification and highlights similarities and differences in primate anatomy and behavior. Part Four (Labs 13–16) focuses on paleoanthropology. It traces our fossil history from the first primates to modern humans. Within each unit is a special section, titled Biological Anthropology in Practice, that highlights the current research of an anthropologist working on topics related to the themes of that unit.

As noted earlier, although the units and labs are arranged in the order in which the topics are often covered in classrooms, we have designed them to be modular, and they can be taught in any order. For courses that have fewer class meetings, labs can be combined or eliminated as necessary. For courses that have more class meetings, labs can be divided across multiple class days. Each lab can be treated as a separate entity, allowing the instructor maximum flexibility in scheduling and lesson planning.

Chapter organization. Within each lab, there are four primary subsections. The first is the **text section**, providing a written overview of the content for the lab. It can be assigned as reading that reviews course information or introduces it for the first time. The text sections are written in a simple and easy-to-follow format, and they are supported with diagrams, images, and realistic examples to better elucidate points. At the end of the text sections of certain labs, we present more advanced concepts that instructors might want to make optional; this material is called out with the heading Exploring Further. The second section is a list of **Concept Review Questions**. These questions target foundational knowledge and are designed to reinforce the learning of basic factual content. They provide a good review of the text portion of the chapter, and they can be assigned as home-work to be completed before class or as pre-lab questions to be completed at the start of class. The third section includes a set of **five to ten Lab Exercises** (the number depending on the type of content covered and the length of the exer-cises). Instructors can choose to assign all the exercises in a lab or only a sample, depending on their classroom needs. The exercises emphasize active and cooperative pedagogy and are designed to target higher levels of learning, such as comprehension and analysis. Instructors with access to casts and skeletal elements can easily integrate their own teaching collections with the Lab Exercises. Instructors who do not have access to casts, or who have gaps in their teaching col-lections, can direct their students to the images provided in the Exercise Image Libraries that accompany the Lab Exer-cises. The final section consists of a list of **Critical Thinking Questions**. This material often targets the highest levels of learning, such as synthesis and evaluation. It provides stu-dents with a review of lab content and a chance to think crit-ically about that content. Instructors can assign this material as follow-up questions to be completed by student groups alongside in-class exercises or individually outside the class-room. Instructors can also use the Critical Thinking Ques-tions and Concept Review Questions as exam questions.

Art and photo program. Biological anthropology is a visual discipline, and we have tried to illustrate this text in the best possible manner. Every chapter has multiple large and detailed figures and photographs. In most cases, to help stu-dents understand the general size of what we picture, we have included scales based on direct measurements of spec-imens or measurements provided in scientific literature. We strive for accuracy in our drawings and represent many bones and fossils with drawings of an almost three-dimensional appearance. The text has been laid out in a step-by-step manner with plenty of white space and a double-column design that promotes easy scanning of pages. We provide a world map and geological time line on the inside front and back covers, respectively.

Tear-out worksheets. All worksheets are designed to be torn out and submitted by students, with plenty of room for answers. Space for student identification is on every page to aid in grading. Some instructors might also like their stu-dents to use the three-hole punched version of this manual, which lets students easily retain worksheets in a binder as they are returned.

Instructor's solutions manual and chapter guidelines. The entire lab manual is supplemented with a special instructor's manual that gives instructors the information they need to implement the manual in their courses. It presents guidelines for the Lab Exercises, including information about materials needed and the length of time suggested for each activity. It also provides instructors with answers to all Concept Review Questions, Lab Exercises, and Critical Thinking Questions.

Image set. Every image, table, and chart from the manual is available for download.

LMS coursepacks. Special LMS coursepacks contain ver-sions of nearly all the Lab Exercises designed to work in your LMS. These versions facilitate online submission and grad-ing of exercises for distance- and blended-learning students (note that students must have the lab manual for access to the Exercise Image Libraries). The Concept Review Ques-tions, Lab Exercises, and Critical Thinking Questions in the coursepack can be selected and modified a la carte by instructors, providing the same flexible implementation as the manual itself. This allows instructors to blend formats—for example, by assigning the Concept Review Questions as easily graded, online, pre-lab homework that is then rein-forced through completion of the Lab Exercises and Critical Thinking Questions in class. The coursepack also provides access to Norton's animation and video resources for biolog-ical anthropology.

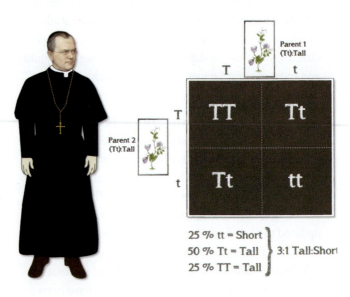

Low-priced versions and bundle discounts. This manual is available in a discounted three-hole punched version, as well as an inexpensive electronic version for your distance-learning students. Discounted bundle prices are also available to keep costs reasonable for students. Please contact your W. W. Norton representative for more information.

FOR STUDENTS

This lab manual is designed to engage you in an exploration of human biology and evolution. The evolution of our species is a vast and complex topic that is studied by biological anthropologists around the world who seek to understand who we are as a species, how we came to be this way, and where we may be headed from here. Biological anthropologists tackle these issues using a range of research questions and methods, and we will investigate these different forms of analysis throughout the text. Each lab in the manual includes text that introduces important information, Concept Review Questions that can be used to test your comprehension of the text, Lab Exercises that ask you to think and act like an anthropologist, and Critical Thinking Questions that ask you to combine all of this knowledge in complex and new ways. There is no set order to the labs, and your instructor may choose to present the labs in any order. No matter where you start or finish, the labs will combine to provide a broad picture of the human species and our evolutionary history.

To facilitate your learning, we engage you as active participants. You will complete tasks, answer questions, and think critically about the information presented. You will get the chance to practice some of the comparative and analytical skills used by biological anthropologists, and you are likely to begin seeing yourself in a whole new light because of it. We provide you with up-to-date information about major topics in biological anthropology, so that you are gaining the most accurate and current knowledge possible. We also describe issues and examples that are interesting and relevant to your own life. We supply you with high-quality photos and drawings of skeletons, fossils, and living animals to illustrate key points and anatomical features throughout the text. Your instructor may then give you access to additional materials, such as skeletal elements and fossil casts, to supplement what you see and learn in the manual.

By the end of this manual and course, you will be thinking and applying analytical skills like a biological anthropologist. You will have learned more about yourself, your place in the world, and your evolutionary history, and you will be armed with this knowledge as you continue life in and outside of anthropology classrooms.

ACKNOWLEDGMENTS

We extend our gratitude to the many people who supported us and generously provided their assistance throughout the process of planning, writing, and publishing this manual. Among them, Elizabeth would especially like to thank her friends and family who supported her during the development of this project, especially the Soluri, Camp, Schneider, and Hayes/Matsunaga families. Elizabeth extends a special thank you to her husband Tsim, who participated in countless conversations about the manual, sharing his ideas and lending his unfailing support every step of the way. Sabrina would especially like to thank Rosemary Joyce, Laurie Wilkie, Ruth Tringham, and Meg Conkey for sharing all their teaching and learning wisdom while formulating ideas for this project. Sabrina also thanks her husband Peter for his support and encouragement over the years in seeing this manual to its fruition.

We greatly appreciate the help and guidance we received from everyone at W. W. Norton & Company. We thank Jack Repcheck for initially approaching us with this opportunity and bolstering us through the early stages of the project. His enthusiasm for the manual was contagious and helped get things off the ground. Eric Svendsen took on the project after Jack, and he expertly steered us through the majority of the writing and publication process. His patience and guidance were instrumental, particularly his insights and assistance during the review, revision, and production processes. We thank Sunny Hwang for her outstanding suggestions for portions of the text and activities, which kept us thinking and exploring new ideas. For the second edition, we benefited from the editorial guidance of Jake Schindel. His dedication to the project helped shepherd the manual through a rigorous revision process that has yielded a new and improved version of the text. We are also indebted to the exceptional editing of Taylere Peterson and Norma Sims Roche, who applied their keen eyes to the project from start to finish. As with the first edition, Rachel Goodman's outstanding organization and attention to detail helped keep the process streamlined and efficient. This text is supported by an excellent media and supplement package, and we thank Miryam Chandler and Ariel Eaton for their careful work in this area. Numerous people helped compile and clear permission for the wonderful images and figures, including Elizabeth Trammell and Travis Carr. Ben Reynolds carefully oversaw the production process. Ashley Lipps contributed her time and expertise in taking beautiful photographs of much of the skeletal material featured in this text. Tiffiny Tung and Melanie Miller generously shared photographs for inclusion in the text. We extend additional thanks to Alison Galloway, Adrienne Zihlman, and Richard Baldwin (Department of Anthropology at the University of California, Santa Cruz) and Chris Conroy (Museum of Vertebrate Zoology, University of California, Berkeley) for providing access to skeletal material for photographic purposes. Clark Larsen encouraged us and offered valuable advice based on his experience. The project would not have been possible without the outstanding support of the entire W. W. Norton & Company team.

A lab manual of this nature is based on our years of teaching this material in 2- and 4-year institutions in the United States and Canada. We thank all of our undergraduate students—past, present, and future—for inspiring and challenging us. We also thank the numerous graduate students and faculty who have taught with us and shared their classroom experiences and suggestions. In particular, we thank the instructors who, as graduate students at the University of California, Berkeley, helped us test some of the activities published here, particularly Patrick Beauchesne, Celise Chilcote, Julie Hui, Ashley Lipps, Melanie Miller, Andrew Roddick, and Julie Wesp. Some activities and questions included here were initially produced with the support of a Pedagogy Improvement Grant from the Graduate Student Teaching and Resource Center of the Graduate Division at the University of California, Berkeley, for which we are especially grateful. We also thank the following colleagues for the various forms of pedagogical support and insights they provided: Martin Covington, Terrence Deacon, Sandra Hollimon, Rosemary Joyce, Susan Kerr, Beth Roselyn, and Linda von Hoene. We offer a special thank you to the four researchers featured in the Biological Anthropology in Practice spotlights in the second edition: Debi Bolter, John Lindo, Vicky Oelze, and Julienne Rutherford. We also extend our special thanks to graduate student teaching assistants, Debra Martin, and Peter Gray, at the University of Nevada, Las Vegas, for their test run of the first edition of the lab manual. Their detailed feedback and ideas were instrumental in shaping the initial product.

The second edition benefited from the feedback and suggestions provided by many reviewers, and we appreciate the time and thought they put into this process.

K. Elizabeth Soluri
Sabrina C. Agarwal

REVIEWERS

Brian Stokes, Allan Hancock College
Dawn Marshall, Blinn College
Lise Mifsud, Cuesta College
Tracy Evans, Fullerton College
Jalpa Parikh, Fullerton College
Corinna Guenther, Grossmont College
Marta Alfonso-Durruty, Kansas State University
Alejandra Estrin Dashe, Metropolitan State University
Peter Warnock, Missouri Valley College
Rachel Messinger, Moorpark College
Erin Blankenship-Sefczek, Ohio State University
Joshua Sadvari, Ohio State University
Timothy Sefczek, Ohio State University
Arion Melidonis, Oxnard College
Susan Cachel, Rutgers University
Renee Garcia, Saddleback College
Scott A. Suarez, San Diego Mesa College
Mario Robertson, Santa Ana College
Phyllisa Eisentraut, Santa Barbara City College
Barbara Wheeler, Santa Rosa Junior College
Nancy Cordell, South Puget Sound Community College

Nasser Malit, State University of New York at Potsdam
Arthur Charles Durband, Texas Tech University
Robert Paine, Texas Tech University
Jessica Cade, University of California, Riverside
Sandra Wheeler, University of Central Florida
Lana Williams, University of Central Florida
Anna Warrener, University of Colorado, Denver
Michael Pietrusewsky, University of Hawaii
Sloan Williams, University of Illinois at Chicago
Alan J. Redd, University of Kansas
Jen Shaffer, University of Maryland
Mary S. Willis, University of Nebraska–Lincoln
Peter Gray, University of Nevada, Las Vegas
Debra Martin, University of Nevada, Las Vegas
Martin Muller, University of New Mexico
Charles P. Egeland, University of North Carolina at Greensboro
David Begun, University of Toronto
Constance Arzigian, University of Wisconsin–La Crosse
Cari Lange, Ventura College
Robert Renger, Ventura College
Lucas Premo, Washington State University

LABORATORY MANUAL AND WORKBOOK FOR BIOLOGICAL ANTHROPOLOGY: ENGAGING WITH HUMAN EVOLUTION

SECOND EDITION

PART ONE

GENETICS AND EVOLUTIONARY THEORY

The genetic code for an organism is stored in its DNA. This DNA is coiled with proteins to form chromosomes. Humans have 23 pairs of chromosomes.

David Marchal/Science Source

LAB 1: BIOLOGICAL ANTHROPOLOGY AND THE SCIENTIFIC METHOD

WHAT TOPICS ARE COVERED IN THIS LAB?

- An introduction to the discipline of anthropology and its four fields
- A closer look at the field of biological anthropology
- A review of science and the scientific method
- An overview of the role of scientific inquiry in biological anthropology research
- An introduction to ethical practices in biological anthropology

LAB 2: GENETICS

WHAT TOPICS ARE COVERED IN THIS LAB?

- An introduction to the cell parts related to processes of evolution and inheritance
- A look at the importance of cell division for evolution
- A review of DNA replication and protein synthesis

LAB 3: INHERITANCE

WHAT TOPICS ARE COVERED IN THIS LAB?

- An overview of Gregor Mendel's research with pea plants
- A consideration of the relationship between dominant and recessive alleles
- A review of genotypes and phenotypes
- An introduction to Punnett squares and pedigree diagrams
- A discussion of Mendelian and non-Mendelian traits
- An examination of sex-linked traits
- An exploration of the ABO blood group in humans to illuminate complex relationships of dominance and recessiveness in real life

LAB 4: FORCES OF EVOLUTION

WHAT TOPICS ARE COVERED IN THIS LAB?

- An introduction to the concept of evolution
- A discussion of the role of genetic recombination in evolution
- A review of the primary forces of evolution (mutation, natural selection, genetic drift, and gene flow)
- Use of the Hardy–Weinberg equation to determine whether evolution is happening

Image BROKER/ Superstock

HANDOUT/KRT/Newscom

Biological anthropologists address a wide range of research topics related to humans and our evolutionary history. This research often includes time in the laboratory and time in the field.

Lab Learning Objectives

By the end of this lab, students should be able to:

- describe the discipline of anthropology in general and compare the four fields of anthropology.

- discuss the similarities and differences between the subfields of biological anthropology.

- explain the scientific method and define "scientific theory."

- discuss how biological anthropologists draw on science and scientific techniques in their work.

- apply the American Association of Physical Anthropologists Code of Ethics.

LAB 1

Biological Anthropology and the Scientific Method

In Germany, a group of researchers examines modern and ancient human DNA to understand human population movements in the past. Meanwhile, researchers in Ethiopia excavate the fossil remains of some of our relatives who went extinct roughly 4 million years ago. In California, a researcher analyzes 7,000-year-old bones for evidence of changes in bone density during life related to both biological sex and gender differences. And in Borneo, other researchers observe orangutans using probing tools to fish for the insects they eat. What do all of these people have in common? They are all conducting biological anthropology research. What does it mean to be a biological anthropologist? What topics do biological anthropologists study? In this lab, we explore answers to these questions.

INTRODUCTION

We begin this lab with an overview of the discipline of anthropology. We discuss the four fields of anthropology, and we pay particular attention

5

to how biological anthropology relates to the other three fields. We outline the subfields of biological anthropology and consider how they overlap and vary. We also explore science more generally, discussing the scientific method, its role in scientific research, and how biological anthropologists employ it in their work. We conclude by examining the ethical considerations involved in anthropological research.

WHAT IS ANTHROPOLOGY?

Anthropology, in the most general sense, refers to the study of people. It can take a variety of forms, including the study of people in the present and of people in the past. There are two ideas that are fundamental to all anthropological work. The first idea is the importance of **context**. Context includes issues of time, space, unique historical and environmental circumstances, and various culturally specific practices. It is important to all anthropological work because it shapes what we study. People do not live in a vacuum. Instead, they are inseparable from the context in which they live. For example, if an anthropologist were to fully understand you, they would have to consider your age, where you live, your gender, your life experience, your cultural practices, your family, your place in the broader biological world, and many other factors specific and unique to you. Where you live determines the environmental resources available to you, your food, and possibly your cultural practices. Your cultural practices influence the way you view the world and your place in it. Your biology, such as your sex or age, may affect your place in your culture. And your life experiences often tell the story of all of these factors. It would be impossible to understand you without understanding as much as possible about these other contextual issues. This emphasis on context and on how different aspects of a study subject interrelate and influence one another is often called a **holistic approach**. With a holistic approach, emphasis is placed on seeing the whole picture because anthropology recognizes that numer-

ous factors and contextual issues contribute to what it means to be human.

The second fundamental idea in anthropology is the use of a **comparative approach**. The comparative approach can take many forms, and anthropological comparisons can be the focus of a research project or only one component of a project. For example, anthropologists often compare different cultural groups, or the same cultural group in different time periods, or people in one region with people in another region, or humans with other species. No matter what anthropologists study, they recognize the importance of considering similarities and differences through comparisons.

Anthropology is a unique field of study because it takes into account how people are shaped by both their biological and their cultural context, and because it explores and compares people in all time periods and geographic regions. Other social sciences, such as psychology and sociology, have minor components of both of these fundamental aspects of anthropology. While many social scientists consider the role of biology and/or culture in human life, most of these disciplines do not emphasize a comparative approach. They study people in the present or people in particular areas of the world. In contrast, anthropological work considers context and employs a broad, comparative perspective.

FOUR FIELDS OF ANTHROPOLOGY

Anthropology is generally divided into four fields (**FIGURE 1.1**). These four fields are united by their consideration of culture and their emphasis on the comparative approach, but they vary in the questions they ask and in the materials they study. One field of anthropology is **cultural anthropology** (often called social anthropology in Europe). Cultural anthropologists study cultural practices, beliefs, economics, politics, gender roles, and so forth; they traditionally studied non-Western groups, although

anthropology the study of people

context the time, space, environment, historical circumstances, and cultural practices within which a subject of anthropological investigation is situated

holistic approach a research approach that emphasizes the importance of all aspects of the study subject and requires a consideration of context to gain an understanding of the broader picture

comparative approach a research approach that emphasizes the importance of comparisons across cultures, times, places, species, and so forth

cultural anthropology the study of the cultural life of living people, including their cultural practices, beliefs, economics, politics, gender roles, and so forth; also called social anthropology

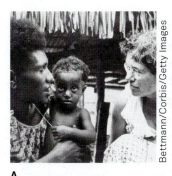

A   B   C   D

FIGURE 1.1 The Four Fields of Anthropology
All four fields of anthropology emphasize the importance of context and apply a comparative approach, but they differ in the specific aspects of humanity that they study. (A) Cultural anthropologists (such as Margaret Mead, seen here with a woman and child in the Admiralty Islands) study the cultural life of living peoples. (B) Linguistic anthropologists (like K. David Harrison, seen here with Anthony Degio and Abamu Degio watching a recording of herself singing a traditional Koro song) study how people make and use language. (C) Archaeologists (like the one seen here excavating an ancient site) study the cultural life of past peoples by examining their material remains. (D) Biological anthropologists study human evolution, and their methods of analysis may be applied to help criminal investigations (as is seen here in the excavation of a war victim in Argentina).

this is not always the case in the field today. Cultural anthropologists study living (or recently living) peoples. These anthropologists make observations, conduct interviews, and examine the things made by the people being studied (their material culture). For example, a cultural anthropologist might study the seasonal rituals practiced by a particular Native American group. She would observe the rituals and the times surrounding them to understand the broader cultural context of the practices. She might interview the people involved in the rituals and the people who observe them, and she might examine the clothing and materials used in the ritual.

A second field of anthropology is **linguistic anthropology**. Linguistic anthropologists study how people make and use language. Like cultural anthropologists, linguistic anthropologists tend to research living (or recently living) peoples, and they traditionally studied non-Western populations. They use observations and interviews to collect data about language production and use. They can also use written documents, where available, and recordings of people speaking the language under study. For example, a linguistic anthropologist might study how language is used differently by men and women in an indigenous group in New Guinea. He would observe people talking with people of their same gender and with people not of their same gender. The anthropologist might also interview people about who taught them their language, how they talk to their children of different genders, and how they talk to different people in their community. He might also listen to recordings of songs made by earlier researchers studying the same group to see if there are differences in men's and women's singing.

A third field of anthropology is **archaeology**. In Europe, archaeology is sometimes treated as a discipline separate from anthropology. In the United States, however, archaeology is considered a subdiscipline of anthropology and is sometimes called anthropological archaeology to highlight this categorization. Archaeologists, like cultural anthropologists, study cultural practices, economics, gender roles, and rituals. However, archaeologists focus on people and cultures in the past. Sometimes they study the distant past, tens of thousands of years ago. Sometimes they study the recent past, maybe only a few decades ago. Archaeologists study both Western and non-Western peoples around the world. Unlike cultural and linguistic anthropology, archaeology primarily examines the material remains left by people to understand their practices and way of life. Material remains

linguistic anthropology the study of how people make and use language

archaeology the study of the cultural life of past people as seen through their material remains, such as architecture, bones, and tools

biological anthropology the study of human evolution, including human biology, our close living and extinct relatives, and current similarities and differences within our species; also called physical anthropology

biocultural approach a research approach that recognizes the close relationship between human biology and culture and attempts to study these two forces simultaneously

human biology the study of human genetics, variation within our species, and how our species is affected by evolutionary processes

forensic anthropology the application of knowledge and methods of skeletal analysis to assist in legal investigations

are things that are made or modified by people and later recovered by an archaeologist. They include things like remnants of houses and ritual buildings, human bones and burials, tools, animal bones and charred plant parts, ceramic vessels, personal ornaments, statues, clothing, and sometimes historical documents. If an archaeologist were studying what Maya people ate in a community in Mexico a thousand years ago, she would probably try to recover and examine animal and plant remains from meals, ceramic vessels that held food and beverages, areas of the community that were used for food storage or preparation, and any documents that might help her understand food use.

The fourth field of anthropology is called **biological anthropology**. Biological anthropology has been traditionally called physical anthropology, with the term "physical" reflecting its traditional focus on the physical measurement of humans. Current trends in the field emphasize methods and theories from biology, such as the growing incorporation of DNA analysis. Thus, while both names are acceptable and continue to be used today, we will use "biological anthropology" to reflect anthropologists' increasing use of biological techniques.

Biological anthropology is the study of human evolution, including our biology, our close primate relatives, our fossil ancestry, and our current similarities and differences. Biological anthropologists study people in the present and in the past. They also study nonhuman species—specifically, our living primate relatives and our extinct fossil relatives. They examine a wide range of materials, including fossils, living primates, skeletons, and DNA. For example, a biological anthropologist studying the primate capacity for language might examine genes that contribute to language production and comprehension. He might also examine the bones of the skeleton related to language production or try to train living primates to produce or understand some form of language. The theme that unifies biological anthropology research is an emphasis on evolution.

One of the things that makes biological anthropology unusual among the sciences is its emphasis on a **biocultural approach**. This approach recognizes that human biology and culture are closely intertwined and need to be examined and understood simultaneously. Thus, biological anthropologists might consider how stone tool use (culture) affected past diets and dietary adaptations (biology) or how mating preferences (culture) affect current population isolation and human variation (biology).

THE SUBFIELDS OF BIOLOGICAL ANTHROPOLOGY

Within biological anthropology, there are several subfields. Each subfield emphasizes different aspects of human evolution and our place in the world. One subfield can be generally referred to as **human biology**. This broad subfield includes research on human genetics, the impact of evolutionary processes on our species, and variation among humans today. It draws heavily on theories and methods from biology. For example, a researcher in human biology might study the evolution of a particular trait, such as adult lactose tolerance. This researcher could explore the effects of different evolutionary processes in shaping this adaptation. She could also consider the genetic basis of the trait and why it might vary in human populations today. Another example of human biology research would be a study of energy demands and nutrition in different human populations. The researcher could observe and interview people in different groups to identify what people eat, how regularly they eat, how they spend their time, and how much energy is required for their lifestyle. He would probably take into account differences in age, gender, and social status that might influence energy demands and nutrition.

Forensic anthropology is an applied area of biological anthropology that has gained popular attention through television programs and crime novels. Forensic anthropology is

LukaTDB/Shutterstock

FIGURE 1.2 Forensic Anthropology
Forensic anthropologists apply methods of human skeletal analysis to aid criminal investigations. They help identify victims and describe circumstances surrounding deaths using clues in human skeletal remains.

related to human biology because it applies methods of skeletal analysis from human biology and anatomy to real-world problems. Forensic anthropologists analyze human skeletons as part of legal investigations. When a criminal investigation uncovers a body that is primarily skeletal, with little soft tissue remaining, investigators call on a forensic anthropologist for assistance (**FIGURE 1.2**). In some cases, forensic anthropologists are asked to help with investigations of war crimes, natural disasters, and other events that involve the identification of numerous victims. These anthropologists are experts on the human skeleton and use various methods and techniques to help identify victims and to suggest the circumstances surrounding their deaths. These methods include examining and measuring bones and teeth to help determine the victim's sex, age, and likely ancestry as well as noting any unusual damage to the bones that might have resulted from injuries sustained around the time of death.

Another subfield of biological anthropology is **primatology**: the study of living primates (**FIGURE 1.3**). Primatologists study similarities and differences across primate species, and they try to understand how, why, and when various primate traits evolved. Because humans are primates, this work is used to help us understand

our broader biological context and evolutionary history. Primatologists draw on biological theories and methods, such as DNA analysis and observations of animals in the wild. They may also design laboratory experiments to test things such as the ability of primates to perform certain problem-solving tasks or learn language. A primatologist might study chimpanzee social interactions in the wild. In doing this, the researcher would stay near a group of chimpanzees for an extended time, observing and documenting their behavior in various social situations, such as sharing food, having sex, and fighting. This type of information could then be used to help us understand human behavior in similar situations today and in the past.

The final subfield of biological anthropology is **paleoanthropology**: the study of the anatomy and behavior of humans and our biological relatives in the past (**FIGURE 1.4**). This subfield uses methods of excavation that are similar to those used by archaeologists, and there is often overlap in the evidence used in paleoanthropology

primatology
the study of living primates, particularly their similarities and differences and why those similarities and differences might exist

paleoanthropology
the study of the anatomy and behavior of humans and our extinct relatives

Penelope Breese/Liaison/Getty Images

FIGURE 1.3 Primatology
Some biological anthropologists, such as Jane Goodall, specialize in primatology.

scientific method
a cycle of scientific practices that helps scientists to gain knowledge and sparks further scientific inquiries

Des Bartlett/Science Source

FIGURE 1.4 Paleoanthropology
Paleoanthropologists examine fossilized remains for information about the anatomy and behavior of our extinct relatives.

and archaeology. However, archaeologists tend to focus on the human species (*Homo sapiens*), whereas paleoanthropologists often focus on our ancient extinct relatives, such as Neanderthals. Paleoanthropologists generally deal with the more distant past, even as far back as several million years ago. They often focus on the analysis of fossilized skeletal remains, and sometimes tools and other artifacts, that have been well preserved across long periods. For example, a paleoanthropologist might study when we first diverged from other primates. She would collect fossil remains from the relevant time period and analyze their anatomical traits and features to identify the extinct species' relationships to humans and other primates. She might explore what kinds of food our early primate relatives ate by examining fossil teeth and comparing them with modern primate teeth. She might also measure fossil limb bones to help determine whether ancient species relied on their arms and primarily moved through trees, or used their legs more and primarily walked on the ground. Work along these lines allows us to trace the evolution of particular human traits, as well as larger evolutionary trends in our history. Paleoanthropologists usually work as part of an interdisciplinary team that brings them together with researchers such as geologists and paleoecologists who study ancient environments. These interdisciplinary partnerships allow paleoanthropologists to gain a more complete picture of the past they study.

THE SCIENTIFIC METHOD

Science is a way of learning about the world. There are many ways of thinking about the world, but science is distinct because it relies on observations and tests to accumulate knowledge about phenomena seen in the natural world. These observations and tests must be repeatable and verifiable by other scientists. Scientists in all scientific disciplines use the scientific method to make their observations.

The **scientific method** is a cycle of scientific practices that helps scientists gain knowledge and sparks further scientific inquiries (**FIGURE 1.5**). There are four key stages to this cycle. The first stage is *observation*. Scientists can make observations of phenomena directly, or they can use observations of phenomena made by other scientists as part of previous research. For example, a researcher may notice that savanna baboons live in larger social groups than do forest-dwelling baboons (**FIGURE 1.6**).

The second stage of the cycle is generating a *hypothesis*. The hypothesis, which is based on the researcher's observations, is a testable explanation of those observations. There can be more than one hypothesis, but the researcher will have to handle them carefully in the next stages of the scientific method to make sure adequate data are collected and evaluated for each one. To generate a hypothesis, the researcher suggests a testable explanation for his observation. Specifically, it should be written as a statement that, if untrue, can be disproved (or falsified) by evidence obtained in data collection. For example, following his observation of savanna baboon groups, a researcher might hypothesize that savanna baboons that live in large groups have greater protection from predators than baboons that live in small groups. This hypothesis is testable because the researcher can observe baboons living in different group sizes and environments and can collect relevant data about their predation risk and rates of survival.

The third stage of the scientific method is *data collection*. During this stage, the hypothesis is actually tested. Data (or evidence) are

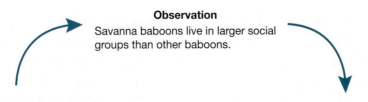

Observation
Savanna baboons live in larger social groups than other baboons.

Hypothesis
Savanna baboons that live in large groups have greater protection from predators than baboons that live in small groups.

Interpretation
Yes, there were more predation injuries and deaths among the baboons that live in small groups than among the baboons that live in larger groups.

Data Collection and Testing
Record the number of predator attacks and resulting injuries and deaths in the different baboon group types.

FIGURE 1.5 The Scientific Method
When conducting research, scientists follow the scientific method. They use previous research and new observations to develop hypotheses. They then collect data to test their hypotheses. They use their data to evaluate the hypotheses and make interpretations. These interpretations then serve as the starting point for further research, and the cycle begins again.

collected through experiments or further observations. What types of data are gathered and how they are collected will depend on the hypothesis being tested. In our baboon example, the researcher must collect data about the number of predator attacks, types of predator attacks, and rates of injury and death in baboon groups of different sizes and in different environments. This kind of data collection is different from traditional experiments that are conducted in laboratories. Laboratory experiments can often be strictly controlled, and the scientist can

Stu Porter/Alamy Stock Photo

FIGURE 1.6 Savanna Baboons
Savanna baboons often form larger social groups than baboons that live in forests.

scientific theory
a scientific explanation supported by substantial evidence

social science a discipline concerned with the study of human society, such as anthropology, psychology, or sociology

target particular variables that will be manipulated or kept in check. This strategy makes it possible to identify what causes certain results relatively clearly. It also makes it easy to repeat and verify the experiments and their outcomes. In contrast, in the natural world, scientists cannot fully control the research situation, and they often have to work around various environmental barriers, such as bad weather, limited daylight, and skittish research subjects. But scientists working in these conditions still follow the basic principles of repeatability and verifiability. They closely document each factor that may affect their results so that researchers in the future can repeat their work as closely as possible to test for similar outcomes.

The final stage of the scientific method is *interpretation*, in which the collected data are used to evaluate the hypothesis. Did the hypothesis adequately explain the early observation? Is there sufficient evidence to support the hypothesis, or should the hypothesis be rejected? Let's return to our baboon example. The researcher finds more predation injuries and deaths among savanna baboons that live in small groups than among savanna baboons living in larger groups or among small groups of forest-dwelling baboons. Thus, the hypothesis is supported. Forest-dwelling baboons do not face as many risks and can get by with a smaller group size. However, baboons on the savanna face more predation, particularly when they form a small group, so savanna baboons tend to form larger groups for safety. Conclusions from this research can then be used as the observations that jump-start another research project in the future. This makes the scientific method an ongoing cycle of knowledge building. Past research feeds current research, which in turn can spark future research with new data and new interpretations.

Because past scientific research becomes the foundation for new research, the scientific method is self-correcting. To explore this concept, let's think about the savanna baboon example. Imagine that the researcher collected data that indicated the rates of predation injuries and deaths were actually the same in both small and large savanna baboon groups. In

this case, the hypothesis would be rejected instead of supported because the larger group size did not protect the baboons from predators. The researcher would then need to revise the hypothesis to come up with a new, testable explanation for why savanna baboons form large social groups. The scientific method allows for knowledge correction because researchers continue to refine and retest hypotheses this way over time. Later scientists may also identify mistakes made in earlier research, and the research can then be performed again.

When the same interpretations are supported by evidence from many different researchers and they are widely accepted by the scientific community, they may become a theory. A **scientific theory** is not a guess. It is an explanation supported by substantial evidence. However, this evidence does not mean that a scientific theory is an absolute truth. A scientific theory is still open to reinterpretation and rejection in the face of new evidence. There are several widely accepted scientific theories today, including the theory of evolution (see Lab 4 for more information).

THE SCIENCE OF BIOLOGICAL ANTHROPOLOGY

Biological anthropologists are scientists. They apply the scientific method to questions about human biology. Because biological anthropologists study human biology in the context of human culture and behavior, biological anthropology is also a **social science**. Biological anthropologists use observations to generate hypotheses, and they accumulate data to evaluate those hypotheses. As previously discussed, some biological anthropology research can be conducted in controlled laboratory settings. Much of the research, however, is conducted by making observations of animals in the wild or observations and analyses of the fossil record. The lack of laboratory experiments does not make biological anthropology unscientific. Remember, the scientific method requires that data be collected to test hypotheses, which is regularly done by biological anthropologists.

ETHICS IN BIOLOGICAL ANTHROPOLOGY RESEARCH

Biological anthropologists often work closely with people and other nonhuman primates. In some cases, they directly study people, both past and present, by methods such as collecting DNA samples to identify and compare genetic traits. In other research contexts, biological anthropologists may hire local people to help observe and collect data about wild nonhuman primates. In still other research projects, biological anthropologists may conduct laboratory experiments with captive nonhuman primates, such as testing a gorilla's ability to use human-like forms of communication. Therefore, biological anthropologists must follow ethical guidelines that outline how to work with these populations safely and fairly.

The American Association of Physical Anthropologists (AAPA; shortly to be renamed the American Association of Biological Anthropologists), the leading professional organization for biological anthropologists in the United States, has outlined a Code of Ethics for biological anthropology work. This Code of Ethics includes the following guidelines:

1. The primary responsibility of anthropologists is to the people, species, and materials they study, as well as the people they partner with in their work. This responsibility takes precedence over responsibilities to others, such as funding agencies.
2. Anthropologists must not harm the people with whom they work.
3. Anthropologists must protect the anonymity of their hosts and of the people providing information if those participants so desire.
4. Anthropologists should also inform the people they are studying about the research and get their consent for the work in advance. This consent process is assumed to be dynamic and ongoing, and anthropologists may need to reobtain consent as their research continues or changes over time. The AAPA Code of Ethics also recognizes that even if anthropologists are not working directly with living people, they should still obtain consent from those who own or control access to their study material. For example, if an anthropologist would like to examine human bones uncovered from an ancient Native American site, he should obtain the informed consent of the living Native American descendants to whom those human remains are related. In many cases, this consent process is mandated by state and federal law.
5. Anthropologists often develop close and lasting relationships with research participants, so it is important to be open and maintain informed consent while also respectfully discussing and agreeing on the limits of those relationships.
6. Anthropologists must not exploit people, animals, or materials while conducting their work. They should also recognize their debt to their research participants and reciprocate in appropriate ways.

Because most biological anthropology research is complex and involves multiple, overlapping steps, biological anthropologists typically work collaboratively with other researchers. For example, a paleoanthropologist will work with other researchers, students, and local people to excavate a fossil site. Then, she will share subsets of the recovered fossil material with other experts who can each focus on specific data sets, such as an expert who examines early human teeth and an expert who studies small rodent bones. The paleoanthropologist will also want to know when the fossil creatures lived at the site, so she will send material to another group of specialists to be chemically analyzed and assigned to a certain time period. As previously discussed, she may also partner with geologists or paleoecologists who can help her understand the ancient landscape. A biological anthropologist is therefore expected to engage in responsible and professional practices as part of a larger scientific research team:

1. Anthropologists must make good-faith efforts to identify and address ethical conflicts before beginning their work.
2. Anthropologists should not falsify, plagiarize, or otherwise misrepresent their work.
3. Anthropologists should preserve opportunities for future scientists to conduct similar work. (Remember, the ability to verify research and refine knowledge is a key part of the scientific method.)
4. Anthropologists should share the results of their research with other scholars whenever possible.
5. Anthropologists should preserve their fieldwork data and seriously consider sharing them with other researchers.

Biological anthropologists conduct work that is relevant and important to the public. Therefore, they are also expected to share their results with funding agencies, students, and nonanthropologists. Anthropologists should explain and contextualize their research so that people will understand it and use the knowledge responsibly. However, anthropologists should limit information sharing if it would interfere with their primary responsibility and could cause harm to their research participants or colleagues.

An important and recent addition to the AAPA's Code of Ethics is its Statement on Sexual Harassment and Assault, which explains the AAPA's commitment to providing safe spaces that are free of harassment and discrimination. The statement also outlines what constitutes harassment and how to proceed should one be the victim of or a bystander to harassment in any professional space, including colleges, laboratories, field contexts, professional conferences, or digital and social media platforms.

CONCEPT REVIEW QUESTIONS

Name: _____   Section: _____

Course: _____   Date: _____

Answer the following questions in the space provided.

1. What are the *two* fundamental ideas in anthropology?

2. Which field of anthropology uses a wide range of data about living and past organisms to study human evolution?

   A. Linguistic anthropology
   B. Archaeology
   C. Biological anthropology
   D. Cultural anthropology

3. What is the biocultural approach in biological anthropology?

4. Which subfield of biological anthropology uses the fossil record to examine the anatomy and behavior of our relatives in the past?

   A. Forensic anthropology
   B. Paleoanthropology
   C. Human biology
   D. Primatology

5. Which subfield of biological anthropology applies methods of skeletal analysis to study humans in a legal context?

   A. Forensic anthropology
   B. Paleoanthropology
   C. Human biology
   D. Primatology

6. During which stage of the scientific method is the hypothesis evaluated?

   A. Observation
   B. Hypothesis generation
   C. Data collection
   D. Interpretation

7. In the context of the scientific method, what is the hypothesis? How is it different from a scientific theory?

8. Are scientific theories absolute truths? Why or why not?

9. Are scientific theories guesses? Why or why not?

10. According to the American Association of Physical Anthropologists (AAPA) Code of Ethics, an anthropologist is primarily responsible to _____ .

LAB EXERCISES

Name: _____   Section: _____

Course: _____   Date: _____

EXERCISE 1   FIELDS OF ANTHROPOLOGY SCENARIOS

Working with a group of your classmates, pick one (or more) of the following scenarios, depending on your instructor's guidelines, and answer the questions that follow. Use a separate sheet of paper if you are completing more than one scenario.

SCENARIO A

Anthropologists have been studying the role of soybean curd and related products in the culture of Hong Kong. The researchers interview people about how frequently they eat soybean products, where they eat them (at home or in restaurants), and during what time of day they eat them. The researchers also ask people about how they prepare soybean products, where they obtain soybean products, and any beliefs they might have about soybean products (such as their nutritional value). The data are used to assess the role of soybean products in the culture. The researchers are also considering how their findings relate to global soybean consumption patterns.

SCENARIO B

An anthropologist has been researching how Native Americans in California were impacted by Spanish missionization from 1776 to 1830. The researcher is particularly interested in how Native Californians may have negotiated their identity and balanced traditional practices with colonial influences. Therefore, the anthropologist excavates material remains from areas where the Native Californians may have gone when they fled the Spanish missions. The materials include things such as stone tools, shell beads, and historic bottle glass. These materials are analyzed and used in conjunction with historical documents to help the researcher better understand what life was like for Native Californians at that time.

SCENARIO C

Building on previous research showing that people of different genders often communicate differently, an anthropologist has been studying how gendered communication affects family interactions. The anthropologist uses recorded conversations from participant families' homes. The anthropologist also uses documentary footage of family interactions. The interactions are analyzed for information about gendered communication, power relationships, and connections between various family members.

SCENARIO D

Anthropologists have been studying Y-chromosomal DNA to understand where and when humans first appeared and when they moved into various areas of the world. The Y chromosome is found only in males, and most of the DNA found on the Y chromosome is passed directly from fathers to sons. Researchers collect Y-chromosomal DNA from living men and measure the amount of genetic difference among populations. Greater amounts of genetic difference indicate longer periods of separation between different groups of people because it takes time to accumulate genetic variations. This Y-chromosomal DNA research has helped anthropologists to understand our species' origin in Africa and our various migrations to other parts of the world.

QUESTIONS:

1. Which scenario did you select?

2. What is the primary field of anthropology addressed in this research?

3. Are there any other fields of anthropology addressed in this research?

4. What aspects of context must be considered as part of this research?

5. How might this research contribute to a comparative approach?

EXERCISE 2 SUBFIELDS OF BIOLOGICAL ANTHROPOLOGY SCENARIOS

Working with a group of your classmates, pick one (or more) of the following scenarios, depending on your instructor's guidelines, and answer the questions that follow. Use a separate sheet of paper if you are completing more than one scenario.

SCENARIO A

Biological anthropologists have discovered a previously unknown fossil species. The species lived about 4.4 million years ago in Africa. The dating of this fossil species places it closer in time to the last common ancestor of humans and chimpanzees than most other known fossil species. This newly discovered species has an interesting mix of traits. For example, it has adaptations for climbing in trees as well as for walking on two legs on the ground. It does not directly resemble any of the living ape species, which suggests the living ape species (including humans) have each become adapted to their own environmental contexts over time.

SCENARIO B

Biological anthropologists have observed several chimpanzees in western Africa making tools to help them hunt. The chimpanzees were seen modifying branches and sticks into spears. They removed any leaves or small branches to make a smooth shaft. They also chewed on the ends of the branches to give them sharp points. They then thrust the sharpened branches like spears into tree trunks, where small primates called galagos make sleeping nests. Although it remains unclear how successful the chimpanzees are in actually killing galagos, multiple members of the chimpanzee group have been observed producing the spears.

Biological anthropologists have studied the relationship between stress and female reproduction in a rural community in Guatemala. The researchers collected regular urine samples from women over the course of 1 year. Stress hormone and reproductive hormone levels from the samples were measured to determine a possible relationship between stress and reproductive function. Results suggest that stress may negatively affect reproductive health.

SCENARIO D

Biological anthropologists in Australia were called on to help identify victims of a series of fires. They analyzed the skeletal material for indicators of sex and age, and they compared this information with medical records and other documents to help identify fire victims. The anthropologists worked as part of an interdisciplinary team that was investigating the mass disaster.

QUESTIONS:

1. Which scenario did you select?

2. What is the primary subfield of biological anthropology addressed in this research?

3. How does this research relate to human evolution? In other words, what can we learn about human evolution from research along these lines?

4. Which other scholarly disciplines outside anthropology do you think might be interested in this research? Why would they find this research relevant?

EXERCISE 3 BIOLOGICAL ANTHROPOLOGY NEWS ARTICLE DISCUSSION

Your instructor has provided you with a news article related to biological anthropology. Read the article and answer the following questions with a group of your classmates.

1. What is the overall topic of your article?

2. How does your article relate to human evolution? In other words, what can we learn about human evolution from the article?

3. Who do you think is the target audience for the article?

4. Is the author an expert biological anthropologist? Did the author interview or quote an expert biological anthropologist?

5. Is there some information that might be missing from the article? If so, what might have been left out?

6. Based on what you have discussed about this article, what biases and other factors should you consider when following popular media coverage of biological anthropology topics?

EXERCISE 4   APPLYING THE SCIENTIFIC METHOD

The following scenarios describe observed phenomena. Working with a group of your classmates, pick one (or more) of the scenarios, depending on your instructor's guidelines, and answer the questions that follow. Use a separate sheet of paper if you are completing more than one scenario.

SCENARIO A (HUMAN BIOLOGY)

Previous research shows that some human populations living at extremely high altitudes have larger lungs. Research also shows that at high elevations the oxygen concentration in the air is lower, and people in these areas are at risk of not getting enough oxygen.

SCENARIO B (FORENSIC ANTHROPOLOGY)

Previous research shows that, in humans, the pelvic opening tends to be wider in females than it is in males.

SCENARIO C (PRIMATOLOGY)

Previous research shows that chimpanzee males form stronger alliances with one another than do chimpanzee females. Research also shows that adult chimpanzee females often split up and go to different areas to feed during the day while adult male chimpanzees spend more time together during the day.

SCENARIO D (PALEOANTHROPOLOGY)

Previous research shows that Neanderthals successfully lived in extremely cold environments during the Ice Age in Europe. Research also shows that toward the end of the Ice Age and around the time that humans (*Homo sapiens*) moved into Europe, Neanderthals quickly became extinct.

QUESTIONS:

1. Generate a hypothesis about what causes the observed phenomena in the scenario.

2. Describe the type or types of data you would ideally collect to test this hypothesis.

3. Describe what hypothetical data might support the hypothesis—for example, "The hypothesis would be supported if we found data that indicated _____."

4. Describe what hypothetical data might cause you to reject the hypothesis—for example, "The hypothesis would be rejected if we found data that indicated _____."

5. If you rejected the hypothesis, how would you refine and rewrite your hypothesis to account for your findings and begin again?

EXERCISE 5 DATA COLLECTION AND INTEROBSERVER ERROR

Have you ever found yourself debating with someone about the size, shape, or color of an object? You think it is a "large" egg, but someone else thinks it is an "extra large" egg. Or, you think a house is painted "moss" green, but someone else thinks the house is painted "avocado" green. These differences of perspective are quite common and can cause real problems in scientific investigations. In science, the difference between how two or more people observe an object or phenomenon is called *interobserver error*. When collecting data, researchers need to consider the possibility of interobserver error and account for it as much as possible, or their results could be skewed and inaccurate.

To explore how dramatic interobserver error can be, complete the following tasks with a group of your classmates.

STEP 1 Collect the data. Each person in the group takes turns measuring the four objects provided by your instructor. Use the measuring implements your instructor gives you (tape measures, rulers, etc.), and enter your measurements in the appropriate column of your own copy of the chart below. Be sure to keep your measurements to yourself as you go so you don't influence other people's outcomes.

INTEROBSERVER ERROR CHART

	Observer 1 (self)	Observer 2	Observer 3	Observer 4
Object One				
Object Two				
Object Three				
Object Four				

STEP 2 Evaluate and compile the data. Now, compare and discuss your results with your group members, and enter their results in the appropriate columns of your chart as well.

1. What differences do you notice?

2. Choose one object with the greatest difference across observers and explain why you think the difference exists (remember to consider the objects being measured, the tool being used, and the people doing the measuring).

EXERCISE 6   DATA COLLECTION AND EVALUATION

Work with a group of your classmates to read this scenario and complete the tasks and questions that follow.

An employee at a shoe store has observed that taller customers have larger shoe sizes than customers who are shorter. She knows that shoe sizes are based on foot length, so she generates a hypothesis: *Compared with shorter people, taller people have longer feet.* Complete the following steps to apply the scientific method and help the sales-person evaluate her hypothesis.

STEP 1 Collect height data. For each person in your group or class, determine the individual's height using tape measures or measuring sticks. *Hint*: It may be easiest to hang a piece of paper on the wall and have each person stand next to the piece of paper. Mark the maximum height (without shoes on). Have the person step away from the wall and then measure from the floor to that mark on the paper. Make sure only one person does all the measuring so you avoid interobserver error.

STEP 2 Collect foot length data. For each person in your group or class, determine the individual's foot length using tape measures or rulers. *Hint*: It may be easiest to have each person remove a shoe and stand on a piece of paper on the floor. While the person is standing, have another person draw around the outside of the foot, keeping the pencil as close to the foot as possible. Have the person step off the paper and then measure the length of the foot outline from the back of the heel to the tip of the longest toe. Make sure only one person does all the measuring so you avoid interobserver error.

STEP 3 Tabulate the data. On a separate sheet of paper, create a list or chart for your data that shows the two sets of data for each person (height and foot length). For example, you can re-create the chart below with your own data:

Name	Height	Foot Length
Eduardo	5 ft 10 inches	10.25 inches
Jane	5 ft 1 inch	8.75 inches
Susan	5 ft 10 inches	10 inches
Devon	6 ft	11 inches
Tim	5 ft 5 inches	9.25 inches
Lily	5 ft	9 inches

STEP 4 Interpretation

1. Look for patterns in the data. Describe any patterns you find.

2. Based on the data you collected, is the hypothesis supported or rejected? Why?

EXERCISE 7 ETHICS CASE STUDY

Working together with a group of your classmates, read this case study and complete the questions that follow. Remember, when making decisions on ethical research, there may be more than one best or correct answer. The key is your ability to justify your choices and highlight how they abide by the AAPA Code of Ethics.

CASE

A paleoanthropologist conducts research at a remote fossil site in eastern Africa. The anthropologist is a researcher based at a major university in the United States, and he spends 6 weeks every summer excavating and cataloging fossil materials at the site. The anthropologist has been working in this area for over 15 years, and he has formed close partnerships with local scholars and residents. His current field team is made up of students from the United States and from Kenya, as well as professional colleagues from both countries. He also hires residents from the local village to help with the excavations and to act as field staff, including drivers, cooks, and guides.

QUESTIONS: In answering each question, be sure to support your choice with relevant information from the AAPA Code of Ethics.

1. In this situation, the anthropologist is studying fossil materials that are over 2 million years old. From whom should he obtain informed consent for his work?

2. If he continues to work here for the next 10 years, how often should he reobtain informed consent? Should this be done at regular time intervals? Or should it be done only when something changes (for example, if he moves to a different excavation area at the site)?

3. Each summer, the anthropologist hires local residents to help at the site. He compensates them with a small wage that is comparable to their local income standards, but much lower than what he would pay similar workers back in the United States. When the field season ends, he and his financial support leave the community until the next summer. Is he adequately reciprocating with the local residents, or do you have recommendations for how he should modify the financial relationship?

4. One summer, the anthropologist returns to the site at the start of a new field season. He discovers that the same local residents who he hires in the summer have allowed their cattle to graze on the site over the winter while he was gone. The cattle have trampled some of the site and have permanently damaged the irreplaceable fossil materials. How should he proceed?

5. The anthropologist is attending the annual conference of the American Association of Physical Anthropologists (AAPA), and he is chatting with another paleoanthropologist named Jane who works at a nearby fossil site in eastern Africa. Jane asks if he will share his fossil data with her so she can compare the information from the two locations. He is hesitant to do so. He has devoted his career to the information uncovered at this site, and he worries that sharing the data with Jane will undermine his authority in the discipline. How should he proceed?

6. The anthropologist is very proud of the work his team is doing, and he would like to share it with a general audience. What formats might he use to spread the word about his work to the general public? What precautions might he take to make sure the information is spread accurately? Is there anything else he should keep in mind when sharing the research with the public?

CRITICAL THINKING QUESTIONS

On a separate sheet of paper, answer the following questions.

1. How are cultural anthropology and linguistic anthropology similar? How are they different?

2. How are archaeology and cultural anthropology similar? How are they different?

3. How are archaeology and biological anthropology similar? How are they different?

4. Find a current news article, or choose one given to you by your instructor, that discusses a biological anthropology topic. Use that article to answer the following questions.
   - What is the overall topic of your article?
   - In which subfield of biological anthropology do you think this topic most belongs?
   - Are there any other fields of anthropology addressed in this research? If so, which ones?
   - Which other scholarly disciplines outside anthropology might be interested in this research? Why would they find this research relevant?
   - What do your answers to the questions above suggest about the broader significance and relevance of biological anthropology research?

5. In the scientific method, why is it important to generate hypotheses before collecting data?

6. In what way is the scientific method a continuous cycle?

7. How does a nonscientist's view of a theory differ from a scientist's view?

8. In Exercise 5, you and a group of your classmates collected data on the size of several objects and considered the resulting interobserver error. If you were going to use similar measurement data in a scientific investigation, how might you avoid interobserver error? If you were working with previously collected data, and there was no way to go back and avoid interobserver error, how might you account for this error in your results and interpretations?

9. In this lab, we explored the Code of Ethics outlined by the American Association of Physical Anthropologists (AAPA). Many anthropological organizations have similar ethical guidelines that may be relevant to biological anthropologists. Review one of the following ethics codes and describe (1) how the code is similar to the AAPA Code of Ethics, (2) how the code is different from the AAPA Code of Ethics, and (3) what changes you might make to the AAPA Code of Ethics based on what you learned.
   - American Anthropological Association: http://ethics.americananthro.org/category/statement/
   - International Primatological Society: http://www.internationalprimatologicalsociety.org/docs/Code%20of _Best_Practices%20Oct%202014.pdf
   - Society for American Archaeology: http://www.saa.org/AbouttheSociety/PrinciplesofArchaeologicalEthics /tabid/203/Default.aspx

BIOLOGICAL ANTHROPOLOGY IN PRACTICE

Exploring How Fetal Environments Shape Reproductive Health

Dr. Julienne Rutherford is a biological anthropologist whose work integrates evolutionary theory with biomedical science to study aspects of human and nonhuman primate biology (see Lab 1). Julienne grew up in a small town near Cleveland, Ohio. By the time she graduated as valedictorian of her high school class, she had developed a strong interest in the life sciences, specifically evolutionary biology. She double-majored in anthropology and zoology at Miami University in Oxford, Ohio, and she earned a Ph.D. in biological anthropology from Indiana University. Her education and research interests have always been interdisciplinary. While in graduate school, she worked on primatological field projects in Nicaragua and Costa Rica. Today, she is an associate professor in the Department of Women, Children and Family Health Science in the College of Nursing at the University of Illinois, Chicago (UIC).

Julienne's research examines the dynamic maternal environment in which a fetus develops. She studies the development, anatomy, and function of the primate placenta in her lab at UIC to answer questions about the effect of maternal ecology (nutrition, life history experience, and behavior) on placental functional morphology and birth outcomes, as well as the consequences for health later in life. For the past 15 years, she has been working with marmoset monkeys, small-bodied primates that have multiple offspring at once (usually twins) (see Lab 10). She has examined how the period of prenatal development in marmosets affects their reproductive development and function into adulthood and subsequent generations. Julienne and her team use body weight and composition, sonograms of uterine growth from birth to adulthood, and biomarkers of energetic, inflammatory, and reproductive status in the monkeys to determine how their intrauterine development affects their adult reproductive function. For example, she has found that a marmoset mother who was a triplet herself loses nearly three times as many offspring to stillbirth, on average, as a female who was a twin (38% vs. 13%). This cutting-edge work demonstrates that the reproductive performance of adult females is shaped by the environments they experienced as fetuses, and it is critical to our understanding and treatment of reproductive dysfunction (such as infertility and pregnancy loss) in women today.

Along with her research interests in biological anthropology, Julienne is deeply passionate about working to eradicate sexual harassment and gender inequity from the sciences. Julienne is one of four co-authors of the Survey of Academic Field Experience (SAFE) studies,[1] who found that sexual harassment and assault are common experiences in field-based sciences (such as anthropology, archaeology, geology, and animal behavior). They found not only that these experiences are common, but also that they contribute directly to the stalling of women's careers. Julienne's research on maternal environments and her work on harassment and gender equity are linked by their shared acknowledgment that nurturing environments early in life, and early in one's career, have lasting consequences for optimal functioning, and both are rooted in premises of social justice.

Julienne's fascinating work requires a strong understanding of human genetics and the processes of inheritance. In Labs 2 and 3, you will get to do your own hands-on work to explore these crucial concepts.

---

[1]Clancy et al. 2014; Nelson et al. 2017.

Dr. Julienne Rutherford prepares a marmoset placenta for microscopic analysis during her doctoral studies at the Southwest National Primate Research Center in San Antonio, Texas.

Courtesy of Dr. Julienne Rutherford

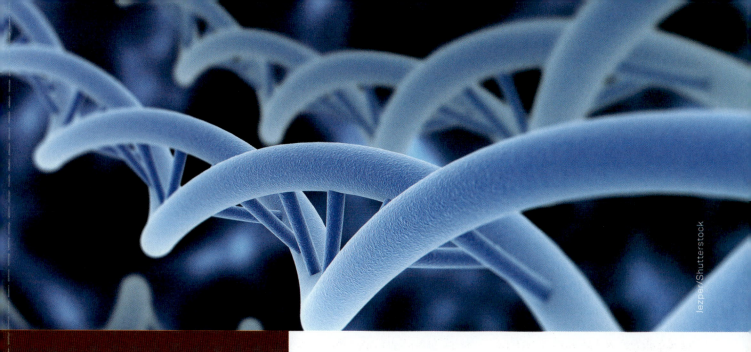

The genetic code for every organism is housed in its DNA.

LAB 2

Genetics

It is early March 1953. Researchers have been working off and on for several years on an interesting scientific problem. They have been trying to determine the structure of DNA. So far, scientists have identified the biological compounds adenine, thymine, guanine, and cytosine in DNA, and they recognize that these compounds appear to follow some sort of pattern: the quantities of adenine and thymine are the same, and the quantities of guanine and cytosine are the same. Thanks to the hard work of Rosalind Franklin **(FIGURE 2.1)**, many X-ray photographs of DNA have been taken, which show that it has a compact, potentially helical structure. These first steps have made a significant contribution to the understanding of DNA's overall shape and components, but many questions still remain. How is so much information kept in such a tiny package, and what could explain the paired quantities of adenine and thymine and of guanine and cytosine molecules?

After months and months, and a few frustrating missteps, researchers in England are about to answer these questions. The team has a new idea. What if the adenine and thymine bond together in the structure, and the guanine and cytosine also bond together? That idea would certainly explain their similar quantities, but is it real or another false lead?

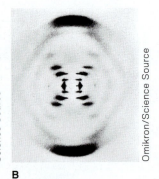

Science Source

Omikron/Science Source

A   **B**

FIGURE 2.1 DNA Pioneers
Much of what we know about DNA and genetics today is possible because of the work of researchers like (A) Rosalind Franklin whose (B) X-ray photographs of DNA helped reveal its underlying structure.

prokaryote organism (such as a bacterium) that has a cell without a nucleus and is often made of only a single cell

eukaryote organism (such as a plant or animal) that is made of many cells that have cell nuclei

nucleus the area inside a eukaryotic cell that contains most of the cell's DNA

DNA (deoxyribonucleic acid) the chemical that acts as the genetic blueprint for an organism

nuclear DNA the DNA found in the nucleus of a cell

organelle a type of cell part with its own function, like an organ of the body

mitochondria (mitochondrion, singular) cell organelles that produce energy for the cell and that contain their own DNA

Two scientists, Francis Crick and James Watson, get to work building, measuring, and refining a model of DNA based on this idea (and other ideas researchers have pieced together over the past year). The model they construct takes the shape of a double helix with bonded pairs of adenine–thymine and guanine–cytosine running along the core. Their excitement mounts, and over the coming days, weeks, and months, their structure is verified by other scientists and supported by further X-ray photography. This group of scientists has just revolutionized our understanding of life on Earth! Their work, which earns them a Nobel Prize, forms the foundation of our modern understanding of genetics and the passing of traits between generations. Understanding these foundational genetics concepts allows us to better understand how evolution happens, and in this lab we review these concepts with this goal in mind.

INTRODUCTION

We begin this lab with an introduction to cells, the basic building blocks of life. This introduction includes a review of the parts of the cell related to genetics and inheritance and an examination of how cells divide and replicate. We also take a close look at the importance of cell division for evolution. We then focus on DNA—the genetic code passed from one generation to the next. We consider how

DNA replicates and how it codes for proteins in the body.

WHAT IS A CELL?

Cells are the most basic units of life. All living organisms are made of cells. Some organisms, such as bacteria, are made of only one cell. The cells of bacteria do not have a cell nucleus, and these organisms are called **prokaryotes**. Other organisms, such as plants and animals, are made of many cells. The cells of plants and animals have a cell nucleus, and these organisms are called **eukaryotes**. We will focus on eukaryotic cells because they are the cells found in humans.

Some of the major parts of eukaryotic cells are the nucleus, the mitochondria, the cytoplasm, and the cell membrane (**FIGURE 2.2**). The **nucleus** contains genetic information in the form of **DNA (deoxyribonucleic acid)**. This **nuclear DNA** holds almost all of the organism's genetic information, which, together with environmental influences, determines the appearance and behavior of an organism. Outside the nucleus, there are various other organelles. **Organelles** are cell parts that have different functions, similar to the special functions of different organs in the body. The *endoplasmic reticulum* is an organelle that holds *ribosomes*, which are important organelles for the production of the body's proteins. **Mitochondria** are organelles that produce "chemical power" for the cell. They take in nutrients and turn them into energy for the cell. Interestingly, mitochondria have their own DNA, separate from the DNA found in the cell nucleus. This DNA is called **mitochondrial DNA (mtDNA)**. This mtDNA has been very useful in attempts to track human lineages and relationships in the past because it is passed directly from a mother to her offspring. The nucleus and the cell organelles, such as mitochondria, are all suspended in the cell in a fluid called *cytoplasm*. Cytoplasmic fluid helps give cells their shape. All of these cell parts are held together by the *cell membrane*. This membrane is a barrier that separates the cell from its surroundings. The

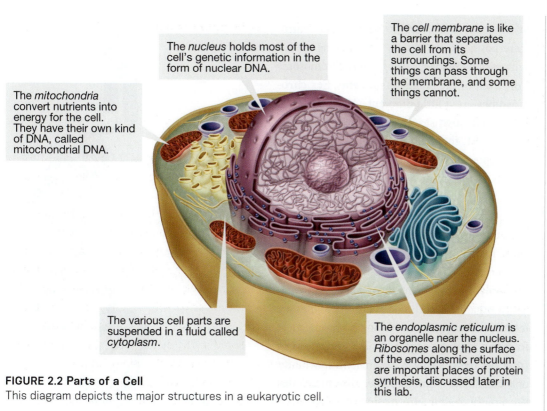

The *nucleus* holds most of the cell's genetic information in the form of nuclear DNA.

The *cell membrane* is like a barrier that separates the cell from its surroundings. Some things can pass through the membrane, and some things cannot.

The *mitochondria* convert nutrients into energy for the cell. They have their own kind of DNA, called mitochondrial DNA.

The various cell parts are suspended in a fluid called *cytoplasm*.

The *endoplasmic reticulum* is an organelle near the nucleus. *Ribosomes* along the surface of the endoplasmic reticulum are important places of protein synthesis, discussed later in this lab.

FIGURE 2.2 Parts of a Cell
This diagram depicts the major structures in a eukaryotic cell.

cell membrane is semipermeable, meaning some things can pass through it while others cannot.

THE GENETIC CODE

The DNA found inside the cell nucleus is the genetic information or blueprint for the organism. DNA is a chemical that is organized into

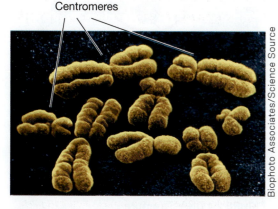

Centromeres

FIGURE 2.3 Chromosomes
These chromosomes, made of paired chromatids, show the diversity of chromosome size and shape. Also, note the different centromere locations on different chromosomes.

chromosomes in the nucleus (**FIGURE 2.3**). These chromosomes are like long threads. A chromosome usually occurs as a single fiber, called a **chromatid**, but chromatids can duplicate and occur in pairs when a cell is about to divide (see below). Chromosomes have an area that is contracted, called a **centromere**. The centromere can be located toward the end of the chromatid or in the middle, depending on the chromosome. This variation makes centromere position a useful tool for identifying chromosomes. Different species have different numbers of chromosomes, but the number of chromosomes found in an organism is not an indicator of an organism's complexity. For example, humans have 46 chromosomes, chimpanzees have 48 chromosomes, and turkeys have 82 chromosomes. None of these organisms is more or less complex than the others.

Types of Chromosomes

There are two types of chromosomes: the autosomes and the sex chromosomes. The **autosomes**, or non-sex chromosomes, exist in homologous pairs. **Homologous pairs** are sets of matching chromosomes with similar types of genetic

mitochondrial DNA (mtDNA) the DNA found in mitochondria, which is passed from mothers to offspring

chromosome a tightly coiled strand of DNA within the cell nucleus

chromatid a single chromosome fiber that duplicates and occurs in pairs when a cell is about to divide

centromere the contracted area of a chromosome, whose position varies from one chromosome to the next and is therefore useful in distinguishing chromosomes

autosome a chromosome other than one of the sex chromosomes

homologous pair a set of two matching chromosomes with similar types of genetic information, similar lengths, and similar centromere positions

Biophoto Associates/Science Source

sex chromosome one of the two different chromosomes (X and Y) involved in the determination of an organism's biological sex

X chromosome the larger of the two sex chromosomes, having genetic information related to a wide range of traits

Y chromosome the smaller of the two sex chromosomes, having genetic information that codes primarily for traits related to maleness

nucleotide a set of linked phosphate, sugar, and nitrogen base molecules in DNA

adenine one of the nitrogen bases in DNA; its complement is thymine

thymine one of the nitrogen bases in DNA; its complement is adenine

guanine one of the nitrogen bases in DNA; its complement is cytosine

cytosine one of the nitrogen bases in DNA; its complement is guanine

information, similar lengths, and similar centromere positions. In sexually reproducing organisms, each homologous pair has one chromosome from each of the organism's parents. **Sex chromosomes** are a little different. Although most people have two sex chromosomes, one from each parent, these chromosomes are not truly homologous like the autosomes. The two different sex chromosomes contribute to an organism's biological sex. The **X chromosome** is larger and has genetic information important to both females and males, such as genes that allow for color vision. The **Y chromosome** is smaller and has genetic information that codes primarily for traits related to "maleness." Generally, organisms with two X chromosomes are female, and organisms with one X chromosome from the mother's egg and one Y chromosome from the father's sperm are male. Importantly, only males have Y chromosomes. This means that the father's genetic information, not the mother's, is responsible for determining the sex of offspring. Only the inheritance of the father's Y chromosome can result in a male offspring. This is particularly interesting when considering that in many cultures, in the past and today, women are held responsible for the successful production of male heirs.

DNA Structure

The genetic information on chromosomes is found in their DNA. The DNA has a double-helix shape, similar to that of a twisting ladder or spiral staircase. The sides of the ladder are formed by phosphates and sugars. The rungs of the ladder are made of nitrogen bases. Each set of linked phosphate, sugar, and nitrogen base molecules is called a **nucleotide**. The nucleotides on the two sides of the helix are held together by hydrogen bonds between the nitrogen bases. There are four possible bases in DNA: **adenine, thymine, guanine,** and **cytosine**. These bases, often abbreviated A, T, G, and C, form complementary base pairs because each one bonds with only one of the other bases. Adenine and thymine always bond together, and guanine and cytosine always bond together **(FIGURE 2.4)**.

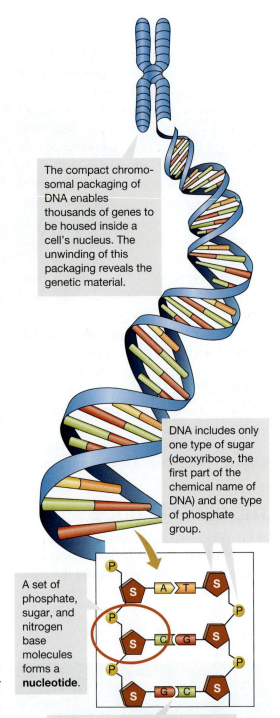

The compact chromosomal packaging of DNA enables thousands of genes to be housed inside a cell's nucleus. The unwinding of this packaging reveals the genetic material.

DNA includes only one type of sugar (deoxyribose, the first part of the chemical name of DNA) and one type of phosphate group.

A set of phosphate, sugar, and nitrogen base molecules forms a **nucleotide**.

DNA includes four different types of nitrogen bases. These bases follow specific pairing rules. Adenine and thymine always pair together, and cytosine and guanine always pair together.

FIGURE 2.4 DNA Structure
DNA has a double helix shape, resembling that of a twisted ladder. The rungs of the ladder are formed by nitrogen bases. The sides of the ladder are formed by phosphates and sugars.

Genes and Alleles

A section of DNA that codes for a particular trait is called a **gene**, and each gene has multiple versions, called **alleles**. For each trait, there are multiple alleles (gene variations). Often, there are even multiple genes for a trait, which multiplies the number of alleles and variations. The genes for particular traits are arranged as part of larger sequences of genes for many traits (**FIGURE 2.5**). These gene sequences are also interspersed with long sections of nucleotides that do not code for traits but instead act as punctuation marks that separate genes from one another and as regulators that can turn nearby genes on and off. All together, the long strands of twisting genes and other nucleotides make up chromosomes. Chromosomes hold the genetic code that determines how our bodies look and function. The chromosomes act in particular ways during cell division to make sure the right amount of genetic information is passed into the replicated cells.

Representing the Genetic Code: Karyotypes

An individual's or species' chromosomal makeup is often represented in a **karyotype**—a picture of the chromosomes, numbered and laid out in their homologous pairs. Karyotypes are produced by staining chromosomes so that some

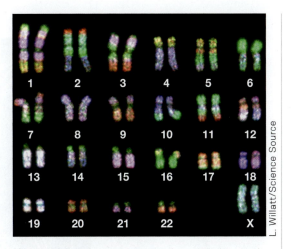

FIGURE 2.6 Human Karyotype
This human karyotype shows 46 chromosomes, arranged in 23 homologous pairs and laid out from largest to smallest. Note that the sex chromosomes are placed at the end of the karyotype. This individual has two X chromosomes, so she is female.

bases (adenine and thymine) show as different colors than other bases (guanine and cytosine). The chromosomes are then matched to their homologous partners based on similarities in size, centromere location, and dye pattern. The homologous pairs are then arranged and numbered in size order, from largest to smallest. In humans, this treatment results in 23 pairs of chromosomes of different sizes (**FIGURE 2.6**). The sex chromosomes are often distinguished from the autosomes and placed at the end of the karyotype, despite their relatively larger size. Karyotypes can be used for a variety of purposes, including identifying chromosomal anomalies or comparing chromosomal information across species for classification purposes.

DNA REPLICATION

DNA replication is the process that allows for the duplication of genetic information. It is the important first step in the cell division processes discussed below. During DNA replication, a strand of DNA is copied, resulting in two identical strands where there was previously one. The replication process is very simple (**FIGURE 2.7**). First, the DNA strand is unzipped by

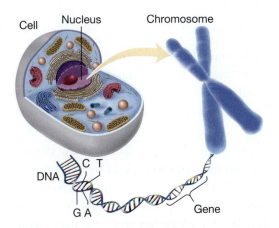

FIGURE 2.5 The Organization of Genetic Material
Sequences of genes form long DNA strands. The DNA strands coil to form the chromosomes in the cell nucleus.

gene a section of DNA that codes for a particular trait

allele an alternative version of a gene

karyotype a picture of an individual's stained chromosomes, arranged in homologous pairs and laid out in order from largest to smallest

DNA replication the process whereby DNA is copied

FIGURE 2.7 DNA Replication
Because all of the bases in a sequence of DNA follow strict pairing rules, one side of a DNA strand can act as the blueprint for a complete strand during DNA replication. The existing nitrogen bases attract complementary free-floating nucleotides.

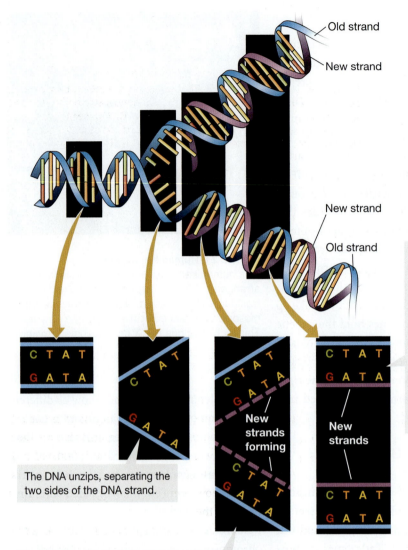

Old strand

New strand

New strand

Old strand

When all the nitrogen bases of the parent strands are paired with (formerly free-floating) nucleotides, replication is complete. There are now two complete DNA molecules, each consisting of one parent strand and one new strand.

C T A T
G A T A

C T A T
G A T A

C T A T
G A T A
C T A T
G A T A

New strands forming

New strands

The DNA unzips, separating the two sides of the DNA strand.

Free-floating nucleotides bond with the exposed nitrogen bases. This bonding follows the pairing rules, with adenine and thymine bonding together and cytosine and guanine bonding together.

an enzyme when replication needs to occur. The bonds holding the two sides of the DNA ladder together weaken and allow the two sides to separate. This exposes the nitrogen bases that were previously bonded together. Second, free-floating nucleotides in the cell (sets of phosphates, sugars, and nitrogen bases) line up with the exposed sides of the DNA strand. The nucleotides bond with the nitrogen bases on the strand, making a two-sided strand of DNA.

Because all of the bases in a sequence of DNA follow strict pairing rules, one side of a DNA strand can act as the blueprint for a complete strand. Each base on a side of DNA can deter-

mine which free-floating nucleotide is bonded to it. Imagine a DNA strand with a hydrogen bond between adenine and thymine. When this strand separates for replication, the adenine and thymine are exposed and open for bonding with free-floating nucleotides. The exposed adenine can bond only with a free-floating thymine, and the exposed thymine can bond only with a free-floating adenine. When these hydrogen bonds are formed with the free-floating nucleotides, the result is two sections of DNA that both have the same adenine–thymine bond. This structured pairing happens for each of the exposed sets of bases along the DNA strand, and each exposed base matches with its appro-

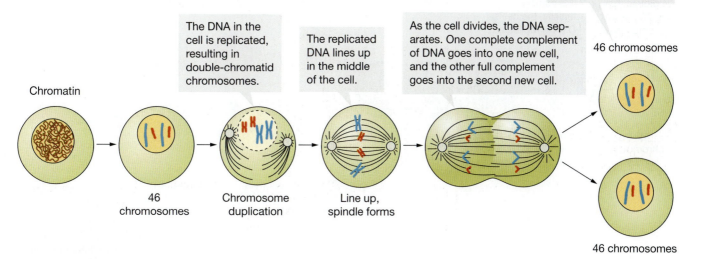

Each new cell has a full set of DNA, with 23 pairs of chromosomes.

The DNA in the cell is replicated, resulting in double-chromatid chromosomes.

The replicated DNA lines up in the middle of the cell.

As the cell divides, the DNA separates. One complete complement of DNA goes into one new cell, and the other full complement goes into the second new cell.

Chromatin

46 chromosomes

46 chromosomes

46 chromosomes

Chromosome duplication

Line up, spindle forms

46 chromosomes

FIGURE 2.8 Mitosis
The process of cell division that takes place in somatic cells is called mitosis. It involves one cell division, and it results in two daughter cells that are exact copies of the original cell.

priate free-floating nucleotide until the strand is duplicated.

CELL DIVISION

Humans have two different types of cells: somatic cells and gametes. **Somatic cells** are also called body cells because they are the cells that make up our different body parts. Hair, organs, bone, fat, and other body parts are made of somatic cells. **Gametes** are called sex cells because they are the cells involved in sexual reproduction. Males have sperm, and females have ova (eggs). New cells are produced through a process called cell division. Generally, cell division in somatic cells occurs through **mitosis**, and cell division in gametes happens through **meiosis**.

In humans, mitosis begins with the 46 single-chromatid chromosomes in a somatic cell. The chromosomes duplicate via DNA replication to form double-chromatid chromosomes. These chromosomes align in the middle of the cell in single file. Then, the chromosomes split apart at their centromeres, and each chromatid goes to a different side of the cell. The cell then pinches in at the middle, leaving two daughter cells that each have a complete set of 46 single-chromatid

chromosomes. This process begins with one cell and ends with two daughter cells that are both exact replicas of the original cell (**FIGURE 2.8**). The process of mitosis creates new somatic cells, which allows for growth and repair of damaged tissue in the body.

Meiosis is a little different (**FIGURE 2.9A**). Meiosis begins with a gamete-forming cell containing 46 single-chromatid chromosomes that replicate to form double-chromatid chromosomes. As in mitosis, these chromosomes then line up in the center of the cell, this time with their homologous partners. In this stage of meiosis, each chromosome can exchange genetic information with its homologous partner. This process is called **crossing-over** because genetic information is exchanged between one chromosome and the other (**FIGURE 2.9B**). After crossing-over, the chromosomes separate for the first time. The double-chromatid chromosomes do not split apart, as they do in mitosis at this stage. Instead, the chromosomes remain intact, and the two members of each homologous pair move to different sides of the cell. Then, the cell pinches in and creates two daughter cells. Remember that because of the crossing-over that occurred earlier, some genetic information has been exchanged, leading to new combinations

somatic cell a non-sex cell that makes up different body parts; also called a body cell

gamete a sex cell (in humans, sperm or egg)

mitosis the process of cell division that occurs in somatic cells

meiosis the process of cell division that produces gametes

crossing-over the stage in meiosis during which genetic information is exchanged between the two chromosomes in a homologous pair

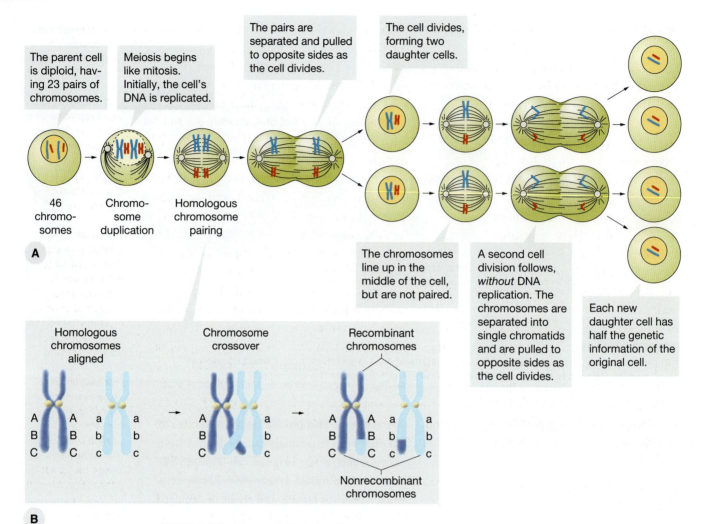

The parent cell is diploid, having 23 pairs of chromosomes.

Meiosis begins like mitosis. Initially, the cell's DNA is replicated.

The pairs are separated and pulled to opposite sides as the cell divides.

The cell divides, forming two daughter cells.

46 chromo-somes

Chromo-some duplication

Homologous chromosome pairing

A

The chromosomes line up in the middle of the cell, but are not paired.

A second cell division follows, *without* DNA replication. The chromosomes are separated into single chromatids and are pulled to opposite sides as the cell divides.

Each new daughter cell has half the genetic information of the original cell.

Homologous chromosomes aligned

Chromosome crossover

Recombinant chromosomes

A   A   a   a
B   B   b   b
C   C   c   c

A   A   a
B   B   b
C   C   c

A   A   a   a
B   B   b   b
C   C   c   c

Nonrecombinant chromosomes

B

FIGURE 2.9 Meiosis and Crossing-Over
(A) The process of cell division that takes place to make gametes is called meiosis. It involves two cell divisions, and it results in four daughter cells that have half the genetic information of the original cell. (B) Early in meiosis, homologous pairs of chromosomes line up in the middle of the cell and swap genetic information during a process called crossing-over.[1]

of genes that were not present before. This means that the daughter cells are not identical to each other or to the original cell. The two daughter cells then undergo a second division. The double-chromatid chromosomes move to the center of the cell. The double-chromatid chromosomes then split apart at their centromeres, as in mitosis. The now single-chromatid chromosomes move to opposite sides of the cell, and the cell pinches in at the middle, leaving two daughter cells. Because there were two daughter cells after the first division that then divided again, meiosis results in a total of four daughter cells. Each of the four cells has 23 single-chromatid chromosomes (half the genetic information of

the original cell) (see Figure 2.9A). The process of meiosis creates gametes (sperm and ova in humans), which are necessary for sexual reproduction.

Meiosis is very important to evolution because it results in **genetic recombination**. This does not mean that entirely new genes are created. It means that the existing genes are mixed up in new combinations. As the chromosomes cross over and the cell is divided, new combinations of genetic information are formed. For example, even if two traits are carried on the same chromosome, they may not necessarily be inherited together. If one of those traits is exchanged with the homologous chromosome during crossing-

genetic recombination the mixing of genetic information into new combinations that occurs during meiosis

[1] Adapted from OpenStax College. 2014. Concepts of biology. OpenStax CNX. cnx.org/contents/b3c1e1d2-839c-42b0-a314-e119a8aafbdd @8.49. Textbook content produced by OpenStax College is licensed under a Creative Commons Attribution License 3.0 license.

over, the two traits become separated. When the cell divides, the two traits will end up in different daughter cells and will not be inherited together. This process leads to genetic variation, and genetic variation plays a key role in evolution. At the same time, each daughter cell created by meiosis carries only half of a parent's possible genes. So, if a person has only one offspring, only half of their genes will be passed to the next generation. If a person has two offspring, there is a greater likelihood of passing on more of their possible genes; however, it is not guaranteed that the parent's entire genome is represented in those two offspring. Remember, the parent's genes are recombined during each meiosis event. There will be some overlap in genes that are passed to both of the offspring, and there will be some genes that are passed to only one offspring and not the other. Even if a person had 100 offspring, some of their genes would never be passed to their children. This variation in genetic recombination and genetic representation across generations is central to evolution.

PROTEIN SYNTHESIS

DNA is the template for proteins in our bodies. Proteins are chemicals that form and regulate tissues in the body, and they are the physical expression of our genetic code. Proteins themselves are made of amino acids, which are produced by the body or obtained through certain foods. The number and combination of amino acids in a protein determine the kind of protein it is. The amino acids that are assembled into a protein are defined by the DNA sequence. So, a sequence of DNA codes for a specific sequence of amino acids, which determines a protein. This process of determining proteins from a DNA sequence is called **protein synthesis**.

There are two primary steps to protein synthesis. The first step is called **transcription**. Nuclear DNA cannot leave the cell nucleus, so the DNA must be transcribed to another form that can leave the nucleus and code for proteins elsewhere (**FIGURE 2.10A**). Transcription, then, is basically a copying process. In fact, it

begins very similarly to DNA replication. First, the DNA strand is unzipped, exposing the two sides of the strand. The exposed bases on one side of the strand attract free-floating nucleotides. However, these nucleotides are not DNA nucleotides. They are **ribonucleic acid (RNA)** nucleotides. RNA is similar to DNA, except that its sugar is slightly different and one of its nucleotide bases is different: instead of thymine, RNA has uracil. Uracil in RNA bonds with adenine, just as thymine in DNA bonds with adenine. The cytosine and guanine in RNA bond with each other, as in DNA. The exposed bases on one side of the unzipped DNA strand—called the template strand—bond with the appropriate free-floating RNA nucleotides, following the same base pairing principles seen in DNA replication. This process forms a single strand of RNA called **messenger RNA (mRNA)**. The mRNA separates from the DNA and moves outside the nucleus to the cell cytoplasm, and the original DNA strand stays inside the nucleus and zips back up.

The second step of protein synthesis is called **translation**. During translation, the RNA is translated (or interpreted) to form the sequence of amino acids that makes up a specific protein. Having moved into the cytoplasm, the mRNA now attaches to ribosomes, the organelles where protein synthesis occurs. Inside the cytoplasm, there is another form of RNA, called **transfer RNA (tRNA)**. Each tRNA molecule contains a triplet of bases called an **anticodon**. These free-floating tRNA molecules seek out complementary mRNA triplets, called **codons**. Again, the basic rules of base pairing apply. Each mRNA codon is a series of three bases that will match only the appropriate series of bases in the complementary tRNA anticodon. For example, an mRNA codon of adenine-guanine-uracil will match with a tRNA anticodon of uracil-cytosine-adenine. Each tRNA molecule carries a specific amino acid that corresponds to its anticodon. The mRNA codons are read in order, like you read a line of text on a page. As each mRNA codon is read, the tRNA with the appropriate anticodon and amino acid is brought over. The amino acids are then linked together into long chains to make proteins (**FIGURE 2.10B**).

protein synthesis the process of determining proteins from a DNA sequence

transcription the first step of protein synthesis where nuclear DNA is transcribed into messenger RNA that can leave the cell nucleus

RNA (ribonucleic acid) a chemical that is similar to DNA, except it contains uracil instead of thymine; it plays vital roles in the process of protein synthesis

messenger RNA (mRNA) the RNA formed in the first stage of protein synthesis (transcription) that brings the genetic information from the cell nucleus to the ribosome

translation the second step of protein synthesis where messenger RNA is translated (or read) to form a sequence of amino acids that makes up a protein

transfer RNA (tRNA) a type of RNA that brings amino acids to a ribosome to form the amino acid chains in the second stage of protein synthesis (translation)

anticodon a triplet of bases in transfer RNA

codon a triplet of bases in DNA (or messenger RNA)

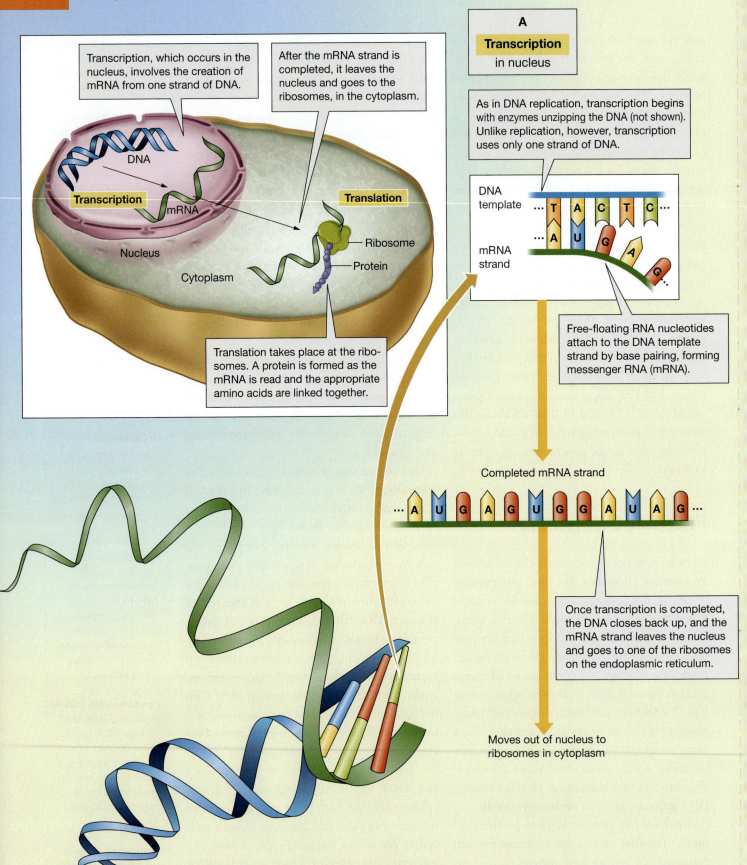

Transcription, which occurs in the nucleus, involves the creation of mRNA from one strand of DNA.

After the mRNA strand is completed, it leaves the nucleus and goes to the ribosomes, in the cytoplasm.

DNA

Transcription

mRNA

Nucleus

Cytoplasm

Translation

Ribosome

Protein

Translation takes place at the ribosomes. A protein is formed as the mRNA is read and the appropriate amino acids are linked together.

A

Transcription
in nucleus

As in DNA replication, transcription begins with enzymes unzipping the DNA (not shown). Unlike replication, however, transcription uses only one strand of DNA.

DNA template ...T A C T C...

mRNA strand ...A U G A G...

Free-floating RNA nucleotides attach to the DNA template strand by base pairing, forming messenger RNA (mRNA).

Completed mRNA strand

...A U G A G U G G A U A G...

Once transcription is completed, the DNA closes back up, and the mRNA strand leaves the nucleus and goes to one of the ribosomes on the endoplasmic reticulum.

Moves out of nucleus to ribosomes in cytoplasm

FIGURE 2.10 Transcription and Translation
(A) The first stage of protein synthesis takes place inside the cell nucleus and results in an mRNA strand that can leave the nucleus. (B) The second stage of protein synthesis takes place at the ribosome. The mRNA is read, forming an amino acid sequence that determines a protein.

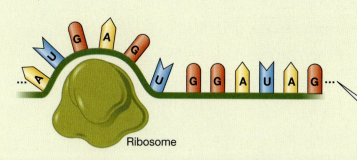

B

Translation

at ribosome

Translation begins as the mRNA binds to a ribosome. In effect, the message carried by the mRNA is translated by a ribosome.

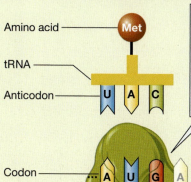

Amino acid — Met

tRNA

Anticodon — U A C

The ribosome reads the mRNA three nitrogen bases at a time. When a codon matches the transfer RNA (tRNA) molecule's anticodon, the tRNA's amino acid is added to the protein chain. For example, if the codon has the bases AUG, then the tRNA with the anticodon of UAC will attach the amino acid methionine to the chain.

Codon — ... A U G A G U G G A U A G ...

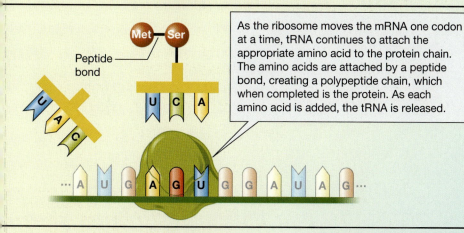

Met — Ser

Peptide bond

U C A

U A C

... A U G A G U G G A U A G ...

As the ribosome moves the mRNA one codon at a time, tRNA continues to attach the appropriate amino acid to the protein chain. The amino acids are attached by a peptide bond, creating a polypeptide chain, which when completed is the protein. As each amino acid is added, the tRNA is released.

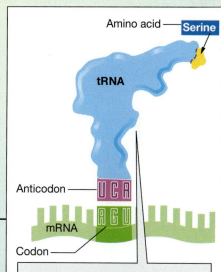

Amino acid — Serine

tRNA

Anticodon — UCA

mRNA — AGU

Codon

At a ribosome, a molecule of tRNA brings the anticodon for each codon on the mRNA. The tRNA carries its anticodon on one end and the associated amino acid on the other.

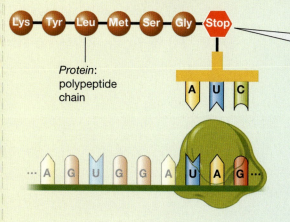

Lys — Tyr — Leu — Met — Ser — Gly — Stop

Protein: polypeptide chain

A U C

... A G U G G A U A G ...

Eventually, a stop codon is reached, which indicates that the protein is completed. The mRNA leaves the ribosome, and the protein is released.

Name: _____   Section: _____

Course: _____   Date: _____

Answer the following questions in the space provided.

1. What is the difference between a prokaryote and a eukaryote?

2. Which of the following cell parts produces energy for the cell and has its own DNA?
   A. Nucleus
   B. Cytoplasm
   C. Cell membrane
   D. Mitochondria

3. What do the two members of a homologous chromosome pair have in common?

4. Following the rules of complementary base pairing, which of these DNA bases could successfully bond with adenine?
   A. Thymine
   B. Guanine
   C. Adenine
   D. Cytosine

5. Following the rules of complementary base paring, which of these RNA bases could successfully bond with adenine?
   A. Thymine
   B. Uracil
   C. Cytosine
   D. Adenine

6. Versions of the same gene are called _____.

7. Mitosis occurs in which type of cell?

8. Meiosis occurs in which type of cell?

9. The genetic information that moves from the nucleus to the cytoplasm of a cell during protein synthesis is called:
   A. mDNA.
   B. tRNA.
   C. mRNA.
   D. tDNA.

10. During protein synthesis, the amino acids are transported by:
    A. mDNA.
    B. tRNA.
    C. mRNA.
    D. tDNA.

LAB EXERCISES

Name: _____   Section: _____

Course: _____   Date: _____

EXERCISE 1   EXTRACT YOUR OWN DNA

In this exercise, you will extract your own DNA from your cheek cells. Although you won't see individual chromosomes or genes with your naked eye, you will see thousands of real DNA molecules all clumped together. Then answer the questions that follow.

STEP 1: Gather your lab materials:
- 3 large cups or beakers (clear cups are best, so you can see inside)
- 1 stir stick
- Measuring cups with metric measurements (or a graduated cylinder or beaker)
- Measuring spoons (like those found in your kitchen)
- 500 mL of drinking water (bottled or tap water is fine)
- 1 tablespoon of salt
- Clear, liquid dish soap
- 100 ml of 70% Isopropyl alcohol (the kind sold in pharmacies for cleaning minor cuts)
- Food coloring (any color)

STEP 2: Remove any gum or candy from your mouth. (For the best results, avoid eating or chewing anything for 30 minutes before completing this activity.)

STEP 3: Mix the 500 mL of water with 1 tablespoon of salt in a cup. Be sure to stir the mixture until the salt is completely dissolved.

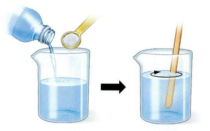

STEP 4: Scoop out 3 tablespoons of the salt water, and place it in a second, separate cup.

STEP 5: Gargle the 3 tablespoons of salt water in your mouth for 1 minute. Be sure to thoroughly swish the liquid around your mouth for the whole time, and try not to swallow any. (During this step, some of your cheek cells will end up in the salt water, so gargling thoroughly will cause more cells to collect in the water and improve the success of later steps.)

STEP 6: Spit the salt water back into the cup.

STEP 7: Add one drop of the clear, liquid dish soap to the salt water. Stir very gently, and try not to make any bubbles. (During this process, the soap is breaking down the cell membranes in your cheek cells. You want to help this process, so the DNA gets released into the water, but you don't want to damage the cells and DNA too much.)

STEP 8: In the third cup, mix 100 mL of 70% isopropyl alcohol and 3 drops of food coloring.

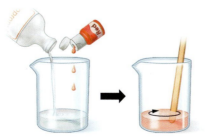

STEP 9: Now, carefully pour the colored alcohol into the salt water cup. Be sure to tilt the salt water cup slightly while you pour. You want the alcohol to form a layer on top of the salt water.

STEP 10: Wait for 2.5 to 3 minutes. While many of the components from your cheek cells stay dissolved in the salt water, DNA will begin to solidify where the alcohol and salt water meet. After several minutes, you will see this solidified DNA (it looks like white clumps and strings). You can use your stir stick to gently move it around and even pull it slightly out of the water! Note: Our mouths are full of lots of bacteria, who have their own DNA, so the DNA in the cup will be a mix of your DNA and the DNA of those bacteria.

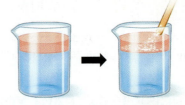

QUESTIONS:

1. In humans, our DNA has two types of chromosomes. What are these two types, and how do they differ from each other? Would you expect both types to appear in the DNA you extracted?

2. In this exercise, you extracted DNA from your cheek cells. If you could magnify the extracted material, how many individual chromosomes from each of these cheek cells would you expect to see? How would this number differ from the number of chromosomes in each of your gametes?

EXERCISE 2 CREATING AND INTERPRETING KARYOTYPES

Your instructor has provided you and a group of your classmates with stained chromosomes from person Z. Complete these steps to create person Z's karyotype and answer the questions that follow.

STEP 1 Match each chromosome to its homologous partner (remember to look for similar sizes, centromere locations, and staining patterns).

STEP 2 Arrange the homologous chromosome pairs in order from largest to smallest.

STEP 3 Match the sex chromosomes provided by your instructor.

1. How many autosomes does person Z have? How many sex chromosomes?

2. Is person Z male or female? Why?

EXERCISE 3   COMPARING KARYOTYPES

Work with a group of your classmates to review the two karyotypes depicted below and answer the questions that follow. Note that these karyotypes depict single chromosomes, rather than homologous pairs.

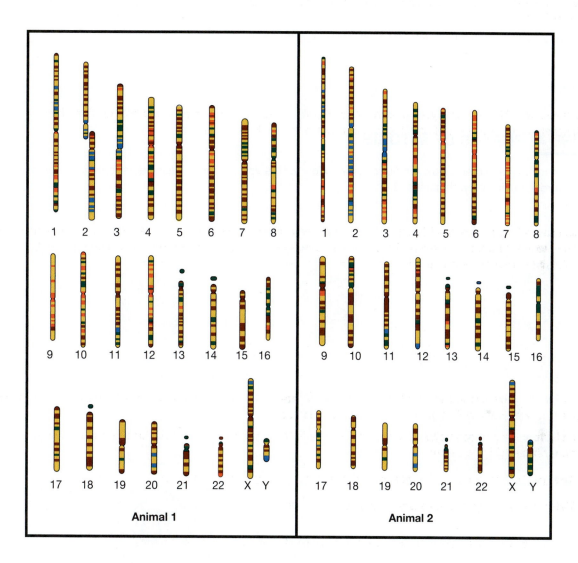

1. Describe two things the two karyotypes have in common.

2. Describe two things that differ between the karyotypes.

3. Which karyotype is from a human? How do you know this?

4. Which karyotype is from a chimpanzee? How do you know this?

The phases of mitosis depicted below are out of order. Work with a group of your classmates to number the phases in their correct order, beginning with number 1.

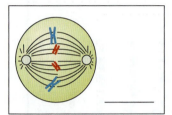
_____

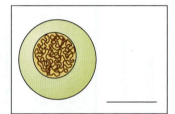
_____

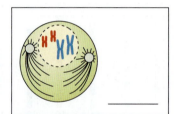
_____

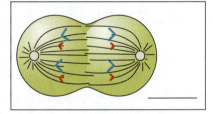
_____

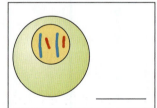
_____

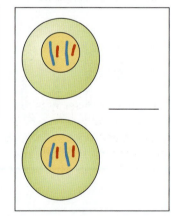
_____

EXERCISE 5 PHASES OF MEIOSIS

The phases of meiosis depicted below are out of order. Work with a group of your classmates to number the phases in their correct order, beginning with number 1.

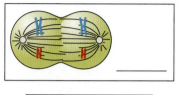

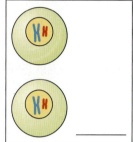

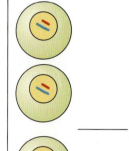

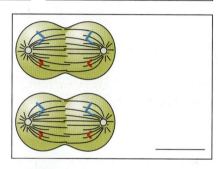

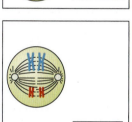

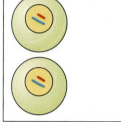

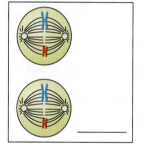

EXERCISE 6 COMPARING MITOSIS AND MEIOSIS

Work with a group of your classmates to review the cell division processes in Exercises 4 and 5 (or the diagrams of mitosis and meiosis in Figures 2.8 and 2.9). Use the information to compare the two processes of cell division, complete the chart below, and answer the questions that follow.

For each of the descriptions on the left, place a mark in the appropriate cell division column on the right.

	Mitosis	Meiosis
Occurs in Gamete-Forming Cells		
Occurs in Somatic Cells		
Has One Cell Division		
Has Two Cell Divisions		
Results in Two Daughter Cells		
Results in Four Daughter Cells		
Results in Daughter Cells with Half the Original Cell's Genetic Material		
Results in Daughter Cells That Are Exact Copies of the Original Cell		

1. Which process of cell division allows for growth and repair of damaged tissue?

2. Which process of cell division produces cells necessary for reproduction?

3. Which process results in recombination of genetic material?

EXERCISE 7 RECOMBINATION

For this exercise, use the set of cards provided at the very back of this manual. There are five pairs of cards in the set, distinguished by color (a pair of white cards, a pair of blue cards, a pair of yellow cards, etc.). Each color pair represents a section of DNA from a particular chromosome.

Color of Card Pair	Chromosome Represented
Blue	Chromosome 4
Red	Chromosome 7
Yellow	Chromosome 10
Green	Chromosome 15
White	Chromosome 20

Within each color pair, one card is labeled "Parental" and the other is labeled "Recombinant." These cards represent some of the DNA an offspring may inherit. If an offspring inherits the parental version of a chromosome card, the DNA was *not* recombined and was transmitted in its original form. If an offspring inherits the recombinant version of a chromosome card, the DNA was recombined and was transmitted in its new form.

STEP 1 Separate your pairs of cards into five piles by color. Pick up the two blue cards and shuffle them. Then, lay both blue cards facedown on the table next to each other. Repeat this process with the other color pairs until all five sets have been shuffled and laid out facedown next to each other.

STEP 2 Randomly select one card from each color pair until you have five different colored cards. These five cards represent the versions of the DNA that were passed to offspring 1. Turn the five cards over to see which versions of the chromosomes offspring 1 inherited. For each chromosome color, indicate whether offspring 1 inherited the parental or recombinant form in the chart below.

STEP 3 Replace the five cards you selected. Reshuffle them with their color partners and lay them facedown again in their color pairs. Repeat Step 2 to determine the versions of the chromosomes inherited by offspring 2. Write your results in the chart.

STEP 4 Continue replacing, shuffling, and reselecting cards for additional offspring until your chart is complete. (*Note*: If you have time, you may run the results for 10 offspring total.)

	Offspring 1	Offspring 2	Offspring 3	Offspring 4	Offspring 5
Blue					
Red					
Yellow					
Green					
White					
Total Percentage Recombinant					

STEP 5 For each offspring, determine what percentage of the group of five chromosomes was inherited in a new, recombinant form. (*Note*: 1/5 = 20%, 2/5 = 40%, 3/5 = 60%, etc.) Write your answers in the space provided in the last row of the chart.

STEP 6 Evaluate your results by answering the following questions.

1. Do all offspring from the same parents inherit the same versions of the available genetic material? Why or why not?

2. How many offspring inherited all 100% of their parent's original DNA?

3. How does recombination affect genetic variation in future generations?

EXERCISE 8   DNA REPLICATION

Work with a partner to complete this exercise.

STEP 1 Review the imaginary strand of DNA below. Note the complementary base pairs.

A G C A A T C C G T C T T G G
T C G T T A G G C A G A A C C

STEP 2 To begin replicating this strand of DNA, draw the two sides of the strand separating.

STEP 3 Now, draw the free-floating bases linking up with the separate sides. Remember to follow the rules of complementary base pairing.

STEP 4 Draw the two resulting DNA strands.

EXERCISE 9   PRINCIPLES OF MAKING PROTEINS

In this lab, we learned that DNA is the template for the proteins in our bodies. During the two steps of protein synthesis, the DNA gets copied and moved to the ribosome (transcription), where it is then read and interpreted (translation). Clusters of three bases (known as codons) correspond to particular amino acids, and the order of those amino acids determines the protein that is made. In this way, translation is like reading letters (bases) that make up words (codons) and eventually form complete sentences (amino acid sequences) that convey ideas (proteins). Follow these steps to see this process in action:

STEP 1   Review the DNA strand seen here. Note the complementary bases.

T C T A G T G A T G C G A G G C A G A A A C C T A A C C T G G T T T A G
A G A T C A C T A C G C T C C G T C T T T G G A T T G G A C C A A A T C

STEP 2   Remember, in protein synthesis, only one side of the DNA strand is copied by mRNA and used in translation. Here, we will use the *top side* of the DNA strand depicted. Review the top side of the DNA strand and list the corresponding mRNA codons in order (be sure to follow the rules of complementary base pairing and to account for the special RNA base, uracil):

STEP 3   Your instructor has distributed a flash card to each student that corresponds to one of the mRNA codons on your list. For each codon, find a classmate that has the appropriate flash card. Line your cards up in order, but do not turn them over; look only at the codon side of the cards. Be sure to include yourself (and your flash card) in the appropriate place in the lineup.

STEP 4   Once you think you have all the codon cards laid out in the correct order, check to see if you were right. Turn them over (in order), and review the words for which they code. If your sentence makes sense, you have successfully coded for a protein! If your sentence has gaps, or the words seem out of place, check your codon sequence and try again.

Write your finished sentence here:

Name: _____   Date: _____

EXERCISE 10 PROTEIN SYNTHESIS

Work with a partner to complete this exercise and answer the questions that follow. You will use the DNA strand from Exercise 8 to make the protein for which it codes.

STEP 1 Review the imaginary strand of DNA below. Note the complementary base pairs.

A G C A A T C C G T C T T G G
T C G T T A G G C A G A A C C

STEP 2 Draw the DNA strand separating down the middle (as in the beginning of DNA replication).

STEP 3 Draw the free-floating RNA bases linking up with the *top side* of the DNA strand. (Remember, in protein synthesis, only one side of the DNA strand is used.) Be sure to follow the rules of complementary base pairing and to account for the special RNA base, uracil.

STEP 4 Draw the new mRNA strand *and* the rezipped DNA strand. Indicate which strand stays in the nucleus *and* which strand moves to the ribosome.

STEP 5 Draw the free-floating tRNA anticodons attracted by the mRNA codons in the ribosome. Be sure to follow the rules of complementary base pairing.

STEP 6 Review the mRNA codons and tRNA anticodons in your drawing above. Remember, each tRNA anticodon will bring a specific amino acid, as indicated by the mRNA codon sequence. Use the mRNA codons and the amino acid table below to write the amino acid sequence for this RNA strand in the space provided.

AMINO ACIDS BY mRNA CODON

		Second Base in Codon			
	U	**C**	**A**	**G**	
U	UUU...Phenylalanine	UCU...Serine	UAU...Tryosine	UGU...Cysteine	U
	UUC...Phenylalanine	UCC...Serine	UAC...Tryosine	UGC...Cysteine	C
	UUA...Leucine	UCA...Serine	UAA...Stop codon	UGA...Stop codon	A
	UUG...Leucine	UCG...Serine	UAG...Stop codon	UGG...Tryptophan	G
C	CUU...Leucine	CCU...Proline	CAU...Histidine	CGU...Arginine	U
	CUC...Leucine	CCC...Proline	CAC...Histidine	CGC...Arginine	C
	CUA...Leucine	CCA...Proline	CAA...Glutamine	CGA...Arginine	A
	CUG...Leucine	CCG...Proline	CAG...Glutamine	CGG...Arginine	G
A	AUU...Isoleucine	ACU...Threonine	AAU...Asparagine	AGU...Serine	U
	AUC...Isoleucine	ACC...Threonine	AAC...Asparagine	AGC...Serine	C
	AUA...Isoleucine	ACA...Threonine	AAA...Lysine	AGA...Arginine	A
	AUG...Methionine; Start codon	ACG...Threonine	AAG...Lysine	AGG...Arginine	G
G	GUU...Valine	GCU...Alanine	GAU...Aspartate	GGU...Glycine	U
	GUC...Valine	GCC...Alanine	GAC...Aspartate	GGC...Glycine	C
	GUA...Valine	GCA...Alanine	GAA...Glutamate	GGA...Glycine	A
	GUG...Valine	GCG...Alanine	GAG...Glutamate	GGG...Glycine	G

First Base in Codon (left) / *Third Base in Codon* (right)

1. Which steps in this exercise re-created the transcription stage of protein synthesis?

2. Which steps in this exercise re-created the translation stage of protein synthesis?

3. Why is it necessary for RNA to be involved in protein synthesis? In other words, why is DNA unable to synthesize proteins on its own?

CRITICAL THINKING QUESTIONS

On a separate sheet of paper, answer the following questions.

1. You have learned that humans have a total of 46 chromosomes and that chimpanzees have a total of 48 chromosomes. Use other textbooks in biological anthropology and biology (or reputable online resources) to find the number of chromosomes in other organisms. Give an organism with considerably more chromosomes than humans. Give an organism with considerably fewer chromosomes than humans. Did your findings surprise you? What did your research suggest about the relationship between chromosome number and organism complexity?

2. Why aren't the X and Y chromosomes considered true homologous partners like the autosomes?

3. What do you think might happen if a person had two X chromosomes and one Y chromosome? Would this person be biologically male or female? What effect might this combination of sex chromosomes have on the person's physical body?

4. Why is it important that mitosis result in daughter cells that contain exact copies of the original cell's 46 chromosomes? Why is it important that meiosis result in daughter cells that have half of the original cell's chromosomes?

5. How are RNA and DNA similar? How are they different?

6. In this lab, we explored how genetic information is translated into proteins in our bodies. However, recent research in a field called *epigenetics* shows that genetic information may be activated and deactivated throughout a person's lifetime. Consider the DNA strand you reviewed in Exercise 9 to form a sentence. Imagine that the second and third codons and the seventh and eighth codons were specifically activated while the others were turned off. What would this new genetic information (sentence) be? Has its meaning been changed? How might epigenetic factors like this affect real-life protein synthesis and the expression of our genes?

7. Describe the difference between the transcription step and the translation step in protein synthesis.

8. Repeat Exercises 8 and 10, using the following DNA strand:

   C G T T A A C T G A C G G A C
   G C A A T T G A C T G C C T G

Courtesy of Teresa Soluri

Courtesy of Sabrina Agarwal

Family members often resemble one another and share physical features. These photos show author Soluri with her sister, father, and brother (*left*) and author Agarwal with her mother (*right*).

Lab Learning Objectives

By the end of this lab, students should be able to:

- describe the work of Gregor Mendel, including the types of data he collected and the laws derived from this research (the law of segregation and the law of independent assortment).

- describe the relationship between dominant and recessive alleles and the relationship between genotypes and phenotypes for traits.

- draw and interpret Punnett squares and pedigree diagrams.

- differentiate Mendelian and polygenic traits using examples from humans.

- discuss the complexities of inheritance exemplified by sex-linked traits and the ABO blood group in humans.

LAB 3

Inheritance

All her life, Dr. Soluri—one of the authors of this text—has been told that she has her father's eyes. When she looks at pictures of herself standing next to her father and siblings, the similarities in their features do appear pronounced. The same is true for Dr. Agarwal—the other author of this text—who bears a strong resemblance to her mother. Is this resemblance an optical illusion? Do people see familial similarities only because they have been told for so long that they exist? Or do people really share some physical traits with members of their families? If we share traits with our parents, how does this come to be? And why do siblings sometimes have the same traits? This lab touches on these issues, allowing us to answer some of these questions and explore larger issues of population changes over time.

INTRODUCTION

In this lab, we begin with the early research on inheritance—the passing of traits from one generation to the next—conducted by Gregor Mendel. We then consider the relationship between dominant alleles and recessive

Gregor Mendel a European monk who conducted tests on pea plants and identified two important principles of classification

law of segregation law stating that the units (or genes) for traits appear separately in the (sex cells of) parents and are then reunited in an offspring

alleles and the relationship between genotypes and phenotypes. We also discuss different ways of representing inheritance using Punnett squares and pedigree diagrams. We distinguish between Mendelian and polygenic traits using examples of these traits in humans, and we explore the patterns of inheritance for sex-linked traits. We conclude with a look at the ABO blood group in humans as an example of how issues of inheritance play out in real life.

GREGOR MENDEL

In the mid-1800s, an Augustinian friar named **Gregor Mendel** conducted a series of tests in a monastery located in the present-day Czech Republic. He crossbred pea plants in the monastery garden and tracked the expression of different characteristics across multiple generations. The traits he studied included flower color, plant height, and pea color (**FIGURE 3.1**). For each of these traits, he identified two possible forms: flowers were purple or white; plants

were tall or short; peas were yellow or green. He noticed that there were regular outcomes when plants with different traits were bred. This observation allowed him to identify two key principles.

The first of Mendel's principles is the **law of segregation**. Many people assumed that traits from two parents were blended in their offspring. This would mean that if a tall pea plant and a short pea plant were bred, we would expect their offspring plants to have an intermediate height. However, Mendel recognized that this was not the case. Most of the offspring plants he observed were, in fact, tall plants. Mendel interpreted this to mean that traits are controlled by distinct units of inheritance. These units occur in pairs, with one inherited from the mother and one inherited from the father. This means that the units for traits (what we now know as *genes*) appear separately in the sex cells of the parents and are brought together in the offspring.

The law of segregation explains why genes from two homologous chromosomes are equally likely to be passed on. Imagine a pea plant that

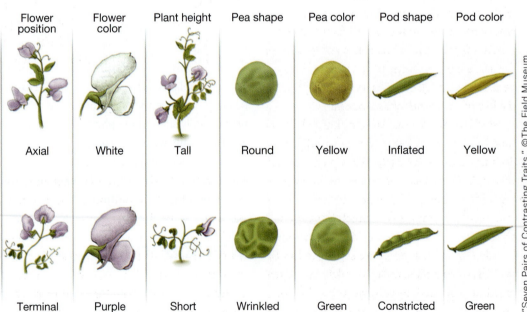

Flower position	Flower color	Plant height	Pea shape	Pea color	Pod shape	Pod color
Axial	White	Tall	Round	Yellow	Inflated	Yellow
Terminal	Purple	Short	Wrinkled	Green	Constricted	Green

"Seven Pairs of Contrasting Traits." ©The Field Museum, Illustration by Greg Mercer. Reprinted with permission.

FIGURE 3.1 Mendel's Pea Plant Traits
Gregor Mendel studied traits in pea plants such as those illustrated here. Through this work, he identified two important principles of inheritance.

has two versions of the gene for plant height: the tall version inherited from one parent and the short version from the other parent. When this pea plant undergoes meiosis and forms gametes, half of those gametes will include the tall variant and half will include the short variant. Which gamete then becomes the next-generation pea plant is random, so the inheritance of tallness or shortness is equally likely. As Mendel suggested, the variants for plant height are separate entities in separate parental gametes; they then come together as part of the homologous pair in an offspring and become separated again when that offspring makes gametes for the next generation. This segregation and reunification occurs over and over from one generation to the next.

The second principle is the **law of independent assortment**. Mendel noticed that pea plant traits were often inherited separately from one another; for example, not all tall plants had yellow seeds. This meant that the units for these traits were sorting independently of one another in the offspring. Today, we understand that this sorting occurs during meiosis. When gametes are formed, the alleles for one trait segregate into the daughter cells independently of the alleles for another trait. This is particularly the case with genes found on different chromosomes. In contrast, when genes are located on the same chromosome, they are more likely to be inherited together and serve as exceptions to the law of independent assortment.

Mendel's work was largely ignored at the time of its publication. It was not until several decades later, in the early 1900s, that his work was rediscovered and integrated with the growing understanding of genetics. Today, we know that genes control traits in much the same way as the units of inheritance Mendel theorized. We also know that genes are segregated in the sex cells during meiosis, as Mendel's law of segregation suggested. Finally, we know that Mendel's law of independent assortment is accurate. If the genes for traits are found on different, nonhomologous chromosomes, they will be independently sorted during meiosis when the nonhomologous chromosomes move to the new cells.

DOMINANCE AND RECESSIVENESS

When conducting his pea plant tests, Mendel noticed that some versions of a trait were more likely to appear in the next generation than others. For example, when he mated a purple-flowered plant and a white-flowered plant, most of the offspring plants had purple flowers. Mendel had discovered that some versions of the traits were **dominant**, while other versions were **recessive**. When we combine his observations with our understanding of genetics today, we recognize that some alleles (alternative forms of a gene) are dominant over other alleles. This does not mean that the dominant alleles are better, stronger, or more common in the population. It simply means that the dominant alleles mask the effects of the recessive alleles. For example, the tall allele is dominant over the short allele in pea plants. The presence of a tall allele will automatically mask a short allele because tallness will manifest itself and obscure shortness. This means that even if you have a pea plant that has one tall allele and one short allele, the plant will look like a tall plant.

GENOTYPE AND PHENOTYPE

This relationship between dominant and recessive alleles highlights an important distinction between the level of genetic makeup and the level of gene expression. An organism's actual genetic material (the alleles it carries) is considered its **genotype**. This genotype is written in a way that indicates the dominant or recessive alleles present. Let's return to our short and tall pea plants. The dominant allele is for tallness, so it will be represented by a *T* in our example. The recessive allele is for shortness, so it will be

law of independent assortment law stating that the units (or genes) for different traits are sorted (and passed on) independently of one another

dominant a dominant allele masks the effects of other alleles for a trait; may also be used in reference to dominant traits or dominant phenotypes

recessive a recessive allele is masked by a dominant allele for a trait; may also be used in reference to recessive traits or recessive phenotypes

genotype the specific alleles an organism has for a trait

homozygous dominant an organism's genotype for a trait when it has two dominant alleles for the trait (such as *RR*)

homozygous recessive an organism's genotype for a trait when it has two recessive alleles for the trait (such as *rr*)

heterozygous an organism's genotype for a trait when it has one dominant allele and one recessive allele for the trait (such as *Rr*)

phenotype the physical expression of an organism's genotype for a trait

Punnett square the method of diagramming inheritance where parental genotypes are used to estimate the probability of various genotypes in a potential offspring

represented by a *t* in our example. Remember, one allele will be inherited from the mother and one from the father. Therefore, each plant should have two alleles for plant height. If a plant has two dominant alleles for the trait, its genotype is written as *TT*, indicating each of the dominant alleles present. This plant is considered to be **homozygous dominant** for the trait because it has two of the same dominant allele. If a plant has two recessive alleles, its genotype is *tt*. This plant is considered to be **homozygous recessive** for the trait because it has two of the same recessive allele. If a plant has one dominant allele and one recessive allele, its genotype is *Tt*. This plant is considered to be **heterozygous** for the trait because it has a mix of alleles (one of each variant).

These same rules for writing genotypes apply to other traits as well: a capital letter indicates the dominant allele and a lowercase letter indicates the recessive allele. Whenever possible, the same letter is used for both alleles. That letter is usually the first letter of the dominant version of the trait, such as *T* for the tallness trait in pea plants. However, because some letters look similar in their capitalized and lowercase forms, they are avoided when possible. For example, the letter *M* is often avoided when writing genotypes.

The genotype represents the molecular level of an organism's genetic makeup, but the physical expression of this genetic material happens at a different level. The actual expression of an organism's genetic material is its **phenotype**. For our tall and short pea plants, there are two possible phenotypes: the dominant phenotype (tall) and the recessive phenotype (short). The homozygous dominant plant will have the dominant phenotype (tall) because it has only dominant alleles to be expressed. The heterozygous plant will also have the dominant phenotype (tall) because the expression of the recessive allele is masked by the dominant allele. The homozygous recessive plant will be the only plant that actually has the recessive phenotype (short) because it is the only plant that lacks the dominant allele.

If you know an organism's genotype for a trait, you can determine its phenotype for that trait, as we did with the tall and short pea plants. It is a bit more difficult to infer genotype from phenotype. If you have an organism with the recessive phenotype, you can be confident that it has the homozygous recessive genotype. However, if you have an organism with the dominant phenotype, the organism could have the homozygous dominant genotype or the heterozygous genotype for the trait. Determining the genotype in these situations requires more information about the organism's relatives, as we will see when we discuss pedigree diagrams below.

PUNNETT SQUARES

There are two possible ways to diagram inheritance. The first is the **Punnett square**, which was devised in the early 1900s by a British biologist named Reginald Punnett. The Punnett square diagrams the possible genotypic outcomes for the mating of two organisms. The diagram consists of a square divided into boxes. One parent's genotype is written above the boxes, and the other parent's genotype is written to the left of the boxes. The boxes are then filled in with the possible allele combinations for an offspring. For example, in the Punnett square shown in **FIGURE 3.2**, one pea plant parent is homozygous dominant (*TT*) for plant height. The other pea plant parent is heterozygous (*Tt*) for the trait. The four boxes indicate the four possible genotypes for one of their offspring. In the box at the top left, there are two dominant alleles, one from each parent. The same is true for the box at the top right. In the box at the bottom left, there is one dominant allele from one parent and one recessive allele from the other parent. The box at the bottom right has the same possible genotype. This means there is a 50% chance the offspring would be homozygous dominant for the trait and a 50% chance the offspring would be heterozygous.

This example shows Mendel's law of segregation in action. Notice that the heterozygous

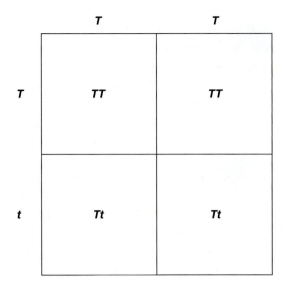

FIGURE 3.2 Punnett Square for Plant Height in Pea Plants
If a homozygous dominant individual (*TT*) mates with a heterozygous individual (*Tt*), there is a 50% chance they will have an offspring that is homozygous dominant (*TT*) and a 50% chance they will have an offspring that is heterozygous (*Tt*).

parent has a 50% chance of passing on its recessive (*t*) allele and an equally likely 50% chance of passing on its dominant (*T*) allele. When its gametes are formed in meiosis, half will have the recessive allele and half will have the dominant allele. Which gamete (and corresponding allele) becomes an offspring is random. Therefore, dominant alleles are not more likely to be inherited and are not necessarily more common in a population.

Punnett squares show genotypes, but you can use this information to determine phenotypes as well. In the example given, both parents have the dominant phenotype. Based on the genotype possibilities for their offspring, we can also say that there is a 100% chance the offspring will have the dominant phenotype.

It is important to remember that the Punnett square is showing you possible outcomes for one mating. It is not showing what outcome would happen if the parents had further offspring. However, the Punnett square (and corresponding outcome chances) would be the same for each separate mating. In the example in Figure 3.2, each time the parents mate, there is a 50% chance of a homozygous dominant offspring and a 50% chance of a heterozygous offspring. Even if the parents have four offspring, they could all be homozygous dominant for the trait because the chances are the same for each separate mating.

PEDIGREE DIAGRAMS

Another way of representing inheritance is through a **pedigree diagram**. Pedigree diagrams show multiple generations of real, related organisms. They are therefore different from the Punnett square, which shows only one real generation (the parents) and one potential generation (the possibilities for a single offspring). In addition, pedigree diagrams show phenotypes for a trait, rather than genotypes. While genotypes can be inferred from this information, we cannot always be 100% confident in those inferences.

Pedigree diagrams use several symbols to represent the real individuals involved. Squares are used to represent males. Circles are used to represent females. Mated pairs (parents) are linked by a horizontal line between their symbols. Offspring are then drawn as descending from their parents' mated pair. When the shape representing an individual is shaded (colored in), the individual expresses the trait in question. When the shape is left uncolored, the individual does not express the trait in question. Either dominant or recessive traits may be shaded in the diagram, depending on what trait is represented. For example, in a pedigree diagram for freckles on the face, a dominant trait in humans, individuals who have freckles (the dominant phenotype) are represented by shaded shapes. In a diagram for attached earlobes, a recessive trait, individuals who have lower earlobes that attach to the side of the head (the recessive phenotype) are represented by shaded shapes.

pedigree diagram
the method of diagramming inheritance that shows the phenotypes of individuals from multiple generations in a family

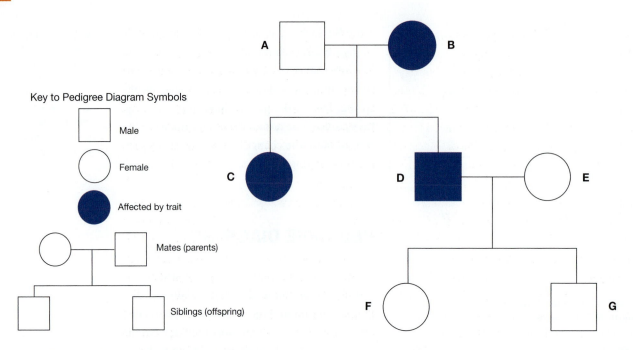

FIGURE 3.3 Pedigree Diagram for Freckles in Humans
As seen in the Key to Pedigree Diagram Symbols (*left*), squares represent males, and circles represent females. Shapes that are colored in reflect individuals who are affected by (or express) the trait of interest. Shapes that are uncolored reflect individuals who are not affected by (or do not express) the trait. In the sample pedigree (*right*), person E is a female who does not express the trait and has the recessive phenotype (no freckles).

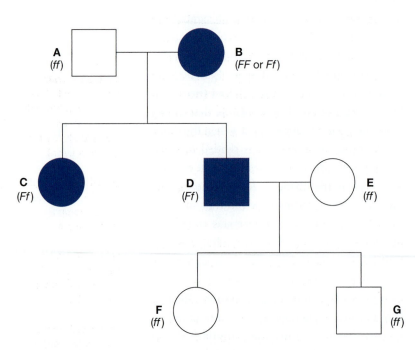

FIGURE 3.4 Pedigree Diagram for Freckles in Humans with Genotypes Added
In this version of the pedigree diagram from Figure 3.3, the genotypes of the individuals, as inferred from their phenotypes, have been added. Note that in some cases, only one genotype is possible, but in other cases, multiple genotypes are possible.

In the sample pedigree diagram in **FIGURE 3.3**, individuals A, D, and G are male. Individuals B, C, E, and F are female. Individuals A and B mated and had two offspring (individuals C and D). Individual D mated with individual E, and they had two offspring (individuals F and G). This sample pedigree diagram shows a human family and its phenotypes for the freckles trait. In humans, having freckles is dominant over not having freckles, so the shaded individuals express freckles (in this case, the dominant phenotype). Individuals B, C, and D have the dominant phenotype, and individuals A, E, F, and G have the recessive phenotype.

Even though pedigree diagrams do not directly show genotypes, we can infer genotypes from the information found in the diagrams. In our sample pedigree, we can confidently say that individuals A, E, F, and G all have the homozygous recessive genotype (*ff*) for freckles because they all have the recessive phenotype (**FIGURE 3.4**). The only way an individual can have the recessive phenotype is if they have the homozygous recessive genotype.

Determining the genotype for the other individuals is more challenging. First, individual C must have the heterozygous genotype (*Ff*) because she has a homozygous recessive father. This father would have passed on a recessive allele to individual C. Because individual C has the dominant phenotype, we know she must also have at least one dominant allele. Therefore, we know individual C is heterozygous because she has one recessive allele from her father and one dominant allele from her mother (see Figure 3.4). Second, because individual D is individual C's brother, the same line of thinking can be used to determine that individual D is also heterozygous (*Ff*) for the trait. Even if we did not know about individual D's parents, we could still use the information about his offspring to come to the same conclusion. Individual D must be heterozygous for the trait because he has homozygous recessive offspring. This indicates that he has a recessive allele in his genotype that was passed on to his offspring. Finally, individual B presents an interesting challenge. Even using the information we have about her offspring, we cannot be sure if individual B is homozygous dominant (*FF*) or heterozygous (*Ff*). Either genotype, when mated with individual A (who is homozygous recessive), could result in the offspring genotypes and phenotypes already determined.

MENDELIAN TRAITS AND POLYGENIC TRAITS

Generally, there are two kinds of traits in humans: Mendelian traits and polygenic traits. **Mendelian traits** are traits that are controlled by one gene. There may be multiple alleles for the gene, but only one **genetic locus** (location of a gene on a chromosome) is involved. For this reason, Mendelian traits are sometimes said to follow a "simple" pattern of inheritance. Humans have some Mendelian traits. For example, attachment of the lower earlobe to the side of the head is a Mendelian trait. The unattached earlobe allele is dominant, and the attached earlobe allele is recessive. Another Mendelian trait in humans is the hitchhiker's thumb. The non-hitchhiker's thumb allele is dominant, and the hitchhiker's thumb allele is recessive. Freckles, as we've seen, are also inherited in Mendelian fashion: freckles are dominant, and the lack of freckles is recessive. The table on the following page depicts some of the Mendelian traits found in humans.

While humans certainly have some Mendelian traits, most of our traits are **polygenic traits**. Polygenic traits are controlled by alleles at multiple genetic loci. Often many genes are involved, and their phenotypic expression is complex (more like a continuum of expression). Human stature (or height) is a good example of this. We do not have just "short" or "tall" people in any given population. Rather, there is a continuum of different heights ranging from short to tall. Skin color, hair color, and eye color are other examples of polygenic traits in humans.

SEX-LINKED TRAITS

So far, we have focused on traits and genes located on the autosomes, but the sex chromosomes also carry important genetic material. Traits that are determined by genes on the sex chromosomes are called **sex-linked traits**, and they have unusual patterns of inheritance and physical expression. As noted in Lab 2, the X and Y chromosomes have key differences in the genes they each carry. The Y chromosome has a limited number of genes, and they are largely tied to traits related to maleness. The X chromosome has many more genes that are important for both males and females. In XX females, two copies of the X chromosome (and any associated genes) are present, so X-linked traits follow the same patterns described for Mendelian traits in general. In XY males, however, only one copy of the X chromosome (and its genes) is present, which may cause unusual patterns of phenotypic expression.

In most Mendelian traits, an individual has two copies of the gene, allowing for the homozygous and heterozygous genotypes previously

Mendelian trait a trait controlled by one gene (although there may be multiple alleles for that one gene)

genetic locus (loci, plural) the location of a gene on a chromosome

polygenic trait a trait controlled by alleles at multiple genetic loci

sex-linked trait a trait coded for by a gene on the X or Y chromosome (although typically used to refer to traits on the X chromosome)

MENDELIAN TRAITS IN HUMANS

Trait	Dominant		Recessive	
Hitchhiker's Thumb	Straight (*S*)	K. Elizabeth Soluri	Hitchhiker (*s*)	K. Elizabeth Soluri
Cleft Chin	Cleft (*C*)	Dean Clarke/Shutterstock	Smooth (*c*)	sirtravelalot/Shutterstock
Freckles	Freckles (*F*)	UfaBizPhoto/Shutterstock	No Freckles (*f*)	Simon Annable/Shutterstock
Attached Earlobes	Unattached (*U*)	Tatjana Romanova/Shutterstock	Attached (*u*)	NADA GIRL/Shutterstock
Widow's Peak	Widow's peak (*W*)	MRAORAOR/Shutterstock	Straight (*w*)	OJO Images Ltd/Alamy Stock Photo

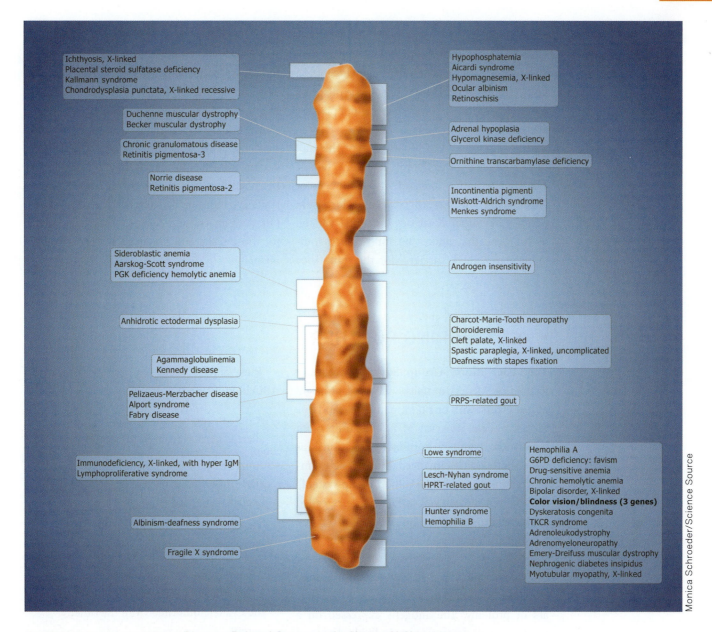

Ichthyosis, X-linked
Placental steroid sulfatase deficiency
Kallmann syndrome
Chondrodysplasia punctata, X-linked recessive

Duchenne muscular dystrophy
Becker muscular dystrophy

Chronic granulomatous disease
Retinitis pigmentosa-3

Norrie disease
Retinitis pigmentosa-2

Sideroblastic anemia
Aarskog-Scott syndrome
PGK deficiency hemolytic anemia

Anhidrotic ectodermal dysplasia

Agammaglobulinemia
Kennedy disease

Pelizaeus-Merzbacher disease
Alport syndrome
Fabry disease

Immunodeficiency, X-linked, with hyper IgM
Lymphoproliferative syndrome

Albinism-deafness syndrome

Fragile X syndrome

Hypophosphatemia
Aicardi syndrome
Hypomagnesemia, X-linked
Ocular albinism
Retinoschisis

Adrenal hypoplasia
Glycerol kinase deficiency

Ornithine transcarbamylase deficiency

Incontinentia pigmenti
Wiskott-Aldrich syndrome
Menkes syndrome

Androgen insensitivity

Charcot-Marie-Tooth neuropathy
Choroideremia
Cleft palate, X-linked
Spastic paraplegia, X-linked, uncomplicated
Deafness with stapes fixation

PRPS-related gout

Lowe syndrome

Lesch-Nyhan syndrome
HPRT-related gout

Hunter syndrome
Hemophilia B

Hemophilia A
G6PD deficiency: favism
Drug-sensitive anemia
Chronic hemolytic anemia
Bipolar disorder, X-linked
Color vision/blindness (3 genes)
Dyskeratosis congenita
TKCR syndrome
Adrenoleukodystrophy
Adrenomyeloneuropathy
Emery-Dreifuss muscular dystrophy
Nephrogenic diabetes insipidus
Myotubular myopathy, X-linked

Monica Schroeder/Science Source

FIGURE 3.5 Location of Some Disease-Related Genes on the Human X Chromosome
The X chromosome has genes for many traits that are not found on the Y chromosome. These X-linked traits are more likely to be expressed in XY males, but both males and females may have and pass on these genes to their offspring.

discussed. However, an XY male who has an unusual X-linked trait on his X chromosome will have no alternative allele on a second X chromosome to compensate for it. Therefore, whatever allele appears at the genetic level on the X chromosome will appear on the phenotypic level in the individual's body. In contrast, an XX female with an unusual allele on one X has another allele on her other X to make up for it. The unusual trait variant is less likely to be expressed in her than in an XY male with the same allele.

The X chromosome has many genes, so numerous traits are X-linked (**FIGURE 3.5**). A classic example is color vision. Humans, like many of our close primate relatives, have tricolor vision that is determined by three separate genes on the X chromosome. If an XY male has an alternative form of one of these genes, it may affect his ability to perceive certain colors, resulting in a condition known as **color blindness**. It is estimated that approximately 5%–8% of males worldwide have the most common form of

color blindness
limited perception of certain colors, which may be the result of variation in the alleles for color vision

color blindness (red-green color blindness). A male that has a color blindness allele may then pass it on to his female offspring who inherit his X chromosome. However, his male offspring inherit his Y chromosome, so he cannot pass the allele to them.

The expression and inheritance of the trait in females is a bit different. If an XX female has an alternative form of one of the color vision genes, she may still have full color vision because her other X carries a normal version of the gene that makes up for it. Such individuals are called "carriers" for the trait. They carry the allele and may pass it on should that X chromosome be inherited by offspring, but they do not express the trait themselves. They may not even know they carry the allele at all. It is possible for XX females to be color blind, but it is very rare, because they would need the same unusual allele on both of their X chromosomes to manifest color blindness at the phenotypic level. For this reason, X-linked traits are more likely to be expressed in males, but both males and females may have alleles for those traits and may pass them on to their offspring.

▶▶▶ EXPLORING FURTHER

The ABO Blood Group System We have focused on Mendelian traits, such as plant height in pea plants, with one dominant allele and one recessive allele. However, Mendelian traits often have more complex dominance relationships between the alleles involved. The classic example in humans is the ABO blood group system.

Different types of cell surface markers, called **antigens**, are found on the surfaces of our red blood cells. In general, an antigen is any substance (such as a bacterium or enzyme, or fragments thereof) that triggers an immune response. Blood group antigens are either sugars or proteins. The antigens expressed on a red blood cell determine an individual's blood type. The main two blood groups are called ABO (with blood types A, B, AB, and O) and Rh (with Rh-positive and Rh-negative blood types). In the ABO blood group system there are two antigens: antigen A and antigen B **(FIGURE 3.6A)**. We know that the A and B blood antigens are sugars, but not much is known about their function in the body today or in our evolutionary past.

The alleles for these antigens are found at one genetic locus, which means that ABO blood type is a Mendelian trait. A person can inherit the A antigen allele, the B antigen allele, or the O allele (which is expressed as having neither antigen on the blood cell surface).

These alleles make six genotypes for the ABO blood system possible:

- A person can be *AA*, with the A antigen allele inherited from both parents.

- A person can be *AO*, with the A antigen allele inherited from one parent and the O allele inherited from the other parent.

- A person can be *BB*, with the B antigen allele inherited from both parents.

- A person can be *BO*, with the B antigen allele inherited from one parent and the O allele inherited from the other parent.

- A person can be *AB*, with the A antigen allele inherited from one parent and the B antigen allele inherited from the other parent.

- A person can be *OO*, with the O allele inherited from both parents.

Interestingly, there are only four corresponding phenotypes or blood types:

- People with the *AA* genotype and the *AO* genotype have A antigens on their red blood cells, giving them blood type A as their phenotype.

antigen (in ABO blood group system) the cell surface marker found on red blood cells that relates to an individual's ABO blood type and triggers antibody reactions to a foreign blood antigen

- People with the *BB* and *BO* genotypes have B antigens on their red blood cells, giving them blood type B as their phenotype.

- People with the *AB* genotype have both A antigens and B antigens on their red blood cells, giving them blood type AB as their phenotype.

- People with the *OO* genotype do not have either type of antigen on their red blood cells, giving them blood type O as their phenotype.

This discrepancy in the number of possible genotypes and phenotypes suggests that the ABO blood group system has a complex pattern of dominance and recessiveness. The A antigen allele is dominant over the O allele. The O allele does not result in antigens, but the presence of the A allele in a heterozygous individual results in the production of the A antigens, giving *AO* individuals the A blood phenotype. The B antigen allele is also dominant over the O allele, with *BO* individuals having the B blood phenotype. The only individuals with a true O blood type are homozygous for the O allele, further suggesting that the O allele is recessive. The relationship between the A antigen allele and B antigen allele is particularly interesting. These two alleles are what we call **codominant**. When the two alleles appear together, as in *AB* individuals, both alleles are expressed in the phenotype. One is not dominant over the other; they are equally dominant. Therefore, when documenting genotypes in codominant traits like human ABO blood type, letters for both alleles are used (*A* and *B*), rather than the same letter in uppercase and lowercase (*A* and *a*).

While much of the function of these red blood cell antigens is still unknown, we do know that exposure to foreign blood antigens triggers a dangerous response from the immune system that can be fatal. The body differentiates between its normal antigens (self-antigens) and foreign antigens. Many foreign antigens, such as bacteria, trigger a protective reaction from the immune system. The body produces **antibodies**, which are special proteins that attack the antigens directly or mark them for attack by other parts of the immune system. This process allows the body to neutralize and fight off infections. In the case of the blood cell surface antigens, the body identifies any foreign blood antigens and produces antibodies to combat them **(FIGURE 3.6B)**. The antibodies attach to the antigens and cause the blood cells to clump together. The coagulated blood does not travel smoothly through the blood vessels, and the body cannot get the blood and oxygen it needs. This condition can result in death.

Because of the antibody response to foreign blood antigens, it is essential that we know an individual's blood genotype and phenotype to choose compatible blood for transfusions. Individuals who have blood type A can receive blood

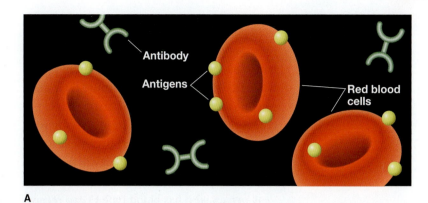

A

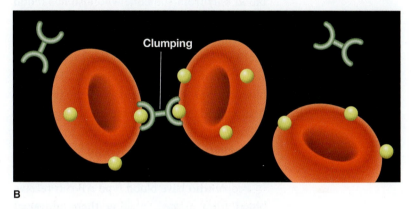

B

FIGURE 3.6 ABO Blood Antigens and Antibodies
(A) The A and B blood antigens are found on the surfaces of red blood cells. When foreign blood antigens are introduced into the body via the transfusion of incompatible blood, antibodies are produced. (B) The antibodies attach to the antigens and cause the blood cells to clump, which can restrict blood flow.

codominant circumstance where multiple alleles are expressed in the phenotype, without one being clearly dominant over the other

antibody a protein that attacks antigens directly or marks them for attack by other parts of the immune system

from people who also have blood type A because their antigens are the same. Individuals who have blood type B can receive blood from people who also have blood type B because their antigens are the same. However, a person with blood type A cannot receive blood from a person with blood type B (and vice versa) because it introduces foreign blood antigens that will trigger an immune response.

A person who has blood type O can receive blood only from someone who also has blood type O. Someone with blood type O doesn't have either type of antigen, so both the A and the B antigens will be considered foreign and will trigger an immune response. However, blood type O is considered to be the universal donor blood. It doesn't have either antigen, so it will not introduce a foreign antigen to the body of a recipient. Anyone can receive blood from a person with blood type O.

People who have blood type AB can receive blood from anyone, making them universal recipients. A person with blood type AB can receive blood from someone else who also has blood type AB, but can also receive blood from someone who has blood type A or someone who has blood type B. Because the A antigen allele and the B antigen allele are codominant, people with blood type AB have both types of antigens in their bodies. When type A blood is introduced, it is accepted, because the A antigen is already present. The same is true for the introduction of type B blood. The introduction of type O blood is also successful because it does not have any antigens that cause clumping.

The complex relationships of dominance and recessiveness among these different antigen alleles create a complicated picture of blood group genotypes and phenotypes, and these genotypes and phenotypes must be understood in order to successfully transfuse blood. Because transfusion reactions can also be triggered by antibody responses to other blood components (such as Rh factor), blood donations are now carefully screened before they are given to recipients to reduce the risk of incompatibility complications. Transfusion patients are also closely monitored for signs of other reactions, such as allergic responses to donated blood, so they can be treated as needed. Interestingly, the ABO blood type alleles seem to have unusual distributions across populations worldwide. We will return to this observation in Lab 8 when we discuss human variation.

CONCEPT REVIEW QUESTIONS

Name: _____ Section: _____

Course: _____ Date: _____

Answer the following questions in the space provided.

1. Name two pea plant traits studied by Gregor Mendel.

2. Define genotype.

3. Define phenotype.

4. Why would a pea plant that is heterozygous for plant height have the dominant phenotype?

5. A pea plant with the recessive phenotype for plant height would have which of the following genotypes?
   A. *TT*
   B. *tt*
   C. *Tt*
   D. *TT* or *Tt*

6. What is the difference between a Mendelian trait and a polygenic trait?

7. Why are females more likely to be carriers for color blindness than to be color blind themselves?

8. Which of the following is a polygenic trait in humans?
   A. Hitchhiker's thumb
   B. Earlobe attachment
   C. Skin color
   D. Freckles

9. In the ABO blood group system, what is/are the possible genotype(s) for a person who has blood type A?

10. In the ABO blood group system, what is/are the possible genotype(s) for a person who has blood type O?

LAB EXERCISES

Name: _____   Section: _____

Course: _____   Date: _____

EXERCISE 1 CREATING PUNNETT SQUARES

Work in a small group or alone to complete this exercise. Trait *F* is the Mendelian trait for freckles. The allele for freckles (*F*) is dominant over the allele for no freckles (*f*).

- Timmy is homozygous dominant for freckles.
- Timmy mates with Sally, who is heterozygous for freckles.
- Timmy's father *and* Timmy's mother are *both* heterozygous for freckles.
- Timmy's maternal grandmother (mother's mother) is homozygous recessive for freckles.
- Timmy's maternal grandfather (mother's father) is homozygous dominant for freckles.

Use the information provided to complete the three separate Punnett squares below.

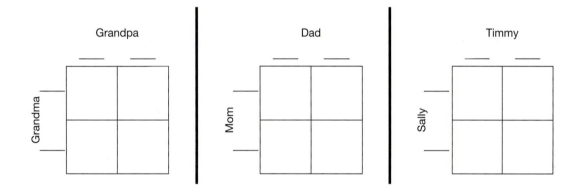

EXERCISE 2 CREATING PEDIGREE DIAGRAMS

Working in a small group or alone, review the information about Timmy's family from Exercise 1. Use this information to create a pedigree diagram for the freckles trait in his family. Be sure to include all three generations and all six people described. Use the space below.

EXERCISE 3   INTERPRETING PUNNETT SQUARES

Work in a small group or alone to complete this exercise. The Punnett square below shows the genotypes of two parents for trait R. Trait R is the Mendelian trait in humans for tongue rolling. The allele for the ability to roll the tongue (R) is dominant over the allele for the inability to roll the tongue (r).

Mom

	R	**r**
R	**RR**	**Rr**
r	**Rr**	**rr**

Dad

1. According to the Punnett square above, what is the mother's genotype? _____

2. What is the mother's phenotype? _____

3. What is the father's genotype? _____

4. What is the father's phenotype? _____

5. What is the likelihood of their daughter Maria having each of the possible genotypes and phenotypes?

   _RR:_ _____

   _Rr:_ _____

   _rr:_ _____

   Dominant phenotype (can roll tongue): _____

   Recessive phenotype (cannot roll tongue): _____

6. Are you 100% sure of Maria's genotype? Why or why not?

7. Are you 100% sure of Maria's phenotype? Why or why not?

INTERPRETING PEDIGREE DIAGRAMS

Work in a small group or alone to complete this exercise using the pedigree diagram below for trait *R* in a family. Trait *R* is the Mendelian trait in humans for tongue rolling. The allele for the ability to roll the tongue (*R*) is dominant over the allele for the inability to roll the tongue (*r*).

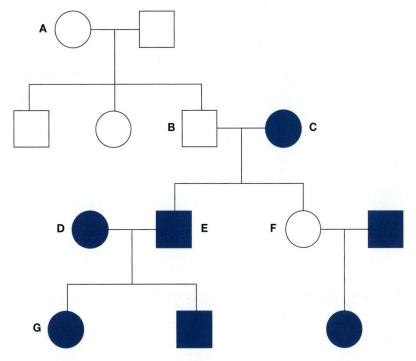

Complete the following chart using the pedigree diagram.

Person	Genotype	Phenotype
A		
B		
C		
D		
E		
F		
G		

1. Are you 100% sure of each person's phenotype? If not, which ones are problematic? Why?

2. Are you 100% sure of each person's genotype? If not, which ones are problematic? Why?

EXERCISE 5   MENDELIAN TRAITS IN HUMANS 1

While most human traits are polygenic, the traits in the chart below have traditionally been considered Mendelian traits. More recent research has disputed the single-gene nature of some of these traits, but for the purpose of this exercise, assume that the following traits are Mendelian.

Work with a partner to help each other determine your own phenotypes and possible genotypes for these traits. Write your answers in the chart. (*Note:* Refer to the table on p. 62 for information about these traits.)

Mendelian Trait	Your Phenotype	Your Possible Genotype(s)
Cleft Chin (Dominant)		
Freckles (Dominant)		
Attached Earlobes (Recessive)		
Hitchhiker's Thumb (Recessive)		
Widow's Peak (Dominant)		

EXERCISE 6   MENDELIAN TRAITS IN HUMANS 2

Some people can taste phenylthiocarbamide (PTC) and similar substances, but some people cannot. PTC tasting is a simple Mendelian trait in humans, where tasting (T) is dominant over nontasting (t).

Your instructor has distributed two taste strips: a control strip and a PTC strip.

STEP 1 Make sure to dispose of any candy, gum, or cough drops you may have in your mouth.

STEP 2 Differentiate the two taste strips by labeling them C (for control) and P (for PTC).

STEP 3 Touch the control strip to your tongue. Do not eat the strip. What do you taste? This is the taste of the paper, without any added substances.

STEP 4 Touch the PTC strip to your tongue. Do not eat the strip. What do you taste?

STEP 5 Discuss your results with several of your classmates. Based on your experience, answer the following questions.

   1. Are you a PTC taster? Do you have the dominant phenotype or the recessive phenotype?

   2. What is your possible genotype(s)?

   3. How do you compare with your classmates?

EXERCISE 7   USING THE SCIENTIFIC METHOD TO INVESTIGATE MENDELIAN TRAITS IN HUMANS

In this lab, we considered several Mendelian traits in humans, including the hitchhiker's thumb trait. We assumed that this trait follows typical Mendelian patterns and has two distinct phenotypic expressions. In this exercise, you will work alone or with a small group to apply the scientific method and test this assumption.

Existing hypothesis: *If the hitchhikers' thumb is a Mendelian trait, then there will be two distinct phenotypic expressions (hitchhiker's thumb and non-hitchhiker's thumb).*

STEP 1 Collect thumb angle data. Use a protractor to measure the angle of at least 10 different people's thumbs. Align the base of the protractor with the center line of the thumb (extending from the wrist through the base and second knuckle of the thumb) as shown in the diagram below. Make sure only one person does all the measuring so you avoid inter-observer error.

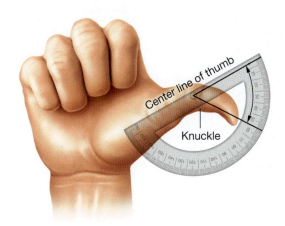

STEP 2 Tabulate the data. Enter your measurements (by individual) in the chart below. The first row has been completed as a demonstration. (If you measure more than 10 people's thumbs, use separate paper to compile the additional data.)

Individual's Name	Thumb Angle
Sasha	75°

STEP 3 Interpretation

1. Look for patterns in the data. Describe any patterns you find.

2. Based on the data you collected, is the hypothesis supported or rejected? Why?

STEP 4 Reflection

3. After investigating this trait more closely, what have you learned about variation in Mendelian traits?

4. Why might this variation exist?

EXERCISE 8   SEX-LINKED TRAITS

Work in a small group or alone to solve this "mating mystery." Then answer the questions that follow.

Mister Poppleton, a cat enthusiast who breeds cats and competes on the Cat Fancier's Association competitive show circuit, has just received quite a shock! His award-winning cat, Emeline, has given birth to some surprising kittens. Of her five kittens, four have black fur, and one has an unexpected coat of fur that is a patchwork of black and orange, known as a tortoiseshell pattern.

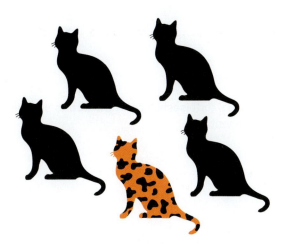

Mister Poppleton was breeding Emeline with an award-winning male cat, named Barnaby, but he is now worried that Emeline may have been having secret sexual relations with a neighborhood stray cat, named Hugo. Mister Poppleton consults with his veterinarian, Dr. Doolittle, for some expert advice.

Dr. Doolittle explains: In cats, there are several genes that determine fur color. One of those genes is found on the X chromosome and codes for whether a cat has orange fur or black fur. Because it is a sex-linked gene, it is expressed a bit differently in males than in females.

In males:

- If a male cat has the orange allele on his X chromosome, he will have orange fur.
- If a male cat has the black allele on his X chromosome, he will have black fur.

In females:

- If a female cat has the orange allele on both of her X chromosomes, she will have orange fur.
- If a female cat has the black allele on both of her X chromosomes, she will have black fur.
- If a female cat has the orange allele on one of her X chromosomes and the black allele on the other X chromosome, she will have a tortoiseshell coat.

With this information in mind, Mister Poppleton takes a closer look at Emeline and the possible fathers (Barnaby and Hugo) of her kittens. Emeline is a female cat with all-black fur. Barnaby is a male cat with all-black fur. Hugo is a male cat with all-orange fur.

1. Who is the father of these kittens? (*Note*: All of the kittens have the same father.) _____

2. How do you know this? Be sure to provide evidence from the scenario and from what you know about patterns of inheritance.

3. Why does only one kitten have the unusual tortoiseshell coat? Be sure to provide evidence from the scenario and what you know about patterns of inheritance.

EXERCISE 9 THE ABO BLOOD SYSTEM

Work with a small group or alone to answer the following questions about the ABO blood group system and blood type compatibility.

1. Can a person with blood type A successfully receive a transfusion from a person who has type O? Why or why not?

2. Can a person with blood type A successfully receive a transfusion from a person who has type B? Why or why not?

3. Can a person with blood type O successfully donate blood to a person who has type AB? Why or why not?

4. Can a person with blood type B successfully donate blood to a person who has type O? Why or why not?

5. Can a person with blood type AB successfully donate blood to a person who has type A? Why or why not?

EXERCISE 10 DIHYBRID CROSS

So far, you have worked on Punnett squares that show monohybrid crosses—likelihoods for an offspring from two parents involving a *single* trait, such as tongue rolling. When conducting his research, Mendel devised a method known as a dihybrid cross, which allowed him to consider *two* different traits. Mendel's work on dihybrid crosses in pea plants helped him realize that traits are inherited separately (the law of independent assortment).

SCENARIO A

Here is an example of a dihybrid cross with Mendel's pea plants. Consider two traits in pea plants: plant height (T) and flower color (P). Tallness (T) is dominant over shortness (t), and purple flowers (P) are dominant over white flowers (p). If a plant that is heterozygous for plant height (Tt) and homozygous recessive for flower color (pp) is mated with a plant that is homozygous dominant for plant height (TT) and for flower color (PP), what are the likelihoods for the offspring's genotypes?

STEP 1 The first step is to determine the parents' genotypes. Here, one plant is *Ttpp* and the other is *TTPP*.

STEP 2 Next, we have to determine all the possible gametes each plant might contribute. To do this, we write down the T and P combinations that may be present in each plant's gametes.

» In plant 1, the possible gametes are *Tp, Tp, tp,* and *tp*.

» In plant 2, the possible gametes are *TP, TP, TP,* and *TP*.

STEP 3 Finally, we mate these possible gametes in a large Punnett square. In this example, the results are as follows:

Plant 1: *Ttpp*

Plant 2: *TTPP*		*Tp*	*Tp*	*tp*	*tp*
	TP	*TTPp*	*TTPp*	*TtPp*	*TtPp*
	TP	*TTPp*	*TTPp*	*TtPp*	*TtPp*
	TP	*TTPp*	*TTPp*	*TtPp*	*TtPp*
	TP	*TTPp*	*TTPp*	*TtPp*	*TtPp*

» There is a 50% chance of an offspring that is *TTPp*.

» There is a 50% chance of an offspring that is *TtPp*.

» On the phenotypic level, there is a 100% chance that the offspring will be tall and have purple flowers.

SCENARIO B

For this exercise, work alone or in a small group to complete the dihybrid cross and answer the questions that follow. Consider two traits in humans: freckles (*F*) and widow's peak (*W*). Having freckles (*F*) is dominant over not having freckles (*f*), and having a widow's peak (*W*) is dominant over not having a widow's peak (*w*).

- Suzy is heterozygous for freckles and widow's peak.
- José is homozygous recessive for freckles and widow's peak.
- Suzy and José are about to have a baby, and they are curious about the likelihood that their child will inherit these traits.

STEP 1 Enter Suzy's and José's genotypes in the Punnett square.

STEP 2 Enter Suzy's and José's possible gametes in the shaded rows and columns.

STEP 3 Complete the Punnett square and answer the following questions.

Suzy's genotype: _____

José's genotype: _____

1. What is the likelihood that Suzy and José's child will have freckles but will not have a widow's peak?

2. What is the likelihood that Suzy and José's child will not have freckles but will have a widow's peak?

3. What is the likelihood that Suzy and José's child will have freckles and a widow's peak?

4. What is the likelihood that Suzy and José's child will not have freckles or a widow's peak?

CRITICAL THINKING QUESTIONS

On a separate sheet of paper, answer the following questions.

1. Describe the two laws of inheritance put forward by Gregor Mendel. For each, also describe how you think modern genetics has clarified or supported these early concepts.

2. Use the Punnett squares you completed in Exercise 2 to answer the following questions.
   - Timmy was homozygous dominant for the freckles trait. Looking at the Punnett square for his parents' mating, what was the probability of Timmy having a different genotype? What was the probability of Timmy having a different phenotype?
   - Timmy's mother was heterozygous for the freckles trait. Looking at the Punnett square for his grandparents' mating, what was the probability of Timmy's mother having a different genotype? What was the probability of Timmy's mother having a different phenotype?

3. Complete the chart below comparing Punnett squares and pedigree diagrams. For each characteristic, indicate whether Punnett squares, pedigree diagrams, or both have that characteristic by placing a mark in the appropriate column.

	Punnett Square	**Pedigree Diagram**
Shows One Mating at a Time		
Shows Multiple Generations at a Time		
Shows Phenotypes		
Requires You to Infer Phenotypes		
Shows Genotypes		
Requires You to Infer Genotypes		
Shows Real Individuals		
Shows Potential Individuals		

4. In this lab, we explored Mendelian traits in humans, and we closely investigated variation within one of these traits (hitchhiker's thumb) in Exercise 7. Now, let's consider another Mendelian trait: earlobe attachment. Review the images on the following page that depict the earlobes of different individuals. Naveen is a biological anthropologist investigating the possibility of variation within this trait. He generates a hypothesis: *If earlobe attachment is a Mendelian trait, then there will be two, distinct phenotypic expressions (attached earlobes and unattached earlobes).* What data would you collect to help Naveen test this hypothesis? (Be sure to specifically describe any potential measurements you would take and what tools would be used to collect these data.) Imagine that you have now collected these data. What patterns in the data would *support* the hypothesis? (For example, "The hypothesis would be supported if we found data that indicated _____.") What patterns in the data would cause you to *reject* the hypothesis? (For example, "The hypothesis would be rejected if we found data that indicated _____.") Based on what you learned in this lab, do you think humans have numerous, clearly Mendelian traits? Why or why not?

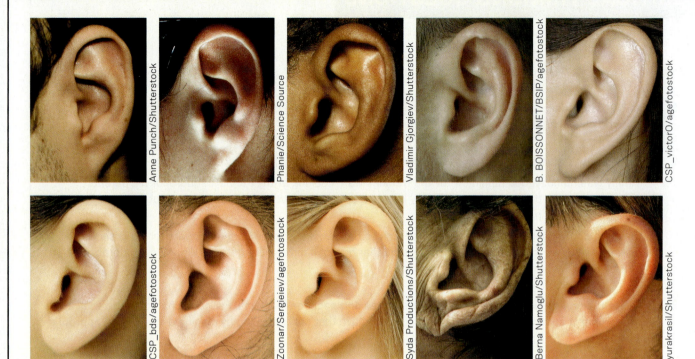

5. In this lab, we explored sex-linked traits. Use books and resources in your classroom (or reputable online sources) to identify another example of a sex-linked trait in humans. What is the trait? What are the genetic variants? How common is the trait in XY males? and in XX females? How does its commonness compare with that of the red-green color blindness example discussed in this lab?

6. Review your results from the dihybrid cross in Exercise 10. Did the inheritance of one trait affect the likelihood of inheriting the other trait? For example, was Suzy and José's child more likely to have a widow's peak if it also had freckles? How does the relationship between the two traits support Mendel's law of independent assortment?

7. Miss Primrose breeds dogs to show in competitions. Her prized female dog, named Stella, recently had an unexpected litter of puppies. Two of the puppies have an unusual coat color called agouti, in which each hair has numerous dark and light bands and a dark tip. Miss Primrose specifically bred Stella with another prize-winning dog named Max, but neither Stella nor Max has the agouti fur trait. Miss Primrose suspects that Stella may have been secretly impregnated by a stray dog she has seen in their neighborhood who does have an agouti coat. Miss Primrose collected the following research and pedigree information on Stella and Max:

- The non-agouti coat trait (*N*) is dominant over the agouti coat trait (*n*).
- Stella does not have an agouti coat.
- Neither of Stella's parents has an agouti coat.
- Stella's maternal grandfather does not have an agouti coat, but Stella's maternal grandmother does have an agouti coat.
- Max does not have an agouti coat.
- Max's mother does not have an agouti coat, but Max's father does have an agouti coat.

Based on this information, is it possible that Max is the father of this litter of puppies? Why or why not? (*Hint*: It might be helpful to make a pedigree diagram of Stella's and Max's families so you can determine their genotypes and the possibility of their having agouti puppies.)

Charles Darwin served as ship's naturalist aboard HMS *Beagle* on a trip around the world in the 1830s. The voyage included stops in the Galápagos Islands, where Darwin's observations of variations in finches, tortoises, and other animals fueled his development of the theory of natural selection.

Lab Learning Objectives

By the end of this lab, students should be able to:

- define evolution.
- describe genetic recombination and how it relates to genetic variation.
- describe the forces of evolution (mutation, natural selection, genetic drift, and gene flow).
- apply the Hardy–Weinberg equation to determine whether a trait is undergoing evolution in a population.

LAB 4

Forces of Evolution

It is October 2, 1836, and HMS *Beagle* has just returned to Falmouth, Cornwall, England, after a 5-year voyage around the world. Captain Robert FitzRoy commanded the ship with the purpose of conducting surveys of the South American coast and improving on existing charts and maps of the area. Charles Darwin served as the ship's naturalist, collecting information about and samples of various plants, animals, and geological features encountered during the voyage. Darwin's experiences have gotten him thinking, and upon his return, he begins to review his extensive notes and samples from the field. With these data and the influence of other contemporary and past scientists, Darwin will develop a theory that will revolutionize science and the way humans perceive the world. He will form an explanation for how we got to be the way we are and how we are related to other organisms, past and present. He will devise a theory of evolution known as natural selection. Today, we know that natural selection, as described by Darwin, is a great force that drives evolutionary change. We also recognize that there are multiple processes, in addition to natural selection, that can bring about evolution. Each of these processes has played (and continues to play) an important role in our own evolutionary history. This lab explores these evolutionary processes to help us further examine our own evolutionary context.

evolution change in allele frequency

INTRODUCTION

We begin with a consideration of evolution in general. We then examine the various processes that drive evolution: mutation, natural selection, genetic drift, and gene flow. For each of these processes, we review the basic concept and how it works, with an eye toward examples in human populations. We conclude by exploring how to determine whether evolution is happening.

WHAT IS EVOLUTION?

In population biology, we define and measure **evolution** as a change in allele frequency. This definition has several important implications. First, we are discussing alleles, which means we are discussing change at the *genetic* level, not just the phenotypic level. Because of the complex relationships that often exist between dominant and recessive alleles, evolution may be occurring subtly at the genetic level without us realizing it at the phenotypic level. This is particularly the case with polygenic traits, where multiple genetic loci are in play at one time.

Second, evolution involves allele *frequencies*. These are ratios of different alleles for a trait. As such, they are always calculated for groups, not individuals. This means that evolution occurs at the population level, not at the level of the individual.

Third, because evolution is about allele frequencies, evolution occurs in *traits*. Within a population at any given time, some traits may be evolving while others remain the same. It is not that the population is evolving. Instead, it is a trait (or suite of traits) that is evolving within a population.

Finally, evolution is a *change* in allele frequency. This means that evolution

occurs across multiple generations. To measure a change in a population's allele frequency for a trait, we must be examining the population over time, from one generation to the next. If a population has an allele frequency of *x* for a trait, the only way to determine whether evolution is occurring or has occurred is to examine the preceding generation or the offspring generation. If either of these generations has a different allele frequency (*y*), we can say that the frequency is changing and that evolution is occurring or has occurred.

Changes in allele frequencies occur all the time in all organisms. But what causes these changes? In other words, how do we explain evolution? There are multiple factors or mechanisms that can bring about changes in allele frequencies. These mechanisms of evolution are often called the *forces of evolution* because they drive evolutionary changes. Although we discuss them separately here, multiple forces of evolution often act simultaneously in real life (**FIGURE 4.1**).

GENETIC RECOMBINATION

In Lab 2, we discussed the process of cell division in gamete-forming cells, called meiosis. Remember, during meiosis, genes from homologous chromosomes cross over and are recombined. This *genetic recombination* results in variation by forming new combinations of genetic material. No new genetic material is created, but new combinations of existing genetic material are produced. Recombination is not considered one of the traditional forces of evolution, but it plays an important role in creating variation, which is the raw material for evolutionary processes.

Example Imagine that a woman is heterozygous for the Mendelian freckle trait (**FIGURE 4.2**). During meiosis, the chromosome that holds the freckle gene lines up with its homologous partner. The first chromosome (inherited from the woman's mother) carries the dominant allele for the trait (*F*), and the homologous chromosome

FIGURE 4.1 Darwin's Finches Charles Darwin noted variation among the finches on the Galápagos Islands. These observations helped him as he developed his theory of natural selection. Today, we have even more evidence in support of Darwin's early ideas.

Ryan M. Bolton/Shutterstock

Stubblefield Photography/Shutterstock

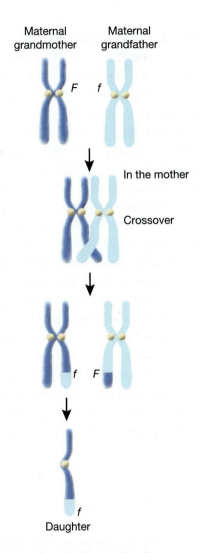

Maternal grandmother   Maternal grandfather

F   f

In the mother

Crossover

f   F

f

Daughter

FIGURE 4.2 Genetic Recombination
Genetic recombination can cause minor genetic variations between generations. In the example depicted here and described in the text, a daughter receives a slightly different combination of genes than was found in her mother's corresponding chromosome.

(inherited from her father) carries the recessive allele (*f*). These two alleles are exchanged during a crossing-over event. This creates a slightly different collection of genetic material on those chromosomes. The first chromosome now has the recessive allele for the freckle trait, and the homologous partner now has the dominant allele for the freckle trait. Now imagine that the first chromosome ends up in a gamete that produces an offspring. The resulting daughter has a slightly different combination of genetic material on this chromosome than her mother

or grandmother. Her mother has the dominant allele for the freckle trait along with the other genes found on this chromosome. The daughter has the recessive allele for the freckle trait (from her grandfather) along with the other genes (from her grandmother). While the mother's and daughter's chromosomes are very similar, there are minor variations, like the switch in the freckle allele, as a result of crossing-over in meiosis.

FORCES OF EVOLUTION—MUTATION

While recombination results in new combinations of genetic material, it does not produce new genes. The only source of entirely new genetic material is **mutation**, or a change in the genetic code. Most mutations occur during DNA replication. Usually this process copies the DNA perfectly, but sometimes there are errors, resulting in mutations. If the errors occur in DNA segments that do not code for traits or play a role in regulating genes, the errors have no real effect. However, sometimes the errors occur in coding DNA, and they can have a profound impact. While mutations can occur in cells throughout the body, the only mutations that can affect evolution are those that occur in gametes (reproductive cells such as the sperm and egg). Remember, these mutations are the only ones that can be passed to the next generation.

Mutations can be very small genetic changes. If a single base pair of DNA is altered, it changes the corresponding codon. Such a change can sometimes result in a different amino acid, which may result in a different protein. These kinds of mutations are called **point mutations** because they occur at a single point in the DNA strand. **Sickle-cell anemia** is an example of a trait caused by a point mutation. One base pair was substituted for another, and a new sickle-cell allele was formed. Expression of this mutated allele produces misshapen red blood cells that cause blockages in blood vessels (for more information on the sickle-cell trait, see Lab 8).

mutation a change in the genetic code that creates entirely new genetic material

point mutation a mutation that occurs at a single point (nitrogen base) in a DNA strand

sickle-cell anemia a disease that results from the sickle-cell allele

Down syndrome
a chromosomal condition that results from an extra chromosome 21

Turner syndrome
a chromosomal condition that results from having a single X chromosome without another sex chromosome

Charles Darwin
often considered the father of evolutionary thinking, who devised the theory of natural selection to explain the process of evolution in the natural world

natural selection
the theory outlined by Charles Darwin to explain evolution; it argues that some traits are more suited to an organism's particular environmental context and are therefore passed on preferentially to the next generation, and these traits become more common in successive generations, resulting in evolutionary shifts in populations

Mutations can also be much larger errors. During the process of meiosis, a large section of a chromosome can be moved elsewhere on the chromosome, or it can be moved to a completely different chromosome. Sometimes whole chromosomes can be duplicated, resulting in an organism with an extra chromosome. This is the case with **Down syndrome** in humans, which is caused by an extra chromosome 21. Other times, a whole chromosome can be lost, leaving the organism with one fewer chromosome. This is the case with **Turner syndrome**, which occurs in individuals with a single X chromosome and no other sex chromosome.

We do not know all of the causes of mutations. Sometimes they are caused by external factors, such as exposure to radiation or specific chemicals. However, most mutations seem to be spontaneous, with no known cause. Also, while we often associate the word "mutation" with negative things, mutations are not always harmful. Many mutations are neutral or even advantageous.

No matter what their cause, mutations create new genetic material, such as entirely new alleles. The variations created by mutation can then be acted on by other evolutionary processes. Thus, mutation works in concert with other forces to bring about evolutionary changes.

FORCES OF EVOLUTION—NATURAL SELECTION

In 1859, **Charles Darwin** published *On the Origin of Species*. This work presented his ideas about evolution and outlined his theory of **natural selection**. This theory offers an explanation for how evolution occurs. Since Darwin's original work, the theory of natural selection has been repeatedly refined to include our growing knowledge of genetics. The basic outline of the theory, however, remains the same. The theory of natural selection states that beneficial alleles increase in frequency over time in a population because of increased survival and reproduction of individuals with those alleles. Let's look more closely at the mechanism behind natural selection.

First, there is always variation in a trait (and thus in the alleles that code for it) within a population. Not every member of the population will have the same version of the trait or allele. Second, there is a tendency toward overreproduction compared with the limited availability of resources. In general, more offspring are produced than can be supported by the resources in the environment (such as food, shelter, and access to mates). This imbalance causes competition for resources, which are always limited. They may be distributed unevenly in an environment or limited seasonally, or there may be some resources that are better (for example, more nutritious or safer) than others. At any given time, members of a population are competing for access to these resources. Third, because of this competition, some versions of a trait will be better suited (or fitted) to the environmental context than other versions. That is, some versions will be advantageous, for example, in helping the organism access food or reproduce efficiently. Other versions will be disadvantageous, perhaps limiting access to food or hindering reproduction. Finally, the organisms with the more helpful traits will outreproduce the other organisms and pass their helpful traits on to the next generation. In other words, the organisms that are more fitted to the environmental context will have greater reproductive success. Over many generations, the population as a whole will have more of the helpful traits because they are being passed on at a greater rate, and the population will become well adapted (or fitted) to the environmental context.

Importantly, natural selection emphasizes traits and alleles, not the individuals carrying those traits and alleles. It is the traits that are advantageous or disadvantageous, and it is the traits and alleles that are passed to the next generation. Also, natural selection highlights the importance of change in allele frequencies over multiple generations, thus incorporating the definition of evolution.

Example Over 50,000 years ago, a group of mammoths (*Mammuthus columbi*) swam approximately 4 miles from the California coast to an island due west in the Pacific Ocean. As the Ice Age came to an end, ice caps and glaciers melted, and sea levels rose around the world. The island became four separate, smaller islands (known today as the California Channel Islands). The food available to the mammoths became more limited. This was particularly problematic in the winter because the mammoths could not migrate to different territories when their local food was scarce. In these times of limited food, mammoths that had smaller body sizes were able to outcompete their larger counterparts (**FIGURE 4.3**). The smaller mammoths needed less food to survive, and their shorter limbs allowed them to climb the steep terrain more efficiently. Thus these small-bodied mammoths were able to stay healthy and produce more small-bodied offspring. Over many generations, the average body size in the population became smaller, and by 13,000 years ago, a new species of pygmy mammoth (*Mammuthus exilis*) had arisen. These dwarfed mammoths were less than half the size of their mainland ancestor; they stood about 4–6 feet high at the shoulder and weighed about 1 ton.

Remember, advantageous traits are not necessarily traits for strength, vitality, wit, and so forth. For example, in the pygmy mammoths described above, smallness was advantageous. Advantageous traits are simply traits that help **reproductive success** (the production of offspring). Similarly, disadvantageous traits are not necessarily injurious or fatal. A disadvantageous trait is merely a trait that limits reproductive success.

FORCES OF EVOLUTION— GENETIC DRIFT

Sometimes allele frequencies change randomly. This process is called **genetic drift**. To understand how genetic drift works, it is helpful to think of it as a statistics problem. Imagine a

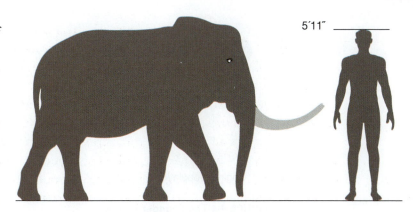

5´11˝

FIGURE 4.3 Pygmy Mammoth
Although mainland mammoths were about 14 feet tall on average, pygmy mammoths on the Channel Islands averaged only 4.5 to 7 feet tall, making them closer in size to a modern human. Their small size was selectively favored on the islands, where there was less food available to support large-bodied mammoths.

population where an equal number of dominant and recessive alleles are represented. You might think that if the members of this population mate, there will be an equal number of dominant and recessive alleles in the second generation. However, when you think of flipping a coin, you realize this is not necessarily the case. When you flip a coin, there is a 50% chance each time you flip it that you will get heads facing up. There is also a 50% chance you will get tails facing up. The results of one coin flip are independent of the results of the next coin flip; these 50% chances are the same *each time* you flip the coin. If a coin is flipped 10 times, the results could be 10 heads or 10 tails in a row. This outcome is unlikely, but it is possible.

Similar patterns emerge in mating. If two heterozygous individuals mate, there is a 50% chance the mother will pass on her dominant allele and a 50% chance she will pass on her recessive allele. The same is true for the father. However, if these individuals produce four offspring, it is entirely possible that the mother will pass on her recessive allele all four times and the father will pass on his recessive allele all four times. While this outcome is unlikely, it is still possible. We could start with a population of two heterozygous individuals and end up with a second generation of all homozygous recessive individuals. This process is called

reproductive success the successful production of viable (fertile) offspring

genetic drift changes in allele frequencies that occur randomly due to factors such as differential reproduction and sampling errors

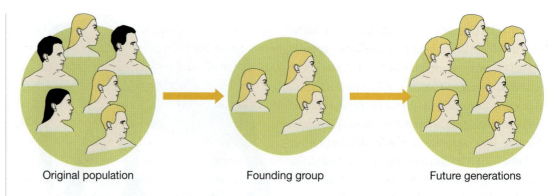

Original population   Founding group   Future generations

FIGURE 4.4 The Founder Effect
A particular type of genetic drift, called the founder effect, occurs when only a subset of a larger population is involved in producing future generations. Depending on the traits carried by the founding group, its future generations can be very different from those of the original population.

founder effect a type of genetic drift that occurs when a subset of a larger population founds the next generation due to substantial population loss or population movement

genetic bottleneck a substantial loss of genetic diversity (often through the founder effect)

genetic drift because, over multiple generations, it may cause a population's allele frequency to drift away from its original allele frequency.

At the same time, not every individual will have the same number of offspring, and this differential reproduction, too, can cause a random shift in allele frequencies. Imagine that one individual, named Devon, has five offspring, and another individual, named Shalyce, has zero offspring. Devon's genetic material will be over-represented in the next generation, and Shalyce's genetic material will be underrepresented in the next generation. Therefore, there will be a slight shift in the population's allele frequencies, with more of Devon's alleles going forward.

A special kind of genetic drift, called the **founder effect (FIGURE 4.4)**, occurs when only a small number of individuals from a larger population are involved in producing the next generation. This can happen when a large percentage of a population dies (for example, from famine or war) and only a few individuals are left to reproduce. It can also happen when a small group of individuals leaves the original population to live somewhere else. These individuals then reproduce in isolation from the original population's gene pool. The "founders" (the individuals involved in reproduction separate from the original, larger population) do not necessarily represent the original, larger population's allele frequencies. So, when they reproduce, they may not generate the original population's allele frequencies, and in effect, they may jump-start genetic drift. The founder effect can lead to what is called a **genetic bottleneck**, meaning that some of the original genetic diversity is lost.

Example In 1608, French settlers moved to the St. Lawrence River area of what is today Canada and established a colony at Quebec City **(FIGURE 4.5)**. Within approximately 70 years, 2,600 settlers had moved to the region. These settlers came from a variety of regions in France, but most came from major Atlantic seaports and areas near Paris. Thus, the founding population

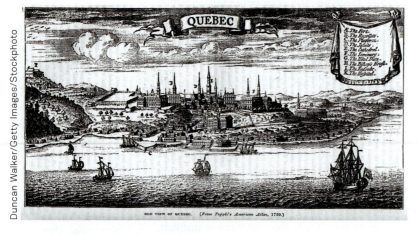

FIGURE 4.5 Colonial Quebec City
Early colonists in Quebec City were a small sample of the larger French population at that time. Many of today's French Canadians in the area are descended from this group of founders, and they have a higher rate of certain genetic traits because these traits were more common among their founding ancestors than in the larger French population.

was a small sample of the original, larger population of France. Today's French Canadian population in the region is largely descended from this small founding population, and because of this founding history, French Canadians have higher rates of certain diseases than other populations. For example, Tay-Sachs disease is more common in French Canadians than in most other groups. This disease is caused by a genetic mutation that must be inherited from both parents. People with Tay-Sachs disease lack a particular protein that is necessary for breaking down a chemical in nerve cells. The lack of this protein causes deafness, blindness, seizures, and other neurological symptoms; it results in death by around age 6. The Tay-Sachs mutation was more common in the founding settler population than in the overall population of France. Because French Canadians are largely descended from this biased founding population, they are more likely to carry alleles for this disease than many other populations.

FORCES OF EVOLUTION— GENE FLOW

A final factor that changes allele frequencies is **gene flow**: the exchange of genes between previously isolated populations. If individuals in population A and population B do not normally mate with one another, populations A and B are considered to be *reproductively isolated*. Now, if some individuals from population A begin mating with individuals from population B, gene flow has occurred between the populations (**FIGURE 4.6**).

Example   Slavery was legal in the United States from colonial times until the ratification of the Thirteenth Amendment of the U.S. Constitution in December 1865. During this period, it is estimated that hundreds of thousands of people were forcibly captured in Africa and transported to America, where they were enslaved and forced to work for Americans of European descent. Although legal restrictions discouraged marriages and mating relationships between the enslaved Africans and European Americans, sexual relationships were common (and often forced on the enslaved people). The African American people of today are descended in part from these relationships, and their DNA shows signs of this mixing of genetic information. The African American population has elevated proportions of European Y-chromosomal DNA (inherited through the male lineage) and African mitochondrial DNA (mtDNA) and X-chromosomal DNA (both inherited through the female lineage). This pattern of sex-linked genetic markers supports countless historical accounts of sexual relationships involving European American men and enslaved African women. Thus, the African American population today carries a combination of African and European

gene flow the exchange of genes between previously isolated populations that begin to interbreed

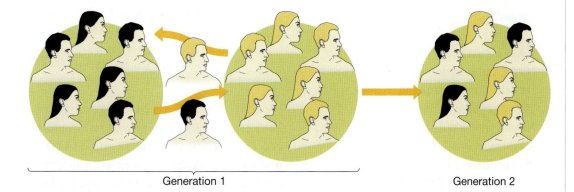

Generation 1   Generation 2

FIGURE 4.6 Gene Flow
Two populations (one with only dark hair and one with only light hair) interbreed. In future generations, both the dark hair and the light hair genes are present.

Hardy–Weinberg equation
the equation
($p^2 + 2pq + q^2 = 1$) outlined by Godfrey Hardy and Wilhelm Weinberg to predict the probable genotype frequencies of a Mendelian trait in the next generation

genes because of the gene flow that occurred many generations ago.

Gene flow can have particularly dramatic consequences when one population has genetic material not found in the other population or when one population is much larger than the other. For example, imagine that population A and population B are interbreeding for the first time and gene flow is under way. Population A has genes for blue eyes, which are not found in population B, but because of gene flow, that trait will be introduced to population B for the first time. This change will dramatically alter the future allele frequencies of population B because this new genetic material will now be present. Also, if population A is 10 times the size of population B, then genes from population A may be found in higher numbers in future generations than genes from population B. This change will also change the future allele frequencies of population B because there will now be more genes from population A present.

HARDY–WEINBERG EQUILIBRIUM

We have discussed what evolution is and how it happens, but how can we tell *when* it is happening? In the early 1900s, both Godfrey Hardy (an English mathematician) and Wilhelm Weinberg (a German physician) recognized that not all traits are evolving all the time. Hypothetically, a trait could be stable, or in a state of equilibrium. They identified seven key conditions that would be necessary for this stability:

1. No mutation is occurring.
2. No natural selection is occurring.
3. No gene flow is occurring.
4. The population is infinitely large.
5. Mating within the population is random.
6. All members of the population mate.
7. All members of the population produce the same number of offspring.

If all of these conditions were true, then the genotype frequencies for the trait would be the same

from one generation to the next. The trait would be in equilibrium and not evolving.

With this in mind, Hardy and Weinberg developed an equation to predict the probable genotype frequencies of a Mendelian trait in the next generation:

$$p^2 + 2pq + q^2 = 1$$

This **Hardy–Weinberg equation** is used for simple Mendelian traits that are determined by one gene with two alleles. When we analyze a trait with one dominant allele and one recessive allele, p is the frequency of dominant alleles for the trait, and q is the frequency of recessive alleles for the trait. Therefore, $p + q = 1$ because the total number of alleles must account for the entire 100% of the gene pool. The chance of being homozygous dominant is p^2, the chance of being homozygous recessive is q^2, and the chance of being heterozygous is $2pq$. The whole gene pool must be the sum of all the possible genotypes, so $p^2 + 2pq + q^2$ must equal 1 (or 100%).

Example 1 Consider the Mendelian plant height trait in pea plants discussed in Lab 3. For this trait, the tall allele (T) is the dominant allele and the short allele (t) is the recessive allele. In one population of pea plants, 60% (0.6) of the alleles are dominant (T) and 40% (0.4) are recessive (t) (**FIGURE 4.7**). We plug this information into the Hardy–Weinberg equation:

$$p = 0.6 \qquad q = 0.4$$
$$p^2 + 2qp + q^2 = 1$$
$$(0.6)^2 + 2(0.6 \times 0.4) + (0.4)^2 = 1$$
$$0.36 + 2(0.24) + 0.16 = 1$$
$$0.36 + 0.48 + 0.16 = 1$$

We have determined that the genotype frequencies in the second generation should be 0.36 (36%) TT, 0.48 (48%) Tt, and 0.16 (16%) tt. If these frequencies are seen in the next generation, the plant height trait is said to be in equilibrium, or not currently evolving. If these frequencies are not seen in the next generation, the trait is evolving.

example, allele *S*). The chance of being homozygous for allele *R* (*RR*) is p^2; the chance of being homozygous for allele *S* (*SS*) is q^2; and the chance of being heterozygous (*RS*) is $2pq$. As is the case with a trait that is not codominant, the whole gene pool here must still be the sum of all the possible genotypes, so $p^2 + 2pq + q^2$ must equal 1 (or 100%).

Example 2 Imagine a plant population where flower color is a Mendelian trait with two codominant alleles coding for white flowers (*W*) and red flowers (*R*). The flowers on these plants may be white (*WW*), red (*RR*), or speckled with white and red (*WR*). In this population, 75% (0.75) of the alleles are for white (*W*) and 25% (0.25) are for red (*R*) (**FIGURE 4.8**). We plug this information into the Hardy–Weinberg equation:

$$p = 0.75 \qquad q = 0.25$$
$$\boldsymbol{p^2 + 2qp + q^2 = 1}$$
$$(0.75)^2 + 2(0.75 \times 0.25) + (0.25)^2 = 1$$
$$0.5625 + 2(0.1875) + 0.0625 = 1$$
$$0.5625 + 0.375 + 0.0625 = 1$$

FIGURE 4.7 Hardy–Weinberg Example 1
In this population of pea plants, there are two plants that are homozygous dominant for plant height (*TT*), two heterozygous plants (*Tt*), and one homozygous recessive plant (*tt*). This means 60% (6 out of 10) of the plant height alleles in the population are dominant (*T*) and 40% (4 out of 10) are recessive (*t*). Using the Hardy–Weinberg equation, we can now determine what the allele frequency should be in the next generation, and we can compare our prediction with actual data to assess whether evolution is under way.

FIGURE 4.8 Hardy–Weinberg Example 2
In this population of plants, there are four plants that are homozygous for white flowers (*WW*), one heterozygous plant with speckled flowers (*WR*), and one plant that is homozygous for red flowers (*RR*). This means 75% (9 out of 12) of the alleles in the population are for white flowers (*W*) and 25% (3 out of 12) are for red flowers (*R*). Using the Hardy–Weinberg equation, we can now determine what the allele frequency should be in the next generation, and we can compare our prediction with actual data to assess whether evolution is under way.

The Hardy–Weinberg equation can also be used to examine a trait with two alleles that are codominant. In this case, *p* is the frequency of one allele (for example, allele *R*), and *q* is the frequency of the other allele for the trait (for

We have determined that the genotype frequencies in the second generation should be 0.5625 (56.25%) *WW*, 0.375 (37.5%) *WR*, and 0.0625 (6.25%) *RR*. As in the previous example, if these frequencies are seen in the next generation, the trait is said to be in equilibrium (not evolving). Again, if these frequencies are *not* seen in the next generation, the trait is evolving. In this way, the Hardy–Weinberg equation can be used to determine whether a trait is evolving (or has evolved) in a population.

The Hardy–Weinberg equation provides a useful tool for examining evolutionary changes across generations. Consider the two types of inheritance diagrams discussed in Lab 3. Punnett squares give valuable information about the probable outcomes for the mating of two individuals, and pedigree diagrams provide helpful information about the inheritance of a trait across numerous individuals from multiple generations within a family. The Hardy–Weinberg equation allows us to predict probable genotypes, as in the Punnett square, but it goes a step further and takes into account entire populations, rather than just two individuals.

Hardy's and Weinberg's work also illustrates an important aspect of the relationship between dominant and recessive alleles. We often assume that dominant alleles are stronger, more common, and more likely to be inherited than recessive alleles. In fact, the word "dominant" is used only to indicate that the allele is more likely to be physically expressed than an alternative (recessive) form of the gene. This likelihood of expression is completely separate from the likelihood of inheriting the allele. Remember from Lab 3 that the level of gene expression (phenotype) is different from the molecular level of genetic makeup (genotype). When a heterozygous individual produces an offspring, it is equally likely to pass on the recessive allele or the dominant allele. The Hardy–Weinberg equation further confirms this principle. In the equation, dominant alleles do not hold a special place as the most frequent alleles, and dominant alleles and recessive alleles are equally likely to become less common in a population over time.

It is important to remember that the Hardy–Weinberg equation is based on a hypothetical state of equilibrium, in which all seven of the conditions noted above are met. In reality, this rarely, if ever, happens. One or more of these conditions almost always does not apply, and traits are usually evolving.

CONCEPT REVIEW QUESTIONS

Name: _____   Section: _____

Course: _____   Date: _____

Answer the following questions in the space provided.

1. How do we measure and define evolution?

2. Evolution occurs:
   A. at the level of the individual.
   B. in traits.
   C. in a single generation.
   D. only at the phenotypic level.

3. The only source of entirely new genetic material is:
   A. natural selection.
   B. mutation.
   C. recombination.
   D. genetic drift.

4. Which of the following is *not* a key component of natural selection?
   A. Traits for strength and vitality are favored over other traits.
   B. Random variation exists for every trait in a population.
   C. There will always be competition for resources.
   D. Those with advantageous traits will outreproduce others.

5. The founder effect is a specific type of:
   A. gene flow.
   B. meiosis.
   C. genetic drift.
   D. mutation.

6. When a substantial amount of genetic variation is lost, we call it a:
   A. genetic die-off.
   B. gene flow.
   C. genetic bottleneck.
   D. gene dam.

7. When two previously isolated populations begin interbreeding and exchanging genes, we call it:
   A. genetic drift.
   B. founder effect.
   C. incest.
   D. gene flow.

8. List two of the seven key conditions necessary for a trait to be in equilibrium.

9. In the Hardy–Weinberg equation, what does p stand for?

10. In the Hardy–Weinberg equation, what does q stand for?

LAB EXERCISES

Name: _____   Section: _____

Course: _____   Date: _____

EXERCISE 1   MUTATION

Work in a small group or alone to complete this exercise. In Lab 2, Exercise 8, you determined the amino acid sequence for the following strand of DNA:

> A G C A A T C C G T C T T G G
> T C G T T A G G C A G A A C C

That strand has mutated. It is now

> A G C A A C C C G T C T T G G
> T C G T T G G G C A G A A C C

Use your knowledge of mutation and protein synthesis to answer the following questions.

1. What mutation has occurred?

2. Will this mutation have a real effect? Why or why not? (*Hint*: You may want to try Exercise 10 from Lab 2 again, using the mutated DNA strand to make the mutated protein.)

EXERCISE 2   NATURAL SELECTION ACTIVITY

Work in a small group to complete this exercise. In this exercise, you will simulate a case of natural selection in a predator–prey situation.

STEP 1   Gather your lab materials. Your group should have:

- 1 fork, 1 knife, 1 spoon, and a length of tape (each will be used to establish the distinct predator "feeding apparatuses")
- 4 cups (each will serve as a distinct predator's "mouth")
- 3 types of prey (such as popcorn, macaroni, and kidney beans)
- 1 clearly delineated habitat (such as a table, a box, or a roped-off area of ground)
- 1 timer that allows for counting by seconds (such as a watch or cell phone)

Note: Your instructor may vary some aspects of your supplies to suit the needs of your class.

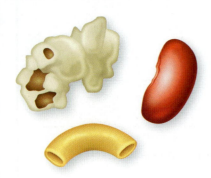

STEP 2 Set up the predators. There is variation in predatory feeding apparatuses in this population. Each group member will choose one of the available predator feeding apparatuses: fork, spoon, knife, or four fingers (with your thumb taped to your hand so that you cannot use it). Each group member will also take a cup, which will represent the predator's mouth. Your goal will be to use your feeding apparatus to collect food and put it in your mouth.

STEP 3 Set up the prey in the environment. Your instructor has provided you with different types of prey that vary in size and shape. Your group should have 100 of each prey type. Your instructor has also provided a delineated habitat for you to use. Distribute your prey evenly in this habitat, and be sure to mix the prey so that each type is found throughout the habitat.

STEP 4 Establish your hypotheses:

1. Which prey type do you think will be the most fit and avoid capture more often than the other prey types?

2. Which predator do you think will be the most fit and succeed in capturing the most prey?

STEP 5 Simulate hunting session 1. Distribute yourselves (the predators) around the habitat full of prey. You will be given 60 seconds to hunt for prey. You must pick up the prey with your feeding apparatus and place it in your cup (your predator's mouth). Your cup must remain flat on the table or ground at all times and cannot be used to help you scrape or scoop up prey. You may hunt prey that is being hunted by other predators. Set a timer for 60 seconds (or use a watch to monitor the time), and begin hunting.

STEP 6 Record your results. After the end of your 60 seconds of hunting, record the number of prey collected by each predator in the appropriate chart provided here. Be sure to identify which prey types you have designated as prey 1, 2, and 3 in the chart. Set these captured prey aside. They are dead and will not produce offspring.

STEP 7 Reestablish the predators. The predators that collected the most prey are well fed and producing offspring. The predator that collected the least amount of prey is underfed and will not produce offspring. This underfed predator will not participate in future hunts, but the group member should still follow along and record the outcomes of the others' hunts in his or her charts. In addition, if any predators have broken their feeding apparatus, they are also underfed and do not produce offspring. They, too, will sit out future hunts, but continue recording results.

STEP 8 Reestablish the environment. Only the prey that have survived the hunt can reproduce. Determine the number of survivors for each prey type. Add in enough of each surviving prey type to double their numbers in the next generation. Be sure to distribute them evenly in the habitat.

STEP 9 Repeat Steps 5 through 8 for two more hunting sessions. Continue to eliminate underfed predators and double surviving prey. Be sure to keep track of your results in the charts provided below for each hunting session.

HUNTING SESSION 1

	Fork	Knife	Spoon	Fingers	Total Prey
Prey 1 _____					
Prey 2 _____					
Prey 3 _____					
Total					

HUNTING SESSION 2

	Fork	Knife	Spoon	Fingers	Total Prey
Prey 1 _____					
Prey 2 _____					
Prey 3 _____					
Total					

HUNTING SESSION 3

	Fork	Knife	Spoon	Fingers	Total Prey
Prey 1 _____					
Prey 2 _____					
Prey 3 _____					
Total					

STEP 10 Use your results to answer the following questions.

3. Which prey type was the best suited to the environmental context? What data do you have to support this conclusion?

4. Which predator was the best suited to the environmental context? What data do you have to support this conclusion?

5. In what ways does this activity demonstrate the process of natural selection and its consequences?

EXERCISE 3   THE FOUNDER EFFECT

Work in a small group to complete this exercise. In this exercise, you will simulate a case of the founder effect.

STEP 1 Gather your lab materials. You should have:

- 1 cup (which will hold the alleles for an entire population—the gene pool)
- 20 red beans (representing the dominant allele (R) for a simple Mendelian trait)
- 20 white beans (representing the recessive allele (r) for the same trait)

Note: You may substitute other everyday objects (such as candies, coins, or paper clips) for the beans, but be sure to designate which objects represent the dominant versus recessive alleles.

STEP 2 Assess the gene pool.

   1. How many alleles of each type are present in your overall population?

STEP 3 Select the subpopulation that will survive an eco-logical catastrophe. Randomly draw out five geno-types (pairs of beans) that will survive. Record the genotypes of these five individuals in the chart below. Remember to use the correct alleles (R and r).

Your genotype pairs should be laid out like this for 5 individuals (pairs), but the specific alleles (bean types) will vary depending on how you randomly pull them from the cup.

Individual	Genotype
1	
2	
3	
4	
5	

2. How many alleles of each type are represented in this surviving population (the founders)?

3. As this surviving population mates, and the popula-tion increases again, will it differ from the original, larger population? Why or why not?

STEP 4 Select a second subpopulation that will survive another catastrophe. Return your alleles (beans) to the gene pool (cup). Now, let's say that only two individuals survive. Randomly draw out two genotypes (pairs of beans) that will survive. Record the genotypes in the chart below. Remember to use the correct alleles (R and r).

Individual	Genotype
1	
2	

4. How many alleles of each type are represented in this surviving population?

5. Does this group of founders differ from the first group of founders above? Why or why not?

6. Does this group of founders differ from the original, larger population? Why or why not?

7. How might the size of the founding group affect genetic drift?

EXERCISE 4 GENE FLOW

Work in a small group to complete this exercise. In this exercise, you will simulate a case of gene flow.

STEP 1 Gather your lab materials. You should have:

- 1 cup (which will hold the alleles for an entire population—the gene pool)
- 24 black beans (representing the dominant allele (*B*) for a simple Mendelian trait)
- 20 white beans (representing the recessive allele (*b*) for the same trait)

Note: You may substitute other everyday objects (such as candies, coins, or paper clips) for the beans, but be sure to designate which objects represent the dominant versus recessive alleles.

   In the twentieth century, a self-isolated group of people living on a small island was joined by a group of explorers from a nearby island.

STEP 2 Create the original, self-isolated population. The self-isolated population consists of six males. Three of them are homozygous recessive, two are heterozygous, and one is homozygous dominant for the simple Mendelian trait. Pull out the appropriate genotypes and set them in front of you.

1. How many recessive alleles are present in this self-isolated population?

2. How many dominant alleles are present in this self-isolated population?

STEP 3 Create the explorer population, based on the model provided keeping the males and females separate. The explorer population consists of two males and eight females, all of whom are homozygous dominant for the same Mendelian trait.

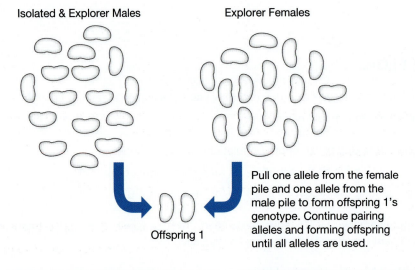

Isolated (males)

Explorer (females)

Explorer (males)

Your genotype pairs should be laid out like this, but check the instructions to identify the specific alleles (bean types) needed in each pair.

3. How many recessive alleles are present in this explorer population?

4. How many dominant alleles are present in this explorer population?

STEP 4 Create the descendant population. Everyone on the island found their perfect mate and decided to have two children. Being sure to keep the male and female alleles separate, mix up the male alleles together, and mix up the female alleles together. Create the next generation by randomly taking one allele from the males and combining it with one allele from the females until 16 new individuals (pairs of alleles) are sitting in front of you. Record their genotypes in the chart below. Remember to use the correct alleles (*B* and *b*).

Isolated & Explorer Males   Explorer Females

Pull one allele from the female pile and one allele from the male pile to form offspring 1's genotype. Continue pairing alleles and forming offspring until all alleles are used.

Offspring 1

Individual	Genotype	Individual	Genotype
1		9	
2		10	
3		11	
4		12	
5		13	
6		14	
7		15	
8		16	

5. How many recessive alleles are present in this descendant population?

6. How does this number vary from the number of recessive alleles present in the explorer population?

7. How many dominant alleles are present in the descendant population?

8. How does this number vary from the number of dominant alleles in the original, self-isolated population?

9. What long-term effects can gene flow have on any two populations that are exchanging genes?

EXERCISE 5 OVERLAPPING FORCES OF EVOLUTION

Work in a small group to complete this exercise. So far, we have treated the forces of evolution somewhat separately, but in reality they may all operate simultaneously, as we will see in this exercise.

STEP 1 Gather your lab materials. You should have:

- 1 cup (which will hold the alleles for an entire population of mice—the gene pool)
- Beans representing a simple Mendelian trait for fur color in mice:
    - » 40 brown beans (representing the dominant allele (*B*) for the trait; *B* codes for brown fur)
    - » 40 white beans (representing the recessive allele (*b*) for the trait; *b* codes for white fur)
    - » 1 black bean (to be used in Step 8)

Note: You may substitute other everyday objects (such as candies, coins, or paper clips) for the beans, but be sure to designate which objects represent the dominant versus recessive alleles.

STEP 2 Create the gene pool by placing all the beans (except the black one) in the cup. Then create a population from the gene pool. Randomly draw out genotypes (pairs of beans) and lay them out in front of you until no more beans remain in the cup. Each pair of beans represents one individual's genotype for fur color. You should have a total of 40 pairs of beans (40 individuals in the population). Record the genotypes of those individuals in the chart below. Remember to use the correct alleles (*B* and *b*).

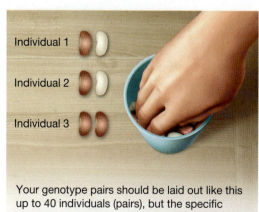

Individual 1

Individual 2

Individual 3

Your genotype pairs should be laid out like this up to 40 individuals (pairs), but the specific alleles (bean types) will vary depending on how you randomly pull them from the cup.

Name: _____   Date: _____

Individual	Genotype	Individual	Genotype
1		21	
2		22	
3		23	
4		24	
5		25	
6		26	
7		27	
8		28	
9		29	
10		30	
11		31	
12		32	
13		33	
14		34	
15		35	
16		36	
17		37	
18		38	
19		39	
20		40	

1. How many recessive alleles are present in your overall population?

2. How many dominant alleles are present in your overall population?

STEP 3 Account for random shifts in allele frequency. Genetic drift is at play in this population and causes random shifts in the allele frequency for fur color. No matter what their fur color is, two of the individuals in the population simply do not produce any offspring. Remove the first and last genotypes (pairs of beans) you laid out for your population, and set them aside. They will not contribute genetic information to future generations.

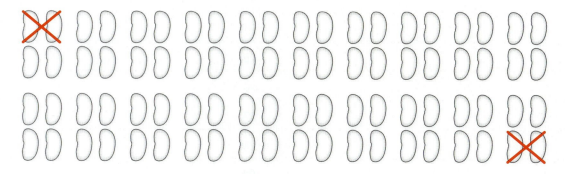

3. What were the two genotypes that were randomly eliminated?

4. Will their elimination influence future allele frequencies in the population? If so, how?

STEP 4 Simulate an environmental change that affects the population. The mice typically live in a rocky environment where their brown fur helps them to blend in and avoid predation, but the environment is cooling, extending the length of the snowy winters. Under these new circumstances, brown fur is a disadvantage because it makes brown-furred mice stand out against the snow and be more susceptible to predation. Review the genotypes remaining after Step 3, and identify which individuals have the dominant brown fur phenotype. Set aside half of these genotypes. These individuals have died and will no longer contribute to the next generation. (If you have an odd number of brown-furred genotypes, remove just under half. For example, if you have 25 brown-furred pairs, remove 12 of them, instead of 12.5.)

STEP 5 Create a descendant population from the survivors. These remaining individuals continue mating, and each couple produces enough offspring to replace themselves in the next generation. So, put the alleles (beans) remaining after Step 4 back into the gene pool (cup), and then randomly draw out new genotypes (pairs of beans) for the next generation. Record the genotypes of this generation in the chart below. Remember to use the correct alleles (*B* and *b*). (*Note:* You may not need all the rows in the chart.)

Name: _____   Date: _____

Individual	Genotype	Individual	Genotype
1		21	
2		22	
3		23	
4		24	
5		25	
6		26	
7		27	
8		28	
9		29	
10		30	
11		31	
12		32	
13		33	
14		34	
15		35	
16		36	
17		37	
18		38	
19		39	
20		40	

5. How many recessive alleles are present in your overall population now?

6. How many dominant alleles are present in your overall population now?

STEP 6 Account for random shifts in allele frequency. Genetic drift is still at play in this population. This time, remove the second and fourth genotypes (pairs of beans) you laid out for your population, no matter what their fur color. They will not contribute genetic information to future generations.

    7. What were the two genotypes that were randomly eliminated?

    8. Will their elimination influence future allele frequencies in the population? If so, how?

STEP 7 Assess the effect of the environmental change on future generations. Mice with brown fur are still more likely to be eaten and are therefore no longer mating. Remove half of the genotypes (pairs of beans) that have the dominant brown fur phenotype. Remate the resulting gene pool for another generation. Record the genotypes of this third generation in the chart below. Remember to use the correct alleles (*B* and *b*). (*Note*: You may not need all the rows in the chart.)

Individual	Genotype	Individual	Genotype
1		21	
2		22	
3		23	
4		24	
5		25	
6		26	
7		27	
8		28	
9		29	
10		30	
11		31	
12		32	
13		33	
14		34	
15		35	
16		36	
17		37	
18		38	
19		39	
20		40	

9. How many alleles of each type are present in your overall population this time?

10. What is happening to the dominant allele?

11. What might eventually happen in this population if the new snowy environment remains and having brown fur continues to harm reproductive success?

12. While natural selection was under way, how did genetic drift simultaneously affect the allele frequency for fur color across generations?

STEP 8 Assess the effect of random mutation on allele frequencies. In this third generation, there is a DNA replication error in one mouse's gametes. A new allele is formed that results in gray fur. Replace one of the brown beans (brown fur alleles) with a black bean to represent the new gray fur allele mutation. Like the brown fur allele, the gray fur allele is dominant over the white fur allele.

13. Consider how the presence of this new fur color allele might influence the future evolution of this population. Under what circumstances might this version of the fur color gene be favored? Under what circumstances might this version of the gene be eliminated from the gene pool?

EXERCISE 6   HARDY–WEINBERG EQUILIBRIUM

Work in a small group or alone to complete this exercise. In human population X, consider the simple Mendelian trait for freckles. *F* is the dominant allele and *f* is the recessive allele. Individuals who are homozygous dominant (*FF*) or heterozygous (*Ff*) for the trait express freckles. Individuals who are homozygous recessive (*ff*) for the trait do not express freckles. In this population, 30% (0.3) of the alleles are recessive (*f*) and 70% (0.7) are dominant (*F*).

1. Use the Hardy–Weinberg equation to determine the genotype frequencies we should *expect* in the next generation. Be sure to show your work.

2. You have collected data on the *observed* genotype frequencies of the next generation. They are 60% *FF*, 30% *Ff*, and 10% *ff*. Based on these observations and your expectations, is this trait currently evolving in this population? Why or why not?

CRITICAL THINKING QUESTIONS

On a separate sheet of paper, answer the following questions.

1. Mutations occur in DNA throughout the cells of our bodies, but mutations do not always lead to evolutionary changes. Describe the circumstances under which mutations *will* have a real evolutionary effect on future generations. Describe the circumstances under which mutations *will not* have a real evolutionary effect on future generations.

2. Describe a hypothetical scenario of natural selection for a trait. Be sure to describe each of the key elements (such as how the trait varies in the population, how the trait factors into resource competition, and how the trait frequency changes over multiple generations).

3. Describe a hypothetical scenario of the founder effect for a trait where substantial genetic variation is lost (causing a genetic bottleneck). Be sure to describe each of the key elements (such as why the founder event occurs, why genetic information is lost, and how the trait frequency changes over multiple generations).

4. Describe a hypothetical scenario of gene flow for a trait. Be sure to describe each of the key elements (such as the trait frequency in the two isolated populations prior to gene flow, why gene flow occurs, and the consequences of the gene flow in future generations).

5. In human population A, hitchhiker's thumb is a simple Mendelian trait. For this trait, *N* is the dominant allele and *n* is the recessive allele. Individuals who are homozygous dominant (*NN*) or heterozygous (*Nn*) express non-hitchhiker's thumbs. Individuals who are homozygous recessive (*nn*) express hitchhiker's thumbs. In this population, 90% (0.9) of the alleles are dominant (*N*) and 10% (0.1) are recessive (*n*).

   - Use the Hardy–Weinberg equation to determine the genotype frequencies we should *expect* in the next generation. Be sure to show your work.

   - You have collected data on the *observed* genotype frequencies of the next generation. They are 70% *NN*, 20% *Nn*, and 10% *nn*. Based on these observations and your expectations, is this trait currently evolving in this population? Why or why not?

6. The flu vaccine (administered as a shot or a nasal spray) is made of a combination of the different types of influenza viruses that research indicates will be most common during the upcoming flu season. For each type of influenza, there are numerous specific viruses that can be selected for use in the vaccine. The vaccine works by introducing small amounts of these influenza viruses to the body. Their presence stimulates the immune system to create antibodies against these specific viruses that help protect the individual from becoming infected with them. Each year, the specific viruses used in the vaccine will vary. Based on what you know of evolution, why might this be the case? Why can't we reuse the same vaccine (and combination of viruses) from year to year?

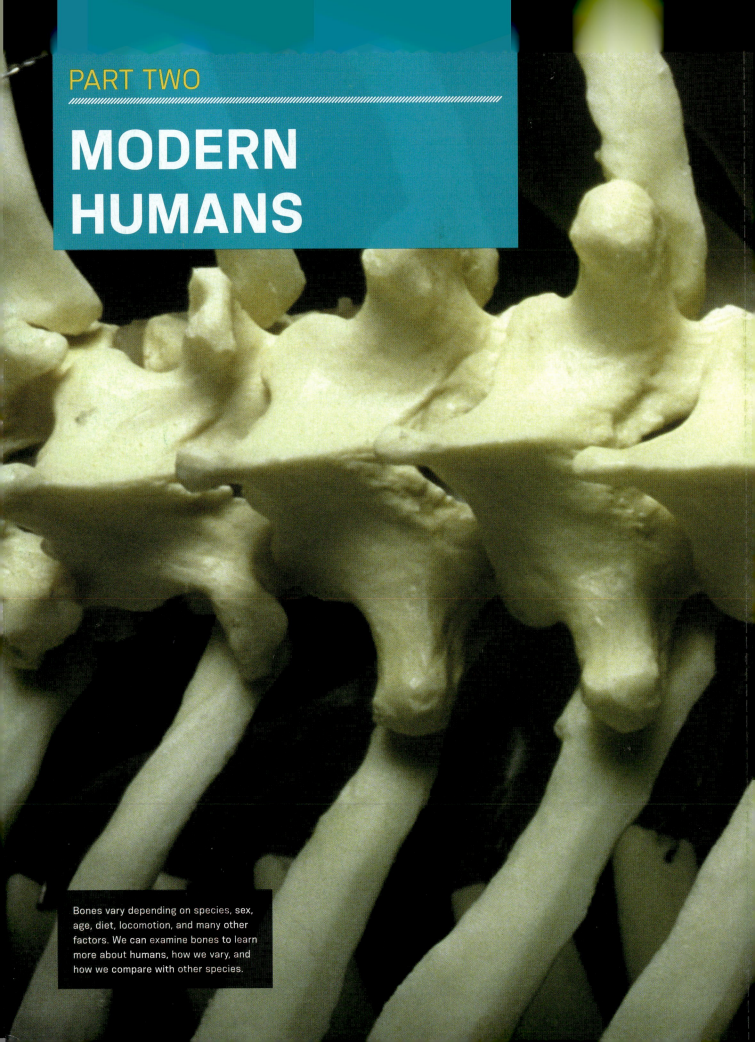

PART TWO

MODERN HUMANS

Bones vary depending on species, sex, age, diet, locomotion, and many other factors. We can examine bones to learn more about humans, how we vary, and how we compare with other species.

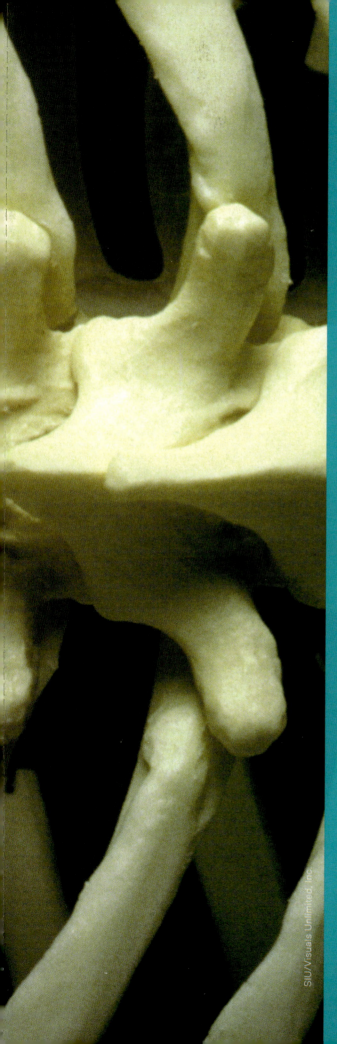

LAB 5: INTRODUCTION TO THE SKELETON

WHAT TOPICS ARE COVERED IN THIS LAB?

- An examination of bone's function in the body and the different types of bone
- A look at how the bone cells work together to make and resorb bone in the body
- An orientation to the skeleton and important directional terminology
- An introduction to the types of bones and key features of bone

LAB 6: BONES OF THE SKELETON

WHAT TOPICS ARE COVERED IN THIS LAB?

- A review of the major bones of the axial skeleton and their defining traits
- A review of the major bones of the appendicular skeleton and their defining traits

LAB 7: BIOARCHAEOLOGY AND FORENSIC ANTHROPOLOGY

WHAT TOPICS ARE COVERED IN THIS LAB?

- An overview of bioarchaeology and the methods used by bioarchaeologists to study past humans
- An introduction to the methods used by forensic anthropologists

LAB 8: MODERN HUMAN VARIATION

WHAT TOPICS ARE COVERED IN THIS LAB?

- A consideration of the biological and cultural basis for "race"
- Modern human adaptation and variation, with particular attention given to:
  - » Skin color
  - » Altitude adaptations
  - » Climatic adaptations (Allen's and Bergmann's rules)
  - » ABO blood system allele frequency distributions
  - » Lactose tolerance
  - » The sickle-cell trait

SIU/Visuals Unlimited, Inc.

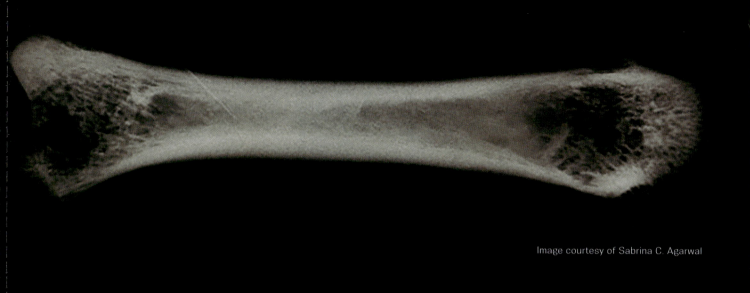

Image courtesy of Sabrina C. Agarwal

When looking at an X-ray, we notice that the exterior edge of the bone appears to be whiter than the inside. This coloration reflects the different composition of the exterior and interior tissue of individual bones.

LAB 5

///

Introduction to the Skeleton

Lab Learning Objectives

By the end of this lab, students should be able to:

- explain the major functions of bone.

- describe the types of bone tissue.

- discuss the bone remodeling process and why it occurs.

- differentiate between the axial and the appendicular skeletal elements.

- use directional terminology, overall bone shape, and bone features to describe bones.

Many of us have had bones in our bodies X-rayed to check for damage and fractures following an injury. Even if you have not seen an X-ray of your own bones, you have probably seen an X-ray of someone else's bones on television, in books, or online. When looking at an X-ray, have you ever wondered why the bone appears brighter white toward the exterior and darker toward the interior? Does it reflect some difference in the density or the structure of the bone tissue? This lab explores the basics of bone biology and provides answers to these questions and more.

Biological anthropologists often work with skeletal material, comparing humans and nonhuman primates, analyzing fossil materials, or examining human remains in forensic settings. As such, biological anthropologists need to have an understanding of bone, its function, and its tissue structures. Biological anthropologists must also be able to describe the relative position and orientation of bones within the skeletons of different primates, and this lab presents the terminology and concepts necessary for these descriptions.

connective tissue
body tissue made of cells, fibers (such as collagen fibers), and extracellular matrix

cartilage a type of flexible connective tissue found at the joints between bones and in the nose and ear

articulation a place where bones meet in the body; a joint

fibrous joint a joint united by irregular, fibrous connective tissue that allows for little to no movement

cartilaginous joint a joint united by cartilage that allows some movement

synovial joint a highly mobile joint held together by ligaments and by irregular connective tissue that forms a fluid-filled articular capsule

INTRODUCTION

In this lab, we begin with an overview of the skeletal system and consideration of the various roles bone plays in the body. We then examine the types of bone tissue and bone cells, and we explore how bone cells work together to make, resorb, and maintain the bones of the body. We continue with an orientation to the skeleton. We differentiate between the axial and appendicular skeletal elements and review important directional terminology. We conclude by describing how bones can be distinguished by their shapes and features.

BONE FUNCTION

Bones play two key roles in our bodies. First, the bones of the skeleton have a *structural function*. They act like the wood frame of a house. The muscles are attached to the bones, like drywall is attached to wood studs. Thus the skeleton gives the muscles the structural support they need and provides a system of levers the muscles can use to move the body. The framing of a house also provides a protected area where the plumbing and the electrical wiring can be erected. Many of the bones in our bodies act as similar protective structures. For example, the rib cage forms a protected area for many vital organs, such as the heart and lungs.

The second major function of the skeleton is a *physiological function*, meaning that the skeleton is an essential part of the normal and healthy functioning of the body. Inside the bones, there is a soft tissue called bone marrow. There are two types of bone marrow: red marrow and yellow marrow. The red marrow is tissue that is capable of producing blood cells for the rest of the body. The yellow marrow is made up mostly of fat cells, and the amount of yellow marrow increases as adults age. In addition, our bones store important nutrients, particularly calcium and phosphorus. When these nutrients are needed elsewhere in the body, they can be released from the bones and sent where necessary. By producing blood cells and storing fat and key nutrients, the skeleton plays a vital role in supporting the overall health of the body.

THE SKELETAL SYSTEM AND BONE TISSUE

Bone and cartilage are two types of **connective tissue** in the skeletal system. Connective tissue is made up of cells, fibers (mostly elastic collagen fibers), and extracellular matrix. **Cartilage** is a flexible type of connective tissue due to its abundance of collagen fibers, but it has no direct blood supply. Cartilage is found in many parts of the human body, including the joints between bones, the ear, the nose, and the bronchial tubes in the airways. In an embryo, the skeleton is made up almost entirely of cartilage, which is replaced by bone tissue during growth and development. By the time the growth period is complete, most of the cartilage in the skeleton has been replaced by bone, except in a few places where it is retained into adulthood, such as in the rib cage and on the surfaces of joints.

Joints are **articulations**, places where two bones meet, or *articulate with,* each other. The articular surface of each bone in a joint is smooth. During life, the articular ends of the bones are separated from each other by a layer of cartilage that helps the joint withstand mechanical impact and movement. There are many joints in the human body, and they are classified by their amount of movement and the type of tissue that connects them. The three main types of joints are fibrous joints, cartilaginous joints, and synovial joints. **Fibrous joints** are united by short, irregular, fibrous connective tissue, and they allow for little or no movement (examples are the suture joints between the flat skull bones). **Cartilaginous joints** are united by cartilage and permit a little movement (such as the joints between vertebrae in the spine, formed by intervertebral disks). **Synovial joints** are the most mobile joints and allow a variety of move-

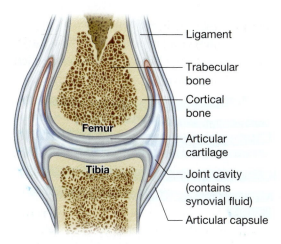

FIGURE 5.1 The Human Knee
At the knee joint, a typical synovial joint, the femur (thighbone) articulates with the tibia (shinbone). Notice that the bones are held together by ligaments.

ments (such as the knee or shoulder joint). The bones of synovial joints are held together along their outer surfaces by ligaments and dense, irregular connective tissue that forms an articular capsule around the ligaments **(FIGURE 5.1)**. Unlike fibrous and cartilaginous joints, synovial joints have a small gap, the joint space, between the articular surfaces of the bones. The capsule is filled with a slippery lubricant called synovial fluid, which flows into the joint space and helps healthy joints move easily.

Bone is a much more rigid connective tissue than cartilage. The bones of the skeletal system work together with many other systems in the body, such as the muscular system and the circulatory system. Approximately one-third of bone tissue is made of organic components, and two-thirds is made of inorganic components. The organic components include proteins like collagen, which helps make up the matrix surrounding the cells in the bone. The inorganic material is primarily carbonated apatite, a mineral made up of calcium, phosphate, and fluoride. While the inorganic components are important for the structural integrity of the bone, the collagen fibers also contribute significantly to the bone's strength and resilience.

There are two main types of bone: woven bone and lamellar bone. **Woven bone** is unorganized bone, primarily seen in immature bones. Juvenile skeletons that are still growing and developing have a lot of woven bone. However, adults can also have woven bone. For example, if you have broken a bone, you will have woven bone at the site of the injury as the bone tries to fill in and repair the break. The other type of bone, **lamellar bone**, is mature bone. An adult's skeleton, when not injured or healing, is made of lamellar bone.

Within lamellar bone, there are two types of bone tissue: cortical bone and trabecular bone **(FIGURE 5.2)**. **Cortical bone** is the compact tissue that makes up the outside surface of a bone. It often appears solid and smooth. In contrast, **trabecular bone** is the spongy or honeycomb-like tissue that makes up the inside of a bone. It appears less solid and rougher than cortical bone, but it is more metabolically active due to the greater amount of surface area in its honeycomb-like structure.

On a microscopic scale, there are three main types of bone cells: osteoblasts, osteocytes, and

woven bone a type of bone tissue that is unorganized and primarily found in immature or healing bone

lamellar bone a type of organized, mature bone

cortical bone the compact tissue that forms the outside surface of a lamellar bone

trabecular bone the spongy (honeycomb-like) tissue that forms the inside of a lamellar bone

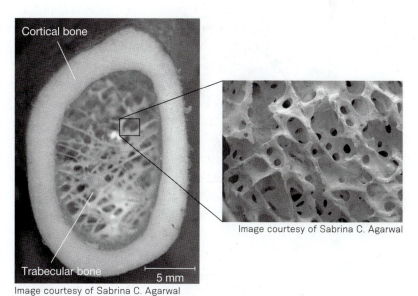

Image courtesy of Sabrina C. Agarwal

FIGURE 5.2 Bone Tissue
Cross section of a mature bone, showing cortical bone on the exterior and trabecular bone in the interior. Notice the honeycomb-like appearance of trabecular bone.

osteoblast a bone cell responsible for forming bone

osteocyte a bone cell responsible for bone maintenance

osteoclast a bone cell responsible for removing bone

bone remodeling the process of bone resorption and formation

osteoclasts. Each of these bone cell types has a different primary function. The **osteoblasts** are responsible for forming bone, the **osteocytes** are responsible for bone maintenance, and the **osteoclasts** are responsible for removing bone. These bone cells work together in a constant process called bone remodeling.

BONE REMODELING

Throughout our lives, our bones are constantly being resorbed and re-formed. In fact, approximately every 10 years, your skeleton is completely replaced by new bone tissue. This process of bone resorption and re-formation is called **bone remodeling** (FIGURE 5.3). In this process, the osteoclasts remove and resorb bone. These osteoclasts are large cells with multiple nuclei. They act almost like cleaning pads that scrub away old bone. Then, the osteoblasts come in to make (or build) new bone. As the osteoblasts

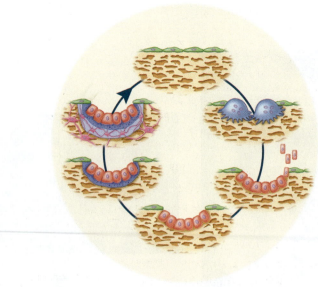

 Osteoclast   Osteoblast   Osteocyte

FIGURE 5.3 Bone Remodeling Cycle
In the bone remodeling cycle, the osteoclasts remove and resorb bone. Then, the osteoblasts build up new bone. Trapped osteoblasts become living bone cells (called osteocytes) that maintain bone.

become trapped in the bone tissue as it mineralizes, they become osteocytes. These osteocytes are the living bone cells that are then left responsible for maintaining the bone tissue.

There are many reasons why this bone remodeling process happens in the skeleton. The first is to allow for normal *growth and development*. As we age from birth to adulthood, our skeletons need to grow, and many osteoblasts lay down tissue to allow for this expansion and growth of bones.

The second reason for bone remodeling is to *extract important nutrients* from the skeleton. Remember, bones store nutrients such as calcium and phosphorus. When those nutrients are needed elsewhere in the body, bone remodeling begins. Tiny gaps are made in the bone to release the trapped nutrients. The tiny gaps are then filled in, and the bone is built back up.

A third reason for bone remodeling is to *repair damage* to the bone. This damage can be large-scale damage, like a bone fracture. But even if you have never had a fracture, your skeleton is still full of small-scale microdamage from everyday use. Like a road that slowly accumulates pits and small cracks, the bones accumulate microscopic damage every day. And if that minor damage goes unrepaired, it can lead to much worse damage. In a road, it can result in potholes and much larger cracks. In your skeleton, neglecting the microdamage can decrease the strength and health of the bone. Thus, in healthy bone, the cells work together continuously to repair damage on multiple scales.

A final reason why bone is remodeled is to *respond to functional and biomechanical challenges* to the bone. A simple phrase is used to highlight this relationship between bone remodeling and the functional needs of the skeleton: Use it or lose it. If you use a part of your body a lot, the muscles in that area will grow larger. When you have larger muscles, you need larger bones for their attachment. So, when you *use* a body part a lot, the corresponding muscles and bones grow bigger. Bone remodeling drives this bone growth. At the same time, if you do not use a part of your body enough, the muscles in that area will become smaller. When there are smaller muscles, less bone is needed for their attachment. So, when you don't use a body part enough, you *lose* muscle and bone mass. Bone remodeling also drives this bone loss.

We see the use it or lose it principle in our lives all the time. For example, you may have noticed that your ring sizes are slightly larger on the hand you write with because you use this hand more frequently. More extreme examples of this principle are found in athletes and astronauts. Athletes often use one arm more than another (think of baseball pitchers, football quarterbacks or tennis players). The bone of the arm that is used more will be larger. Astronauts are an opposite example. After spending extended time in outer space, astronauts often lose significant muscle and bone mass because of the lack of mechanical force on their muscles and bones in the zero gravity environment.

AXIAL SKELETON AND APPENDICULAR SKELETON

Now that we have talked about bone function and composition, it is important to contextualize this information with an overall orientation to the skeleton. The human skeleton can be divided into two parts: the axial skeleton and the appendicular skeleton (FIGURE 5.4). The **axial skeleton** is composed of all of the bones that lie along the midline (or central axis) of the body. It includes the bones of the cranium, the mandible, the rib cage, and the vertebral column. All of these bones lie on the central axis of the body.

The **appendicular skeleton** is composed of all of the bones of the appendages (arms and legs). It includes the bones of the arm, wrist, and hand, as well as the bones of the leg, ankle, and foot. Importantly, bones are considered to be part of an appendage if they are essential to the function of that appendage. This means there are some bones that appear to lie on the central axis but are actually part of the appen-

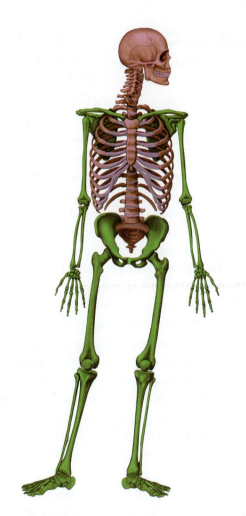

FIGURE 5.4 The Axial and Appendicular Skeletal Elements
In the human skeleton, the bones that run along the midline (central axis) of the body are considered part of the axial skeleton (red). The bones that make up the limbs (appendages) are considered part of the appendicular skeleton (green).

dicular skeleton. For example, the hip bones (or pelvis) might appear to be the base of the body's midline, as if they were part of the axial skeleton. However, the primary function of the pelvis is to act as an area of muscle attachment for leg muscles. This makes the pelvis part of the appendicular skeleton. Similarly, the clavicle and scapula, bones that help make up the shoulder, appear to be on the midline of the body. However, these two bones are primarily involved with arm muscle attachment and stability, which makes them part of the appendicular skeleton.

axial skeleton the bones that lie along the midline (central axis) of the body

appendicular skeleton the bones of the appendages (arms and legs)

DIRECTIONAL TERMINOLOGY

In addition to distinguishing between the axial and appendicular skeletal elements, it is also possible to describe the locations and positions of bones (and other bony parts or features) using directional terminology. Any description of the bones begins with the body in what is called the anatomical position. By using the anatomical position as the starting point to describe the body, we can refer to different elements of the skeleton regardless of their position. In humans, which are bipedal (walk upright), the standard anatomical position is with the head and body facing forward and standing up, with the arms close to the sides of the body and the palms of the hands facing forward. When describing animals that are quadrupedal (walk on four legs), the standard anatomical position is with all four feet touching the ground and with the belly of the animal parallel to the ground. The anatomical position of the skull has its own international convention, called the Frankfurt plane, in which the lower margins of the orbits (the sockets in which the eyes and their appendages sit) and the upper margins of the ear canals all lie in the same horizontal plane. This is the approximate position the skull is in when someone is standing upright and facing forward. The Frankfurt plane is used to compare the skulls of living and fossil human and nonhuman primates.

The directional terms used to describe the locations and positions of bones all make up pairs of opposites, where the two terms in a pair describe two alternate positions and each term must be used in relation to other parts of the body. For example, a bone cannot simply be called superior, but it can be said to be positioned superiorly in relation to another bone. Most of these positions are relative to the midline or different sides of the body. **Superior** and **inferior** are used to refer to relative positions along the longitudinal axis of the body in the anatomical position **(FIGURE 5.5)**. Bones that are superior are located higher on this axis (closer to the top of the head) than bones that are inferior. For example, the cervical vertebrae (in the

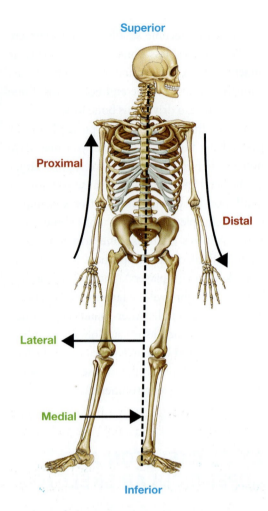

FIGURE 5.5 Superior–Inferior, Medial–Lateral, and Proximal–Distal
Directional terminology describes the relative positions of bones in the skeleton. Notice that bones higher along the axis are more superior, and bones lower along this axis are more inferior. Lateral bones are farther from the central axis (like those in the pinky toe), while medial bones are closer to this axis (like those in the big toe). Finally, if a bone (or end of a bone) is closer to the trunk, it is more proximal. If the bone (or end of a bone) is farther from the trunk, it is more distal.

neck) are superior to the lumbar vertebrae (in the lower back).

Medial and lateral are used to refer to positions relative to the midline of the body, but they are different from superior and inferior (see Figure 5.5). With superior and inferior, the focus is on a position along the central axis. However, with medial and lateral, the focus is on what is closer to or farther from the longitudinal axis. **Medial** refers to being closer to the midline, and

superior relative location higher on the body's axis

inferior relative location lower on the body's axis

medial relative location closer to the midline of the body

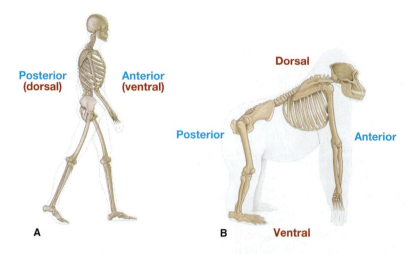

FIGURE 5.6 Anterior–Posterior and Ventral–Dorsal
(A) In the human, the front of the body is both the anterior and the ventral side, and the back of the body is both the posterior and the dorsal side. (B) In the ape, the underside of the body (closest to the ground) is the ventral side; the top of the body (closest to the sky) is the dorsal side; the front of the body (closer to the face) is the anterior side; and the rear of the body is the posterior side.

lateral refers to being farther from the midline (more to the side). For example, the pinky toe is lateral to the big toe.

Proximal and distal are also used to refer to positions relative to the middle of the body, but here the emphasis is on being toward the trunk or away from the trunk (see Figure 5.5). These terms are often used to describe different ends of bones, particularly in the arms and legs. The **proximal** end is the end nearest to (in greatest proximity to) the trunk. The **distal** end is the end that is farthest (most distant) from the trunk. For example, the shoulder end of the humerus (the upper arm bone) is the proximal end, and the elbow end of the humerus is the distal end.

Anterior and posterior are used to refer to sides of the body (**FIGURE 5.6A**). **Anterior** refers to the front, and **posterior** refers to the back. Thus, the anterior surface of a bone is the surface that faces the front of the body. The posterior surface of a bone is the surface that faces the back of the body. For example, the anterior surface of the cranium is made up of the face bones, and the posterior surface is made up of the bone at the back of the skull, called the occipital bone. Similarly, when a bone feature has an anterior position, it is located closer to the front of the bone. If the feature has a posterior posi-

tion, it is located closer to the back of the bone. For example, the eye sockets are positioned more anteriorly on the skull than the external auditory meatus (the holes that serve as the openings for the ear canals).

In the case of quadrupedal vertebrates, the terms dorsal and ventral are also used to refer to sides of the body (**FIGURE 5.6B**). **Ventral** refers to the belly side, and **dorsal** refers to the back side. You can think of dolphins that have a dorsal fin on their backs. In humans, these terms are synonymous to anterior (front) and posterior (back). The ventral surface of a bone is the same as the anterior surface, and the dorsal surface of a bone is the same as the posterior surface.

DISTINGUISHING BONES: SHAPES

Vertebrate organisms have a large number of different bones. Humans, for example, have a total of 206 bones (**FIGURE 5.7**). With so many bones, how do we distinguish among them? One way to do this is by looking at their overall shape. The bones of the human skeleton can be classified into four different categories based on

lateral relative location farther from the midline of the body

proximal relative location closer to the trunk of the body

distal relative location farther away from the trunk of the body

anterior relative location toward the front of the body

posterior relative location toward the rear of the body

ventral relative location toward the belly of the body

dorsal relative location toward the back of the body

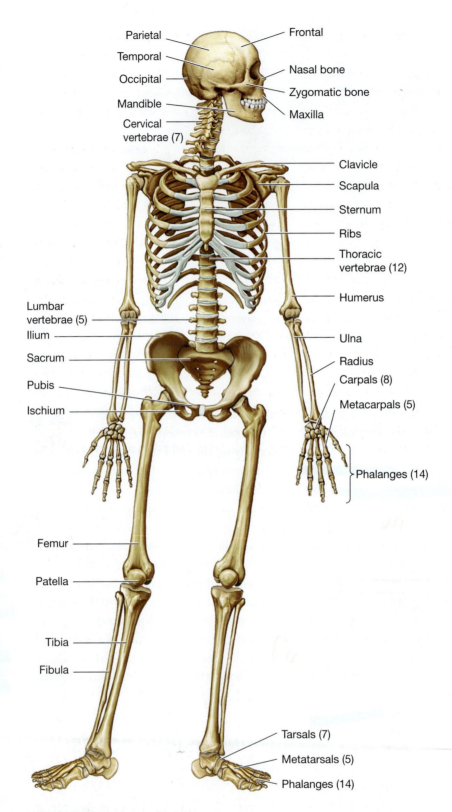

FIGURE 5.7 The Human Skeleton
The major bones in this diagram of the human skeleton are labeled.

their shape: long bones, short bones, flat bones, and irregular bones.

Long bones are made of a central shaft with distinct, slightly larger ends on each side **(FIGURE 5.8)**. The long bones, joints, and associated muscles work together to help the arms and legs achieve their maximum potential when engaged in daily activities, such as bearing weight, facilitating movements such as flexion (bending) and extension (straightening), and carrying loads. In particular, having longer muscles in the arms and legs allows for a greater range of motion, and these longer muscles require longer bones for support and extension. A classic example of a long bone is the femur in your thigh. It has a long shaft in the middle and two distinct ends. Importantly, while the femur is a measurably long and large bone (typically the largest bone in the human body), not all long bones are large. For example, the long bones of the hand and fingers are much smaller than the femur, but they are still considered long bones because of their shape and how they grow. The ends of the long bones (called the *epiphyses*) have growth plates that separate them from the shaft to allow the bone to grow in length until the end of puberty (see Lab 7 for more information).

In contrast to long bones, **short bones** do not have a clear shaft. Instead, short bones are more cube-like in shape, with width and length dimensions that are similar **(FIGURE 5.9)**. These short bones are often found in compact areas, and the presence of multiple, tightly packed short bones limits the range of motion in those areas. The bones of the wrist (the carpals) are classic short bones. They are cube-like, appearing relatively similar on most sides, and there are several of them packed into a small area, which limits mobility and gives stability within the wrist.

Flat bones are thin, platelike bones that make up a small proportion of the bones in the body **(FIGURE 5.10)**. They consist of a layer of trabecular bone sandwiched between two thin layers of flat cortical bone. Flat bones may serve as broad

long bone a bone with an elongated middle shaft and distinct, slightly larger ends

short bone a bone with a cube-like shape, with similar width and length dimensions

flat bone a platelike bone consisting of a layer of trabecular bone sandwiched between two thin layers of flat cortical bone

FIGURE 5.8
A Long Bone
The human femur (thighbone) is a typical long bone. Notice the elongated shape with a middle shaft and two distinct ends.

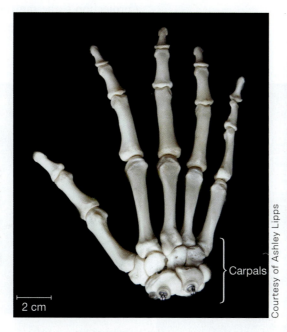

FIGURE 5.9 A Short Bone
Human carpals (wrist bones) are typical short bones. Notice the cube-like shape. Remember, though, that the hand and finger bones (the metacarpals and phalanges) are long bones, despite their small size.

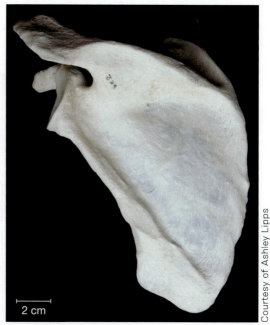

FIGURE 5.10 A Flat Bone
The human scapula (shoulder blade) is a typical flat bone. The generally flat shape that allows for extensive muscle attachment.

irregular bone a bone with a complex shape that is not easily classified as long, short, or flat

projection an area of bone that protrudes from the main bone surface

sagittal crest a ridge of bone along the midline of the cranium that allows for the attachment of extra-large chewing muscles

depression a hollow or depressed area of a bone

fossa (**fossae**, plural) a shallow depression in a bone

groove a furrow along the surface of a bone

areas for muscle attachment (as in the shoulder blade, or scapula) or as platelike protection for delicate structures (as in the bones of the skull, or cranium).

Irregular bones do not readily fit into any of the other three categories. They have complex and varied shapes (**FIGURE 5.11**). The bones of the spine, called vertebrae, are good examples of irregular bones. They are clearly not long bones because they do not have anything resembling a shaft. We can also rule out a classification of vertebrae as flat bones because they are too thick and fat to be part of the platelike group of bones. At first they might appear to be short bones because of the cube-like shape of the vertebral body. However, on closer consideration, it becomes apparent that the specialized spines sticking out of the vertebrae (which serve to anchor key ligaments of the spine) make the overall shape of these bones highly unusual and less cube-like. The vertebrae don't qualify as long bones, short bones, or flat bones; therefore, they are placed in the catchall category of irregular bones.

DISTINGUISHING BONES: FEATURES

Distinguishing among bones does not stop with their overall shape. Multiple bones can be placed into each of the shape categories (long, short, flat, and irregular). How can we further distinguish the bones within these broad categories? Another way to describe bones is by using the landmarks and features on them. Remember, bone is a responsive tissue, so influences from surrounding tissues, such as attaching muscles, will leave marks on the skeleton. Because each bone will have slightly different markings depending on how it relates to and interacts with other nearby tissues, we can use these markings (bone features) to help us further identify specific bones.

There are numerous specific types of bone features, but we will focus on three major types: (1) projections; (2) depressions, fossae, and grooves; and (3) foramina and canals. **Projections** are areas of bone that stick out from the rest of the bone surface. These bumps or ridges vary in size and usually serve as sites for muscle and tendon attachment. An extreme example of a projection is the **sagittal crest** (**FIGURE 5.12**), an extra ridge of bone that runs along the mid-

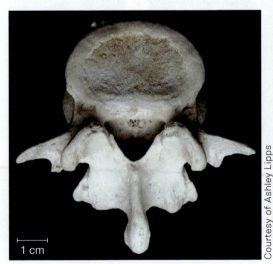

Courtesy of Ashley Lipps

FIGURE 5.11 An Irregular Bone
A human vertebra (back bone) is a typical irregular bone. It does not easily fit into the other shape categories because it is not elongated, cube-like, or flat. It has a unique, irregular shape.

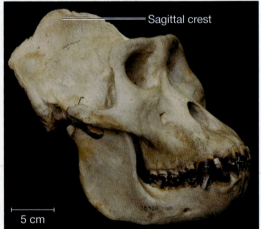

Sagittal crest

Courtesy of Ashley Lipps

FIGURE 5.12 Sagittal Crest
The sagittal crest on a gorilla is an example of a bone projection. It is an area of bone that projects from the surface of the cranium (skull) and allows for the attachment of large chewing muscles.

line of the cranium in some primates, such as gorillas. It allows for the attachment of extra-large chewing muscles.

Depressions, fossae, and **grooves** are indentations on the bone surface. These indentations often accommodate nerves, blood vessels, muscles, or other structures. For example, there is a large indentation called the iliac fossa on the anterior of the ilium (the upper bone of the pelvis) (**FIGURE 5.13**). This indentation accommodates the iliac muscle, which attaches in that area.

nels in bone, like tunnels. These holes in the bone are usually associated with nerves or vessels. For example, the **foramen magnum** is the large hole at the base of the cranium (**FIGURE 5.14**). It allows for the brain stem (descending from inside the cranium) to connect to the spinal cord (inside the vertebral column).

foramen (foramina, plural) a hole in a bone

canal a narrow tunnel or tubular channel in a bone

foramen magnum the large hole at the base of the cranium that allows the brain to connect to the spinal cord

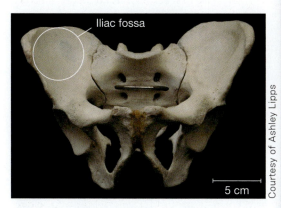

Courtesy of Ashley Lipps

Iliac fossa

5 cm

FIGURE 5.13 Iliac Fossa
The iliac fossa on the anterior surface of the ilium (upper portion of the pelvis) is an example of a fossa. It is an indented area of bone where the iliac muscle attaches.

Foramina and **canals** are holes in the bone. Foramina (*foramen,* singular) are usually simple holes, while canals are often narrow, tubular chan-

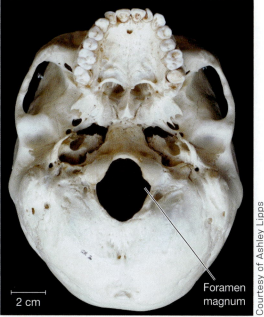

Courtesy of Ashley Lipps

Foramen magnum

2 cm

FIGURE 5.14 Foramen Magnum
The foramen magnum on the underside of a human cranium (skull) is an example of a bone foramen. It is a large hole in the cranium that allows the brain to connect to the spinal cord.

CONCEPT REVIEW QUESTIONS

Name: _____   Section: _____

Course: _____   Date: _____

Answer the following questions in the space provided.

1. Describe one of the main functions of the skeleton inside the body.

   It is a structural function, sort of like a wooden frame.

2. What are the two main types of bone tissue in lamellar bone?

3. How much of the skeleton is made of organic components?
   A. 2/3
   B. 1/4
   C. 1/3
   D. All of it

4. Which type of bone cell is responsible for making bone?
   A. Osteoblast
   B. Osteoclast
   C. Osteodon
   D. Osteocyte

5. Which type of bone cell is responsible for removing bone?
   A. Osteodon
   B. Osteocyte
   C. Osteoblast
   D. Osteoclast

6. Describe one reason why bone is remodeled.

7. Name one bone that is part of the appendicular skeleton.

8. Compared with the cervical (neck) vertebrae, the lumbar (lower back) vertebrae are positioned more:

   A. anteriorly.
   B. inferiorly.
   C. ventrally.
   D. laterally.

9. You are examining a bone that has a shaft in the middle and distinct ends on each side. What type of bone is this?

   A. Flat bone
   B. Long bone
   C. Irregular bone
   D. Short bone

10. A hole in the bone that is associated with a nearby nerve or vessel is usually called a:

   A. depression.
   B. fossa.
   C. foramen.
   D. projection.

LAB EXERCISES

Name: _____   Section: _____

Course: _____   Date: _____

EXERCISE 1 BONE REMODELING

Work in a small group or alone to complete this exercise.

1. Describe one hypothetical situation that illustrates the "use it" portion of the use it or lose it principle. Description of the situation/behavior:

   Explanation for why *more* bone is present under these circumstances:

2. Describe one hypothetical situation that illustrates the "lose it" portion of the use it or lose it principle. Description of the situation/behavior:

   Explanation for why *less* bone is present under these circumstances:

EXERCISE 2 AXIAL AND APPENDICULAR SKELETON

Work in a small group or alone to complete this exercise. Review the skeleton diagram provided below.

1. On the diagram, draw *circles* around bones that are part of the axial skeleton.

2. On the diagram, draw *boxes* around bones that are part of the appendicular skeleton.

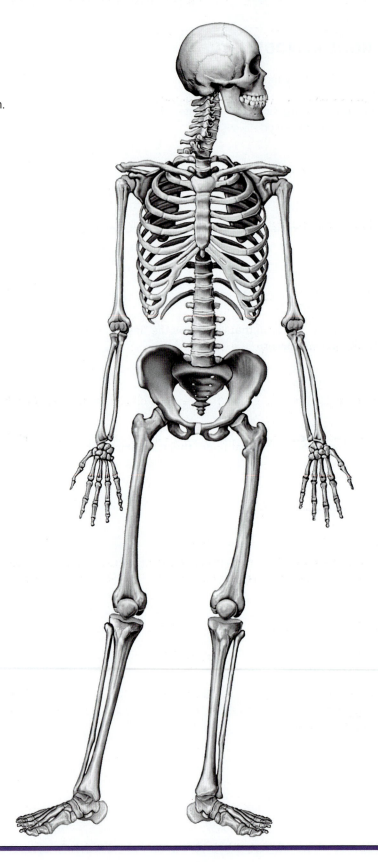

EXERCISE 3 DIRECTIONAL TERMINOLOGY

Work in a small group or alone to complete this exercise. Use the skeletal material provided by your instructor (or the diagram in the Lab 5 Exercise Image Library on p. 130) to answer the following questions.

1. Name three (3) bones that are proximal to the carpals.

2. Name two (2) bones that are anterior to the occipital bone.

3. Name one (1) bone that is superior to the temporal bone.

4. Name four (4) bones that are distal to the femur.

5. Name one (1) bone that is posterior to the sternum.

6. Name one (1) bone that is inferior to the cervical vertebrae.

7. On the diagram in the Exercise Image Library, draw a circle around the toe of each foot that is the most medial.

8. On the diagram in the Exercise Image Library, draw a box around the toe of each foot that is most lateral.

EXERCISE 4 BONE SHAPES

Work in a small group or alone to complete this exercise.

STEP 1 For each of the four bone shapes, choose a different color. Be sure to consider which colors might stand out well against one another. Indicate your color choices in the spaces provided:

- Long bones = _____
- Flat bones = _____
- Short bones = _____
- Irregular bones = _____

STEP 2 Now, review the skeleton diagram provided in Exercise 2 on p. 126. Classify each of the bones on the skeleton diagram as one of the four bone shapes. Color each bone on the diagram the appropriate color based on your color choices above.

EXERCISE 5 BONE FEATURES

Work in a small group to complete this exercise. This exercise is to help you begin to understand the terminology we use to identify the general landmarks and features on bones (you will learn the specific bones of the skeleton and their features in greater detail in Lab 6). Use the skeletal material provided by your instructor (or the photos in the Lab 5 Exercise Image Library on p. 131) to complete the following tasks.

1. Examine the cervical vertebra (neck vertebra). Locate the features boldfaced and described below, and write the corresponding letters in the blanks provided on the image on p. 131.

   A. The *transverse* **foramen** (one on each side of the vertebra) transmits the vertebral arteries that send blood to the brain.

   B. The posterior end of the vertebra has a *spinous* **process** to which muscles and ligaments attach.

   C. The foramen posterior to the body of the vertebra creates the *vertebral* **canal** for the spinal cord to pass through when the vertebrae are stacked up on one another in the spine.

2. Examine the humerus (upper arm bone). Locate the features boldfaced and described below, and write the corresponding letters in the blanks provided on the image on p. 131.

   A. On the posterior side of the distal end of the humerus, there is a feature called the *olecranon* **fossa**. This is where the elbow-forming projection of the ulna (one of the lower arm bones) sits when the lower arm is extended.

   B. The medial side of the distal humerus has a small projection you can feel on the inside of your arm, called the *medial* **epicondyle**.

   C. On the shaft of the humerus there is a projection called the *deltoid* **tuberosity** where the deltoid muscle attaches.

3. Examine the sacrum, shinbone (tibia), and hip bone (pelvis). For each bone, state whether the bone feature indicated (either by your instructor or by a red circle on the photo in the Lab 5 Exercise Image Library on p. 132) is a **projection**, **depression/groove**, or **foramen/canal**.

   A.

   B.

   C.

CRITICAL THINKING QUESTIONS

Use a separate sheet of paper to answer the following questions.

1. The skeleton is an integral part of the body. It works with other major body systems to help the body function and stay healthy. The bones are also shaped by their relationships with other body systems. How does the skeleton specifically work with and relate to the muscular system? How does the skeleton specifically work with and relate to the circulatory system? (Be sure to consider things like bone remodeling and bone features as well as general bone function.)

2. Under what circumstances would an adult have woven (or unorganized) bone?

3. Review your work in Exercise 1 above. Describe an additional hypothetical situation that illustrates the "use it" portion of the use it or lose it principle. Be sure to describe the situation/behavior and explain why more bone is present under these circumstances. Also, describe an additional hypothetical situation that illustrates the "lose it" portion of the use it or lose it principle. Be sure to describe the situation/behavior and explain why less bone is present under these circumstances.

4. Why is a bone like the scapula (shoulder blade) considered part of the appendicular skeleton and not the axial skeleton?

5. Use directional terminology to describe the relationship between the following pairs of bones in the *human* skeleton. Use the skeleton diagram provided in Figure 5.7 (on p. 118) to help you.

   Cranium–pelvis   Femur–tarsals

   Tibia–fibula   Pinky toe phalanges–big toe phalanges

   Sternum–thoracic vertebrae   Occipital–frontal

   Radius–humerus   Lumbar vertebrae–cervical vertebrae

6. Use the skeleton diagram from Exercise 2 (on p. 126) to help you visualize the different bone shapes in the human body. Why are short bones well suited to an area like the wrist? Why are long bones more suited to areas like the lower arm?

7. Consider the mandibular canal pictured here. It is located inside the mandible (lower jawbone), extending posteriorly from the mental foramen. Based on what you know of bone features, what do you think this canal is for? Why would we need a hollow space in this area of this bone?

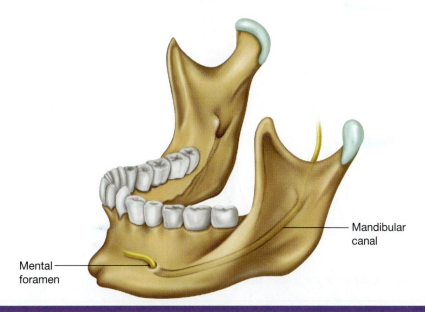

Mandibular canal

Mental foramen

LAB 5 EXERCISE IMAGE LIBRARY
Students should use these images only if directed to by their instructor.

EXERCISE 3 DIRECTIONAL TERMINOLOGY

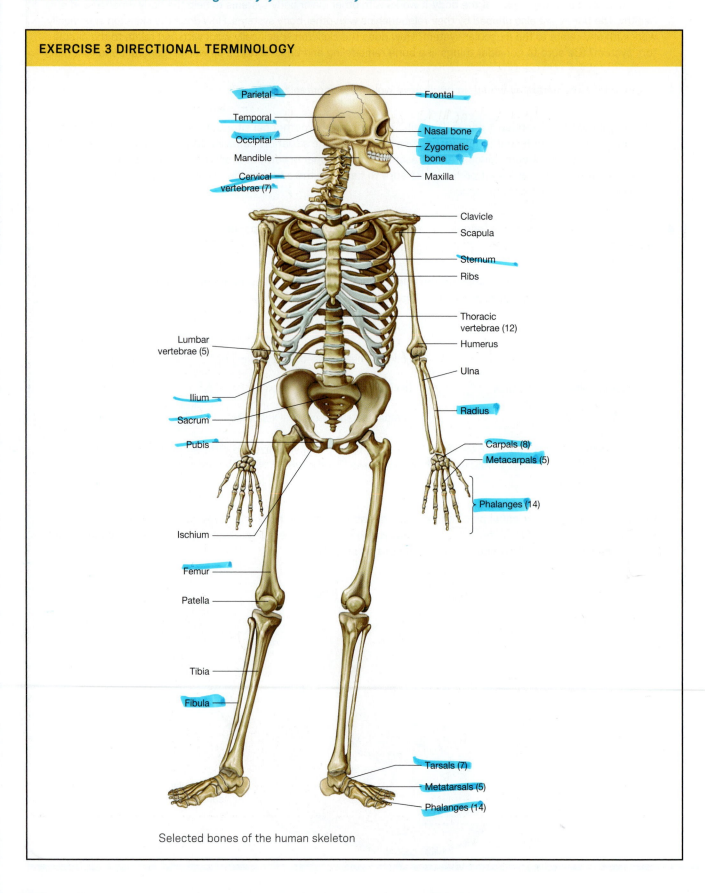

Selected bones of the human skeleton

EXERCISE 5 BONE FEATURES

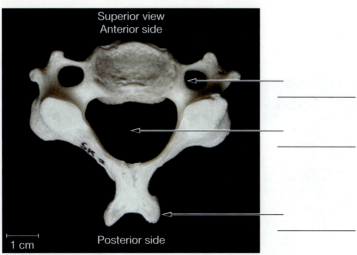

Superior view
Anterior side

Posterior side

1 cm

Courtesy of Ashley Lipps

1. Cervical vertebra

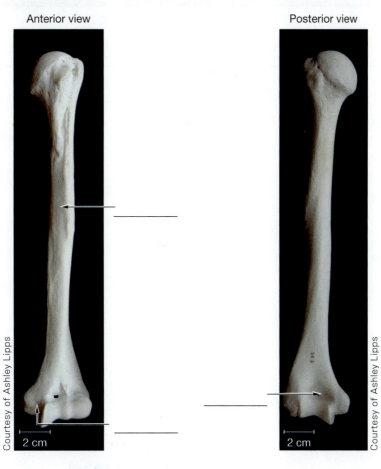

Anterior view

Posterior view

2 cm

2 cm

Courtesy of Ashley Lipps

Courtesy of Ashley Lipps

2. Left humerus (upper arm bone)

EXERCISE 5 BONE FEATURES (CONTINUED)

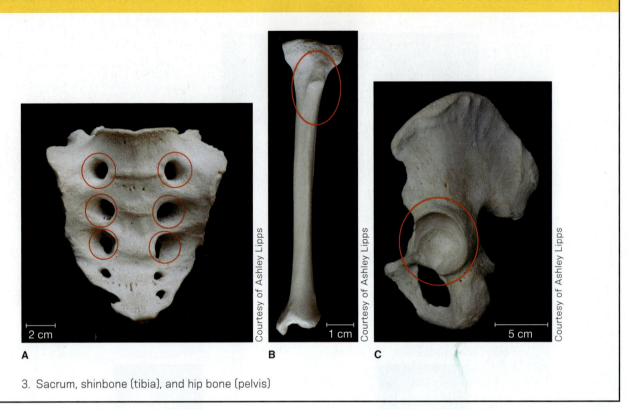

A

2 cm

Courtesy of Ashley Lipps

B

1 cm

Courtesy of Ashley Lipps

C

5 cm

Courtesy of Ashley Lipps

3. Sacrum, shinbone (tibia), and hip bone (pelvis)

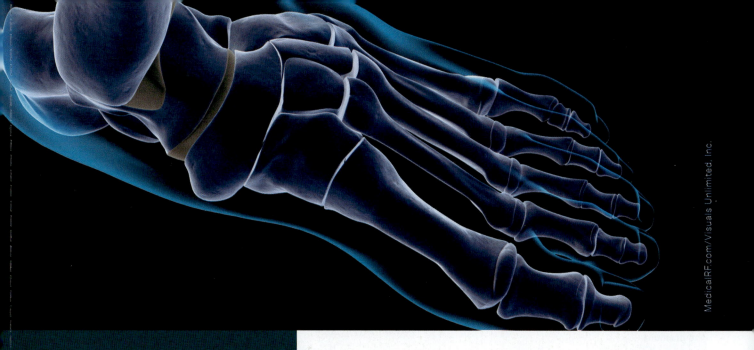

A traditional spiritual called "Skeleton Bones" became a popular children's song used to orient children to the basic parts of the human body, such as the bones of the foot and leg. Biological anthropologists need a more in-depth, scientific understanding of the skeleton for their work.

LAB 6

//

Bones of the Skeleton

Lab Learning Objectives

By the end of this lab, students should be able to:

- identify the major bones of the human skeleton using their defining features.

- identify the teeth of the human skeleton using their defining features.

- compare different bones and discuss how any observable similarities or differences relate to functional similarities or differences.

Many people are familiar with the song "Dem Bones" (also called "Skeleton Bones"). It was originally written as a traditional spiritual and was later recorded by numerous rhythm and blues and jazz musicians. By the mid-1900s, the song had also become a children's standard, which today makes for a classroom game where children can sing the song and point to the various areas of the body it describes:

> With the toe bone connected to the foot bone,
> And the foot bone connected to the ankle bone,
> And the ankle bone connected to the leg bone, . . .

This is a great way for small children to learn the different parts of their bodies, but this song is clearly a simplified description of the bones of the skeleton. There are actually multiple toe bones, and in fact there are multiple foot bones, ankle bones, and leg bones as well. Biological anthropologists must have an accurate and detailed understanding of the skeleton. Familiarity with the human skeleton allows us to better understand skeletal similarities and differences among living primate species, and it provides us with the knowledge we need to analyze fossilized skeletal material from our extinct relatives. In addition, a comprehensive understanding of the human skeleton is essential in the applied field of forensic anthropology. This lab lays the groundwork for these goals by exploring the fundamentals of human skeletal anatomy.

cranium the skull without the jawbone

frontal bone the most anterior bone of the cranium

brow ridge a bony ridge located above the eye orbits

parietal bone one of the paired bones posterior to the frontal bone that forms the top of the cranium

INTRODUCTION

This lab closely examines the major bones of the human skeleton (**FIGURE 6.1**). We begin with a consideration of the bones in the axial skeleton, then turn to the bones of the appendicular skeleton. We discuss the relative location and position of each bone within the body as well as the identifying features on each bone.

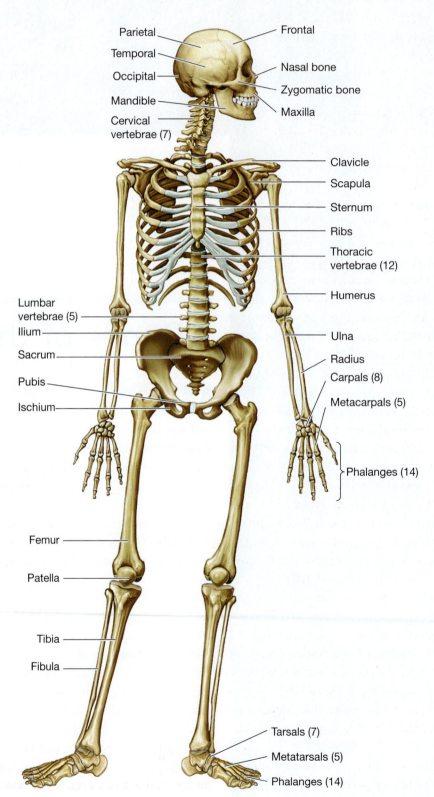

FIGURE 6.1 The Human Skeleton
The major bones in this diagram of the human skeleton are labeled.

Parietal
Temporal
Occipital
Mandible
Cervical vertebrae (7)
Frontal
Nasal bone
Zygomatic bone
Maxilla
Clavicle
Scapula
Sternum
Ribs
Thoracic vertebrae (12)
Humerus
Lumbar vertebrae (5)
Ilium
Sacrum
Pubis
Ischium
Ulna
Radius
Carpals (8)
Metacarpals (5)
Phalanges (14)
Femur
Patella
Tibia
Fibula
Tarsals (7)
Metatarsals (5)
Phalanges (14)

PART 1: THE AXIAL SKELETON

Remember, the *axial skeleton* is made up of the bones that lie along the midline (or central axis) of the body. We will discuss each of the major bones along this axis in humans, beginning at the superior end of the body and working our way down.

The Cranium and Mandible

The skull (the entire bony structure of the head and jaw) is perhaps the most complex element of the skeleton. The **cranium** (that is, the skull without the jawbone) houses many of the key organs of the senses as well as the brain. The skull is also of major interest to biological anthropologists because it is critical in age and sex determinations and is a key structure in understanding the evolutionary history of primates. Although it appears to be a single, complex structure, the cranium is actually made up of many smaller bones that fuse together as we grow (**FIGURE 6.2** and **FIGURE 6.3**). It is important to understand the different bones of the cranium because they have different features and functions.

One of the most anterior bones of the cranium is the **frontal bone**, also called just the *frontal* (see Figures 6.2A and 6.3A). This bone is what makes up your forehead and the superior (top) part of your eye sockets (*eye orbits* or just *orbits*). The frontal bone is one of the largest and thickest cranial bones. It is distinguished by a number of key landmarks, including the *supraorbital foramen* (sometimes called the *supraorbital notch*), which is a small hole above each eye orbit for blood vessels and nerves; and the *frontal eminences* (or *bosses*), which are the paired, raised areas on the bony forehead (**FIGURE 6.4**). Two other important landmarks are the *supraorbital margins*, which are the upper edges of the orbits, and the **brow ridge** (or *superciliary arches*), which are the bony ridges above the orbits that are often larger in males than females.

Posterior to the frontal bone are the paired **parietal bones**, or *parietals* (see Figures 6.2B

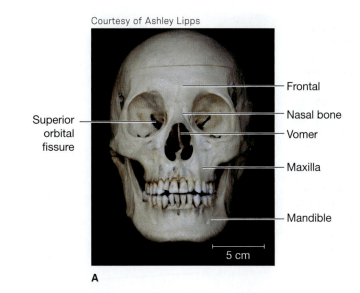

Courtesy of Ashley Lipps

Superior orbital fissure — Frontal — Nasal bone — Vomer — Maxilla — Mandible

5 cm

A

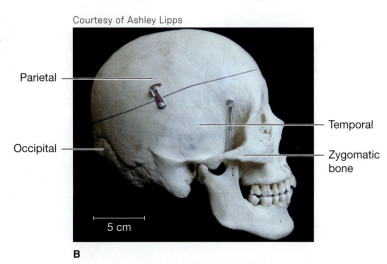

Courtesy of Ashley Lipps

Parietal — Occipital — Temporal — Zygomatic bone

5 cm

B

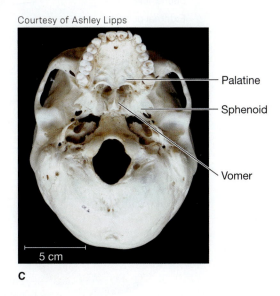

Courtesy of Ashley Lipps

Palatine — Sphenoid — Vomer

5 cm

C

FIGURE 6.2 The Cranium
(A) Frontal view, (B) lateral view, and (C) basilar (underside) view of a human skull. Note the major bones labeled.

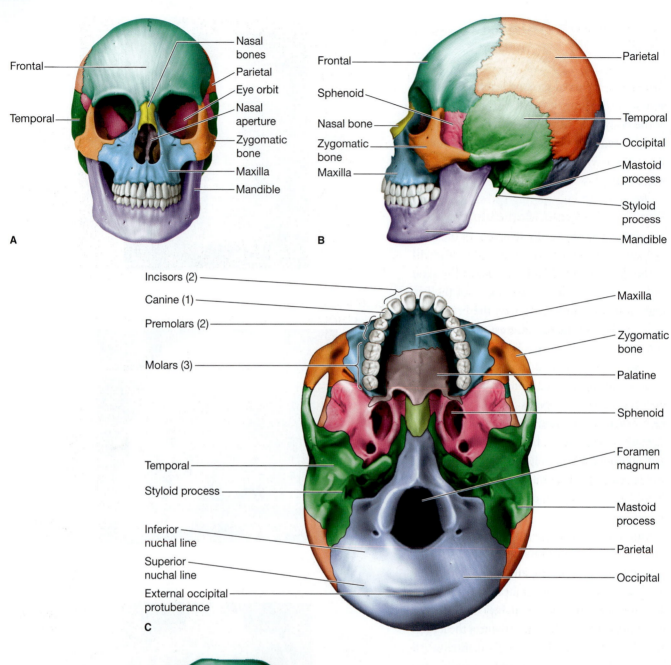

A

Frontal
Temporal

Nasal bones
Parietal
Eye orbit
Nasal aperture
Zygomatic bone
Maxilla
Mandible

B

Frontal
Sphenoid
Nasal bone
Zygomatic bone
Maxilla

Parietal
Temporal
Occipital
Mastoid process
Styloid process
Mandible

C

Incisors (2)
Canine (1)
Premolars (2)
Molars (3)
Temporal
Styloid process
Inferior nuchal line
Superior nuchal line
External occipital protuberance

Maxilla
Zygomatic bone
Palatine
Sphenoid
Foramen magnum
Mastoid process
Parietal
Occipital

D

Frontal
Coronal suture
Parietal
Sagittal suture
Lambdoidal suture
Occipital

Sagittal suture
Occipital
Mastoid process

Parietal
Lambdoidal suture
Nuchal line

FIGURE 6.3
The Cranium
(A) Frontal view, (B) lateral view, and (C) basilar (underside) view of the human skull. (D) Cranial and posterior view of sutures, which form where cranial bones fuse together.

and 6.3B). There is one on each side; together, they form the superior and lateral sides of the cranium. The parietals are square-shaped bones that have an overall uniform thickness. They are the largest bones of the cranium.

The **occipital bone**, or *occipital*, forms the posterior surface and base of the skull (see Figures 6.2B and 6.3B), and it has a number of key landmarks (**FIGURE 6.5**). The *foramen magnum* is the large opening through which the brain stem passes to enter the vertebral canal. The *occipital condyles* are two projections with oval articular (joint) surfaces on either side of the foramen magnum. They articulate with the first cervical vertebra in the neck. Just superior to each of the occipital condyles are the *hypoglossal canals*, which are small openings on either side of the foramen magnum for the 12th cranial nerves that innervate (supply nerves to) the tongue. On the external surface of the occipital, we also see the horizontal *nuchal lines*, which are bony ridges to which the neck (or nuchal) muscles attach. We also find the *external occipital protuberance*, which looks like a bump on the midline of the external surface of the occipital. Highly variable in size, it is often larger in males than females.

Inferior to the parietal bones are the **temporal bones**, or *temporals*, one on each side of the cranium (see Figures 6.2B and 6.3B). The temporal bones form the upper portion of the jaw joint and also house the organs and delicate bones used for hearing. The temporal bone has a number of key features on the outside (or ectocranial) surface (**FIGURE 6.6A**). The flat, smooth area of the bone is called the *squamous portion*. It articulates superiorly with the parietal bone. The *zygomatic process* is a thin projection that forms half of the zygomatic arch (what we can feel as our cheekbone). The **zygomatic arches** form a space for the jaw muscles, which attach to the mandible below and the temporal bones above. The zygomatic arches are important to biological anthropologists because they vary in size depending on a primate's dietary adaptations. The small depression seen just below the root of the zygomatic process is called the *mandibular fossa*. This is where the mandible articulates and forms the *temporomandibular*

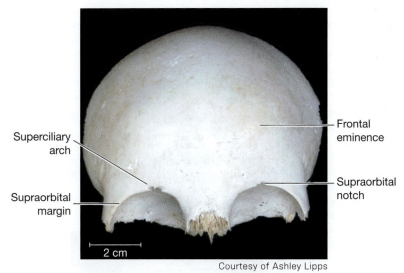

FIGURE 6.4 The Frontal Bone
Anterior (ectocranial) view of a human frontal bone. Note the important features that distinguish this bone.

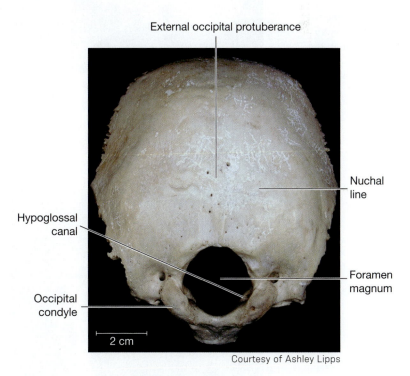

Courtesy of Ashley Lipps

FIGURE 6.5 The Occipital Bone
Posterior (ectocranial) view of a human occipital bone with important features labeled.

joint (*TMJ*) during life. The small external opening or hole just behind the mandibular fossa is the opening to the external ear canal and is called the *external auditory* (or *acoustic*) *meatus*. Posterior to the auditory meatus is the **mastoid process**, which is a small bony bump you can feel just below and behind your ear. The mastoid process is a point of attachment for neck

occipital bone the bone that forms the back and base of the cranium

temporal bone one of the pair of bones inferior to the parietal bone on each side of the cranium

zygomatic arch
cheekbone area formed by numerous small bones, allowing a space for the jaw muscles that attach to the mandible below and the temporal bone above

mastoid process
the bony projection located posterior to the ear that allows for the attachment of neck muscles

auditory ossicles
the three tiny bones that help form each middle ear

sphenoid bone the butterfly-shaped bone between the cranial vault and the face bones

muscles that rotate, flex, and extend the head. Males often have larger mastoid processes than females.

On the inside (or endocranial surface) of the temporal bone, we see the *petrous portion* (or pyramid), a region of dense bone that encloses the fragile organs and tiny ear bones used for hearing (**FIGURE 6.6B**). The ear bones are called the **auditory ossicles**, and they are the smallest

bones in the human body (**FIGURE 6.7**). On each side of the cranium, there are three ear bones: the *malleus* (hammer), the *incus* (anvil), and the *stapes* (stirrup). The malleus is connected to the eardrum, and the remaining bones are located more medially in each ear.

The **sphenoid bone**, or *sphenoid*, is a bat- or butterfly-shaped bone, and it is perhaps the most complex bone of the cranium (**FIGURE 6.8**). It is

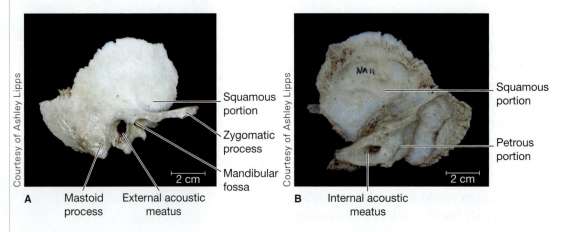

Courtesy of Ashley Lipps

Squamous portion
Zygomatic process
Mandibular fossa
A Mastoid process   External acoustic meatus
2 cm

Courtesy of Ashley Lipps

Squamous portion
Petrous portion
B Internal acoustic meatus
2 cm

FIGURE 6.6 The Temporal Bone
(A) Lateral (ectocranial) view and (B) medial (endocranial) view of a human right temporal bone.

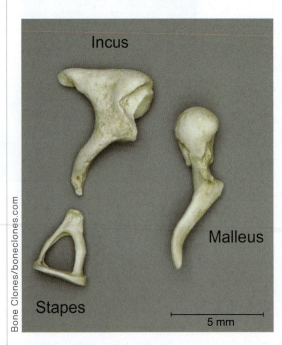

Incus

Malleus

Stapes

5 mm

Bone Clones/boneclones.com

FIGURE 6.7 The Auditory Ossicles
Note the differences in shape among the three "tiny" human ear bones (or auditory ossicles) that are found inside the middle ear.

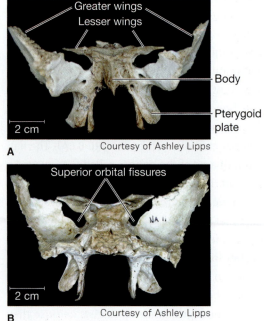

Greater wings
Lesser wings
Body
Pterygoid plate
2 cm
A   Courtesy of Ashley Lipps

Superior orbital fissures
2 cm
B   Courtesy of Ashley Lipps

FIGURE 6.8 The Sphenoid Bone
(A) Anterior view and (B) posterior view of a human sphenoid bone. Note the important features that distinguish this bone.

difficult to see in its entirety in the skull because it sits deep between the face bones and the cranial vault (the bones surrounding the brain). However, you can see parts of it from the side of the cranium or by looking inside the orbits. The sphenoid has many small openings that conduct important cranial nerves and blood vessels to and from the face. It has four basic parts: the pterygoid plates, the body, and the greater and lesser wings. The *pterygoid plates* can be seen only from below or from the side of the cranium. They are thin plates of bone that serve as sites of muscle attachment. The *body* is the substantial portion of the bone lying on the midline. It has a saddle-like depression on it called the *sella turcica*, which holds the hormone-secreting pituitary gland. There are two *greater wings* (one on each side), which lie anterior to the temporal bones and can be seen through the eye orbits. There are also two *lesser wings*, which are much smaller and provide partial support for the anterior of the brain. Because of its location in the cranium, the sphenoid also has two other features associated specifically with the eye. The *superior orbital fissures* are long fissures between the lesser and greater wings. These fissures, which are visible through the eye orbits (see Figures 6.2A and 6.3A), allow nerves and blood vessels to connect to the eye. The small, round opening superior to each orbital fissure, called the *optic foramen*, is the opening to the *optic canal*. This canal accommodates the optic nerve and blood vessels as they pass to the eye.

The **ethmoid**, or *ethmoid bone*, is a small, delicate, cube-shaped bone. It is centered along the midline between the frontal and sphenoid bones. Due to its position in the skull, it articulates with many bones. It forms the medial wall of the eye orbits and the roof of the nasal cavity. Several features can be seen in the disarticulated bone (**FIGURE 6.9**). The *cribriform plate* is a horizontal area of bone that forms the roof of the nasal cavity. It looks like a sieve with its many tiny perforations, which allow the olfactory nerves to pass from the nose to the brain. The small projection perpendicular to the cribriform plate is the *crista galli*. A part of the outer covering of the brain attaches to this projection.

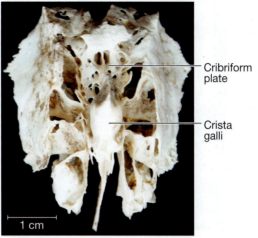

Courtesy of Ashley Lipps

FIGURE 6.9 The Ethmoid
Note the important features that distinguish a human ethmoid.

The olfactory bulbs (organs for smell) sit on the cribriform plate on either side of the crista galli.

The **maxillae** (**maxilla**, singular) are paired bones (one on each side of the face) that hold the roots of the upper (maxillary) teeth. These bones form the face, the floor of the nasal cavity and orbits, and the roof of the mouth (hard palate) (see Figures 6.2A and 6.3A). The maxilla has four key features (**FIGURE 6.10**). The *alveolar process* is the inferior portion that contains the teeth; the *zygomatic process* forms part of the cheek; the *palatine process* forms most of the hard palate and floor of the nasal cavity; and the long, thin *frontal process* articulates with the frontal bone and other facial bones.

The **palatines**, or *palatine bones*, are a pair of small, L-shaped bones that sit just posterior to the palatine processes of the maxillae (**FIGURE 6.11**). They form the most posterior part of the hard palate.

The **zygomatic bones** are paired bones that lie between the maxillae and the temporal bones (see Figures 6.2B and 6.3A). They form the most prominent part of the cheeks. The *temporal process* articulates with the temporal bone, the *maxillary process* articulates with the maxilla, the *frontal process* articulates with the frontal bone, and the *infraorbital margin* forms the lower outside (inferolateral) corner of the orbits (**FIGURE 6.12**).

ethmoid the small, cube-shaped bone between the frontal and sphenoid bones in the cranium

maxilla (maxillae, plural) one of the pair of bones that forms the face and holds the upper teeth

palatine one of the pair of bones that forms part of the hard palate in the mouth

zygomatic bone one of the bones that forms the zygomatic arch

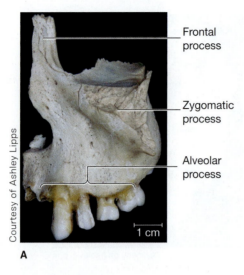

Frontal process

Zygomatic process

Alveolar process

Courtesy of Ashley Lipps

A

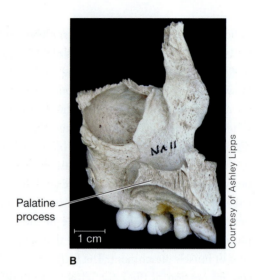

Palatine process

Courtesy of Ashley Lipps

B

FIGURE 6.10 The Maxilla
(A) Anterior view and (B) posterior view of a human left maxilla with the four key features labeled.

Courtesy of Ashley Lipps

FIGURE 6.11 The Palatine
Posterior view of a human left palatine.

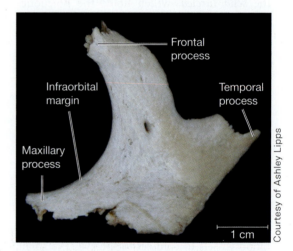

Frontal process

Infraorbital margin

Temporal process

Maxillary process

Courtesy of Ashley Lipps

FIGURE 6.12 The Zygomatic Bone
Anterior view of a human left zygomatic bone.

Courtesy of Ashley Lipps

FIGURE 6.13 The Inferior Nasal Concha
Lateral view of a human left inferior nasal concha.

nasal bone one of a pair of small bones that forms the bridge of the nose

vomer a small, thin bone inside the nasal cavity

inferior nasal concha (**conchae**, plural) one of a pair of scroll-like bones inside the nasal cavity

mandible the bone that holds the lower teeth and is primarily responsible for chewing; also called the jawbone

The **nasal bones** are small, rectangular bones that lie along the midline, just below the frontal bone. They form the bony bridge of the nose (see Figures 6.2A and 6.3A).

The **vomer** is a small, thin, plow-shaped bone that is located in the midline of the nasal cavity and forms the inferior part of the nasal septum (see Figures 6.2A and 6.2C).

The **inferior nasal conchae** are a pair of delicate, scroll-like bones found inside the nasal cavity inferior to the ethmoid. Sometimes called the *turbinate bones*, they are important in moistening inhaled air (**FIGURE 6.13**).

The lower jawbone, or **mandible**, sits below the anterior of the cranium (see Figures 6.2 and 6.3). It is primarily responsible for chewing, so it holds the lower teeth and includes areas for the attachment of chewing muscles (**FIGURE 6.14**). The main part of the mandible is its horizontal *body*, which is thick and strong to support the teeth. A *vertical ramus* extends upward on each side of the mandible, and the end of each vertical ramus is marked by a mandibular condyle. The *mandibular condyles* are round processes that articulate with the fossae on the temporal bones to make the *temporomandibular joint* (*TMJ*). On each side of the mandible, anterior and superior to the vertical ramus, there is another bony projection called the *coronoid process*. This thin, flat, triangular process serves as an attachment site for a chewing muscle. The protuberance at the midline of the mandible is called the *mental protuberance* (or *eminence*) and forms the bony chin.

All of the individual bones of the cranium articulate with one another by means of immovable fibrous joints called **sutures**. When we are born, the spaces between the sutures are incompletely fused to allow for growth of the brain and cranium. Some of the spaces between these sutures are so big that there are noticeable soft spots on the superior and posterior surfaces of a baby's head, called **fontanelles**. There are cartilaginous membranes here that will eventually grow and harden into bone **(FIGURE 6.15)**. The different sutures have different names. The *metopic suture* (or *frontal suture*) runs down the center of the frontal bone. The *sagittal suture* is seen along the midline of the skull between the pari-

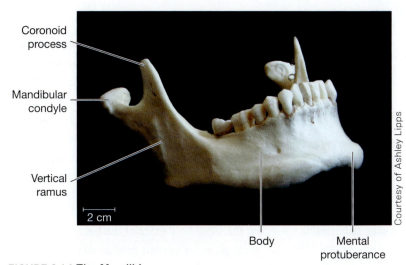

Courtesy of Ashley Lipps

FIGURE 6.14 The Mandible
Anterolateral view of a human mandible with important features labeled.

etal bones. The *coronal suture* lies between the frontal bone and the parietal bones. The *lambdoidal suture* separates the occipital bone from the two parietal bones, and the *squamosal suture* is between the temporal and the parietal bones. There are also many other smaller sutures that are simply named after the bones they run between, such as the *zygomaticomaxillary sutures*, which run between the zygomatic bones and maxillae, or the *frontonasal suture*, which is the small suture between the frontal and nasal bones.

suture an immovable fibrous joint between individual bones of the cranium

fontanelle a soft spot on a baby's head where the space at a suture is particularly big

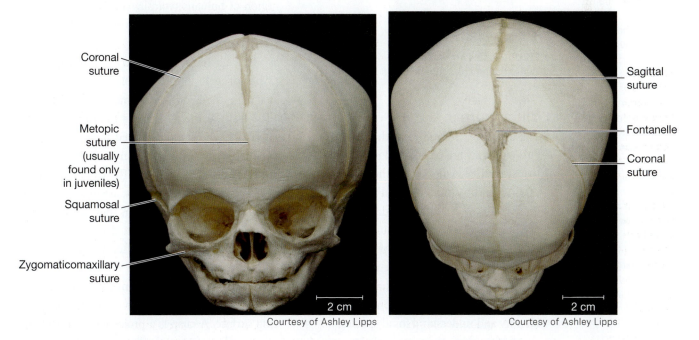

Courtesy of Ashley Lipps   Courtesy of Ashley Lipps

FIGURE 6.15 The Newborn Cranium
We are born with spaces between our cranial sutures, like those that are visible in this newborn cranium. These spaces are called fontanelles.

hyoid bone the small, U-shaped bone suspended in the throat below the cranium

dentition the teeth

enamel the hard mineralized tissue on the exterior surface of a tooth

dentin a calcified tissue found inside a tooth, beneath the enamel surface

deciduous teeth the first set of teeth, also called baby or milk teeth, that are later replaced by permanent teeth

permanent teeth the second set of teeth, also called adult teeth, that replace the earlier deciduous teeth

incisor a spatula-shaped tooth at the front of the mouth

canine a pointy tooth between the incisors and premolars

premolar a tooth with two cusps, between the canines and molars

cusp a rounded (or slightly pointed) projection on a tooth's chewing surface

molar a large, multi-cusped tooth at the back of the mouth

The Hyoid Bone

The **hyoid bone** is a small, U-shaped bone suspended in the throat below the cranium. It is unusual because it does not articulate with any other bones. However, it does articulate (via ligaments) with the numerous cartilages that form the *larynx*, which is involved in swallowing and speech. The hyoid has three main parts (**FIGURE 6.16**). The *body* is the larger, central area of the bone; the *greater horns* form the posterior ends; and the *lesser horns* are small projections on the superior surface of the body. All of these areas allow for various muscle attachments that help move the larynx and tongue.

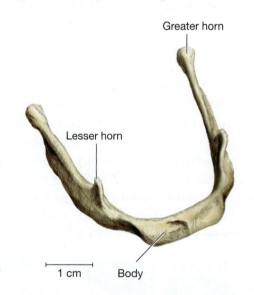

FIGURE 6.16 The Hyoid Bone
Superior view of a human hyoid bone.

The Dentition

The teeth are referred to as the **dentition**, and although they are considered part of the digestive system, we will discuss them here because of their utility for biological anthropologists. They relate to our dietary adaptations, can be used to help classify us and our living and fossil relatives, and can indicate aspects of our social behavior. And the teeth are more easily preserved in the fossil record than other parts of the body. This means we often rely on them to identify and understand fossil species.

All teeth share the same basic structure (**FIGURE 6.17**). The three main regions of the tooth are the crown, the neck, and the root. The *crown*

is the area we see above the gum line, the *neck* is the constricted area just below the crown, and the *root* is the area that extends below the gum line and anchors the tooth. The exterior of the crown is covered by a hard substance called **enamel**, which is made up mostly of minerals and is the hardest substance in the human body. The enamel is the tooth's protective covering. A layer of dentin lies beneath the enamel. The **dentin** contains a slightly higher proportion of organic material than the enamel, so it is softer and more subject to decay. However, dentin is still largely inorganic and provides support for the tooth. The central area of the tooth is the *pulp*, which is a soft tissue that contains nerves and blood vessels.

Like most mammals, humans have two sets of dentition during the course of our lives. First, we have 20 **deciduous teeth**, which are also called baby or milk teeth because they are the first teeth that come in when we are babies. The deciduous dentition of humans typically consists of 8 incisors, 4 canines, and 8 molars. We then have another set of 32 teeth that grows in and replaces the deciduous teeth as we get older. These teeth, commonly called the adult teeth, are the **permanent teeth**. The permanent dentition of humans typically consists of 8 incisors, 4 canines, and 12 molars plus an additional 8 premolars (or bicuspids).

In each set of teeth, there are four different types of teeth (**FIGURE 6.18**). These tooth types vary in their position, shape, and function. The teeth at the anterior of the mouth are the **incisors**. The spatula-shaped incisors are used primarily for biting. Behind the incisors are the cone-shaped **canines**. The canines in some animals, such as carnivores, are used for shredding. In primates, however, they are used primarily in aggressive threat displays and male competition behaviors. After the canines, we find the **premolars**, which are used for chewing. These teeth are sometimes called bicuspids because they each have two cusps on the chewing surface. A **cusp** is a projection on the chewing surface of a tooth that is usually rounded or slightly pointed. The teeth in the posterior of the mouth are the **molars**. Like the premolars, the molars are used for chewing. The molars are generally similar to premolars but tend to be larger, squarer, and have more cusps.

Dental Formulas

Different animal species have different numbers of each kind of tooth. Species that are closely related tend to have the same numbers of each kind of tooth, so determining tooth numbers is an important tool used in classification. The numerical count of the different tooth types in a species is called its **dental formula**. To determine a species' dental formula, you must focus on one quadrant of the mouth of an individual at a time. You begin with an upper quadrant, either the upper right or the upper left. You then count the number of each type of tooth in the quadrant, working from the anterior of the mouth toward the posterior. You write these numbers in order, separating them with periods. You then do the same for the corresponding lower quadrant of the mouth. For example, if you first used the upper right quadrant, you now examine, count, and write down the tooth numbers in the lower right quadrant. Again, be sure to separate the numbers with periods. The two sets of numbers are then written on top of each other, such that the upper quadrant numbers are above the lower quadrant numbers. Many species have the same tooth counts on the top and bottom, so their dental formulas can be simplified to only one set of numbers (the top or bottom). However, in some species, the counts vary by one or two teeth between the top and bottom, so both sets of numbers must be reported.

Let's use the dentition in Figure 6.18 to practice determining a dental formula. We will begin in the upper right quadrant. When we count the teeth from anterior to posterior, we find two incisors, one canine, two premolars, and three molars. We find the same numbers when we count from anterior to posterior in the lower right quadrant: two incisors, one canine, two premolars, and three molars. This dental formula is written as follows:

2.1.2.3
2.1.2.3

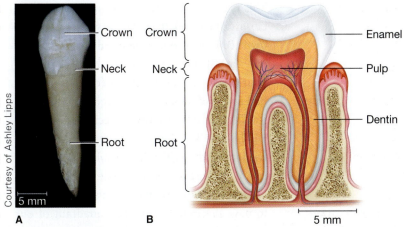

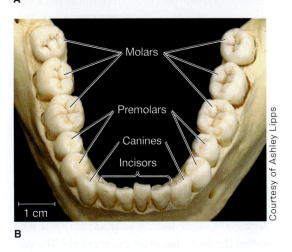

FIGURE 6.17 Tooth Structure
(A) Human canine tooth, showing the three main regions visible from the exterior of the tooth. (B) Cross section of the human tooth.

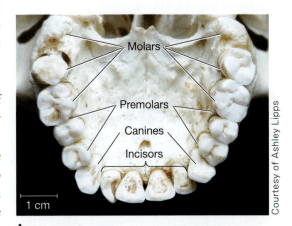

**FIGURE 6.18
The Dentition**
Note the different tooth types in the (A) maxillary and (B) mandibular dentition.

Or, because the top and bottom are the same, the dental formula can be simplified to

2.1.2.3

dental formula a numerical count of the different tooth types in an animal

This is the dental formula for humans and our close primate relatives. So, if you count your own teeth in a mirror, you will probably find you have this dental formula. If you have had your wisdom teeth removed (or if you never had any), your teeth will not represent the typical dental formula for our species because you will have only two molars, instead of three. The wisdom teeth are the third molars and are the last to erupt. They usually come in during your late teens or early twenties. As a species, we tend to have three molars in each quadrant of our mouths. However, it is becoming increasingly common for some people (in populations with access to dental care) to have the third molars removed because they do not have enough room in their mouths for them.

The Vertebral Column

As we work our way down the body from the cranium, we first encounter the vertebral column. The **vertebral column** is the vertical stack of bones that make up what we commonly call our spine or backbone. It includes the twenty-four individual vertebrae, the sacrum, and the coccyx. These bones protect the spinal cord as it runs from the base of the cranium to the lower body. In humans, the vertebral column takes an unusual S shape due to a curve in the neck and a curve in the lower back **(FIGURE 6.19)**. This shape is an adaptation we have to help with our unique form of bipedal locomotion (see Lab 14 for more information).

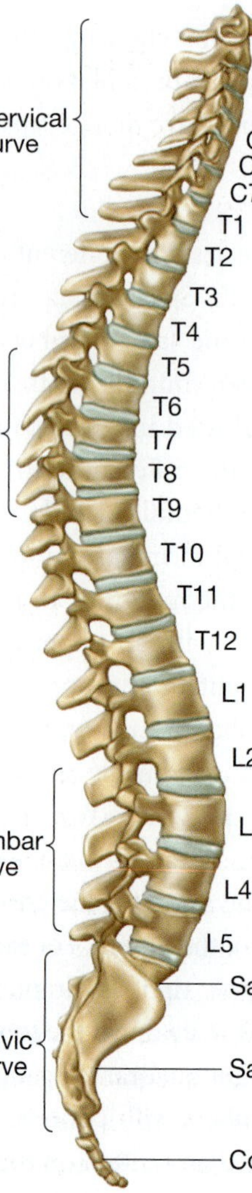

The **vertebrae** (**vertebra**, singular) are the irregularly shaped bones that make up most of the vertebral column. They are separated by *intervertebral discs*, which form cartilaginous joints that allow for mobility and also cushion and absorb shock in the spine. In general, the vertebrae share the same basic structures **(FIGURE 6.20)**. They have a large, cylindrical area called the *body* that extends anteriorly. The *vertebral arch* extends posteriorly from the body. This arch forms an opening called the *vertebral foramen*, which holds the spinal cord. On either side of the vertebral arch, *transverse processes* extend laterally. On the posterior surface of the

FIGURE 6.19 The Vertebral Column
Lateral view of the human vertebral column. Note the different types of vertebrae and the curvature of different areas of the spine. These curves give humans a uniquely shaped vertebral column, as discussed in greater detail in Lab 14.

vertebral arch, there is a *spinous process* that extends out along the midline. These various processes help with muscle attachment and/or articulation with other bones.

There are three types of vertebrae superior to the pelvis; they are differentiated based on their position in the vertebral column and their function. The **cervical vertebrae** are found in the neck. They are the smallest vertebrae in humans. There are seven cervical vertebrae, and

---

vertebral column the row of bones that form the backbone

vertebra (**vertebrae**, plural) an irregularly shaped bone that is part of the vertebral column

cervical vertebra one of the seven vertebrae (C1–C7) that form the neck

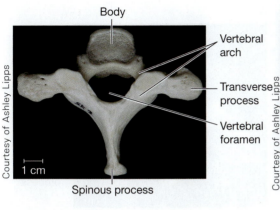

Courtesy of Ashley Lipps

FIGURE 6.20 A Typical Vertebra
A thoracic vertebra (superior view) represents a typical human vertebra. Note the major bony features that are shared by most vertebrae.

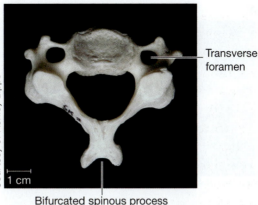

Courtesy of Ashley Lipps

FIGURE 6.21 A Typical Cervical Vertebra
Superior view of a typical cervical vertebra. Note the major bony features that are shared by most cervical vertebrae.

atlas the unusually shaped C1, a vertebra that works with the axis to allow for head movement and rotation

axis the unusually shaped C2, a vertebra that works with the atlas to allow for head movement and rotation

thoracic vertebra one of the 12 vertebrae (T1–T12) that articulate with ribs in the chest area

lumbar vertebra one of the five vertebrae (L1–L5) that form the lower back

they are numbered based on their order from the most superior to the most inferior. Thus, C1 (cervical 1) is the most superior cervical vertebra, and C7 is the most inferior cervical vertebra. The cervical vertebrae have some unusual features (**FIGURE 6.21**). Each transverse process on these vertebrae has a *transverse foramen* that allows arteries to pass through the neck to supply blood and oxygen to the brain. In addition, most cervical vertebrae have short spinous processes with *bifurcated* (or *forked*) *ends*, meaning that the end splits into two separate branches. The first two cervical vertebrae are particularly unusual. The first cervical vertebra (C1) is called the **atlas** (**FIGURE 6.22A**). Unlike other vertebrae, it does not have a body. Instead, it has an *anterior arch* and a *posterior arch* that give it a ring-like shape. It also has a *superior articular facet* on each of the transverse processes. These facets articulate with the protruding *occipital condyles* at the base of the cranium. The second cervical vertebra (C2) is called the **axis** (**FIGURE 6.22B**). The axis has a small body with a perpendicular structure called the *odontoid process* (or *dens*), which extends superiorly. This structure acts as the pivot on which the atlas rotates. These two cervical vertebrae work together to allow for head movement and rotation, which is why they have unusual shapes that provide more mobility (**FIGURE 6.22C**).

Interestingly, almost all mammals have seven cervical vertebrae, no matter how long their necks. For example, humans, giraffes, and cows all have seven cervical vertebrae. Giraffes do not have a longer neck because they have more cervical vertebrae than other mammals. Rather, their cervical vertebrae are larger and longer than those of many other mammals.

Inferior to the cervical vertebrae are the **thoracic vertebrae**, which form the backbone in the chest area. There are twelve thoracic vertebrae, numbered T1 (most superior) to T12 (most inferior), which articulate with ribs. In addition to being a little larger than cervical vertebrae, the thoracic vertebrae can be distinguished by a few key features (**FIGURE 6.23**). On each side of the body of a typical thoracic vertebra, there are two *costal facets*, one superior and one inferior, along the vertebral body. These facets articulate with the heads of the ribs. In addition, the spinous processes on most thoracic vertebrae are long and oriented so that they point downward and overlap one another. However, the lowest thoracic vertebrae have spinous processes that more closely resemble those of lumbar vertebrae.

Finally, inferior to the thoracic vertebrae are the **lumbar vertebrae**. There are five lumbar vertebrae, numbered L1 (most superior) to L5 (most inferior). They are the largest vertebrae

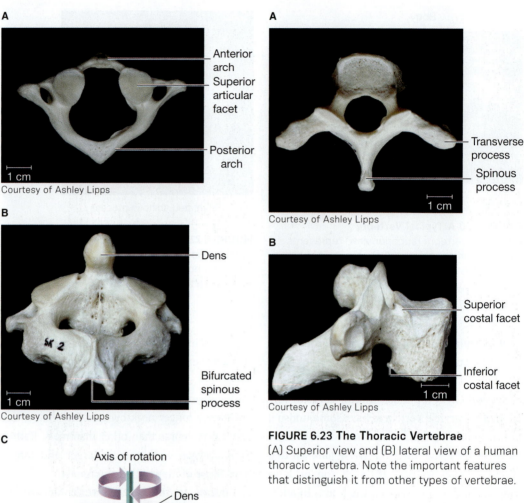

A

Anterior arch
Superior articular facet
Posterior arch

1 cm

Courtesy of Ashley Lipps

B

Dens

Bifurcated spinous process

1 cm

Courtesy of Ashley Lipps

C

Axis of rotation

Dens

Atlas

Transverse ligament

Axis

Atlantoaxial joint

Reprinted by permission from *Anatomy & Physiology* 7th edition. © 2015 McGraw Hill.

FIGURE 6.22 The Atlas and the Axis
(A) Superior view of a human atlas, with important features that distinguish it from other cervical vertebrae labeled. (B) Posterior view of a human axis, with important features that distinguish it from other cervical vertebrae labeled. (C) The atlas and the axis work together at the atlantoaxial joint to allow for head movement and rotation.

A

Transverse process
Spinous process

1 cm

Courtesy of Ashley Lipps

B

Superior costal facet

Inferior costal facet

1 cm

Courtesy of Ashley Lipps

FIGURE 6.23 The Thoracic Vertebrae
(A) Superior view and (B) lateral view of a human thoracic vertebra. Note the important features that distinguish it from other types of vertebrae.

in humans because they support the weight of the upper body. They are relatively generalized and lack the special features seen in the other vertebrae **(FIGURE 6.24)**. For example, lumbar vertebrae do not have the transverse foramen found in cervical vertebrae or the costal facets found in thoracic vertebrae. Lumbar vertebrae also have short, blunt spinous processes.

The remainder of the vertebral column is made of two bones: the sacrum and the coccyx. The **sacrum** is a large, triangular bone at the base of the vertebral column **(FIGURE 6.25)**. Overall, the bone curves slightly, creating a concave anterior surface and convex posterior surface; and it has numerous small holes (called *sacral foramina*) that allow for the passage of nerves and blood vessels. The sacrum is composed of five vertebrae that begin fusing together in the teen years and are fully fused in adults. The flared

sacrum the large, triangular bone at the base of the vertebral column and between the two hip bones

A

— Transverse process

1 cm

Courtesy of Ashley Lipps

B

Spinous process

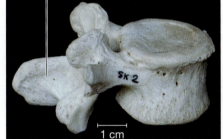

1 cm

Courtesy of Ashley Lipps

FIGURE 6.24 The Lumbar Vertebrae
(A) Superior view and (B) lateral view of a human lumbar vertebra, with important features that distinguish it from other types of vertebrae labeled.

sides of the sacrum (called *alae*; *ala*, singular) are formed by the fusion of the transverse processes, and they articulate with the ilia on the pelvis to form the *sacroiliac joints*. The superior surface of the sacrum articulates with the last lumbar vertebra (L5), and the inferior surface of the sacrum articulates with the superior surface of the coccyx. The **coccyx** is a small bone that anchors a few muscles and ligaments **(FIGURE 6.26)**. It is formed by the fusion of three to five rudimentary vertebrae (the *coccygeal vertebrae*), and it is known commonly as the tailbone because it is the remnant of a vestigial tail that is lost very early in our embryonic development. The *cornua* project from the superior surface of the coccyx and articulate with the sacrum.

A

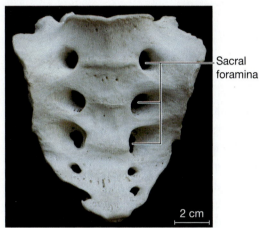

— Sacral foramina

— Median spine (crest)

2 cm

Courtesy of Ashley Lipps

B

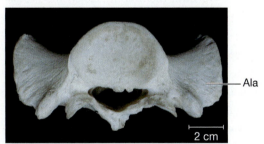

— Sacral foramina

2 cm

Courtesy of Ashley Lipps

C

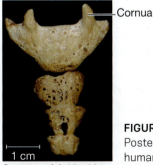

— Ala

2 cm

Courtesy of Ashley Lipps

— Cornua

1 cm

Courtesy of Ashley Lipps

FIGURE 6.25
The Sacrum
(A) Anterior view, (B) posterior view, and (C) superior view of a human sacrum. Note the important features that distinguish this bone.

FIGURE 6.26 The Coccyx
Posterior view of a human coccyx.

coccyx a small bone that articulates with the inferior end of the sacrum, also called the tailbone

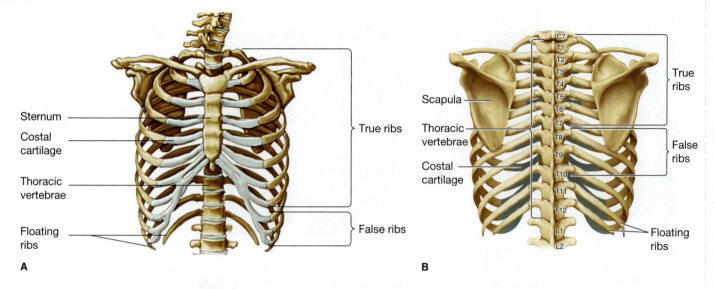

FIGURE 6.27 The Thoracic Cage
(A) Anterior view and (B) posterior view of a human thoracic cage (or rib cage). Note the different bones that make up this important structure.

The Ribs and Sternum

The vital organs of the chest, such as the heart and lungs, are enclosed and protected by the thoracic cage, or rib cage **(FIGURE 6.27)**. The posterior of the thoracic cage is formed by the articulation of the ribs with the thoracic vertebrae. The ribs then curve around to the anterior, where they attach to the sternum (via cartilage) to form the anterior of the thoracic cage.

The **sternum** (commonly called the breastbone) is formed by three bones that fuse together later in life **(FIGURE 6.28)**. The most superior of these bones is the *manubrium*. It is a triangular bone that has a *clavicular notch* on each side to articulate with the clavicles. It also has a *jugular notch* in the center that can be felt just at the base of your throat. The second bone of the sternum, the *sternal body*, is inferior to the manubrium. It is more elongated and oval-shaped. It has *costal notches* along each side, where the ribs articulate (via cartilage). The most inferior bone is the *xiphoid process*. It is the cartilaginous inferior point of the sternum that becomes mineralized into bone later in life.

There are twenty-four **ribs** arranged in pairs, with twelve ribs on each side of the thoracic cage **(FIGURE 6.29)**. All of these ribs articulate with the thoracic vertebrae posteriorly, but they do not all articulate with the sternum anteriorly (see Figure 6.27). The first seven pairs of ribs are called *true ribs* because they articulate with the sternum directly via *costal cartilage*. The next three pairs of ribs are called *false ribs* because they join with the costal cartilage of the

sternum a bone formed by the fusion of three separate bones in the chest, also called the breastbone

rib bone one of the 12 long bones that form each side of the rib cage (or thoracic cage)

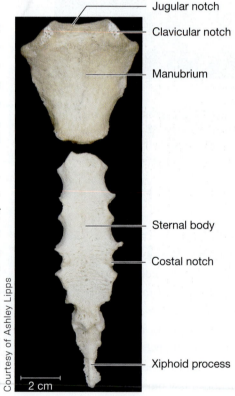

Courtesy of Ashley Lipps

FIGURE 6.28 The Sternum
Anterior view of a human sternum, showing the three bones that fuse to form this bone.

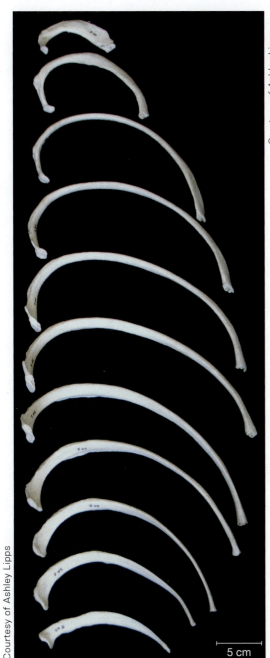

Courtesy of Ashley Lipps

FIGURE 6.29 The Ribs
Note the variation in size and curvature of the ribs, which depend on their anatomical position.

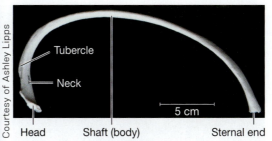

Courtesy of Ashley Lipps

Tubercle

Neck

5 cm

Head   Shaft (body)   Sternal end

FIGURE 6.30 A Typical Rib
Superior view of a typical human left rib. Note the important features that ribs share.

tubercle along the *neck* of the rib that articulates with the transverse process of the same thoracic vertebra. The main part of the rib is called the *shaft* (or *body*). The shaft is the elongated, flat area that curves around to the anterior of the thoracic cage. While the superior (top) of this shaft is rounded, the inferior (underside) of this shaft has a sharp, tapering edge. This shape can be helpful when trying to determine to which side of the body a rib belongs. You can identify the sharp surface (underside) and can then orient the rib correctly to determine if it is from the right or left side of the thoracic cage.

PART 2: THE APPENDICULAR SKELETON

Now that we have discussed the bones of the axial skeleton, we turn to the bones of the appendicular skeleton. Remember, the *appendicular skeleton* is made up of the bones that form the appendages (arms and legs) on each side of the body. It includes some bones that appear to be along the body's central axis but are considered appendicular because they are functionally tied to the appendages. We will discuss each of the major bones of the human appendicular skeleton, beginning with the upper limb.

The Clavicle

The **clavicle** is commonly referred to as the collarbone. It helps to stabilize the shoulder, providing structural support and areas for muscle attachment. The clavicle is a slightly curved,

ribs above, rather than directly to the sternum. The last two pairs of ribs do not connect to the sternum at all, so they are called *floating ribs*. These floating ribs are sometimes considered to be a specific kind of false ribs. All ribs share the same key features (**FIGURE 6.30**). They have a *head* on the posterior end that articulates with the body of a thoracic vertebra, and they have a

clavicle a slightly curved bone that helps stabilize each shoulder; also called the collarbone

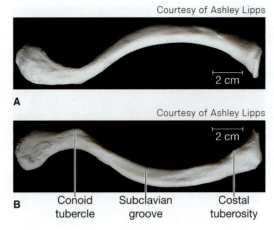

Courtesy of Ashley Lipps

2 cm

A

Courtesy of Ashley Lipps

2 cm

B

| Conoid tubercle | Subclavian groove | Costal tuberosity |

FIGURE 6.31 The Clavicle
(A) Superior view and (B) inferior view of a human left clavicle. Note the important features that distinguish this bone.

somewhat S-shaped bone (**FIGURE 6.31**). You can feel the curve in your own clavicle if you run your fingers along it from one end to the other. The medial end of the clavicle is rounded, and it articulates with the sternum. The lateral end of the clavicle is flatter, and it articulates with the scapula. The *conoid tubercle* is an area for ligament attachment located on the lateral end of the posteroinferior surface. There is also a long, shallow depression (called the *subclavian groove*) that runs along the inferior side of the clavicle's central shaft. This area accommodates nearby blood vessels. Finally, on the medial inferior end, there is a rough surface called the *costal tuberosity* for the attachment of another ligament.

The Scapula

The **scapula** is commonly called the shoulder blade (**FIGURE 6.32**). It is a large, flat, triangular bone. It is fairly mobile, and you can feel it move around on your back as you move your arm. In humans and some other primates, the scapula is positioned on the posterior surface of the rib cage. In other primates and animals, the scapula is typically positioned more to the side of the rib cage (see Lab 12 for more information). Each edge of the triangular scapula has a name. The *superior border* runs along the superior edge; the *vertebral border* runs along the medial edge, parallel to the vertebral column; and the *axil-*

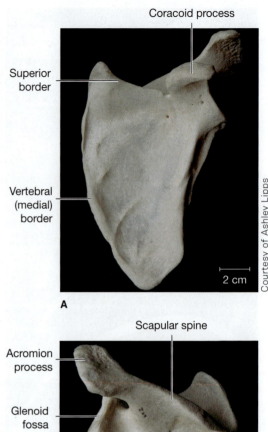

Coracoid process

Superior border

Vertebral (medial) border

Courtesy of Ashley Lipps

2 cm

A

Scapular spine

Acromion process

Glenoid fossa

Axillary (lateral) border

Courtesy of Ashley Lipps

2 cm

B

FIGURE 6.32 The Scapula
(A) Anterior view and (B) posterior view of a human left scapula, with important features labeled.

lary border runs along the lateral edge, near the armpit. On the posterior surface of the scapula, there is a ridge of bone that runs roughly parallel to the superior border. This ridge is called the *scapular spine*. At the lateral edge of the scapular spine, there is a projection called the *acromion process*, which articulates with the clavicle. Near the acromion process along the superior border, there is another large projection called the *coracoid process* that is an area for arm muscle

scapula a large, flat bone that forms part of each shoulder joint; also called the shoulder blade

attachment. Where the axillary and superior borders meet, there is a round depression called the *glenoid fossa*. This shallow depression articulates with the head of the humerus (upper arm bone) to form the highly mobile shoulder joint.

The Humerus

The upper arm bone, called the **humerus**, is a typical long bone (**FIGURE 6.33**). The proximal end of the humerus is called the *head*. It has a rounded shape, and it is the part of the humerus

humerus the upper bone in each arm

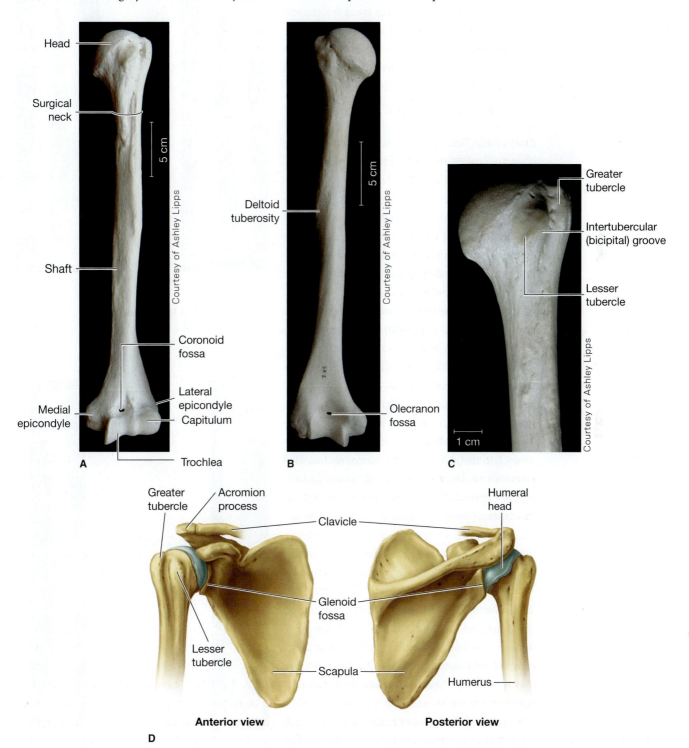

FIGURE 6.33 The Humerus
(A) Anterior view, (B) posterior view, and (C) close-up of the proximal end of a human left humerus. (D) The humerus shown in articulation at the shoulder joint. Note the important features that distinguish this bone.

that articulates with the glenoid fossa of the scapula. Near the head of the humerus, there are two important projections. The *lesser tubercle* is the more anterior and smaller of the two, while the *greater tubercle* is the more posterior and larger. Both tubercles are areas for muscle attachment. Between these two projections, there is an indentation called the *intertubercular* (or *bicipital*) *groove*. This groove accommodates a tendon of the biceps muscle. Below the head, there is an area called the *surgical neck*, which joins the head to the shaft. Further down the shaft of the bone on the lateral surface, there is an area called the *deltoid tuberosity*, which is where the deltoid muscle attaches.

At the distal end of the humerus, there are several key features. The *capitulum* is a rounded projection on the lateral side, and it articulates with the radius (a lower arm bone). The *trochlea* is an area that is shaped like a spool of thread. It is medial to the capitulum and articulates with the ulna (the other lower arm bone). Lateral (and slightly proximal) to the capitulum is a projection called the *lateral epicondyle*. A slightly larger projection, called the *medial epicondyle*, is positioned medial (and slightly proximal) to the trochlea. Both epicondyles are areas for ligament and/or muscle attachment for the lower arm. In addition to these various projections, the distal end of the humerus has two pronounced depressions. The *olecranon fossa* is a large depression on the posterior surface, and the *coronoid fossa* is a smaller depression on the anterior surface. Both of these depressions articulate with the ulna as part of the elbow joint.

The Radius and Ulna

The lower arm is made up of two long bones: the radius and the ulna (**FIGURE 6.34**). The proximal ends of both the radius and the ulna articulate with the humerus. The distal ends of these two lower arm bones articulate with the carpals to form the wrist. With your arm at your side and the palm of your hand facing forward, the **radius** is the more lateral and shorter of the two lower arm bones (**FIGURE 6.35**). Its proximal end has a round depression called the *head*, which articulates with the capitulum of the humerus. Below the head, there is a pro-

radius the more lateral of the two lower bones in each arm

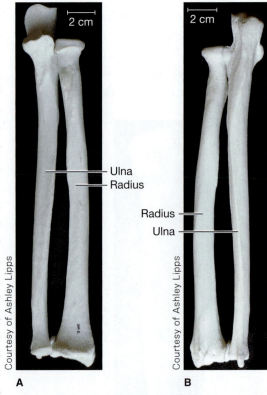

Courtesy of Ashley Lipps

FIGURE 6.34 The Radius and Ulna
(A) Anterior view and (B) posterior view of a human left radius and ulna in anatomical position.

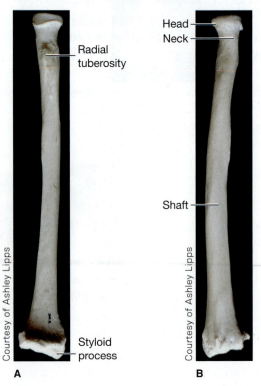

Courtesy of Ashley Lipps

FIGURE 6.35 The Radius
(A) Anterior view and (B) posterior view of a human left radius. Note the important features that help to distinguish this bone.

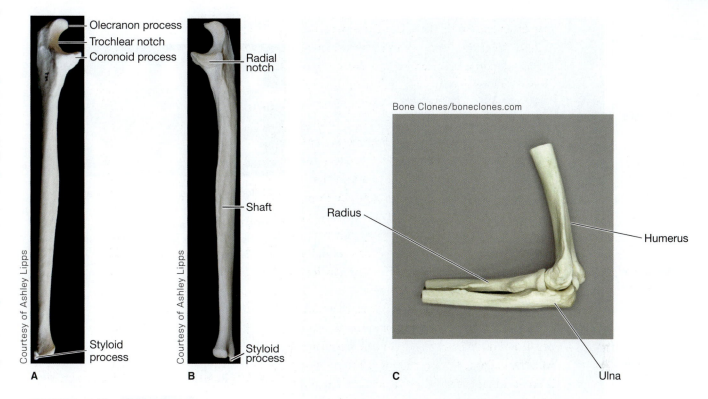

FIGURE 6.36 The Ulna
(A) Lateral view and (B) medial view of a human left ulna. (C) The ulna shown in articulation at the elbow joint. Note the important features that distinguish this bone.

jection on the anteromedial surface called the *radial tuberosity*. It is an area of attachment for the biceps muscle. Between the head and the radial tuberosity, the bone is constricted (narrower) in an area called the *neck* of the radius. The *shaft* of the radius extends from the neck to the distal end of the bone. At the distal end, there is a sharply pointed area called the *styloid process* on the lateral side of the bone.

With your arm at your side and the palm of your hand facing forward, the **ulna** is the more medial and longer of the two lower arm bones (see Figure 6.34). It has a unique, wrench-shaped proximal end formed by several key features **(FIGURE 6.36)**. The *olecranon process* is a large projection that accommodates muscle attachment and fits in the olecranon fossa of the humerus when the arm is extended. It is the large bony area that we often think of as the tip of the elbow. Just below the olecranon process, there is an area called the *trochlear notch*, which is a C-shaped notch that articulates with the rounded trochlea of the humerus. At the base of the trochlear notch on the anterior surface, there is a pointy projection called the *coronoid*

process that articulates with the coronoid fossa of the humerus. The ulna articulates with the radius at the *radial notch*, which is located on the lateral end of the coronoid process. As with the radius, the main length of the ulna is called the *shaft*, and the distal end is marked by a pointy projection called a *styloid process*. However, in the ulna, the styloid process is located on the medial side of the bone, rather than the lateral side.

The Bones of the Wrist and Hand

The bones of the wrist and hand take three basic forms: carpals (wrist bones), metacarpals (palm or hand bones), and phalanges (finger bones) **(FIGURE 6.37)**. There are eight **carpals** in each hand. They are typical short bones, appearing generally cube-like in shape **(FIGURE 6.38)**. They provide support and limit mobility in the wrist area. They are positioned such that they form two rows, with four bones in each row. The proximal row includes (from lateral to medial) the *scaphoid*, the *lunate*, the *triquetral* (or *triquetrum*), and the *pisiform*. The distal row includes (again from lateral to medial) the *trapezium*, the

ulna the more medial of the two lower bones in each arm

carpal one of the eight short bones of each wrist

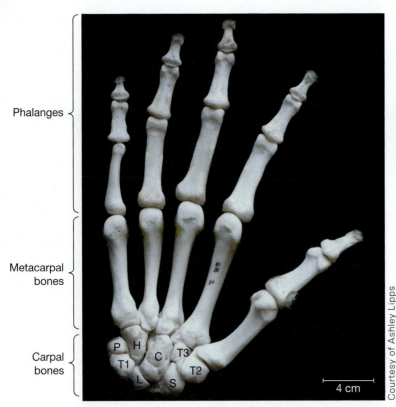

Courtesy of Ashley Lipps

FIGURE 6.37 The Bones of the Hand and Wrist (Right Hand)
Palmar view of the bones of the right hand and wrist in anatomical position.
Carpals: S = scaphoid, L = lunate, T1 = triquetral, P = pisiform, T2 =
trapezium, T3 = trapezoid, C = capitate, H = hamate.

Hamate   Capitate   Trapezoid   Trapezium

Pisiform   Triquetral   Lunate   Scaphoid

Courtesy of Ashley Lipps

FIGURE 6.38 The Carpals
Note the similarities and differences among
individual human left carpal bones.

trapezoid, the *capitate,* and the
hamate. Notice that while all of
these bones have a general cube-
like shape, they vary in their exact
shape and size.

The bones of the hand, or
palm, are called the **metacarpals**
(**FIGURE 6.39**). There are five metacarpals in each hand, one corresponding to each finger. The
metacarpals are numbered from
1 to 5, with 1 corresponding to
the thumb and 5 corresponding
to the pinky finger. The proximal
end of a metacarpal is somewhat square-shaped and concave,
and it articulates with one or
more rounded carpal surfaces.
In humans, the proximal ends
of metacarpals 2 through 5 also
articulate with the adjacent metacarpals. The distal end of a meta-

metacarpal one of
the five bones that
form the palm of
each hand

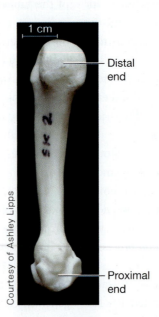

Distal
end

Proximal
end

Courtesy of Ashley Lipps

**FIGURE 6.39 The
Metacarpals**
Anterior view of a typical
human left metacarpal
bone. Note the difference
between the proximal
and distal ends.

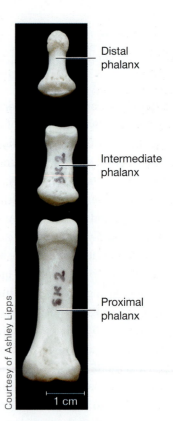

Distal
phalanx

Intermediate
phalanx

Proximal
phalanx

Courtesy of Ashley Lipps

FIGURE 6.40 The Finger Bones
Anterior view of the three
hand phalanges (or finger
bones) from one left finger.
Each of the four fingers has
three phalanges like those
shown here. The thumb has
only two phalanges.

carpal is more rounded, and it articulates with a phalanx (finger bone).

The finger bones are called **phalanges** (**phalanx**, singular). The thumb has only two phalanges, but the other fingers each have three phalanges (**FIGURE 6.40**). From the metacarpal to the fingertip, the three phalanges of each finger are referred to as the proximal phalanx, the intermediate phalanx, and the distal phalanx. The thumb has only a proximal phalanx and a distal phalanx; it lacks the intermediate phalanx. In general, the hand phalanges get smaller as they approach the fingertip, with the proximal phalanges being the largest and the distal phalanges being the smallest. The distal phalanges have flattened distal ends that correspond to the pads on our fingertips.

The Pelvis

Having considered the upper limb, we now turn to the lower limb. The pelvis (or *pelvic girdle*) appears to be one large bone, but it is actually composed of three bones. The posterior of the pelvis is formed by the sacrum, which is considered part of the axial skeleton. The sides and anterior are formed by the two **ossa coxae** (**os coxa**, singular), also called **innominate bones** or hip bones (**FIGURE 6.41**). The ossa coxae articulate with the sacrum posteriorly at the *sacroiliac joints*, and they articulate with each other anteriorly at the *pubic symphysis joint*. Each os coxa is in turn formed by the fusion of three bones: the ilium, the ischium, and the pubis. The **ilium** is the large, bladelike area that you can feel when you put your hands on your hips. The **ischium** forms the underside upon which we sit. The **pubis** is the anterior region, and it is the area where the two ossa coxae articulate with each other.

The pelvis is an important area for the attachment of muscles, such as the gluteal muscles that help move the leg and stabilize the body during locomotion. The pelvis is also useful for determining an individual's sex because it varies considerably between males and females. Because the pelvis has numerous significant features, we discuss them for each component bone, beginning with the features of the ilium

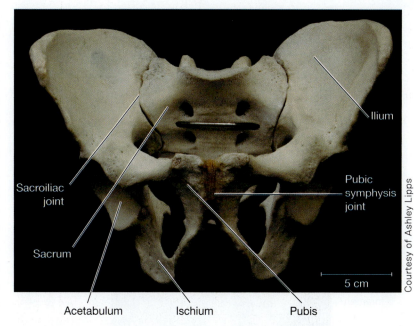

Sacroiliac joint

Sacrum

Ilium

Pubic symphysis joint

Acetabulum   Ischium   Pubis

Courtesy of Ashley Lipps

5 cm

FIGURE 6.41 The Pelvic Girdle
Anterior view of a human pelvic girdle. Note the three different bones that form an articulated pelvic girdle.

(**FIGURE 6.42**). On the medial surface of the ilium, there is an ear-shaped area called the *auricular surface*. This is where the os coxa articulates with the sacrum to form the sacroiliac joint. The superior edge of the ilium, called the *iliac crest*, is an attachment area for numerous abdominal muscles. The *anterior superior iliac spine* is found at the anterior end of the iliac crest, and the *posterior superior iliac spine* is found at the posterior end of the iliac crest. Both are areas for muscle attachment. The *greater sciatic notch* is located inferior to the posterior superior iliac spine, and it accommodates muscles and nerves that run through the pelvis to the lower limb. The *acetabulum* is the large, cuplike depression on the lateral surface of the os coxa. It is located anterior and slightly inferior to the greater sciatic notch, and it is the area of the pelvis that articulates with the femur head to form the hip joint. It is also the area where the ilium, ischium, and pubis fuse together.

The ischium has additional important features (see Figure 6.42). Posterior to the acetabulum and inferior to the greater sciatic notch, we find the *ischial spine*. The *lesser sciatic notch* is located just inferior to the ischial spine, and it accommodates an important leg muscle. The

phalanx (**phalanges**, plural) one of the fourteen bones that form the fingers and toes on each hand or foot

os coxa (**ossa coxae**, plural) one of the paired bones that forms the sides and front of the pelvis, resulting from the fusion of the ilium, ischium, and pubis; also known as the **innominate bone**

ilium (**ilia**, plural) the large, bladelike area of each os coxa (hip bone)

ischium the bone that forms the underside (posteroinferior side) of an os coxa

pubis the bone that forms the front (anterior) of an os coxa; also called the pubic bone

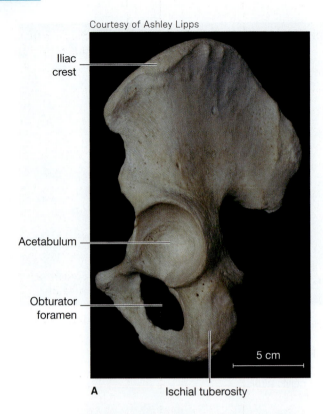

Courtesy of Ashley Lipps

Iliac crest

Acetabulum

Obturator foramen

5 cm

A Ischial tuberosity

large, rough area of bone just below the lesser sciatic notch is called the *ischial tuberosity*. It forms the posteroinferior corner of the pelvis, and it is an attachment point for several leg muscles.

Finally, on the pubis, we see still other important features (see Figure 6.42). The *superior pubic ramus* joins the pubis to the ilium in the acetabulum, and the *inferior pubic ramus* joins the pubis to the ischium. Together with the ischium, these two rami form a large hole, called the *obturator foramen*, which allows for the passage of nerves and blood vessels between the pelvis and leg. The pubic symphysis joint is the relatively immobile cartilaginous joint where the pubis bones of the two ossa coxae

FIGURE 6.42 The Os Coxa
(A) Lateral view and (B) medial view of a human left os coxa. Note the important features of the ilium, ischium, and pubis. (C) These three bones fuse to form each os coxa.

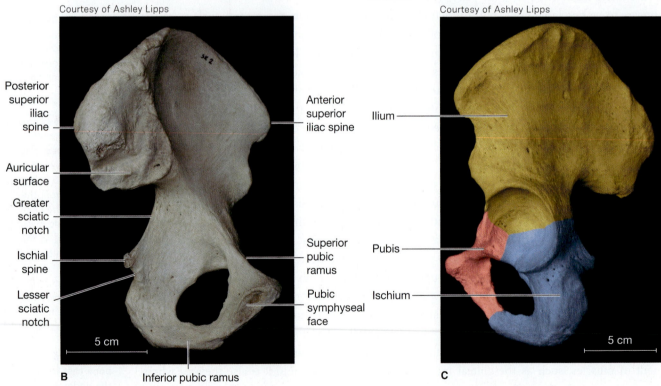

Courtesy of Ashley Lipps

Posterior superior iliac spine

Auricular surface

Greater sciatic notch

Ischial spine

Lesser sciatic notch

Anterior superior iliac spine

Superior pubic ramus

Pubic symphyseal face

5 cm

B Inferior pubic ramus

Courtesy of Ashley Lipps

Ilium

Pubis

Ischium

5 cm

C

articulate. The surface of the pubis that is involved in this articulation is called the *pubic symphyseal face*, and it is an important area used to estimate age from a skeleton.

The Femur and Patella

The large and heavy thigh bone is called the **femur** (**FIGURE 6.43**). The proximal end of the femur has a round *head* that articulates with the acetabulum of the pelvis. The head of the femur has a small depression in the center, called the *fovea capitis*. An important ligament runs between here and the acetabulum to help keep the femur in place in the hip joint. Below the head, there is a constricted area, called the *neck* of the femur, which joins the head and shaft. On the lateral side of the proximal end of the femur, there is a large projection called the *greater trochanter*. This projection is a muscle attachment site for gluteal muscles that originate

femur the bone that forms the thigh of each leg

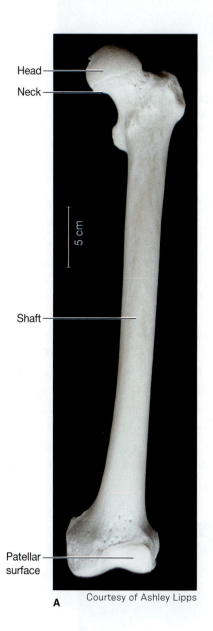

Head
Neck

5 cm

Shaft

Patellar surface

A Courtesy of Ashley Lipps

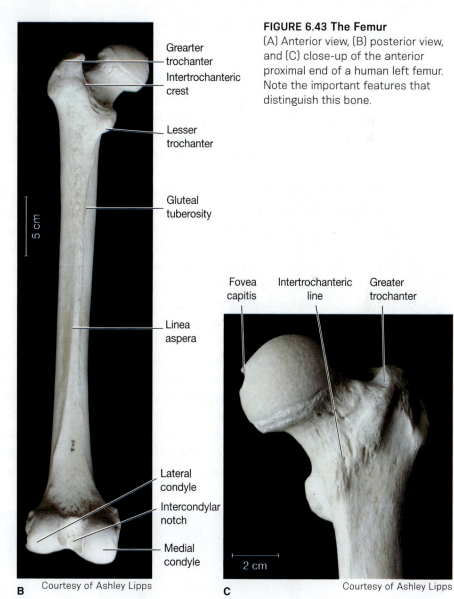

Grearter trochanter
Intertrochanteric crest

Lesser trochanter

Gluteal tuberosity

5 cm

Linea aspera

Lateral condyle
Intercondylar notch

Medial condyle

B Courtesy of Ashley Lipps

FIGURE 6.43 The Femur
(A) Anterior view, (B) posterior view, and (C) close-up of the anterior proximal end of a human left femur. Note the important features that distinguish this bone.

Fovea capitis · Intertrochanteric line · Greater trochanter

2 cm

C Courtesy of Ashley Lipps

patella the small, slightly triangular bone that helps form each knee joint; also called the kneecap

tibia the larger and more medial of the two bones in each lower leg; also called the shinbone

fibula the thinner and more lateral of the two bones in each lower leg

on the pelvis. Just below where the femur neck meets the shaft on the posterior surface, there is another projection, called the *lesser trochanter*. This projection is an area of attachment for muscles from the pelvis and lower back. Between the greater and lesser trochanters, on the posterior surface of the femur, there is a raised ridge called the *intertrochanteric crest*. Between the trochanters on the anterior surface, there is a less pronounced line in the bone called the *intertrochanteric line*. Extending down the femur shaft from the greater trochanter on the posterior, lateral surface is an area called the *gluteal tuberosity*. It can be a pronounced projection or appear as simply a rough area of the bone. As its name suggests, the gluteal tuberosity is an area for gluteal muscle attachment. Beginning at the inferior end of the gluteal tuberosity and extending down much of the posterior shaft surface, there is a ridge of bone, called the *linea aspera*, that is an important area for the attachment of the hamstring muscles. At the distal end of the femur are two large, rounded projections. The more medial projection is called the *medial condyle*, and the more lateral projection is called the *lateral condyle*. These two condyles articulate with the proximal end of the tibia (shinbone) to form the knee joint. On the posterior surface between these two condyles, there is a depression called the *intercondylar fossa* or *notch*. On the anterior surface between the condyles, there is a depression called the *patellar surface*, which is where the patella articulates and moves back and forth during knee movement.

The **patella** (commonly called the kneecap) is a small bone that is somewhat triangular in

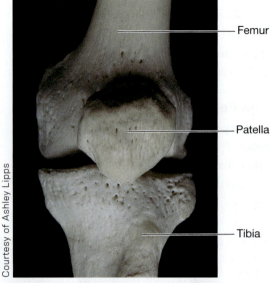

FIGURE 6.44 The Patella and Femur
Anterior view of a human left patella, femur, and tibia in anatomical position.

Courtesy of Ashley Lipps

shape. The patella is the largest sesamoid bone in the body. A sesamoid bone is a bone that is embedded within a tendon and is typically very tiny. The patella articulates with the patellar surface on the anterior side of the distal femur **(FIGURE 6.44)**. It moves up and down along this surface as the knee moves, helping to both protect the knee and facilitate its function. The patella has three key features **(FIGURE 6.45)**. The distal tip of the patella comes to a slight point, called the *apex*. On the posterior surface, the patella has two depressions that articulate with the distal surface of the femur. The medial depression is called the *medial articular facet*, and the lateral depression is called the *lateral articular facet*.

FIGURE 6.45 The Patella
(A) Anterior view and (B) posterior view of a human left patella. Note the important features that distinguish this bone.

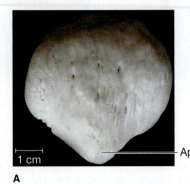

A

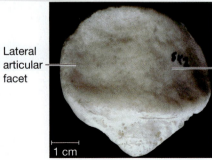

B

Courtesy of Ashley Lipps

The Tibia and Fibula

The lower leg is made up of two long bones: the tibia and the fibula. The **tibia** is commonly called the shinbone, and it is the thicker and more medial of the two lower leg bones (**FIGURE 6.46**). The proximal end of the tibia is marked by a relatively flat surface, called the *tibial plateau*, which articulates with the distal end of the femur (**FIGURE 6.47**). The medial side of the tibial plateau is formed by the *medial condyle*, and the lateral side of the tibial plateau is formed by the *lateral condyle*. These condyles are separated by a small, raised area called the *intercondylar eminence*. Toward the posterior of the lateral condyle, there is a small facet called the *superior fibular articular facet*, which is where the proximal ends of the tibia and fibula articulate. Inferior to the tibial plateau on the anterior surface, there is a projection called the *tibial tuberosity* that is an area of attachment for the quadriceps muscle. Along the anterior surface of the central tibia shaft is a sharp crest of bone called the *anterior crest*. This is the area of bone you can feel when you run your fingers down your shin. At the distal end of the tibia, there is a projection on the medial side called the *medial malleolus*. This is the large knob of bone you can feel on the inside of your ankle. On the lateral side of the distal tibia is the *inferior fibular articular surface* (or *fibular notch*), which is where the distal ends of the tibia and fibula articulate.

The **fibula** is the thinner and more lateral of the two lower leg bones (see Figure 6.46). Unlike the tibia, the fibula is not involved in the knee joint. At the proximal end, the fibula has a rounded *head* that articulates with the tibia (**FIGURE 6.48**). The *shaft* of the fibula is long and thin. The distal end of the fibula is somewhat flatter than the rounded head, and it is marked by a projection at the tip of the bone called the *lateral malleolus*. This projection is the knob of bone you can feel on the outside of your ankle.

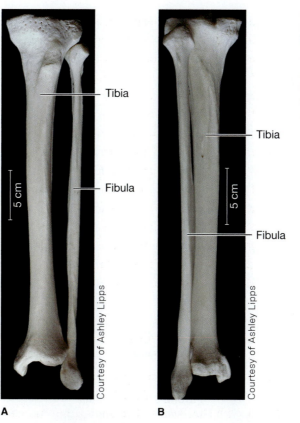

FIGURE 6.46 The Tibia and Fibula
(A) Anterior view and (B) posterior view of a human left tibia and fibula in anatomical position.

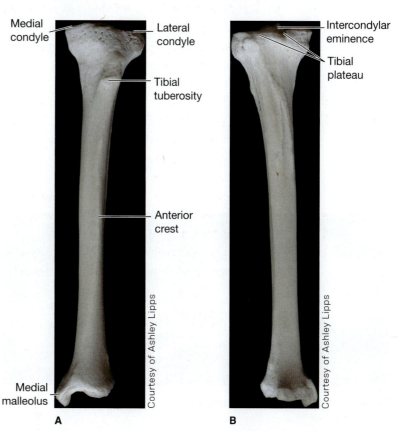

FIGURE 6.47 The Tibia
(A) Anterior view and (B) posterior view of a human left tibia. Note the important features that distinguish this bone.

tarsal one of the seven short bones that form each ankle

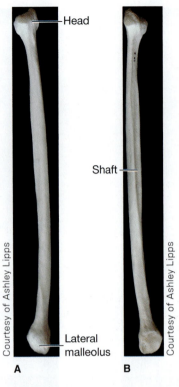

Head

Shaft

Lateral malleolus

Courtesy of Ashley Lipps

Courtesy of Ashley Lipps

A   B

FIGURE 6.48 The Fibula
(A) Anterior view and
(B) posterior view of a
human left fibula, with
important features labeled.

The Bones of the Ankle and Foot

Like those of the wrist and hand, the bones of the ankle and foot take three basic forms: tarsals (ankle bones), metatarsals (foot bones), and phalanges (toe bones) **(FIGURE 6.49)**. There are seven **tarsals** in each foot, and, like the carpals, they are generally cube-shaped **(FIGURE 6.50)**. However, tarsals are larger than carpals, and they are not positioned in two rows. The largest tarsal bone is the *calcaneus*, which forms the heel of the foot. The second largest tarsal is the *talus* (often called the astragalus in non-humans). It is medial and superior to the calcaneus and articulates with the tibia and fibula to form the ankle. The third largest tarsal is the *cuboid*. It lies between the calcaneus and metatarsals and is the most regularly cube-shaped tarsal. The *navicular* is positioned medial to the cuboid, between the talus and the remaining tarsals—the cuneiforms. There are three cuneiforms: the *medial cuneiform*, the *intermediate cuneiform*, and the *lateral cuneiform* (listed from most medial to most lateral). Notice that while most of these bones have a general cube shape, they vary considerably in their exact shape and size. The calcaneus and talus have particularly unusual shapes.

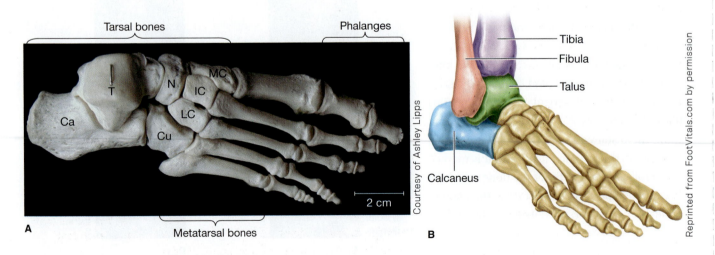

Tarsal bones   Phalanges

MC
N   IC
LC
Ca
Cu

2 cm

A   Metatarsal bones

Courtesy of Ashley Lipps

Tibia
Fibula
Talus

Calcaneus

B

Reprinted from FootVitals.com by permission

FIGURE 6.49 The Bones of the Foot and Ankle
(A) Superior view of the bones of the human right foot and ankle in anatomical position. Tarsals: Ca = calcaneus, T = talus, N = navicular, Cu = cuboid, MC = medial cuneiform, IC = intermediate cuneiform, LC = lateral cuneiform. (B) Bones of the foot shown in articulation with the lower leg bones at the ankle joint.

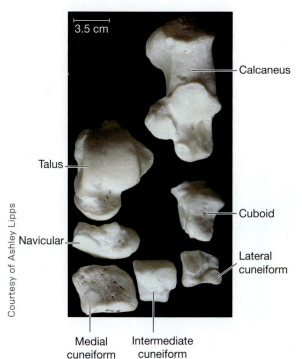

Courtesy of Ashley Lipps

FIGURE 6.50 The Tarsals
Note the similarities and differences among these human left tarsal bones, all from the same individual.

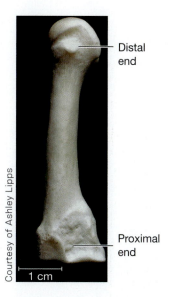

Courtesy of Ashley Lipps

FIGURE 6.51 The Metatarsals
Anterior view of a typical human left metatarsal. Note the difference between the proximal and distal ends.

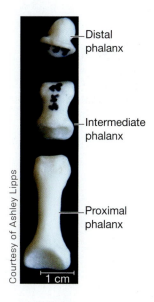

Courtesy of Ashley Lipps

FIGURE 6.52 The Toe Bones
Anterior view of the three human left foot phalanges (or toe bones) from one toe. The four toes each have three phalanges, such as those here. The hallux (big toe) has only two phalanges.

The bones of the foot are called the **metatarsals**. The foot is laid out similarly to the hand. There are five metatarsals in each foot, with one metatarsal corresponding to each toe. The metatarsals are numbered from 1 to 5, with 1 corresponding to the big toe (or **hallux**) and 5 corresponding to the pinky toe. The proximal end of a metatarsal is somewhat square-shaped and concave, and it articulates with a complementary tarsal surface. The distal end of a metatarsal is more rounded, and it articulates with a phalanx (**FIGURE 6.51**). In humans, the first metatarsal (for the hallux) is much thicker than the other metatarsals.

Like the finger bones, the toe bones are called phalanges (phalanx, singular). Again, the layout and organization of the foot phalanges are similar to that of the hand phalanges (**FIGURE 6.52**). The hallux has only two phalanges, but the other toes each have three phalanges. From the metatarsals to the ends of the toes, the three phalanges of each toe are referred to as the proximal phalanx, the intermediate pha-

lanx, and the distal phalanx. The hallux has only a proximal phalanx and a distal phalanx; it lacks the intermediate phalanx. In general, the toe phalanges get smaller as they approach the end of the toe. In humans, the toe phalanges are usually smaller than their counterparts in the fingers.

metatarsal one of the five bones that form each foot

hallux the biggest and most medial of the toes on each foot

CONCEPT REVIEW QUESTIONS

Name: _____   Section: _____

Course: _____   Date: _____

Answer the following questions in the space provided.

1. Name the bone that forms the posterior (back) of the cranium.

2. Name the four types of teeth found in primates.

3. Which of the following bones is found in the neck?
   A. Cervical vertebra
   B. Sacrum
   C. Lumbar vertebra
   D. Thoracic vertebra

4. Which of the following bones articulates with ribs?
   A. Sacrum
   B. Lumbar vertebra
   C. Cervical vertebra
   D. Thoracic vertebra

5. How many ribs articulate directly with the sternum? How many ribs articulate with the sternum indirectly? How many ribs do not articulate with the sternum at all?

6. Name the three bones that articulate with the humerus.

7. How many phalanges are in the typical human hand?
   A. 8
   B. 14
   C. 15
   D. 5

8. Name the three fused bones that make up each os coxa.

9. Name the three bones that articulate with the femur.

10. The tarsals are found in which area of the body?

   A. The upper back
   B. The ankle
   C. The knee
   D. The wrist

LAB EXERCISES

Name: _____ Section: _____

Course: _____ Date: _____

EXERCISE 1 CRANIUM

Work in a small group or alone to complete this exercise.

PART A

Refer to the skeletal material provided by your instructor (or the photos of a human cranium in the Lab 6 Exercise Image Library on p. 172). Some of the major bones of the cranium have been assigned numbers. For each number, provide the appropriate bone name in the space below.

1.

2.

3.

4.

5.

6.

7.

PART B

Refer to the skeletal material provided by your instructor (or the photos of a human cranium in the Lab 6 Exercise Image Library on p. 172) and label (or identify) the following key features of the cranium:

1. External auditory (acoustic) meatus

2. Mental protuberance

3. Mastoid process

4. Alveolar process

5. Foramen magnum

6. Occipital condyle

EXERCISE 2 DENTITION

Work in a small group or alone to complete this exercise. Refer to the skeletal material provided by your instructor (or the mystery animal dentition photo in the Lab 6 Exercise Image Library on p. 172) to calculate the dental formula for the animal and write it in the space below.

Dental formula:

EXERCISE 3 VERTEBRAL COLUMN

Work in a small group or alone to complete this exercise.

PART A

Refer to the skeletal material provided by your instructor (or the human vertebral column diagram in the Lab 6 Exercise Image Library on p. 173). The major bones of the vertebral column have been assigned numbers. For each number, provide the appropriate bone name in the space below:

1.   4.

2.   5.

3.

PART B

Refer to the skeletal material provided by your instructor (or the photo of a typical human vertebra in the Lab 6 Exercise Image Library on p. 173) and label (or identify) the following key features of the vertebra:

1. Vertebral body   3. Spinous process

2. Vertebral foramen   4. Transverse process

PART C

Refer to the skeletal material provided by your instructor (or the photos of three mystery vertebrae in the Lab 6 Exercise Image Library on p. 173) to answer the following questions.

1. Which mystery vertebra is a cervical vertebra? Describe two features that helped you determine this.

2. Which mystery vertebra is a thoracic vertebra? Describe two features that helped you determine this.

3. Which mystery vertebra is a lumbar vertebra? Describe two features that helped you determine this.

EXERCISE 4 THORACIC CAGE (RIB CAGE)

Work in a small group or alone to complete this exercise. Refer to the skeletal material provided by your instructor (or the diagram of the human rib cage in the Lab 6 Exercise Image Library on p. 174) and label (or identify) the following bones of the rib cage:

1. Manubrium

2. Sternal body

3. Xiphoid process

4. True ribs

5. False ribs

6. Floating ribs

EXERCISE 5 UPPER LIMB AND LOWER LIMB COMPARISON

Work in a small group or alone to complete this exercise.

PART A

Refer to the skeletal material provided by your instructor (or the photo of human upper limb bones in the Lab 6 Exercise Image Library on p. 175). The major bones have been numbered. For each number, provide the appropriate bone name in the space below.

1.

2.

3.

4.

5.

6.

PART B

Refer to the skeletal material provided by your instructor (or the photo of human lower limb bones in the Lab 6 Exercise Image Library on p. 175). The major bones have been numbered. For each number, provide the appropriate bone name in the space below.

1.

2.

3.

4.

5.

6.

EXERCISE 6   UPPER LIMB

PART A

Refer to the skeletal material provided by your instructor (or the photos of a human humerus in the Lab 6 Exercise Image Library on p. 176) and label (or identify) the following key features of the humerus:

1. Head
2. Lesser tubercle
3. Greater tubercle
4. Intertubercular groove

5. Lateral epicondyle
6. Medial epicondyle
7. Olecranon fossa
8. Coronoid fossa

PART B

Refer to the skeletal material provided by your instructor (or to Figure 6.37 on p. 154). Review the bones of the hand. Describe two things that make the first finger (the thumb) different from the other fingers.

EXERCISE 7   LOWER LIMB

Work in a small group or alone to complete this exercise.

PART A

Review the skeletal material provided by your instructor (or the photo of a human pelvis in the Lab 6 Exercise Image Library on p. 177). The major bones and features have been numbered. For each number, provide the appropriate name in the space below.

1.

2.

3.

4.

5.

6.

7.

PART B

Review the skeletal material provided by your instructor (or the photos of a human femur in the Lab 6 Exercise Image Library on p. 177) and label the following key features of the femur:

1. Head
2. Neck
3. Greater trochanter
4. Lesser trochanter

5. Lateral condyle
6. Medial condyle
7. Patellar surface

PART C

Refer to the skeletal material provided by your instructor (or to Figure 6.49 on p. 160). Review the bones of the foot. Describe two things that make the first toe (the big toe) different from the other toes.

EXERCISE 8   SURFACE ANATOMY OF THE SKELETON

Work in a small group or alone to complete this exercise.

Use your own body (in anatomical position) to identify the following bones and features of the skeleton. Name the specific bone(s) [and feature(s) if possible] for each.

1. Your chin

2. The bump behind the bottom of your ear

3. The dip at the bottom midline of your neck between your two collarbones

4. The tip of your elbow

5. The sides of your elbow

6. The protrusion or bump on the back of your wrist

7. The protrusion or bump you can feel on the corner of your wrist (palmar surface)

8. The protrusion or ridge at the front and top of your hips

9. The protrusion or bump on your outer ankle

10. The protrusion or bump on your inner ankle

CRITICAL THINKING QUESTIONS

Use a separate sheet of paper to answer the following questions.

1. Why do you think there are so many bones in the cranium? Why do you think we are born with separate cranial bones that later fuse together as we grow and develop?

2. Review the vertebral column and individual vertebrae from Exercise 3. What similarities and differences do you notice between the three major types of vertebrae? Why might these similarities exist? Why might these differences exist? Humans do not have tails, so we do not have caudal vertebrae (the vertebrae that make up the tail). However, many other primates do have these vertebrae. Based on what you know about the other kinds of vertebrae, what would you expect caudal vertebrae to look like? Compare your estimation with images of caudal vertebrae in your classroom, online, or in books. How accurate was your estimation?

3. The ribs articulate to the sternum through lengths of costal cartilage. This means that much of the anterior side of the rib cage is cartilage. Why do you think it is important that so much of the rib cage is made of cartilage and not bone?

4. Review the upper limb from Exercise 5. Compare the shoulder joint and the elbow joint. What do you notice is similar? What do you notice is different? How do these similarities and differences relate to similarities and differences in the function and mobility of these joints?

5. Review the upper and lower limbs from Exercise 5. Consider the joints, the types of bones, and the overall layout of the bones. What do you notice is similar? What do you notice is different? How do these similarities and differences relate to similarities and differences in the function and mobility of these appendages?

6. The human hands and feet have similar types and numbers of bones. However, hands and feet are very different in their appearance. What physical differences do you notice between the hands and feet? How might these differences relate to differences in the function of these body parts? Would you expect other primates to have hands and feet that differed like this? Why or why not?

LAB 6 EXERCISE IMAGE LIBRARY
Students should use these images only if directed to by their instructor.

EXERCISE 1 CRANIUM

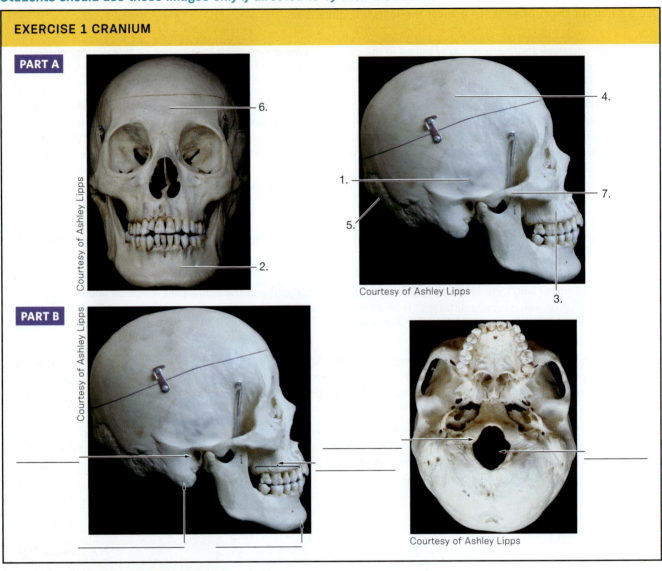

PART A

6.

2.

4.

1.

5.

7.

3.

Courtesy of Ashley Lipps

Courtesy of Ashley Lipps

PART B

Courtesy of Ashley Lipps

Courtesy of Ashley Lipps

Courtesy of Ashley Lipps

EXERCISE 2 DENTITION

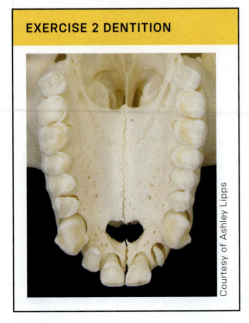

Courtesy of Ashley Lipps

EXERCISE 3 VERTEBRAL COLUMN

PART A

PART B

Courtesy of Ashley Lipps

PART C

A   Courtesy of Ashley Lipps

B   Courtesy of Ashley Lipps

C   Courtesy of Ashley Lipps

EXERCISE 4 THORACIC CAGE (RIB CAGE)

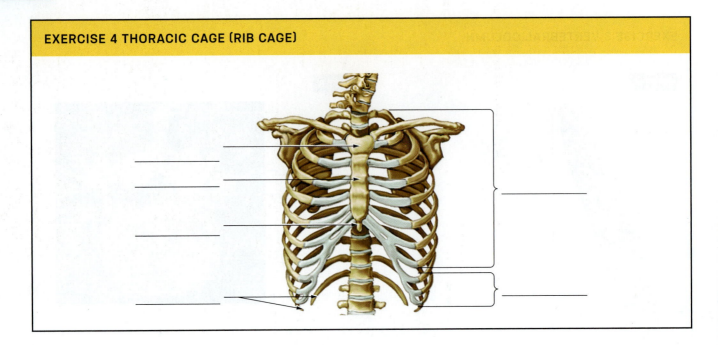

EXERCISE 5 UPPER LIMB AND LOWER LIMB COMPARISON

PART A

Courtesy of Ashley Lipps

5.

4.

1.

2.

3.

6.

PART B

Courtesy of Ashley Lipps

1.

2.   5.

6.

4.   3.

EXERCISE 6 UPPER LIMB

PART A

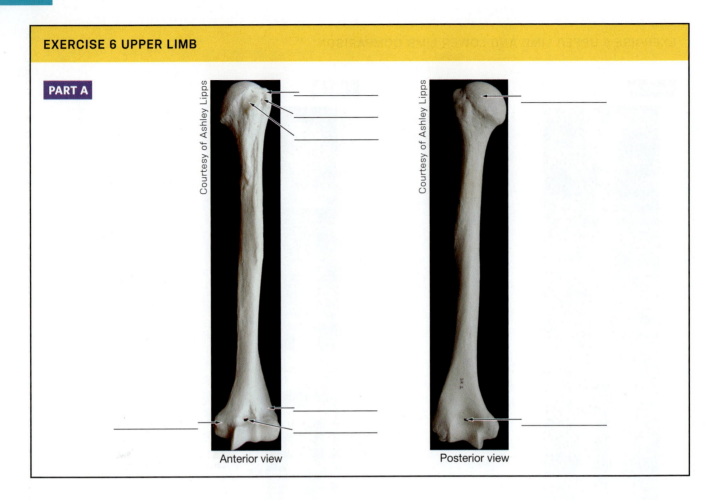

Anterior view

Posterior view

Courtesy of Ashley Lipps

EXERCISE 7 LOWER LIMB

PART A

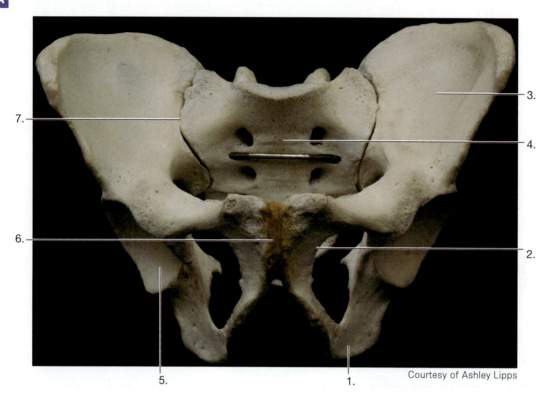

7.

3.

4.

6.

2.

5.

1.

Courtesy of Ashley Lipps

PART B

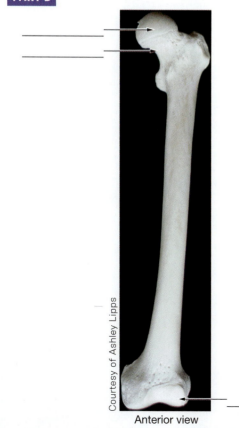

Courtesy of Ashley Lipps

Anterior view

Courtesy of Ashley Lipps

Posterior view

The conditions in the Amazon rainforest lead to rapid decomposition, and human remains found in this area are often mostly skeletal (with little soft tissue). In these cases, a forensic anthropologist may be called on to assist in police investigations.

LAB 7

Bioarchaeology and Forensic Anthropology

Lab Learning Objectives

By the end of this lab, students should be able to:

- discuss the similarities and differences between forensic anthropology and bioarchaeology.

- distinguish between human and animal bone.

- determine the minimum number of individuals represented by a bone assemblage.

- estimate the likely sex and age at death of individuals using their bones.

- make stature estimations using measurements of long bones.

- identify and distinguish between key types of antemortem and perimortem pathology.

- discuss methods and problems of determining ancestry from skeletal material.

In August 2006, two tourists were reported missing in the Ecuadorian area of the Amazon rainforest. Between December 2006 and March 2007, dismembered human remains were recovered from three separate locations in the area. Because the body parts were highly decomposed, with little soft tissue available for identification or analysis, a forensic anthropologist was called in to assist with the examination of the remains. Using her expert knowledge of the human skeleton, she was able to identify the victims and reconstruct some of the circumstances surrounding their deaths.

The anthropologist determined that the remains belonged to two separate individuals. From there, she tried to reconstruct the identity of the victims. She estimated the sex, age, and stature (height) of the victims and identified some unique characteristics, such as the individuals' dental health and history. Based on this research, the victims were successfully identified as the two missing tourists. In addition, the anthropologist studied marks on the bones and learned that the victims had been dismembered using a chainsaw. This information, along with other forensic evidence (such as fibers and possible murder weapons recovered from the sites), will be used in the trial of the suspected perpetrators.

bioarchaeology the study of skeletal remains from archaeological contexts

Although coroners and other related experts have a valuable understanding of human soft tissue, there are sometimes situations where soft tissue evidence is limited or unavailable. In these situations, understanding the nuances of the human skeleton can be particularly useful. In this lab, we examine how forensic anthropologists use skeletal remains to reconstruct a victim's identity and the circumstances surrounding his or her death. We also discuss how bioarchaeologists use similar pieces of information from skeletons to reconstruct information about individuals and populations in the past.

INTRODUCTION

This lab closely explores the procedures and methods used by bioarchaeologists and forensic anthropologists. We begin with an introduction to the field of bioarchaeology. We then turn to the related field of forensic anthropology. Next, we consider the primary steps used in both fields to analyze the skeletal remains of individuals. For each step, we review the techniques

used and the key skeletal elements needed. We also discuss more detailed aspects of forensic anthropology protocol that can obtain more specific information and lead to the identification of individuals. Both bioarchaeology and forensic anthropology, and the methods associated with them, are important parts of the discipline of biological anthropology. Many biological anthropologists are employed in these fields, and work along these lines has been popularized through hit television series and best-selling novels.

WHAT IS BIOARCHAEOLOGY?

Bioarchaeology is the study of human skeletal remains from archaeological sites (**FIGURE 7.1**). Bioarchaeologists are not involved in contemporary legal cases; they are more broadly interested in understanding the past lifeways of historical and prehistoric people through the analysis of their skeletons. Bioarchaeological studies attempt to reconstruct past human activities, diets, diseases, and overall health patterns. Because bioarchaeologists apply methods of skeletal analysis to archaeological contexts, they bridge the gap between biological anthropology and archaeology. Like many other fields, bioarchaeology is often interdisciplinary and overlaps with other disciplines, such as demography, chemistry, and medicine.

How much bioarchaeologists can learn from archaeological skeletal remains depends on their state of preservation. Preservation of remains is affected by multiple factors, including how old the remains are and in what type of environment they are buried. In addition, the study of ancient skeletal remains carries important ethical and legal obligations. In many countries, including the United States, there are laws that prioritize the rights of descendant communities and their religious beliefs and cultural heritage over the study and disturbance of skeletal remains. Bioarchaeologists are always keenly aware of their ethical responsibilities and the need to treat human remains with respect.

Photo courtesy of Melanie Miller

FIGURE 7.1 Bioarchaeology
Bioarchaeologists such as Melanie Miller, seen here, use methods of skeletal analysis to understand what life was like for past (archaeological) populations. This excavation focused on 5,000-year-old skeletons in Ubate, Colombia. Miller used gloves, a face mask, and aluminum foil packets to avoid contaminating the DNA recovered from the archaeological context.

The bioarchaeologist compiles as much information as possible from ancient skeletal remains to reconstruct the life of the individual (age at death, sex, signs of disease, etc.). Ultimately, however, bioarchaeologists are also interested in reconstructing the lives of groups of people and communities, not just individuals. They may study the life histories of individual skeletons to get a sense for how the larger group lived and to answer broader questions: Were there differences in the ways males and females, young people and old people, or people of different statuses lived? Bioarchaeologists apply many of the same methods and techniques as forensic anthropologists, and when presented with archaeological skeletal remains, they follow many of the same protocol steps.

WHAT IS FORENSIC ANTHROPOLOGY?

Forensic anthropology is the branch of biological anthropology that applies specialized methods of skeletal analysis to human skeletal remains during the course of legal investigations. For example, if a victim's body was buried for many years, or was severely burned, much of the victim's soft tissue may no longer be available. In cases such as these, a forensic anthropologist is called on to analyze the remaining skeletal material. The primary job of the forensic anthropologist in these situations is to build a profile that will help in identifying the victim and, if possible, help in determining the circumstances surrounding the victim's death.

Although popular television shows and books suggest that forensic anthropologists spend all of their time investigating individual victims, this is not always the case. Forensic anthropologists often work on cases of mass death, such as genocide, war crimes, and natural disasters. In addition, many forensic anthropologists participate in investigations only part-time. They spend the rest of their time teaching or conducting research.

When forensic anthropologists are investigating skeletal material in legal contexts, they follow a protocol that lays out steps in a meaningful order to help them identify an individual. Often, one step cannot be accurately completed without the completion of prior steps. These steps include determining the age, sex, and stature of the individuals as well as examining indications of pathology before death and estimating the amount of time since death.

SKELETAL BIOLOGICAL VARIATION

Like all biological anthropologists, bioarchaeologists and forensic anthropologists are interested in examining aspects of human variation, particularly aspects of skeletal variation. Differences in age, biological sex, height, or response to disease are all aspects of human variation that we can examine in the skeleton. For example, the skeletons of males and females can differ in shape and size. Similarly, the bones grow larger, and teeth erupt at different ages and at different times, in male and female children, and the bones of older adults degenerate in a regular fashion and appear different from the bones of younger adults.

We have two primary ways to study the variation in skeletons. The first is by using *qualitative* methods, where we observe the variation of the bones by visual inspection. This approach is called **anthroposcopy**. For example, when we look at differences in the shape of the pelvis between males and females, or the presence of certain tooth shapes, such as the shovel-shaped incisors seen in some populations, these are qualitative observations. The second way we can assess variation in skeletons is by using *quantitative* methods, where we actually measure characteristics of the bones or teeth. For example, we may measure variation in the length of individuals' femurs, which contributes to our variation in height, or we may measure the sizes of the molar teeth, which vary between the sexes, among different human species, and even among modern human populations. The quantitative approach of measuring human proportions is called **anthropometry**, and the approach of

forensic anthropology the application of knowledge and methods of skeletal analysis to assist in legal investigations

anthroposcopy the observation of physical bodily characteristics by inspection as opposed to exact measurement

anthropometry the scientific study of the measurements and proportions of the human body

osteometry
the study and measurement of the human or animal skeleton, especially in an anthropological context

specifically measuring bones is called **osteometry**. Both qualitative and quantitative approaches are used in bioarchaeology and forensic anthropology to learn more about the lives and identities of individuals from their skeletal remains, and you will have a chance to learn both groups of methods here.

METHODS USED IN THE ANALYSIS OF SKELETAL REMAINS

Many of the steps and methods used in the analysis of skeletal remains are the same in forensic and in archaeological contexts. Typically, once the basic steps of analysis are complete, additional methods are used to gain more specific and specialized information. For example, chemical analysis (isotope analysis) may be used to get data on the diets of archaeological populations; analysis of skeletal morphology or modification may be used to infer lifestyles or cultural behaviors; or DNA analysis may be used to help identify individual victims in forensic cases. We discuss here the primary steps taken in analyzing skeletal material.

Some Key Steps in Analyzing Human Skeletal Remains

1. Distinguish between human and animal bone.
2. Determine the minimum number of individuals present.
3. Estimate the sex of each individual.
4. Estimate the age at death for each individual.
5. Estimate the stature of each individual.
6. Identify indicators of pathology or stress for each individual.

Additional Steps Specific to Forensic Contexts

7. Determine the likely ancestry of each individual.
8. Calculate the postmortem interval.

DISTINGUISHING BETWEEN HUMAN AND ANIMAL BONE

There are many human bones that resemble the bones of other animals. For example, the bones of a human hand and the bones of a bear paw are very similar (**FIGURE 7.2**). This means that human bones can be mistaken for those of other animals, and vice versa. Such errors are even more likely to occur when the skeletal material is fragmented and incomplete. It is important for both bioarchaeologists and forensic anthropologists to make sure they are working with human bone before they proceed with their analyses.

There are two considerations when determining if a bone is human. First, you must consider its size. Is the bone the appropriate size to be that of a juvenile or adult human? Even though there is a lot of variation in human size, there are many animals that are considerably larger or smaller. For example, cattle are very large and have large, robust bones. This robusticity is clear even in some bone fragments, so it can be used to differentiate cattle bones from more gracile (slender) human bones. Similarly, dog bones are relatively gracile but smaller than human bones. This smallness can be used to differentiate them from larger human bones.

Second, you must consider unique human adaptations. For example, humans have chins and foreheads whereas other animals do not. If a mandibular fragment is found with a mental protuberance (chin), it must be human. Similarly, if a tall, vaulted frontal bone is found, it must be human. Humans also have a generally large braincase with a smaller face, a shorter snout, and smaller canines in comparison with other animals, which have smaller braincases, larger projecting snouts, and in the case of carnivores especially, larger, saber-like canine teeth (**FIGURE 7.3**). We also have a series of specialized adaptations for bipedal locomotion (walking upright on two limbs) that make our skeletons unusual (see Lab 14 for more details). If a bone is found with any of these adaptations, it must be human.

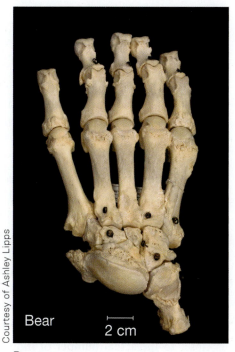

FIGURE 7.2 Human or Nonhuman?
Some human skeletal elements are very similar to those of other animals. For example, this human hand (A) is similar to this bear paw (B). Bioarchaeologists and forensic anthropologists must be able to recognize when they are working with human bone.

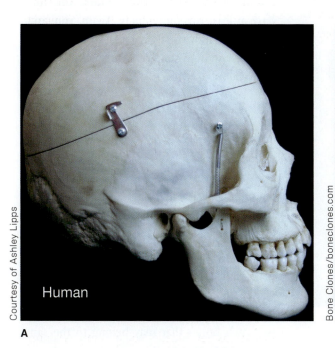

FIGURE 7.3 Human and Nonhuman Skulls
Human skulls (A) have a noticeably large braincase relative to the face and lack a projecting snout, as compared with other animals, which have a smaller braincase and a long projecting snout, as seen in this pit bull dog skull (B).

DETERMINING THE MINIMUM NUMBER OF INDIVIDUALS

In most bioarchaeological contexts and in many forensic contexts, the recovered bones are from multiple individuals. It is then up to the bioarchaeologist or forensic anthropologist to determine how many people are actually represented by the bones in the **assemblage** (collected material). Because there are many bones in the human body that could be recovered, it is often impossible to determine *exactly* how many people are represented. Instead, biological anthropologists focus on determining the **minimum number of individuals (MNI)** possibly represented by the bone assemblage. The MNI gets us closer to the actual number of individuals without overestimating that number. It also helps the researcher to distinguish skeletal elements from different people and focus further analysis on separate individuals. There are three steps to this process. In practice, determination of the MNI can be tricky, as recovered bones are often fragmentary and not well preserved.

Step 1: Are There Any Bones That Are Unique in the Human Body?

There are certain bones that are unique in a human body, such as the mandible. Because there is only one mandible in each human, if your assemblage has two mandibles, you must have *at least* two people. You could have more than two people because there could be people whose mandibles were removed or destroyed. But you definitely have at least two people.

Step 2: Are There Any Bones That Are from the Same Side of the Body?

Some bones in the human body are not unique, but they are sided. For example, the human body has two femurs; the femur is not a unique bone. But the right femur and the left femur are different; the femur is sided **(FIGURE 7.4)**. If your assemblage has two right femurs, you must have at least two individuals. Again, you could have more individuals whose right femurs are not present, but you know you have at least two individuals.

Step 3: Can You Match Any of the Bones to the Same Individual?

The final step is trying to match the bones together. Imagine that your assemblage has two right femurs and two right pelvises. Based on Step 2, you might think you have four individuals. However, it is possible that at least one of your right femurs and one of your right pelvises belong to the same individual. Because of this possibility, biological anthropologists try to match bones that may belong to the same person **(FIGURE 7.5)**. Bones that appear to join with each other (such as the right femur and pelvis) can be articulated to see if they fit correctly. If they do, the femur and pelvis belong

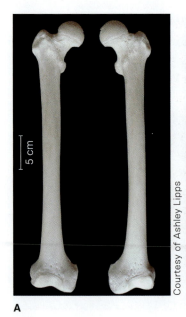

A   B

FIGURE 7.4 One Person or Two?: Paired Bones
Bones such as the femur are paired in the human body. If an assemblage contains a right femur and a left femur (A), they might be from the same person. However, if an assemblage contains two right femurs (B), a biological anthropologist knows she is examining at least two individuals.

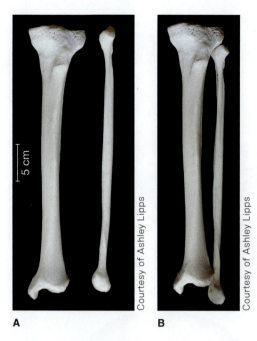

5 cm

Courtesy of Ashley Lipps

A   B

Courtesy of Ashley Lipps

FIGURE 7.5 One Person or Two?: Articulation
When a biological anthropologist recovers two bones that might articulate together, such as the tibia and fibula (A), he or she must try to articulate them to see if they match. If the two bones articulate correctly (B), they probably came from the same person. If the two bones do not articulate correctly due to differences in size or shape, they probably came from two different people.

to the same person, not to two different people. Biological anthropologists can also determine whether multiple bones might belong with each other based on their state of preservation, age, sex, or pathology. Bones from the same body and area of the skeleton are often in a similar state of preservation and of similar age and sex. The bones may also show the same disease or pathology if they are found in the same area of the body or if the pathology is spread throughout the body.

ESTIMATING SEX

After determining that the bones in question are indeed human and estimating the number of individuals, one of the first things that a bioarchaeologist or forensic anthropologist must try to determine is the biological sex of the individual(s) in question; this step is called

sexing. Identification of sex from skeletal remains is based on **sexual dimorphism**, which is the variation between adult male and adult female bodies. In the case of sexual dimorphism in the skeleton, we are specifically looking at differences in bone morphology (size and shape). It is important to remember that the sex of skeletons is relative and exists on a continuum: an individual is more male or less male, or more female or less female. Sexing is not a cut-and-dried determination with only two choices; rather, it is an estimation of where an individual falls along the sex continuum. Further, sexing estimates the likely biological sex of an individual, but it does not speak to the sexual orientation or gender of an individual. Finally, it is important to keep in mind that sexing can be done only on adult skeletons (individuals that are postpubescent). Prior to this age, the skeleton is still growing and developing; many of the biologically based sex differences, which develop later in puberty due to hormones, are not yet present or are difficult to identify. Sexing typically relies on the two skeletal areas with the clearest sex-based differences: the cranium and the pelvis.

In general, there is a slight size difference between modern human males and females, with males tending to be larger. Males tend to be taller than females, so they tend to have longer bones than females. Males tend to be heavier and more muscular than females, so they tend to have more robust bones and more rugged bony features than females. Of course, there are always individuals that do not follow this general pattern. There are taller, more muscular females and shorter, more gracile males. Further, populations differ in their average skeletal size and degree of sexual dimorphism (see Lab 8 for more information about human variation).

Sex Estimation Based on Traits of the Cranium

The cranium is often used in sex estimation because there can be pronounced differences in the sizes and shapes of male and female cranial

sexing the process of estimating the likely sex of an individual based on skeletal remains

sexual dimorphism the physical differences between adult males and adult females of a species

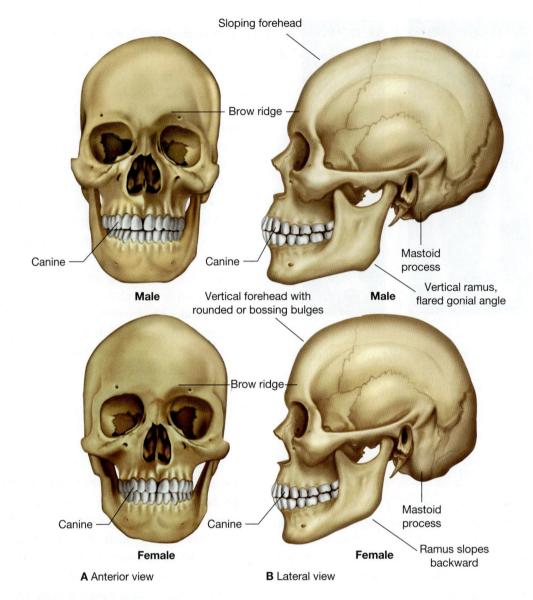

Sloping forehead

Brow ridge

Canine

Canine

Mastoid process

Male

Vertical forehead with rounded or bossing bulges

Male

Vertical ramus, flared gonial angle

Brow ridge

Canine

Canine

Mastoid process

Female

Female

Ramus slopes backward

A Anterior view

B Lateral view

FIGURE 7.6 Cranial Sexing
(A) Anterior and (B) lateral views of human skulls show cranial features used to estimate an individual's probable sex. Numerous cranial features vary in size between males and females, with males generally being more robust.

features (some of which are listed in the table on the next page) that can be examined quantitatively and qualitatively. In general, males often have larger skulls than females. Cranial features and areas of muscle attachment are more pronounced and robust in males than in females (**FIGURE 7.6**). For example, males have more pronounced or larger features such as *brow ridges* and larger areas of muscle attachment such as *mastoid processes*. Similarly, the occipital (back) region of the skull has a more pronounced and

rougher *nuchal area* (for the nuchal muscles) in males than in females. In addition, the *superior margin* of the eye orbit in males is usually rounded and blunt, but is sharper in females. The bony *forehead* of males tends to slope back. In females, the forehead tends to be more vertical and rounded with *bossing*, or slight bulges. Males also tend to have a broad, square-shaped *mandible* and chin, and females tend to have a rounder mandible and a more pointed chin. The vertical side of the mandible, or *ramus* (*rami*,

SAMPLE OF ANTHROPOSCOPIC TRAITS USED FOR ESTIMATING BIOLOGICAL SEX FROM THE CRANIUM

Cranial Trait	Males	Females
Overall size	Larger	Smaller
Skull robusticity	More pronounced	Less pronounced
Brow ridges	Larger and/or thicker	Smaller
Shape of forehead	Sloping	Vertical and rounded with "bossing" bulges
Occipital and nuchal area of skull	Rougher and more pronounced	Smoother and less pronounced
Mastoid process	Larger	Smaller
Superior margin of eye orbits	Rounded, blunt	Sharper
Shape of mandible/chin	Square	Rounded and pointed
Mandibular ramus	Ramus vertical, with flared gonial angle	Ramus sloping backward
Canine teeth	Larger, more pronounced	Smaller, less pronounced

plural), in males tends to be vertically oriented, with flared *gonial angles* on the lower posterior of the rami, while female mandibles have rami that tend to slope backward. Finally, males tend to have slightly larger and more pronounced *canine teeth*, while females have smaller and less pronounced canines.

Sex Estimation Based on Traits of the Pelvis

There are also differences between male and female skeletons related to functional differences between the sexes that can be assessed both quantitatively and qualitatively (some of which are listed in the table on the next page). The sexes have evolved to complement each other in sexual reproduction; therefore, their skeletons have functional differences related to their different roles in the reproductive process. Specifically, females can give birth, so the female bony pelvis must accommodate the passing of a fetus during childbirth. Males cannot give birth, and their pelvises cannot accommodate the passing of a fetus.

Looking more closely at the pelvis, we see a number of specific traits that vary between females and males due to this functional difference (**FIGURE 7.7**). For example, the female *pubic bone* is shorter *superoinferiorly* (from top to bottom) but rectangular or wider mediolaterally (from side to side), while the male pubic bone is longer superoinferiorly but triangular or narrower mediolaterally. The *subpubic angle* (the angle formed below the pubic symphysis) is wider in females and is sharper and narrower in males. The *greater sciatic notch* (a notch on the inferior side of the ilium) is narrower superoinferiorly and deeper anteroposteriorly (from front to back) in females, so that it resembles a boomerang in shape. In males, the greater sciatic notch is deeper superoinferiorly and narrower anteroposteriorly, so that it has a candy cane shape. In addition, the *pelvic opening* (the large hole in the center of the pelvis that is formed by the articulation of the two ossa coxae and the sacrum) is wider and heart-shaped in females and narrower in males. The larger female pelvic opening allows for the fetus to pass through

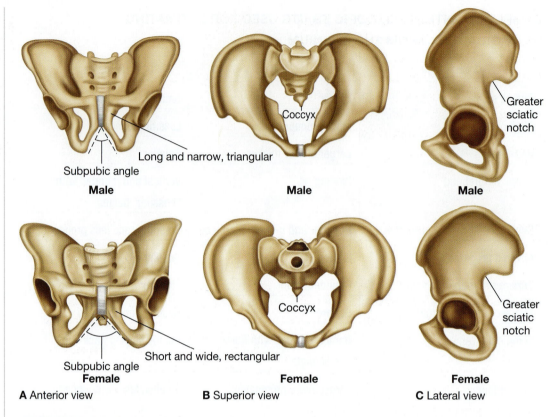

FIGURE 7.7 Pelvic Sexing
(A) Anterior, (B) superior, and (C) lateral views of human pelvises show pelvic features used to estimate an individual's probable sex. Several features differ between males and females. These differences primarily relate to the female's ability to give birth through the pelvic opening.

SAMPLE OF ANTHROPOSCOPIC TRAITS USED FOR ESTIMATING BIOLOGICAL SEX FROM THE PELVIS

Pelvic Trait	Males	Females
Overall size and robusticity	Larger and more pronounced	Smaller and less pronounced
Pelvic opening	Smaller and narrower	Larger and wider and heart-shaped
Coccyx position	Curves ventrally (anteriorly)	Curves dorsally (posteriorly)
Pubic bone	Longer superoinferiorly but triangular or narrower mediolaterally	Shorter superoinferiorly but rectangular or wider mediolaterally
Subpubic angle	Sharper and narrower	Wider
Greater sciatic notch	Candy cane shape (deeper superoinferiorly and narrow anteroposteriorly)	Boomerang shape (narrow superoinferiorly and deeper anteroposteriorly)

the pelvis during childbirth. Passage through the birth canal is also facilitated by the position of the *coccyx* (tailbone) in females. In males, this bone curves ventrally (anteriorly) and partially obstructs the pelvic opening. In females, the bone is positioned more dorsally (posteriorly), so that the female pelvic opening is less obstructed than in males.

Sex Estimation Using Osteometric Traits

Because size differences between males and females are often observed across elements of the human skeleton, we can also estimate biological sex using measurements of the skull and postcranial skeleton (the elements that compose the skeleton apart from the skull). For example, we may measure the breadth and length of the skull or the length of individual features, such as the mastoid process. Similarly, we can measure a limited number of postcranial elements that typically differ between males and females. For example, we can measure the diameter of the head of the humerus or femur (see the table below). Generally, femoral or humeral head diameters that are less than 42.5 mm indicate a probable female, while femoral or humeral head diameters above 47.5 mm indicate a probable male. However, there is an indeterminate range in between, and it is also important to note that these estimates have been made only for skeletons of white European ancestry. Other postcranial elements may be used for sex estimation as well. For example, a maximum scapula length of less than 14 cm usually indicates a female, while a length of 17 cm or more usually indicates a male; and if the length of the glenoid fossa of the scapula is above 36 mm, it usually indicates a male, while a length below this usually indicates a female (**FIGURE 7.8**). However, these mea-

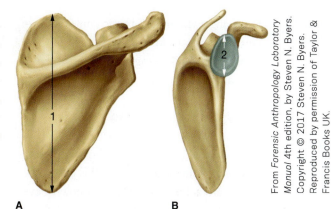

From *Forensic Anthropology Laboratory Manual* 4th edition, by Steven N. Byers. Copyright © 2017 Steven N. Byers. Reproduced by permission of Taylor & Francis Books UK.

FIGURE 7.8 Scapular Sexing
Measurement of the scapula can be used to estimate sex. (A) The maximum length of the scapula (line 1) is determined by measuring the maximum straight distance between the superior and inferior borders. (B) The maximum length of the glenoid fossa (line 2) is determined by measuring the maximum length or height at the superior and inferior margins. Both measures are made using calipers.

surements, again, vary with ancestry, and as with all qualitative and quantitative measures, there is variation in the degree of sexual dimorphism among different human populations.

ESTIMATING AGE AT DEATH

After separating out individuals and estimating their biological sex, both bioarchaeologists and forensic anthropologists typically move on to estimating the ages of those different individuals; this step is called **aging**. Here, we are talking about estimating the biological age of the individual at the time of death. Age information is particularly important to law enforcement officers because it is tracked through public records, such as driver's licenses, and can be helpful in

aging the process of estimating an individual's age at death based on skeletal remains

BIOLOGICAL SEX ESTIMATES FROM FEMORAL AND HUMERAL HEAD DIAMETER

Probable female (F+)	Possible female (F–)	Indeterminate sex (?)	Possible male (M–)	Probable male (M+)
Under 42.5 mm	42.5–43.5 mm	43.5–46.5 mm	46.5–47.5 mm	Over 47.5

Note: From Stewart 1979; estimates are for white European ancestral groups.

juvenile a physically immature individual whose body is still growing and developing

adult an individual that has reached physical maturity

ossification the process of bone mineralization and fusion that occurs as an individual develops into a physically mature adult

epiphyseal fusion the process of ossification where the ends of a long bone fuse to its shaft, the extent of which can be used to age a juvenile skeleton

epiphysis (**epiphyses**, plural) the area at the end of a long bone that forms separately from and fuses with the shaft of the bone during growth and development

diaphysis the central area (shaft) of a long bone that forms separately from and fuses with the ends of the bone (epiphyses) during growth and development

cranial suture closure the process of ossification where the cranial bones fuse together at the sutures, the extent of which can be used to age a skeleton

identifying a victim in forensic contexts. Aging takes two primary forms: age estimation based on developmental changes and age estimation based on metamorphic changes.

Age Estimation Based on Developmental Changes

The rates at which the human body grows and develop are known. We can use this information to compare a skeleton with the known developmental stages and determine the likely age of that individual. This method is suitable for aging **juveniles**—young individuals who are undergoing growth and development—because their bodies are still undergoing developmental changes. The skeleton of an **adult**—an individual who is no longer developing—cannot be aged using this method.

There are also known rates of bone **ossification**—the process of bone mineral solidification and fusion that occurs as a juvenile develops into an adult. Knowing the stages of ossification provides us with another useful aging method. For example, the long bones of the body undergo a particular ossification process known as **epiphyseal fusion**. In this process, the ends of the bone (**epiphyses**) fuse to the shaft of the bone (**diaphysis**) over time (**FIGURE 7.9**). If a long bone is recovered that has partially fused epiphyses, the extent of fusion can be used to determine age (**FIGURE 7.10**). The more complete the fusion is, the older the individual. The epiphyses of the various long bones of the body fuse at different ages, with the clavicle (collarbone) fusing last by the early twenties. Therefore, different long bones are suited for determining different ages.

Rates of ossification for the skull (or cranial) bones are also known. Recall from Lab 6 that the cranium is actually composed of many flat bones that fuse together as the body grows and develops. The extent of **cranial suture closure** at the areas where the bones come together and form sutures can be used to determine age. In general, if the bones are separate, the individual is very young (**FIGURE 7.11A**). If the bones are fusing but the suture lines are very distinct, the individual is older (**FIGURE 7.11B**). If the suture

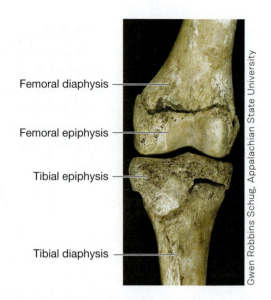

Femoral diaphysis

Femoral epiphysis

Tibial epiphysis

Tibial diaphysis

Gwen Robbins Schug, Appalachian State University

FIGURE 7.9 Epiphyseal Fusion
In the long bones of juveniles, like the femur and tibia seen here, the diaphysis (central shaft) is separate from the epiphyses (ends). These parts grow together and fuse as the child ages. If a biological anthropologist has long bones with unfused or partially fused ends, she knows she is examining a juvenile. In addition, the bones fuse at known rates, so the extent of fusion can help identify the ages of juveniles.

lines are less distinct or almost obliterated, the individual is even older (**FIGURE 7.11C**).

In addition to known rates of bone ossification, there are known rates of **dental eruption**—the process whereby the teeth grow into the mouth (**FIGURE 7.12**). The *deciduous teeth* (baby teeth) and *permanent teeth* (adult teeth) come in at different ages as the body develops (**FIGURE 7.13**). This is something we have all experienced. New parents talk about the time when their child is *teething*—when the deciduous teeth are breaking the bone and gum surface and growing in. Most of us are also familiar with the development of the permanent teeth. This process forces the deciduous teeth to fall out to make room for the permanent teeth. Many people remember when they lost their first tooth or have photos of themselves with missing teeth during their elementary school years. The different teeth erupt at different ages and in a particular order. In general, the middle (or central) incisors are first, and the remaining teeth appear mostly from the front to the back of the

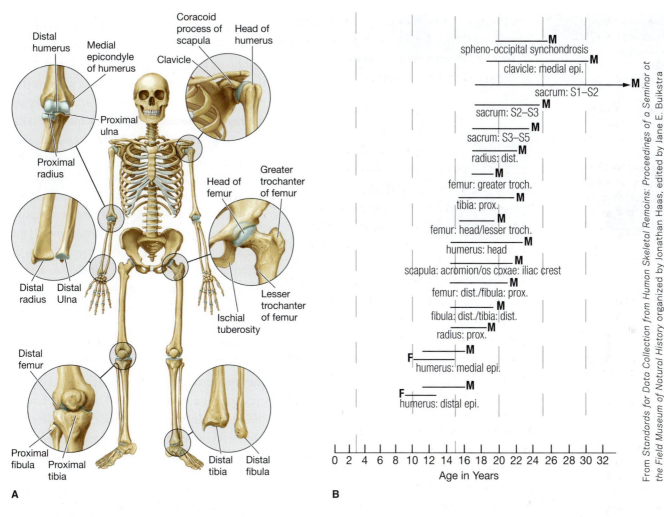

From *Standards for Data Collection from Human Skeletal Remains: Proceedings of a Seminar at the Field Museum of Natural History* organized by Jonathan Haas, edited by Jane E. Buikstra and Douglass H. Ubelaker (Arkansas Archaeological Survey, 1994), reprinted with permission of the Arkansas Archaeological Survey.

A

B

FIGURE 7.10 Ages of Epiphyseal Fusion in Different Skeletal Elements

(A) The positions of epiphyses in humans. (B) This graph shows the relative timing of fusion of epiphyses in various skeletal elements. The black bars show when fusion normally begins and ends. Data given are for males (M) and females (F) as indicated.

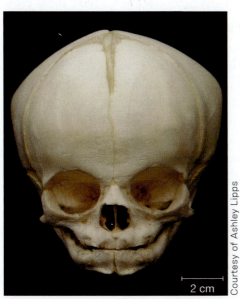

Courtesy of Ashley Lipps

A

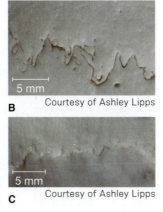

5 mm

Courtesy of Ashley Lipps

B

5 mm

Courtesy of Ashley Lipps

C

FIGURE 7.11 Cranial Suture Closure

Babies are born with separate cranial bones (A). These individual bones then fuse together over time (B) until they become completely joined (C). If a biological anthropologist recovers a cranium with bones that are not fully fused, their degree of fusion can be used to determine the age of the individual.

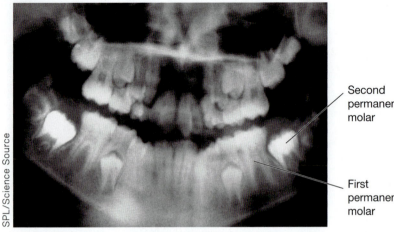

SPL/Science Source

FIGURE 7.12 Dental Eruption
Our permanent teeth form in early childhood and later erupt to replace the deciduous teeth that came before them. The formation and eruption of these teeth occur at known ages, so a biological anthropologist can use this information to age juvenile skeletons.

Second permanent molar

First permanent molar

mouth. The last teeth to come in are the last (or third) molars of our permanent dentition, which usually erupt during our late teens or early twenties. We call these molars the *wisdom teeth* because they come in at a much later age than the other teeth.

Age Estimation Based on Metamorphic or Degenerative Changes

Bone undergoes structural metamorphic changes as we age, and we can use the rates of these changes to make age estimations. These methods are suitable for aging adults, as their skeletons and joints begin to undergo degeneration over time. Juvenile skeletons, however, are too young to have accumulated these changes, so these methods are not suitable for aging them.

Most of these metamorphic changes are observed on bone joint surfaces that have little to no movement during life. For example, the degree of age-related metamorphic change can be quantified on the joint at the sternal end of a rib (where the rib and sternum join), and on the auricular joint surface of the ilium (where the ilium joins the sacrum). One of the primary areas for observing age-related metamorphic changes is the pubic bone. Changes occur specifically on the *pubic symphysis* (the joint where the two pubic bones meet anteriorly along the

midline) that can be observed on the symphyseal surface of the pubic bone. Many age estimation methods have been developed from the morphological changes of the pubic symphysis. One of the most recent and best aging methods is the **Suchey–Brooks method** **(FIGURE 7.14)**, named after the researchers that developed it. In general, as age increases, the prevalence of prominent and regular ridges on the symphyseal face decreases, the prevalence of rimming and bony nodules on the symphyseal face increases, and the symphyseal face becomes more concave. These changes occur at differing rates for males and females, so different ranges are used to estimate the age at death of male and female individuals, as shown in the table on p. 195.

Another method for aging adults is analysis of **dental wear** **(FIGURE 7.15)**. Over time, the chewing surfaces of our teeth are worn down by continual use **(FIGURE 7.16)**. Unlike the bones, the teeth do not undergo remodeling. They are a finite resource, and once they are formed, they cannot be naturally repaired or re-formed. This means we can use the extent of tooth wear as a general or relative age indicator: in general, the more wear on the tooth, the longer and more extensively it has been used. While it cannot tell us an exact age, dental wear can be used to tell us the relative age of an individual. It is important to note that some diets and activities can result in more tooth wear than others, so this aging method is not as precise as some of the other methods we've discussed. In general, recent human populations have a fairly refined diet that results in little tooth wear. As such, dental wear is not a precise enough aging method for use in forensic anthropology. However, in the case of historical or prehistoric populations, it is often possible to use estimated rates of dental wear for aging.

In general, it is important to remember that when determining the age of a skeleton, more precise estimates can be obtained for juveniles than for adults, particularly when the determination is based on developmental changes in the skeleton. This is because the stages of development are relatively precise and take place over

Suchey–Brooks method a method of aging adult skeletons that relies on changes to the symphyseal surface of the pubic bone

dental eruption the process whereby the deciduous teeth (and later the permanent teeth) grow into the mouth, the extent of which can be used to age juvenile skeletons

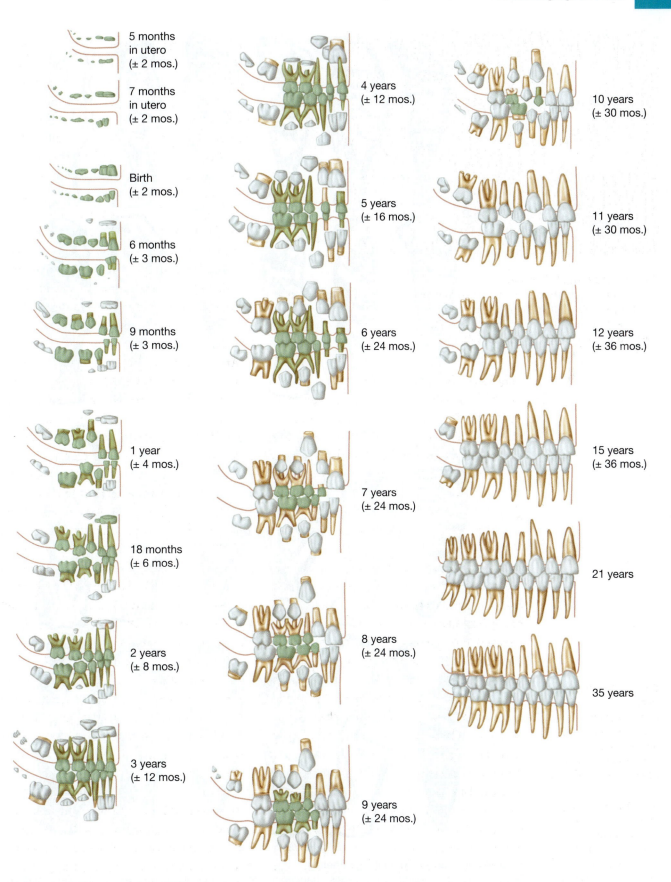

FIGURE 7.13 Dental Eruption Age Stages
The deciduous and permanent teeth form and erupt through the gums at specific ages. Thus, the extent of dental eruption can be used to help determine an individual's age at death using estimated known ages of eruption. (Adapted from Ubelaker 1989.)

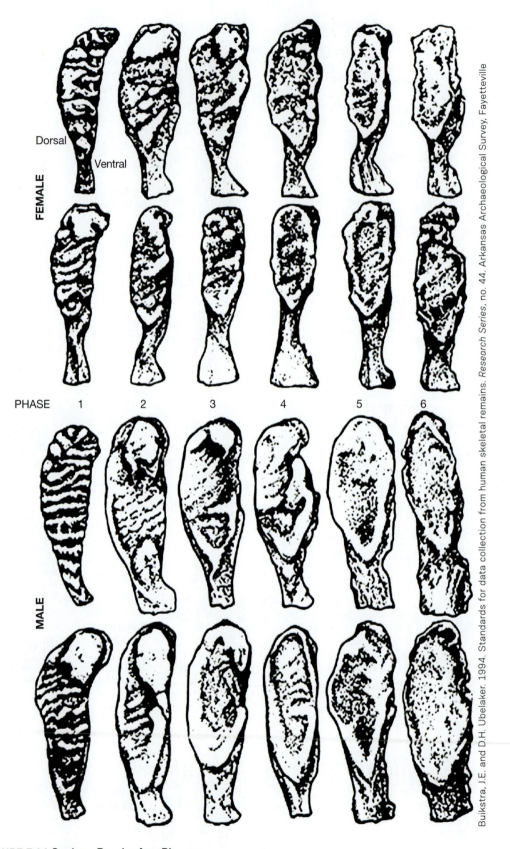

Buikstra, J.E. and D.H. Ubelaker. 1994. Standards for data collection from human skeletal remains. *Research Series*, no. 44. Arkansas Archaeological Survey, Fayetteville

FIGURE 7.14 Suchey–Brooks Age Phases

The pubic symphyseal face undergoes changes as we age. Thus, it can be used to help determine an individual's age at death. This figure shows six phases of age-related change, labeled 1–6. Note that the age phases differ slightly for females and males. For each sex, the top image shows morphology at the start of the given phase, while the bottom image shows morphology at the end of the given phase.

SUCHEY–BROOKS AGE PHASES

Phase	Mean Age at Death, Female (n = 273)	Standard Deviation, Female	95% Range, Female	Mean Age at Death, Male (n = 739)	Standard Deviation, Male	95% Range, Male	Description
1	19.4 years	2.6	15–24 years	18.5 years	2.1	15–23 years	Symphyseal face has a billowing surface composed of ridges and furrows which includes the pubic tubercle. The horizontal ridges are well marked. Ventral beveling may be commencing. Although ossific nodules may occur on the upper extremity, a key feature of this phase is the lack of delimitation for either extremity (upper or lower).
2	25.0 years	4.9	19–40 years	23.4 years	3.6	19–34 years	Symphyseal face may still show ridge development. Lower and upper extremities show early stages of delimitation, with or without ossific nodules. Ventral rampart may begin formation as extension from either or both extremities.
3	30.7 years	8.1	21–53 years	28.7 years	6.5	21–46 years	Symphyseal face shows lower extremity and ventral rampart in process of completion. Fusing ossific nodules may form upper extremity and extend along ventral border. Symphyseal face may either be smooth or retain distinct ridges. Dorsal plateau is complete. No lipping of symphyseal dorsal margin or bony ligamentous outgrowths.
4	38.2 years	10.9	26–70 years	35–2 years	9.4	23–57 years	Symphyseal face is generally fine-grained, although remnants of ridge and furrow system may remain. Oval outline usually complete at this stage, though a hiatus may occur in upper aspect of ventral circumference. Pubic tubercle is fully separated from the symphyseal face through definition of upper extremity. Symphyseal face may have a distinct rim. Ventrally, bony ligamentous outgrowths may occur in inferior portion of pubic bone adjacent to symphyseal face. Slight lipping may appear on dorsal border.
5	48.1 years	14.6	25–83 years	45.6 years	10.4	27–66 years	Slight depression of the face relative to a completed rim. Moderate lipping is usually found on the dorsal border with prominent ligamentous outgrowths on the ventral border. Little or no rim erosion, though breakdown possible on superior aspect of ventral border.
6	60.0 years	12.4	42–87 years	61.2 years	12.2	34–86 years	Symphyseal face shows ongoing depression as rim erodes. Ventral ligamentous attachments are marked. Pubic tubercle may appear as a separate bony knob. Face may be pitted or porous, giving an appearance of disfigurement as the ongoing process of erratic ossification proceeds. Crenellations may occur, with the shape of the face often irregular.

FIGURE 7.15 Dental Wear Age Stages
The surface of the tooth wears down with use, exposing the inner dentin layer (indicated here in pink). Generally, older individuals have used their teeth for more years, and thus have more dental wear, than younger individuals. Each column shows three stages of wear within each age category for M1 (first adult molar), M2 (second adult molar), and M3 (third adult molar).

Age Span		17–25			25–35			35–45			45+
Tooth		M1	M2	M3	M1	M2	M3	M1	M2	M3	
Wear Pattern	or / or			No dentin exposed							More advanced wear

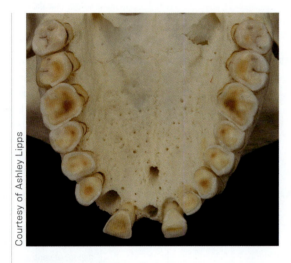

FIGURE 7.16 Dental Wear
These teeth are very worn down and belonged to an older individual.

Courtesy of Ashley Lipps

dental wear the wearing down of tooth surfaces with continued use, the extent of which can be used to age adult skeletons

stature an individual's overall body height

osteometric board an instrument used to measure bones

a short period. The stages of wear on the body, however, take place over a longer time and can vary within and among individuals and populations depending on external factors, such as diet and activity patterns.

ESTIMATING STATURE

A person's **stature** (body height) is based in large part on the size of the bones. A person with longer bones will be taller overall, and a person with shorter bones will be shorter overall. For this reason, we can use bone measurements to help us determine a person's stature during life.

This information, like estimated age, is useful in forensic cases because height is often tracked in public records, such as driver's licenses.

A number of researchers have developed formulas to estimate stature from bone measurements in both bioarchaeological and forensic contexts. Although some formulas are based on measurement of various bones from the whole skeleton, most researchers use measurements of long bones. Long bones (particularly those of the arms and legs) are used to estimate stature because their length strongly correlates with overall stature. The forensic anthropologist measures the bone's maximum length using an instrument called an **osteometric board** (FIGURE 7.17), but a tape measure can be used if necessary. This measurement is entered into a formula that is dependent on the individual's sex and ancestry. The result is a stature estimate

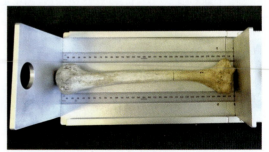

Image courtesy of Sabrina C. Agarwal

FIGURE 7.17 Osteometric Board
An osteometric board may be used to measure the maximum length of a long bone for stature estimation.

EQUATIONS USED TO ESTIMATE STATURE FROM THE LONG BONES OF VARIOUS GROUPS OF INDIVIDUALS BETWEEN 18 AND 30 YEARS OF AGE

Males of European Descent					Males of African Descent				
3.08	×	Hum	+	70.45	± 4.05	3.26	×	Hum	+	62.10	± 4.43
3.78	×	Rad	+	79.01	± 4.32	3.42	×	Rad	+	81.56	± 4.30
3.70	×	Uln	+	74.05	± 4.32	3.26	×	Uln	+	79.29	± 4.42
2.38	×	Fem	+	61.41	± 3.27	2.11	×	Fem	+	70.35	± 3.94
2.68	×	Fib	+	71.78	± 3.29	2.19	×	Fib	+	85.65	± 4.08
Females of European Descent						**Females of African Descent**					
3.36	×	Hum	+	57.97	± 4.45	3.08	×	Hum	+	64.67	± 4.25
4.74	×	Rad	+	54.93	± 4.24	2.75	×	Rad	+	94.51	± 5.05
4.27	×	Uln	+	57.76	± 4.30	3.31	×	Uln	+	75.38	± 4.83
2.47	×	Fem	+	54.10	± 3.72	2.28	×	Fem	+	59.76	± 3.41
2.93	×	Fib	+	59.61	± 3.57	2.49	×	Fib	+	70.90	± 3.80
Males of East Asian Descent						**Males of Mexican Descent**					
2.68	×	Hum	+	83.19	± 4.25	2.92	×	Hum	+	73.94	± 4.24
3.54	×	Rad	+	82.0	± 4.60	3.55	×	Rad	+	80.71	± 4.04
3.48	×	Uln	+	77.45	± 4.66	3.56	×	Uln	+	74.56	± 4.05
2.15	×	Fem	+	72.57	± 3.80	2.44	×	Fem	+	58.67	± 2.99
2.40	×	Fib	+	80.56	± 3.24	2.50	×	Fib	+	75.44	± 3.52

From Trotter 1970.

Note: All bone lengths are maximum lengths (Hum = humerus, Rad = radius, Uln = ulna, Fem = femur, Fib = fibula length, all in centimeters). The tibia is not included because of historical inconsistencies in the measurement of and formula for this bone. To estimate the stature of older individuals, subtract $0.06 \times$ (age in years − 30) cm. To estimate cadaveric stature, add 2.5 cm.

with a range, or standard error (SE), that gives an idea of how much error is possible in the measurement. This means that the real stature is probably very close to the resulting number, but not necessarily the same number. The measurements used in these formulas are taken using the metric system and reported in centimeters (cm). To get a value in English units (U.S. customary units), you divide stature estimates in centimeters by 2.54 to get inches. You can then divide the inches value by 12 to get a stature estimate in feet.

The formulas used for stature estimates are different for each long bone because the rela-tionship between each bone's length and over-all stature varies. In addition, all formulas vary between males and females because body pro-portions and overall stature vary slightly with sex. The formulas also vary for people of dif-ferent ancestry. Again, as discussed in greater detail in Lab 8, body sizes and proportions vary slightly among populations from different regions and climates, so this variation must be accounted for by different formulas. The table above shows stature formulas for the major long bones by sex and ancestry.

There are some issues with stature estimation that must be kept in mind. First, many of the

pathology disease, or the changes that disease causes in the body

antemortem pathology pathology that developed at any time prior to an individual's death

perimortem pathology pathology and trauma that developed around the time of an individual's death and may have contributed to that death

manner of death the circumstances surrounding death that may have contributed to death, such as traumatic injuries

cause of death a medical determination of the physiological reason for an individual's death

dental enamel hypoplasia a gap or horizontal line on a tooth that has less enamel than surrounding areas

dental caries areas of the teeth that have undergone demineralization and decay due to acid exposure; also called cavities

formulas for stature estimation were developed using museum collections of skeletons from people that died in the 1900s (such as the Terry Collection at the Smithsonian). There have been gradual changes in body size and height among populations in the last century, and it is unclear if those skeletal measurements are accurate for use in more recent forensic cases. Second, the formulas for the tibia are probably not as precise as the formulas for other bones. The original tibial formulas were developed without including the distal medial malleolus in the tibial measurement. Excluding this area of the bone during measurement can change the accuracy of the measurement.

IDENTIFYING PATHOLOGY

Bioarchaeologists and forensic anthropologists are also interested in any indicator on an individual's skeleton that is not related to normal variation but rather to **pathology** (disease) or metabolic stress. Further, they must distinguish between antemortem pathology and perimortem pathology. **Antemortem pathology** is pathology that developed at any point prior to an individual's death. **Perimortem pathology** is pathology or trauma that developed around the time of an individual's death and may have contributed to that death. This distinction is a particularly important one for the forensic anthropologist to make, as she may be asked to comment on the manner of a victim's death in a legal proceeding. The **manner of death** includes circumstances surrounding death that may have contributed to death, such as traumatic injuries. However, the forensic anthropologist does *not* determine official cause of death. The **cause of death** is a medical determination made by a medical examiner or coroner, often in conjunction with information from the forensic anthropologist. For example, the forensic anthropologist may recognize that the victim's hyoid bone has been broken, indicating likely strangulation. Yet, the official cause of death given by the coroner would be asphyxiation. To properly identify possible factors contributing to the victim's death,

the forensic anthropologist must be able to distinguish pathology that occurred earlier in life and did not contribute to death.

Antemortem Pathology

While antemortem pathology does not necessarily inform us about the manner of death, it can give us valuable information about how an individual lived and what their overall health was like during life. For the bioarchaeologist, antemortem pathology tells about the health of one person, and antemortem pathology indicators in many individuals in a population can help him build a picture of overall stresses on the population and its lifestyle in the past. Stress indicators are routinely used in the analysis of skeletal remains from bioarchaeological contexts. For the forensic anthropologist, looking at antemortem pathology can aid in the identification of a victim.

In general, there are several categories of antemortem pathology. The first includes pathology related to overall health and metabolic stress. Often, when the body is under nutritional stress due to lack of food or severe illness, it compensates by slowing down bone growth and focusing metabolic energy elsewhere. When the nutritional stress is over, the bone then begins growing regularly again. A classic example of this process is seen in the teeth. If an individual has a period of nutritional stress while the teeth are growing during childhood, enamel will stop forming on the tooth crowns for a time. When the period of stress has passed, the enamel-forming process will resume where it ordinarily should be, not where it left off. The result is a gap or horizontal line with reduced enamel, called a **dental enamel hypoplasia (FIGURE 7.18)**. Because we have specific knowledge of when the teeth and enamel are formed, we can use the locations of dental enamel hypoplasias to obtain an accurate estimate of the age at which the nutritional or illness-related stress occurred.

Another nutrition-related pathology is the presence of dental caries. **Dental caries**, also called cavities, are areas of the teeth that have undergone demineralization and decay due to

Image courtesy of Sabrina Agarwal

FIGURE 7.18 Dental Enamel Hypoplasia
These horizontal ridges on the teeth indicate that the individual suffered stress (nutritional or health problems) while the tooth was being formed in early childhood. This antemortem pathology reflects health problems in early life.

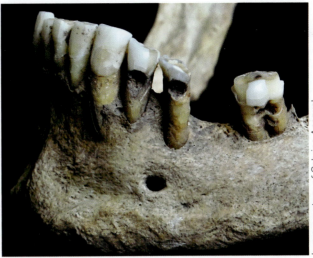

Image courtesy of Sabrina Agarwal

FIGURE 7.19 Dental Caries
These areas of tooth decay (also known as cavities) are related to acid levels in the mouth. This antemortem pathology can develop at any time prior to death.

acid exposure **(FIGURE 7.19)**. The acid is formed naturally by oral bacteria as the mouth begins to break down food to start digestion. However, if the acids are produced in high quantities (due to what is eaten) or not properly cleaned away through proper dental hygiene, caries can form. The prevalence of dental caries is much higher in populations with an agricultural lifestyle than it is in populations with a foraging lifestyle. This is because an agricultural lifestyle is often based on a diet high in carbohydrates, which results in more acid in the mouth.

In addition to pathology associated with nutrition, there is pathology associated more specifically with disease. For example, **iron-deficiency anemia** is a condition caused by a severe lack of iron in the body. This lack of iron is often due to disease or parasites in the body (and is also potentially related to dietary stress). The primary indicator of this condition is a type of bone destruction called **porotic hyperostosis (FIGURE 7.20)**, which is usually seen on the cranial bones. Porotic hyperostosis results from an expansion of the bone marrow cavity, which causes the smooth cortical bone of the cranium to look porous and spongy.

In addition to nutritional and disease-related pathology, there are also pathologies associated with chronic conditions. For example, **osteoarthritis**, a condition where accumulated wear and tear on the joints results in the loss of their

Bone Clones/boneclones.com

FIGURE 7.20 Porotic Hyperostosis on the Cranial Vault
Most commonly found in the cranium, this type of bone destruction results in a spongy bone surface. It indicates iron-deficiency anemia, a type of antemortem pathology.

cartilage linings, is common among humans. This loss of cartilage causes changes (both bone formation and bone loss) in the underlying bone **(FIGURE 7.21)**. Without healthy cartilage as a cushion between the bones, bone surfaces at a joint end up contacting each other directly. This contact can result in **eburnation**, in which an area of bone becomes polished and shiny

iron-deficiency anemia a condition caused by a severe lack of iron in the body

porotic hyperostosis a form of bone destruction that usually presents in the cranial bones as porous and spongy bone surfaces

osteoarthritis a condition where trauma or accumulated wear and tear on the joints results in loss of their cartilage lining

eburnation the polishing of a bone surface caused by repeated direct contact between bones at a joint

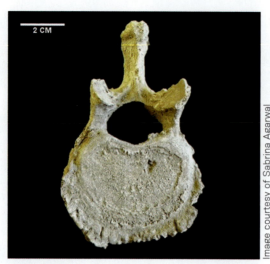

FIGURE 7.21 Osteoarthritis
In this form of antemortem pathology, accumulated wear and tear on the joints causes changes in the bone. Note the osteophytes, extra spicules of bone, around the edges of these vertebrae.

osteophyte a spicule of bone that often forms around the margin of a joint surface when the cartilage at the joint is worn down

knife wound an injury caused by a sharp, bladelike instrument, which often leaves telltale nicks or cut marks on bone

cut mark an indentation left on bone by a sharp instrument, such as a knife or stone tool

blunt force trauma injury caused by contact with a blunt object, such as a club, which often creates depressions in the bone that are surrounded by small fractures

gunshot wound injury caused by bullets shot from various small arms (guns), which may create holes or nicks in bone, depending on where the bullet enters and exits the body; also called projectile trauma

due to repeated direct contact between bones at the joint. The bone may also respond to dwindling cartilage by forming extra spicules of bone, called **osteophytes**, around the margin of the joint surface. Osteoarthritis is common in highly mobile joints such as those in the hip, knee, and lower back.

Perimortem Pathology

As with antemortem pathology, there are different types of perimortem pathology. The examination of perimortem pathology in skeletal remains is particularly important in the forensic context. Most perimortem pathology is obviously distinguishable from antemortem pathology because it involves severe, traumatic injuries. For example, **knife wounds** are often indicated by large cuts or nicks in a bone. When a hard blade makes contact with bone tissue, it leaves behind small **cut marks** (indentations). For instance, if an individual has been stabbed repeatedly in the chest, this is likely to leave a series of cut marks on the ribs. The size (length and depth) and shape of the cut marks can indicate the size and type of blade used, and the orientation of the cut marks can indicate the angle of the thrusts.

Another traumatic injury that can be seen in bones is **blunt force trauma**. This type of trauma results from coming in contact with a blunt object, and it can occur through falling or through being hit with an object, such as a baseball bat. Blunt force trauma is indicated by the presence of a depression in bone at the point of impact (**FIGURE 7.22**). There can also be small bone cracks or fractures that radiate out from the depressed area due to the force of impact.

Gunshot wounds (or projectile trauma) can be very obvious in the skeleton. For example, if an individual has been shot, there may be clear points of bullet entry and exit, indicated by holes in the bone. The entry hole is smaller and has more discrete edges than the exit hole, which is larger and has an inward-sloping, beveled edge (when viewed from the outer surface of the bone). The size of the entry wound can be used to determine the maximum possible bullet size, and the orientation of the entry and exit wounds can be used to indicate the trajectory of the shot. Sometimes, however, gunshot

FIGURE 7.22 Blunt Force Trauma
This form of perimortem pathology is indicated by a depression in bone near the point of impact, such as the depression and radiating fracture lines seen on the posterior right parietal here. These bones, from the Monqachayoq sector at Huari in Ayacucho, Peru, are dated ca. AD 1275–1400.

wounds are less obvious. If, for example, a victim was shot in the chest, there is unlikely to be a clear entry or exit hole because the rib cage is not a solid mass through which the bullet must pass. The bullet may have slipped between two ribs and skimmed a bone only along the edge, leaving a nick or mark in the bone similar to a cut mark. This nick would have to be examined closely to distinguish it from a knife-related injury.

Some traumas leave very distinct damage to particular bones. For example, choking, or **strangulation**, requires that a lot of force be applied to the throat. The small, fragile hyoid bone in the neck is likely to acquire damage as a result of this force. Therefore, an unhealed fracture of the hyoid bone is usually indicative of choking or strangulation.

Often, we experience traumatic injuries that do not contribute to death. These injuries must be distinguished from other injuries to understand the manner of death. For example, a person may have suffered a fracture of the arm 2 years before dying. This trauma needs to be distinguished from any injuries that may have actually contributed to death. The distinction can be made by whether the bone has healed through remodeling **(FIGURE 7.23)**. If the injury was treated well initially, the bone may have remodeled very cleanly, leaving little evidence of the fracture. If, however, the injury was not treated well, the bone may have healed incorrectly. The two sides of the bone may not line up together (they may be offset), or there may be extra bone formation in the area of the fracture. Either way, if the bone shows signs of remodeling, it indicates that the damage occurred long enough before death that the body could begin the healing process.

ADDITIONAL STEPS OFTEN EMPLOYED IN FORENSIC CONTEXTS

Determining Likely Ancestry

Often, forensic anthropologists are asked to determine a victim's likely ancestry because this information can aid in the attempt to identify

FIGURE 7.23 Fracture
When bones experience traumatic injuries, such as fractures, the body will attempt to repair the damage through bone remodeling. If the bone does not remodel cleanly, it may leave behind extra bone, or offset areas of bone, near the injury site. This tibia shows a midshaft oblique fracture that has healed offset.

Bone Clones/boneclones.com

an unknown victim. Bioarchaeologists may also be interested in determining ancestry in archaeological populations when studying past migrations or population movements, familial relationships, and other population trends. As we will see in Lab 8, on modern human variation, people from different parts of the world have different biological morphologies, which are the combined result of population genetics and human adaptation. Group differences in morphology can also be seen in skeletons. These skeletal differences are superficial, and they have developed very recently in the deep time of human evolution. Nevertheless, they can often be used to roughly identify a person's regional ancestry.

There are two types of traits that can be used as morphological indicators of ancestry: metric traits and nonmetric traits. **Metric traits** are osteometric quantitative traits that are measurable on the skeleton, such as the length or breadth of certain bones. Typically, dozens of measurements of different skeletal areas are taken, and these measurements are incorporated into complex statistical analyses to determine the most likely ancestral group. The use of metric traits is based on the principle that people in different regions have different sizes, proportions, or degrees of robusticity (again, see Lab 8).

Nonmetric traits are anthroposcopic qualitative traits that are not measurable. Instead, they are traits that an individual either has or does not have. They are scored as either present or absent. Different ancestral groups are

strangulation the forcible choking of another individual, which often results in damage to the hyoid bone

metric trait a measurable osteometric trait of the skeleton

nonmetric trait an anthroposcopic qualitative trait of the skeleton that cannot be measured, but instead is either present or absent

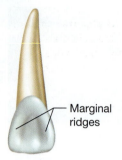

Marginal ridges

FIGURE 7.24 Shovel-Shaped Incisors
Some traits, like shovel-shaped incisors, are more common in some human populations than in others. Shovel-shaped incisors have a distinct shovel shape on their back (tongue side) and are more common in some Asian and Native American populations.

likely to have different combinations (or suites) of these traits. For example, the shovel-shaped incisor trait is a nonmetric trait **(FIGURE 7.24)**. The term refers to a unique incisor shape, in which the lingual (tongue side) surface of the tooth has distinct indentations that make it look like the spade of a shovel. This tooth shape is most commonly found in people with Asian or Native American ancestry. Another nonmetric trait is the malar tubercle, which is a bony projection extending from the inferior edge of the zygomatic bone **(FIGURE 7.25)**. This tubercle is pronounced in people of Asian ancestry, but it is usually absent in people of European and African ancestry. In addition to these traits, anthropologists may also look for nonmetric variations in the shapes of skeletal features. For example, the nasal root (superior nasal margin) is low and rounded in African populations, high and peaked in European populations, and low and peaked in Asian populations (see Figure 7.25). Anthropologists can study suites of traits like these to try to determine a person's possible ancestry.

It is important to emphasize that there is individual and within-population variation in both metric and nonmetric traits. This means that within an ancestral group, not everyone will have the exact same measurements or all the same nonmetric features. Further, traits that may indicate biological ancestry do not inform us about the cultural or ethnic affiliation of a person during life. Finally, we are dealing with ranges, and the ranges of different populations overlap. For this reason, some anthropologists prefer to emphasize nonmetric traits when possible because they result in less ambiguous identifications.

Although the determination of ancestry from skeletal remains is far from straightforward, forensic anthropologists can use skeletal measurements and traits to help them build a profile of an otherwise unknown victim in a legal investigation. Additionally, anthropologists are always looking at suites of multiple traits. The anthropologist does not make an ancestry determination based on only one trait. She tries to use a combination of metric and nonmetric traits

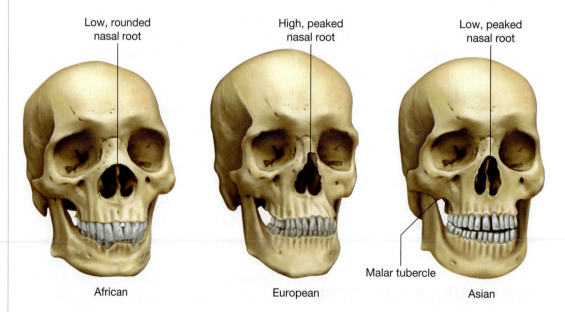

Low, rounded nasal root

High, peaked nasal root

Low, peaked nasal root

Malar tubercle

African   European   Asian

FIGURE 7.25 Metric and Nonmetric Traits
The malar tubercle is a nonmetric trait used in ancestry determination. This trait is more common in Asian populations than in European and African populations. Another nonmetric trait is nasal root shape. In African populations, the nasal root is low and rounded. In European populations, the nasal root is high and peaked. In Asian populations, the nasal root is low and peaked. These skulls also have clear differences in size and morphology, and some of these differences can be quantified as metric differences that relate to biological ancestry.

from throughout the body to improve the accuracy of the determination.

Calculating the Postmortem Interval

The forensic anthropologist is also usually asked to estimate the **postmortem interval** for a victim. This term refers to the time that has elapsed since death. Generally, as more time elapses, it becomes more difficult to estimate the time since death. During the early stages of decomposition, there are regular phases of insect activity, so if insects are present on the body, they can be used to determine postmortem interval. Similarly, soft tissue decays fairly quickly and at known rates, so the degree of soft tissue decay can be used to estimate the time since death as well. However, if enough time has passed that there is no longer soft tissue or insect activity on the body, determining the postmortem interval becomes much more challenging. Bones decay too gradually to be used alone for calculating elapsed time intervals.

Calculating the postmortem interval is further complicated by variations in environmental and depositional conditions. If the body has been in an area that is conducive to rapid decay, such as an open and humid environment with a lot of insect activity, it may appear that more time has elapsed because the body will show advanced decomposition. If the body is in a setting that is less conducive to decay, such as under cover in a dry environment, it may appear that less time has elapsed because the body will show less decomposition. The forensic anthropologist will attempt to take these factors into account and provide a rough estimate (range of time) for when the victim died.

postmortem interval
the time that has elapsed since an individual died

CONCEPT REVIEW QUESTIONS

Name: _____   Section: _____

Course: _____   Date: _____

Answer the following questions in the space provided.

1. Define bioarchaeology.

2. Define forensic anthropology.

3. What is the first step in analyzing skeletal remains in both bioarchaeological and forensic contexts?
   A. Determine the minimum number of individuals.
   B. Estimate the sex of each individual.
   C. Calculate the postmortem interval.
   D. Distinguish between human and animal bone.

4. After skeletal remains have been identified as human, what step usually comes next in bioarchaeological and forensic investigations?
   A. Identify pathology in each individual.
   B. Estimate the age at death for each individual.
   C. Determine the minimum number of individuals.
   D. Estimate the sex of each individual.

5. Name one bone that is useful in estimating sex.

6. Describe a method for aging a juvenile skeleton. Be sure to note which bone or bones are necessary for this method.

7. Describe a method for aging an adult skeleton. Be sure to note which bone or bones are necessary for this method.

8. What bone or bones are best suited for stature estimates? Why?

9. Describe the difference between manner of death and cause of death.

10. Compared with antemortem pathology, perimortem pathology:
    A. occurs closer to the time of death.
    B. is less likely to have contributed to death.
    C. is less useful in determining manner of death.
    D. is more likely to have healed before death.

LAB EXERCISES

Name: _____   Section: _____

Course: _____   Date: _____

EXERCISE 1   ANIMAL OR HUMAN?

Work in a small group or alone to complete this exercise. Refer to the skeletal material provided by your instructor (or the photos in the Lab 7 Exercise Image Library on p. 217) and answer the following questions.

PART A

1. Which of the skeletal elements is human?

2. Describe *one* trait that helped you make this distinction:

PART B

1. Which of the skulls is human?

2. Describe *two* traits that helped you make this distinction:

EXERCISE 2   MINIMUM NUMBER OF INDIVIDUALS

Work in a small group or alone to complete this exercise. Refer to the skeletal material provided by your instructor (or the mystery assemblage in the Lab 7 Exercise Image Library on p. 218) to answer the following questions.

1. List the bones depicted. (Be as specific as possible, including the side of the body that the bone is from, if applicable.)

2. What is the minimum number of individuals in this assemblage?

EXERCISE 3 AGING

Work in a small group or alone to complete this exercise. Review the skeletal material provided by your instructor (or the images in the text and in the Lab 7 Exercise Image Library) to answer the following questions.

1. Examine the X-ray of a juvenile upper and lower jaw in Figure 7.12 (on p. 192) and compare it with the dental eruption age stages in Figure 7.13 (on p. 193). What is the approximate age of this individual?

2. Examine the skeletal material (or the image in the Lab 7 Exercise Image Library on p. 218), which is from a female and shows the symphyseal face of the pubis. Compare it with the Suchey–Brooks age phases provided in Figure 7.14 (on p. 194). What is the approximate age of this individual?

EXERCISE 4 SEXING

Work in a small group or alone to complete this exercise. Review the traits used for estimating biological sex from the cranium and the pelvis in the tables on p. 187 and p. 188. Use the skeletal material provided by your instructor (or the images in the Lab 7 Exercise Image Library on pp. 219–220) to complete the following exercise.

PART A

Estimate the sex of the three crania using the chart below. For each cranial feature on the list, score it as either M, F, or ? (if you are unsure or the feature is not visible). Compare the crania with one another, other crania you have in the classroom, or the crania depicted in Figure 7.6 (on p. 186). Once you have completed the chart, tally the total number of Ms and Fs for each cranium and determine the estimated sex.

Cranial Feature	Cranium A	Cranium B	Cranium C
Overall size			
Skull robusticity			
Brow ridges			
Shape of forehead			
Occipital and nuchal area of skull			
Mastoid process			
Superior margin of eye orbits			
Shape of mandible/chin			
Mandibular ramus			
Canine teeth			
Total Ms			
Total Fs			
Total ?s			
Final sex estimate			

PART B

Estimate the sex of the three pelvises using the chart below. For each pelvic feature on the list, score it as either M, F, or ? (if you are unsure or the feature is not visible). Compare the three pelvises with one another, other pelvises you have in the classroom, or the pelvises in Figure 7.7 (on p. 188). Once you have completed the chart, tally the total number of Ms and Fs for each pelvis and determine the estimated sex.

Pelvic Trait	Pelvis A	Pelvis B
Overall size and robusticity		
Pelvic opening		
Coccyx position		
Pubic bone		
Subpubic angle		
Greater sciatic notch		
Total Ms		
Total Fs		
Total ?s		
Final sex estimate		

PART C

Use the skeletal material (or measurements) provided by your instructor to complete the following exercise.

1. Measure the maximum humeral head diameter (assume the bone is of white European ancestry). Record your measurements in the chart below and use the table on p. 189 to determine an estimated sex (M, M+, ?, F−, F+).

	Humerus A	Humerus B	Humerus C
Maximum Humeral Head Diameter			
Any Other Indicators of Sex Based on Size and Robusticity (Pronounced Muscle Markings)?			
Estimate of Sex (M, M+, ?, F−, F+)			

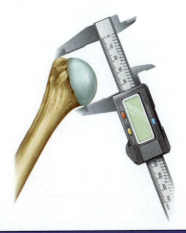

2. Measure the maximum femoral head diameter (assume the bone is of white European ancestry). Record your measurements in the chart below and use the table on p. 189 to determine an estimated sex (M−, M+, ?, F−, F+).

	Femur A	Femur B	Femur C
Maximum Femoral Head Diameter			
Any Other Indicators of Sex Based on Size and Robusticity (Pronounced Muscle Markings)?			
Estimate of Sex (M, M+, ?, F−, F+).			

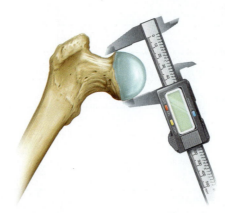

3. Measure the scapula length and length of the glenoid fossa (following the guidelines provided in Figure 7.8 on p. 189). Record your measurements in the chart below and use the numeric markers described in the text to determine an estimated sex (M−, M+, ?, F−, F+).

	Scapula A	Scapula B	Scapula C
Length of Scapula			
Length of Glenoid Fossa			
Estimate of Sex (M, M+, ?, F−, F+).			

EXERCISE 5 ANCESTRY

Work in a small group or alone to complete this exercise. Refer to the skeletal material provided by your instructor (or the images in the Lab 7 Exercise Image Library on p. 221) to answer the following questions.

1. Which individual has shovel-shaped incisors?

2. Which individual has a malar tubercle?

3. What might these two traits indicate about these individuals' ancestry?

4. Are these two traits alone enough to make an ancestry determination? Why or why not?

EXERCISE 6 STATURE

Work in a small group or alone to complete this exercise. Review the skeletal material provided by your instructor (or the description below) and complete the following exercise.

A forensic anthropologist has determined that a female victim has a maximum femur length of 49.5 cm. The anthropologist has also determined that the victim is of African ancestry. Use the table on p. 197 to estimate this individual's stature. (Be sure to give the estimation in feet and inches, using the conversion information provided in the text.)

EXERCISE 7 PATHOLOGY

Work in a small group or alone to complete this exercise. Review the skeletal material provided by your instructor (or the images in the Lab 7 Exercise Image Library on p. 222) and answer the following questions.

PART A

1. What bone is this?

2. What pathology is indicated on this bone?

3. Describe *one* trait you used to make this pathology identification.

4. Is this pathology antemortem or perimortem?

PART B

1. What bone is this?

2. What pathology is indicated on this bone?

3. Describe *one* trait you used to make this pathology identification.

4. Is this pathology antemortem or perimortem?

EXERCISE 8 FRAGMENTARY REMAINS

Work in a small group or alone to complete this exercise. Refer to the skeletal material provided by your instructor (or the images in the Lab 7 Exercise Image Library on p. 223). These partial remains have been found in a shallow grave in a wooded lot. Use this information to answer the following questions.

1. What bones are present?

2. What is the MNI?

3. What is the age of the individual(s), and how did you determine this?

EXERCISE 9 TYING IT ALL TOGETHER

Work in a small group or alone to complete this exercise. A collection of skeletal remains has just been unearthed at a crime scene. You have been asked to help law enforcement officials in their investigation of this skeletal material. Refer to the skeletal material provided by your instructor (or the mystery assemblage in the Lab 7 Exercise Image Library on p. 224) to answer the following questions.

1. Is any of this skeletal material nonhuman? If so, which bone(s) is/are nonhuman? Why do you think this?

2. List all of the human skeletal elements, being as specific as possible. What is the minimum number of individuals (MNI) represented?

3. Does any of the skeletal material appear to be juvenile? If so, which bone(s)? Why do you think this?

4. Can any of the skeletal material be used to determine the biological sex of the victim(s)? If so, which bone(s)? What is the sex you determined? What evidence supports that conclusion?

5. Bone I in the assemblage has been measured with an osteometric board. It has a maximum length of 35.7 cm. You have determined the individual is of European ancestry. Based on this information and what you know about this person's sex, what is the estimated stature of this individual? (Be sure to give the estimation in feet and inches.)

6. Based on the materials recovered, can you make any suggestions for additional analyses you might use to further understand the circumstances surrounding the death of the victim(s)?

CRITICAL THINKING QUESTIONS

On a separate sheet of paper, answer the following questions.

1. You have been asked to examine a bioarchaeological assemblage. You have identified the bones and made the following list of the material:

   - 1 left femur with unfused epiphyses
   - 1 right femur with fused epiphyses
   - 2 adult sacrums
   - 1 cranium with extensive tooth wear
   - 1 mandible with some teeth erupted and others unerupted

   What is the minimum number of individuals for this assemblage?

2. Why are age estimates for adults less accurate than age estimates for juveniles?

3. In Exercise 6, you determined the stature of an individual based on femoral measurements. Imagine that you also recovered this individual's right humerus. The maximum length of the humerus is 35.1 cm. What is the individual's estimated stature based on the humeral data? (Again, use the table on p. 189 and be sure to convert your estimate into feet and inches.) Is this result consistent with the estimation you made using the femur measurement? Why or why not?

4. What is the difference between antemortem pathology and perimortem pathology? Why must a forensic anthropologist be able to distinguish between the two types of pathology?

5. How are forensic anthropology and bioarchaeology similar? How are they different?

6. A combination of economic disparity, political instability, and shifting immigration policy in recent years has resulted in a humanitarian crisis along the border between the United States and Mexico. A striking number of undocumented migrants who attempt to cross illicitly from Mexico into the United States die during their journey. Scholars and nonprofit agencies estimate that approximately 2,200–2,649 deaths occurred between the years 2000 and 2015 along the Arizona border alone, and the estimated death count during the past 14 years along the entire U.S. border with Mexico is more than 6,000 individuals.[1] Forensic anthropologists have played an instrumental role in examining the remains of individuals found along this border. Using information found in your classroom, online, or in books, answer the following questions: What specific analyses do forensic anthropologists conduct when they are looking at the human remains of border migrants? What are the forensic anthropologists hoping to find out? What impact does this work have on the broader community on both sides of the border?

7. Imagine that you are working with a team of bioarchaeologists that has just excavated a medieval cemetery site in Italy. The cemetery has over 200 graves, with all sexes and ages represented in the skeletal sample. You are interested in knowing whether there were gender differences in health among members of the medieval community. How would you answer this question using the skeletal remains? What analyses would you need to conduct with the skeletons, and what health indicators might you look for in the bones?

[1] Fleischman et al. 2017.

8. Two forensic anthropologists, named Julia and Marco, have identified the skeletal remains shown in the photos below as belonging to the same individual. Both anthropologists have examined the pelvis and cranium for indicators of the victim's biological sex. Julia argues the individual was male, but Marco argues that the individual was female. Why might the anthropologists disagree? Which anthropologist do you think is correct? Provide evidence from the skeletal material to support your conclusion.

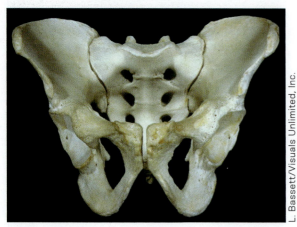
L. Bassett/Visuals Unlimited, Inc.

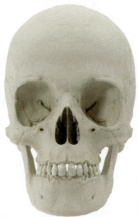
Andrey Simonenko/Alamy Stock Photo

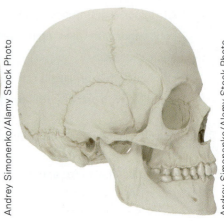
Andrey Simonenko/Alamy Stock Photo

9. As part of a forensic analysis, you have been asked to determine an individual's ancestry using skeletal indicators. The metric measurements you collect indicate that the individual is of European ancestry, but you see several nonmetric traits in the cranium that are typically found in individuals of Asian ancestry. Why might the two methods give different results? Be sure to consider the differences between metric and nonmetric traits as well as other factors that might contribute to individual skeletal variation.

LAB 7 EXERCISE IMAGE LIBRARY

Students should use these images only if directed to by their instructor.

EXERCISE 1 ANIMAL OR HUMAN?

PART A

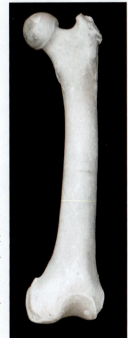

Courtesy of Ashley Lipps

Courtesy of Ashley Lipps

A

B

PART B

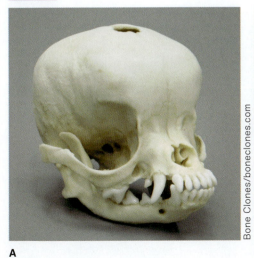
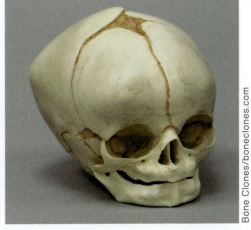

Bone Clones/boneclones.com

Bone Clones/boneclones.com

A

B

EXERCISE 2 MINIMUM NUMBER OF INDIVIDUALS

Courtesy of Ashley Lipps

EXERCISE 3 AGING

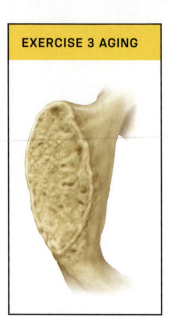

EXERCISE 4 SEXING

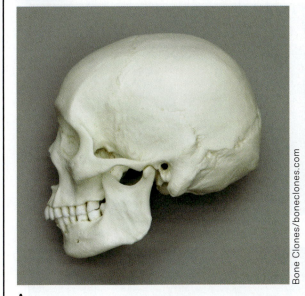

A

B

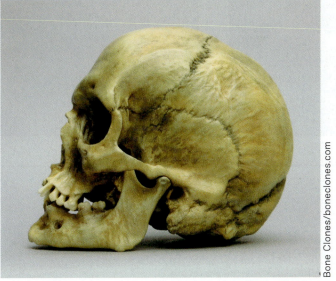

C

EXERCISE 4 SEXING (CONTINUED)

Courtesy of Ashley Lipps

Courtesy of Ashley Lipps

A

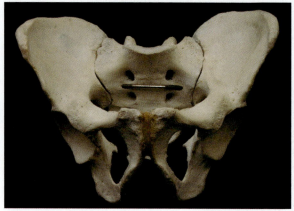

Courtesy of Ashley Lipps

Courtesy of Ashley Lipps

B

EXERCISE 5 ANCESTRY

Individual A

Courtesy of Ashley Lipps

Individual B

Ira Block/National Geographic Creative

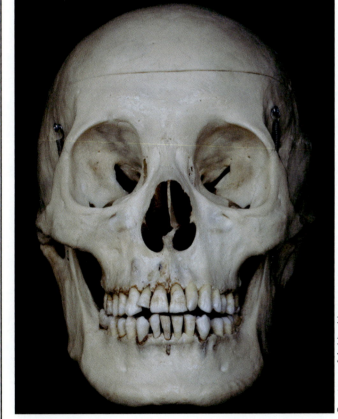

Individual A

Courtesy of Ashley Lipps

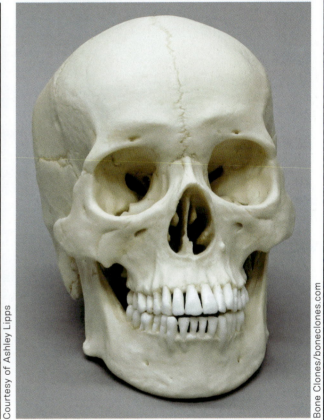

Individual B

Bone Clones/boneclones.com

EXERCISE 7 PATHOLOGY

PART A

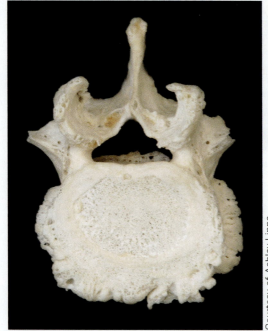

Courtesy of Ashley Lipps

PART B

Courtesy of Tiffiny Tung

EXERCISE 8 FRAGMENTARY REMAINS

EXERCISE 9 TYING IT ALL TOGETHER

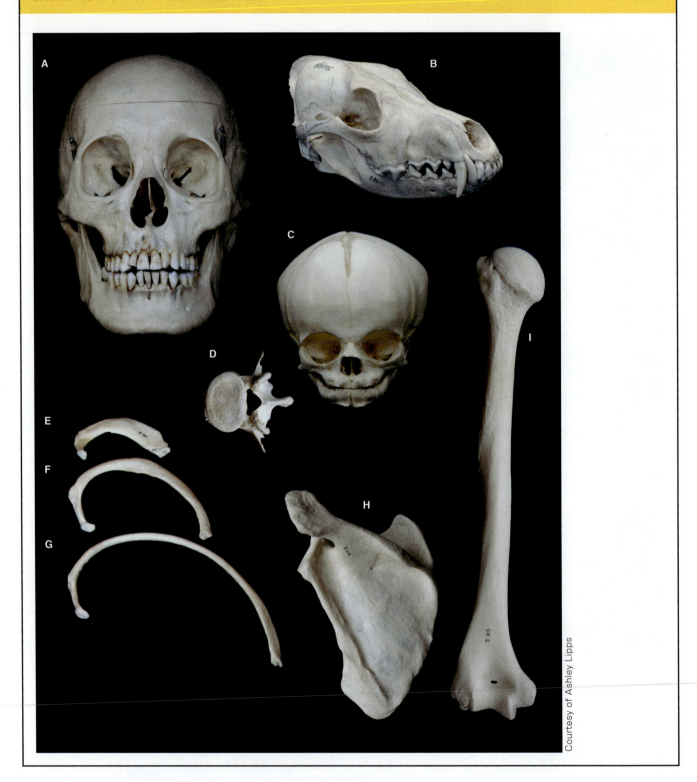

BIOLOGICAL ANTHROPOLOGY IN PRACTICE

Using Ancient DNA to Tell the Story of a People

Dr. John Lindo is a biological anthropologist who specializes in ancient DNA research to understand human population histories and evolution (see Lab 8). John's interest in ancient DNA started back in 1993, when he saw the movie *Jurassic Park*. He was captivated by the idea of "going back in time" with genetics to witness the grandeur of long-extinct animals. After the Neanderthal genome was published, he decided to pursue his true passion in science and attended graduate school to study biological anthropology. New molecular methods and computational power had created a new frontier in ancient DNA studies by opening up the possibility of working with entire ancient genomes, instead of small fragments that provided limited information. Researchers like John now had access to hundreds of thousands of years of evolution, which allowed them to study complex population movements and to detect natural selection.

Today, John's research focuses on identifying molecular traits related to changes in human population density, adaptation to high altitude, and the consequences of interactions between indigenous people and Europeans (such as disease, warfare, and social alterations). In one of his early research projects, John worked with indigenous tribes from the Americas to better understand the genetic impacts of European colonization, especially in relation to diseases. In grade school, John had been taught that European-borne diseases, such as smallpox, had largely devastated Native American and First Nations populations. However, John felt that there was more to this story. To investigate further, he collaborated with the Tsimshian tribe of British Columbia, who allowed him to sample DNA both from modern living tribal members and from bone samples from ancient individuals (see Lab 7). With this information, John studied the population before and after their interactions with Europeans. He sequenced genomes and looked for evidence of natural selection. With these data, John found that the true story, at least for the Tsimshian, was not one of susceptibility, but of resilience. John found that the ancient Tsimshian had adapted to pathogens that were present in their environment before the arrival of Europeans. When Europeans brought smallpox to the area in the 1800s, those who survived may have been aided by earlier selection for a gene variant that provided a form of protection from the virus. Importantly, John partners with the communities he studies and gives them a say in how his work is conducted. Before publishing his recent work, John sought the approval of Tsimshian leaders, and he shared authorship with tribal representatives to ensure that his publications respected the tribe's culture and history.

John continues to work with Native American tribes in community-engaged research, as well as with people living in the United States with "Hispanic" or Latin American ancestry. He hopes that evolutionary studies can help reinforce both groups' cultural links to their ancestors and reveal their unique population histories via specific adaptations to their environments and ways of life. In Lab 8, it's your turn to explore human variation and genetic adaptations to a variety of different environments.

Dr. John Lindo has worked to cultivate research projects that are of interest and benefit to indigenous communities, such as the Tsimshian in British Columbia.

People are not all the same. We have different skin colors, body types, heights, and so on.

LAB 8

Modern Human Variation

When we look around at a crowd of people, we notice that people look different from one another. Some people are taller, and others are shorter. Some people have darker hair and skin color, and others have lighter hair and skin color. Some people are lean, and others are stocky. Are these differences significant? Can we group people by their similarities and differences? If we *can*, are these groupings universal, or do the groups vary depending on what traits we emphasize? If we *cannot* group people by their similarities and differences, does that mean these physical traits are biologically meaningless? Or do physical similarities and differences tell us something about the people who carry them? Can we reconstruct the evolutionary history of a group using this kind of information? This lab examines these issues of modern human variation.

INTRODUCTION

We begin this lab with a consideration of race. In this consideration, we specifically explore whether there is a biological basis for race in humans. We then turn to an exploration of other key dimensions of human variation, including skin color, altitude adaptations, climate adaptations, ABO blood alleles, and lactose tolerance. For each of these dimensions of variation, we focus on the adaptive significance of the variation and what it

Lab Learning Objectives

By the end of this lab, students should be able to:

- describe the difference between the variation found *within* human populations and the variation *between* human populations, and explain how this difference relates to issues of race.

- explain the adaptive significance of variation in skin color, altitude adaptations, and climate adaptations.

- use variations, such as differences in ABO blood group allele frequencies, to discuss the effect of evolutionary forces on our species.

- discuss the role of cultural practices in shaping human variations, such as adult lactose tolerance and sickle-cell trait frequencies.

David Grossman/Alamy Stock Photo

227

tells us about human population histories. We conclude with a closer examination of the sickle-cell trait as an example of the complexity of human variations.

RACE

Since early naturalists began classifying organisms centuries ago, various scientists have attempted to subdivide the human species into distinct racial categories. Historically, biological anthropologists contributed to this work, especially through the use of various skeletal traits for racial affiliation. Much of this research was conducted by Europeans, who created hierarchical schemes of human variation that suggested they (Europeans) were superior to other groups of people (non-Europeans). Often, physical traits were linked with personality traits in racial classifications, such that different racial groups were linked with different levels of intelligence, propensities toward violence, and degrees of "savagery." Governments and other ruling bodies often used these racial categories and the behavioral traits associated with them to justify the subjugation or systematic extermination of certain groups. For example, many colonial powers used the classification research of anthropologists to justify their unfair treatment of colonized indigenous populations. The historical roots of racial categorization and racism formed the basis for our misunderstanding of human biological variation. Today, anthropologists are trying to both better understand human variation and prevent the misuse of their research. With this in mind, we must recognize the history of the discipline and the complications surrounding racial categorization while simultaneously examining the nuances of human variation and its significance.

Dividing people into distinct racial categories begins with the false assumption that people from different groups are biologically distinct. For example, in many racial classifications, people from Europe are differentiated from people from Africa. It is assumed that there are numerous biological distinctions between these two populations. Traditionally, racial classification was based on obvious physical characteristics, such as skin color, stature, and eye color. These traits were readily observable and seemed to vary between populations. In more recent years, we have been able to analyze underlying genetic data, and these genetic data have presented us with a very different picture of human variation that directly challenges the notion of a genetic basis for race. Comparisons of genetic information show that most of human variation is actually found *within* populations, rather than between populations. For example, in many traditional racial classifications, all people from Africa are treated as one population that is distinct from populations from other continents. However, newly studied genetic data show us that the greatest variation is actually within this broad African population (**FIGURE 8.1**).

This greater degree of within-population genetic variation makes sense in terms of the evolutionary history of our species. First, it is important to note that humans are a very recent species. As we will see in later labs, our species became distinct from other species no more than 200,000 years ago. While this may seem like a long time, it is very little time in terms of evolution. Human populations have not had enough time to accumulate a lot of biological changes, which makes them very genetically similar. Second, humans have a tendency toward mobility and interbreeding. People are not as deterred by mountain ranges and bodies of water as other primates. People move between environments and territories regularly, and they often mate with people they find in other areas. This means human populations have not been subject to as much reproductive isolation as many other primate species. Humans have been undergoing gene flow regularly throughout their evolutionary history, which has made them more genetically similar to one another.

Our species today certainly has some genetic differences between populations; however, most of our genetic differences are minor variations within populations. We have a great deal of underlying genetic similarity, even across great geographic distances. This suggests that any differences we see between populations are relatively superficial. They have evolved recently,

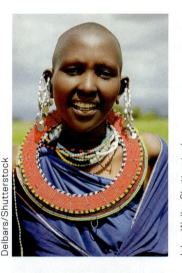 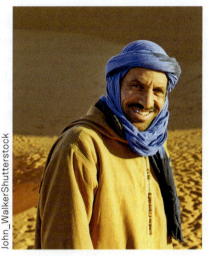 

FIGURE 8.1 Human Variation within Groups
Humans show a lot of variation not only among groups, but also within groups, such as the wide phenotypic variation among African people seen here.

sometimes only within the last few thousand years, and often reflect recent adaptations to particular environmental or cultural circumstances. Beneath it all, all humans are very similar biologically, and we cannot readily divide humans into distinct racial groups. There is no biological basis for these large-scale classifications. However, our superficial variations can be used to better understand the nuances of our ancestry. We can apply our knowledge of evolutionary processes to understand patterns of variation that reflect population movement (the **founder effect**), interbreeding (**gene flow**), and adaptation (**natural selection**).

Despite this understanding of the role of complex evolutionary forces in crafting human genetic variation, the biological differences we see in our species continue to be misinterpreted. Some of this misinterpretation has been perpetuated by modern biomedical research and ancestry testing kits available to the general public. While these increasingly popular ancestry tests offer to help people find out about their racial history and the geographic origins of their ancestors, the marketing of the kits only reinforces misconceptions. The tests have several limitations about which consumers are not clearly informed. For example, these tests sample only a small amount of the test taker's DNA (about 1%), and in order to identify genetic ancestry, companies use their own limited comparative data sets of genetic markers that fail to capture the full range of genetic diversity in a particular geographic region or population.

Genetic tests for the risk of disease outcomes and the use of biomedical testing to study racial disparities in health also reinforce the idea that there are genetic differences between human races. While it is true that there are differences among populations in the frequency of conditions such as cardiovascular disease, diabetes, or certain cancers, there is clear evidence that social inequality, racism, and environmental conditions over the life course, rather than underlying biological differences, shape these health discrepancies between communities. Humans are biologically flexible organisms, and as such, they are influenced by the environments in which they develop from birth, through childhood, and into adulthood—and these biocultural experiences are also key to understanding the variation we see in human groups today. Through an understanding of the role of adaptation in our species as a whole, and of the importance of life experiences in shaping our individual and group biology, we can move beyond a rigid structure of racial categorization to a more fluid understanding of evolutionary history and ancestry.

Finally, it is crucial to note that while genetics suggests that there is no biological basis for distinct racial categories, this does not mean racial

founder effect a type of genetic drift that occurs when a subset of a larger population founds the next generation due to substantial population loss or population movement

gene flow the exchange of genes between previously isolated populations that begin to interbreed

natural selection the theory outlined by Charles Darwin to explain evolution: it argues that some traits are more suited to an organism's particular environmental context and are therefore passed on preferentially to the next generation, and these traits become more common in successive generations, resulting in evolutionary shifts in populations

clinal distribution
a distribution of trait variations that has a continuous gradation across a geographic area

categories lack cultural significance. Many people self-identify with a particular racial group or groups. Race often helps in the forging of group identities and provides a sense of solidarity among people. At the same time, race is still central to discrimination and disenfranchisement around the world. People continue to be mistreated due to their perceived or self-ascribed racial identity. As we have seen, distinct racial categories misrepresent the complexity of human variation, and genetic evidence suggests that human populations are often more similar than different. Nevertheless, race does exist as a cultural phenomenon and is fundamental to many aspects of human cultural life.

In the context of this exploration of biological anthropology, we take a nuanced (and biologically based) view of human variation. As such, we trace the variation of a few key traits. We pay particular attention to what these variations may tell us about the evolutionary history of the populations who carry them.

When we are discussing human variations seen in people today, we are actually reconstructing ancestral histories and adaptations. There has been significant population movement via colonization and globalization in recent centuries, and it is difficult at present to track the effects of these recent trends. Instead, we focus on the variants people carry from their ancestral population. For example, when thinking about the ancestral variations of people in the United States, we might be considering the variations of indigenous Native Americans, descendants of enslaved Africans, or a wide range of recent immigrant populations from around the world. We must be clear about which *ancestral* group we are studying. Throughout this lab, we will generally be dealing with data and information about indigenous populations. Therefore, when we are talking about variations in American populations, we are discussing Native American populations. When we are discussing variations in African populations, we are discussing indigenous African populations. We are not including recent immigrants and descendants of colonizers in these populations unless explicitly stated as such.

SKIN COLOR

Skin color has been widely used as a trait for distinguishing human races throughout history. However, the use of this trait to categorize races is very problematic. First, it misrepresents the nature of skin color variation. Using skin color to differentiate distinct races assumes that skin color variation can be neatly divided into distinct groups of colors. In reality, skin color has a **clinal distribution**, which means that there is continuous and progressive gradation of the trait over a geographic region. In the case of skin color, we see that long-term residents of the tropics have the most pigmentation in their skin, while long-term residents of Arctic regions have the least pigmentation (**FIGURE 8.2**). However, the transition of pigmentation from the tropics to northern parts of the globe is very gradual—if you were to walk across the continents from the equator northward, you would not see sudden changes in skin color from one group to the next.

The second problem with the use of skin color to differentiate races is that it ignores the adaptive significance of skin color variation. Darker skin color is more common closer to the equator, and lighter skin color is more common farther from the equator. When we are exposed to the sun, we are also exposed to the sun's ultraviolet (UV) rays. These rays can have harmful consequences for our bodies, including cell death (such as that experienced in a sunburn) and skin cancer. Darker skin color provides greater protection from damaging ultraviolet radiation (UVR). But the evolution of human skin pigmentation is more complex. It is related not only to levels of UVR, but also to two unrelated nutrients, vitamin D and folate, that are both key to human biology. Vitamin D is unique in humans because it is the only vitamin that we produce in our skin following exposure to UVR. Vitamin D is important in almost every body system, and its primary function is to influence calcium absorption and storage in our bones, intestines, and kidneys as part of our bodies' system for regulating calcium levels. Folate is important for cell division, growth and

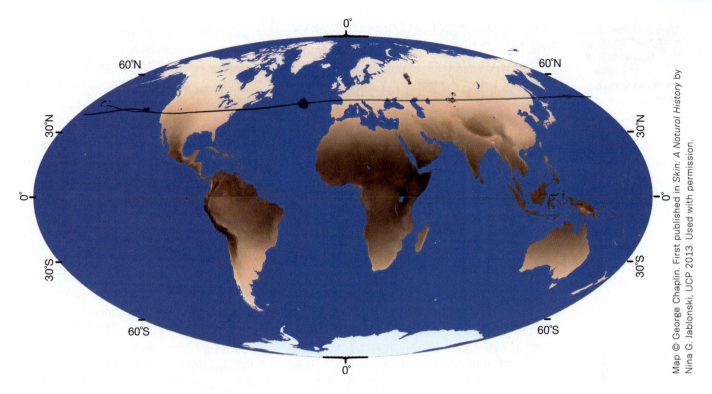

Map © George Chaplin. First published in *Skin: A Natural History* by Nina G. Jablonski, UCP 2013. Used with permission.

FIGURE 8.2 Regional Skin Color Variation

This map shows predicted human skin color variation, which has been confirmed by measurements of skin reflectance across indigenous populations. Note that human skin color varies geographically. Darker skin colors are more common near the equator, and lighter skin colors are more common away from the equator. Remember, although the map seems to show distinct color categories, each of the color gradients on the map accounts for a range of skin color variants that have been grouped together to simplify the map.

development, and reproductive functions such as sperm production. Folate and vitamin D have different sensitivities to UVR; while vitamin D is synthesized (produced) in our skin in response to UVR exposure, folate is degraded (lost) in skin exposed to UVR.

The close relationship between these two nutrients, UVR, and the degree of skin pigmentation is the basis for one of the main theories explaining the evolution of human skin color: the **vitamin D–folate hypothesis**. Because UVR depletes the folate stored in our bodies, we require more protection from the sun's destructive UV rays in regions where sun exposure is high throughout the course of the year, such as near the equator. Over countless generations, populations from these areas have adapted by producing more protective **melanin** in their skin. Melanin is a pigment that helps give skin its brownish color. In general, the more melanin that is present in the skin, the darker the skin color. The increased melanin—and corresponding darker skin color—seen in populations near the equator acts as a natural shield, blocking some of the sun's UV rays from penetrating deeply into the body.

This protective function of melanin explains why dark skin color evolved in human populations who lived near the equator for many generations. But how does this theory explain the light skin color found in populations who lived for many generations in nonequatorial regions? While exposure to the sun increases harmful UVR exposure, it is also necessary begin the process of vitamin D synthesis is vital to our health. As such, in area as sun exposure is limited throughout from it is in temperate and Arctic reg?d to be the equator, human populatio᭄r limited able to maximize the benef?ᵒper levels sun exposure and maint˒have lived in of vitamin D. Populati᭄

vitamin D–fol᭄ hypothesis᭄ ᭄ry of the p᭄ns for the expla᭄ of human ev᭄olor, arguing ᭄ darker skin ᭄otects from folate loss in regions of high sun exposure and lighter skin fosters vitamin D production in regions of low sun exposure

melanin a pigment that helps to give skin its brownish color

hypoxia a condition where one cannot take in enough oxygen to meet the body's needs

acclimatization a short-term, temporary adjustment the body makes to better suit its current environmental context

vasodilation the expansion of the blood vessels near the surface of the body to help heat escape the body

vasoconstriction the constriction (narrowing) of the blood vessels near the surface of the body to help maintain heat in the body's core

these areas for generations have skin with less melanin and a lighter color so as to take in as much UV energy as possible when it is available, as well as the ability to tan for protection when UVR exposure is unusually high. These changes resulted in lighter skin color variants in nonequatorial populations.

The evolution of human skin color was a balancing act. Each population needed to adapt by acquiring the appropriate skin color variant to suit its ancestral region. Our earliest ancestors in Africa would have been covered in body hair that protected them from the sun. As human populations in this equatorial region lost their body hair, they needed to have enough melanin to protect themselves from the harmful effects of UVR while still allowing for vitamin D synthesis. When human populations left Africa and settled in latitudes with less sun exposure, dark skin color was not necessary for protection, and it was more important to possess light skin color to allow vitamin D synthesis. Interestingly, the evolution of lighter skin color appears to have occurred independently in various regions. For example, lighter skin color evolved in Europeans and East Asians separately at different times, and its evolution was probably also affected by population migration and genetic bottlenecks. This complex evolutionary history contributes to the clinal distribution we see in skin color today. Equatorial and Arctic populations have extreme differences in skin color because of the extreme differences between their environments. Other populations distributed between these regions have adapted by evolving the skin color that is best suited to their particular, intermediate environment.

TITUDE

Hun...
enviro... all over the world, often in extreme
is found One such extreme environment
level you li... titudes. The farther above sea
body. You are re stress is placed on your
more intense so to colder temperatures,
often more difficu... on, more wind, and
addition, oxygen

concentrations in the air continuously decrease the farther above sea level you go. Low oxygen concentrations can lead to **hypoxia**, a condition where you cannot take in enough oxygen to meet the metabolic needs of your body. In its mildest form, it can result in dizziness, headaches, and nausea. However, prolonged or intense hypoxia at high altitudes has the potential to cause much more serious stress and damage to the heart, lungs, and brain.

In general, there are two primary ways that humans respond to physiological stress. The first type of response is called **acclimatization**. This term refers to short-term, temporary adjustments our bodies make to suit the current environmental context better. A suntan, for example, is an acclimatization that builds a layer of protection from UVR exposure. Another example is the **vasodilation** we may experience in hot temperatures. This term refers to the expansion of the blood vessels near the surface of the body to help heat escape the body's core. Alternatively, in cold temperatures, we may experience **vasoconstriction**. This happens when the blood vessels near the surface of the body constrict to help maintain heat in the body's core. All of these acclimatizations are short-term, helping people adjust to their temporary environmental circumstances and then reverting back to their normal state.

People visiting high altitudes will undergo certain acclimatizations that help them function better in these extreme environments. For example, you might experience increased respiration in a high-altitude environment, taking in extra air through deeper and more frequent breaths to get the oxygen you require. Your lung capacity might increase, so you can take in more air with each breath. You might make extra red blood cells to facilitate the transportation of oxygen through the body. Each of these responses is temporary. They will set in relatively quickly to help you avoid hypoxia, but they are reversible.

This process of acclimatization to high altitude can also help athletes train for major events. Often, athletes who live at low altitudes will train at high altitudes for a few weeks or months before an event. By doing this, the athletes expose their bodies to the extreme altitude and trigger the acclimatization process. When the athletes return to a lower altitude for their events, they will maintain the acclimatizations for a short time before their bodies revert to their prior states. The athletes will now have more efficient respiration and oxygen distribution during their events thanks to their acclimatization to their training environments. Similarly, if an athletic event is taking place at high altitudes, athletes will train at high altitudes before the event to gain the acclimatizations they need to avoid hypoxia during the event.

In addition to temporary acclimatizations, humans also have **adaptations**. These responses are permanent, and they are the result of natural selection acting on traits over many generations. Adaptations are often more extreme than acclimatizations. For example, populations that have lived at high altitude for many generations often have special adaptations to help them in this stressful environment **(FIGURE 8.3)**. Like altitude acclimatizations, these adaptations help them to maximize their use of the limited supply of oxygen and avoid hypoxia. However, unlike altitude acclimatizations, these traits appear to be inherited and permanent. Classic examples are found in indigenous populations from two mountain ranges, the Himalayas and the Andes. Tibetans have adaptations of the circulatory system that support higher blood flow and oxygen movement than in low-altitude populations. Andeans have adaptations that allow them to take in more oxygen when breathing, and they have a higher proportion of red cells in their blood to facilitate oxygen movement through their bodies. It is believed that these two populations evolved different adaptations to their similar high-altitude environments because of differences in their genetic makeup and because of the different lengths of time they have inhabited their respective regions. The Himalayas were settled around 25,000 years ago, and the Andes were settled more recently (around 11,000 years ago). This means the Himalayan populations have had a longer time to adapt to their high-altitude environment and may have developed different traits as a result. In addition, the found-

Courtesy of Cynthia Beall

FIGURE 8.3 Life at High Altitudes
People who live at high altitudes, like this farmer in Tibet, have adaptations to maximize their oxygen intake. These adaptations include traits such as larger hearts and lungs, which result in a broad chest.

ing populations in these two regions were different and probably carried different genetic variants to the respective locations. The variants present in the founders of each population would have limited the possible trajectories of natural selection and adaptation in that population.

CLIMATE

In addition to adaptations to UVR exposure and altitude, humans have adaptations to different climates. Populations with a long history of living in hot climates have different body proportions than populations with a long history of living in cold climates. The principles associated with these adaptations were outlined by two different researchers. Carl Bergmann outlined a relationship between overall body size and climate. This relationship is called Bergmann's rule. Joel Allen identified a relationship between limb proportions and temperature, called Allen's rule.

Bergmann's rule recognizes that as volume increases, surface area also increases, but at a slower rate. Imagine a cube that measures 1 unit in all directions **(FIGURE 8.4)**. This cube has a volume of 1 cubic unit and a surface area of

adaptation a trait that has been favored by natural selection and helps a population be better suited to its environmental context

Bergmann's rule the principle that, because volume increases more rapidly than surface area, a large, thick body is well adapted for cold climates because it has relatively less surface through which body heat can be lost

Allen's rule the principle that, because equiaxed shapes have less surface area than elongated shapes, long limbs are well adapted for hot climates because they have relatively more surface to help vent excess body heat

antigen (in ABO blood group system) the cell surface marker found on red blood cells that relates to an individual's ABO blood type and triggers antibody reactions to a foreign blood antigen

lactose a sugar found in milk

lactase an enzyme required in order to properly digest the lactose in milk

6 square units. When we increase the size of the cube to measure 2 units in all directions, we find that this larger cube has a volume of 8 cubic units and a surface area of 24 square units (see Figure 8.4). This means the volume has increased by eight times, while the surface area has increased by only four times. Bergmann's rule applies this scaling principle to body size. It argues that larger, thicker bodies are better adapted for cold climates because they have more volume relative to surface area. Having less surface area translates to less heat loss, so a larger body with less surface area helps conserve body heat in cold temperatures.

Allen's rule recognizes that an equiaxed shape (one with approximately equal dimensions in all directions, like a cube) has less surface area than an elongated shape of the same volume (like a rectangular prism). Imagine an equiaxed cube that measures 2 units in all directions (**FIGURE 8.5**). It has a volume of 8 cubic units and a surface area of 24 square units. Now, imagine an elongated shape that measures $4 \times 1 \times 2$ units (see Figure 8.5). It also has a volume of 8 cubic units, but its surface area is 28 square units. Both shapes have the same volume, but the elongated shape has a larger surface area. Allen's rule applies this principle to limb proportions. It suggests

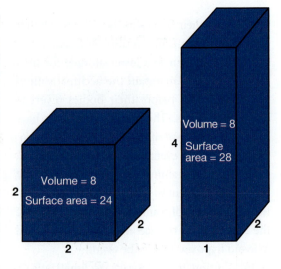

FIGURE 8.5 Allen's Rule
An equiaxed shape (*left*) has less surface area than an elongated shape (*right*). In this example, both shapes have the same volume, but the elongated shape has more surface area. According to Allen's rule, elongated limbs are well adapted to hot climates. This shape allows for more surface area, and more surface area means more venting of body heat.

that elongated limbs are well adapted for hot climates because they have a greater surface area. This increased amount of surface area allows for greater venting of body heat in hot temperatures.

THE ABO BLOOD GROUP

In Lab 3, we introduced the ABO blood group system and discussed the different blood **antigen** alleles that determine ABO blood type. The A allele results in the A antigen, and the B allele gives the B antigen. The O allele produces neither antigen. One allele is inherited from each parent, giving offspring one of six possible genotypes, referred to as *AA, AO, BB, BO, AB,* and *OO*. Each of these genotypes corresponds to a different phenotype.

Interestingly, when we track the distribution of these alleles across indigenous populations worldwide, we find noteworthy patterns. First, the A allele is most common in Europe, parts of Australia, and some far northern areas of North America (**FIGURE 8.6A**). The B allele is most

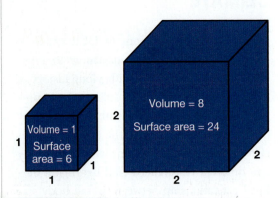

FIGURE 8.4 Bergmann's Rule
As volume increases, surface area increases at a slower rate. In this example, we increase the volume of the cube to be eight times larger (from 1 to 8 cubic units). However, the surface area has increased by only four times (from 6 to 24 square units). According to Bergmann's rule, a stocky build is a good adaptation for a cold climate. This body type allows for more body mass relative to surface area, and less surface area means less body heat loss.

abundant in northern and central Eurasia (**FIG-URE 8.6B**). Finally, the O allele is very common in the Americas and parts of Australia (**FIG-URE 8.6C**). In fact, in some parts of North and South America, almost 100% of the indigenous population has the O allele.

These allele distributions can tell us a lot about the evolutionary history of different populations. Areas with high concentrations of one allele may be the result of the founder effect. Imagine a population that has a relatively even distribution of the blood antigen alleles. A subgroup of this population moves away to settle a new area and found a new population. If the founding subgroup has a disproportionate number of one of the alleles, we are likely to see an unusually high frequency of that allele in the descendant population. Blood antigen allele distributions may also be the result of gene flow. If the frequencies of an allele are similar across a large geographic area, it may suggest that the populations in that area were mobile and experienced a lot of interbreeding.

LACTOSE TOLERANCE

The human variations discussed so far give us a variety of clues about our evolutionary history. Skin color, altitude adaptations, and climate adaptations reflect how natural selection helps to balance the different needs of populations living in different environmental circumstances. Variations in ABO blood allele frequencies reflect the processes of genetic drift (the founder effect) and gene flow (interbreeding). In considering these traits, we have emphasized the significance of factors such as population movement and adaptation to natural environmental conditions. In some cases, however, human variation is more the result of cultural factors than of strictly environmental factors. An example of such variation is lactose tolerance in humans.

Milk contains a sugar called **lactose**. To digest milk, therefore, you need a particular enzyme called **lactase**. All mammalian babies have a gene that codes for lactase, which allows them

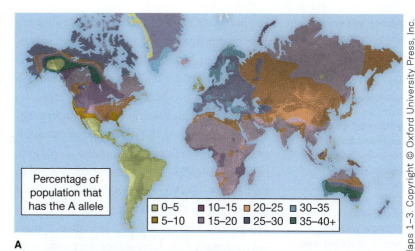

A

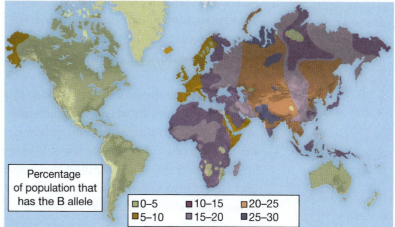

B

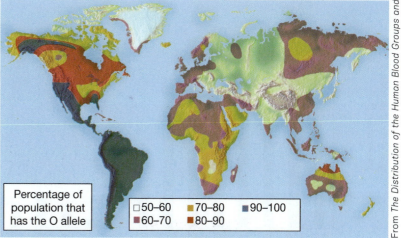

C

FIGURE 8.6 Relative Distributions of the ABO Blood Antigen Alleles Vary Geographically
(A) The A allele is most common in parts of Europe, Australia, and far northern North America. (B) The B allele is most common in Central Asia. (C) The O allele is most common in the Americas and parts of Australia.

lactose intolerance
a condition common to all mammals where adults cannot properly digest lactose

lactose tolerance an unusual condition in some humans where adults can properly digest lactose

pastoralism
a lifestyle where raising domesticated herd animals is central to the diet and economy

to produce the enzyme early in life so they are able to digest their mother's milk in infancy. As mammals grow and are weaned from their mother's milk, the gene for lactase is turned off, and they stop producing the enzyme; thus, as mature adults, they are no longer able to properly digest lactose. Interestingly, most adult humans follow this typical mammalian pattern: their lactase production gene is turned off as they mature, and they become less able to digest lactose. When they attempt to consume dairy products during adulthood, they often experience a range of digestive discomforts. We refer to this condition as **lactose intolerance**. Despite Western popular cultural ideas to the contrary, lactose intolerance is the norm for our species, and most humans worldwide are lactose intolerant as adults.

Why, then, are there some exceptions to this rule? Why are some people able to enjoy milk, and milk products such as ice cream and cheese, well into adulthood? When we look at populations around the world, we find that some populations have unusually low frequencies of lactose intolerance (**FIGURE 8.7**). Their adult populations have high **lactose tolerance**, meaning that adults are still producing lactase and

are capable of digesting lactose. Interestingly, the populations with the highest levels of adult lactose tolerance are primarily descended from northern European and East African groups. These populations have a long history of **pastoralism**. This term refers to a lifestyle where raising domesticated herd animals is central to the diet and economy. Animal domestication is very recent, occurring within the last 10,000 years or so, and it is found in various parts of the world, from the mountains of South America to the grasslands of East Africa. However, not all people practicing pastoralism use their animals for the same purposes. Often, domesticated animals are used as work animals or for their raw materials, such as their meat, hides, and dung. In some cultures, though, there is a history of using the animals specifically for their milk products. In these populations, we see higher frequencies of adult lactose tolerance.

It seems that populations in parts of Europe and Africa have been using animal milk products for many, many generations. People who had a genetic variant—a random mutation—that allowed for continued lactose digestion into adulthood could take advantage of this available food source throughout their lives. Over time, this genetic variant was selectively favored, such that descendants of these populations today have higher frequencies of adult lactose tolerance than other populations. What is interesting is that lactose tolerance evolved separately in different parts of the world. In fact, the genetic mutations for this ability were slightly different in each of these regions. When one version of the ability randomly appeared in a part of Europe that practiced dairy farming, it was selectively favored in that population; and when a different genetic mutation resulted in the same ability in a population in Africa with dairying traditions, it was selectively favored and maintained in that region. Note that in both cases, the start of the ability is a random genetic mutation. It is then passed to future generations at a high rate because it is useful in a population that has dairy animals on hand. It is *not* the result of eating dairy products. Rather, it is a happy coincidence that a mutation randomly

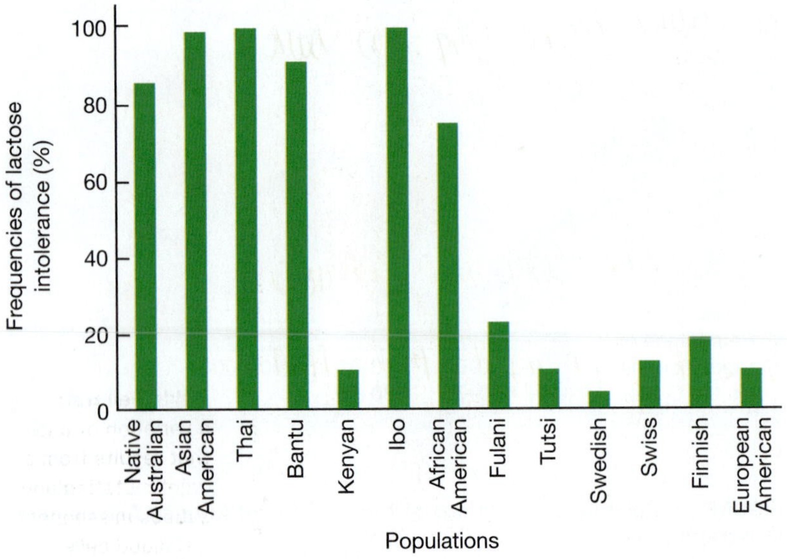

FIGURE 8.7 Adult Lactose Intolerance Frequency
Most adult humans are lactose intolerant. Lactose tolerance, which is unusual, is seen in populations with a long history of raising animals for their dairy products (such as some European and African populations).

appeared in a population of dairy farmers who could put the trait to use.

Variation in lactose tolerance has profound implications for the understanding of our evolutionary history. First, it indicates that the evolutionary history of organisms is influenced by their diets and the adaptations that evolve to suit their dietary needs. We will see further examples of such influences as we trace the connections between diet and dietary adaptations in later labs about primates and our fossil ancestors. Second, today's distribution of human lactose tolerance exemplifies the complex relationship between human culture and biology throughout our evolutionary history. In this case, humans modified their diet through a cultural shift toward pastoralism and the incorporation of dairy products. This new diet created a new environmental context, which then selectively favored the lactose tolerance mutation when it randomly appeared. Through culture, humans have the ability to alter their environment so much that those alterations influence their biological evolution.

▶▶▶ EXPLORING FURTHER

The Sickle-Cell Trait Often, human variations are the result of evolution that balances complex factors simultaneously, as we saw with skin color. Another classic example of an evolutionary balancing act is seen with the **sickle-cell trait**. The sickle-cell allele causes the body to form misshapen red blood cells that take the form of a sickle (**FIGURE 8.8**). These misshapen cells cannot properly transport oxygen. People who are heterozygous for the trait (carrying one sickle-cell allele and one normal allele) suffer few effects on their health and reproduction. However, people who are homozygous for the trait (carrying two sickle-cell alleles) have a lot of misshapen red blood cells in their blood vessels. Their presence reduces oxygen transportation and causes a severe form of anemia called **sickle-cell anemia**. The high numbers of misshapen cells can also cause blockages in blood vessels that can be fatal. Under most circumstances, a trait with severe negative consequences, such as the sickle-cell trait, would be weeded out by natural selection. In some populations, however, the sickle-cell trait has been selectively favored despite the obvious disadvantages.

Why has the sickle-cell trait been maintained in these populations? The answer lies in the relationship between the sickle-cell trait and a deadly disease called malaria. Malaria is an infection caused by a parasite that is transmitted via mosquitoes; therefore, it is common in tropical areas, where mosquito populations are high. The malaria parasite infects red blood cells and can be fatal if untreated. Interestingly, malaria cannot take hold in people who are heterozygous for the sickle-cell trait. Individuals with the sickle-cell trait have red blood cells that are a little

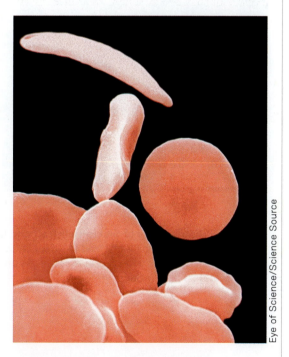

Eye of Science/Science Source

FIGURE 8.8 The Sickle-Cell Phenotype
The sickle-cell allele causes red blood cells to be misshapen. They take a semicircular form, like a sickle, instead of the normal rounded, disk form.

sickle-cell trait
a variation of a gene that results from a point mutation and causes misshapen red blood cells

sickle-cell anemia
a disease that results from the sickle-cell allele

balanced polymorphism
a situation where multiple alleles for a trait are maintained in balance because natural selection favors the heterozygous condition

smaller than normal cells, so they are not good hosts for the malaria parasite. In populations that live where the risk of malaria is high, the sickle-cell trait has been maintained (**FIGURE 8.9**). Individuals with two sickle-cell alleles risk death from sickle-cell anemia, and individuals with two normal alleles risk death from malaria. However, many individuals are heterozygous, having one sickle-cell allele and one normal allele. These people do not have enough misshapen red blood cells to have sickle-cell anemia, but their red blood cells are small enough to protect them from malaria. This situation is called a **balanced polymorphism** because as natural selection favors the advantageous heterozygous condition, multiple variants of the trait (the sickle-cell and normal alleles) are maintained in balance in the population.

The sickle-cell trait is particularly frequent in some African populations. These populations live in tropical areas that provide a natural habitat for mosquitoes. In addition, these populations have a history of practicing slash-and-burn agriculture, where large areas of land are rapidly cleared to create fields for domesticated crops. This clearing causes extensive damage to the soil and results in large pools of stagnant water. Because these pools of water are ideal environments for mosquitoes, they boost mosquito numbers and exacerbate the risk of malaria. As with the lactose tolerance trait, human cultural practices (slash-and-burn agriculture) have modified the environment (increasing mosquito concentration and malaria risk), which has then influenced selection for particular traits (the sickle-cell trait).

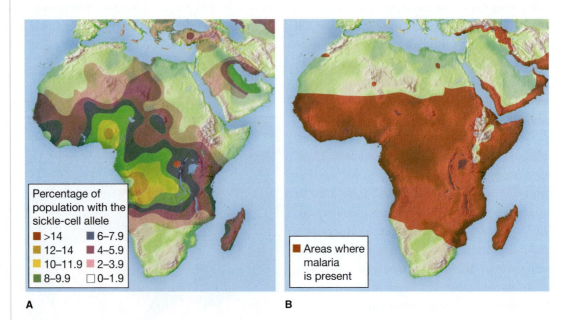

Percentage of population with the sickle-cell allele
- >14
- 12–14
- 10–11.9
- 8–9.9
- 6–7.9
- 4–5.9
- 2–3.9
- 0–1.9

Areas where malaria is present

A   B

FIGURE 8.9 Distributions of Sickle-Cell Trait and Malaria in Africa
The frequency of the sickle-cell trait (A) is higher where malaria risk is also high (B). The sickle-cell trait has been selectively favored in these areas and maintained in populations because it provides some protection from malaria.

CONCEPT REVIEW QUESTIONS

Name: _____   Section: _____

Course: _____   Date: _____

Answer the following questions in the space provided.

1. Which of the following geographic areas is home to people with the darkest skin colors?

   A. East Asia
   B. Central Africa
   C. Northern Europe
   D. Eastern North America

2. Adaptations are:

   A. permanent traits that may result from natural selection.
   B. temporary responses to physiological stress.
   C. the same as acclimatizations.
   D. reversible, short-term adjustments.

3. Define hypoxia.

4. Why is hypoxia common at high altitudes?

5. According to Bergmann's rule, which trait is advantageous in a cold climate?

   A. Smaller body size
   B. Equiaxed shape
   C. Larger body size
   D. Elongated shape

6. The B blood antigen allele is most frequent in which region?

   A. South America
   B. Australia
   C. Southern Africa
   D. Central Eurasia

7. Describe the difference between lactose and lactase.

8. Lactose tolerance is common among:

   A. people that live near the equator.
   B. populations that have a history of raising dairy animals.
   C. all adult humans worldwide.
   D. groups that live in extremely cold climates.

9. Where do we find populations with high frequencies of the sickle-cell trait?

10. Where do we find populations with high exposure to malaria?

Africa + Asia

LAB EXERCISES

Name: _____   Section: _____

Course: _____   Date: _____

EXERCISE 1 CLINAL DISTRIBUTIONS

Work in a small group or alone to complete this exercise. We learned in this lab that skin color has a clinal distribution. This is true for many of our other traits as well.

1. Identify one human trait, other than those discussed in this lab, that you think has a clinal distribution.

2. Why do you think this trait varies among different individuals and populations? (Does it provide advantages in certain environments, or might it improve reproductive success?)

3. How would you study this hypothesis? What data would you collect about the trait?

4. What data would you collect about the evolutionary context of the trait (such as the environment or reproductive rates)?

EXERCISE 2 SKIN COLOR VARIATION

Work in a small group or alone to complete this exercise. Recent research has identified a gene (*SLC45A2*) that codes for a protein that affects melanin production in humans and other animals. A mutation in this gene has given rise to two variant alleles. The *L374* allele correlates with darker pigmentation, and the *F374* allele correlates with lighter pigmentation. Researchers collected DNA samples from people in 14 European, Asian, and African populations and identified the frequency of the *F374* allele in these groups. Review the data in the chart below and answer the questions that follow.

No.	Population*	*n* (Number of Individuals Studied)	Frequency of *F374* (Lighter Pigmentation)
1	German (Germany)	241	0.965 (96.5%)
2	French (France)	98	0.893 (89.3%)
3	Italian (Italy)	97	0.851 (85.1%)
4	Turkish (West Germany)	200	0.615 (61.5%)
5	Indian (India)	51	0.147 (14.7%)
6	Bangladeshi (Bangladesh)	118	0.059 (5.9%)
7	Khalha (Mongolia)	173	0.113 (11.3%)
8	Buryat (Mongolia)	143	0.115 (11.5%)
9	Han (China)	89	0.028 (2.8%)
10	Han (China)	119	0.000 (0%)
11	Han (China)	111	0.005 (0.5%)
12	Japanese (Japan)	87	0.000 (0%)
13	Indonesian (Indonesia)	105	0.005 (0.5%)
14	African (Germany, Japan)	17	0.000 (0%)

Modified from Yuasa et al. 2006.

*The place name in parentheses following the population name indicates where members of the population were living when they were sampled; for example, population 4 consisted of Turks who had emigrated to Germany.

1. In what populations do we see the highest frequencies of the *F374* allele for lighter pigmentation?

2. In what populations do we see the lowest frequencies of the *F374* allele for lighter pigmentation?

3. The map below shows the ancestral locations of the populations studied, superimposed on Figure 8.2, a map of regional skin color variation. Are these results what you would expect based on the skin color information in the map? Why or why not?

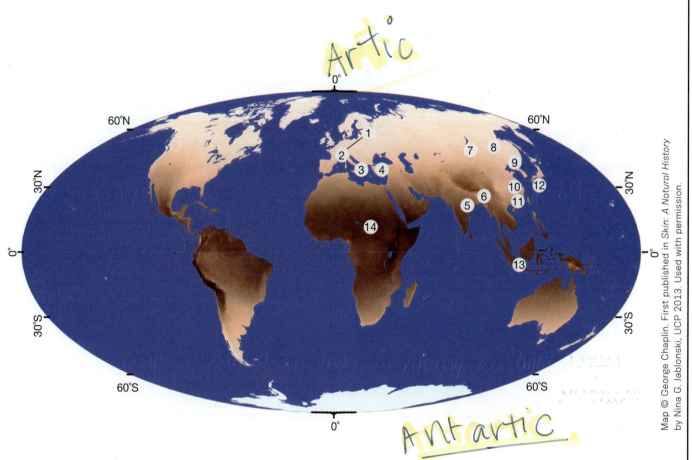

Artic

Antartic

4. Why might some light-skinned populations, such as the Japanese, be missing the *F374* allele for lighter skin pigmentation? (*Hint*: Consider the various forces of evolution that may be at play.) (#12 on the map)

Name: _____ Date: _____

EXERCISE 3 ALTITUDE ADAPTATION

Work in a small group or alone to complete this exercise. You and your classmates have decided to take a vacation to the Andes in South America. You plan to spend 2 weeks hiking, camping, and exploring the area.

1. While you are there, you can expect to undergo some acclimatization to this high-altitude environment. Describe *one* of these possible acclimatizations. less oxygen intake.

   (increased respiration)

2. Why would your body undergo such a change? What benefit or benefits does this acclimatization afford while you are vacationing at high altitude? avoid hypoxia.

   ↓

   greater oxygen intake.

3. Several weeks after you have returned home from your vacation, will you still have this acclimatization? Why or why not? No. Acclimatizations will slowly go away w/ time to what you're normally used to.

4. While you are in the Andes, you notice that local people seem to be better adapted to the high-altitude conditions than you are. Describe *one* of their possible adaptations.

   higher blood red cell proportion in blood to facilitate oxygen movement.

5. If someone with this adaptation were to visit you at a lower altitude, would they lose their adaptation? Why or why not? No, adaptations are more extreme and permanent.

   It is a trait that their body has evolved to have.

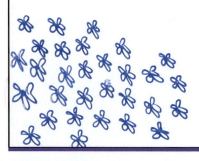

EXERCISE 4   CLIMATE ADAPTATION

Work in a small group or alone to complete this exercise. Examine the images provided by your instructor (or the images in the Lab 8 Exercise Image Library on p. 254) and answer the following questions.

PART A

1. Is this person adapted for a cold climate or a hot climate? *Hot*

2. Describe *one* trait that helped you make this determination.

   Long limbs
   Heavier skin tone
   dignter body set

3. Is this trait related to Bergmann's rule or Allen's rule?

   Allen's Rule.

PART B

1. Is this person adapted for a cold climate or a hot climate? *Cold*

2. Describe *one* trait that helped you make this determination.

   Short limbs
   Lighter skin tone
   Heavier body type & set.

3. Is this trait related to Bergmann's rule or Allen's rule?

   Bergmann's Rule.

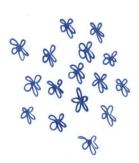

EXERCISE 5 ABO BLOOD GROUP

Work in a small group or alone to complete this exercise. Review Figure 8.6 (on p. 235). Use this information, as well as your understanding of the forces of evolution, to answer the following questions.

1. Many populations throughout central Eurasia share high frequencies of the B allele. What does this pattern suggest about the evolutionary history of these populations? Describe the evolutionary force that probably caused this trait distribution.

2. The O allele is unusually frequent in the Americas. What does this pattern suggest about the evolutionary history of these populations? Describe the evolutionary force that probably caused this trait distribution.

EXERCISE 6 OVERLAP OF MULTIPLE TRAITS

Work in a small group or alone to complete this exercise. You are conducting a survey of human variation at a bus station. While conducting your survey, you meet a very large tour group of adult college students. The tour group has a high number of people who are carriers of the sickle-cell trait and a high number of people who are lactose tolerant.

1. Why would a population have a high number of people who are carriers of the sickle-cell trait? (Consider factors such as economic practices, location in the world, and history.)

2. Why would a population have a high number of adults who are lactose tolerant? (Consider factors such as economic practices, location in the world, and history.)

3. Based on these adaptations, what can you suggest about the group's geographic or cultural background? (Be as specific as possible.)

4. If you had data about only one of these traits (sickle-cell *or* lactose tolerance), how might your answer to Question 3 above be different?

EXERCISE 7   THE SICKLE-CELL TRAIT AND G6PD DEFICIENCY

Work in a small group or alone to complete this exercise. Glucose-6-phosphate dehydrogenase deficiency (G6PD deficiency) is an inherited disorder where either the body has less of the G6PD enzyme than normal or the available G6PD is not functioning correctly. This deficiency affects red blood cell function and may result in anemia (the destruction of red blood cells) when people with the condition have infections, are taking certain medications, or eat certain foods. People with G6PD deficiency may have some protection from malaria because their abnormal red blood cells interfere with the reproduction of the malaria parasite in their bodies.

1. Consider the prevalence of G6PD deficiency estimated by the World Health Organization (WHO), as shown in the map below.

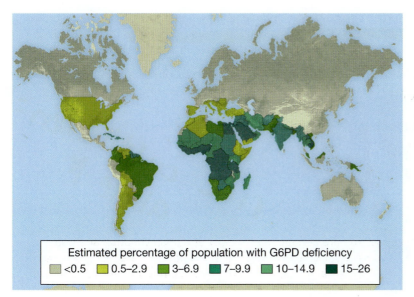

Estimated percentage of population with G6PD deficiency
◻ <0.5   ◻ 0.5–2.9   ◼ 3–6.9   ◼ 7–9.9   ◼ 10–14.9   ◼ 15–26

Compare the distribution of G6PD deficiency with the distributions of the sickle-cell trait and malaria shown in Figure 8.9 (on p. 238). What similarities between these distributions do you notice? What differences do you notice?

2. Why might these similarities and differences exist? Be sure to consider the evolutionary context (including the natural environment, cultural practices, and interbreeding).

EXERCISE 8 VARIATION IN THE *ADH1B* GENE

Work in a small group or alone to complete this exercise. The *ADH1B* gene is one of the genes that codes for alcohol dehydrogenase (ADH)—an enzyme that helps in the digestion of alcohol. A variant of this gene, called the *ADH1B*47His* allele, helps metabolize alcohol faster than other variants of the gene, thus reducing the amount of alcohol that saturates the bloodstream. It also causes a negative side effect, where a person's face flushes red when he or she consumes alcohol. This allele is rarely found in African or European populations, but it is very frequent in East Asian populations, where it is often found in more than 50% of the population and may even be found in almost 100% of people in certain populations. These East Asian populations also have a history of growing rice and making fermented rice beverages that extends as far back as 12,000 years before the present (BP). The map below shows the frequency of the *ADH1B*47His* allele in East Asia. Sites where evidence of rice cultivation has been found are superimposed on the map.

Given what you know about the evolutionary forces behind human variations, how would you explain the distribution of the *ADH1B*47His* allele? Why do you think this allele is common in East Asian populations? Do you see a relationship between rice cultivation and allele frequency? *Hint*: Consider the benefits and drawbacks of consuming alcoholic beverages and how this might factor into the evolution of the *ADH1B*47His* allele.

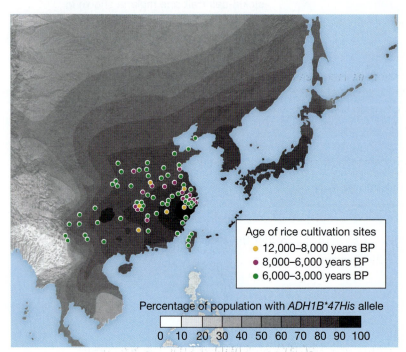

Age of rice cultivation sites
- 12,000–8,000 years BP
- 8,000–6,000 years BP
- 6,000–3,000 years BP

Percentage of population with *ADH1B*47His* allele

0 10 20 30 40 50 60 70 80 90 100

rice cultivation = allele ↑

more years = more allele.

EXERCISE 9 BODY MASS INDEX

Work in a small group or alone to complete this exercise. In this lab, we considered various human adaptations. It is important to remember that many of these adaptations evolved to suit environmental circumstances of the past, and that they may be less helpful (or even maladaptive) in today's world. For example, humans are adapted to store fat in the body for later use. This is very helpful during times when food is limited (such as during extended droughts) because it allows us to live on the fat stores of our bodies. However, in much of the world today, there is food abundance rather than food scarcity. In the face of food abundance in many populations today, our ability to store fat becomes maladaptive and contributes to obesity and related health problems (type 2 diabetes, heart disease, etc.). One way to measure obesity and other weight categories is called body mass index (BMI). Calculate your own body mass index using this formula:

[Weight in pounds / (height in inches × height in inches)] × 703 = BMI

For example, if you are 5 feet 6 inches tall and weigh 120 pounds, your BMI is

$$[120/(66 \times 66)] \times 703 = 19.4$$

STEP 1 Calculate your BMI. Using the formula above, calculate your own body mass index (BMI). If you have access to a scale and measuring tools, take current measurements of your weight and height to generate the most accurate determination. If you do not have access to these tools, use your best guess. Show your measurements and calculation in the space provided here.

Weight (in pounds) =   Height (in inches) =

Calculation (show your work):

Body mass index =

STEP 2 Make comparisons. To answer the following questions, use the BMI database compiled by the World Health Organization at **http://gamapserver.who.int/gho/interactive_charts/ncd/risk_factors/bmi/atlas.html**. This site shows mean (average) BMI data for adults in countries around the world. If you scroll over or click on a country in the map, it highlights that country's data on each chart.

1. How does your BMI compare with the mean (average) for adults in the United States?

2. A person is considered overweight if their BMI is ≥ 25. How does the mean (average) for adults in the United States compare to this standard?

3. Looking at the world map for mean (average) adult BMI, what regional trends do you notice?

4. Why might there be regional differences in BMI?

5. What are the implications of these trends for worldwide health now and in the future?

CRITICAL THINKING QUESTIONS

On a separate sheet of paper, answer the following questions.

1. Various cultures designate racial categories differently, and they often base these categories on very different traits. For example, some cultures use nose shape as one of the defining traits for a racial group. Other cultures do not use nose shape in defining racial groups, but use hair color instead. Conduct a survey in person on your campus, via your social media accounts online, or among your friends and family. Ask at least 20 people what *five traits* they think are most important when distinguishing racial groups. Document the responses, and then review the data. Did every person use the same traits? What do differences in racial classification such as these suggest about the universality of race and racial groupings?

2. Review Figure 8.2 (on p. 231). Note that skin colors are a little lighter in equatorial parts of the Americas than they are in equatorial Africa. Why might this be the case? (*Hint*: Think about the possible effects of evolutionary forces other than natural selection.)

3. In Exercise 3, you considered the adaptations of people living in the Andes. What other adaptations do you think would be beneficial to indigenous people who live in similar high-altitude environments? Are there any other places in the world where you might expect to find populations with these adaptations to high altitude? (Use information found in your classroom, online, or in books to answer this question.)

4. Bergmann's and Allen's rules apply to many animals, not just humans. Use material in your classroom, online, or in books to locate images of a black-tailed jackrabbit (*Lepus californicus*) and a snowshoe hare (*Lepus americanus*). Based on what you can see in the images, which of these hares is adapted for a cold climate? Which is adapted for a hot climate? What adaptations do they have to suit their respective environments? Do humans living in similar climates share the same adaptations?

5. Humans are unusual because our cultural practices can actually change our environmental circumstances. We can change the environment in which natural selection acts on our traits. Describe how this process has played out in the evolution of adult lactose tolerance. Describe how this process has played out in the maintenance of the sickle-cell trait. Can you hypothesize any similar situations where our future evolution may be influenced by cultural practices we have today?

6. As we saw in Exercise 6, human adaptations do not exist independently of one another. In real life, of course, each population, and each individual within that population, has numerous coexisting adaptations. Ignore what you know of your family history and consider only your own physical traits for the following adaptations: skin color, lactose tolerance, and body shape. Place marks on the map on the next page to show in which parts of the world each of these traits may have originated in your ancestors. (Be sure to label the marks to indicate which trait is being mapped.) Do all three of your traits suggest similar ancestry? For each trait, explain why you think the trait may have evolved in your ancestors. (Think about all the forces of evolution that might impact your unique history, such as natural selection, gene flow, and the founder effect.)

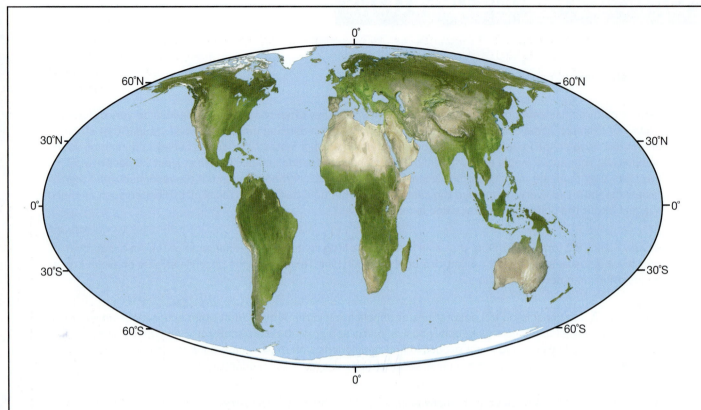

7. Recent research has shown that a variant of the *HERC2* gene affects the expression of the nearby *OCA2* gene, limiting the amount of melanin produced in the iris and resulting in blue eye color. The map below shows the distribution of this blue-eye genetic variant (with darker colors representing higher frequencies in a population and lighter colors representing lower frequencies).

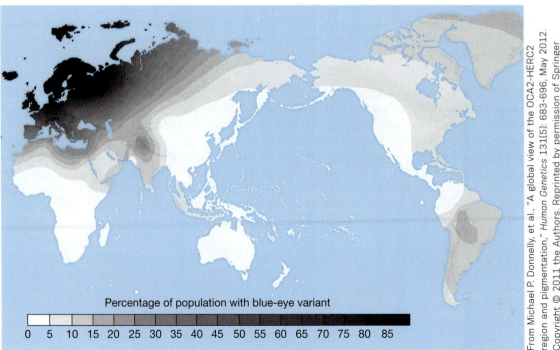

Percentage of population with blue-eye variant

0 5 10 15 20 25 30 35 40 45 50 55 60 65 70 75 80 85

Compare this distribution map with the map below showing regional skin color variation and the table in Exercise 2 (on p. 243) showing the distribution of the *F374* allele for lighter skin pigmentation. What do you notice is similar about the distribution of the *HERC2* variant for blue eyes and the *F374* allele for lighter skin pigmentation? Based on what you know about skin color and human variation, what evolutionary circumstances might have caused this distribution of the blue-eye variant?

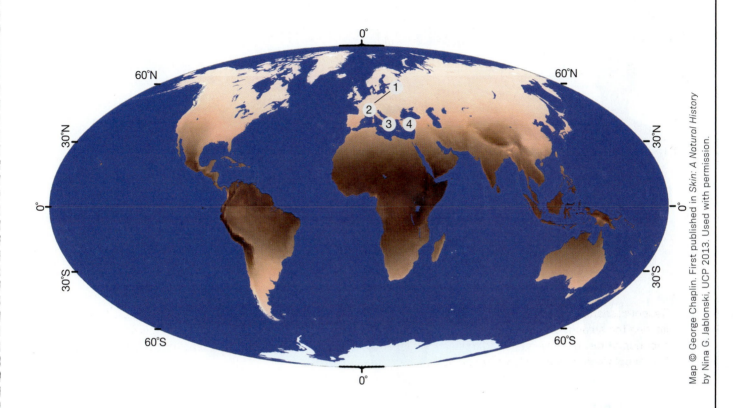

LAB 8 EXERCISE IMAGE LIBRARY
Students should use these images only if directed to by their instructor.

EXERCISE 4 CLIMATE ADAPTATION

PART A   **PART B**

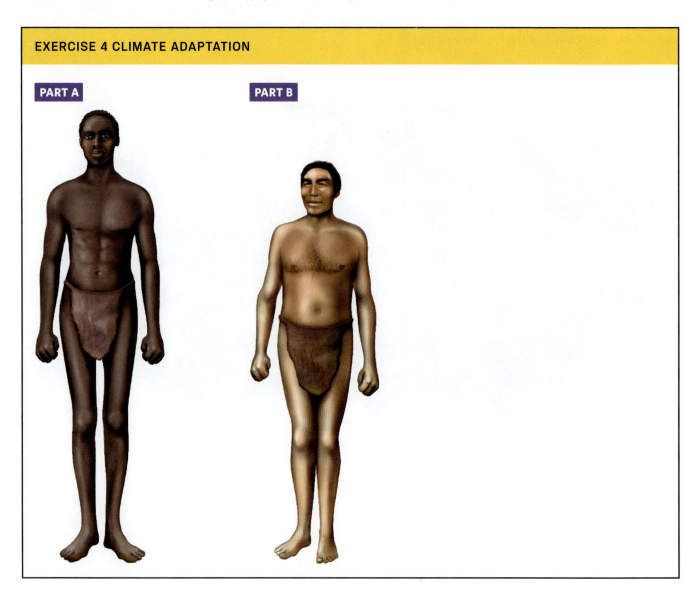

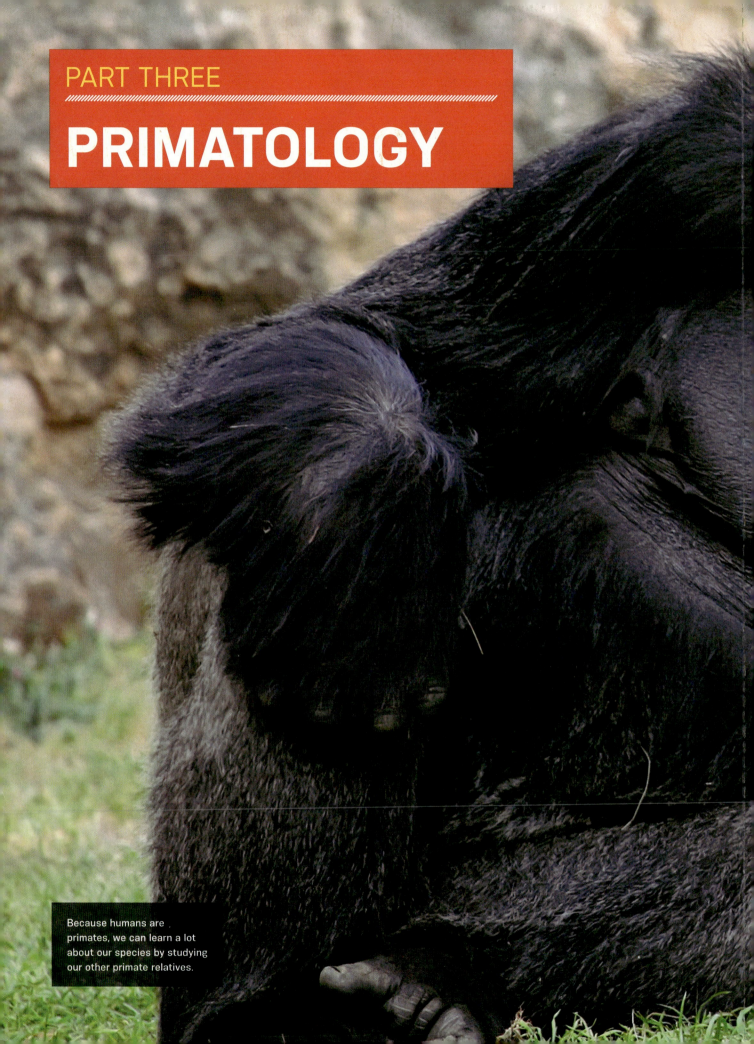

PART THREE
PRIMATOLOGY

Because humans are primates, we can learn a lot about our species by studying our other primate relatives.

LeonP/Shutterstock

We categorize supermarket produce to help shoppers find what they want in the store. We classify living organisms to better understand how they relate to one another.

Lab Learning Objectives

By the end of this lab, students should be able to:

- differentiate biological species and write genus and species names in their scientific format.

- distinguish between homologous and analogous traits, using examples.

- compare the different types of homologies, using examples.

- apply cladistic classification methods.

LAB 9

Classification

Imagine you are standing in the produce section of a supermarket. All around you, the produce is clustered into groups on tables or shelves. The oranges are next to the lemons and the grapefruit on a table; the romaine lettuce and iceberg lettuce are next to each other on a shelf; organic produce is clustered together on a separate table. Why is the produce arranged this way? There are numerous reasons. It helps shoppers to easily identify what they need, and it helps the store managers to keep track of their inventory so they can easily restock shelves when necessary.

Just as the supermarket clusters similar fruits (such as citrus fruits) in one area, the biologist clusters similar organisms into a group. A small group of organisms can also be clustered together with other small groups to make a larger classification cluster of related organisms. Like the supermarket's categories that help shoppers find the produce they want in the store, the biologist's classifications help us to identify the organism we are studying and to understand how it fits into a larger biological picture. Classification allows us to place an organism into the context of its close and distant relatives. This context gives us a better sense of the evolutionary history of the organism, and it allows us to make more accurate and relevant comparisons across groups of organisms. Classification is an essential element of biology and biological anthropology, and it is the focus of this lab.

genus (**genera**, plural) the level of classification that includes multiple related species

species one of the most specific levels of classification uniting related organisms

family the level of classification that includes multiple related genera

order the level of classification that includes multiple related families

class the level of classification that includes multiple related orders

phylum (**phyla**, plural) the level of classification that includes multiple related classes

kingdom the highest level of classification, which includes multiple related phyla

INTRODUCTION

This lab begins with a consideration of the different levels of classification and how we distinguish between organisms at the most specific level of classification—the biological species. We then look at the types of traits used to classify organisms. We pay particular attention to traits known as homologies because these traits are the most helpful when we are trying to reconstruct the relationships between organisms. We conclude with a look at the approaches to classification used by anthropologists today.

WHAT ARE THE LEVELS OF CLASSIFICATION?

In the 1700s, a Swedish naturalist named Carl von Linné (also known by his Latinized name, Carolus Linnaeus) assigned all plants and animals two levels of classification: the genus and the species. The **genus** was a more general level of classification, and the **species** was a more specific level of classification. Each type of organism had its own species, and species that were similar shared a common genus. Later, additional levels of classification were added to incorporate broader levels of relationship.

Today, the major levels of classification, based on Linnaeus's system, begin with the species—the most specific classification. Similar species are grouped into the same genus to reflect their relationship to one another. Similar genera (the plural of genus) are then clustered into the same **family**, and similar families are clustered into the same **order**. Related orders are grouped together in the same **class**, and related classes are grouped together in the same **phylum**. The highest level of classification is the **kingdom**, which is made up of related phyla (plural of phylum). Every known organism belongs to a group at each major level of classification (**FIGURE 9.1**). These groups reflect how the organism is related to other organisms. There are also levels of classification that fall between these major levels. For example, in addition to the order, researchers can place organisms in a suborder.

These additional levels allow for even more specific classifications (see Lab 10 for more information on the classification of living primates).

What's in a Name?

Each known type of organism has a two-part scientific name (or *binomial*), made up of the organism's genus name and species name. The names often tell us something about the organism. For example, *Homo erectus* means "upright man." The names also follow certain rules, particularly in terms of how they are written. The scientific name is written with the genus name first, followed by the species name. The genus name is always capitalized, the species name is always lowercase, and both words are italicized (or underlined if they are written by hand).

If you are referring to the same species repeatedly, you can abbreviate the genus name to the first initial, followed by a period. The letter is still capitalized, as it is when the whole genus name is written out completely. This type of abbreviation can be used only if you have already written out the entire genus name earlier in the work. For example, since we have already written *Homo erectus* above, we could now shorten it to *H. erectus*. If we are writing about two genera that start with the same first letter, we can abbreviate the genera to the first letter (capitalized) and the second letter (lowercase), followed by a period. For example, if we are writing an article about *Australopithecus afarensis* and *Ardipithecus ramidus*, we can abbreviate those names (after their first use) to *Au. afarensis* and *Ar. ramidus*.

THE BIOLOGICAL SPECIES CONCEPT

One of the most fundamental levels of classification is the species, but what is a species? How do we know if two organisms are from the same species or from different species? There is ongoing debate about the meaning of the word "species," and dozens of definitions of that word are used by biologists today. It is particularly difficult to define a species in the case of plants or

Taxonomic Category	Taxonomic Level	Common Characteristics
Kingdom	Animalia	Mobile multicellular organisms that consume other organisms for food and develop during an embryo stage.
Subkingdom	Eumetazoa	All major animals (except sponges) that contain true tissue layers, organized as germ layers, which develop into organs in humans.
Phylum	Chordata	Group of vertebrate and invertebrate animals that have a notochord, which becomes the vertebral column in humans and other primates.
Subphylum	Vertebrata	Animals with vertebral columns or backbones (including fish, amphibians, reptiles, birds, and mammals).
Superclass	Tetrapoda	Vertebrate animals with four feet or legs, including amphibians, birds, dinosaurs, and mammals.
Class	Mammalia	Group of warm-blooded vertebrate animals that produce milk for their young in mammary glands. They have hair or fur and specialized teeth.
Subclass	Theria	Group of mammals that produce live young without a shelled egg (including placental and marsupial mammals).
Order	Primates	Group of mammals specialized for life in the trees, with large brains, stereoscopic vision, opposable thumbs, and grasping hands and feet.
Infraorder	Anthropoidea	Group of primates, including monkeys, apes, and humans. They have, in general, long life cycles and are relatively large-bodied.
Superfamily	Hominoidea	Group of anthropoids, including humans, great apes, lesser apes, and humanlike ancestors. They have the largest bodies and brains of all primates.
Family	Hominidae	Great apes, humans, and humanlike ancestors.
Genus	*Homo*	Group of hominids including modern humans, their direct ancestors, and extinct relatives such as Neanderthals. They are bipedal and have large brains.
Species	*sapiens*	Modern and ancestral modern humans. They have culture, use language, and inhabit every continent except Antarctica.

FIGURE 9.1 The Classification of Humans
This chart shows how humans are classified in Linnaeus's system. Note that we are assigned to a group at each classification level, from the kingdom to the species.

microorganisms (such as bacteria). In biology, the **biological species concept** is often used to address the issue of delineating and differentiating species. This definition is not universally applied, but it is the most practical definition used, particularly in the case of vertebrate animals. According to the biological species concept, two organisms are from the same species if they can produce **viable offspring**, and two organisms are from different species if they cannot produce viable offspring. We might assume that "viable offspring" means *living* offspring. In biology, though, viable offspring must be living *and* be capable of reproduction. So it is not enough that the two organisms produce a living offspring. Their living offspring must also be capable of reproduction to be considered viable.

A classic example will illustrate this point. Horses have 64 chromosomes, and donkeys have 62 chromosomes. When a female horse and a male donkey mate, each contributes half of their genetic information. So, their offspring receives 32 horse chromosomes and 31 donkey chromosomes. This chromosomal combination can produce a living offspring—a mule (**FIGURE 9.2**). However, the presence of the unmatched chromosome interferes with meiosis (the cell division involved in producing gametes), so all male mules (and most female mules) are infertile. Despite the fact that the mule is alive, it is not considered a biologically viable offspring because it cannot reproduce. Therefore, accord-

ing to the biological species concept, horses and donkeys are separate species.

Distinguishing species based on the biological species concept is challenging when we are trying to distinguish **paleospecies**—extinct species. To do this, we are dependent on the fossil record. We cannot place two fossils in a room, encourage them to mate, and see if they produce viable offspring. Instead, we are forced to use physical traits as indicators of the relationship between specimens. These physical traits also reflect behaviors, such as diets and forms of locomotion. So, we can use physical traits to determine if two fossils have both anatomical and behavioral similarities. The more similar the fossils are, the more likely they are to be related. We can also take into account the geographic distribution of the fossils and their dates. If two similar fossil specimens are from the same time period at the same site, they are more likely to be related than two similar fossil specimens that are from different continents and are separated by vast time spans.

HOMOLOGY VERSUS ANALOGY

What kinds of traits do biological anthropologists consider when they classify organisms? There are generally two types of trait similarities

A

B

C

FIGURE 9.2 Biological Species Concept
When female horses (A) and male donkeys (B) mate, they produce mules (C). Even though mules are living offspring, they are not considered viable because they are infertile. So horses and donkeys are considered to be different species.

A   B

FIGURE 9.3 Analogous Traits
Colobus monkeys (A) and cows (B) both have complex digestive systems. However, this similarity is not due to common ancestry. It is the result of similar adaptations to a plant-based diet. Having complex digestive systems is an analogy in these species.

between organisms. They are called homologies and analogies. In both cases, we are dealing with traits that are shared between organisms. However, shared traits may come about for different reasons, and homologies and analogies are the result of two different processes.

Analogies are traits that are similar across organisms due to similar adaptations. These traits are the result of homoplasy. **Homoplasy** refers to the evolutionary development of similar traits in unrelated organisms. It can often result from circumstances such as similarities in diet and environmental conditions. For example, consider the complex stomachs of colobus monkeys and cows (**FIGURE 9.3**). Both colobus monkeys and cows eat a lot of plants, which are difficult to digest and require specialized digestive tracts. The common ancestor of colobus monkeys and cows did not have a complex stomach. The trait evolved separately in the colobus monkey and cow lineages. Thus, the fact that both colobus monkeys and cows have long, complex digestive tracts is the result of adaptation to similar diets, rather than something that was inherited from a common ancestor.

When we classify organisms, we are trying to group them according to their biological relationships to one another. If we simply look for

similarities, without considering the underlying reasons for those similarities, we may be misled in our classifications. If we had simply observed that colobus monkeys and cows had similarly complex stomachs, we might have classified them as being more closely related than they really are. This is why biological anthropologists have to distinguish between analogies, which can be misleading, and homologies, which are actually helpful for classification.

Homologies are traits that are similar among organisms that share common ancestry because they were passed down from a common ancestor to its descendants. These traits reflect real, ancestral relationships between organisms, so they are much more helpful for classification than misleading analogies. Even so, there are different types of homologies, and some of these homologies may be more helpful than others.

TYPES OF HOMOLOGIES

Ancestral traits (or plesiomorphies) are traits that are inherited by two organisms from a relatively distant common ancestor. For example, humans and ring-tailed lemurs both have mammary glands (**FIGURE 9.4**). This is a shared

analogy a trait that is similar across organisms due to similar adaptations

homoplasy the evolutionary development of similar traits in unrelated organisms

homology a trait that is similar across organisms because the organisms share common ancestry

ancestral trait a trait that is shared by two organisms and inherited from a relatively distant common ancestor; also called a plesiomorphy

derived trait a trait that is a modification of an ancestral form; also called an apomorphy

shared derived trait a modified trait that is shared by two or more organisms; also called a synapomorphy

unique derived trait a modified trait that is unique to one group; also called an autapomorphy

Millard H. Sharp/Science Source

Chris Meier/doc-stock/ Visuals Unlimited, Inc.

A

B

FIGURE 9.4 Ancestral Traits
Ring-tailed lemurs (A) and humans (B) both have mammary glands. This trait was shared by their last common ancestor, so having mammary glands is an ancestral trait (a type of homology) in these species.

trait that was found in the common ancestor of humans and lemurs. The mammary gland trait is useful in that it supports the idea that humans and ring-tailed lemurs are somehow related. However, it is a trait that is found in all mammals and can be traced to the last common ancestor of this entire group of animals. It is not particularly useful in helping us actually distinguish between humans and ring-tailed lemurs. For this reason, biological anthropologists often focus on the other kinds of homologies, called derived traits.

Derived traits (or apomorphies) are traits that are modifications of ancestral forms. There are two types of derived traits: shared derived traits and unique derived traits. **Shared derived traits** (or synapomorphies) are modified traits *shared* by two different groups of organisms. For example, apes and Old World monkeys have the same dental formula (numbers and types of teeth) **(FIGURE 9.5)**. This dental formula is a modification of an ancestral trait, a dental formula that was slightly different. Thus, it is a derived trait. Because it is a modification that is shared between the two organisms, it is a shared derived trait. The second type of derived trait is the unique derived trait. **Unique derived traits** (or autapomorphies) are modified traits *unique* to one group. For example, humans have an unusual pelvis that is very round and bowl-shaped **(FIGURE 9.6)**. This trait is a modification of an ancestral pelvis that was flatter. Thus, it is a derived trait. Because the modification is unique to humans, it is a unique derived trait.

So far, we have considered only physical (or morphological) characteristics. In reality, researchers today also use genetic analysis to help them classify organisms. Anthropologists may examine DNA or amino acid sequences to look for similarities and differences between organisms. Like physical similarities, genetic similarities are used to infer ancestral relationships. The more similar two organisms' genes are, the more closely related they are assumed to be. In Lab 10, we will see how genetic analysis has influenced the classification of some of the living primates, particularly tarsiers.

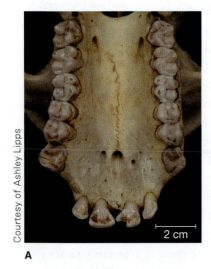
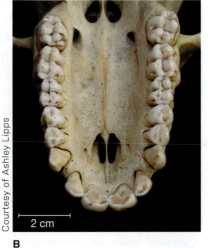

Courtesy of Ashley Lipps

Courtesy of Ashley Lipps

2 cm

2 cm

A

B

FIGURE 9.5 Shared Derived Traits
Apes (A) and Old World monkeys (B) both have the same dental formula. This dental formula is a modification of an ancestral form with more teeth, so it is a shared derived trait.

THE PROCESS OF CLASSIFICATION

As we saw at the start of this lab, people have been interested in classifying organisms for a long time. This classification of life is called **taxonomy**, and it forms the basis for **systematics**: the study of the relationships between organisms. Biological classification today usually falls under the heading of systematics, as it takes into account the biological relationships between the organisms being classified. In modern systematics, biological anthropologists use two primary approaches to classification.

The first and longest-running approach to classification is called **evolutionary systematics**. This approach emphasizes both derived traits and ancestral traits as useful tools in classification. The second and more recent approach to classification is called **cladistics** (or phylogenetic systematics). This approach emphasizes derived traits and de-emphasizes ancestral traits. Proponents of this view argue that the more derived traits are more useful in distinguishing groups. Note that both approaches to classification emphasize homologies and avoid misleading analogies. The difference between the approaches is the type of homology emphasized.

Imagine that a researcher has just used cladistics to identify the biological relationships among a set of primates. How will she share this classification with others? The easiest way to do this is to create a diagram of the relationships. The type of diagram used to represent cladistic classifications is called a **cladogram**. A cladogram lists every organism included in the classification at one level (usually in a row along the top). The organisms are then connected by a series of lines. The fewer the lines between two organisms, the more closely related they are.

Let's review an example of a primate cladogram prepared by a hypothetical researcher (**FIGURE 9.7**). The four primates represented are the black-and-white colobus monkey, the red colobus monkey, the chimpanzee, and the human. The two types of colobus monkeys connect to each other at point A on the diagram. This point represents their common ancestor, and it shows

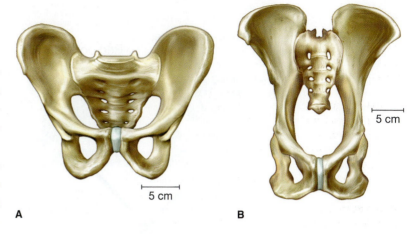

FIGURE 9.6 Unique Derived Traits
The human pelvis (A) is a modification of an ancestral form that is unlike the pelvis of other living primates (B). The rounded pelvis is a unique derived trait.

that they are more closely related to each other than they are to the other primates in the cladogram. Similarly, the chimpanzee and the human are closely related to each other. They also connect to each other before they connect to any of the other primates, showing their common ancestry (point B on the diagram). All four primates are distantly related. That is why they all connect at point C to show their common ancestry.

Cladograms like Figure 9.7 are constructed through a process of cladistic analysis that begins with identifying potential homologies. The presence or absence of these traits (or characters) is identified and then recorded in a matrix that includes each organism under investigation (see the table on the next page). The data matrix allows researchers to quickly identify whether the traits are shared across many of the organisms (ancestral traits), shared by some of the organisms (shared derived traits), or unique to one organism (unique derived traits). With this information, researchers can then begin grouping the organisms based on their relationships. In real life, researchers consider so many traits that they use computers to analyze data matrices for patterns.

When we return to our sample cladogram, we can see how the traits studied helped the researcher to both cluster and distinguish the organisms. All the organisms have a narrow

taxonomy the classification of organisms

systematics the study of the relationships between organisms

evolutionary systematics an approach to classification that emphasizes both derived traits and ancestral traits

cladistics an approach to classification that emphasizes derived traits and de-emphasizes ancestral traits; also called phylogenetic systematics

cladogram a diagram used to represent cladistic classifications, where lines are used to link organisms with different degrees of relationship to one another

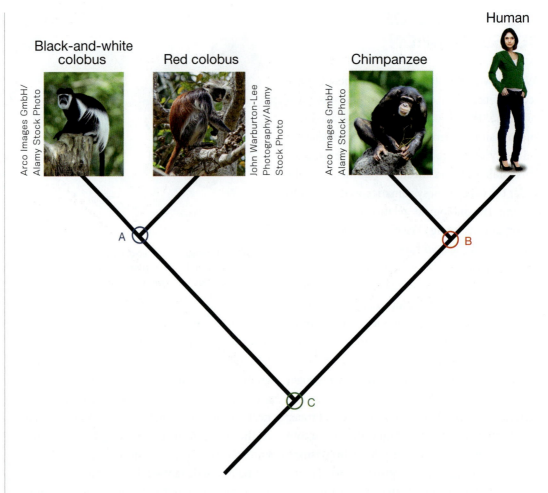

FIGURE 9.7 Sample Cladogram
In this cladogram, the black-and-white colobus and the red colobus are closely related and share a common ancestor (point A). The chimpanzee and the human are also closely related and share a common ancestor (point B). Both groups are also related to each other and share a common ancestor (point C).

SAMPLE DATA MATRIX

	Narrow Nose	Multicolored Fur	Broad Chest	Fur-Covered Body
Black-and-White Colobus	Yes	Yes	No	Yes
Red Colobus	Yes	Yes	No	Yes
Chimpanzee	Yes	No	Yes	Yes
Human	Yes	No	Yes	No

nose. This is an ancestral trait that demonstrates they are all related to one another via a common ancestor. The black-and-white colobus and the red colobus both have multicolored fur. This is a shared derived trait that indicates these two organisms are more closely related to each other than they are to the other organisms. Similarly, the chimpanzee and the human share a broad chest. This is a shared derived trait that reflects their close relationship to each other. Finally, the human seems to be unusual because it is the only organism without fur all over its body. This is a unique derived trait that distinguishes the human from even its closest relative (the chim-

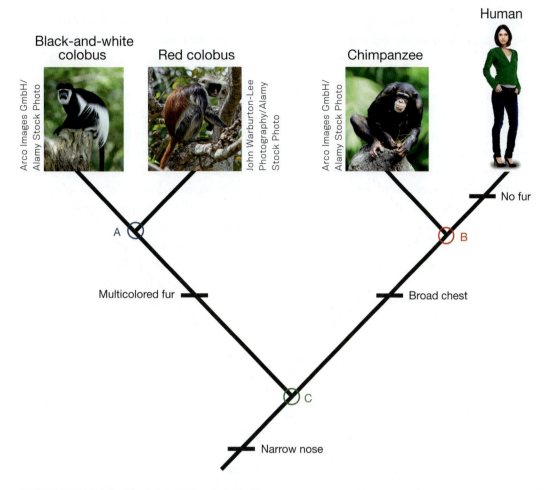

Human

Black-and-white colobus

Red colobus

Chimpanzee

A

No fur

B

Multicolored fur

Broad chest

C

Narrow nose

FIGURE 9.8 Sample Cladogram Showing Traits
Here, we can see how the researcher used particular traits to cluster and differentiate the organisms in the cladogram.

panzee). These four traits can be placed on the cladogram to show which organisms have each trait (**FIGURE 9.8**). Each trait is placed below the point that represents the common ancestor of all the organisms with that trait, which signifies that all organisms above that point possess the trait.

Another type of diagram that can be used to show evolutionary relationships is the **phylogram**. This type of diagram is similar in style and meaning to a cladogram, but it also accounts for the amount of evolutionary change (which usually correlates with time) through varying branch lengths. For example, a longer branch is used to indicate a greater amount of change, and thus a longer time span, since the split between two organisms. Both types of diagrams—cladograms and phylograms—are used by biological anthropologists to convey important information about the relationships among organisms. They tell us which species are closely related to one another and how other relationships extend out beyond different pairs of species.

CONFLICTING CLASSIFICATIONS

Many people assume that classifications are exact, with only one "right answer." However, there is often disagreement about how to classify organisms, particularly when dealing with fossils, which cannot be genetically tested or directly observed for interbreeding potential. Some researchers are considered "lumpers" because they tend to

phylogram a diagram used to represent evolutionary relationships that also accounts for the amount of change (and usually length of time) separating organisms

group (or lump) organisms into a few large groups. They emphasize the similarities between organisms and often interpret differences as minor variations within a group. Other researchers are considered "splitters" because they tend to divide (or split) organisms into numerous smaller groups. They emphasize the differences between organisms and often interpret differences as substantial variations between the behavior, ecology, and adaptations of separate species. These two perspectives on classification often result in two very different interpretations of the same evidence, which is why there is not always agreement on how to classify organisms, particularly fossil species.

At the same time, there are additional points of disagreement and departure in classification schemes. For example, anthropologists may choose different traits to analyze. In our earlier cladogram (see Figures 9.7 and 9.8), we chose four traits for analysis, but there were numerous other traits we could have used instead. The traits we use will influence the conclusions we come to. If we had not chosen the broad chest trait, we might not have recognized the relationship between the chimpanzee and the human. Without this connection between the chimpanzee and the human, we might have classified the chimpanzee as more closely related to the black-and-white colobus and red colobus because they all have fur.

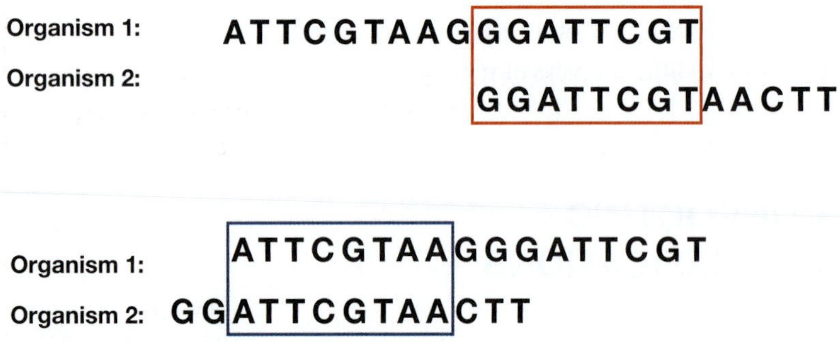

In some cases, it is difficult to distinguish traits. We often see this in genetic analysis. For example, imagine that a researcher has sequenced the DNA from two organisms, and she is now looking for stretches of DNA that are similar and thereby indicate an ancestral relationship between the organisms. This task requires her to align the stretches of DNA from both organisms and look for overlap. Because overlap in bases may occur at multiple points (**FIGURE 9.9**), the anthropologist must make a judgment call and decide which alignment is accurate and shows a meaningful similarity between the DNA. Other anthropologists may make different judgments about where the DNA strands are similar, so they may come to different conclusions about the relationship between the organisms.

In other situations, as we discuss in Lab 15, anthropologists may choose the same traits but interpret them differently. For example, two anthropologists agree that individual A has more robust (dense, heavy) bony facial structures than individual B. The first anthropologist argues that individual A is the male of the species, which explains why he has larger facial structures than individual B, who is interpreted as female. This anthropologist considers the differences in robusticity to be minor, and he interprets the individuals to be from the same species. In contrast, the second anthropologist argues that individual A has a more robust face because it has a diet that requires more chewing and physical exertion than the diet of individual B. This anthropologist thinks the differences in robusticity reflect significant differences in ecology and adaptation, and she interprets the individuals to be from two different species. In this situation, the anthropologists agree on the traits, but come to different conclusions.

It is important to remember that the process of classification is full of choices, and that those choices may lead researchers to different conclusions. The overall perspectives of individual researchers, the traits they use, and how they interpret those traits will all affect the final classifications they make.

Organism 1: **A T T C G T A A** **G G A T T C G T**
Organism 2: **G G A T T C G T** **A A C T T**

Organism 1: **A T T C G T A A G G G A T T C G T**
Organism 2: **G G A T T C G T A A C T T**

FIGURE 9.9 Variations in DNA Analysis
The DNA strands from the two organisms studied appear to be similar at two different places (outlined by the red box and the blue box), depending on how the strands are aligned. The anthropologist must judge where the DNA strands actually align and whether the strands are similar due to common ancestry.

CONCEPT REVIEW QUESTIONS

Name: _____   Section: _____

Course: _____   Date: _____

Answer the following questions in the space provided.

1. List the major levels of classification in order from the most general to the most specific.

2. According to the biological species concept, the phrase "viable offspring" refers to:
   A. only female offspring.
   B. offspring that survive to adulthood.
   C. living offspring that are capable of reproduction.
   D. offspring that are alive.

3. When classifying paleospecies, anthropologists use:
   A. geographic distribution.
   B. physical traits.
   C. ability to reproduce.
   D. location, time period, and physical traits.

4. What is the correct abbreviation for *Pan troglodytes* (chimpanzee)?
   A. *P. Troglodytes*
   B. P. troglodytes
   C. *P. troglodytes*
   D. *p. Troglodytes*

5. Beetles and hummingbirds have wings, but these organisms are not related to each other. The fact that they both have wings is an example of:
   A. an analogy.
   B. an ancestral trait.
   C. a unique derived trait.
   D. a shared derived trait.

6. Humans and baboons have noses with nostrils that face downward, but many other primates have noses with nostrils that face out to the sides. Humans and baboons are also more closely related to each other than they are to primates with outward-facing nostrils. Therefore, the fact that both humans and baboons share the downward-facing nostril orientation is an example of:
   A. a unique derived trait.
   B. a shared derived trait.
   C. an analogy.
   D. an ancestral trait.

7. An anthropologist is using cladistics to classify living primates, so she:
   A. focuses on similarities that resulted from homoplasy.
   B. uses analogies to group similar primates.
   C. emphasizes derived traits.
   D. emphasizes ancestral traits.

For questions 8–10, refer to the baboon-gorilla-human cladogram below.

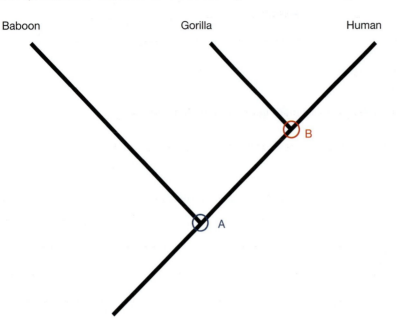

Baboon   Gorilla   Human

A

B

8. In the cladogram, which two primates are most closely related to each other?

9. In the cladogram, what does point A represent?

    A. The ancestor of gorillas and humans
    B. The ancestor of humans only
    C. The ancestor of gorillas and baboons
    D. The ancestor of baboons, gorillas, and humans

10. In the cladogram, what does point B represent?

    A. The ancestor of gorillas and humans
    B. The ancestor of humans only
    C. The ancestor of gorillas and baboons
    D. The ancestor of baboons, gorillas, and humans

LAB EXERCISES

Name: _____   Section: _____

Course: _____   Date: _____

EXERCISE 1 SCIENTIFIC NAMES

Work in a small group or alone to complete this exercise. (Remember to underline scientific names when writing them by hand.)

For each of the following scientific names, identify what is wrong with the way it is currently written. Then, provide the correct format.

Scientific Name	What Is Wrong?	Correct Format
Homo Sapiens		
Pan paniscus		
pan troglodytes		

Complete the following chart by providing the appropriate abbreviation for each of the scientific names.

Scientific Name	Correct Abbreviation
Homo habilis	
Gorilla gorilla	
Hylobates agilis	
Homo neanderthalensis	

Use the chart of abbreviations above to answer the following questions.

1. If you were writing about *Homo habilis* and *Homo neanderthalensis* at the same time, would you need to change your abbreviations? Why or why not? If you needed to change them, what would the new abbreviations be?

2. If you were writing about *Hylobates agilis* and *Homo neanderthalensis* at the same time, would you need to change your abbreviations? Why or why not? If you needed to change them, what would the new abbreviations be?

EXERCISE 2 HOMOLOGOUS STRUCTURES

Work in a small group or alone to complete this exercise.

In this lab, we discussed homologous traits. In addition to specific traits that reflect common ancestry, there are also general traits (such as the basic organization and layout of body parts) that reflect shared ancestry. These general similarities due to common ancestry are called *homologous structures*. In this exercise, you will examine homologous structures in the limbs of several different animals.

1. Examine the limb specimens provided by your instructor (or the images in the Lab 9 Exercise Image Library on p. 276) and complete the chart below.

    » For bone length, indicate whether you think the animal's limb bones are relatively long, short, or intermediate *for its overall body size*. Use the drawings of the complete animals and shading of the bone elements as a guide. (For example, a kangaroo would be described as having long legs for its body.)

    » For bone robusticity, indicate whether you think the animal's bones are robust (heavy and dense), gracile (lightweight and slender), or intermediate.

Animal	Bone Length	Bone Robusticity
Frog		
Dog		
Bird		
Pig		

2. What do you notice is generally similar across all the specimens?

3. What do you notice is generally different across the specimens?

4. How do these similarities and differences relate to the evolutionary relationships between these species?

5. What similarities and differences in adaptation (for example, different locomotor needs or different weight-bearing needs) may also relate to the similarities and differences you see across these specimens?

EXERCISE 3   TYPES OF HOMOLOGIES

Work in a small group or alone to complete this exercise.

Review the materials provided by your instructor (or the images in the Lab 9 Exercise Image Library on p. 276), which represent different organisms that need to be classified. The first step in classification is identifying useful homologous traits. Examine the objects and use them to answer the following questions. (Your instructor may request that you provide more traits than asked for in this exercise.)

1. Describe *one* trait that all the objects have in common (an ancestral trait).

2. Describe *two* traits that some of the objects share but other objects do not (shared derived traits).

3. Describe *one* trait that is particularly unusual, perhaps found in only one object (a unique derived trait).

You may find it useful to complete a data matrix to help you see patterns in the traits. Remember to indicate what your traits are, and add more rows as needed for additional objects.

	Trait 1: _____	Trait 2: _____	Trait 3: _____	Trait 4: _____
Object 1				
Object 2				
Object 3				
Object 4				
Object 5				

EXERCISE 4   INFERRING RELATIONSHIPS FROM TRAITS

Work in a small group or alone to complete this exercise.

The second step of classification is using homologous traits to determine the relationships between organisms. Based on the traits you identified in Exercise 3, it should now be possible to group some of the objects together. Objects that share a derived trait are related to one another, and they should be grouped together. Objects that share *multiple* shared derived traits are closely related, and they should be subgroups within larger related groups.

Draw your groups here:

EXERCISE 5 MAKING A CLADOGRAM

Work in a small group or alone to complete this exercise.

The final step in classification is to diagram the relationships you have identified. Using the groups you made in Exercise 4, identify the nested relationships among the objects. Consider which objects are most closely related, and which object or objects are the next most closely related.

Draw the cladogram of these relationships in the space below. Show which objects possess which traits by labeling your cladogram with the traits you used (as in Figure 9.8 on p. 267).

On a separate sheet of paper, answer the following questions.

1. Use material in your classroom, online, or in books to identify the species, genus, family, order, class, phylum, and kingdom for humans. Be sure to check at least two different sources. Do your sources agree on all of these levels of classification? Why might there be some disagreement about how we (or any other species) are classified?

2. Humans have 46 chromosomes, and chimpanzees have 48 chromosomes. Based on what you know about the mating of donkeys and horses, what do you think would happen if a human and a chimpanzee mated? Would they produce a living offspring (a "humanzee")? Would they produce a viable offspring in the biological sense? Would humans and chimpanzees no longer be considered separate species?

3. In Exercise 2, you examined the hind limbs of four animals as examples of homologous structures. What other body structures do you think these animals share due to their common ancestry (homologies)?

4. For each of the following traits, identify whether you think the trait is an analogy or a homology, and why.
   A. Dolphins and sharks have fins.
   B. Horses and zebras have hooves.
   C. Turtles and snails have shells.
   D. Some snakes and spiders have venom.
   E. Crabs and lobsters have claws.

   Now, use material in your classroom, online, or in books to verify your answers about whether the traits are due to similar adaptations or common ancestry. Why is it important to distinguish between analogies and homologies when we classify organisms?

5. Today, classification research incorporates more and more genetic data. Why might this genetic information sometimes reinforce previous classification schemes? Why might it sometimes force us to rethink previous classification schemes? What data do you think researchers should use to make the most accurate classifications?

6. In Exercises 3, 4, and 5, you classified objects representing different organisms. Repeat these exercises using the objects illustrated below.

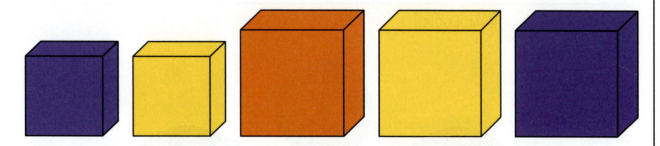

7. Review your work from Exercises 3, 4, and 5 (or your work from Question 6 above). How do you think a lumper would approach the classification of the objects? How do you think a splitter would approach the classification of the objects? What would be similar and different in the classifications these two researchers produced? (*Hint*: Does each object need to be considered a separate species?)

LAB 9 EXERCISE IMAGE LIBRARY
Students should use these images only if directed to by their instructor.

EXERCISE 2 HOMOLOGOUS STRUCTURES

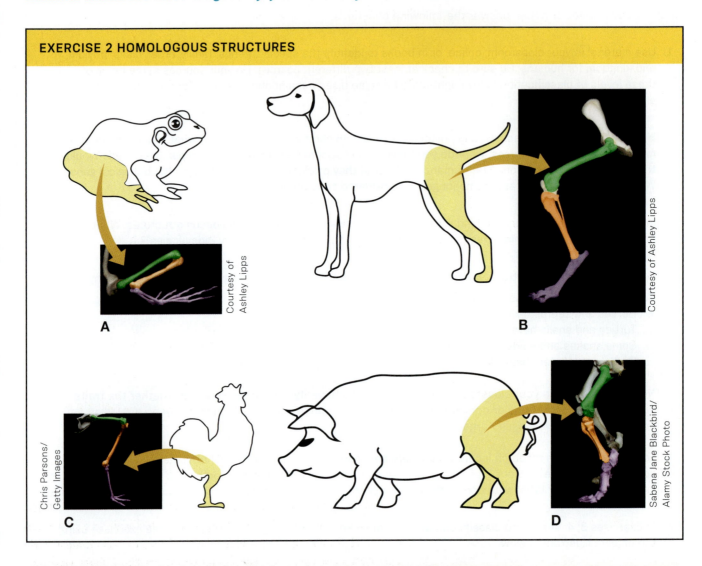

A   Courtesy of Ashley Lipps

B   Courtesy of Ashley Lipps

C   Chris Parsons/Getty Images

D   Sabena Jane Blackbird/Alamy Stock Photo

EXERCISE 3 TYPES OF HOMOLOGIES

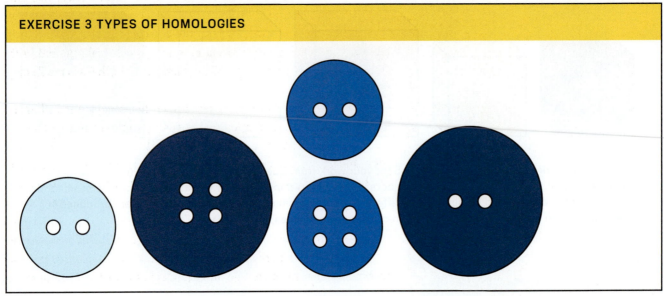

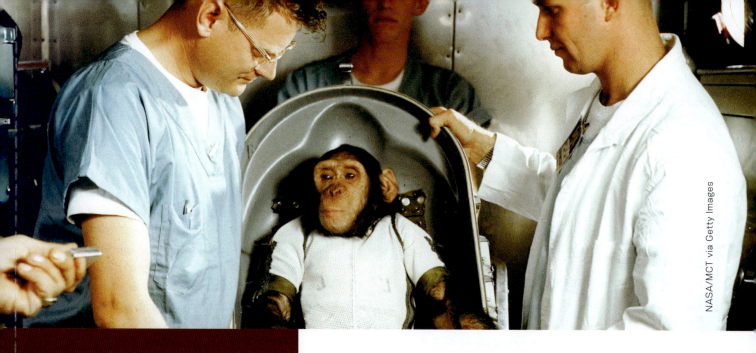

NASA/MCT via Getty Images

Ham, the chimpanzee seen here, was one of several chimpanzees sent into space in the early 1960s.

Lab Learning Objectives

By the end of this lab, students should be able to:

- describe the key features that differentiate primates from other mammals.

- recognize and describe the defining features of the major primate groups.

- classify primates using their defining features.

LAB 10

Overview of the Living Primates

In late January 1961, a 4-year-old chimpanzee named Ham was sent into space aboard a rocket. Ham was brought from his birthplace in western Africa to Holloman Air Force Base in New Mexico to participate in early rocket tests for space travel. Although it was short, Ham's flight was similar to later ones taken by the first human astronauts. After the flight, data were collected about Ham's health. This information was invaluable for planning manned missions to space. Ham was eventually retired to the National Zoo in Washington, DC (and later, the North Carolina Zoological Park).

Why send a chimpanzee into space before attempting to send a human? Test animals were common on rocket missions in the United States and the former Soviet Union prior to Ham's flight. The earliest efforts sent mice, and later rocket tests often used dogs or monkeys. However, researchers believed that to thoroughly test the viability and safety of human space travel, chimpanzees made the best test subjects. Chimpanzees are our closest living biological relatives, so they were thought to be good models for what might happen to humans under space flight conditions.

Today, there is significant debate about the use of nonhuman primates in experimental research, and strict guidelines exist for these practices

277

mammary gland a milk-producing gland in female mammals

terrestrial living on the ground

arboreal living in trees

nocturnal active primarily during the night hours

diurnal active primarily during the daylight hours

(see Lab 1). No matter where one stands in that debate, there is no denying the great biological similarity between humans and chimpanzees. In addition to the features we share as primates, we share numerous shared derived traits with great apes. In this lab, we explore the living primates to help us situate humans in the appropriate biological context.

INTRODUCTION

In this lab, we explore the living primates to better understand the biological context of our own human species. We begin with a look at what distinguishes primates from other mammals. We then discuss some of the debates regarding primate classification. Finally, we review each of the major groups of primates and their defining characteristics.

WHAT IS A PRIMATE?

Primates is an order of mammals that evolved over the last 65 million years. We will explore this evolutionary history in greater detail in Lab 13. Here, we focus on the living members of the primate order. There are hundreds of known nonhuman primate species today, although some are critically endangered (see Lab 11 for more information). Nonhuman primates are found in tropical and subtropical areas around the world (FIGURE 10.1). Humans, of course, have a worldwide distribution. As mammals, all primates share some mammalian traits, such as fur, the development of the fetus in the womb, giving birth to live offspring, and the presence of **mammary glands**, which produce milk for the offspring. The primates also share several anatomical and behavioral traits that differentiate them from other mammals.

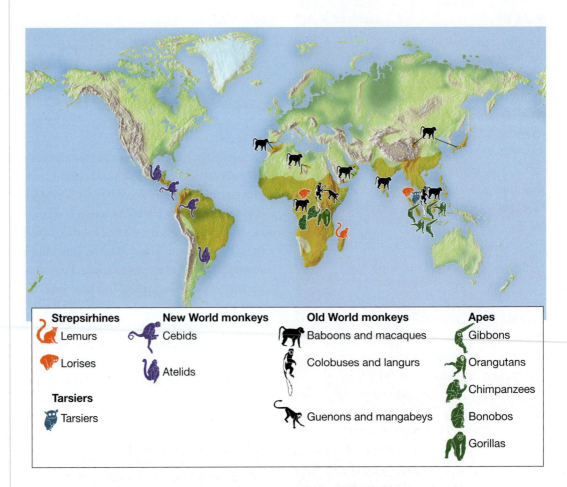

FIGURE 10.1 Geographic Distribution of the Living, Nonhuman Primates
Today, the nonhuman primates primarily inhabit tropical and subtropical forests.

We will begin with behavioral similarities. While a few primate species are **terrestrial** (live on the ground), most primates are **arboreal**, spending the majority of their time in trees. This means many primates live in densely forested environments. Primates tend to have generalized diets. They eat a range of foods, rather than eating just meat or just plants. For this reason, primates have a generalized dentition, with four different types of teeth that are each suited to a variety of biting and chewing tasks (see Lab 6 for more information). However, within the range of possible food sources, individual primate species focus on particular resources more than others, so they have some minor differences in their dentition and other anatomy (see Lab 12 for more information). While a few primates are **nocturnal** (active primarily at night), most primates tend to be **diurnal**, meaning they are active in the daytime.

Most primates are relatively social, spending much of their time in groups made up of multiple individuals. Even the primates that do not eat together usually socialize and sleep together. Most primates are **uniparous**, meaning they give birth to one offspring at a time, and primate offspring tend to take longer than other mammals to reach reproductive age. Because of this, primates are limited in the number of offspring they can have in a lifetime. This means that most primates, especially females, invest a lot of time and energy into caring for and raising their offspring.

In addition to these behavioral similarities, primates share important anatomical similarities. Primates usually have relatively **opposable** thumbs and big toes that can be placed opposite the other fingers and toes. This trait gives primates the ability to grasp objects and tree branches (**FIGURE 10.2**). Primates have a sensitive sense of touch, particularly in the tactile pads on the tips of their fingers and toes; primate hands and feet also usually have nails instead of the claws seen in many other mammals. In addition to an enhanced sense of touch, most primates have an enhanced sense of vision. Primates have **forward-facing eyes** that provide better depth perception because

the fields of vision from the two eyes overlap in the center (**FIGURE 10.3**). They also have more bone around their eyes than other mammals. In addition, most primates have color vision. These traits—depth perception, structural eye support, and color vision—all provide primates with a better sense of vision than many other mammals. There has been a trade-off between the senses, however, such that primates tend to emphasize seeing and touching over smelling and hearing. They have shorter snouts, and are less sensitive to smells, than many other mammals (**FIGURE 10.4**).

Primates also have larger brains relative to their body size than many other mammals. If we compare a primate and a nonprimate mammal of

FIGURE 10.2 Grasping Hands Primates have opposable thumbs that give them the ability to grasp things, such as tree branches and food.

FIGURE 10.3 Forward-Facing Eyes Primates have forward-facing eyes. This position makes the fields of vision from the two eyes overlap, giving primates enhanced depth perception.

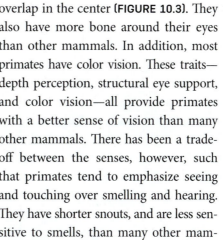

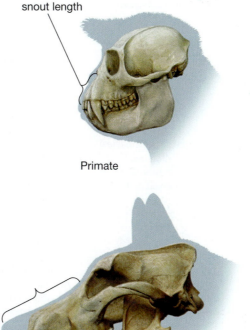

FIGURE 10.4 Reduced Snout Compared with many other mammals (such as dogs), primates have less reliance on their sense of smell. Accordingly, primates have shorter snouts than many other mammals.

uniparous producing one offspring at a time

opposable digit a thumb or big toe capable of being positioned opposite the other digits (fingers or toes), which confers the ability to grasp objects

forward-facing eyes eyes that are positioned at the front of the face and point directly ahead

FIGURE 10.5 Primate Taxonomy
This classification provides an overview of the relationships among living primates. It has gained support from growing knowledge about living primate DNA.

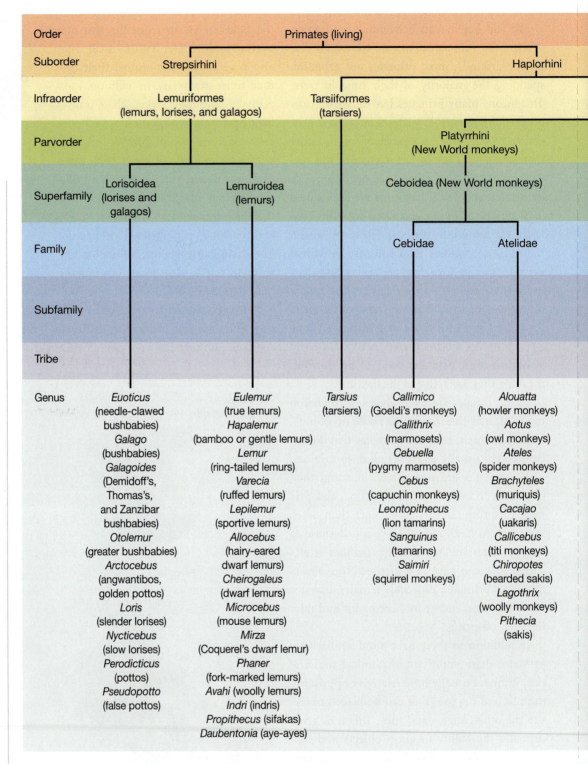

approximately the same body size, the primate will probably have a larger brain. However, not all sections of the primate brain are enlarged. For example, the areas of the brain associated with the sense of smell (the olfactory bulbs) are much smaller in primates than in many other mammals, which correlates with primates' reduced sense of smell.

PRIMATE TAXONOMY

As discussed in Lab 9, there are many debates surrounding classification. Experts may identify or emphasize different traits, which can lead to totally different classification schemes. In biological anthropology, there has been a significant amount of debate surrounding how best to clas-

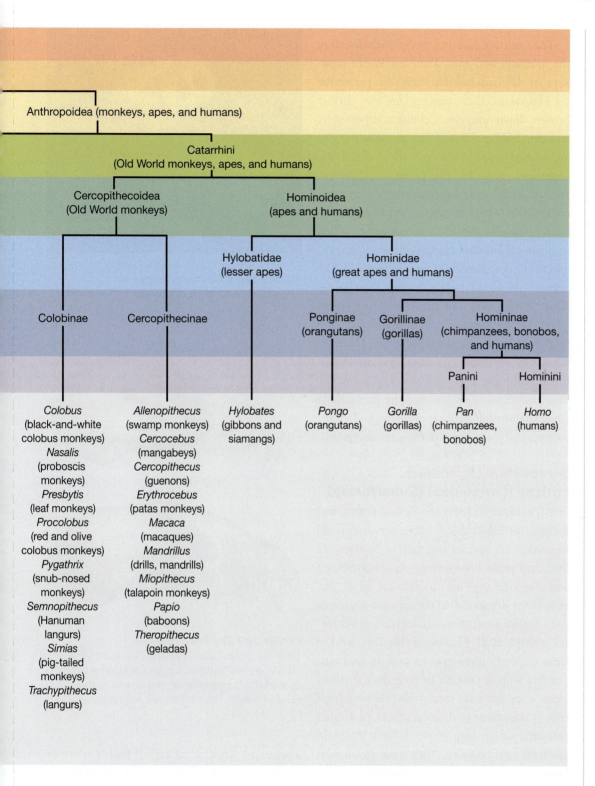

Anthropoidea (monkeys, apes, and humans)

Catarrhini
(Old World monkeys, apes, and humans)

Cercopithecoidea
(Old World monkeys)

Hominoidea
(apes and humans)

Hylobatidae
(lesser apes)

Hominidae
(great apes and humans)

Colobinae

Cercopithecinae

Ponginae
(orangutans)

Gorillinae
(gorillas)

Homininae
(chimpanzees, bonobos,
and humans)

Panini

Hominini

Colobus
(black-and-white
colobus monkeys)
Nasalis
(proboscis
monkeys)
Presbytis
(leaf monkeys)
Procolobus
(red and olive
colobus monkeys)
Pygathrix
(snub-nosed
monkeys)
Semnopithecus
(Hanuman
langurs)
Simias
(pig-tailed
monkeys)
Trachypithecus
(langurs)

Allenopithecus
(swamp monkeys)
Cercocebus
(mangabeys)
Cercopithecus
(guenons)
Erythrocebus
(patas monkeys)
Macaca
(macaques)
Mandrillus
(drills, mandrills)
Miopithecus
(talapoin monkeys)
Papio
(baboons)
Theropithecus
(geladas)

Hylobates
(gibbons and
siamangs)

Pongo
(orangutans)

Gorilla
(gorillas)

Pan
(chimpanzees,
bonobos)

Homo
(humans)

sify the primates. Here, we will be using the approach that is increasingly common in biological anthropology, which takes into account physical characteristics as well as genetic similarity.

The primate order is divided into the suborders Strepsirhini (the strepsirhines) and Haplorhini (the haplorhines) (FIGURE 10.5). The strepsirhine group includes the lemurs (Lemuroidea) and the lorises (Lorisoidea), and the haplorhine group includes the tarsiers (Tarsiiformes) and the anthropoids (Anthropoidea). While there has been some debate about whether the tarsiers should be included with the lemurs and lorises, current research suggests tarsiers are more closely related to anthropoids than they are to lemurs or lorises; this taxonomy reflects that relationship.

postorbital bar a bar of bone that sits lateral to the eye but does not fully enclose the eye in a bony pocket

rhinarium a damp pad at the end of the nose

The Anthropoidea infraorder includes all of the monkeys and apes. The New World monkeys are differentiated into their own parvorder: the Platyrrhini. These monkeys are then further broken down into the Ceboidea superfamily and the Cebidae and Atelidae families. The Old World monkeys and the apes are placed in the Catarrhini parvorder. This group is further differentiated into the superfamilies Cercopithecoidea (Old World monkeys) and Hominoidea (apes). The Old World monkeys are classified into two subfamilies: the Colobinae (colobines) and the Cercopithecinae (cercopithecines). The apes are classified into two families: the Hylobatidae (lesser apes) and the Hominidae (great apes). The great apes are further differentiated into three subfamilies: the Ponginae (orangutans), the Gorillinae (gorillas), and the Homininae (chimpanzees, bonobos, and humans). This classification emphasizes the particularly close relationship between humans and chimpanzees and places them in the same subfamily.

Strepsirhini (*Suborder*)
Lorises (Lorisoidea) (*Superfamily*)

The Lorisoidea includes the lorises, pottos, and galagos (or bushbabies). Here, we discuss all these primate species together as "lorises," in the broad sense, because they are closely related and classified together. Lorises are small primates that are found in Africa and Southeast Asia. Unlike most primates, lorises are nocturnal (**FIGURE 10.6**). Because of this, they tend to have relatively large eyes to take in as much ambient light as possible in their dark environment. They also have more rods (photoreceptor cells in the retina) in their eyes than most other primates, which help improve their vision in low-light environments. They have an unusual bony eye structure called a **postorbital bar**, which provides more structural support than is found in most mammals but is less supportive than the full enclosure seen in many other primates (**FIGURE 10.7**). The postorbital bar is a bar of bone that is lateral to the eye but does not fully enclose the eye in a bony pocket. Despite having this additional support in their eye region, lorises are not as reliant on their vision as many other primates. Vision is not as useful

Martin Harvey/Getty Images

FIGURE 10.6 A Nocturnal Loris
The lorises tend to be nocturnal (active at night).

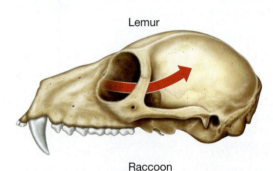

Lemur

Raccoon

FIGURE 10.7 The Postorbital Bar
Most mammals (such as raccoons) have very little bony eye support. Lorises and lemurs have postorbital bars posterior and lateral to their eyes. However, their orbits are still hollow.

a sense for a nocturnal animal that is active in the dark. Instead, lorises have longer snouts and a **rhinarium**—a damp pad at the end of the nose, similar to what is found in a cat or dog—which gives them a stronger sense of smell (see Figure 10.10 for a similar snout and nose in a lemur).

Lorises tend to eat a lot of insects, often stalking their prey very slowly before pouncing. They usually eat alone, but they will come together to socialize and sleep. Some lorises move very slowly on all fours. Others move more rap-

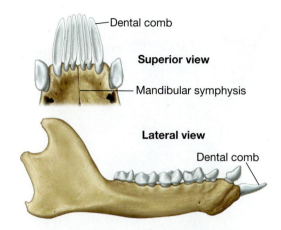

Dental comb

Superior view

Mandibular symphysis

Lateral view

Dental comb

FIGURE 10.8 The Loris and Lemur Mandible
Lorises and lemurs have dental combs formed by the elongation and protrusion of their lower incisors and canines. They also have unfused mandibles attached by cartilage at the mandibular symphysis.

idly, leaping through the trees. Lorises have a mix of nails and claws, and they often use their claws to groom their fur. They have a 2.1.3.3 dental formula and a special type of tooth structure called a **dental comb** (FIGURE 10.8). The dental comb is made up of the lower incisors and canines, which project out from the face. These teeth are elongated and slender, and they are positioned very closely together. This makes the teeth resemble the tines on a comb. Lorises use the dental comb primarily for feeding (to scrape at tree bark and extract tree gums), but also for grooming (much as you would use a comb on your hair). Lorises also have an **unfused mandible**, meaning that the mandible is made

of two separate bones that are attached by cartilage at the midline (called the **mandibular symphysis**). The mandible appears to be a single bone, but in reality it is not. Unfused mandibles are common in mammals, both primate and nonprimate.

Strepsirhini (*Suborder*)
Lemurs (Lemuroidea) (*Superfamily*)

Lemurs are closely related to lorises, and the two groups share many traits. Lemurs are a very diverse group of primates (FIGURE 10.9). Restricted to Madagascar, they adapted to a wide variety of environmental contexts on the island, resulting in an extensive diversity of species. Some lemurs are very similar to lorises: they are small, nocturnal, and eat a lot of insects. Other lemurs are more unusual. For example, some species are medium-sized animals with a diurnal lifestyle and a diet that includes more leaves and fruit. Lemurs also form a wide range of social groups. Some species are similar to lorises and are only limitedly social. Other species, such as ring-tailed lemurs, are very social and live in large groups of many individuals (see Figure 10.9A). Lemurs also have very different forms of locomotion depending on their environmental contexts. Most lemurs are arboreal, and they either move on all fours or leap through the trees. A few species, again, such as the ring-tailed lemur, are more terrestrial and spend a lot of time on all fours on the ground.

dental comb a tooth structure made of elongated and closely positioned lower incisors and canines that project out from the front of the face

unfused mandible a mandible (jawbone) made of two separate bones that are attached by cartilage along the midline

mandibular symphysis the area where the two sides of an unfused mandible are attached by cartilage

A

Millard H. Sharp/Science Source

B

Nigel J. Dennis/Science Source

FIGURE 10.9 Lemur Diversity
Although they are found only on the island of Madagascar, modern lemurs are a diverse group, including species as different as ring-tailed lemurs (A) and aye-ayes (B).

Robert Ross/Getty Images

FIGURE 10.10 The Lemur Snout and Nose
Unlike many other primates, the lemurs and lorises are still somewhat dependent on their sense of smell and have longer snouts than other primates. They also have a wet nose (called a rhinarium), seen here in a black-and-white ruffed lemur, that resembles the nose of a dog or cat.

Cheryl Ravelo/Reuters/Newscom

FIGURE 10.11 Tarsiers
Because they are nocturnal, tarsiers have very large eyes. They also have very long legs and feet to help them leap through the trees.

Despite this great diversity within the lemur group, all lemurs share some key traits with lorises. They have postorbital bars, but they are often less reliant on vision than monkeys and apes. This is especially true of the nocturnal lemur species. Lemurs also tend to be more dependent on smell and have long snouts and a rhinarium (**FIGURE 10.10**). Most lemurs have a 2.1.3.3 dental formula, although some species have fewer teeth, such as the unusual aye-aye (see Figure 10.9B), with an upper dentition of 1.0.1.3 and a lower dentition of 1.0.0.3. Lemurs have dental combs in their lower dentition, and they have unfused mandibles. They also have a mix of claws and nails. All of these similarities between lemurs and lorises reflect their close relationship.

Haplorhini (*Suborder*)
Tarsiers (Tarsiiformes) (*Infraorder*)

Tarsiers are small primates that live in Southeast Asia (**FIGURE 10.11**). Tarsiers share a few traits with lemurs and lorises. They are generally small and eat primarily insects. They are nocturnal, and they live in small social groups. They leap through the trees, like galagos and some lemurs. They also have a mix of claws and nails. However, tarsiers also share traits with the anthropoid primates. For example, they have more enclosed bony orbits, instead of a postorbital bar, and they lack the dental comb seen in lemurs and lorises. Like anthropoids, tarsiers have a short snout and a dry nose instead of a wet rhinarium. They also have a more anthropoid-like inner ear structure. And tarsiers share more genetic similarity with anthropoids than with lemurs and lorises. Because of these similarities, tarsiers are classified as being more closely related to anthropoids.

Tarsiers also have some unusual traits that set them apart from all other primates. First, they have a unique dental formula. Their upper dentition is 2.1.3.3, as in lorises and most lemurs. However, their lower dentition is 1.1.3.3, unlike what is seen in lorises and lemurs. Second, tarsiers have remarkably large eyes. While many lorises have enlarged eyes to aid their nocturnal lifestyle, tarsiers have a more extreme adaptation for their nocturnal activity pattern. The eyes of a tarsier are so large that they dominate its face, and a single tarsier eye is larger than the animal's entire brain. In addition to their exaggerated eyes, tarsiers have highly mobile necks. They can turn their heads almost 180° in each direction, which gives them the ability to rotate their heads almost 360°. Tarsiers also have incredibly long legs and feet. In fact, the origin of the name "tarsier" is related to their very large tarsal (foot) bones. They also have unusual lower leg bones, in which the tibia and fibula are fused together. These leg and foot features help tarsiers leap through the trees (see Lab 12 for more information on locomotor adaptations).

Haplorhini (*Suborder*)
Anthropoids (Anthropoidea) (*Infraorder*)

The remaining primate species (the monkeys and apes) are all anthropoids. The anthropoid primates are generally larger than the lemurs, lorises, and tarsiers. They also tend to have bigger brains for their body size. Almost all anthropoids are diurnal and rely more on their vision than their sense of smell. They lack the olfactory adaptations of a longer snout and rhinarium that are present in lemurs and lorises. Instead, anthropoids have several traits related to their enhanced vision. They usually have color vision, and they have full bony enclosures for their eyes (**FIGURE 10.12**). They also have eyes that are closer together in the front of the face, providing even more overlap between the fields of vision.

New World Primates (Platyrrhini) versus Old World Primates (Catarrhini)

The anthropoid group is subdivided into the New World primates (platyrrhines) and the Old World primates (catarrhines). The New World primates are the monkeys that inhabit the Americas (or **New World**). The Old World primates are the monkeys and apes that inhabit Africa and Asia (the **Old World**). These two groups can be distinguished by a few key traits. First, the New World monkeys have broad noses, with nostrils that face out to the sides and a wide **septum** (the

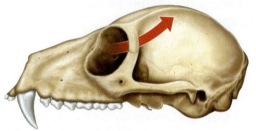

Gibbon

Lemur

FIGURE 10.12 Fully Enclosed Bony Orbits
Whereas lemurs and lorises have postorbital bars, anthropoids such as gibbons have full bony enclosures for their eyes. Therefore, anthropoids' orbits are less open than those of lemurs and lorises.

soft tissue between the nostrils). In contrast, the Old World monkeys and apes have narrower noses, with nostrils that face downward and a narrow septum (**FIGURE 10.13**). Their names

New World a name traditionally assigned to the American continents (North and South America)

Old World a name traditionally assigned to the majority of the non-American continents, specifically Africa, Asia, and Europe

septum the soft tissue between the nostrils

Ann Kakaliouras, Whittier College

Bill Coster/Alamy Stock Photo

Platyrrhines
New World

Catarrhines
Old World

FIGURE 10.13 New World Primates versus Old World Primates
New World monkeys (platyrrhines) have broad noses with nostrils that are far apart and face outward. Old World monkeys and apes (catarrhines) have narrow noses with nostrils that are close together and face downward.

prehensile tail a tail with the ability to grasp objects and act like a fifth limb

highlight this distinction. Platyrrhini is from the Greek for "broad-nosed," and Catarrhini is from the Greek for "hook-nosed." The second key difference between these primate groups is their dentition. New World monkeys tend to have three premolars in each quadrant of the mouth, while the Old World monkeys and apes have two.

Haplorhini (*Suborder*)
New World Monkeys (Ceboidea) (*Superfamily*)

The New World monkeys live in the forests of Central and South America. As noted above, they have the platyrrhine nose structure and three premolars in each quadrant of the mouth. The number of molars differs between species, such that some New World monkeys have a 2.1.3.3 dental formula while other species have a 2.1.3.2 dental formula. There are many species of New World monkeys, and they vary considerably. Most are arboreal and diurnal. However, one genus—comprising the owl monkeys (*Aotus*)—is nocturnal. The New World monkeys have a variety of diets. Some of the smaller monkeys rely largely on insects or tree gums. Other, larger New World monkeys rely more on fruits or leaves. They tend to be relatively social,

and some species live in very large groups. Most of the New World monkeys move through the trees on all fours, but some New World monkeys have a special form of locomotion facilitated by a **prehensile tail**. This tail has the ability to wrap around and grasp things, such as tree branches, so it can be used as a fifth limb (**FIGURE 10.14**). In contrast, none of the Old World monkeys has a prehensile tail.

Capuchin monkeys are perhaps the most famous of the New World monkeys (**FIGURE 10.15**). They regularly appear in television shows and films as pets. They are also trained as service animals, like service dogs, to help disabled people. Howler monkeys are well known for their incredibly loud "howling" vocalizations (**FIGURE 10.16**). Some of the most unusual New World monkeys are the tamarins and marmosets (**FIGURE 10.17**). These are the smallest New World monkeys, and they tend to eat a lot of tree gums and insects. They typically give birth to twins, which is rare among primates, and they sometimes live in a highly unusual *polyandrous* social group with more adult males than adult females (see Lab 11).

Dietmar Nill/naturepl.com

FIGURE 10.15 Capuchin Monkeys
Well known for their appearances in television shows and films as pets, capuchins are sometimes trained as service animals to help disabled people.

Kevin Schafer/Getty Images

FIGURE 10.14 Prehensile Tails
Some New World monkeys (such as the woolly spider monkeys seen here) have prehensile tails that can grab onto tree branches and be used like a fifth limb.

FIGURE 10.16 Howler Monkeys
One of the loudest animals on Earth is the howler monkey. These New World monkeys make howling vocalizations to mark and defend their territories and mates.

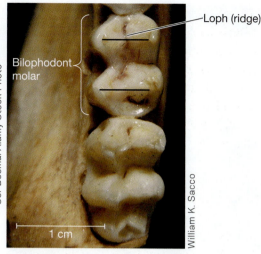

FIGURE 10.18 Bilophodont Molars
All Old World monkeys have unusual molars with cusps that are organized into two parallel ridges. These teeth are called bilophodont molars.

FIGURE 10.17 Tamarins
Tamarins (such as the lion tamarin seen here) are very unusual New World monkeys. They are very small, often give birth to twins, and often live in unusual social groups with more adult males than adult females.

Haplorhini (*Suborder*)
Old World Monkeys (Cercopithecoidea) (*Superfamily*)

The remaining primates (the Old World monkeys and the apes) are catarrhines. They all have the catarrhine nose structure, as well as two premolars in each quadrant of the mouth (giving a dental formula of 2.1.2.3). The Old World monkeys (also called cercopithecoids) live in various habitats in Africa and Asia. In general, Old World monkeys are diurnal, usually live in large social groups, and move on all fours (whether they are arboreal or terrestrial). They have unique molars, called **bilophodont molars** (**FIGURE 10.18**). These molar teeth have four cusps that are arranged in two parallel ridges (or lophs), hence *bi-loph-o-dont* (two-ridged teeth). Old World monkeys also have special patches of roughened skin on the buttocks, called **ischial callosities** (**FIGURE 10.19**). "Ischial" refers to the area of the pelvis that one sits on, and "callosity" refers to the callus-like, roughened skin. There are two subgroups of Old World monkeys: the colobines and the cercopithecines.

Colobines (Colobinae) The colobine group includes monkeys such as the langur, the colobus monkey, and the proboscis monkey (**FIGURE 10.20**). Most colobines live in Asia, but a few species, such as the black-and-white colobus (**FIGURE 10.21**), are found in Africa. The monkeys of the colobine group tend to be medium-sized and have long tails. They are usually arboreal and eat a lot of leaves. Many colobines have special adaptations for their leaf-eating diet,

bilophodont molar
a molar with four cusps arranged in two parallel ridges (or lophs)

ischial callosity a roughened patch of skin located in the ischial area (on the buttocks)

Courtesy of Joan Silk

FIGURE 10.19 Ischial Callosities
All Old World monkeys have special rough patches of skin on the buttocks, called ischial callosities.

Fredrik Stenström/Alamy Stock Photo

FIGURE 10.20 Proboscis Monkeys
The proboscis monkeys are Asian colobines with unusually long noses.

Kevin Schafer/Getty Images

FIGURE 10.21 Colobus Monkeys
Colobus monkeys, such as the black-and-white colobus seen here, are among the colobines that live in Africa.

cheek pouch a pouch in the cheek and neck area that can expand to store food

such as complex stomachs (see Lab 12 for more information on dietary adaptations).

Cercopithecines (Cercopithecinae) The cercopithecine group includes monkeys that are often larger than the colobines, such as the baboons

and macaques. Many of the cercopithecines, including most baboon species, are found in Africa (**FIGURE 10.22**), but some species live in Asia. Many of the cercopithecines are terrestrial and have relatively short tails. However, some cercopithecines are arboreal and have long tails like colobines. Cercopithecines tend to have a more diverse diet, containing more fruit, than the leaf-eating colobines. They also have special **cheek pouches** that allow them to store food, comparable to those of some rodents. These cheek pouches help cercopithecines collect a lot of food in a short time and store it for later.

Haplorhini (*Suborder*)
Apes (Hominoidea) (*Superfamily*)

Humans are apes that have a worldwide distribution, but the other apes are restricted to central Africa and Southeast Asia. The apes (or hominoids) are catarrhines, like the Old World monkeys, so they have several catarrhine traits in common with the cercopithecoids. They have two premolars in each quadrant of the mouth (and a dental formula of 2.1.2.3). If you examine your own teeth in the mirror, you will discover that you have this same dental formula because you are an ape. However, if you do not have your wisdom teeth, you will be missing the third molars found in most humans. Although some people have had their third molars removed (or have third molars that never came in), as a species we tend to maintain the 2.1.2.3 dental formula of all apes and Old World monkeys. In addition to the catarrhine dentition, apes also have the catarrhine nose structure. Again, you can observe this on your own nose. Your nostrils face downward, are positioned relatively close together, and are separated by a narrow septum.

While apes share some traits with Old World monkeys, they also have numerous traits that differentiate them from their close relatives. All apes have a special type of molar called the **Y-5 molar** in the lower dentition (**FIGURE 10.23**). Remember, Old World monkeys have bilophodont molars with four cusps arranged in two rows. In apes, the lower molars each have five cusps that are positioned such that a pronounced Y-shaped groove forms between them. The upper molars are slightly different and tend to have four cusps without the Y-shaped groove. In addition to these unusual molars, apes have faces that are flatter (more **orthognathic**), while other primates have faces that are more projecting (**prognathic**). Compared with other primates, apes also tend to have larger brains for their body size.

The apes are diurnal and usually live in heavily forested areas, where they spend at least some of their time in the trees. In fact, all apes retain adaptations for swinging through the trees. We see this in their long arms and long, curved fingers. However, for some of the larger apes, such as gorillas, a more terrestrial lifestyle is necessary. One of the most defining characteristics that distinguishes apes from other primates is their lack of a tail. Remember, most primates have a tail. The lack of a tail in all apes (including humans) is an important shared derived trait that highlights their close evolutionary relationship. The apes are divided into two families: the lesser apes (Hylobatidae) and great apes (Hominidae).

Gibbons and Siamangs (Hylobatidae) The gibbons and siamangs are also called the lesser apes, and they are classified together in the hylobatid family (see Figure 10.5). There are numerous species of gibbons and one species of siamang living in the forests of Southeast Asia (**FIGURE 10.24**). These species are called lesser apes because they have smaller body sizes, and correspondingly smaller brain sizes, than the other apes. They are diurnal, eat a lot of fruit, and live in small social groups. Both males and females help to defend their territory through complex vocalizations, often referred to as songs. In some species, the males and females also share parenting responsibilities and help take care of offspring.

The lesser apes primarily move around by swinging through the trees, more so than any other type of primate. Their bodies are smaller and more **gracile** (with thin, light musculature and bone) than those of the other apes, and they have even longer arms and longer, more curved fingers to help with arboreal locomotion. In addition, their thumbs are very short

FIGURE 10.22 Olive Baboons
Many of the cercopithecines are baboon species that live in Africa (as do the olive baboons seen here).

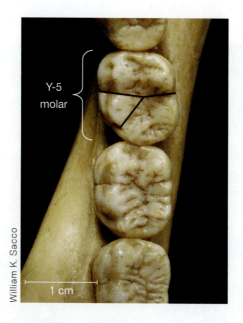

FIGURE 10.23 Y-5 Molars
All apes have special molars in their lower dentition. These molars have five cusps that are arranged such that a Y-shaped groove is present between the cusps. These teeth are called Y-5 molars.

and do not interfere with the apes' rapid arboreal swinging, and they have strong shoulders with a lot of mobility.

Orangutans (Ponginae) Orangutans (genus *Pongo*) are great apes found exclusively on the

Y-5 molar a molar in the lower dentition that has five cusps positioned such that a pronounced Y-shaped groove forms between the cusps

orthognathic having a flat face

prognathic having a projecting or protruding face

gracile having thin, light musculature and bone

robust having thick, dense, heavy musculature and bone

dish-shaped face a somewhat concave face formed by a sloping upper face and protruding lower face

FIGURE 10.24 Gibbons
The lesser apes include gibbons (such as the one seen here) and siamangs. They are smaller than the other apes, which is why they are called "lesser."

FIGURE 10.25 Orangutans
Orangutans are large-bodied apes that live only on the islands of Borneo and Sumatra in Southeast Asia.

islands of Borneo and Sumatra (**FIGURE 10.25**). Orangutans are classified in the family Hominidae and subfamily Ponginae (see Figure 10.5). Although we traditionally recognized two species of orangutans (one species for each island population), new research indicates that Sumatra is actually home to two distinct species of orang-

utans that became completely isolated around 10,000 to 20,000 years ago. This means there are now three known orangutan species (one on Borneo and two on Sumatra) (see p. 292 for more detail). Orangutans are known for their unusual orange fur and for the extreme size difference between the males and females, or *sexual dimorphism* (see Lab 12). They move through their dense forest habitats using a form of slow climbing. They are diurnal and eat a lot of fruit, and they spend most of their time alone. However, on occasions when food is more abundant, they are known to congregate temporarily.

The orangutan cranium is relatively **robust** (thick, dense, and heavy). The orbits are large, particularly from the superior to inferior edge, and they sit relatively close together in the face. The upper portion of the face angles in slightly, creating what is called a **dish-shaped face**: when seen in profile, the orangutan face appears to be shaped like the edge of a dish (or plate). In addition to this unusual facial structure, orangutans have lateral incisors that are considerably smaller than their medial incisors.

Gorillas (Gorillinae)   Another type of great ape is the gorilla (genus *Gorilla*) (**FIGURE 10.26**). Gorillas are classified in the hominid family along with orangutans, but they are placed in a separate subfamily (Gorillinae) (see Figure 10.5). Gorillas live in forests in equatorial Africa. Some gorillas live in highlands, while others live in lowlands; thus, they have some minor differences in their lifestyles and features. In general, gorillas (especially the males) are very large; they are actually the largest of the primates. Since they are so large, they are more terrestrial than many of the other apes. There are significant differences between male and female gorillas, including the trademark silver fur color seen on the backs of adult males, but not females. Gorillas are diurnal and live in relatively large social groups. They also eat a lot of leaves, far more than any other ape. The gorilla cranium is very robust. This robusticity mostly relates to their heavy plant diet and the extensive chewing it requires.

Chimpanzees and Bonobos (Panini)   Chimpanzees and bonobos are great apes in the family Hominidae. They are the closest living relatives of humans, and they are classified with humans in the subfamily Homininae to reflect this. Within the hominine subfamily, both chimpanzees and bonobos belong to the tribe Panini and the genus *Pan*, indicating their particularly close relationship to each other (see Figure 10.5). Chimpanzees (**FIGURE 10.27**) are classified as *Pan troglodytes*, and bonobos (**FIGURE 10.28**) are classified as *Pan paniscus*.

Both chimpanzees and bonobos live in equatorial Africa, but the chimpanzee is found in several areas (including parts of western equatorial Africa) while the bonobo is limited to a particular area of the Democratic Republic of the Congo. The two species are separated by the Congo River (known in the past as the Zaire River), and they are not found in overlapping areas. Chimpanzees often live in territories shared by gorillas, but gorillas do not live in the area where bonobos are found.

Chimpanzees and bonobos are smaller than the other great apes, but larger than the lesser apes. They are diurnal and spend some of their time in the trees and some on the ground. Both species eat a wide variety of foods, including fruit, leaves, nuts, insects, and small animals. Their crania are relatively robust, but not nearly as robust as those of gorillas. They live in large social groups, and there are some differences between adult males and females of the same species.

There are some important physical and behavioral differences between bonobos and chimpanzees that help distinguish them as different species. Bonobos tend to have longer, leaner bodies than chimpanzees. They are also a little more arboreal than chimpanzees. The major differences between the two species relate to their levels of aggression and sexual activity. Chimpanzees tend to be more violent and have fewer sexual interactions. In contrast, bonobos tend to be less violent and have frequent (often nonreproductive) sexual interactions.

Humans (Hominini)   Humans (*Homo sapiens*) are apes too! As described above, humans are classified in the same hominine subfamily as chimpanzees and bonobos. Humans are then

FIGURE 10.26 Gorillas
Gorillas are large-bodied apes that inhabit equatorial forests in Africa, where they eat a lot of leaves.

FIGURE 10.27 Chimpanzees
One of the best-known apes, chimpanzees live in equatorial African forests. Sometimes their territories overlap with gorilla ranges.

separated from these other species in the tribe Hominini (see Figure 10.5). Compared with other primates, humans have larger brains relative to their body size, faces that are flatter (more orthognathic), and smaller relative tooth sizes.

Martin Harvey/Alamy Stock Photo

Roy Toft/National Geographic Image Collection/Getty Images

Michael Nichols/National Geographic Image Collection/Getty Images

FIGURE 10.28 Bonobos
Found only in a particular area of the Democratic Republic of the Congo, bonobos are a little more arboreal, and have longer, leaner bodies, than chimpanzees.

They have generalized diets, limited sexual dimorphism, and numerous adaptations for walking on two legs. Because many of the labs in this text are devoted to humans, we will not discuss them at length here. We do, however, want to highlight that humans are apes that fit within the broader context of living primate groups.

ONGOING PRIMATE TAXONOMY RESEARCH

As we saw earlier in this lab and in Lab 9, classification can be tricky, and researchers do not always agree on classification schemes. This situation is further complicated by ongoing research that results in the identification of new species. How could there be new primate species? Haven't we been all over the world and documented all of them already? Sometimes, even if scientists and communities have lived in or visited an area for many years, the nonhuman primates in that region are difficult to observe. Perhaps they are very small, are active only at night, or live high up in trees. Any of these characteristics would make it unlikely that the primate would be well known to humans.

As we have seen here, the primate order has continued to evolve and diversify throughout its 65-million-year history (**FIGURE 10.29**). At the same time, it is possible that the populations are so small, and the differences between species so subtle, that it takes years for scientists to collect enough data to distinguish the groups. This was the case with the orangutan species (*Pongo tapanuliensis*) recently identified in Sumatra. The Tapanuli orangutan was first discovered in 1997, but it took two decades to systematically study the small population and compare it with other orangutans. Researchers collected data on the orangutans' physical traits, behaviors, and genetics before concluding that this population of fewer than 800 orangutans living in the Batang Toru ecosystem of North Sumatra was in fact a distinct species that first diverged from other Sumatran orangutans around 3.4 million years ago, then became completely isolated around 10,000 to 20,000 years ago.

Similar discoveries have been made in recent years in other primate groups. For example, after noting that the hoolock gibbons in China's Yunnan Province had different vocalizations and physical traits than other hoolock gibbons, scientists began studying and comparing their features and genes. They discovered that these gibbons were a distinct species (*Hoolock tianxing*), commonly now referred to as the Skywalker hoolock gibbon, in reference to both the *Star Wars* films and the Chinese characters of its species name, meaning "Heaven's movement." Although Skywalker hoolock gibbons were known and had been photographed 100 years earlier, their status as a separate species was determined only recently (in 2017) after those systematic comparisons and genetic analyses.

Note that in both the orangutan and gibbon cases, people knew of the primates long before scientific research confirmed their distinct spe-

FIGURE 10.29 Evolutionary Overview of the Primate Order
The different types of primates evolved gradually over time.

cies designations. Because scientific research is a painstaking process that relies on multiple lines of evidence and the accumulation of extensive data, it often takes a great deal of time to thoroughly document separate species. Research progress may be further delayed by limited access to particular data sets, such as skeletal material that is collected only after animals have died in the wild. The slow pace of research may also be compounded by remote habitats and low population numbers among the studied groups. Both the Tapanuli orangutan and Skywalker hoolock gibbon have incredibly small wild populations, and the Tapanuli orangutan is officially recognized as critically endangered. This status draws additional attention to primate conservation issues (see Lab 11 for more information).

CONCEPT REVIEW QUESTIONS

Name: _____ Section: _____

Course: _____ Date: _____

Answer the following questions in the space provided.

1. List *three* traits found in primates that distinguish them from other mammals.

2. Which of the following primate groups is most closely related to lemurs?
    A. Lorises
    B. Tarsiers
    C. Humans
    D. New World monkeys

3. Lorises:
    A. rely heavily on their vision.
    B. have large bodies.
    C. eat a diet of mostly leaves.
    D. are nocturnal.

4. What is the only place on Earth where you can find lemurs living in the wild?

5. Describe *one* trait that tarsiers share with lorises and lemurs. Describe *one* trait that tarsiers share with the anthropoids.

6. Describe *one* trait that distinguishes the platyrrhines and catarrhines. (Be sure to describe how the trait differs between the two groups.)

7. Which of the following traits is found in some New World monkeys and none of the Old World monkeys?
    A. Arboreal lifestyle
    B. Diet emphasizing fruit
    C. Prehensile tail
    D. Ischial callosities

8. I live in the forests of central Africa. I am arboreal and have a long tail. I have bilophodont molars, and I have a diet that includes a lot of leaves. What type of primate am I?
    A. Ape
    B. Colobine
    C. New World monkey
    D. Cercopithecine

9. List *two* traits that are found in apes but not in other primates.

10. I live in the forests of Southeast Asia. I am arboreal and swing through the trees. I have Y-5 molars, and I eat a lot of fruit. I live in small social groups, where males and females work together to defend the territory and raise offspring. What type of primate am I?

    A. Orangutan
    B. Gorilla
    C. Bonobo
    D. Gibbon

LAB EXERCISES

Name: _____   Section: _____

Course: _____   Date: _____

EXERCISE 1 DISTINGUISHING MAMMALS AND PRIMATES

Work in a small group or alone to complete this exercise. Use the mystery mammals provided by your instructor (or the photos in the Lab 10 Exercise Image Library on p. 303) to complete the chart below. Identify whether the mystery mammal is a primate and list *at least one* trait that helped you make this determination. (Your instructor may request that you provide more distinguishing traits.)

	Primate (Yes or No)?	Trait(s)
Mystery Mammal A		
Mystery Mammal B		

EXERCISE 2 LORISES AND LEMURS

Work in a small group or alone to complete this exercise.

PART A

Use the primate material provided by your instructor (or the photos in the Lab 10 Exercise Image Library on p. 304) to complete the chart below. Identify whether the primate is nocturnal or diurnal and list *at least one* trait that helped you make this determination. (Your instructor may request that you provide more distinguishing traits.)

	Nocturnal or Diurnal?	Trait(s)
Primate A		
Primate B		

PART B

Use the primate crania provided by your instructor (or the photos in the Lab 10 Exercise Image Library on p. 304) to complete the chart below. Identify whether the primate is a lemur or an anthropoid and list *at least one* trait that helped you make this determination. (Your instructor may request that you provide more distinguishing traits.)

	Lemur or Anthropoid?	Trait(s)
Primate A		
Primate B		

EXERCISE 3 TARSIERS

Work in a small group or alone to complete this exercise. Review the material provided by your instructor (or the photos in the Lab 10 Exercise Image Library on p. 305).

1. Tarsiers have an unusual mix of anatomical features. Describe *at least one* anatomical trait that is unique to tarsiers.

2. Are tarsiers more closely related to lemurs and lorises or to monkeys and apes? Describe *three* anatomical traits that can be used as evidence to support your answer.

EXERCISE 4 DISTINGUISHING NEW WORLD MONKEYS AND OLD WORLD MONKEYS

Work in a small group or alone to complete this exercise. Use the monkey crania provided by your instructor (or the photos in the Lab 10 Exercise Image Library on p. 305) to answer the following questions.

1. Which of these monkeys is a New World monkey?

2. Which of these monkeys is an Old World monkey?

3. Describe *at least two* traits you used to make these determinations. (Be sure to describe how each trait differs between the two monkeys.)

EXERCISE 5 DISTINGUISHING OLD WORLD MONKEYS AND APES

Work in a small group or alone to complete this exercise.

PART A

Use the primate crania provided by your instructor (or the drawings of lower premolar and molar teeth in the Lab 10 Exercise Image Library on p. 306) to complete the chart below. Identify whether the primate is an Old World monkey or an ape and list *at least one* dental trait that helped you make this determination. (Your instructor may request that you provide more distinguishing traits.)

	Old World Monkey or Ape?	Dental Trait(s)
Primate A		
Primate B		

 Name: ______________ Date: ________

PART B

Use the primate material provided by your instructor (or the photos in the Lab 10 Exercise Image Library on p. 306) to complete the chart below. Identify whether the primate is an Old World monkey or an ape and list *at least one* nondental trait that helped you make this determination. (Your instructor may request that you provide more distinguishing traits.)

	Old World Monkey or Ape?	Nondental Trait(s)
Primate A		
Primate B		

CRITICAL THINKING QUESTIONS

On a separate sheet of paper, answer the following questions.

1. Use material in your classroom, online, or in books to find images and descriptions of two nonprimate mammals (such as dogs, horses, dolphins, or raccoons). What traits do these animals share with primates? What important primate traits do they lack?

2. Most primates are arboreal, and living in this environmental context poses great challenges. Describe at least one specific problem or challenge a primate might encounter in a forested environment (consider things like movement, finding/accessing food, and finding mates). Now, identify at least one trait that primates have that helps them solve this problem. Which of these traits (if any) do you have? What does this suggest about your ancient primate relatives?

3. Nocturnal primates often have larger eyes and better senses of smell than do other primates. Choose one nocturnal primate species or group. Describe its eyes and its traits related to olfaction (smell). Why would these primates have these traits? Consider their environmental context and lifestyle, and describe the adaptive significance of each trait (how does it help them?).

4. The National Primate Research Center at the University of Wisconsin-Madison has assembled taxonomic information about living primates into "primate factsheets" on the following website: http://pin.primate.wisc.edu/factsheets. Visit this website and choose a factsheet for one primate species (or genus). Describe the geographic distribution of this primate and a few of its anatomical and behavioral traits. Then, identify its larger taxonomic group (loris, lemur, tarsier, New World monkey, Old World monkey, or ape). Finally, describe how its geographic distribution and traits justify its classification as a member of this taxonomic group.

5. This lab began with the story of Ham, a chimpanzee who was sent into space by NASA in the 1960s as part of early test flights for space travel. Since this time, we have gained a greater appreciation for how closely related we are to chimpanzees and how similar we are in behaviors and intelligences. With this knowledge in mind, do you think that chimpanzees should still be used in research of this type today? Why or why not? Do you think the same rules should apply to all primates (those that are less closely related to humans, such as monkeys, as well as those that are more closely related to humans, such as apes)? Why or why not? Do you think we should limit the use of nonhuman primates in research—for example, by using them only in lifesaving medical research? Why or why not? Visit the website of the American Society of Primatologists and explore its ethical guidelines (https://www.asp.org/society/resolutions/EthicalTreatmentOfNonHumanPrimates.cfm). Use this information to support your answers.

6. In this lab, we reviewed several different primate groups and the traits that distinguish them. To help you make comparisons across these primate groups and understand larger trends in primate traits, complete the following Living Primate Chart.

7. Use your completed Living Primate Chart (on next page) to answer the following questions.

   A. Identify one geographic region that has numerous types of nonhuman primates living there today. What primates live there?
   B. Identify one geographic region that does not have any wild nonhuman primates living there today. Why might nonhuman primates be rare there?
   C. Choose one strepsirhine primate and one haplorhine primate, and list at least two traits they have in common. List at least two traits that distinguish them. What do these traits suggest about their evolutionary relationship and classification?
   D. Choose any two haplorhine primate groups, and list at least two traits they have in common. List at least two traits that distinguish them. What do these traits suggest about their evolutionary relationship and classification?
   E. Identify a diet that is found in more than one primate group. Which primates have this diet?
   F. Identify a form of locomotion that is found in more than one primate group. Which primates have this locomotion?
   G. With which nonhuman primate group do you have the most in common? Which traits do you share? What do these traits suggest about your evolutionary relationships and classification?

LIVING PRIMATE CHART

Primate Group	Geographic Location	3 to 5 Anatomical Traits	Diet	Primary Locomotion
Lorises (Strepsirhini: Lorisoidea)				
Lemurs (Strepsirhini: Lemuroidea)				
Tarsiers (Haplorhini: Tarsiiformes)				
New World Monkeys (Haplorhini: Ceboidea)				
Old World Monkeys (Haplorhini: Cercopithecoidea)				
Gibbons and Siamangs (Haplorhini: Hominoidea)				
Orangutans (Haplorhini: Hominoidea)				
Gorillas (Haplorhini: Hominoidea)				
Chimpanzees and Bonobos (Haplorhini: Hominoidea)				

LAB 10 EXERCISE IMAGE LIBRARY

Students should use these images only if directed to by their instructor.

EXERCISE 1 DISTINGUISHING MAMMALS AND PRIMATES

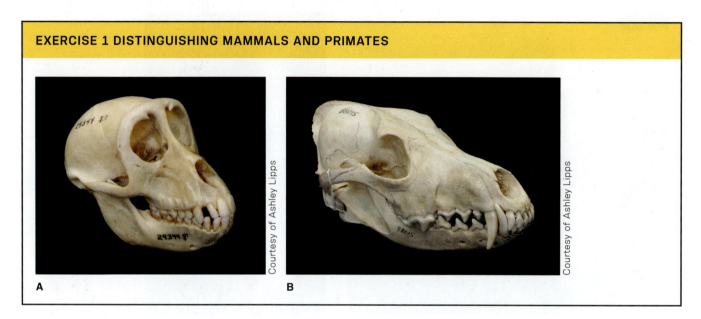

A

B

Courtesy of Ashley Lipps

Courtesy of Ashley Lipps

EXERCISE 2 LORISES AND LEMURS

PART A

A

Frederick Mark Sheridan-Johnson/Alamy Stock Photo

B

DLILLC/Corbis/VCG/Getty Images

PART B

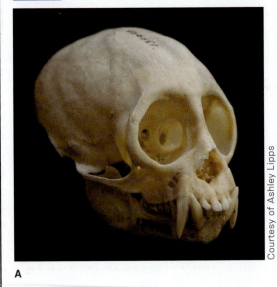

A

Courtesy of Ashley Lipps

B

Courtesy of Ashley Lipps

Note: *These crania are shown at the same scale.*

EXERCISE 3 TARSIERS

A

Harri Pekkinen/Alamy Stock Photo

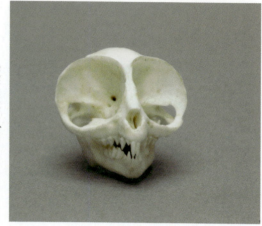

B

Bone Clones/boneclones.com

EXERCISE 4 DISTINGUISHING NEW WORLD MONKEYS AND OLD WORLD MONKEYS

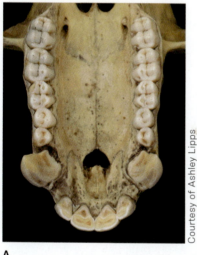

A

Courtesy of Ashley Lipps

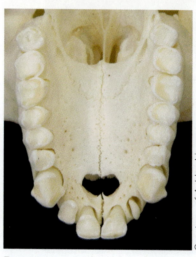

B

Courtesy of Ashley Lipps

EXERCISE 5 DISTINGUISHING OLD WORLD MONKEYS AND APES

PART A

A   B

Note: *These drawings show the lower premolars and molars from two mystery primates.*

PART B

apple2499/shutterstock

raliand/Shutterstock

A   B

BIOLOGICAL ANTHROPOLOGY IN PRACTICE

Climbing Trees and Conducting Biochemical Analyses to Learn about Our Ape Relatives

Dr. Vicky Oelze is a biological anthropologist who uses biochemical analyses to better understand primate ecology and behavior (see Labs 11 and 12). Growing up, Vicky was fascinated by animals and their behavior. As she got older, she questioned the differences between humans and other animals and wondered why animals were not afforded more of the same rights as people. Biological anthropology was the perfect discipline to help her explore these issues and learn more about great ape culture and social intelligence.

In Vicky's current work, she uses chemical analysis to help detect behaviors in nonhuman apes that are difficult or impossible to observe directly in the field. For her, it is particularly important to limit interference with the animals and their natural environment, so she uses creative and noninvasive methods to collect the data she needs. Vicky and her research collaborators collect samples of hair and feces that are left behind naturally by the apes being studied. This often requires climbing into trees to collect samples from ape sleeping nests after the animals have left for the day. In this way, the researchers can collect the samples they need without disturbing the primates or exposing them too much to humans, who might inadvertently interfere with their behaviors or spread diseases.

After the samples are collected, they are brought to Vicky's lab at the University of California, Santa Cruz, where they are carefully prepared and then processed through a mass spectrometer, a device that measures the relative masses of atoms. These data are compared with a known standard to determine an isotopic signature, which represents the relative proportion of isotopes (or variants) for a specific element (such as oxygen, carbon, or nitrogen). In Lab 13, we discuss how radioactive isotopes are used to help date fossil sites, but nonradioactive (or stable) isotopes can be used in anthropological research as well. Stable isotope ratios vary based on climate, type of food consumed, and the local environment, so archaeologists and paleoanthropologists can use stable isotope analysis to reconstruct past climates, diets (see Lab 15), and migration patterns.

Vicky uses stable isotopes ratios from ape hair and feces to reconstruct what the apes are eating in the present day. For example, she tries to detect how much monkey meat a chimpanzee eats after hunting and meat sharing (see Lab 11). This information provides valuable insights into ape social behavior and nutrition that would be difficult to obtain using only direct observations. Similarly, it can be challenging to observe young primates who are nursing from their mothers while sitting high up in trees, but Vicky uses stable isotopes collected from the feces of juvenile bonobos to determine the age at which the bonobos are weaned from their mothers' milk. Vicky's reconstructions of great ape diets also help us understand broader patterns of primate ecology, such as how gorillas and chimpanzees can coexist in the same forest by having different dietary specializations (see Lab 12 for more on primate diets).

By combining field observations and quantitative lab work, Vicky and her team have contributed to our knowledge of the lives of great apes. In Labs 11 and 12, you, too, will perform a mix of observational and quantitative research to assess primate behavior and ecology.

Dr. Vicky Oelze climbs trees to collect African chimpanzee hairs left behind after the apes depart their sleeping nests, but she also collects plant samples in the tree canopy, as seen here.

Gorillas are often portrayed as aggressive and beastly, along the lines of the exaggerated character in the movie *King Kong*. In reality, however, gorillas are usually peaceful and calm.

Lab Learning Objectives

By the end of this lab, students should be able to:

- describe the differences between laboratory and field primate studies.

- make observations of primate behavior, collecting both quantitative and qualitative data.

- discuss how primate ecology affects primate social life.

- differentiate between the forms of primate social organization.

- describe examples of "cultural" behaviors in nonhuman primates.

LAB 11

Primate Behavior

With the release of the film *King Kong* in 1933, gorillas stormed the popular imagination as aggressive and frightening beasts. In the most famous scene of the film, an oversized gorilla-like creature kidnaps a woman and climbs the Empire State Building in New York City with the woman in tow. The great marauding beast is then brought down by biplanes firing a rain of bullets. For many people this was the first popular and iconic image of gorillas, and it has been reinforced by contemporary media representations, including militant gorillas in the *Planet of the Apes* franchise and a kidnapping gorilla in the *Donkey Kong* video game series. Yet the true nature of gorillas is far from this fictionalized exaggeration.

Through the fieldwork of Dian Fossey and other primatologists beginning in the late 1960s, we have gained a much clearer understanding of gorilla behavior. Gorillas do engage in some aggressive and violent behaviors, particularly when their infants are threatened or when a new male assumes control of a group, but this violence is relatively uncommon. Instead, they are among the gentlest nonhuman primates. Gorillas spend most of their time eating leafy vegetation and resting. They regularly engage in soft vocalizations that symbolize their contentment and social bonds, and they form strong attachments to other members of their social group, particularly infants.

The realities of primate behavior are often very different from our fictitious imaginings. The raging King Kong character that kidnaps women

captive primate study research conducted with primates in captivity (in laboratories or zoos)

field primate study research conducted with primates in their wild habitat

is very unlike the real male gorilla who sits contentedly with his offspring during an afternoon period of rest in the African forests. As biological anthropologists, it is important that we move beyond popular stereotypes and try to understand the true behaviors of our various primate relatives. These behaviors provide the context necessary to understand our own behaviors and how we are similar to and different from other primates.

INTRODUCTION

In this lab, we explore the behavior of living primates to better understand our own biological context. We begin with a look at how researchers study primates in captivity and in the wild. We then outline typical affiliative and aggressive primate behaviors. We also consider the various forms of social organization found in primates, as well as how food availability affects these social groups. We discuss primate sexual behavior, with a particular look at the unusual practices of bonobos, and we review some of the

learned practices among nonhuman primates that resemble human culture. We conclude with a consideration of the complexity of primate field research in the face of rapidly declining primate population sizes and growing primate species endangerment.

STUDYING PRIMATES

There are generally two different contexts for conducting primate research: captive contexts and field contexts. Each research context has benefits and drawbacks, and each is more or less suitable for different research topics. A **captive primate study** is a research program that is conducted with primates in captivity (in laboratories or zoos). These contexts provide a controlled environment. The researcher can often work with a primate or group of primates for their whole lives, and the researcher can carefully select primates of the appropriate age and sex to study. In captive contexts, researchers can also expose nonhuman primates to human-like tasks and skills to test their capability for human-like thought processing and behavior. For these reasons, captive studies are often used to assess such things as nonhuman primate language capacity and problem-solving skills.

Captive contexts are not well suited to researching more "natural" behaviors and circumstances that occur in the wild, such as group interactions, resource use, territory defense, and primate health. For research along these lines, primatologists turn to field studies (**FIGURE 11.1**). A **field primate study** is a research program conducted with primates in their wild habitat. Field studies are conducted in less controlled environments than captive studies. The researcher may have trouble locating and observing primates that travel often or live at high levels of the forest canopy. The researcher may also have little choice about the age and sex of the primates available for study. For example, a primatologist may set out to research the interactions between infants and their mothers in the wild and then be unable to find any infants in the study area. While the lack of control can make field studies challenging,

Courtesy of Dawn Kitchen

FIGURE 11.1 Primate Field Studies
In order to understand how nonhuman primates behave in the wild, primatologists conduct primate field studies.

these contexts are well suited to investigations of wild primate behaviors. Researchers can observe primate social interactions, food-gathering processes, territory defense, vocalization patterns, and any other behaviors that occur in wild, natural settings. Of course, even in the wild, non-human primates are impacted by encroaching human populations (see the Exploring Further section in this lab) and the presence of the human researchers themselves. However, field studies are the closest we can get to a "natural" nonhuman primate context.

Whether conducting primate research in the captive context or in the field context, the primatologist must consider two things: (1) Will the data collected be qualitative or quantitative? (2) Will observations be made of a primate group or an individual? The answers to these two questions will often depend on the primatologist's hypotheses (or research questions), and how the primatologist answers them will dramatically affect how the work is conducted. **Qualitative data** are descriptive and center on the *qualities* that are observed (such as appearance and smell). This kind of data often provides rich detail and additional contextual information. For example, observations of a primate and detailed descriptions of its appearance and all its behaviors would be qualitative data. The details of the behavior may not be readily comparable with data from other primates, but those details can be helpful in providing more contextual information for making interpretations. Qualitative data are helpful for research that is descriptive, such as reporting previously unknown behavior.

In contrast, **quantitative data** are more focused and clearly measurable. These data are the measurable *quantities* observed (such as the number of instances of a behavior). They often provide information that is good for making comparisons. For instance, observations of a primate that note when and how many times the primate performs specific behaviors (such as grooming or vocalizing) would constitute quantitative data. A record of how many times a primate vocalizes within a time period can be easily compared with similar records for other primates. Quantitative data are helpful for research

that emphasizes comparisons, such as contrasting the behavior patterns of males and females or of young and old primates.

In many instances, researchers use a combination of qualitative and quantitative data. For example, a primatologist that is researching vocalization patterns between mothers and their infants may collect qualitative data about the vocalizations that describe the sounds and corresponding gestures or body language that are made. The primatologist might also collect quantitative data about how often the mothers and infants vocalize at certain times of day or under certain circumstances.

In addition to deciding whether quantitative data, qualitative data, or a combination of both will be used, the primatologist must also consider whether to observe a group of primates or focus on individual primates. As with the type of data collected, there are benefits and drawbacks to each option. When primatologists observe the behavior of multiple primates simultaneously, they are conducting a **group observation**. Group observations allow researchers to collect data about how primates interact with one another, such as how they share food, have sex, build social bonds, and communicate. However, it is often difficult to observe numerous primates at one time, so a single researcher is likely to miss some behaviors and individual variations that occur outside the line of sight. Instead, the primatologist could choose to do a **focused observation** by focusing attention on the behaviors of a single individual at a time. Focused observations allow researchers to collect data about individual behavioral variations, such as unusual practices seen in a particular primate. Focused observations are also useful for observing behaviors that may be more private and conducted alone, such as giving birth or collecting food. However, when researchers are focusing on one primate, they may miss some of the broader social context and important social interactions of a larger group. As with qualitative and quantitative data, primatologists often use a combination of group and focused observations. For example, if researchers wanted to study chimpanzee diets, they would probably

qualitative data
descriptive data about the qualities that are observed

quantitative data
focused and clearly measurable data

group observation
the observation of many individuals simultaneously

focused observation
the observation of a single individual at a time

affiliative behavior
behavior that is generally cooperative

grooming the removal of foreign objects (such as insects or plant parts) from another primate's fur

affiliative communication
verbal or nonverbal communication that reinforces social relationships.

vocalization a verbal communication

aggressive behavior behavior that challenges, threatens, or harms others

threat display an action (such as flashing the teeth) that seeks to threaten others from a distance

conduct group observations of chimpanzees congregating to eat leaves. However, the researchers would also probably want to observe chimpanzees collecting and eating other resources, such as ants. This would require focused observations because chimpanzees tend to collect these resources independently, rather than in large groups.

AFFILIATIVE BEHAVIOR

What types of behaviors do primates practice? In general, primatologists tend to characterize primate social behavior as one of two types: affiliative behavior and aggressive behavior. **Affiliative behavior** is behavior that is generally cooperative. It reinforces social bonds and affiliations. The most common form of affiliative behavior in primates is **grooming (FIGURE 11.2)**. Primates often pick through each other's fur and remove insects or plant parts. Sometimes they eat the removed materials, such as the insects. Grooming generally promotes good health and hygiene by keeping the fur clean and free of pests. In addition, grooming is a soothing behavior that relaxes the primate

being groomed and reinforces social bonds. Often lower-ranking individuals will groom higher-ranking individuals as a sign of submission, and males and females will groom each other to reinforce mating relationships. Humans also engage in grooming behavior to promote social bonds. Parents often make a ritual or game out of bath time and hair brushing. This relaxes the children and strengthens their bonds with their parents. Similarly, adults often find themselves relaxed by the experience of having their hair washed at the salon and are more open to conversation with the hair stylist afterward.

In addition to grooming, primates engage in a range of **affiliative communications**. These communications, which reinforce social relationships, may be verbal or nonverbal. Nonverbal communications often take the form of embracing gestures, such as the grooming hand clasp seen in some chimpanzees. This gesture is a combination of typical grooming behavior and hand holding. The action communicates social connectedness and bonding. Verbal communications usually take the form of **vocalizations**, particular sounds that communicate different types of information. Many primates, such as gorillas, have particular vocalizations that indicate contentment and satisfaction. These sounds are made when individuals are relaxed, and they reinforce the general sense of social connection between the primates involved.

AGGRESSIVE BEHAVIOR

The second category of primate behavior is **aggressive behavior**. Aggressive behavior is anything that challenges, threatens, or harms the primates involved. The most common types of aggressive behaviors are threats. Direct violence is dangerous, and any primates directly involved or in close proximity can be injured. Therefore, most primates try to avoid fighting and use **threat displays** instead. These displays are actions that highlight the actor's strength from a distance. They are meant to threaten potential enemies and scare them into submission before

Duncan McKay/Alamy Stock Photo

FIGURE 11.2 Chimpanzee Grooming
Primates often engage in grooming as a way to strengthen social bonds and maintain good hygiene. Grooming is an example of an affiliative behavior.

violence breaks out. Threat displays take a variety of forms. One of the most common is the **threat yawn**, which is an opening of the mouth that displays the teeth (**FIGURE 11.3**). It is called a yawn because it involves wide opening of the mouth, not because it is a motion triggered by being tired. This display allows the yawner to warn others that a fight would expose them to the dangers of the yawner's very large teeth. Many primates engage in threat yawns or similar displays of teeth, such as flipping the upper lip to expose the top teeth. Other threat displays take a variety of forms, including stomping up and down, thrashing tree branches, or banging fists on the ground. In all of these cases, the loud noise and violent body movements are meant to herald the potential for further violence.

Not all aggressive encounters end with threats. Many primate species regularly engage in direct violence. This is particularly true when males are fighting one another for access to females or territory. Chimpanzees are perhaps the most violent primates in the wild. They often engage in violent attacks. These attacks are usually per-

petrated by adult males against other adult males and females; however, adult females also attack other adult females with some frequency. In addition, adults of both sexes are known to attack adolescents and juveniles. But in general, males attack more often than females. The most violent chimpanzee attacks are usually directed at outsider chimpanzees from nearby groups. Chimpanzee males have even been known to patrol the boundaries of their territory and attack stray chimpanzees found near their borders. Violent attacks often involve biting, scratching, and beating, and they can result in serious injury and death.

In some primates, aggressive behavior includes a practice known as **infanticide**. This term refers to the killing of infants or young members of the species. Unlike the infanticide occasionally seen in humans, where a person kills his or her own children, infanticide in nonhuman primates usually involves killing the offspring of another individual. In most of these cases, the infanticide seems to be related to the reproductive potential of the infant's mother. When a nonhuman primate is breast-feeding, she is less fertile and less likely to become pregnant. (Note that in human primates, breast-feeding does not necessarily suppress fertility in the same way.) When a new male takes over a group that includes females who are breast-feeding their offspring, the male is likely to kill those offspring. The male did not sire these infants because he is new to the group and has not had sex with the females. As long as the females are breast-feeding, they will not produce any offspring with the new male. Therefore, the male kills the present infants, and the females become capable of producing his offspring. We also see infanticide when a new female with an infant migrates into an existing group. Again, the male or males of the group know the infant is not their own, and it is killed to allow the incoming female to mate with the male or males of the group. The practice of infanticide may have been selected because it increases the reproductive success of the perpetrators. Males who kill infants that are not their own are able to mate with the newly lactating mothers and pass on their genes more frequently.

threat yawn an opening of the mouth that displays the teeth in a threatening manner

infanticide the killing of infants or young members of the species

Norbert Rosing/National Geographic Creative

FIGURE 11.3 Baboon Threat Yawn
Primates often use threat displays to warn off enemies. This baboon's threat yawn is a common example of this type of aggressive behavior.

primate ecology
the study of the relationship between primates and their environments

fission–fusion
a type of social organization that involves the fission of a large group into smaller groups to pursue sparsely distributed resources and the fusion of the smaller groups back into a large group at other times

social hierarchy
the assignment and distribution of different social status positions in a group

PRIMATE ECOLOGY

Primates lead complicated social lives, and as with most animals, their social lives are affected to some extent by their environmental circumstances. Understanding these relationships falls under the heading of **primate ecology**. This term refers to the study of the relationship between primates and their environments. Primate ecology research has shown that primate group structure in particular is influenced by food availability and the risk of predator attacks.

In situations where food is scarce, there are not enough resources to support large primate groups. For example, primates that hunt insects as their primary food source tend to live in smaller groups because insects are scarce. One stick insect or beetle will not feed a large group. Even a tree full of many insects will still not provide enough food for a large group to regularly eat together. Similarly, primates that eat a lot of fruit may live in smaller groups, depending on the availability of fruit in their area. While we often assume that a tropical forest is full of fruit trees that provide food year-round, in reality fruit trees may be scattered throughout the forest and bear fruit infrequently. Thus, small groups are common among fruit eaters. Occasionally, we see primates take another approach to dealing with sparse resources. Some primates, such as chimpanzees, will spend most of their time in a large group but will separate into smaller groups when they pursue food that is sparsely distributed in their territory. This type of social organization is called a **fission–fusion** structure. The group fissions into smaller subgroups when they seek sparsely distributed foods, and they fuse back together when they seek other foods or sleep at night.

In contrast to the small social groups we usually find when food is sparse, primates often form much larger social groups when their food is abundant. For example, many primates that emphasize leaves and plants in their diets follow this pattern. These primates tend to live in forests or grasslands where plant food is abundant, so they can form large groups that eat and live together. Even primates that do not normally live in large groups may congregate in large groups when food is temporarily abundant. For example, adult orangutans usually spend their time alone because the fruit they eat is very sparsely distributed in their environment and does not normally support multiple adults at one time. Sometimes, however, there is a temporary abundance of fruit in a particular tree or location. In these instances, many adults from the extended area will congregate in a much larger social group for as long as the food lasts.

In addition to resource distribution, primate group size is influenced by predation risk. Most primates have numerous predators to fear in their habitats, including big cats, birds of prey, large reptiles, and sometimes other primates. If there is a high risk of attack by predators in an area, a larger social group is favored because it provides extra eyes and ears to detect danger. It also decreases the chance that a particular individual will be killed. If you live in a group of 3 and are attacked by a predator, there is a 1 in 3 chance you will be the one killed. If you live in a group of 30 and are attacked by a predator, there is now only a 1 in 30 chance you will be the one killed.

Like other animals, primates must always strike a balance between having a large enough group to protect against predation and a small enough group that everyone has access to food. For some primates, resource availability is more important, especially if predation risk is low. For other primates, predation risk is more important, especially if food is abundant.

PRIMATE SOCIAL ORGANIZATION

Within most primate social groups, especially large ones, there is a complex **social hierarchy**. As in our own societies, some individuals have a higher status than other individuals. Often this status is inherited, and an infant is born into a higher or lower status based on the rank of its mother or father. These hierarchies are important because they affect a primate's access to food and mating partners. Generally, individuals of higher status have better access to food and mates, while individuals of lower status have less access to food and mates. Primate social hierarchies are not completely set in stone. There is usually some room for changing one's social status.

Often, forming **coalitions** facilitates negotiating the social hierarchy within large, complex social groups. Multiple individuals may work together in a coalition against others outside the coalition. For example, the individuals in a coalition may work together to overthrow others and assume their status, or they may work together to maintain their own social status and avoid being overthrown by others. Perhaps the best-known coalitions are those formed by male chimpanzees. These coalitions involve complex social relationships. They may be temporary and fluid, depending on individual needs at a given time, or they may be long-lasting alliances. These coalitions are often reinforced through affiliative behavior, such as grooming and sharing food.

Primates are very social animals, and primate social groups can take a variety of forms. Sometimes group structure will vary from one species to the next, and sometimes primates from the same species will have very different group structures due to differences in their local food availability and predation risk. Here, we will describe the six types of primate social organization: solitary, monogamy, polyandry, single-male polygyny, multimale polygyny, and bachelor groups. For each type of social organization, we will describe the general pattern and provide examples of primates who practice this pattern in the wild.

Solitary

A **solitary** social structure is one where adults spend most of their time alone (**FIGURE 11.4**). Adult females (and their offspring) occupy separate, individual territories. An adult male will occupy a territory that overlaps with female territories, giving him access to the females as mating partners. There may also be free-ranging adults that do not occupy a specific territory. These free-ranging adults may have less access

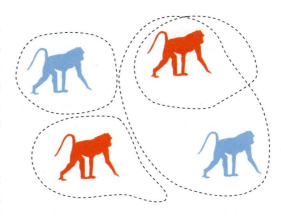

FIGURE 11.4 Solitary Social Organization
In solitary primates, each adult female (red), along with her offspring, occupies a separate territory (dashed lines). An adult male (blue) occupies a territory that overlaps with the territory of one or more females. There may also be free-ranging adults.

to food and mates than adults in specific territories. When studying primates with a solitary social structure, a researcher is unlikely to see multiple adults together in the wild. However, even though these adults spend a lot of time alone, they are not asocial. They often engage in social behavior and interactions, particularly if they temporarily congregate in larger groups when food is more abundant. The solitary social structure is seen in orangutans as well as in some lemurs and lorises.

Monogamy

Monogamy is a social structure where groups are composed of one adult male, one adult female, and their offspring (**FIGURE 11.5**). A mated pair

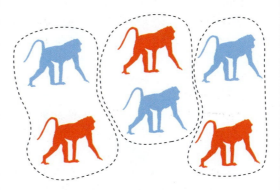

FIGURE 11.5 Monogamous Social Organization
In monogamous primates, an adult female (red), an adult male (blue), and their offspring occupy a territory together. Their territory is separate from the territories of other adult pairs.

coalition a group of primates that work together against other members of their social group

solitary spending most of one's time alone; refers to a form of social organization where adult females (and their offspring) occupy separate territories, and an adult male occupies a territory that overlaps with those of several females

monogamy a form of social organization where one adult male, one adult female, and their offspring live together

polyandry a form of social organization where one adult female, multiple adult males, and their offspring live together

polygyny a form of social organization where there are multiple adult females for each male

single-male polygyny a form of social organization where one adult male, multiple adult females, and their offspring live together

multimale polygyny a form of social organization where multiple adult males, multiple adult females, and their offspring live together

lives together, sometimes for most of their reproductive lives. They often work together to raise their offspring and defend their territory against outsiders. Some lemurs and many tarsiers practice monogamy. In addition, some of the New World monkeys, especially several types of marmosets, live in monogamous groups. Among the apes, the gibbons and siamangs (the lesser apes) have a monogamous social structure as well.

Polyandry

Poly means "multiple," and *andry* refers to males. **Polyandry** is a particularly rare form of social organization where one adult female, multiple adult males, and their offspring live together (**FIGURE 11.6**). This form of social organization is seen only in some New World monkeys, especially the tamarins. These primates are very small and often give birth to twins. Having an additional male or males in the group allows for each offspring to be looked after by an adult while leaving at least one adult unencumbered and able to feed or defend the group as needed. If the additional adults were females, they would have the potential to produce additional twins, which would further burden the social group. So, instead, there are additional males who can contribute to raising the offspring without burdening the group with more infants. All the males will copulate with the female, so at any

time, a male will not know if he is taking care of his own offspring.

Polygyny

Here, *poly* means "multiple," and *gyny* refers to females. **Polygyny** is a type of social organization where there are multiple females for each male in a group. Polygyny can take two forms. The first form is **single-male polygyny**, where one male, multiple females, and their offspring live together (**FIGURE 11.7**). This type of social group is seen in some New World monkeys, such as the howler monkey. It is also seen in some Old World monkeys, such as geladas and colobus monkeys. Among the apes, many gorillas live in single-male polygynous groups.

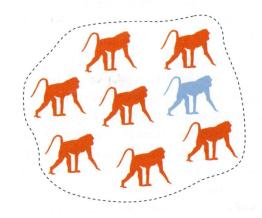

FIGURE 11.7 Single-Male Polygynous Social Organization
In single-male polygynous primates, a single adult male (blue), multiple adult females (red), and their offspring occupy a territory together.

The second form of polygyny is **multimale polygyny**, where multiple males, multiple females, and their offspring live together (**FIGURE 11.8**). This type of polygyny is seen in ring-tailed lemurs and some New World monkeys, such as the squirrel monkey. Many Old World monkeys, such as savanna baboons and most macaques, also practice it. Among the apes, both the bonobos and the chimpanzees live in multimale polygynous groups.

Bachelor (All-Male) Groups

In solitary and single-male polygynous species, such as gorillas, one male is paired with numerous females. However, in these species, a rela-

FIGURE 11.6 Polyandrous Social Organization
In polyandrous primates, an adult female (red), multiple adult males (blue), and their offspring occupy a territory together.

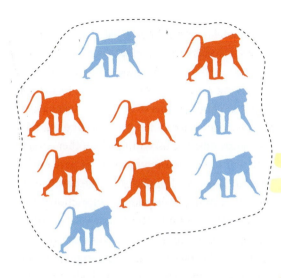

FIGURE 11.8 Multimale Polygynous Social Organization
In multimale polygynous primates, multiple adult males (blue), multiple adult females (red), and their offspring occupy a territory together.

tively equal number of males and females exist across the entire population. This means many of the males of the species are living without a group of females. These males often form social groups together, called **bachelor groups** (**FIGURE 11.9**). These all-male groups often roam the landscape because they do not yet control a territory or a group of females. When an opportunity arises to take over a territory or group of females from a reigning male leader, males from the bachelor group may work together to fight off the current leader and gain control.

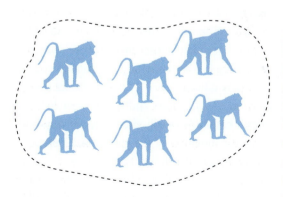

FIGURE 11.9 Bachelor Groups
In some primate species, males who do not control a territory or a group of females live together in all-male groups.

PRIMATE SEXUAL BEHAVIOR

To fully understand primate behavior, we must consider primate sexual and reproductive practices. Male and female primates often have different reproductive strategies. For most male primates, emphasis is placed on getting access to females for mating. This strategy is often accomplished through competition with other males, and its success may be related to a male's status within the social hierarchy and the strength of his male coalition. For most female primates, emphasis is placed on getting access to resources for supporting offspring. This strategy is also influenced by competition, and its success may be related to a female's status in the social hierarchy. In both instances, primates are competing with other primates of the same sex. Males compete with males for female mating partners; females compete with females for resources.

Competition and reproductive behavior can influence primate anatomy. Many primates, particularly the Old World monkeys, have special coloring that indicates from a distance whether one is facing a male or female of the species. Males sometimes even have brightly colored fur around their genitals, which calls further attention to their maleness. As we will discuss further in Lab 12, male primates may also be larger than their female counterparts and have larger canine teeth. All of these traits indicate to competitors that they are facing another male, and they facilitate aggressive competition for mates.

In some primates, such as chimpanzees and savanna baboons, female anatomy is also influenced by competition and sexual behavior. In these species, females have extreme swelling in their genital region around the time of ovulation. This phenomenon is called **estrus swelling** because it is timed with the female estrus (or fertility) cycle. A female's estrus swelling indicates to everyone in the group that she is ovulating and sexually receptive. Primate species that display pronounced estrus swelling tend to live in large, multimale polygynous groups where males compete over access to females in estrus. Conversely, pronounced estrus swelling is not

bachelor group an all-male social group where multiple adult males live together, without females or offspring

estrus swelling the swelling of the female genital region around the time of ovulation

alarm call a vocalization that indicates a particular threat

seen in social groups where male access to female mates is guaranteed, such as in single-male polygynous groups or monogamous groups. Thus, female estrus swelling relates to male–male competition.

For almost all primates, reproduction is a central component of social life, and sexual interactions emphasize reproduction. This is true for most animals, so it is not unusual that primates also follow this reproduction-centered pattern. In fact, one thing that makes humans different is that we break with this typical pattern and regularly engage in sexual activities that are non-reproductive. We are not alone in this, however. There are a few other nonhuman primates that also engage in nonreproductive sexual activities.

For example, the bonobos participate in a wide range of sexual behaviors. Bonobo sexual encounters cross age groups and can involve adults and even juveniles. They have male–female sex in numerous positions, including ventral–ventral mating where both parties face each other (which is extremely rare in nonhuman animals). Bonobos also engage in male–male genital stimulation and female–female genital stimulation, and they are known to practice self-stimulation. This diversity of sexual behavior distinguishes the bonobos from all other primates, apart from humans. Why do the bonobos behave this way?

Bonobos seem to use sexual activity as a relatively standard affiliative behavior. Like grooming, it is used to reinforce social bonds and avoid escalating tensions. This may help to explain why the combinations of sexual partners are so varied. If everyone in the group is forming relationships and bonds with one another, everyone will use sexual interactions as part of this bonding process. Bonobo social groups tend to be close-knit with few violent interactions. This is in stark contrast to their close relatives—the chimpanzees—whose social groups are marked by limited sexual interactions, competing male coalitions, and considerably more violence.

PRIMATE COMMUNICATION AND CULTURE

We previously discussed how primates use some forms of vocalization to reinforce social bonds. Primate vocalizations may serve other purposes as well. For example, many primates use vocalizations as a way to mark their territory and warn off intruders. In gibbons, a paired male and female make particular sounds, similar to a duet song, together. When the duet is sung, it warns others to stay away from their territory. Similarly, howler monkeys in Central and South America engage in regular vocalizations (reminiscent of howls) that mark their territory and inform intruders of their presence (**FIGURE 11.10**). Many primates also have specific **alarm calls**. Alarm calls are vocalizations that indicate a particular threat. When these vocalizations are made, other primates are informed that danger is approaching. A primate species may have different alarm calls for different threats, such as one for lions and another for birds of prey. These calls usually elicit different responses from the members of the group, each appropriate to the specific threat. For example, the reaction to the lion call may be very different from the reaction to the bird call because avoiding these different types of predators requires different behaviors. Interestingly, primate species that regularly live side by side with others often

David Tipling/Getty Images

FIGURE 11.10 Howler Monkey Vocalization
Howler monkeys use loud, howling vocalizations to mark their territorial boundaries.

understand the alarm calls of their neighboring primate species. This allows multiple species to form something similar to a "neighborhood watch," where the alarm sounded by one individual sparks a response in all of the local primates.

In addition to complicated forms of communication, many nonhuman primates have behavioral practices somewhat reminiscent of those of our own cultures. Human culture is unique to our species and perhaps some of our most closely related fossil relatives (see Lab 16). Human culture is a multifaceted phenomenon that encompasses our beliefs, practices, languages, and all other learned aspects of our social lives. In contrast, **nonhuman primate culture** is defined more simply as group-specific learned behavior. When we refer to "culture" in nonhuman primates, we do not mean to suggest that these primates have culture on a scale anywhere near what is seen in humans. Instead, we are highlighting some of the similarities between human and nonhuman primate behaviors. For example, in both cases, we find that cultural behaviors vary from one local group to another. Also, in both human and nonhuman primates, culture is centered on learned behavior, rather than natural or innate behavior.

In nonhuman primates, culture can take a variety of forms. Research traditionally emphasizes the wide range of tool use seen among the great apes. While many animals are known to make and use rudimentary tools, such as crows, elephants, and sea mammals, the level of complexity in the manufacturing and use of tools is particularly notable in nonhuman primates. For example, orangutans select twigs, remove the leaves, and use the modified sticks to extract insects and honey from holes in trees. Chimpanzees also shape twigs into tools that they use to extract ants and termites from trees and insect mounds **(FIGURE 11.11)**. Several chimpanzee groups also use particular methods of cracking nuts to access the edible meat inside the shells. Some of these groups use wood hammers and anvils, while other groups use rocks instead. Research has also begun to track cultural behavior in monkeys. For example, capuchin monkeys (New World monkeys)

© the Jane Goodall Institute / By Bill Wallauer

FIGURE 11.11 Chimpanzee Insect Fishing
Many chimpanzees form twigs into tools with which they can collect insects. This skill must be learned, and juveniles may spend years observing and practicing before they master the skill.

follow a list of steps to harvest and extract the meat from clams, and Japanese macaques (Old World monkeys) have been observed washing food to remove undesirable sand particles. In addition, some monkeys are known to use tools similar to those used by apes. Capuchin monkeys use rocks to crack seeds or nuts and use sticks to extract insects from trees. In addition, long-tailed macaques in Thailand (Old World monkeys) use rocks as hammerstones to crack open oil palm nuts.

As anthropologists have started to learn more about nonhuman primate tool use, a new type of research, called primate archaeology, has been established in recent years. Primate archaeologists use data collected from observations of living primates along with data obtained through surveys and excavations of ancient primate tool sites. Together, these data shed light on how tool use may have started, been maintained, and been modified in nonhuman primate species, which in turn helps us better understand

nonhuman primate culture group-specific, learned behavior in nonhuman primates

Ian C. Gilby

FIGURE 11.12 Chimpanzee Hunting
Chimpanzees often hunt other animals, such as monkeys. The hunt requires cooperation, and the distribution of the meat is based in part on social status and affiliations. In this way, hunting plays an important social role in chimpanzee life.

tives, but primate archaeology is demonstrating that they may be common practices in other tool-using primates as well.

In all of these examples of nonhuman primate culture, the primates are learning the behavior through an extended process of observing others and practicing on their own. Often it will take years to learn the behavior, and some individuals will never master the technique. This is particularly true with tool use in which a raw material must be carefully selected and then modified. For example, in making an insect fishing tool, a twig of the appropriate size and strength must be chosen and the leaves removed before it is ready for use.

A final category of nonhuman primate culture includes social hunting practices (FIGURE 11.12). While chimpanzees are most famous for their hunting, similar practices are seen in capuchin monkeys (New World monkeys) and some baboons (Old World monkeys). The primates work together in the hunt, often by herding prey toward an ambush. While adult males are usually the hunters, they share the meat with females and juveniles of the group. This meat distribution is often based on social status and affiliations. The choreography involved in the hunt must be learned, and the strategy and preferred prey vary among groups. At the same time, the meat obtained in hunts is usually only a small dietary supplement, making the hunt at least as important socially as nutritionally.

these behaviors in our own human lineage. For example, primate archaeologists have documented similar tool use practices across ape and monkey species. These practices include transporting tools from one place to another and using tools in a place frequently enough that discrete tool use sites form. These behaviors were once considered hallmarks of tool use among humans and our extinct hominin relations.

►►► EXPLORING FURTHER

Primate Conservation   If primatologists are to conduct field studies, there must be primate populations living in the wild. Unfortunately, finding substantial populations of nonhuman primates is becoming increasingly difficult, especially for particular species. For example, bonobos, chimpanzees, gorillas, and orangutans are all endangered or critically endangered. Almost all gibbons and the siamang are endangered as well. We are facing a great loss of diversity as these and other primate populations decline and

face extinction. In addition, the surviving primate groups are smaller and often hide deeper in the forest. This makes it more difficult to locate, count, study, and conserve these fractured primate populations.

What is causing nonhuman primate population declines? There are a number of factors involved, and any combination of them may be present at any particular location. The two most significant factors are habitat loss and hunting. Many nonhuman primates live in tropical forests, which are increasingly under threat of deforestation. To support themselves and their families, many of the humans in these areas cut down the forest to make room for villages and farmland. As the forests shrink, fewer habitats are available for forest-dwelling nonhuman primates. In addition, as global climate change continues, forests will shrink more and more. These changes will exacerbate the already troubling situation and lead to even further habitat loss. Similar circumstances of habitat loss are at play in some unforested environments, which will impact nonhuman primates living in these locations as well.

The second factor contributing to nonhuman primate population decline is hunting. Humans often hunt nonhuman primates. The juveniles are collected and sold in the illegal pet trade, and adults that defend their juveniles are killed in the process. Some nonhuman primates are killed and eaten by local people desperately in need of food or sold to international markets. Still others are accidentally caught and fatally injured in snares and traps meant for other animals living in their habitats.

What is being done to conserve nonhuman primates? In most of the countries where these problems occur, laws already exist banning some of these practices. For example, in many countries, it is illegal to keep an endangered primate as a pet. However, the laws are not always strongly enforced. In many parts of the world where nonhuman primates are at risk, the humans are facing numerous challenges themselves. Many of these places are war-torn countries where individuals are simply trying to survive and support their families. There is rarely enough money and infrastructure to fully enforce the existing conservation laws.

In addition to law enforcement, efforts have focused on establishing protected habitats (parklands and preserves) where nonhuman primates can live. Again, maintaining enough park personnel and equipping them to properly enforce the laws and restrictions of the park can be challenging. There are also efforts to form rehabilitation areas where primates rescued from the illegal pet trade can be rehabilitated and eventually released back into the wild. Of course, this approach requires financial and personnel support for the rehabilitation facility, as well as habitats where primates can be successfully released.

In support of nonhuman primate conservation efforts, many primatologists advocate more outreach to local human populations. Primatologists often give presentations to local groups or hire local workers to help with their research. In doing this, they are spreading knowledge about and interest in the nonhuman primates of the area. Primatologists also sometimes advocate providing local human populations with economic opportunities, such as employment in ecotourism, that decrease their reliance on deforestation and hunting, particularly in protected parkland.

Field primate studies are an important component in our efforts to understand who we are as a species. These research projects help us to understand how primates negotiate social status, obtain and distribute food, and work together to defend territories or mates. By learning about these behaviors in other primates, we may also learn more about similar behaviors in our ancestral species and ourselves. The world of primate field research today is complex. Primatologists face numerous research challenges, especially as it becomes harder to find primate populations to study. In addition, primatologists face ethical challenges as they attempt to balance the conservation needs of nonhuman primates with the survival needs of humans in the same areas. Undoubtedly these challenges will continue into the future, and primatologists will continue to tackle them to gain more knowledge about us and our primate relatives.

Name: _____   Section: _____

Course: _____   Date: _____

Answer the following questions in the space provided.

1. Is research conducted with primates in a zoo considered a field primate study? Why or why not?

2. A primatologist is watching numerous primates at once and collecting easily measurable information that facilitates comparisons. This researcher is:

   A. conducting a focused observation and collecting quantitative data.
   B. conducting a group observation and collecting quantitative data.
   C. conducting a focused observation and collecting qualitative data.
   D. conducting a group observation and collecting qualitative data.

3. You are observing two juvenile chimpanzees. When they first meet, they embrace. They then begin tickling each other and wrestling mildly. Would you characterize this behavior as affiliative or aggressive?

4. What size groups do primates tend to form when food is sparsely distributed?

5. I am an adult female primate. I live in a territory with my offspring. My territory is separate from those of other females, so I don't see them often. An adult male has a territory that overlaps with mine, but we hardly ever spend time together. What type of social organization do I participate in?

   A. Polygynous
   B. Monogamous
   C. Solitary
   D. Polyandrous

6. I am an adult female primate. I live in a territory with two adult males and our offspring. What type of social organization do I participate in?

   A. Solitary
   B. Polyandrous
   C. Monogamous
   D. Polygynous

7. Which of the following statements about primate sexual behavior is **true**?

   A. Most male primates have to compete with one another, but females never do.
   B. Most female primates emphasize getting access to mates for reproduction.
   C. Most male primates are ranked in a social hierarchy, but females are not ranked.
   D. Most female primates emphasize getting access to resources for their offspring.

8. Compared with chimpanzees, bonobos have:

    A. a wider range of sexual practices.

    B. more violent behavior.

    C. a higher degree of male–male competition.

    D. less social bonding between individuals.

9. Define nonhuman primate culture.

10. Describe *one* of the threats to wild primate populations today.

LAB EXERCISES

Name: _____   Section: _____

Course: _____   Date: _____

EXERCISE 1 CAPTIVE AND FIELD STUDIES

Work in a small group or alone to complete this exercise. Review the research projects in each scenario below. For each project, identify whether you think it is best studied in captivity or in the field and the reason(s) for your choice.

SCENARIO A

Do chimpanzees have the ability to learn and use language? This research project will attempt to teach chimpanzees how to use sign language. They will be taught a certain number of signs and then evaluated on their ability to use the signs in innovative combinations and settings.

   1. Is this topic best studied in a captive study or field study?

   2. Why?

SCENARIO B

Do capuchin monkeys use meat sharing to reinforce social bonds? This research project will observe how capuchin monkeys distribute meat from hunts. Data will be collected about who obtains meat, how much they receive, and in what order they receive their shares.

   1. Is this topic best studied in a captive study or field study?

   2. Why?

SCENARIO C

Do bonobos use sexual interactions to avoid or mediate conflict? This research project will observe bonobo sexual behavior. Particular attention will be paid to situations when sexual interactions occur around the time of social conflicts. Data will be collected about the type of sexual act and degree of conflict observed, who is involved, and the length of time elapsed between the sexual behavior and the conflict.

   1. Is this topic best studied in a captive study or field study?

   2. Why?

EXERCISE 2 OBSERVING PRIMATES

The following two pages provide observation forms for qualitative and quantitative data collection. Use these forms to record your observations of human primates in a public place, or nonhuman primates at a local zoo or online via zoo cams.

QUALITATIVE PRIMATE OBSERVATION FORM

Date: _____   Start time: _____   End time: _____

Location: _____

Weather: _____

Primate species: _____

Check one: Group observation ☐   Focused observation ☐

Number of adult males: _____ Number of adult females: _____ Number of juveniles: _____

Description of study primate(s): Describe each primate, including its size, coloring, and unusual features. If you are studying a group, assign each primate a code, such as F1 for female 1, F2 for female 2, and J1 for juvenile 1. Then use the codes to streamline your note taking.

_____

_____

_____

Observations: Choose a time interval, such as every 2 minutes. Record your choice below. Then after each time interval, describe the behaviors you observe in that instant.

Length of time interval: _____

Time interval 1: _____

_____

_____

Time interval 2: _____

_____

_____

Time interval 3: _____

_____

_____

Time interval 4: _____

_____

_____

QUANTITATIVE PRIMATE OBSERVATION FORM

Date: 2/15/2022   Start time: ~~XXXXXXXXX~~ 12:00 PM   End time: 12:08 PM

Location: Utica Zoo

Weather: ~~18~~ 17°F (feels like ~~12~~°F). Cloudy weather and windy (~~XX~~ 3.5 mph) light Snow!

Primate species: Tamarins

Check one: Group observation ☑   Focused observation ☐

Number of adult males: 2   Number of adult females: 1   Number of juveniles: _____

Description of study primate(s): Describe each primate, including its size, coloring, and unusual features. If you are studying a group, assign each primate a code, such as F1 for female 1, F2 for female 2, and J1 for juvenile 1. Then use the codes to streamline your note taking.

F1 has white/brownish fur. small bodies, long tails. F1 is older, body is slightly bigger.

M1 white/brownish fur. small bodies, long tails.

M2 white/brownish fur. small bodies, long tails.   All these tamarins look almost if not completely, identical.

Observations: Choose a time interval, such as every 2 minutes. Record your choice below. Then after each time interval, write the primate's code in the appropriate box in the chart if it is practicing that behavior in that instant.

Length of time interval: 2 minutes

Behavior	Interval 1	Interval 2	Interval 3	Interval 4
Grooming or Scratching	✓ (M1 +M2)	✓ (M1+M2)	✓ (M1+M2)	✓ (M1+M2)
Playing		(M1+M2)		
Affiliative Vocalization				
Threat Display				
Violence				
Aggressive Vocalization				
Food Collecting				
Eating				
Food Sharing				
Tool Use				
Courtship or Soliciting Sex				
Sex				
Sleeping	✓ (F1)	✓ (F1)	✓ (F1)	
Caring for Juvenile				
Moving or Locomotion				
Other (Please Describe)			✓ (All)	✓ (All)

looking around

Name: _____ Date: _____

EXERCISE 3   AFFILIATIVE VERSUS AGGRESSIVE BEHAVIOR

Work in a small group or alone to complete this exercise.

PART A

Examine the primate behavior depicted in the photo provided by your instructor (or in the Lab 11 Exercise Image Library on p. 334).

1. Do you think this is affiliative behavior or aggressive behavior?

2. Why?

PART B

Examine the primate behavior depicted in the photo provided by your instructor (or in the Lab 11 Exercise Image Library on p. 334).

1. Do you think this is affiliative behavior or aggressive behavior?

2. Why?

PART C

Consider your own experiences with human behavior.

1. How are human affiliative and aggressive behaviors similar to what is seen in nonhuman primates? Provide specific examples.

2. How are human affiliative and aggressive behaviors different from what is seen in nonhuman primates? Provide specific examples.

EXERCISE 4   PRIMATE ECOLOGY AND GROUP SIZE

Work in a small group or alone to complete this exercise. Match each of the mystery primates in the column on the left to the description of its environment in the column on the right.

Primate 1 _____
The majority of my diet consists of fruit, and I live in a monogamous social group.

A. Tropical Forest (Southeast Asia)
Trees are everywhere in this habitat, but fruit trees produce fruit sporadically and are sparsely distributed throughout the forest.

Primate 2 _____
I eat mostly insects (such as beetles and moths) that I hunt at night. I am mostly solitary.

B. Highlands (Ethiopia)
Large fields are tucked among rocky hillsides and steep slopes. These fields contain a range of grasses, herbs, and small plants.

Primate 3 _____
I eat a range of foods, including a lot of grass and flowers. I live in a polygynous group.

C. Savanna Woodland (Southern Africa)
Pockets of wooded areas are interspersed in an open, grassy landscape. The wooded areas offer a variety of trees and shrubs that appeal to a range of insects, birds, and small mammals.

EXERCISE 5   PRIMATE SOCIAL ORGANIZATION

Work in a small group or alone to complete this exercise.

PART A

Examine the primate group depicted in the photo provided by your instructor (or in the Lab 11 Exercise Image Library on p. 335).

1. What type of social group do you think this is?

2. Why?

PART B

Examine the primate group depicted in the photo provided by your instructor (or in the Lab 11 Exercise Image Library on p. 335).

1. What type of social group do you think this is?

2. Why?

EXERCISE 6 NONHUMAN PRIMATE CULTURE

Work in a small group or alone to complete this exercise.

Research has found that chimpanzees in one area make spears to help them hunt bushbabies (African lorises). The chimpanzees locate a tree trunk in which the bushbabies live. They then select a tree branch, trim off the leaves and side branches, and trim the end of the branch to form a sharpened tip. The chimpanzees thrust these branches, like spears, into the tree to try to stab bushbabies (see the Lab 11 Exercise Image Library on p. 336 for associated images).

1. Is this behavior an example of nonhuman primate culture?

2. Why or why not?

CRITICAL THINKING QUESTIONS

On a separate sheet of paper, answer the following questions.

1. In Exercise 2 (on p. 326), you completed observations of primates. Write a brief reflection based on your experience. What behaviors were common? Would these behaviors be common in other primates? Did you see anything unusual or surprising? How might your experience be different if you were researching nonhuman primates in the field? Did you prefer collecting quantitative data or qualitative data? Why? What did you learn by doing this assignment?

2. In this lab, we reviewed different examples of affiliative behavior and aggressive behavior in primates. To help you make comparisons and better understand the similarities and differences between these behaviors, complete the Primate Behavior Chart on p. 332. Describe two examples of affiliative behavior and two examples of aggressive behavior. For each example, be sure to specify the primate or primates involved. Use material in your classroom, online, or in books and films to supplement what you learned in this lab if necessary.

3. In this lab, we also reviewed the different types of primate social groups. To help you make comparisons and better understand the similarities and differences between these groups, complete the Primate Social Organization Chart on p. 333. For each type of social group, be sure to describe the group's members (proportions of adult males, adult females, and juveniles) and specify the primate or primates involved.

4. In this lab, we also reviewed different examples of nonhuman primate culture. To help you make comparisons and better understand the general pattern of these behaviors, complete the Nonhuman Primate Culture Chart on p. 333. Describe three examples of nonhuman primate culture. Try to include examples from apes and monkeys. For each example, be sure to specify the primate or primates involved. Use material in your classroom, online, or in books and films to supplement what you learned in this lab if necessary.

5. In this lab, we explored primate communication and culture, and we learned that many of our human behaviors are similar to those found in nonhuman primates. Using your knowledge of primates, consider this recent real-world legal case. In 2011, David J. Slater, a photographer from the United Kingdom, set up his camera equipment among a group of crested black macaques (*Macaca nigra*) on the island of Sulawesi, Indonesia. He then sat nearby while a few of the monkeys took the camera and began playing with it. They made faces and bared their teeth into the reflective surface of the lens while also pressing buttons on the camera. The result was a series of "selfie" photographs (see next page for an example). Slater later claimed copyright on the images, publishing some himself and licensing others to media outlets. Two legal battles then unfolded over the next several years. Some entities, like Wikimedia Commons, claimed that the images must be in the public domain because they were taken by the monkeys themselves, and nonhuman animals cannot hold copyrights under the law. Others, like People for the Ethical Treatment of Animals (PETA), claimed that the monkeys should be given copyright to the photos because they created them. Meanwhile, Slater argued that he should be able to claim the copyright because the images were taken using his equipment with his photographic settings. What do you think?

   A. Does the monkeys' behavior constitute a form of nonhuman primate culture? Why or why not?
   B. Should nonhuman primates be granted additional privileges under the law because of their social and behavioral similarities with humans? Why or why not?
   C. Should these monkeys be granted the copyright for their "selfie" photos? Why or why not?
   D. What did the courts decide in this case? (Review the information available from reputable sources online to determine the United States Copyright Office's requirements for authorship and what the United States Court of Appeals for the Ninth Circuit ruled about PETA's attempt to give the monkeys copyright in *Naruto v. David Slater*, https://www.ca9.uscourts.gov/opinions/)

David Slater/Caters

6. As discussed in this lab, nonhuman primate conservation is a growing concern, particularly as many primate populations are rapidly declining. Locate a recent news article (from the last 5 years) about the conservation of a primate. You can use an article about an ape species (such as those discussed in this lab) or a non-ape species. Popular news sources could include magazines (such as *Discover, Scientific American*, and *National Geographic*) or newspapers (such as the *New York Times* or *San Francisco Chronicle*). Read the article and answer the following questions: What primate is being discussed? Why does this primate need to be conserved (what is negatively impacting its population)? How is this primate being conserved (what is being done to try to protect this primate from further population decline)?

PRIMATE BEHAVIOR CHART

	Example	Primate(s)
Affiliative Behavior 1		
Affiliative Behavior 2		
Aggressive Behavior 1		
Aggressive Behavior 2		

PRIMATE SOCIAL ORGANIZATION CHART

	Description	Primate(s)
Solitary		
Monogamy		
Polyandry		
Single-male Polygyny		
Multimale Polygyny		

NONHUMAN PRIMATE CULTURE CHART

Example	Primate(s)

LAB 11 EXERCISE IMAGE LIBRARY
Students should use these images only if directed to by their instructor.

EXERCISE 3 AFFILIATIVE VERSUS AGGRESSIVE BEHAVIOR

PART A

Courtesy of Joan Silk

PART B

K. G. Preston-Mafham/Premaphotos Wildlife

EXERCISE 5 PRIMATE SOCIAL ORGANIZATION

PART A

Ger Bosma/Alamy Stock Photo

PART B

Holger Ehlers/Alamy Stock Photo

EXERCISE 6 NONHUMAN PRIMATE CULTURE

Reprinted from *Current Biology*, Volume 17, Jill D. Pruetz and Paco Bertolani, "Savanna Chimpanzees, *Pan troglodytes verus*, Hunt with Tools," pp. 412–17. © 2007, with permission from Elsevier.

2.54 cm

Dr. Paco Bertolani

Robert Marien/Corbis

Ken Lucas/Visuals Unlimited, Inc.

Although there are slight differences between human males and females (*left*), in other primates, such as orangutans (*right*), the differences between males and females can be extreme.

LAB 12

Comparative Primate Anatomy

Lab Learning Objectives

By the end of this lab, students should be able to:

- define the four major primate diets, as well as their corresponding adaptations, and give primate examples.

- define the major types of primate locomotion, as well as their corresponding adaptations, and give primate examples.

- identify males and females of a primate species using their physical features.

- identify the social organization of a primate group by its degree of sexual dimorphism.

Human males and females look physically different. While these biological differences begin to be manifest early in life, they become even more pronounced at puberty. For example, females generally grow tall and gain body fat during adolescence. Meanwhile, males grow even taller, gain more muscle mass, and gain more body and facial hair than females. These physical differences are most obvious when we see a typical adult human male and female standing next to each other. Men are usually slightly larger and more robust, while women are usually slightly smaller and more gracile. While this is a generalization, and many individuals show variation in physical morphology, these general differences in skeletal size and robusticity between males and females often enable forensic anthropologists to estimate the probable sex of a skeleton.

Physical differences between the sexes are often even more pronounced in nonhuman primates. Many nonhuman primates follow the general pattern seen in humans, with males being larger and more robust than females. In addition, the sexes of some species have differences in tooth size, fur coloration, or other features. For example, adult male gorillas are considerably larger and have more robust cranial features than female gorillas. Adult male gorillas also have silver-gray fur on their backs that is not seen in female gorillas. The differences between orangutan males and females are also extreme. Besides being much larger than females, adult male orangutans have additional fat pads around their faces that are not seen in females. Why would some primates, such as gorillas and orangutans, have such pronounced differences between the sexes? This is one of the questions we address in this lab about the relationship between primate behavior and anatomy.

INTRODUCTION

In this lab, we discuss the relationship between primate behavior and anatomy. This information helps us to identify patterns that we can use to interpret the fossil record and better understand our evolutionary history. We begin with a look at the major types of primate diets and their corresponding anatomical adaptations. We then consider the major forms of primate locomotion and the anatomical traits that correspond to each type of locomotion. We conclude with a discussion of the physical, biological differences between males and females of a species and what these differences can tell us about the primates' social organization.

PRIMATE BEHAVIOR AND ANATOMY

Some anatomical traits are better suited to a specific behavior than others. Therefore, if a population practices the same behavior for many generations, we find that particular anatomical traits are selectively favored and become more prevalent in the population. Biological anthropologists identify particular anatomical adaptations that correspond to particular primate behaviors. They then use these patterns as analogies for interpreting the fossil record.

When we study extinct fossil species, we do not have the opportunity to directly observe the behavior of the animals or ask them about their behavioral practices. We are left with only their fossil remains—traces of their skeletal anatomy.

This would seem to limit our research to anatomical questions. However, we can use what we know about living primate anatomy and behavior to help us interpret the fossil record. For example, imagine you have found a fossil species that has large molar teeth. You are unable to observe the fossil species to see what significance this trait may have for its behavior, but you do know of several living primates with similar molar teeth. You have information about the behavior of these primates because they have been observed in the present day. This research has shown that primates with molars of this type tend to have a diet that requires a lot of chewing, such as a plant-based diet. Even though you cannot travel to the past and observe the fossil species actually eating these foods, you can hypothesize that its large molars served this purpose because there is a strong pattern of association between large molars and plant eating in living primates today. You have used a pattern of behavior and anatomy seen in living primates to interpret your fossil data. In this lab, we discuss the three most important patterns of behavior and anatomy: those related to diet, locomotion, and social organization.

DIET AND DIETARY ADAPTATIONS

One of the most important patterns of behavior and anatomy is the relationship between diet and dietary adaptations. Some foods are more difficult to digest than others, so they require special adaptations to facilitate digestion. Primates with different diets often have different tooth forms and digestive tracts. This variation is particularly useful when interpreting the fossil record because many dietary adaptations are found in teeth, and teeth are the most commonly preserved element found in the fossil record. In addition, some foods provide small bursts of energy, while others provide slow-burning energy. Because of this variation, primates with different diets often have different body sizes, depending on the energy available from their food.

Most primates eat a wide range of foods, including things such as fruits, leaves, insects, and even meat. However, each primate tends to emphasize some types of food over others. For example, orangutans eat fruit, leaves, honey, and insects. Of these various foods, fruit makes up the majority of their diet, with leaves, honey, and insects serving as supplements. A primate has anatomical adaptations that suit its dietary emphasis. For example, orangutans have adaptations for fruit eating, as opposed to leaf eating or insect eating, because fruit is their dietary emphasis. Among the primates, there are four different dietary emphases: insectivory, gummivory, folivory, and frugivory.

Insectivory

Insectivory is a diet that emphasizes insects, such as beetles and moths. These foods provide small packets of energy. A large-bodied primate would need to eat massive quantities of insects to obtain enough energy to meet its metabolic needs, which is not feasible. Thus, insectivorous primates tend to have small bodies that can survive more efficiently on these small packets of energy. In addition, insects have exoskeletons: skeletons on the outside of the body, rather than the inside. To get to the squishy food inside an insect, a primate must first break through the exoskeleton. Insectivorous primates have teeth with very pointy cusps that help them crunch through the hard exteriors of insects (**FIGURE 12.1**). Chewing insects is relatively easy with the help of these pointy teeth, so insectivorous primates typically have medium-sized to small mandibles and jaw muscles. Once an insect has

been broken into smaller pieces by chewing, it is swallowed and sent down the digestive tract. Insects are very easy to digest, so the digestive tracts of insectivores are simple and short. Many of the lorises and tarsiers are insectivorous, as are some of the marmosets (New World monkeys).

Gummivory

Gummivory is a diet that emphasizes tree gum (or sap). In many trees, sap oozes out of the bark of a stem or trunk. Think of the maple tree sap that humans collect and turn into maple syrup and maple sugar candy. Some nonhuman primates also eat tree sap. Like insects, tree gums provide small bursts of energy, so gummivorous primates tend to be small-bodied. However, gums do not provide necessary proteins, so many gummivores supplement their diet with insects. Tree gums are trapped inside the tree bark, and the bark must be gnawed to expedite the release of gums. Gummivorous lemurs and lorises often have *dental combs* (**FIGURE 12.2**) that help them scrape tree bark to encourage gum seepage. Once a primate laps up the seeping tree gum, it doesn't really need to chew it, so gummivores typically have small mandibles and jaw muscles. Gums are easy to digest, like insects, so gummivorous primates also have relatively simple and short digestive tracts. In addition to some lemurs and lorises,

insectivory a diet that emphasizes insects

gummivory a diet that emphasizes tree gums (or sap)

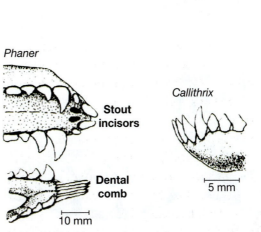

FIGURE 12.2 Gummivore Dentition
Gummivorous primates often have a special tooth structure, called a dental comb, formed by the elongation and protrusion of the lower incisors and canines.

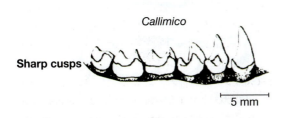

FIGURE 12.1 Insectivore Dentition
Insectivorous primates have teeth with sharp cusps to help them crunch through insect exoskeletons.

folivory a diet that emphasizes leaves (foliage) and other plant parts

sagittal crest a ridge of bone along the midline of the cranium that allows for the attachment of extra-large chewing muscles

frugivory a diet that emphasizes fruit

many marmosets (New World monkeys) are gummivorous.

Folivory

Folivory is a diet that emphasizes leaves (foliage) and other plant parts, such as stems. Plants, particularly leaves, can be difficult to digest because they are often highly fibrous. Before they can be swallowed, plants often require extensive chewing to break them apart. We encounter this challenge with plants in our own diet. When we eat celery, for example, it requires a lot of extra chewing to break through the long plant fibers. Similarly, when we eat a raw spinach salad, we have to chew the leaves to break them up into pieces we can swallow. Because their diet emphasizes chewing rather than biting, many folivorous primates have large molars and smaller incisors (**FIGURE 12.3**). Their molars also have special shearing crests. When folivorous primates chew, the shearing crests of their top molars work with the shearing crests of their bottom molars to shred fibrous plant material, like a pair of scissors. These primates also tend to have large mandibles and jaw muscles to help with chewing. Large jaw muscles sometimes require extra areas of bone for muscle attachment. For example, folivorous gorillas have a **sagittal crest**: an extra ridge of bone along the midline of the cranium that allows for the attachment of powerful jaw muscles (see Figure 5.12).

Even after leafy material has been shredded in the mouth, it still requires extensive digestion to maximize the extraction of available nutrients. Because of this, folivorous primates often have special adaptations in their digestive tracts. Many leaf-eating primates have elongated intestines that help them digest plant material. The folivorous colobus monkeys (Old World monkeys) even have special complex stomachs (similar to those of cows) that contain bacteria to help break down leaves. Leaves provide limited, slow-burning energy, and leaf eating requires a longer digestive tract. Thus, folivorous primates tend to have large bodies. The classic example is the folivorous gorilla, the largest living primate. Other folivorous primates include colobines, such as the langur and black-and-white colobus (leaf-eating Old World monkeys), as well as the howler monkey (New World monkeys).

Frugivory

Frugivory is a diet emphasizing fruit. Fruit is relatively easy to digest and provides an intermediate amount of energy. Frugivorous primates tend to have medium-sized bodies and relatively simple digestive tracts. To properly crush fruit, frugivores have molars with low, rounded cusps that act like juicers to squeeze the fruit and help reduce it to pulp (**FIGURE 12.4**). Chew-

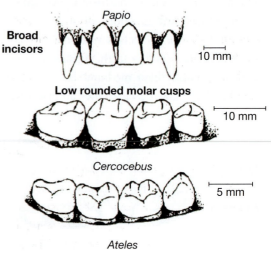

FIGURE 12.4 Frugivore Dentition
Frugivorous primates have large incisors and low, rounded molars to help them bite into and chew fruits.

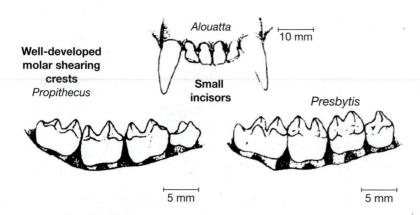

FIGURE 12.3 Folivore Dentition
Folivorous primates have small incisors and large, shearing molars to help them shred leafy material.

ing fruit is much easier than chewing leaves, so the molars of a frugivore are not as large as the molars of a folivore. At the same time, biting is more important to a frugivore than it is to a folivore. While a folivore can fold leaves and wad them into the mouth, a frugivore often has to take bites of fruit before it can be chewed and digested. This biting emphasis results in wider incisors in frugivores than in folivores. Because frugivores rely less on chewing than do folivores, they have medium-sized mandibles and jaw muscles compared with folivores. Most primates are frugivorous, including some lemurs and lorises, most New World monkeys, numerous cercopithecines (a group of Old World monkeys), and many of the nonhuman apes, such as gibbons and orangutans.

A

B

FIGURE 12.5 Vertical Clinger and Leaper Skeleton
Vertical clingers and leapers have very long legs and feet to help them leap from one tree to the next.

LOCOMOTION AND LOCOMOTOR ADAPTATIONS

Another important pattern of primate behavior and anatomy is the relationship between locomotion and locomotor adaptations. The term **locomotion** refers to an animal's form of movement—how it travels from one place to another. There are different forms of locomotion, and each form of locomotion requires different things of the body. For example, some locomotor strategies may rely more on the arms (**forelimbs**), while other strategies rely more on the legs (**hind limbs**). Because these areas of the body are used differently in each form of locomotion, the anatomical adaptations for locomotion vary as well.

Vertical Clinging and Leaping

One of the more unusual forms of primate locomotion is called **vertical clinging and leaping**. In this form of locomotion, the body is oriented vertically, and movement occurs by leaping from tree to tree. The primate begins by clinging upright to a tree trunk (or similar surface). It then pushes off the tree with its legs and leaps through the air. It lands on another nearby tree in an upright clinging position. In vertical cling-

ing and leaping, the legs do most of the work—both leaping and absorbing some of the shock of landing. Thus, vertical clingers and leapers have very long legs and feet (**FIGURE 12.5**). This form of locomotion is unusual and is practiced only by some lemurs and lorises, as well as the tarsiers. The adaptations for vertical clinging and leaping are perhaps most extreme in the tarsiers, whose ankles are so elongated that these primates have been named for their dramatic foot (tarsal) bones. Tarsiers also have unusual tibia and fibula bones that are fused together at the distal end, providing extra support and shock absorption.

locomotion an animal's form of movement in traveling from one place to another

forelimb the upper or front limb (commonly called the arm)

hind limb the lower or back limb (commonly called the leg)

vertical clinging and leaping a form of locomotion where the body is oriented vertically and movement occurs by leaping from tree to tree

Anton Ivanov/Alamy Stock Photo

Suspensory Locomotion (Brachiation, Semibrachiation)

suspensory locomotion a form of locomotion where the body is suspended (or hanging) below tree branches

brachiation a form of suspensory locomotion where movement occurs through arm-over-arm swinging

semibrachiation a form of suspensory locomotion where movement occurs through the use of the arms and a specially adapted prehensile tail, which can grasp tree branches

Some primates practice forms of **suspensory locomotion**, meaning that they hang (or suspend themselves) below tree branches. There are two types of suspensory locomotion: brachiation and semibrachiation. **Brachiation** refers to a form of suspensory locomotion where movement occurs through arm-over-arm swinging. This form of locomotion is very similar to the movements humans make to cross the monkey bars on a playground. In brachiation, movement is dependent on the arms, so brachiators have very long arms (**FIGURE 12.6**). They also have long, curved fingers to help the body hang from tree branches. Brachiators need to have mobile shoulder joints to have full range of motion in their arms, so these primates have scapulas positioned on the posterior surface of the rib cage rather than on the lateral surfaces. This frees up some of their shoulder area and allows for more mobility. Some brachiators, such as the gibbon, also have mobile wrists that allow the hand to stay in place holding a tree branch while the arm and body rotate in different directions. Finally, most brachiating primates have broad chests and short lumbar areas that improve stability and decrease movement in the trunk while they are suspended from tree branches.

Interestingly, humans have many of these features. When we relax our hands, we find that our normal hand position is slightly curved. In addition, our scapulas are positioned on the back of the rib cage and allow for a full 360° rotation in our arms. Humans have these features because our ancestors were brachiators, and we have maintained some of these adaptations from our evolutionary past. In fact, all apes have adaptations for brachiation, because the last common ancestor of all apes was probably a brachiator. Today, the only apes that regularly practice brachiation are the gibbons and siamangs (the lesser apes), and true brachiation is not seen in any of the non-ape primates. So, in reality, those monkey bars on the playground should probably be called "lesser ape bars."

FIGURE 12.6 Brachiator Skeleton
Brachiators have long arms and long, curved fingers. In addition, their scapulas are positioned on the back of their rib cage, and they have mobile shoulder joints.

The second type of suspensory locomotion is called **semibrachiation**. Semibrachiation is a form of suspensory locomotion where movement occurs through the use of the arms and tail. It is similar to brachiation because it involves hanging from tree branches, but it is not true brachiation because it does not involve arm-over-arm swinging. Semibrachiation requires a *prehensile tail* (FIGURE 12.7). This type of tail has the ability to grasp, so it can act as an additional hand. In fact, semibrachiators can hang from a tree branch using only the tail and keep their arms free for feeding and other activities. Because semibrachiators do not practice arm-over-arm swinging, they do not have the skeletal adaptations seen in true brachiators, such as highly mobile shoulder joints. Instead, the semibrachiator skeleton resembles that of a quadrupedal primate with the addition of a prehensile tail (compare Figures 12.7 and 12.8). Semibrachiation is seen only in some of the New World monkeys, such as the howler monkeys, the spider monkeys, the woolly monkeys, and the capuchin monkeys.

Quadrupedalism (Arboreal and Terrestrial, and Knuckle-Walking)

The most common form of primate locomotion is **quadrupedalism**. *Quad* means "four," and *pedal* refers to feet (think of pedals for your feet on a bicycle). Quadrupedalism refers to locomotion that uses all four limbs (or is "four-footed"). There are two major types of quadrupedalism in primates: arboreal quadrupedalism and terrestrial quadrupedalism. **Arboreal quadrupedalism** is quadrupedalism that is practiced in the trees. Arboreal quadrupeds walk and run along the horizontal surfaces of tree branches and jump from branch to branch. While arboreal quadrupeds frequently use both their arms and their legs, their legs may be slightly longer to facilitate leaping between tree branches (FIGURE 12.8). An arboreal quadruped's hands and feet are prehensile and have relatively long fingers and toes to help them hold onto tree branches. Most of these primates also have a long tail to help with balance. Arboreal quadrupeds have narrow chests with scapulas positioned laterally on the rib cage. Their trunks are

quadrupedalism a form of locomotion that uses all four limbs

arboreal quadrupedalism a form of quadrupedalism that is practiced in the trees

FIGURE 12.8 Arboreal Quadruped Skeleton
Arboreal quadrupeds have long tails to help them balance. They also sometimes have legs that are slightly longer than their arms to help them jump between tree branches.

FIGURE 12.7 Semibrachiator Skeleton
Semibrachiators have prehensile tails that can grasp tree branches and act like a fifth hand.

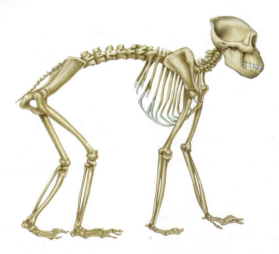

FIGURE 12.9 Terrestrial Quadruped Skeleton
Terrestrial quadrupeds have short tails and arms and legs of relatively equal length.

therefore similar to the trunks of many other quadrupedal animals. Most primates are arboreal quadrupeds, including some lemurs, most New World monkeys, and the colobines (arboreal Old World monkeys).

The other major type of quadrupedalism in primates is **terrestrial quadrupedalism**. This term refers to quadrupedalism that is practiced on the ground. Terrestrial quadrupeds walk and run along the surface of the ground. This form of locomotion uses the arms and legs relatively equally. In contrast to arboreal quadrupedalism, leaping is rare in terrestrial quadrupedalism, so a terrestrial quadruped's arms and legs are more similar in length (**FIGURE 12.9**). Compared with an arboreal quadruped, a terrestrial quadruped has shorter and more robust hands and feet, which are well suited for bearing weight and supporting the body on the ground. Terrestrial quadrupeds do not need long tails for balance, so they have much shorter tails than arboreal quadrupeds. The trunk of a terrestrial

quadruped is very similar to that of an arboreal quadruped, with a narrow chest and scapulas positioned laterally on the rib cage. Terrestrial quadrupedalism is less common than arboreal quadrupedalism and is mostly found in the cercopithecines (terrestrial Old World monkeys).

There is one type of quadrupedalism that is particularly rare. It is called **knuckle-walking**, and it is seen only in the gorillas, chimpanzees, and bonobos. This form of terrestrial quadrupedalism involves walking on the knuckles of the hands (**FIGURE 12.10**). Chimpanzees, bonobos, and gorillas are unusual because they maintain adaptations for brachiation, but they spend a lot of their time on the ground. This apparent contradiction forces these apes into a locomotion compromise. They must balance their ancestral brachiation traits with their current terrestrial quadrupedal behaviors. Unlike other terrestrial quadrupeds, these apes do not have arms and legs of similar length or short fingers. Their brachiator arms are much longer than their legs, so their chests are elevated high off the ground when their hands are on the ground (**FIGURE 12.11**). Because they do not have the short fingers optimal for terrestrial locomotion, they walk instead on the dorsal (back) surfaces of the middle phalanges of their hands, with their knuckles supporting their weight. Their fingers naturally curl toward their palms while they knuckle-walk because they have the curved fingers of a brachiator. The phalanges (finger bones) of their hands are robust and help support their weight.

Quantifying Locomotor Adaptations

In addition to observing the general characteristics previously discussed (such as the robust phalanges of knuckle-walkers), primatologists may collect quantitative data to help them identify locomotor adaptations. Notice that when we reviewed many of the forms of locomotion, we observed that they correspond to different arm and leg lengths. For example, vertical clingers and leapers have long legs to aid in pushing off and landing as they leap from tree trunk to tree

terrestrial quadrupedalism a form of quadrupedalism that is practiced on the ground

knuckle-walking a form of terrestrial quadrupedalism that involves walking on the knuckles of the hands

Juniors Bildarchiv GmbH/Alamy Stock Photo

FIGURE 12.10 Knuckle-Walking
When they knuckle-walk, primates such as gorillas walk on the dorsal (back) surface of the middle phalanges of all four fingers. Their knuckles support the weight of their upper body.

FIGURE 12.11 Knuckle-Walker Skeleton
Knuckle-walkers have the long arms and curved hands of a brachiator. They also have robust finger bones.

Intermembral Index	Primary Locomotion
50–80	Vertical clinging and leaping
80–100	Quadrupedalism
100–150	Brachiation (and knuckle-walking)

trunk. Primate limb proportions follow quantifiable patterns, which allows anthropologists to correlate limb measurements with locomotion type. The most commonly used measurement is the intermembral index. *Inter* means between, and *membral* refers to limbs, so the **intermembral index** is a ratio of forelimb length to hind limb length.

To calculate the intermembral index, primatologists measure the length of the humerus and the length of the radius. The sum of these measurements is the overall forelimb length. They then measure the length of the femur and the length of the tibia. The sum of these measurements is the overall hind limb length. The overall forelimb length is divided by the overall hind limb length, and the result is then multiplied by 100 to generate the intermembral index.

$$\frac{(\text{humerus length} + \text{radius length})}{(\text{femur length} + \text{tibia length})} \times 100$$

If the resulting intermembral index value is less than 100, it indicates that the animal has long hind limbs. If the value is greater than 100, it indicates that the animal has long forelimbs, and if the value is close to 100, it indicates that the animal has forelimbs and hind limbs of relatively equal length.

As discussed above, different forms of primate locomotion use the forelimbs and hind limbs in different ways. Returning to vertical clingers and leapers, we notice that these species have elongated hind limbs to help with their leaping movement, so vertical clingers and leapers have intermembral index values less than 100. On the other end of the spectrum, brachiators rely heavily on their arms to swing from tree branch to tree branch, so they have elongated arms that result in intermembral index values that are greater than 100.

SOCIAL ORGANIZATION AND SEXUAL DIMORPHISM

The third important pattern of primate behavior and anatomy is the relationship between social organization and sexual dimorphism. *Di* means "two," and *morph* refers to form. So, **sexual dimorphism** refers to the physical differences between the male form and the female form within a species. This difference often manifests as larger overall body size in adult males than in adult females (**FIGURE 12.12**), as well as larger canine teeth and more robust cranial features in adult males than in their female counterparts (**FIGURE 12.13**). Humans have only slight sexual dimorphism, particularly when compared with other primates. Human males tend to be a little

intermembral index
a ratio of forelimb length to hind limb length that is often used to quantify locomotor adaptations

sexual dimorphism
the physical differences between adult males and adult females of a species

FIGURE 12.12 Sexual Dimorphism in Body Size
Some primates have pronounced sexual dimorphism in body size. In baboons, for example, males are much larger than females.

Steffen Foerster/Shutterstock

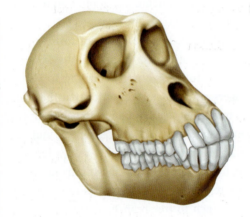

Female

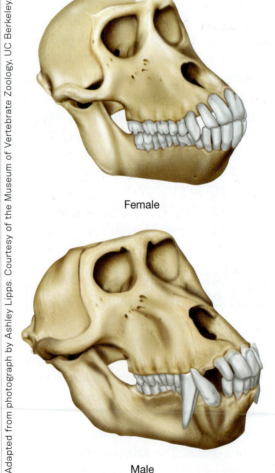

Male

Adapted from photograph by Ashley Lipps. Courtesy of the Museum of Vertebrate Zoology, UC Berkeley.

FIGURE 12.13 Sexual Dimorphism in the Cranium and Dentition
Some primates have pronounced sexual dimorphism in their crania and dentition, where males have more robust cranial features and larger canine teeth than females. These crania are shown at the same scale.

larger and more robust than females, and size differences are used by forensic anthropologists to help them sex skeletons (see Lab 7 for more information). But why, as we asked at the start of this lab, do some primate species have more pronounced sexual dimorphism than others?

Degrees of sexual dimorphism relate to degrees of male–male competition within a species. Primate species with more male–male competition have more pronounced sexual dimorphism. In contrast, primates with less male–male competition have less sexual dimorphism. To understand why this relationship exists, we must consider why sexual dimorphism may have evolved. It is important to recognize that sexual dimorphism is the result of an increase in and exaggeration of male body size and traits. It is not that female body types are smaller versions of male types. Rather, male body types are enlarged versions of female types. The enlarged and exaggerated traits of males are selectively favored because they improve male reproductive success. Bigger, more robust males outreproduce their smaller, more gracile male competitors. Their enlarged size and features may help them to win direct competitions with smaller males, so that they are able to maintain access to females for reproduction. Furthermore, a male with enlarged traits may be able to maintain access to females by simply threatening other males at a distance and avoiding direct competition entirely. In either case, the exaggerated traits of robust males are passed on preferentially to the next generation. Over time, we end up with populations with extreme differences in male and female body types.

Because sexual dimorphism relates to male–male competition, it also relates to social organization. Some types of primate social groups have more intense male–male competition than others. Therefore, in some types of social groups, we are likely to see more pronounced sexual dimorphism than in others. In monogamous social groups, male–male competition is limited. Most adult males will be partnered with an adult female and be successfully reproducing. The males do not need to compete for mating partners. We see the least amount of sexual

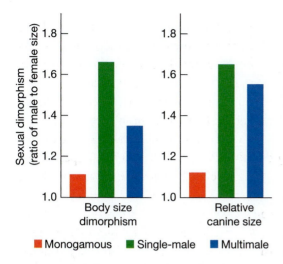

FIGURE 12.14 Sexual Dimorphism and Social Organization
The degree of sexual dimorphism in a primate species relates to its social organization. Primates in monogamous groups have little male–male competition and very little sexual dimorphism (near a ratio of 1.0, which represents no dimorphism). Primates in single-male groups have intense male–male competition and the highest levels of sexual dimorphism. Primates in multi-male groups have relatively high male–male competition and relatively high sexual dimorphism.

dimorphism in these monogamous groups (**FIGURE 12.14**).

In single-male polygynous groups (and some solitary groups), male–male competition is extremely high. One adult male will have access to a group of females. This leaves many other adult males wandering around without sexual partners. These unpartnered males will regularly challenge a male with females and attempt to take over his group or territory. In addition, there is little to limit the intensity of the competition. At the end of the day, the males competing with one another live separately and do not need to maintain a social relationship. Competition in these circumstances can be particularly violent. Consequently, sexual dimorphism is extremely pronounced in species with single-male social groups (see Figure 12.14).

Finally, in multimale polygynous groups, male–male competition is relatively high. An adult male will have access to multiple females within his group, but access to mates may be hindered by his position in the social hierarchy. Higher-status males will have access to more mating partners of the right age and fertility. Thus, competition exists between males trying to improve their social status and their consequent access to females. In contrast to the single-male polygynous group, there is, however, a limit to the competition within a multimale group. At the end of the day, these males do often continue to live together and maintain social relationships. This usually prevents the competition from becoming particularly violent. As a result, sexual dimorphism in multimale polygynous groups is pronounced, but not as extreme as in single-male groups (see Figure 12.14). By understanding the relationship between sexual dimorphism and social organization, biological anthropologists can use the degree of sexual dimorphism present in a population to hypothesize about and infer its likely social organization (just as they can use dietary adaptations to infer diet and locomotor adaptations to infer mode of locomotion).

CONCEPT REVIEW QUESTIONS

Name: _____   Section: _____

Course: _____   Date: _____

Answer the following questions in the space provided.

1. I have molars with pointy cusps and a simple digestive system. What type of diet do I have?

   A. Insectivorous
   B. Gummivorous
   C. Frugivorous
   D. Folivorous

2. A gummivorous primate is likely to have which of these traits?

   A. Large mandible
   B. Molars with shearing crests
   C. Large body size
   D. Small body size

3. I have molars with shearing crests and a complex stomach. What type of diet do I have?

   A. Frugivorous
   B. Insectivorous
   C. Folivorous
   D. Gummivorous

4. Define brachiation.

5. Semibrachiation is made possible by the presence of what trait?

6. What is the difference between arboreal quadrupedalism and terrestrial quadrupedalism?

7. I have arms and legs of similar length, robust hands and feet, and a short tail. What type of locomotion do I practice?

   A. Terrestrial quadrupedalism
   B. Brachiation
   C. Arboreal quadrupedalism
   D. Vertical clinging and leaping

8. I have long arms, mobile shoulders, and very robust finger bones. What type of locomotion do I practice?

   A. Brachiation
   B. Arboreal quadrupedalism
   C. Vertical clinging and leaping
   D. Knuckle-walking

9. Describe *one* sexually dimorphic trait in primates. Be sure to note how the trait appears in females and in males.

10. Which of these social groups is likely to have the most pronounced sexual dimorphism?
    A. Multimale polygynous group
    B. Single-male polygynous group
    C. Monogamous group
    D. None: All groups have the same degree of sexual dimorphism

LAB EXERCISES

Name: _____   Section: _____

Course: _____   Date: _____

EXERCISE 1   TOOTH TYPES

In this lab, we learned about different primate diets and dietary adaptations. Here, we will explore the types of teeth found in primates and how they function to help primates eat.

Work in a small group or alone to complete the following tasks.

STEP 1 Generate hypotheses. Review the types of food provided by your instructor and answer the following questions to generate your initial hypotheses.

1. Which food type(s) do you hypothesize will require biting?

2. Which food type(s) do you hypothesize can be eaten without biting?

3. Which food type do you hypothesize will require the most chewing?

4. Which food type do you hypothesize will require the least chewing?

STEP 2 Collect the data. Take each food one at a time. Eat the food as you normally would, taking bites if appropriate and chewing it until you are comfortable swallowing. As you do so, enter the relevant data in the chart below. Be sure that one person eats all four foods to avoid inconsistencies in eating styles and resulting data.

FOOD TYPES AND TEETH CHART

	Number of Bites Taken (0 or More)	Teeth Used to Bite (if Relevant)	Number of Chews per Bite (Up and Down Jaw Movement = 1 Chew)	Teeth Used to Chew (if Relevant)
Leafy Food				
Soft Fruit Food				
Crunchy Food				
Gooey Food				

STEP 3 Evaluate the data. Now, review your results with your group members, and use the data to evaluate your hypotheses.

5. Which food type(s) required biting? How do these data compare to your earlier hypotheses?

6. Which food required the most chewing? Which food required the least chewing? How do these data compare to your earlier hypotheses?

7. Which types of teeth were primarily used for biting? Which teeth were primarily used for chewing?

8. If you were to further test how different types of teeth correspond to different diets, what types of teeth would you hypothesize to be enlarged in primates whose diets emphasize each of these food types? Why?

EXERCISE 2 TOOTH SHAPE AS ADAPTATION

As we learned in this lab and in Exercise 1, the sizes and shapes of primates' teeth are often adaptations that help them eat particular types of food. Here, we will explore this relationship further.

Work in a small group or alone to complete the following tasks.

STEP 1 Review the primate diets discussed in this lab. Match each of the diets below to its primary obstacle.

1. Insectivory _____
2. Gummivory _____
3. Folivory _____
4. Frugivory _____

A. Food is soft and needs to be gently pulped
B. Food is surrounded by thin crunchy layer
C. Food is trapped behind tough tree bark
D. Food is tough and fibrous

STEP 2 To explore the relationship between shape and function, examine the everyday objects provided by your instructor (or those depicted in the Lab 12 Exercise Image Library on p. 359) and answer the following questions.

5A. Which object would you use to gently squash or squeeze something?

5B. What aspects of this object's shape would help you perform this task?

6A. Which object would you use to slice something?

6B. What aspects of this object's shape would help you perform this task?

7A. Which object would you use to pierce or puncture something?

7B. What aspects of this object's shape would help you perform this task?

8A. Which object would you use to scrape something?

8B. What aspects of this object's shape would help you perform this task?

STEP 3 Use your answers to reflect on the relationship between tooth shape and primate diet.

9A. What tooth shapes would be most useful for an insectivore?

9B. Why would these shapes be useful?

10A. What tooth shapes would be most useful for a gummivore?

10B. Why would these shapes be useful?

11A. What tooth shapes would be most useful for a folivore?

11B. Why would these shapes be useful?

12A. What tooth shapes would be most useful for a frugivore?

12B. Why would these shapes be useful?

EXERCISE 3   DIET AND DIETARY ADAPTATIONS 1

Work in a small group or alone to complete this exercise. Refer to the mystery primate dentitions provided by your instructor (or the photos in the Lab 12 Exercise Image Library on p. 360) to complete the chart below. Describe the incisors, molars, and muscle attachment on the mandible of each mystery primate. Then, using this trait information, determine the likely diet of each mystery primate, and give an example of one primate that has this diet.

	Mystery Primate A	Mystery Primate B	Mystery Primate C	Mystery Primate D
Incisors				
Molars				
Mandible Size and Muscle Attachment				
Diet				
Example Primate				

EXERCISE 4   DIET AND DIETARY ADAPTATIONS 2

Work in a small group or alone to complete this exercise. Review the primate descriptions below. For each primate, describe the primate's likely body size and digestive tract.

1. Primate A is an insectivore that eats a lot of moths, stick insects, and grasshoppers. These foods provide small packets of energy that are easy to digest.

    » Body size:

    » Digestive tract:

2. Primate B is a frugivore that eats a lot of berries, figs, and other tree fruits. These foods provide moderate packets of energy that are relatively easy to digest.

    » Body size:

    » Digestive tract:

3. Primate C is a gummivore that eats a lot of tree sap. This food provides small packets of energy that are easily digested.

    » Body size:

    » Digestive tract:

4. Primate D is a folivore that eats a wide variety of leaves, stems, and young plant shoots. This food provides limited, slow-burning energy and is difficult to digest.

    » Body size:

    » Digestive tract:

EXERCISE 5 LOCOMOTION AND LOCOMOTOR ADAPTATIONS 1

Work in a small group or alone to complete this exercise. Use the mystery primate skeletons provided by your instructor (or the photos in the Lab 12 Exercise Image Library on p. 361) to complete the chart below. Identify the scapular position, calculate the intermembral index, and describe the tail of each mystery primate. Then, using this trait information, determine the likely form of locomotion of each mystery primate, and give an example of one primate that has this form of locomotion.

	Mystery Primate A	Mystery Primate B
Scapular Position		
Intermembral Index*		
Tail		
Locomotion		
Example Primate		

*To calculate the intermembral index, use the formula provided on p. 345 of the text. Remember to use maximum bone lengths determined using a tape measure, ruler, or osteometric board (if available).

EXERCISE 6 LOCOMOTION AND LOCOMOTOR ADAPTATIONS 2

Work in a small group or alone to complete this exercise. Use the mystery primate skeletons provided by your instructor (or the photos in the Lab 12 Exercise Image Library on pp. 362–363) to complete the chart below. Identify the scapular position, calculate the intermembral index, and describe the tail of each mystery primate. Then, using this trait information, determine the likely form of locomotion of each mystery primate, and give an example of one primate that has this form of locomotion.

	Mystery Primate A	Mystery Primate B	Mystery Primate C
Scapular Position			
Intermembral Index*			
Tail			
Locomotion			
Example Primate			

*To calculate the intermembral index, use the formula provided on p. 345 of the text. Remember to use maximum bone lengths determined using a tape measure, ruler, or osteometric board (if available).

EXERCISE 7   SEXUAL DIMORPHISM

Work in a small group or alone to complete this exercise. Examine the mystery primate crania provided by your instructor (or the photos in the Lab 12 Exercise Image Library on p. 364) and answer the following questions. These crania represent adult individuals from the same species.

1. Which mystery primate is female?

2. Which mystery primate is male?

3. Describe *two* traits you used to make this distinction.

EXERCISE 8   SOCIAL ORGANIZATION AND SEXUAL DIMORPHISM

Work in a small group or alone to complete this exercise. Examine the mystery primate crania provided by your instructor (or the photos in the Lab 12 Exercise Image Library on p. 365) and answer the following questions. These crania represent an adult male and an adult female from two mystery primate species, A and B.

1. Which mystery primate species has a single-male polygynous social structure?

2. Which mystery primate species has a multimale polygynous social structure?

3. Describe *one* trait you used to make this distinction.

CRITICAL THINKING QUESTIONS

On a separate sheet of paper, answer the following questions.

1. Imagine that a biological anthropologist 10,000 years in the future is examining our fossil remains. The anthropologist notices that humans have broad incisors and molars with rounded cusps. How do you think the anthropologist would interpret these traits—what diet would the traits indicate? Would this interpretation be accurate? Why might humans have these traits, as opposed to the specialized teeth we see in primates with other diets?

2. What adaptations for brachiation do you have in your body today? Why do humans have these adaptations? What adaptations for brachiation are you missing? Why do you lack some of the adaptations for brachiation seen in gibbons?

3. Consider the degree of sexual dimorphism in humans. What does it suggest about our social organization in the present? Many of our fossil relatives have more sexual dimorphism than we do; what does this observation suggest about our ancestral social organization?

4. You come across a primate living in the grassy highlands of eastern Africa. She has arms and legs that are relatively equal in length, and a short tail. She has small incisors and large, bilophodont molars. This primate is female, but males of her species have much larger bodies and canine teeth than females. Males also have extra fur around their chests and heads that is not seen in females. What is the likely diet of this primate species? Give one trait that supports your determination. What is the likely form of locomotion of this primate species? Give one trait that supports your determination. What is the likely social organization of this primate species? Give one trait that supports your determination.

5. In this lab, we learned about the intermembral index and how this calculation correlates with locomotor adaptations. Measure the human skeletal material provided by your instructor (or in the image at right). Remember to measure the maximum bone length using a tape measure, ruler, or osteometric board (if available).

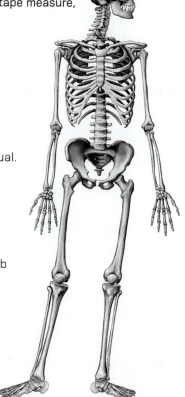

    Humerus: _____

    Radius: _____

    Femur: _____

    Tibia: _____

Use these measurements to calculate the intermembral index for this individual. Use the formula provided on p. 345 of the text.

    Intermembral index: _____

What does this intermembral index suggest about the limb proportions of humans? What other primates have similar intermembral index values and limb proportions, and for what form of locomotion are they adapted? Do humans move the same way? Why do you think humans and these other primates have similar limb proportions and intermembral index values?

6. In this lab, we reviewed primate diets and dietary adaptations, as well as forms of locomotion and locomotor adaptations. To help you make comparisons and better understand the general pattern of these behaviors, complete the two charts that follow. In the Primate Diet Chart on p. 358, describe

the adaptations associated with each diet and give an example of a primate that has this diet. Similarly, in the Primate Locomotion Chart below, describe the adaptations associated with each form of locomotion and give an example of a primate that practices this form of locomotion.

PRIMATE DIET CHART

	Adaptations	Primate(s)
Insectivory		
Gummivory		
Frugivory		
Folivory		

PRIMATE LOCOMOTION CHART

	Adaptations	Primate(s)
Vertical Clinging and Leaping		
Brachiation		
Semibrachiation		
Arboreal Quadrupedalism		
Terrestrial Quadrupedalism		
Knuckle-Walking		

LAB 12 EXERCISE IMAGE LIBRARY

Students should use these images only if directed to by their instructor.

EXERCISE 2 TOOTH SHAPE AS ADAPTATION

A

Panther Media GmbH/ Alamy Stock Photo

B

Nop1/Shutterstock

C

Bubbers BB/Shutterstock

D

Michael Burrell/Alamy Stock Photo

A

Bone Clones/boneclones.com

B

Courtesy of Ashley Lipps

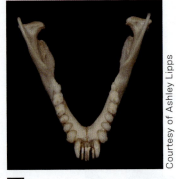

C

Courtesy of Ashley Lipps

D

Courtesy of Ashley Lipps

EXERCISE 5 LOCOMOTION AND LOCOMOTOR ADAPTATIONS 1

Note: *These images are not to scale. However, because intermembral index calculations are an internal comparison of the ratio of bone lengths within a single skeleton, the calculations may still be used accurately.*

Courtesy of Ashley Lipps

A

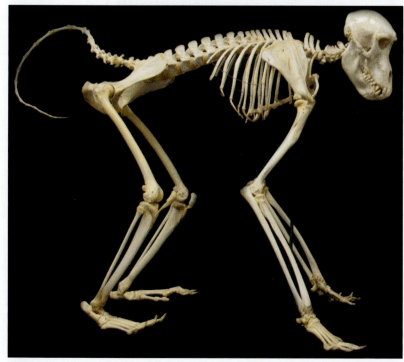

Courtesy of Ashley Lipps

B

EXERCISE 6 LOCOMOTION AND LOCOMOTOR ADAPTATIONS 2

Note: *These images are not to scale. However, because intermembral index calculations are an internal comparison of the ratio of bone lengths within a single skeleton, the calculations may still be used accurately. In addition, the limbs of Primate A are slightly distorted by the position of the skeleton. When measuring the limb bones of Primate A, we encourage you to use the specimen's right femur and left tibia to obtain the most accurate measurements.*

Courtesy of Ashley Lipps

A

EXERCISE 6 LOCOMOTION AND LOCOMOTOR ADAPTATIONS 2 (CONTINUED)

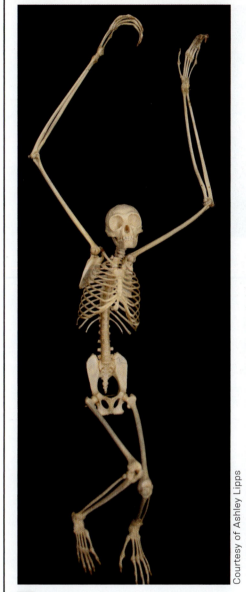

Courtesy of Ashley Lipps

B

Courtesy of Ashley Lipps

C

EXERCISE 7 SEXUAL DIMORPHISM

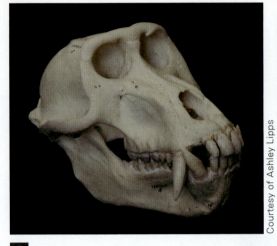

Courtesy of Ashley Lipps

A

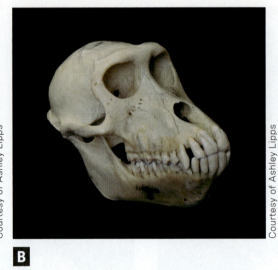

Courtesy of Ashley Lipps

B

EXERCISE 8 SOCIAL ORGANIZATION AND SEXUAL DIMORPHISM

Ted Thai/The LIFE Picture Collection/ Getty Images

Courtesy of Ashley Lipps

A

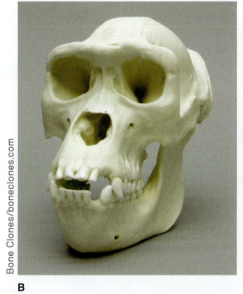

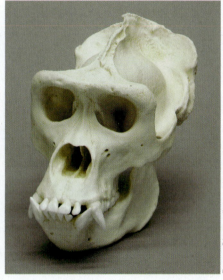

Bone Clones/boneclones.com

Bone Clones/boneclones.com

B

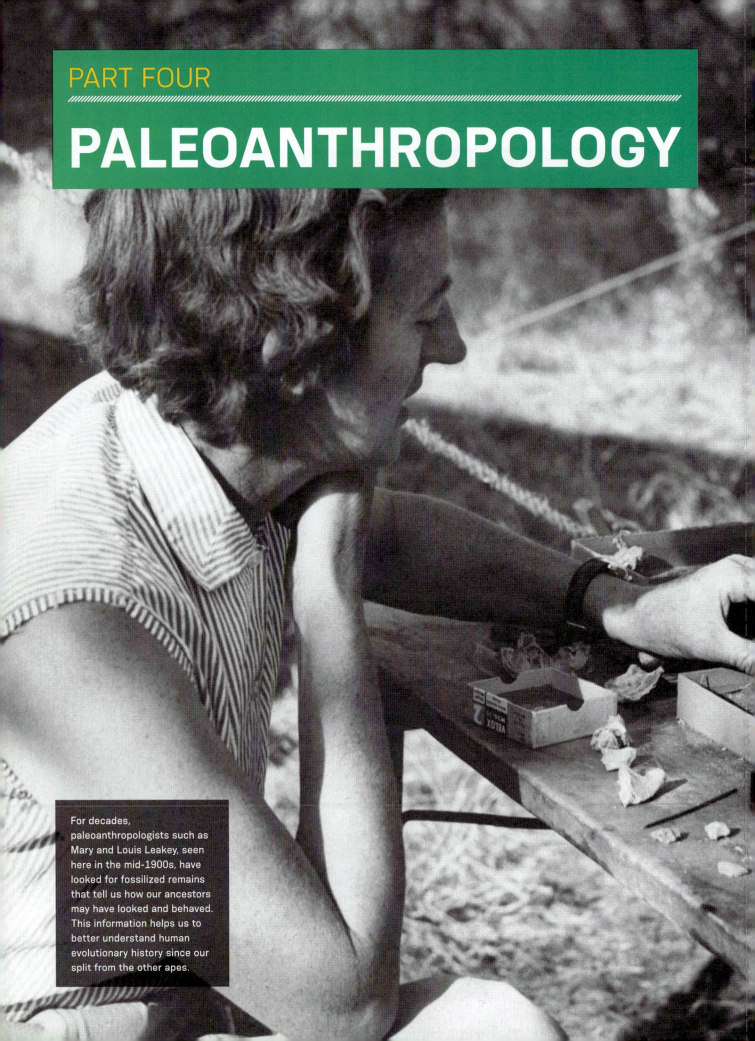

PART FOUR

PALEOANTHROPOLOGY

For decades, paleoanthropologists such as Mary and Louis Leakey, seen here in the mid-1900s, have looked for fossilized remains that tell us how our ancestors may have looked and behaved. This information helps us to better understand human evolutionary history since our split from the other apes.

Bettmann/Getty Images

LAB 13: PRIMATE EVOLUTION

WHAT TOPICS ARE COVERED IN THIS LAB?

- An introduction to the process of fossilization
- An overview of mammalian evolution
- A review of the major fossil finds in primate evolution
- An introduction to the methods used to date fossil sites

LAB 14: IDENTIFYING THE HUMAN LINEAGE

WHAT TOPICS ARE COVERED IN THIS LAB?

- A critical review of different approaches to identifying the human lineage
- An introduction to bipedalism and its associated skeletal adaptations
- A look at our earliest possible ancestors since our split from the other apes

LAB 15: THE AUSTRALOPITHS AND EARLY MEMBERS OF THE GENUS *HOMO*

WHAT TOPICS ARE COVERED IN THIS LAB?

- An overview of the major fossil *Australopithecus* species
- A comparison of the different australopiths
- An overview of the first species in the *Homo* genus and a look at the debate surrounding their classification

LAB 16: LATER MEMBERS OF THE GENUS *HOMO*

WHAT TOPICS ARE COVERED IN THIS LAB?

- An overview of the later species in the *Homo* genus
- A review of the migration of our ancestors out of Africa
- A comparison of alternative explanations about the origin and spread of our species
- A consideration of the relationship between Neanderthals and humans

Evidence from the large Chicxulub crater in Mexico shows that an asteroid crashed to Earth around 66 mya. This impact led to the extinction of many of the dinosaurs, but small, nocturnal mammals alive at that time survived and became the diverse group of animals we know today.

LAB **13**

Primate Evolution

Lab Learning Objectives

By the end of this lab, students should be able to:

- describe the major changes throughout mammalian evolution.

- describe at least one fossil primate for every major group of living primates, including its temporal and spatial distribution, main features, and relationship to living primates.

- identify the key trends in primate evolution and place these trends in chronological order.

Imagine Earth 66 million years ago (mya)—it is the Mesozoic era, the Age of Reptiles. Flowering plants are proliferating, and reptiles, including dinosaurs, live throughout the world. For the past 200 million years, a group of small animals have lived side by side with their more famous dinosaur contemporaries. These overlooked animals are generally small, covered in fur, and have specialized teeth. They come out at night to find food—primarily insects. They are less subject to predation at night, so their nocturnal lifestyle is helping them to survive in the dinosaur-dominated landscape. However, they are by no means thriving. Reptiles occupy most of Earth's habitats, and they are stiff competition for these small, nocturnal mammals.

At around this time, something unexpected happens. A large asteroid crashes into Earth, leaving a 180-kilometer-wide crater near the Yucatán Peninsula of Mexico. The crash causes massive clouds of dust that block sunlight for months (or possibly years) and trigger a dramatic drop in temperatures. Many organisms are ill adapted to these new environmental conditions, and 50% of the world's animal families (including many of the dinosaurs) go extinct. In contrast, the small nocturnal mammals begin to flourish. As the dinosaurs go extinct and vacate various habitats, the mammals move in. Once in a new habitat, they adapt to their current environmental circumstances, undergoing rapid diversification. Some become well suited to tree dwelling, while others are more suited to open

fossil the traces or remains of an organism preserved in rock

fossilization the process of fossil formation that occurs under certain conditions

continental drift the shifting of the continents that is caused by the movement of Earth's continental plates

deserts. Others become better suited for life in water, and still others become suited to life in the air. This formerly struggling group quickly becomes a diverse and successful class of organisms. The Age of Reptiles is over, and the Age of Mammals begins.

INTRODUCTION

In this lab, we discuss the important fossil species and major trends of primate evolution. This information helps us place our own evolutionary history in a broader chronological context. We begin with an introduction to the process of fossilization. We then briefly consider the major trends in mammalian evolution. Next, we examine primate evolution more specifically. Then we review the key fossil species associated with the major groups of living primates. We conclude with a discussion of the complexities of dating fossil sites.

WHAT IS A FOSSIL?

Fossils are the traces or remains of organisms preserved in rock. In some cases, fossils are preserved impressions left by organisms, such as their footprints or tracks. In other cases, fossils are formed as the organic materials of an organism decay and are slowly replaced by minerals from the surrounding environment. Any organic material can become a fossil, but fossils that are of interest to paleoanthropologists are usually formed from bones and teeth. It is important to remember that fossils are basically rocks. For this reason, they often lack organic material and DNA. Although some remains are only partially fossilized and do contain small pockets of DNA, such remains are uncommon. Trace amounts of DNA are more likely to be found in remains that have fossilized more recently (see Lab 16 for an example).

Not all organisms become fossilized when they die. The remains of an organism will undergo the **fossilization** process only under very specific conditions (**FIGURE 13.1**). Its organic material

must decay slowly to be successfully replaced by surrounding minerals. Conditions that speed up decay are not good for fossilization. For example, if an organism dies and is left exposed to weather or predators, decomposition will occur more rapidly. Similarly, if an organism dies in an oxygen-rich environment with abundant bacteria, its remains will decay quickly. In these situations of rapid decomposition, fossilization is unlikely. At the same time, soil and geological conditions are big factors in the fossilization process. If the surrounding soil is too acidic or has too much groundwater, organic material will dissolve too quickly for fossilization to take place. In addition, if there is too much geological pressure or activity, the bones and teeth may be deformed so much that the fossil is greatly distorted or not formed at all.

There are several key biases in the fossil record that we must always take into account. First, the distribution of fossils is not uniform across time and space. As we've discussed, fossilization requires specific environmental conditions. In many parts of the world, at many different times, the environment has not been conducive to fossilization. These conditions cause big gaps in the fossil record. For example, we have virtually no fossil record for the time interval when the last common ancestors of humans and the other great apes were alive. These ancestral African species would have lived in rainforests, where conditions do not readily allow for fossilization. Similarly, even in time intervals where we have extensive fossil data from one area, we might not have any fossil data from a nearby area. For example, we have a lot of fossil material from our ancestors from eastern and southern Africa, but virtually none from western and northern Africa. Our ancestors probably lived throughout the vast continent, but ideal conditions for fossilization at that time were found only in the eastern and southern regions.

The issue of fossil distribution is further complicated by continental drift. In the past, all of the land on Earth was concentrated in one very large landmass (**FIGURE 13.2**). This landmass then broke up into separate pieces (continents) that began shifting apart. This process of shifting is known as **continental drift**, and it conti-

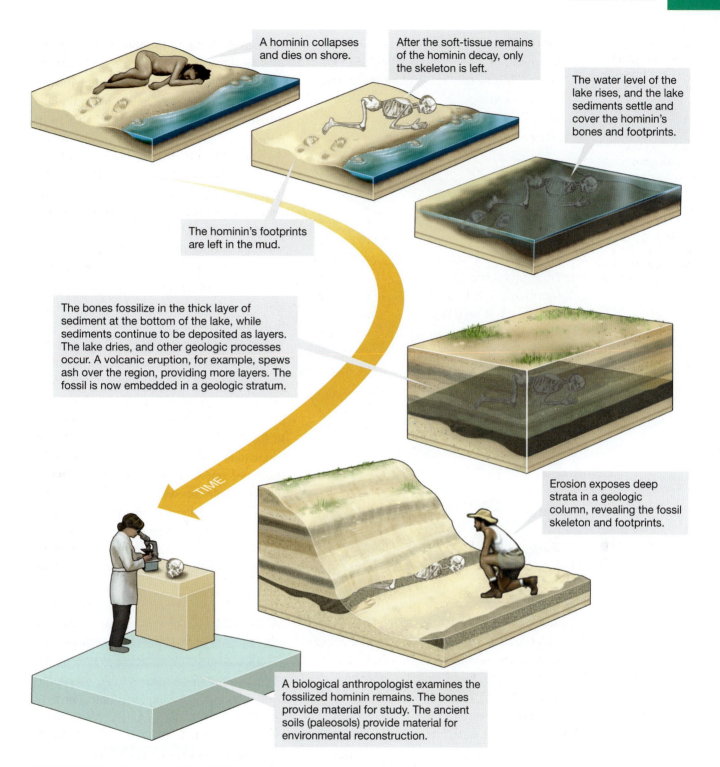

A hominin collapses and dies on shore.

After the soft-tissue remains of the hominin decay, only the skeleton is left.

The water level of the lake rises, and the lake sediments settle and cover the hominin's bones and footprints.

The hominin's footprints are left in the mud.

The bones fossilize in the thick layer of sediment at the bottom of the lake, while sediments continue to be deposited as layers. The lake dries, and other geologic processes occur. A volcanic eruption, for example, spews ash over the region, providing more layers. The fossil is now embedded in a geologic stratum.

TIME

Erosion exposes deep strata in a geologic column, revealing the fossil skeleton and footprints.

A biological anthropologist examines the fossilized hominin remains. The bones provide material for study. The ancient soils (paleosols) provide material for environmental reconstruction.

FIGURE 13.1 The Process of Fossilization
Only a handful of organisms become fossils when they die. Fossilization requires specific environmental conditions and processes.

nues today. As the continental plates drift, their movement causes earthquakes and other geological events. At different times in the past, the continents we know today were in very different places. These former locations, along with larger variations in climate, allowed for very differ-

ent primate distributions in the past than we see today. For example, around 50 mya, similar early primate species were distributed throughout North America and Europe. Just before that time, the two continents were connected and shared similar environments, so ancestors of these

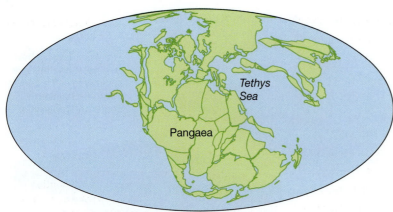

Early Jurassic (about 200 mya)

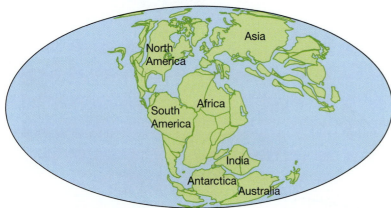

Late Jurassic (about 150 mya)

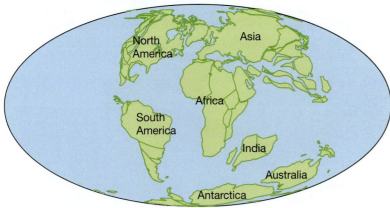

Late Cretaceous (about 70 mya)

FIGURE 13.2 Continental Drift
Throughout Earth's history, the continental plates have shifted. In the past, the continents we know today were in very different locations around the world.

sil materials, leading to more gaps in the fossil record. For example, one site may have a lot of fossil material for a particular time interval, but it may have nothing for the interval immediately after. Events that occurred after fossilization may have randomly destroyed some of the fossils, but not others. Of course, geological events that occurred after fossilization may also help paleoanthropologists today. For example, Olduvai Gorge is a well-researched location in Tanzania with fossil remains from many of our ancestral species. Erosion and other geological forces in this area in recent years (postfossilization) created the gorge, which has exposed lower levels of sediment and improved access to deeply buried fossils.

Finally, we as researchers bias the fossil record. We tend to look in a limited number of places for fossil remains. Part of the reason is that many researchers have found fossils in those areas before, so we know those areas are conducive to fossilization. However, any decision about where to look is also based on our own preferences, our emphasis on certain time intervals or regions, or current events in a region. For example, researchers interested in a particular species may return to the same regions where others have located the species in the past. While the researchers are likely to find more fossils in that same area, they may be overlooking fossils in other areas. Furthermore, a researcher may be forced to abandon or avoid research in certain areas because of local political conflict or war. The choices made about where to look for fossils may result in some areas being overstudied while others are left completely untouched.

BEFORE THE PRIMATES

Earth's history is divided into different time spans. The smallest chunks of time are the *epochs*. Numerous epochs form *periods*, which in turn form *eras*; multiple eras then form an *eon*. Each of these divisions is given a name, and increasing detail is provided for more recent times. This time scale is used by geologists, biological anthropologists, and other scientists to help organize the history of Earth and of its living creatures.

primate species could easily move between regions and live in either area.

In addition to these issues affecting fossil distribution, we must also take into account the fact that even if fossils are formed, they are not necessarily well preserved. Later geological activity, such as earthquakes, may shift or destroy fos-

Although numerous plants, fish, insects, and amphibians flourished in the Paleozoic era (541 to 252 mya), the Mesozoic (252 to 66 mya) is the more famous era in Earth's history **(FIGURE 13.3)**. Often referred to as the Age of Reptiles, the Mesozoic is known for the proliferation of reptiles, particularly dinosaurs. During this same era, however, the very first mammals appeared around 220 mya. These mammals were small, rodent-like animals that were usually nocturnal. As discussed at the beginning of this lab, a large asteroid crashed to Earth and altered environmental conditions around 66 mya. Many of the Earth's animals, including many of the dinosaurs, went extinct as a result. This event marked the end of the Mesozoic and the beginning of the Cenozoic (66 mya to present), and it is known as the **K–Pg (Cretaceous–Paleogene) boundary**, formerly the K–T (Cretaceous–Tertiary) boundary.

During the Cenozoic era, the mammals thrived and proliferated. They moved into the habitats vacated by the dinosaurs and other extinct animals, and they quickly diversified in

K–Pg (Cretaceous–Paleogene) boundary (formerly known as the Cretaceous–Tertiary (K–T) boundary) the temporal boundary between the Mesozoic and Cenozoic eras; marked by the large extinction event when many dinosaurs went extinct

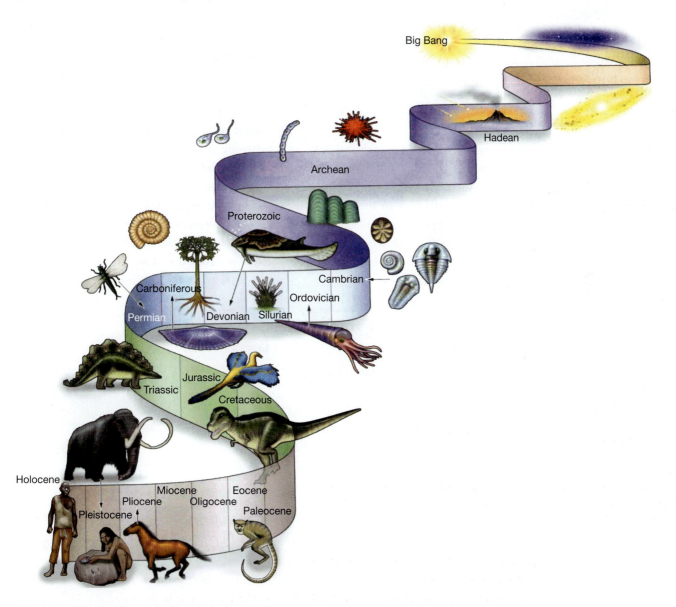

FIGURE 13.3 Major Events in the Evolution of Life
Many early plants, fish, insects, and amphibians lived in the Paleozoic era (the Cambrian through Permian periods). The Mesozoic era (the Triassic through Cretaceous periods) was the Age of Reptiles, when dinosaurs flourished and early mammals first appeared on Earth. Our recent evolution as primates and humans occurred in the Cenozoic era (the Paleocene through Holocene epochs).

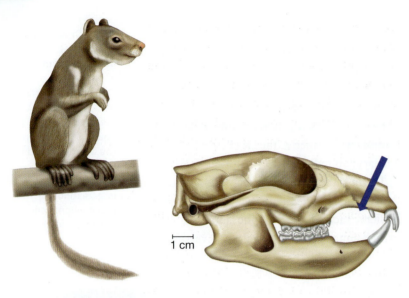

FIGURE 13.4 *Plesiadapis*
Early plesiadapiforms, such as *Plesiadapis*, would probably have been more rodent-like than many modern primates. They had long snouts and specialized front teeth separated from their back teeth by a toothless gap (arrow).

plesiadapiform
one of a group of diverse primate-like mammals that lived over 56 mya and may be among the first primates

adapiform one of a group of early primates that lived between 56 and 34 mya

postcranial relating to the bones below or behind the head

omomyoid one of a group of early primates that lived between 56 and 34 mya

their new environments. Most of the major mammal groups that we know today, such as bats, rodents, horses, and whales, were formed as a result. The mammals were so successful in the Cenozoic that the era is often called the Age of Mammals. During this time, when mammals as a whole were rapidly diversifying, the first primates appeared on Earth.

PRIMATE EVOLUTION

There is a lot of debate about what species qualify as the very first primates. During the Paleocene epoch (66 to 56 mya), a diverse group of primate-like mammals lived in North America, Europe, and Asia. These mammals are called **plesiadapiforms**. These species were initially interpreted as the first primates because they share some features with primates, such as generalized molar teeth. The later plesiadapiforms often share additional traits with primates, such as long fingers and short palms. However, many researchers have pointed out that despite some similarities, the plesiadapiforms lack several important primate features. For example, many plesiadapiforms do not have bony eye orbits, nails, grasping hands and feet, or a large brain for their body size—all characteristic traits of

primates. In addition, plesiadapiforms, such as the genus *Plesiadapis*, often have an elongated snout with specialized front teeth separated from their other teeth by a toothless gap (**FIGURE 13.4**).

The Early Lemurs and Lorises

While the earliest primates are not clearly identifiable in the fossil record, by the Eocene (56 to 34 mya), we see numerous fossil species in North America and Europe that have clear, defining primate features. These fossils, known as the **adapiforms**, are generally small to medium-sized (similar to modern lemurs). The adapiforms, such as the genus *Adapis*, have forward-facing eyes, postorbital bars, grasping hands and feet, nails instead of claws, and larger brains relative to their body size than other mammals (**FIGURE 13.5**). Although some adapiforms have large eyes that suggest nocturnal behavior, most adapiforms have relatively small eyes and appear to have been diurnal. Their **postcranial** traits (those below the head) suggest arboreal locomotion, such as climbing and leaping. Many researchers believe the adapiforms are related to living lemurs or lorises. However, the adapiforms lack some key lemur and loris traits (such as the dental comb), so the relationship is unclear.

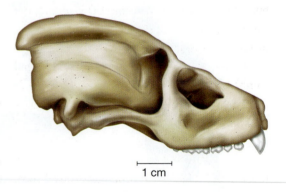

FIGURE 13.5 *Adapis*
Adapiforms, such as the *Adapis* specimen seen here, had forward-facing eyes, postorbital bars, and relatively large brains for their body size. Many adapiforms had small eyes, suggesting a diurnal lifestyle.

The Early Tarsiers

During the Eocene, we also see another group of primates, known as the **omomyoids**, throughout North America and Eurasia. Similar to the

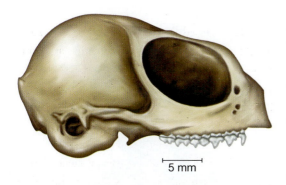

FIGURE 13.6 *Shoshonius*
Omomyoids, such as the *Shoshonius* specimen seen here, had forward-facing eyes, postorbital bars, and relatively large brains for their body size. Many omomyoids have large eyes, suggesting a nocturnal lifestyle. They also have shorter snouts than adapiforms.

adapiforms, the omomyoids are definite primates with forward-facing eyes, postorbital bars, grasping hands and feet, nails instead of claws, and large brains. However, compared with adapiforms, omomyoids (such as the genus *Shoshonius*) have shorter snouts and smaller bodies (**FIGURE 13.6**). The teeth of different species indicate various diets, including frugivory and insectivory. Omomyoids tend to have very large eyes, indicating nocturnal behavior. They also have some postcranial indicators for a leaping form of locomotion. Some researchers consider the omomyoids to be related to modern lorises, but other researchers consider them to be more closely related to tarsiers. As with the adapiforms, the omomyoids lack some of the key traits seen in modern lorises (such as the dental comb) or in modern tarsiers (such as some of the special leaping adaptations), so the relationship remains unclear.

The Early Anthropoids

It is unclear whether anthropoids evolved from adapiforms, omomyoids, or another primate group. What is apparent is that by the end of the Eocene, we see primates with true anthropoid traits. For example, the genus *Eosimias*, found in China, dates to around 42 mya. It includes some of the smallest known primate species (living or extinct), with dental and postcranial traits that suggest they are anthropoids. The classification and significance of *Eosimias* and its Eocene relatives are debated. Some research-

ers believe it is the earliest anthropoid genus because of its anthropoid-like traits, such as a New World monkey–like dental formula and foot adaptations for arboreal quadrupedalism. Other researchers argue it is more closely related to nonanthropoids because of features such as its insectivorous diet and incredibly small body size (individuals were estimated to weigh less than half a pound).

Anthropologists have recovered numerous anthropoid fossils dating from the end of the Eocene and during the Oligocene (34 to 23 mya). Many of these anthropoid species can be found in the Fayum region of Egypt. Today this area is a desert, but in the early Oligocene it was a forested swampland and home to countless species of plants and animals, including many anthropoids. Perhaps the best-known of these anthropoids is *Aegyptopithecus*, a genus with one known species, *Aegyptopithecus zeuxis* (**FIGURE 13.7**). Dating to around 30 mya, *Aegyptopithecus* has several general anthropoid traits, such as full bony enclosure of the orbit and a fused mandible. It also has quite a few specifically catarrhine-like traits. For example, it has a 2.1.2.3 dental formula and a larger brain than earlier fossil primates. It has a body size similar

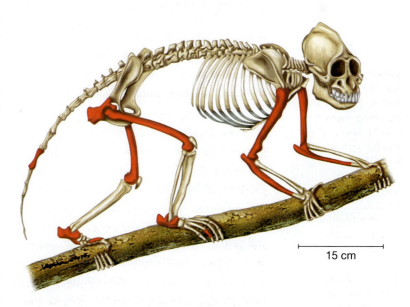

FIGURE 13.7 *Aegyptopithecus*
Parts of the *Aegyptopithecus* cranium and some postcranial bones (shown in red) have been recovered. This skeletal evidence suggests that *Aegyptopithecus* was an early anthropoid with full bony enclosure of the eye orbits and a fused mandible. In addition, it had a 2.1.2.3 dental formula and a large brain for its body, like modern catarrhines.

to that of many living monkeys and postcranial traits that suggest it was an arboreal quadruped. Its dental traits indicate a frugivorous diet, although it also has a sagittal crest and correspondingly large chewing muscles. It appears to have been sexually dimorphic, which may indicate some form of polygynous social organization. This combination of traits suggests that *Aegyptopithecus* was an early catarrhine anthropoid.

The Early New World Monkeys

While catarrhines probably evolved from *Aegyptopithecus* or something similar in the Old World, the evolution of the New World primate lineage is less clear. One of the oldest known South American primates is called *Branisella* (**FIGURE 13.8**). This primate is found in Bolivia and dates to around 26 mya (late Oligocene). It shares several dental traits with living New World monkeys, such as the presence of three premolars in each mouth quadrant. Its teeth also indicate a frugivorous or folivorous diet. Numerous Miocene (23 to 5.3 mya) New World monkeys have been discovered as well. Unfortunately, the New World monkey fossil record is very challenging to interpret.

First, while some fossil species have been discovered, the primate fossil record of Central and South America is relatively sparse. Second, it is particularly difficult to determine the place of origin for the New World monkeys. Are they descended from the adapiforms and omomyoids that lived in North America? If so, why are there so few primate fossils in the millions of years between the early Eocene (about 50 mya) primates of North America and the late Oligocene to Miocene (26 to 5.3 mya) primates of South America? Alternatively, are the New World primates descended from an anthropoid from the Old World? If this is the case, how did that ancestral primate get from Africa to South America when the continents were already separated by the Atlantic Ocean? The two continents were closer together in these ancient time intervals than they are today, but could a primate that was washed out to sea on debris during a storm in Africa survive a journey of many days to the shores of South America?

FIGURE 13.8
Branisella
The earliest known platyrrhine is *Branisella*. It had three premolars in each mouth quadrant and low, rounded molar cusps that suggest a frugivorous diet.

Low, rounded cusps

2 mm

Takai et al. 1996. New specimens of the oldest fossil platyrrhine, *Branisella boliviana*, from Salla, Bolivia. *American Journal of Physical Anthropology* 99:301–314. Copyright © 1996, Wiley-Liss, Inc.

Drawing by Jorge Antonio Gonzalez

FIGURE 13.9 *Perupithecus*
The recently discovered *Perupithecus* lived in the Americas around 36 mya and had traits similar to African species alive at the same time. This supports the hypothesis that New World monkeys originated in Africa.

A recently discovered fossil species from the rainforest of Peru provides new evidence in support of the hypothesis that monkeys inadvertently rafted from Africa to the Americas. *Perupithecus*, which dates to around 36 mya, was about the size of a modern-day tamarin and had monkey-like teeth (**FIGURE 13.9**). It predates *Branisella* by 10 million years and pushes the appearance of monkeys back much earlier in the Americas. Most interestingly, the molar teeth of *Perupithecus* are somewhat similar to those of a species of monkey from North Africa that lived at the same time (*Talahpithecus*). This similarity suggests that the two species may be related, which strengthens the hypothesis that the ancestors of New World monkeys evolved in Africa and rafted across the then-smaller ocean, rather than originating in North America and working their way south.

The Early Old World Monkeys

Returning to the Old World, remember that the catarrhines probably evolved from something along the lines of *Aegyptopithecus*. Early catar-

cercopithecine-like terrestrial lifestyle. Within the Pliocene (5.3 to 2.6 mya) and Pleistocene (2.6 mya to 12 kya—that is, 12,000 years ago), the fossil species become more similar to the distinct Old World monkey groups seen today. These more recent fossils often resemble living Old World monkeys so much that they are assigned to the same genera as their living counterparts, such as *Macaca* (living macaques and their extinct relatives) and *Colobus* (living colobus monkeys and their extinct relatives).

The Early Apes

Like the Old World monkeys, the apes probably evolved from an early catarrhine, such as *Aegyptopithecus*. As they split from Old World monkeys, early apes would have probably evolved specific ape traits, such as Y-5 molars, suspensory adaptations, and the lack of a tail. Perhaps the best-known early ape is the genus *Proconsul* (**FIGURE 13.11**). It was found in Africa from 22

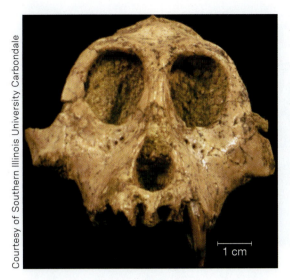

FIGURE 13.10 *Victoriapithecus*
One of the earliest members of the distinct Old World monkey lineage, *Victoriapithecus* had bilophodont molars and dental adaptations for a frugivorous diet.

rhines would have then split into the two distinct groups we recognize today: the Old World monkeys and the apes. The oldest genus in the distinct Old World monkey lineage is *Victoriapithecus*, with one known fossil species, *Victoriapithecus macinnesi* (**FIGURE 13.10**). Although *Victoriapithecus* first appears in Africa around 19 mya (early Miocene), it is primarily known from a site in Kenya that dates to around 15 mya (middle Miocene). *Victoriapithecus* has the bilophodont molars found in modern Old World monkeys, and it generally has a mix of colobine-like and cercopithecine-like features. It has wide incisors and low molar cusps, suggesting a frugivorous diet. However, it also has a sagittal crest, suggesting prominent chewing muscles and a dietary emphasis on hard fruits (rather than soft fruits). Its postcrania indicate at least some adaptations for terrestrial quadrupedalism.

After the split from apes, Old World monkeys evolved into the distinct groups we recognize today—the colobines and cercopithecines. The exact nature and timing of this split is unclear, but numerous fossils of each group appear throughout Africa and Asia at the end of the Miocene. The earliest of these fossils often have an unusual mix of traits, such as colobine-like adaptations for folivory paired with a more

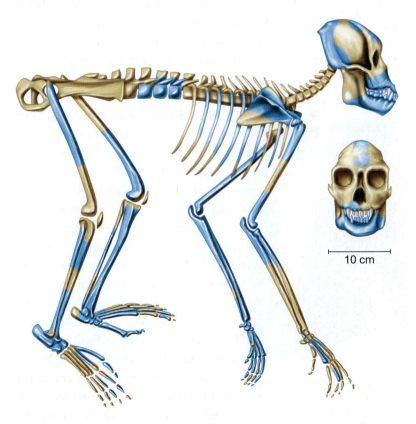

FIGURE 13.11 *Proconsul*
One of the earliest apes, *Proconsul* had Y-5 molars and was tailless. However, it was not a brachiator. Note that the bones shown in blue have actually been recovered, while the other bones are reconstructions based on available information.

A   **B**

FIGURE 13.12 *Nyanzapithecus alesi*
(A) In 2017, researchers led by Isaiah Nengo (holding fossil) unearthed (B) an infant skull of *Nyanzapithecus alesi* with preserved, ape-like teeth and bony ear structures. This find (nicknamed Alesi) adds evidence supporting the hypothesis that apes originated in Africa.

to 17 mya (early Miocene). It has dental traits that suggest a frugivorous diet, and its postcranial traits indicate that it was probably an arboreal quadruped. Although it is an early fossil that still shares many features with earlier Oligocene catarrhines, it has some important apelike traits. For example, it is tailless, has a large brain for its body size, and has Y-5 molars. The exact relationship of *Proconsul* to living apes is unclear, but it is likely that living apes evolved from a common ancestor similar to *Proconsul*.

By 13 mya (middle Miocene), the apes had become a diverse group of species distributed throughout much of Europe and Asia as well as Africa. The fossil record for Africa at this time is quite limited compared with that of Eurasia. However, researchers hypothesize that the apes were common in Africa throughout the Miocene. The gap in the African fossil record probably exists because the apes were living in areas that were not conducive to fossilization (as discussed above). One unusual exception is the recently discovered species *Nyanzapithecus alesi*, recovered from a middle Miocene site in Kenya in 2017. Adding to its unusual

preservation conditions, the specimen (nicknamed Alesi) is a nearly complete skull from an infant, which is particularly rare in the fossil record (**FIGURE 13.12**). Studies of the external features and internal morphology (via sophisticated X-ray imaging) indicate that Alesi had apelike teeth and bony ear structures. It was part of the nyanzapithecine ape group that first appeared in Africa around 25 mya, and its discovery supports the hypothesis that apes originated and began diversifying in Africa before expanding out to other continents.

Outside of Africa in Europe, we find the genus *Dryopithecus* (**FIGURE 13.13**). Apes of this genus lived around 12 to 8 mya (late Miocene) and had apelike canines and Y-5 molars. Both their brain and body sizes were comparable to those of a modern chimpanzee, and they may have had some adaptations for suspensory locomotion (such as long arms). Around 8 to 7 mya (late Miocene) in Europe, we find the genus *Oreopithecus* (**FIGURE 13.14**). This fossil ape was closely related to the nyanzapithecine ape group (including Alesi) that originated earlier in Africa. It had teeth with tall cusps for folivory and a medium body size. It also had long, mobile arms suited for suspensory locomotion. Both *Dryopithecus* and *Oreopithecus* are related to living apes, but

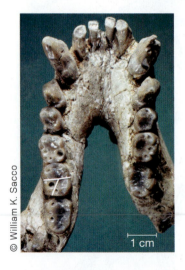

FIGURE 13.13 *Dryopithecus*
Dryopithecus, an early European ape, had Y-5 molars (shown here), a relatively large brain for its body size, and possibly some adaptations for brachiation.

neither of them appears to be in the direct lineage of any particular modern ape species. It is perhaps more helpful to think of them as branches in the bushy ape family tree that did not survive to the present day.

Around the same time in Asia, we also find numerous ape species. The genus *Khoratpithecus* lived in Thailand around 9 to 6 mya (late Miocene). It had broad incisors and other dental traits that indicate a frugivorous diet and a close relationship to modern orangutans. At 8 mya in Asia, we also find the largest primates that ever lived. Some of these huge primates are estimated to have weighed as much as 300 kg (or 660 lb) and have been aptly classified into the genus *Gigantopithecus* (FIGURE 13.15). *Gigantopithecus* had thick enamel on its teeth, like many other fossil apes. It also had very large molars and mandibles, suggesting a diet requiring a lot of chewing. Some research has suggested that *Gigantopithecus* may have eaten a lot of bamboo. Perhaps the most interesting thing about *Gigantopithecus* is that it lived in parts of Asia until as recently as 300 kya. This means it lived side by side with *Homo erectus*, an early member of our genus. While *Khoratpithecus* is probably a close relative of living orangutans, *Gigantopithecus*, with its several unique specializations, is a more distant relative of living great apes.

The evolutionary history of the primate order is difficult to interpret. For some time intervals we have many fossil primate species, even more than are living today, and for other time intervals we have very few. As discussed earlier, these patterns of fossil distribution may be the result of past environmental conditions, circumstances of preservation, or researcher bias. There may also have been times when primates thrived and diversified and other times when they struggled and dwindled. The gaps in the fossil record leave us with unanswered questions about primate evolution. Further complicating matters, we may recognize that a fossil group is generally related to a living primate but may not be able to decipher the details of this relationship. Fossil primates are not exact copies of living species. They often have their own unique combinations of traits and

FIGURE 13.14 *Oreopithecus*
Oreopithecus, an early European ape, had dental adaptations for folivory and long, mobile arms for brachiation.

FIGURE 13.15 *Gigantopithecus*
Gigantopithecus, an early Asian ape, was incredibly large and had large molars and mandibles for a diet that emphasized chewing. Some research suggests that it may have eaten a lot of bamboo.

adaptations. The fossil record does not allow us to draw neat lines that connect extinct and living primates like highways connecting cities on a road map. Instead, we often find a complicated web of overlapping lineages, dead ends, and unclear relationships. As we will see in the remaining labs, the same is true of our unique human evolutionary history after our split from the other apes.

relative dating any dating method that provides the age of something relative to the age of something else, rather than as a numerical age

law of superposition a law stating that material from lower geological layers must be older than material from higher geological layers

stratigraphy the study of the deposition of geological and cultural layers (or strata)

comparative stratigraphy a relative dating method based on the assumption that things found in the same strata (or layers) will be from the same time interval because they were deposited together

▶▶▶ EXPLORING FURTHER

Dating Fossil Sites   While the fossil record is difficult to interpret, we are somewhat aided by being able to place fossils in their temporal context. By obtaining good estimates of the time intervals when fossil species were alive, we can better understand their likely relationships and evolutionary histories. How do we come up with these dates? There are two broad types of dating: relative dating and chronometric dating.

Relative dating is any dating method that provides the age of something relative to the age of something else—as in X is older than Y. For example, one would say that the American Civil War happened before (is older than) World War II, or that the Great Pyramid of Giza is older than the Empire State Building. Relative dating methods for fossils are usually based on the law of superposition. Over time, sediment and rock build up in layers on Earth's surface. Like the layers in a layer cake, the bottom layers are formed first and the top layers are formed last. The **law of superposition** uses this principle to argue that material from lower (deeper) geological layers must be older than material from higher (shallower) geological layers (**FIGURE 13.16**).

One of the most common relative dating methods is comparative stratigraphy. **Stratigraphy** is the study of the deposition of layers (or strata). **Comparative stratigraphy** assumes that things found in the same strata are from the same time interval because they were deposited together. This assumption can help us to get a sense of the relative ages of materials at a site. Following the law of superposition, all materials found in the lowest layer will be older than all the materials found in the highest layer. This method can also be used to get relative ages for materials at different sites. Often, the same geological events leave similar strata at different sites. For example, a large volcanic explosion may leave a similar layer of ash at multiple sites in a region. Using comparative stratigraphy, we can argue that materials found in the ash layer at one site should be the same age as materials found in the same ash layer at another site. This method is useful in that it gives us a rough estimate for how old or young things are in relation to one another. It can also be used along with other dating methods to get even more accurate dates. For instance, a particular material in a layer may be able to be dated by another method. Its age can then be assigned to that particular material, all other materials in that layer at the site, and materials found in the same layer at other sites. Stratigraphy, however, can be very difficult to interpret. An earthquake may shift strata, a rodent may burrow through layers and mix up the materials, or a human may plow layers together to prepare for planting or building.

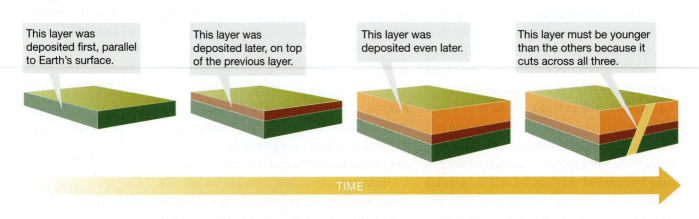

This layer was deposited first, parallel to Earth's surface.

This layer was deposited later, on top of the previous layer.

This layer was deposited even later.

This layer must be younger than the others because it cuts across all three.

TIME

FIGURE 13.16 The Law of Superposition
According to the law of superposition, material from lower geological layers must be older than material from higher geological layers because the lower layers were deposited first.

These and numerous other events could disturb the strata and lead to misinterpretation.

The other main type of dating is called **chronometric dating**. As opposed to simply indicating whether something is older or younger than something else, chronometric dating methods provide a numerical age estimate for the material involved. For example, one would say that the American Civil War started in 1861 and World War II started in 1939, or that the Great Pyramid was built about 4,500 years ago and the Empire State Building was built about 85 years ago. Because these methods give a numerical age, they are sometimes called **absolute dating** methods. This name is misleading, though, because it suggests that we are absolutely certain of the precise age assigned. In reality, we are not completely certain, and we often get age ranges instead of one precise date.

There are two kinds of chronometric dating methods: radiometric dating and nonradiometric dating. **Radiometric dating** is any dating method that uses the principles of radioactive isotope decay to determine numerical age. **Isotopes** are variations of an element that differ in the number of neutrons in the nucleus. For example, carbon has three isotopes that have different numbers of neutrons: carbon-12 has six neutrons and six protons (for a total mass number of 12), carbon-13 has seven neutrons and six protons (a total of 13), and carbon-14 has eight neutrons and six protons (a total of 14). While many isotopes are stable and remain unchanged indefinitely, other isotopes are radioactive, which means that they decay over time. These radioactive isotopes decay until they become a stable isotope of the same element or of another element. The length of time it takes for half of the original amount of isotope to decay is called the **half-life** of that isotope. We can measure the ratio of the amount of radioactive isotope to the amount of its stable counterpart and determine how many half-lives have passed. Importantly, different isotopes have different half-lives. Isotopes with long half-lives are good for dating older material, and isotopes with shorter half-lives are good for dating more recent material.

The most famous radiometric dating method is **radiocarbon dating**. This method relies on the radioactive isotope carbon-14. Carbon is found in all living organisms and in the atmosphere. When organisms are alive, the ratio of radioactive carbon (carbon-14) to stable carbon (carbon-12) in their tissues is constant. When organisms die, however, the carbon-14 decays to nitrogen-14. Radiocarbon dating requires organic material, such as bone, shell, or wood. It is a particularly useful method because it provides a date for the actual material, rather than the surrounding rocks or soil. It also tells us when an organism died, as opposed to when the surrounding geological layer was formed. However, the half-life of carbon-14 is 5,730 years. Therefore, radiocarbon dating is well suited for recent material from between about 2 and 50 kya, but it is not useful for older material because current technologies cannot detect the trace amounts of carbon-14 left after this time.

A similar radiometric dating method depends on radioactive potassium isotopes. This method, called **potassium–argon dating**, measures the decay of potassium-40 to argon-40 in volcanic rocks. The half-life of potassium-40 is very long: 1.3 billion years. This means that potassium–argon dating is not useful for material from less than 200 kya, but it can be used for anything older, even for material from as far back as the formation of Earth (4.5 billion years ago). Potassium–argon dating can provide ages for volcanic rocks, which is useful because many of the strata associated with primate evolution contain volcanic rocks. As we saw in our discussion of comparative stratigraphy, the date for volcanic rocks in a layer can then be assigned to the fossil material found in that layer. However, potassium–argon dating does not give an age for the actual fossil material. Another related method is called **argon–argon dating**. In this method, a volcanic rock sample is irradiated to convert the potassium-39 in the sample to argon-39, and the ratio of the two argon isotopes, argon-39 and argon-40, is then measured. This method has a date range similar to that of potassium–argon dating, and it can be run on a much smaller sample.

chronometric dating (absolute dating) any dating method that provides a numerical age estimate for the dated material

radiometric dating any dating method that uses the principles of radioactive isotope decay to determine numerical age

isotope a variation of a chemical element that has a different number of neutrons in its nucleus than other variations of the same element

half-life the length of time it takes for one-half of an amount of a radioactive isotope to decay

radiocarbon dating a radiometric dating method that relies on carbon-14, an isotope with a half-life of 5,730 years

potassium–argon dating a radiometric dating method that relies on radioactive potassium isotopes with a half-life of about 1.3 billion years

argon–argon dating a radiometric dating method that relies on the ratio of two argon isotopes and has a date range similar to that of potassium–argon dating

nonradiometric dating any chronometric dating method that is not based on the principles of radioactive isotope decay

paleomagnetic dating a nonradiometric dating method based on changes in Earth's magnetic polarity

Nonradiometric dating methods are chronometric techniques that are not based on radioactive isotope decay. **Paleomagnetic dating** is a nonradiometric technique that is based on changes in the magnetism of the planet. Throughout Earth's history, the magnetic poles have shifted back and forth, with magnetic north becoming magnetic south and vice versa. When rocks are formed, their metal particles arrange themselves in relation to the direction of Earth's magnetic field—its polarity—at the time. If we examine rock from a geological layer, we can determine what the polarity was at that time. The dates of these shifts in polarity have been documented using other methods, such as potassium–argon dating, so we can determine the time interval during which the rock was probably formed. Paleomagnetic dating is useful for material from about 750 kya (when the last major polarity shift occurred) to 200 mya (the extent of our polarity mapping to date). Again, this method can be used to date the rocks from a site, but it cannot be used to date the actual fossils.

Each dating method has its advantages and disadvantages. Paleoanthropologists must understand what materials are available for dating and roughly how old the materials may be before they choose a dating method. If they have organic material that is roughly a few thousand years old, they would be likely to pursue radiocarbon dating. If, however, they have volcanic rock that is roughly a few million years old, they would be more likely to pursue potassium–argon dating. The limitations associated with each dating method make choosing the right one a complicated process. In addition, we often find ourselves in situations where we cannot date the layer we would prefer. For example, we may have fossils in one layer that are not associated with the right kinds of organic materials or rocks for dating. We may have to date material from the layers above and below our fossil layer. Using the law of superposition in combination with chronometric dating methods, we can determine a date range for the fossil layer. If the layer below the fossils dates to 1.5 mya and the layer above the fossils dates to 1 mya, we know the fossil species lived between 1.5 and 1 mya. Dating fossil contexts is complex, and the timing of events in our evolutionary history can sometimes be vague. However, our methods are constantly being refined, and our dates are regularly reevaluated and adjusted when new information becomes available.

CONCEPT REVIEW QUESTIONS

Name: _____   Section: _____

Course: _____   Date: _____

Answer the following questions in the space provided.

1. Define fossil.

2. Compared with living primates, ancient plesiadapiforms were more likely to have:

    A. grasping hands and feet.
    B. a toothless gap between their front and back teeth.
    C. bony (enclosed) eye orbits.
    D. large brains for their body sizes.

3. Compared with adapiforms, omomyoids:

    A. are usually more nocturnal.
    B. have longer snouts.
    C. are usually larger.
    D. have more enclosed bony orbits.

4. Describe *one* trait found in *Aegyptopithecus* that suggests it was an early catarrhine.

5. I lived in Africa around 15 mya. I had bilophodont molars and a frugivorous diet. I had some adaptations for terrestrial quadrupedalism. What fossil primate am I?

    A. *Aegyptopithecus*
    B. *Khoratpithecus*
    C. *Dryopithecus*
    D. *Victoriapithecus*

6. *Proconsul* lived in Africa around 20 mya. It had Y-5 molars and a frugivorous diet. It also had some adaptations for arboreal quadrupedalism and was tailless. What living primate group is its closest living relative?

    A. Tarsiers
    B. Old World monkeys
    C. Apes
    D. New World monkeys

7. What is the genus assigned to the largest primate that ever lived?

8. Which category of dating methods provides a more precise numerical age for fossil sites: relative dating or chronometric dating?

9. According to the law of superposition, are deeper geological layers older or more recent than layers near the surface?

10. What type of material would you need to conduct radiocarbon dating?

LAB EXERCISES

Name: _____   Section: _____

Course: _____   Date: _____

Note: When completing these exercises, it may be useful to refer back to Labs 10–12 for information about living primates.

EXERCISE 1 PLESIADAPIFORMS

Work in a small group or alone to complete this exercise. Use the images and information provided here to answer the questions that follow.

In 2002, researchers reported the discovery of a partial skeleton from the genus *Carpolestes*. It lived in North America around 56 mya. It was about the size of a mouse and had a pronounced snout. It also had grasping hands and feet and a mix of nails and claws. It did not have a postorbital bar (instead, the eye socket had very little bony support). This fossil (depicted below) has been classified as a plesiadapiform.

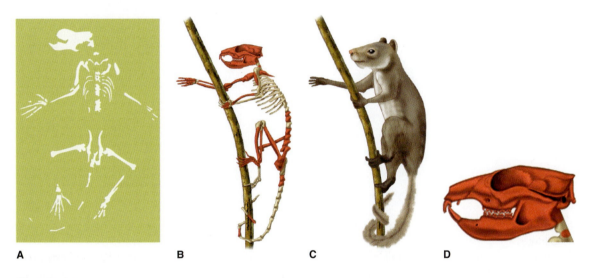

A   **B**   **C**   **D**

Carpolestes
(A) Drawing of *Carpolestes* fossil remains recovered. (B) Reconstruction of skeleton with recovered material in red. (C) Reconstruction of specimen. (D) Close-up of the reconstructed skull.

1. Describe *at least one* feature that *Carpolestes* shares with other plesiadapiforms such as *Plesiadapis*.

2. Describe *at least one* feature that makes it different from most other plesiadapiforms.

3. Do you think this new find forces us to reconsider the relationship between plesiadapiforms and primates? Why or why not?

EXERCISE 2   ADAPIFORMS AND OMOMYOIDS

Work in a small group or alone to complete this exercise. Use the fossil descriptions here and the material provided by your instructor (or the images in the Lab 13 Exercise Image Library on p. 396) to answer the questions that follow.

Mystery fossil genus A lived in North America in the mid-Eocene. Its teeth had shearing crests, indicating a folivorous diet.

Mystery fossil genus B lived in North America in the early Eocene. Its teeth suggest it was insectivorous.

1. Which of these mystery fossils is an adapiform?

2. Which of these mystery fossils is an omomyoid?

3. Describe *at least two* traits you used to make these identifications. (Be sure to describe how each trait differs between the two mystery fossils—for example, fossil A has this trait, but fossil B does not.)

EXERCISE 3   *DARWINIUS*

Work in a small group or alone to complete this exercise. Use the images and information provided here to answer the questions that follow.

In 2009, a new fossil species, called *Darwinius masillae*, was identified in Germany, represented by a nearly complete skeleton nicknamed Ida (depicted on next page). It lived around 47 mya. It had a small brain, short protruding snout, large eyes, and postorbital bar. Its diet probably included a lot of fruit and leaves. It did not have a dental comb. It had nails instead of claws and was probably an arboreal quadruped. Researchers disagree about whether the fossil is more similar to living haplorhines (tarsiers, monkeys, and apes) or more similar to strepsirhines (lemurs and lorises). The skeleton is about 23 inches (58 cm) long including the tail, and has a body length of about 9 inches (24 cm) without the tail.

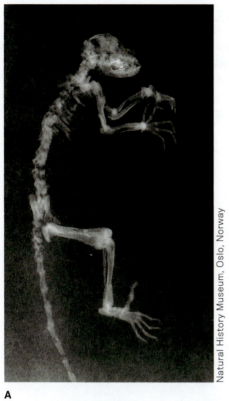

Darwinius
(A) X-ray of the *Darwinius masillae* specimen nicknamed Ida. (B) Photo of same specimen.

1. Describe *at least two* features that *Darwinius* shares with living haplorhines.

2. Describe *at least two* features that the fossil shares with living strepsirhines.

3. Would you classify *Darwinius* as a haplorhine relative or a strepsirhine relative? Why?

EXERCISE 4 FOSSIL NEW WORLD AND OLD WORLD MONKEYS

Work in a small group or alone to complete this exercise. Use the fossil descriptions and images here and any supplemental material provided by your instructor to answer the questions that follow.

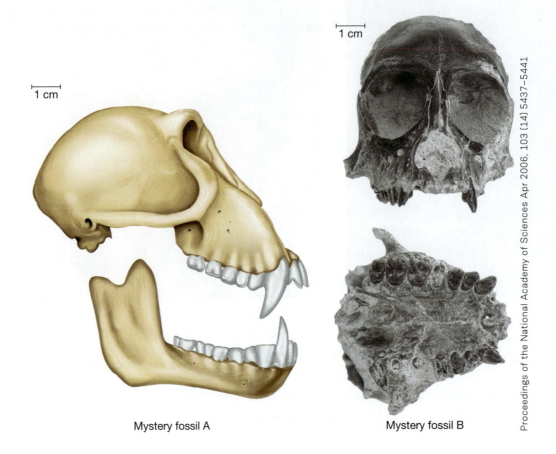

Mystery fossil A   Mystery fossil B

Proceedings of the National Academy of Sciences Apr 2006, 103 (14) 5437–5441

Mystery fossil genus A has been dated to the late Pliocene and early Pleistocene. Its canines were sexually dimorphic, and it had bilophodont molars. Its postcranial traits indicate that it was a terrestrial quadruped, and its overall body size was over 55 lb (25 kg).

Mystery fossil genus B has been dated to the early Miocene. It is estimated that adults weighed around 2 lb (1 kg), with some sexual dimorphism possible in body weight and canine size.

1. Which of these mystery fossils is a fossil Old World monkey?

2. Which of these mystery fossils is a fossil New World monkey?

3. Describe *at least two* traits you used to make these identifications. (Be sure to describe how each trait differs between the two mystery fossils—for example, fossil A has this trait, but fossil B does not.)

EXERCISE 5 *THEROPITHECUS*

Work in a small group or alone to complete this exercise. Use the fossil description and images here to answer the questions that follow.

Theropithecus lived in Africa at the end of the Pliocene and in the early Pleistocene. It had two premolars in each mouth quadrant and bilophodont molars. Its teeth indicate an unusual diet that emphasized grasses. It had larger canines and a much larger body size than its living primate relatives. Its postcranial traits suggest it was a well-adapted terrestrial quadruped.

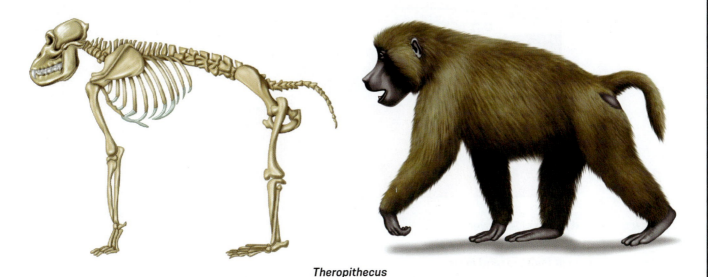

Theropithecus

1. Do you think this fossil has more in common with living colobines or with living cercopithecines?

2. Describe *at least one* trait you used to make this classification.

EXERCISE 6 *SIVAPITHECUS*

Work in a small group or alone to complete this exercise. Use the fossil description here and any supplemental material provided by your instructor (or the photos in the Lab 13 Exercise Image Library on p. 396) to answer the questions that follow.

Sivapithecus lived in Asia from about 12 to 8 mya. It had a 2.1.2.3 dental formula and adaptations for chewing hard food such as seeds and nuts. It had very few postcranial adaptations for suspensory locomotion, but it did have long fingers. It also had tall orbits that sat close together.

1. Is *Sivapithecus* more similar to living Asian great apes or to living African great apes?

2. Describe *at least two* traits you used to make this distinction.

EXERCISE 7 DATING METHODS

Work in a small group or alone to complete this exercise. Use the stratigraphy drawing provided below to answer the questions that follow.

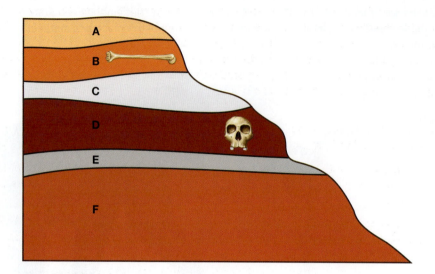

1. Draw a star next to the oldest layer.

2. Circle the youngest (most recent) layer.

3. In layer B, you find an unfossilized bone. What chronometric dating method could you use to date this layer? For what date range would this method be appropriate?

4. In layer D, you find a fossilized bone. Layer C and layer E are made of volcanic rock. Given what is available at the site, what strategy will you use to determine a chronometric date for layer D? (Be sure to specify the exact dating method or methods used and the corresponding applicable age ranges.)

CRITICAL THINKING QUESTIONS

On a separate sheet of paper, answer the following questions.

1. As we discussed, plesiadapiforms were initially interpreted as being the first primates. They were then interpreted as being outside the direct primate lineage because they lacked many of the key traits that define the primate order. This debate continues today. Given what you know about the defining traits found in most living primates, describe four traits you think should be found in the earliest primates. What advantages would these traits have provided the first primates? Are any of these traits found in plesiadapiforms? (Use resources in your classroom, credible online sources, or books to help you.)

2. Below are descriptions of five mystery fossil primates. Use the information provided to determine which of these mystery fossil primates is an adapiform, an omomyoid, a New World monkey, an Old World monkey, or an ape.

   Mystery fossil primate A lived in the early to middle Miocene in South America. It had an enclosed bony orbit, three premolars in each mouth quadrant, and dentition suggesting a frugivorous and folivorous diet. Its postcrania indicate that it was a quadruped.

   Mystery fossil primate B lived in the early Eocene in North America. It had an unfused mandible, long snout, and small forward-facing orbits. It had sexually dimorphic canines and teeth that suggest a frugivorous diet. Its postcrania indicate some leaping behaviors.

   Mystery fossil primate C lived in the late Miocene and Pliocene in Africa. It had two premolars in each mouth quadrant, bilophodont molars, and dental adaptations for folivory. Its postcrania suggest it practiced a combination of arboreal and terrestrial quadrupedalism.

   Mystery fossil primate D lived in the middle Miocene in Europe. It had two premolars in each mouth quadrant. It had a flexible wrist, a broad chest, and short fingers. It is likely that its scapulas were positioned on the back of its rib cage.

   Mystery fossil primate E lived in the middle and late Eocene in Europe. It had a postorbital bar, very large orbits, and a short snout. Its dentition suggests an insectivorous diet, and its postcrania indicate that it did a lot of leaping.

3. Given your knowledge of living and fossil primates, what traits do you think define the anthropoid group? What traits define the catarrhine group? What traits define the ape group? For each list of traits, underline the traits that are most likely to be preserved in the fossil record.

4. In this lab, we reviewed important fossil primates related to each of the major living primate groups. To help you make comparisons across groups and understand the general patterns of primate evolution, complete the Fossil Primate Chart on pp. 393–394. For each fossil primate, provide its date and location, its important anatomical traits, its behavior (such as diet and locomotion), and its most closely related living primate group.

5. Use your completed Fossil Primate Chart (on pp. 393–394) to answer the following questions.
   A. What geographic region(s) have numerous fossil primate discoveries? Why might fossil primates be common in these places?
   B. Identify one geographic region that has few or no fossil primates. Why might fossil primates be rare here?
   C. Choose one strepsirhine-like fossil primate and one haplorhine-like fossil primate, and list at least two traits that distinguish them. What do these traits suggest about their classification and relationship to living primates?
   D. Choose any two haplorhine-like fossil primates and list at least two traits that distinguish them. What do these traits suggest about their classification and relationship to living primates?

6. In this lab, we reviewed several important dating methods used by paleoanthropologists. To help you make comparisons between these methods, complete the Dating Methods Chart on p. 395. For each dating method, identify whether the method is a relative or chronometric method, the material needed for analysis, and the approximate date range covered by the method.

7. Use your completed Dating Methods Chart (on p. 395) to answer the following questions.

    A. What materials are most commonly used for dating?
    B. Given their date ranges, which dating method(s) are most useful for anthropologists studying early primate evolution? Why?
    C. Given their date ranges, which dating method(s) are most useful for anthropologists studying our lineage since the split from other primates (within the last 9 million years)? Why?

FOSSIL PRIMATE CHART

Fossil Group or Species	Dates and Locations	Anatomical Traits	Behavior	Relationship to Living Primates
Plesiadapiform (*Plesiadapis*)				
Adapiform (*Adapis*)				
Omomyoid (*Shoshonius*)				
Aegyptopithecus				
Branisella				
Perupithecus				

FOSSIL PRIMATE CHART *(continued)*

Fossil Group or Species	Dates and Locations	Anatomical Traits	Behavior	Relationship to Living Primates
Victoriapithecus				
Proconsul				
Nyanzapithecus alesi				
Dryopithecus				
Oreopithecus				
Khoratpithecus				
Gigantopithecus				

DATING METHODS CHART

Dating Method	Relative or Chronometric?	Material Needed	Date Range
Comparative Stratigraphy			
Radiocarbon			
Potassium–Argon and Argon–Argon			
Paleomagnetism			

LAB 13 EXERCISE IMAGE LIBRARY

Students should use these images only if directed to by their instructor.

EXERCISE 2 ADAPIFORMS AND OMOMYOIDS

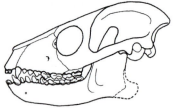
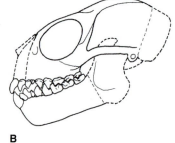

Figure 3 from Rose, Kenneth D. 1994. The earliest primates. *Evolutionary Anthropology* 3(5):159–173. Copyright © 1994 Wiley-Liss, Inc., A Wiley Company. Reprinted with permission of Wiley-Liss, Inc., a subsidiary of John Wiley & Sons, Inc.

A

B

EXERCISE 6 *SIVAPITHECUS*

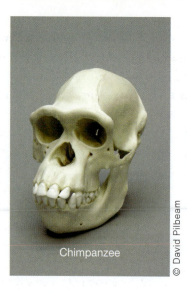

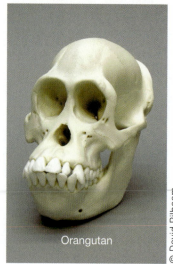

Chimpanzee

Sivapithecus

Orangutan

Sivapithecus (center) *is compared with a modern chimpanzee* **(left)** *and a modern orangutan* **(right).**

John Reader/Science Source

In Laetoli, Tanzania, paleoanthropologists uncover tracks made around 3.5 mya as numerous animals, including our extinct relatives, traversed an open grassland covered by a layer of damp ash. When the ash hardened, it preserved the tracks of the animals that had walked through the area.

LAB 14

//

Identifying the Human Lineage

Lab Learning Objectives

By the end of this lab, students should be able to:

- differentiate between the three types of bipedalism, using examples.

- describe the major skeletal adaptations for bipedalism, as well as the advantages afforded by each of these adaptations.

- describe different hypotheses for the evolution of bipedalism and how pre-australopith finds fit into these explanations.

It is a warm day in Laetoli, Tanzania. The dry season is coming to an end in the open savanna. The rhinoceroses, rabbits, antelopes, and birds that have lived in this grassland for months are wandering the landscape. Other animals, such as horses and baboons, are starting to venture into the area in anticipation of the coming rains.

A recent volcanic explosion has covered the land with a layer of ash. As it starts to rain, the ash layer becomes damp and muddy; the animals crossing the savanna leave tracks in the damp ash. These tracks will soon harden and preserve the overlapping paths taken by antelopes, elephants, cats, pigs, horses, and other animals. Among these animals, there is a small group of apes. A large ape and a small ape leave a trail of parallel tracks in the ash. A second small ape leaves a trail that overlaps and partially obscures the tracks of the large ape.

About 3.5 million years later (in 1978), a team of paleoanthropologists uncovers these tracks. The anthropologists soon realize that the tracks made by the group of apes are remarkable. They resemble human footprints and indicate that these apes practiced an unusual form of locomotion—they walked on two legs. Although they are now extinct, these upright, walking apes were among the earliest members of our human lineage.

hominin the classification group (tribe) containing humans and our extinct relatives since the split from other apes

cranial capacity the amount of space available in the cranium for the brain

bipedalism a form of two-footed locomotion where movement occurs primarily through the use of the hind limbs

INTRODUCTION

In this lab, we discuss how paleoanthropologists identify fossil species in the human lineage. Information from these fossils helps us to understand our unique evolutionary history since our split from the other apes. We begin with a reflection on the utilization of brain size and tool use as hallmarks of the species in our lineage. We then discuss bipedalism, which may be the key component of our lineage. We introduce the three types of bipedalism, and we discuss the major skeletal adaptations for bipedalism and the advantage each of these adaptations affords. We conclude by discussing why our ancestors may have become bipedal and how recent research is challenging our long-standing assumptions about the evolutionary shift to bipedalism.

HOW DO WE KNOW IF A FOSSIL SPECIES IS PART OF OUR HUMAN LINEAGE?

Over the years, several different traits have been used as the hallmark indicator that a fossil species is a **hominin**: a member of the group including humans and our fossil relatives since the point at which we split from the other apes. For example, a large *brain size* was long considered to be the defining characteristic of humanness. However, most researchers today recognize that emphasis on brain size is problematic for several reasons. First, brain tissue does not fossilize, so researchers are forced to work with indirect indicators of brain size. For example, we can use measurements of a fossil species' **cranial capacity** (the amount of space available in the cranium for a brain) to estimate brain size. In addition, we can use indentations and ridges on the inside of the cranium to estimate the sizes of different brain regions, but these estimates are often imprecise and do not tell us about brain organization. Second, having a large brain is not actually unique to humans. Numerous animals, such as elephants, have brains that are larger than ours, as brain size is generally pro-

portional to body size. Moreover, although we have large brains relative to our body size, this characteristic is not unique to humans either. Other animals (such as mice) have brains that are even larger for their body size than ours are. Therefore, it is not enough to say that humans (and our extinct relatives) are special because we have large brains; rather, our uniqueness is a matter of what our brains do—how they are organized and function—which is often difficult to assess in fossils. Finally, as we will see in the coming labs, the increase in brain size to the modern human range is a relatively recent development in our evolutionary history; if we used brain size as the defining characteristic for our lineage, we would miss several million years of that history. For all of these reasons, large brains may not be a good indicator of membership in our lineage.

Another trait that has often been used to distinguish hominins is *tool use*. But use of this trait, too, is problematic. First, this approach has traditionally emphasized stone tools because they preserve well and are visible in the fossil record. However, this emphasis downplays the potential significance of tools made from less durable materials, such as plants, and may inadvertently exclude from our lineage numerous species that used plant-based tools. Second, as discussed in Lab 11, research has demonstrated widespread tool use in nonhuman apes and some monkeys. These observations suggest that tool use is not limited to humans and our closely related ancestors. Rather, it is a common behavior of primates in general. For these reasons, tool use may not be a unique characteristic of our lineage.

In light of the problems associated with these traits, a different characteristic needs to be used to identify hominins. The best characteristic for this purpose is **bipedalism**. Here, *bi* means "two," and *pedal* refers to feet. Thus, bipedalism is a form of two-footed locomotion where movement occurs primarily through the use of the hind limbs (legs). It is an unusual form of locomotion among primates, and as we will see in the coming labs, it appears very early in our evolutionary history.

TYPES OF BIPEDALISM

Although bipedalism defines our lineage, it is not restricted to our species. In fact, many primates practice some sort of bipedalism. What distinguishes us is that we practice a particular kind of bipedalism, called obligate bipedalism. There are two other kinds of bipedalism, called occasional bipedalism and habitual bipedalism. To fully understand our own bipedalism, we must understand all three types of bipedalism seen in primates.

Occasional bipedalism is bipedal locomotion that is practiced sometimes (or occasionally). Occasional bipeds rely on a different form of locomotion as their primary means of movement, but they resort to bipedalism under certain circumstances. For example, nonhuman apes will sometimes move bipedally on the ground when they are using their hands to carry things (FIGURE 14.1). In these situations, the hands cannot be used in locomotion because they are otherwise occupied, so the primate uses only its legs and moves bipedally. Because the primate rarely practices bipedalism, it has few, if any, anatomical adaptations for bipedalism. Instead, it is anatomically adapted for its primary form of nonbipedal locomotion. Chimpanzees and bonobos are good examples of occasional bipeds. Although they occasionally move bipedally, they are not really adapted for bipedalism. Rather, they are anatomically adapted for their primary form of locomotion: knuckle-walking (see Lab 12 for more information).

Habitual bipedalism is bipedal locomotion that is practiced regularly (or habitually). Habitual bipeds may also rely on a different form of locomotion, but they use bipedalism and their other locomotion strategy more equally than occasional bipeds do. For example, many of the early members of our lineage practiced habitual bipedalism. The australopiths that produced the Laetoli footprints discussed at the beginning of this lab are classic examples of habitual bipeds (see Lab 15 for more examples). They were still somewhat arboreal and spent a lot of time climbing in trees. On the ground, however, they often practiced bipedalism. Habitual bipeds have a mix of locomotor adaptations. They are bipedal enough that they have some selectively favored bipedal adaptations. However, they also use an alternative form of locomotion (such as arboreal climbing) enough that they have some selectively favored adaptations for that form of locomotion as well.

Obligate bipedalism is bipedal locomotion that is practiced all the time. Obligate bipeds are obliged to move around bipedally. Unlike occasional or habitual bipeds, obligate bipeds have no other realistic locomotor option. Humans today are obligate bipeds, as were all of our ancestors since *Homo erectus* about 1.8 mya (million years ago) and perhaps even *Homo habilis* about 2.5 mya (see Labs 15 and 16 for more information). We can cover short distances by crawling on all fours, and we can climb trees and practice arm-over-arm swinging. However, we cannot do these things comfortably for any length of time without special training and practice. Once we reach a certain age and body size,

FIGURE 14.1 Occasional Bipedalism
Nonhuman apes sometimes walk short distances bipedally while they carry things in their hands.

Gudkov Andrey/Shutterstock

occasional bipedalism bipedal locomotion that is practiced sometimes (or occasionally)

habitual bipedalism bipedal locomotion that is practiced regularly (or habitually)

obligate bipedalism bipedal locomotion that is practiced all the time

foramen magnum
the large hole at the base of the cranium that allows the brain to connect to the spinal cord

vertebral column the row of bones that form the backbone

we are anatomically obliged to walk on two legs. While we maintain a few adaptations for other forms of locomotion, such as the adaptations for suspensory locomotion shared by all apes (as described in Lab 12), most of our locomotor adaptations are for bipedalism. Our bodies are more suited for bipedal locomotion than for any alternative.

When we analyze the fossil record, we are testing our hypotheses about a fossil species and how it lived. We examine the physical traits of the fossils (data), and we then use these data to interpret the behavior of the species. Thus, when we are trying to determine whether a fossil species was a member of our lineage, we look for anatomical traits for bipedal locomotion. Bipedal anatomical traits indicate that a species was at least habitually bipedal, practicing bipedalism frequently enough that natural selection favored traits that facilitated this form of locomotion. These habitual bipeds were more bipedal than members of nonhuman primate lineages and therefore belong in our human lineage.

BIPEDAL ADAPTATIONS

There are numerous adaptations for bipedalism that can be seen in our skeletons (and therefore also in the fossilized skeletons of our ancestors). Here we discuss the major bipedal adaptations and the advantages they afford, working our way from the head to the toes. Beginning in the cranium, the position of the foramen magnum is an indicator of bipedalism (**FIGURE 14.2**). As discussed in Lab 6, the **foramen magnum** is the large hole at the base of the cranium that allows the brain to connect to the spinal cord. In a quadruped, the foramen magnum is positioned more posteriorly (toward the back of the cranium). This position allows the vertebral column to remain parallel to the ground while extending outward from the braincase. In a biped, the body has a more upright orientation, and the vertebral column is perpendicular (rather than parallel) to the ground. Thus, the *foramen magnum of a biped is positioned more anteriorly* (toward the front of the cranium) *and inferiorly* (on the underside of the cranium). This position helps to center the head over the upright vertebral column. If a biped had a more posteriorly positioned foramen magnum, its normal relaxed head orientation would be tilted slightly upward because its upright vertebral column would extend down from the back of its skull. This would require the biped to constantly use its neck muscles to pull its head down to look forward. Instead, because the anteriorly and inferiorly positioned foramen magnum centers the head over the upright vertebral column, the normal, relaxed head position of a biped has the eyes facing forward, and its neck muscles are not overworked to orient the head correctly.

Moving down the body, the next major bipedal adaptation is found in the **vertebral column**. Bipeds have an *S-shaped vertebral column* with curves in the thoracic and lumbar regions (**FIGURE 14.3**). In the thoracic region, the vertebral column curves back, creating a convex dorsal (or posterior) surface. In the lumbar region, the vertebral column curves forward, creating a convex ventral (or anterior) surface. When looking at the right side of the body, these two

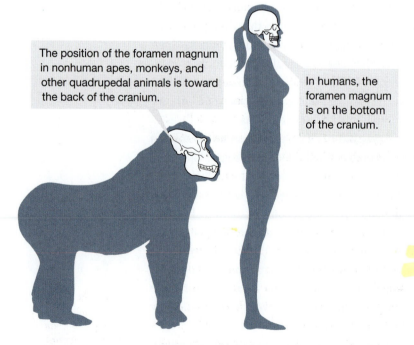

The position of the foramen magnum in nonhuman apes, monkeys, and other quadrupedal animals is toward the back of the cranium.

In humans, the foramen magnum is on the bottom of the cranium.

FIGURE 14.2 Position of the Foramen Magnum
The foramen magnum (the hole at the base of the cranium through which the brain connects to the spinal cord) is positioned differently in a quadruped and in a biped.

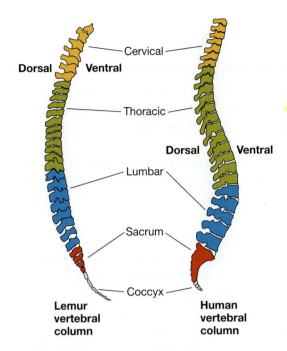

Cervical

Dorsal **Ventral**

Thoracic

Dorsal **Ventral**

Lumbar

Sacrum

Coccyx

Lemur vertebral column

Human vertebral column

FIGURE 14.3 The Vertebral Column
In most primates (such as the lemur shown here) the vertebral column forms one gradual curve down its length from the head to the sacrum. In bipeds, the vertebral column curves back in the upper chest and curves toward the front at the lower back. This gives the bipedal vertebral column an S-shape.

curves resemble the two curves of the letter *S*. In nonbipeds, the vertebral column is straighter, with a single curve that gradually forms a long, convex dorsal surface. The presence of the lower lumbar curve in bipeds helps to shift the upper body weight forward and center it over the pelvis and lower body. In addition, bipeds have *large lumbar vertebrae*. These vertebrae support the weight of all the body parts above them, so they often have large vertebral bodies to accommodate this function.

The pelvis of bipeds, which has an unusual bowl shape, is also specially adapted for bipedalism (**FIGURE 14.4**). The *bowl-shaped pelvis* is largely the result of differences in the two **ilia** (**ilium**, singular). In a biped, the ilia are short and broad, and they are positioned more laterally in the pelvis. This shape is related to adaptations in the leg muscles of bipeds. While we are all probably familiar with the gluteus maximus muscle of the buttocks, we are probably less familiar with two related muscles: the glu-

teus minimus and the gluteus medius. These muscles attach to the ilium on one end and the femur on the other. In quadrupeds, these muscles straighten the thigh, acting as powerful extensors for quadrupedal locomotion. In bipeds, these muscles perform a very different function. When we walk, we have only one foot on the ground at a time. This foot and leg need help to remain steady and balanced during walking. In bipeds, the gluteus medius and minimus serve to stabilize the pelvis when all of the weight of the body is on the balancing leg. Because these muscles serve a different function in bipeds than in quadrupeds, they have a different shape and position. In turn, the biped pelvis is shaped differently to accommodate these unusual gluteal muscles. Overall, the bowl-shaped pelvis and corresponding gluteal muscles help us to maintain a stable and efficient bipedal gait (rather than a teetering gait that wobbles from side to side). In addition to its more significant muscle-attachment function, the bowl-shaped pelvis helps support our intestines and other organs when our bodies are positioned upright.

Bipeds also have overall body proportions different from those of nonbipeds. In Lab 12, we often found that the largest body parts of primates were also the parts they used most for their form of locomotion. For example, a leaping tarsier has incredibly long legs and feet to help with jumping, but a brachiating gibbon has incredibly long arms and hands to help with swinging. Bipeds follow this same pattern. Compared with our living ape relatives, we have much *longer legs* (**FIGURE 14.5**). Their length is largely the result of our elongated femurs, tibias, and fibulas.

In addition to being longer, the biped **femur** has an unusual angled position (see Figure 14.5). In most primates, the femur extends relatively straight from the pelvis to the knee. This position keeps the knee toward the lateral side of the body. In contrast, bipeds have an *angled femur* that extends down and medially (inward) from the femur to the knee. This position centers the knees (and lower legs) under the body and near its midline, which improves our balance and

ilium (**ilia**, plural) the large, bladelike area of each os coxa (hip bone)

femur the bone that forms the thigh of each leg

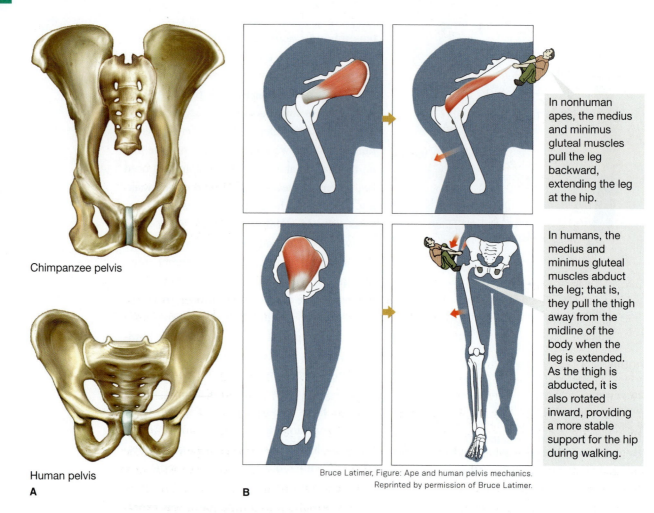

Chimpanzee pelvis

Human pelvis

A

B

In nonhuman apes, the medius and minimus gluteal muscles pull the leg backward, extending the leg at the hip.

In humans, the medius and minimus gluteal muscles abduct the leg; that is, they pull the thigh away from the midline of the body when the leg is extended. As the thigh is abducted, it is also rotated inward, providing a more stable support for the hip during walking.

Bruce Latimer, Figure: Ape and human pelvis mechanics.
Reprinted by permission of Bruce Latimer.

FIGURE 14.4 The Pelvis
(A) The biped pelvis is shorter, broader, and more bowl-shaped than the pelvis of a quadruped. The two pelvises are shown at the same scale. (B) This difference in shape is the result of differences in the muscles that attach to the pelvis.

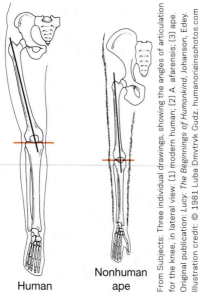

Human

Nonhuman ape

From Subjects: Three individual drawings, showing the angles of articulation for the knee, in lateral view: (1) modern human; (2) A. afarensis; (3) ape.
Original publication: *Lucy: The Beginnings of Humankind*, Johanson, Edey.
Illustration credit: © 1981 Luba Dmytryk Gudz, humanoriginsphotos.com

FIGURE 14.5 The Femur
Bipeds have femurs that angle in toward the midline of the body and center the knees under the body. The other apes have straight femurs and knees positioned more toward the lateral sides of their bodies.

walking efficiency. As we move forward, the body follows a central path, rather than wobbling from side to side. In addition, when we briefly balance on one foot each time we take a step, the lower leg is closer to the midline and thus more stable.

In bipeds, the feet are incredibly important: they support the entire weight of the body and are the only areas to make contact with the ground while we are moving. Therefore, they have several key adaptations. First, bipeds have *short toes* (**FIGURE 14.6A**). Unlike other primates, we do not use our toes for grasping. Instead, we use our toes for support while standing and to help push off when we step forward. Our toes are much shorter than the toes of other primates for these reasons. Interestingly, our big toe (the

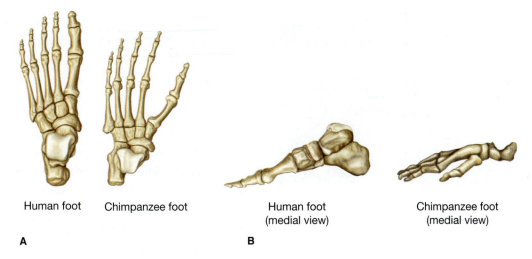

FIGURE 14.6 The Foot
(A) Bipeds have short toes and a nondivergent hallux (big toe), but other primates have long toes and a divergent hallux. (B) Bipeds also have longitudinal arches in their feet, whereas other primates have flatter feet. These feet are shown at the same scale.

hallux) is larger than our other toes, which is the opposite of what is seen in most primates. Our relatively enlarged hallux helps with bearing weight and transmitting force as we take steps. Second, bipeds have a *nondivergent hallux* that is in line (parallel) with the other toes (see Figure 14.6A). Again, since we do not use our feet for grasping, we do not need the opposable hallux seen in other primates. Instead, our hallux is lined up with the other toes to provide better balance and pushing-off ability. Third, the biped foot has a *longitudinal arch* that extends down the length of the foot from the base of the toes to the heel (**FIGURE 14.6B**). This arch helps with shock absorption as we walk, and it helps to direct our body weight and energy to create a smooth push-off while stepping forward.

WHY DID BIPEDALISM EVOLVE?

Bipedalism is a unique and central component of our lineage. As such, researchers have often asked why bipedalism evolved. What happened in our evolutionary history that led to our unusual locomotion? Numerous explanations have been put forward and have gained varying amounts of support in the scholarly community. Perhaps the most famous of these explanations

is the savanna hypothesis. This explanation was supported by Raymond Dart, the early paleoanthropologist who first identified *Australopithecus africanus* (see Lab 15 for more information on this species). The **savanna hypothesis** argues that bipedalism was selectively favored as open grassland environments expanded throughout Africa. Around 8 to 5 mya, Earth was experiencing a period of dramatic cooling. Some of Earth's water became trapped in glaciers at the poles, and conditions were much drier than they had been in the past. In Africa, many of the forested areas shrank and were replaced by **savanna environments**—open grasslands interspersed with pockets of trees.

The shift to savanna environments was further facilitated by geological activity in eastern Africa. Continental plates were splitting apart (or rifting), causing landscape changes that contributed to more dramatic differences between wet and dry seasons. These seasonal changes, combined with overall drying, encouraged the expansion of grassland habitats in the region. According to the savanna hypothesis, bipedalism evolved as a favorable adaptation that facilitated life in these grasslands, where earlier forms of arboreal locomotion would be less helpful and an upright posture would have allowed our ancient ancestors to see over the tall grasses of the savanna environment. Researchers supported

hallux the biggest and most medial of the toes on each foot

savanna hypothesis an explanation for the evolution of bipedalism that argues bipedalism was selectively favored as open grassland environments expanded throughout Africa in the past

savanna environment open grassland interspersed with pockets of trees

patchy forest hypothesis an explanation for the evolution of bipedalism that argues bipedalism was selectively favored because it was more energy efficient than quadrupedalism in the patchy forest environment of Africa

thermoregulation hypothesis an explanation for the evolution of bipedalism that argues bipedalism was selectively favored because it helped early hominins to stay cool during the hottest times of the day

provisioning hypothesis an explanation for the evolution of bipedalism that argues bipedalism was selectively favored because it helped males to provision females and improve reproductive success

postural feeding hypothesis an explanation for the evolution of bipedalism that argues bipedalism was favored as a way to more efficiently reach hanging fruit in small trees

FIGURE 14.7 East African Tree Cover
Two anthropologists, Rodman and McHenry, argue that bipedalism was favored during the late Miocene and early Pliocene in East Africa as tree cover in the region became patchy (similar to the tree cover seen here).

the savanna hypothesis for many years, but since the 1990s, paleoanthropologists have discovered numerous fossils of early hominins which challenge the validity of this explanation. Many of these earliest species may not have lived in savannas at all. Thus, alternative hypotheses for the evolution of bipedalism must be considered as well.

Like the savanna hypothesis, the **patchy forest hypothesis**, put forward by anthropologists Peter Rodman and Henry McHenry, ties the evolution of bipedalism to environmental changes. Rodman and McHenry argue that bipedalism would have been more energy efficient than quadrupedalism as the environment in Africa transitioned to a patchy forest over the several million years from the end of the Miocene into the Pliocene (**FIGURE 14.7**). Today, bipedal humans are more energy efficient in these types of environments than are quadrupedal chimpanzees, but it is unclear if the first bipeds would have had the same efficiency benefits that we do. As we will see in Lab 15, the transition to obligate bipedalism was gradual, and not all of our bipedal traits evolved at the same time. The earliest bipeds in our lineage would probably not have benefited from increased efficiency when walking upright.

Another explanation based on environmental changes is the **thermoregulation hypothesis**, proposed by Peter Wheeler. This model argues that bipedalism was favored because it helped our early ancestors to manage their body temperature and stay cool during the heat of the day. An upright posture would have lifted much of the body up into a slightly cooler zone of air above 3 feet (1 m) off the ground. It would also expose their bodies to more wind and air circulation to help with cooling. Critics of this hypothesis have noted that the earliest hominins lived in environments that still afforded plenty of tree cover in which to find shade during the hottest times of day, so an upright posture was not necessary.

The **provisioning hypothesis**, first proposed by biological anthropologist Owen Lovejoy, argues that bipedalism evolved in early humans that were monogamous, specifically to allow male human fathers to carry food and resources to their female partners. Typically, ape mothers spend years providing for a single offspring before it reaches an age when it can provide for itself and the mother can have another infant. If a male provides a mother with food, it may allow her to raise multiple offspring at a time. So provisioning would reduce birth spacing, increase the overall number of offspring a female produced in her lifetime, and improve reproductive success. Thus, according to the provisioning hypothesis, bipedalism evolved to free the hands so males could carry food back to females. However, the validity of this hypothesis has been challenged, particularly because it assumes a particular social structure (specifically, monogamy) for early humans, whose social structure is not clearly known.

In a final example, the **postural feeding hypothesis**, presented by Kevin Hunt, is also based on the feeding benefits associated with bipedalism, although it does not assume provisioning or particular social relationships. Instead, Hunt argues that an upright posture helps apes (such as chimpanzees today) to more effectively reach hanging fruit in the small trees typical in African woodland environments. The earliest bipeds in our lineage became upright not because of walking, but because of standing to collect these fruits (**FIGURE 14.8**). Once our ancestors had adapted a few traits that helped with bal-

complete support of the paleoanthropological community. This may mean that additional alternatives are needed, or it may mean that bipedalism evolved for a complex combination of reasons that cannot be easily reduced to a single determining factor. As more bipedal fossils are discovered and analyzed in the coming years, anthropologists will continue testing and refining hypotheses for the evolution of bipedalism.

THE FIRST APPEARANCE OF BIPEDALISM: PRE-AUSTRALOPITHS

When did bipedalism first appear, and by extension, when did the human lineage first diverge from that of the other apes? For almost a hundred years, we believed that the first hominins were a group of fossil species in the genus *Australopithecus.* However, four new fossil species (classified in three different genera) have been identified since the 1990s that possess the bipedal adaptations unique to members of our lineage. These species lived between 7 and 4.4 mya, which pre-dates the famous *Australopithecus* (and related) species, so they are called the pre-australopiths. The pre-australopith species have a mix of adaptations for bipedalism and arboreal climbing, showing that the evolution of bipedalism was probably gradual and occurred in a mosaic fashion, with different bipedal adaptations evolving separately over time instead of simultaneously.

The first of the pre-australopith species is *Sahelanthropus tchadensis.* It lived around 7 to 6 mya (late Miocene) in the modern-day central African country of Chad. This location is particularly unusual because it is over 1,000 miles from the better-known fossil sites of eastern Africa. Known largely from the remains of one fossil cranium, nicknamed Toumaï, this species has a pronounced brow ridge and a small cranial capacity (around 350 cubic centimeters), similar to that of living nonhuman apes (**FIGURE 14.9**). However, some researchers argue that its foramen magnum is positioned more

FIGURE 14.8 Upright Feeding Postures
As seen here, chimpanzees sometimes stand upright, balancing on two legs, while they reach overhead to collect fruit. They may then shuffle on two feet to another nearby feeding location. Kevin Hunt argues that this same behavior may have led to bipedalism in our hominin ancestors.

ancing in an upright posture, additional traits that helped with walking upright became favored as well. What began as an adaptation to slowly shuffle from one tree to the next eventually became the full bipedalism we know today. However, it is unclear how much of the diet would have come from these fruits and, therefore, how important the ability to collect them would have been among our ancestors. Critics argue that this one food source alone would not have been enough to drive such large evolutionary changes.

Of the numerous current explanations proposed for the evolution of bipedalism, no one hypothesis has irrefutable evidence and the

FIGURE 14.9 *Sahelanthropus tchadensis*
The species *Sahelanthropus tchadensis* is primarily known from this fossil cranium (nicknamed Toumaï). The foramen magnum of this specimen appears to be positioned more anteriorly, suggesting that this hominin used bipedal locomotion.

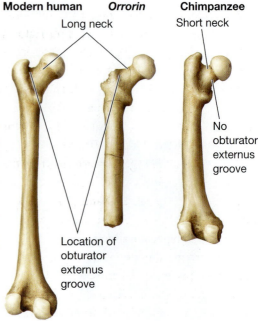

FIGURE 14.10 *Orrorin tugenensis*
The femur of *Orrorin tugenensis* has the obturator externus groove that is present in bipedal humans and absent in quadrupedal chimpanzees. This trait suggests that *Orrorin* was a biped.

anteriorly, indicating more human-like bipedal locomotion. *Sahelanthropus* also has a smaller, less prognathic face than nonhuman apes. This mixture of facial and bipedal traits, as well as the early date for *Sahelanthropus*, suggest that it may have been the earliest member of our unique lineage or a common ancestor of humans and other apes, such as chimpanzees.

The second pre-australopith is *Orrorin tugenensis*. This species was found in the Tugen Hills of Kenya (eastern Africa) and dates to around 6 mya. While its teeth are more similar to those of nonhuman apes than to those of humans, it appears to have had adaptations for bipedalism. Although the available fossil fragments cannot be used to determine whether its femurs were angled, the available proximal ends of a few *Orrorin* femurs have bipedal traits **(FIGURE 14.10)**. The femurs have long necks as well as a groove for the obturator externus muscle, which helps to stabilize and rotate the leg. Both of these features are seen in modern bipedal humans, but not in modern chimpanzees. These traits suggest that *Orrorin* was another early bipedal hominin.

The last two pre-australopiths have both been classified as members of the genus *Ardipithecus*.

Both species were found in the Middle Awash region of Ethiopia (eastern Africa). *Ardipithecus kadabba*, the older of the two species, lived around 5.5 mya (latest Miocene). The teeth of this species appear to have some modern human–like features and some chimpanzee-like features, and its early date makes it a possible ancestor of humans and chimps **(FIGURE 14.11)**. The other species, *Ardipithecus ramidus*, is more recent, living around 4.4 mya (early Pliocene). More is known about this *Ardipithecus* species because fossilized remains of at least 35 individuals have been recovered. The most famous of these is the partial skeleton of a single individual, nicknamed Ardi.

Like its *Ar. kadabba* cousin, *Ar. ramidus* had short canines with wear on the tips, but it lacked the intermediate honing complex that helped *Ar. kadabba*'s upper canines to be slightly sharpened against the lower premolars. Thus, the teeth of *Ar. ramidus* are even more typical of members of our lineage than the teeth of other apes. *Ar. ramidus* had a small cranial capacity and short stature (around 4 ft tall) **(FIG-**

URE 14.12A). It had very long arms and long, curved fingers, but other upper limb features indicate that it probably practiced more arboreal climbing than suspensory locomotion. It also had bipedal adaptations, such as a shorter and wider pelvis. Its foot is particularly interesting because it has a mixture of locomotor adaptations (FIGURE 14.12B). The toes are long, and the hallux is divergent, suggesting that the feet were still frequently used for arboreal grasping. However, the muscles and bones of the feet would have been rigid and more suited for pushing off in bipedal walking.

As a group, the pre-australopith species share two important features. First, the pre-australopiths are habitual bipeds with a mix of adaptations for bipedal and arboreal locomotion. This means that they practiced arboreal locomotion, but also practiced bipedalism frequently enough that bipedal adaptations were selectively favored as well. Second, from analyses of animal (and sometimes plant) remains from pre-australopith sites, we know that they lived in forested environments. When taken together, these features of pre-australopith life directly challenge the long-standing savanna hypothesis. The pre-australopiths were bipedal

FOSSIL CREDIT: Housed in National Museum of Ethiopia, Addis Ababa.
PHOTO CREDIT: 2003 © Tim D. White, humanoriginsphotos.com

FIGURE 14.11 *Ardipithecus kadabba*
Ardipithecus kadabba (*right*) had a honing complex similar to that seen in chimpanzees today (*left*), in which the upper canines are naturally sharpened by rubbing against the lower premolars when the mouth is opened and closed.

in the forest, so the evolution of bipedalism was not the result of living in open savannas. Rather, bipedalism must have evolved for a different reason. As paleoanthropologists continue to find even more fossil specimens from this time interval, new light will undoubtedly be shed on this pivotal time in our evolutionary history.

A

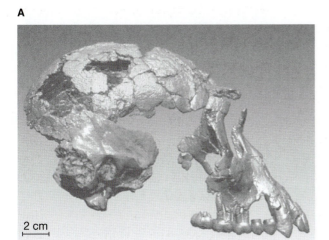

2 cm

B

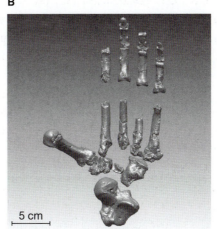

5 cm

FOSSIL CREDIT A and B: Original fossils in National Museum of Ethiopia, Addis Ababa. DIGITAL RENDER CREDIT A and B: © 2009 White, Suwa, et al., humanoriginsphotos.com

FIGURE 14.12 *Ardipithecus ramidus*
Ardipithecus ramidus had a small cranial capacity (A) and a mix of bipedal and arboreal traits, such as the adaptations for grasping and bipedal walking seen in its foot (B).

CONCEPT REVIEW QUESTIONS

Name: _____   Section: _____

Course: _____   Date: _____

Answer the following questions in the space provided.

1. When studying the brains of our fossil relatives, why do we rely on indirect evidence (cranial capacity) instead of direct evidence (brain tissue)?

2. Is tool use unique to members of our own human lineage? If not, name at least one other animal that makes tools.

3. The kind of bipedalism practiced by a living chimpanzee is called:

    A. random bipedalism.
    B. habitual bipedalism.
    C. occasional bipedalism.
    D. obligate bipedalism.

4. In a biped, the foramen magnum is positioned more:

    A. anteriorly at the base of the skull.
    B. posteriorly at the back of the skull.
    C. laterally to the side of the skull.
    D. dorsally at the rear of the skull.

5. The S shape of the human vertebral column is formed by two curves. Describe where these two curves are located.

6. How is the human pelvis different from the pelvis of a nonbipedal primate?

7. Describe the bipedal adaptations that can be found in the human femur.

8. What is the savanna hypothesis?

9. The pre-australopiths lived around:

    A. 8 mya to 5 mya.

    B. 7 mya to 4.4 mya.

    C. 6 mya to 3 mya.

    D. 9 mya to 6.5 mya.

10. Which of the following adaptations for bipedalism is *not* known to be present in the currently known pre-australopith fossils?

    A. *S*-shaped vertebral column

    B. Anteriorly positioned foramen magnum

    C. Obturator externus muscle groove on femur neck

    D. Short, broad pelvis

LAB EXERCISES

Name: _____   Section: _____

Course: _____   Date: _____

EXERCISE 1 BIPEDAL ADAPTATIONS OF THE CRANIUM

Work in a small group or alone to complete this exercise. Examine the skeletal material provided by your instructor (or the photos in the Lab 14 Exercise Image Library on p. 421).

1. Which mystery primate is a biped?   A

2. Describe *one* adaptation seen *in this primate's cranium* that indicates bipedal locomotion.

   The foramen magnum is located more anteriorly

3. How does this adaptation help the primate to move bipedally?

   helps center the head over the vertebral column, helping w/ balance + stability

EXERCISE 2 BIPEDAL ADAPTATIONS OF THE VERTEBRAL COLUMN

Work in a small group or alone to complete this exercise. Examine the skeletal material provided by your instructor (or the drawings in the Lab 14 Exercise Image Library on p. 421).

1. Which mystery primate is a biped?   A

2. Describe *two* adaptations seen *in this primate's vertebral column* that indicate bipedal locomotion.

   verbal column forms (1) gradual curve down its length from the head to their cranium. gives the spine an "s" shape like feature.

3. How do these adaptations help the primate to move bipedally?

   helps primate obtain more stability as they walk.

EXERCISE 3 BIPEDAL ADAPTATIONS OF THE PELVIS

Work in a small group or alone to complete this exercise. Examine the skeletal material provided by your instructor (or the photos in the Lab 14 Exercise Image Library on p. 422).

1. Which mystery primate is a biped?   A

2. Describe *two* adaptations seen *in this primate's pelvis* that indicate bipedal locomotion.

   ilium of the pelvis is short + broad.
   walls of pelvis are facing laterry.

3. How do these adaptations help the primate to move bipedally?

helps primate by encreasing area which helps stabilize
the torso

EXERCISE 4 THE BIPEDAL GAIT

Work in a group to complete this exercise. In this lab, you learned that bipeds have elongated legs. In this exercise, we will examine this trait and why it might have evolved. It is hypothesized that *longer legs result in longer strides, so that a long-legged biped may cover a greater distance in fewer steps.*

   You will now collect and analyze data to test this hypothesis.

STEP 1 Collect leg length data. For each person in your group or class, determine the individual's leg length using tape measures or measuring sticks. *Hint*: Take the measurements while the person is standing upright with their shoes off. Remember to measure from the hip joint (where the hip bends) instead of the hip bones (the top of the pelvis/ilium). The hip joint will be several inches lower than the top of the ilium. Once you have located the hip joint, measure straight down to the floor. To avoid interobserver error, use the same measuring tools for each person and have one person do all the measuring.

STEP 2 Collect stride data.

   A. Lay out a long length of paper (at least 15 ft, or 4.5 m); tape it to the floor; and lay out a long tape measure alongside the paper.

   B. Pour a small amount of water into a shallow basin.

   C. Have one student step in the basin of water and wet their feet or apply an even amount of water to their bare feet. Then, have the student walk normally across the length of the paper, leaving their footprints behind. (Remember to use caution when walking, so you do not slip on your wet feet.)

   D. Measure the length of each stride the student has taken using the tape measure laid out alongside the footprints. One stride length is the distance from one footprint heel to the next footprint heel from the same foot. For example, if a student took the first step with the right foot, you would measure from the back of the *right* footprint heel to the back of the next *right* footprint heel ahead of it to determine one stride length.

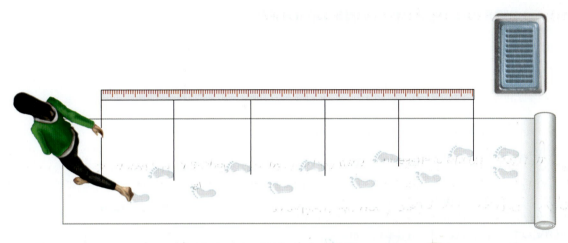

E. Once you have all of the individual strides for this student measured, calculate the average length of that student's strides. Add all of the stride measurements together and then divide by the number of strides that were measured. This gives you the average stride length for this person.

F. Repeat Steps 2C through 2E for each remaining student in the group. Be sure that everyone starts from the same point and uses their normal, comfortable gait (walking pattern).

STEP 3 Tabulate the data. On a separate sheet of paper, create a list or chart for your data that shows the two sets of data for each person (leg length and average stride length). For example, you can re-create the chart below with your own data:

Name	Leg Length (cm)	Average Stride Length (cm)
Ken	88.9	73.78
Caitlyn	78.75	65
Isabel	88.9	73.4
Deshawn	91.5	75.9
Julio	82.5	68.47

STEP 4 Interpretation

1. Look for patterns in the data. Describe any patterns you find.

2. Based on the data you collected, is the hypothesis supported or rejected? Why?

3. In thinking about the evolution of bipedalism, describe at least one advantage that longer legs may have provided to our ancestors.

EXERCISE 5   BIPEDAL ADAPTATIONS OF THE FEMUR

Work in a small group or alone to complete this exercise. Examine the skeletal material provided by your instructor (or the photos in the Lab 14 Exercise Image Library on p. 422).

1. Which mystery primate is a biped? *B*

2. Describe *one* adaptation seen *in this primate's femur* that indicates bipedal locomotion.

   femur angled ~~toward~~ inwards unlike other primates

3. How does this adaptation help the primate to move bipedally?

   helps center the knee, which improves balance + ~~better~~ ~~walking~~ walking efficiency.

EXERCISE 6   BIPEDAL ADAPTATIONS OF THE FOOT

Work in a small group or alone to complete this exercise. Examine the skeletal material provided by your instructor (or the photos in the Lab 14 Exercise Image Library on p. 423).

1. Which mystery primate is a biped?   *B*

2. Describe *two* adaptations seen *in this primate's foot* that indicate bipedal locomotion.

   2 arches.
   - short toes
   - non-divergent hallux (big toe)

3. How do these adaptations help the primate to move bipedally?

   longitudinal arch allows transmission of weight from heel to big toe. transverse arch acts as a shock absorber + distributes weight when standing or 2 feet.

EXERCISE 7   THE PRE-AUSTRALOPITHS

Work in a small group or alone to complete this exercise.

PART A

Match each of the pre-australopiths named below to its corresponding description.

Sahelanthropus tchadensis ___2___

Orrorin tugenensis ___1___

Ardipithecus ramidus ___3___

1. I lived about 6 mya in eastern Africa. My femurs had long necks with grooves for my obturator externus muscles.

2. I lived about 7 to 6 mya in central Africa. I had a small cranial capacity, a large brow ridge, and an anteriorly positioned foramen magnum.

3. I lived about 4.4 mya in eastern Africa. I had long arms and fingers and a relatively short, broad pelvis.

Examine the material provided by your instructor (or the photo in the Lab 14 Exercise Image Library on p. 423). What adaptations for bipedalism are seen in this *Ardipithecus ramidus* pelvis?

Shorter + wider pelvis

The pre-australopith fossils are especially significant because they challenge some of the long-standing explanations of our evolutionary history. Describe *two* reasons the pre-australopiths force us to rethink the savanna hypothesis in particular. (*Hint*: Think about the anatomical traits of the pre-australopiths and the environmental and temporal context in which they lived.)

. adaptions of bipedal + arboreal locomotion.
* -flexible wrist to cling to trees, lack stiff wrists +*
stronger upper torso to swing branch to branch.
*   - stiff outer foot like humans, large toe to grip branches.*

EXERCISE 8 THE EVOLUTION OF BIPEDALISM: THERMOREGULATION

Work in a small group or alone to complete this exercise.

In this lab, we considered several different explanations for the evolution of bipedalism. In this exercise, we will take a closer look at the thermoregulation hypothesis.

Your instructor has provided you with a lamp (representing the sun) and a doll (representing one of our extinct relatives). Using these tools, follow the steps below to further explore the thermoregulation hypothesis.

STEP 1 Position the lamp so it is above the doll and facing directly downward (as if the sun were directly overhead).

STEP 2 Position the doll so that it is on all fours under the lamp, in a position similar to that of a baboon wandering the open savanna. Note the amount of sun exposure the doll receives in this position.

STEP 3 Position the doll so that it is standing on two legs under the lamp, in a position similar to that of a human wandering the open savanna. Note the amount of sun exposure the doll receives in this position.

STEP 4 Answer the following discussion questions.

1. In which position did the doll have the least sun exposure?

2. Why might having less sun exposure be an advantage in a warm environment?

3. In which position do you think the doll has the most exposure to wind and air circulation?

4. Why might having more exposure to the wind be an advantage in a warm environment?

5. Based on this test, do you think the thermoregulation hypothesis might provide a valid explanation for the evolution of bipedalism? Is it challenged by the pre-australopith finds?

EXERCISE 9 THE EVOLUTION OF BIPEDALISM: POSTURAL FEEDING

Work in a small group or alone to complete this exercise.

In this lab, we considered several different explanations for the evolution of bipedalism. In this exercise, we will take a closer look at the postural feeding hypothesis. According to the postural feeding hypothesis, *bipedalism evolved as an extension of existing upright feeding postures common among apes*. If this hypothesis is correct, it would mean that bipedalism evolved initially to suit feeding from trees, rather than to suit a terrestrial lifestyle.

STEP 1 Review the data provided in the table below. (These data come from several different research studies, which were compiled by biological anthropologist Kevin D. Hunt. They provide a general sense of the patterns of posture and locomotion among living ape species.)

Type of Primate	Environment	Percentage of Posture That Is Suspensory Arm-Hanging	Percentage of Posture That Is Bipedal Standing	Percentage of Movement That Is Bipedal Walking
Papio anubis (baboon)	Open forest/savanna	0.2	0.1	0
Hylobates syndactylus (siamang)	Closed forest/dense tree cover	61.7	0	11
Pongo pygmaeus (orangutan)	Closed forest/dense tree cover	17.8	3.8	0
Pan paniscus (bonobo)	Closed forest/dense tree cover	5	0	8
Pan troglodytes (chimpanzee)	Open forest/savanna	5.3	0.4	1.2

STEP 2 Analyze the data and look for patterns.

1. In general, which primates engage in more suspensory arm-hanging: the baboon or the apes?

    Apes (61.7) vs baboon (0.2)

2. Which two primates engage in the most suspensory arm-hanging? What environment do they live in?

    orangutans + siamangs.

    closed forests / dense tree cover

3. Which primate engages in the most bipedal standing? What environment does it live in?

    orangutan, closed forest + dense tree cover.

4. Which two primates engage in the most bipedal walking? What environment do they live in?

    Siamang and bonobo.

    closed forest + dense tree cover.

STEP 3 Interpret the data.

5. Based on the patterns you identified above, do you think the ape lineage was more likely to become bipedal than the other primates? Why or why not?

    Yes. The ape lineage has the highest percentage of arm hanging and the best posture alignment that supports bipedal standing.

6. Based on the patterns you identified above, is an open forest (or savanna) environment necessary for the evolution of bipedalism? Why or why not?   NO.

    Open savanna is not necessary for the evolution of bipedalism. The baboon has little to no proof of bipedal walking despite living in an open savanna, but the chimpanzee has a much higher percentage, even higher than primates who live in a closed forest.

7. Do the data presented here support the postural feeding hypothesis? Why or why not?

    - upright posture helps apes to reach more hanging fruit.

    yes, apes have a high % of bipedal standing posture and bipedal walking.

CRITICAL THINKING QUESTIONS

On a separate sheet of paper, answer the following questions.

1. Describe the three different types of bipedalism. For each one, be sure to discuss the frequency of bipedal loco-motion, describe the extent of bipedal adaptations, provide at least one sample primate that practices this type of bipedalism, and describe why the sample primate uses this form of bipedalism.

2. Although bipedalism is unusual, humans are not the only living bipeds. For example, some flightless birds are also bipedal. Identify a living nonprimate animal that is also a biped. Then, compare its bipedalism with our bipedalism. Try to consider how it moves and some of its possible adaptations (such as limb length). Use resources in your classroom, credible online sources, or books to help you if necessary.

3. A paleoanthropologist has uncovered a fossilized pelvis in Africa. She has sent you the drawing below and wants your opinion. Was this individual bipedal? Provide two traits that support your interpretation.

Front   Top

4. At the start of this lab, we discussed the footprints discovered at Laetoli in Tanzania. These footprints have been interpreted as belonging to our relatives because they show bipedal adaptations. Examine the photo of one of these footprints below. Compare it with the footprints that you made in Exercise 4. Describe two of the bipedal adaptations visible in the Laetoli footprint. Is this footprint identical to yours? If not, what makes it different?

J. Reader/Science Source

5. In some cases, our bipedal adaptations have changed areas of our bodies so much that it is difficult (if not impossible) for these areas to perform other functions. For example, the human pelvis provides the areas of muscle attachment we need for bipedal locomotion, but its unusual shape makes human childbirth more diffi-cult. The foot is another area that reflects the effects of bipedal specialization. What foot traits and correspond-ing functions seen in other primates have been lost in our feet? Why would we have lost helpful features such as these?

6. In this lab, we discussed several explanations for the evolution of bipedalism. Each hypothesis has its draw-backs and has been criticized. It's your turn to hypothesize why our lineage evolved bipedalism. Describe some of the advantages of bipedalism (be sure to think about what life would have been like for our ancestors millions of years ago when bipedalism evolved, including their risk of predation, food availability, environment, etc.). Are there any disadvantages to bipedalism? If so, what are they? Taking into account these possible advantages and disadvantages, why do you think bipedalism might have evolved?

7. In this lab, we reviewed several important adaptations for bipedalism. To better understand these adaptations, complete the following Bipedal Adaptations Chart. For each skeletal element, describe the features you would expect to find in a bipedal primate and in a nonbipedal primate.

8. Use your completed Bipedal Adaptations Chart to answer the following questions.
   A. Do we have more adaptations for bipedalism in the upper body or the lower body? Why might this be the case?
   B. Draw a star next to any of the bipedal traits that help with balance while walking or standing. What do these traits suggest about the challenges of moving bipedally?
   C. Draw a circle around any of the bipedal traits that reflect skeletal changes in response to soft tissue (such as nerves, muscles, or organs). What do these traits suggest about the functional relationship between the skeleton and the rest of the body?

BIPEDAL ADAPTATIONS CHART

	Bipedal Primate	Nonbipedal Primate
Cranium		
Vertebral Column		
Pelvis		
Legs		
Feet		

LAB 14 EXERCISE IMAGE LIBRARY

Students should use these images only if directed to by their instructor.

EXERCISE 1 BIPEDAL ADAPTATIONS OF THE CRANIUM

Note: Skulls are not to scale.

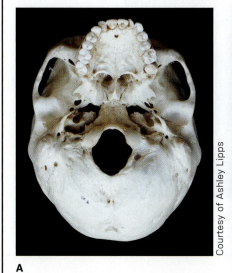

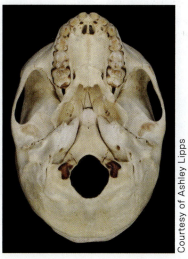

A

B

Courtesy of Ashley Lipps

Courtesy of Ashley Lipps

EXERCISE 2 BIPEDAL ADAPTATIONS OF THE VERTEBRAL COLUMN

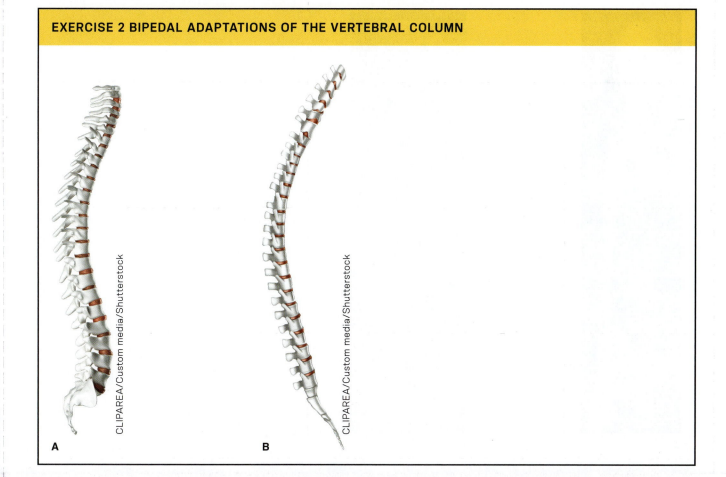

A

B

CLIPAREA/Custom media/Shutterstock

CLIPAREA/Custom media/Shutterstock

EXERCISE 3 BIPEDAL ADAPTATIONS OF THE PELVIS

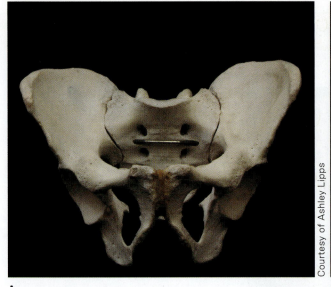

A

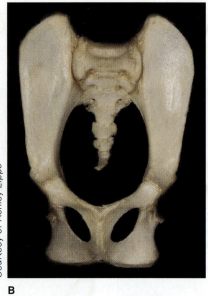

B

Courtesy of Ashley Lipps

Courtesy of Ashley Lipps

EXERCISE 5 BIPEDAL ADAPTATIONS OF THE FEMUR

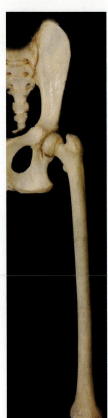

A

Courtesy of Ashley Lipps

B

Bone Clones/boneclones.com

EXERCISE 6 BIPEDAL ADAPTATIONS OF THE FOOT

Courtesy of Ashley Lipps

A

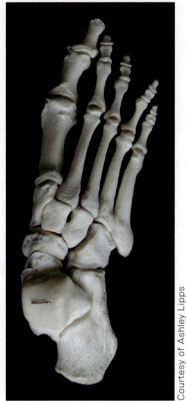

Courtesy of Ashley Lipps

B

EXERCISE 7 THE PRE-AUSTRALOPITHS

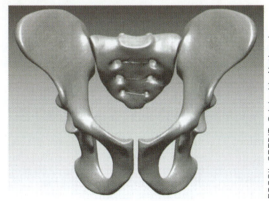

FOSSIL CREDIT: Original in National Museum of Ethiopia, Addis Ababa. DIGITAL RENDER CREDIT: © 2009 White, Suwa, et al., humanoriginsphotos.com

BIOLOGICAL ANTHROPOLOGY IN PRACTICE

Investigating Clues in Early Human Teeth

Dr. Debi Bolter is a biological anthropologist whose work bridges primatology (see Part 3) and paleoanthropology (Part 4). Debi grew up in a small town in Northern California, and she first became interested in anthropology after taking an introductory course in the discipline, which started her thinking about humans in new and fascinating ways. She then pursued this early interest by earning degrees and conducting research in anthropology. During her doctoral work at the University of California, Santa Cruz, she became an expert in growth and development patterns in primate teeth and skeletons. In recent years, she has applied this knowledge and skill set to paleoanthropological investigations. Debi uses nonhuman primate developmental stages as a model for studying and interpreting juvenile remains of fossil hominin species, such as *Australopithecus sediba* and *Homo naledi* from South Africa. Because fossil hominins seem to have had accelerated developmental stages compared with those of humans today, nonhuman primate models are essential for accurately identifying and studying juvenile hominin fossil specimens.

In 2015, Debi joined the Rising Star research team that was investigating over 1,500 *Homo naledi* fossils discovered in a South African cave (see Lab 16). She led the team that determined the life stages of the fossils. This effort included a lot of work with the fossil teeth. Because teeth have a stronger mineral composition than bones, they are more likely to be preserved in the fossil record and are less likely to be damaged or degraded. As described in Lab 7, teeth have the added benefit of being very useful in making age estimations. In mammals, each type of tooth in both sets of dentition (deciduous teeth and permanent teeth) erupts at specific rates. This means that biological anthropologists can check the dentition of a specimen, identify which teeth are in which stages of eruption, and then estimate how old the individual was at death. Debi and her team used this process to analyze the *Homo naledi* fossils recovered from the Rising Star cave and determine the number of individuals and their life stages.

After carefully analyzing the available fossil data, Debi and the other researchers were able to determine that at least 15 fossilized individuals had been recovered from the cave chamber. The cave remains included those of infants, juveniles, young adults, and even an older adult with very worn teeth. Working with researchers from Spain, England, Australia, China, Ethiopia, Tanzania, and South Africa, the Rising Star teams were able to help reconstruct important information about life stages, anatomical adaptations, and intentional disposal behaviors in these members of a newly discovered, 300,000-year-old fossil hominin species.

Debi's work on hominin fossils sharpens our picture of what life was like for some of our earliest ancestors. In Labs 15 and 16, it's your turn to apply what you learn to identify and describe early hominin species.

Photo by Dr. Adrienne Zihlman, University of California, Santa Cruz

Dr. Debi Bolter examines nonhuman primate skeletal and dental material for evidence of growth and developmental stages that can then be used to help interpret similar stages in fossil hominins.

Donald Johanson (and his colleagues) found the famous Lucy fossil specimen unexpectedly.

LAB 15

Lab Learning Objectives

By the end of this lab, students should be able to:

- describe the key australopith groups (genera and species), including their distributions and defining characteristics.

- compare and distinguish the various australopiths.

- discuss why some researchers classify the robust australopiths in their own genus.

- describe the first species of our own genus, including its distribution and defining characteristics.

- compare and distinguish between australopith genera and members of the *Homo* genus.

The Australopiths and Early Members of the Genus *Homo*

It is a late November day in 1974, and Donald Johanson's field season has been under way for several weeks. Johanson is a paleoanthropologist helping to lead a team of researchers in Hadar, Ethiopia. As on most other days, he wakes up and enjoys his morning coffee just after dawn. It is already a balmy 80°F, and it will reach 110°F by lunchtime. He is a little edgy and anxious to get to work. Johanson agrees to show a colleague named Tom Gray a part of the research area with which Tom is less familiar. After a bumpy ride in their Land Rover, the two men work in the area for a couple of hours. They are about to return to camp (before the heat of the day becomes too intense) when they spot fossil fragments scattered along an exposed slope of land. They quickly recognize parts of bones from an arm, skull, pelvis, and leg. The fragments seem to be laid out in order, as if they belong to a single individual, and they have telltale traits that suggest the individual was an early hominin.

The two men are incredibly excited and begin jumping up and down, shouting, and embracing. They return to camp and immediately share the news with the rest of the research team. The whole camp celebrates with

425

music and dancing. They listen to the Beatles song "Lucy in the Sky with Diamonds" over and over again. After their initial excitement, the researchers spend the next 3 weeks returning to the site every day. They slowly uncover the fossilized remains first spotted by Johanson and Gray so that the discovery and its significance can be better understood. They call the individual Lucy, after the Beatles song that figured prominently in their celebration. Today, Lucy is one of the best-known fossils ever reported, but over 3 million years ago, she was just one among many members of the species *Australopithecus afarensis*.

INTRODUCTION

In this lab, we continue our exploration of our fossil relatives. We introduce the most important australopith species and their defining charac-

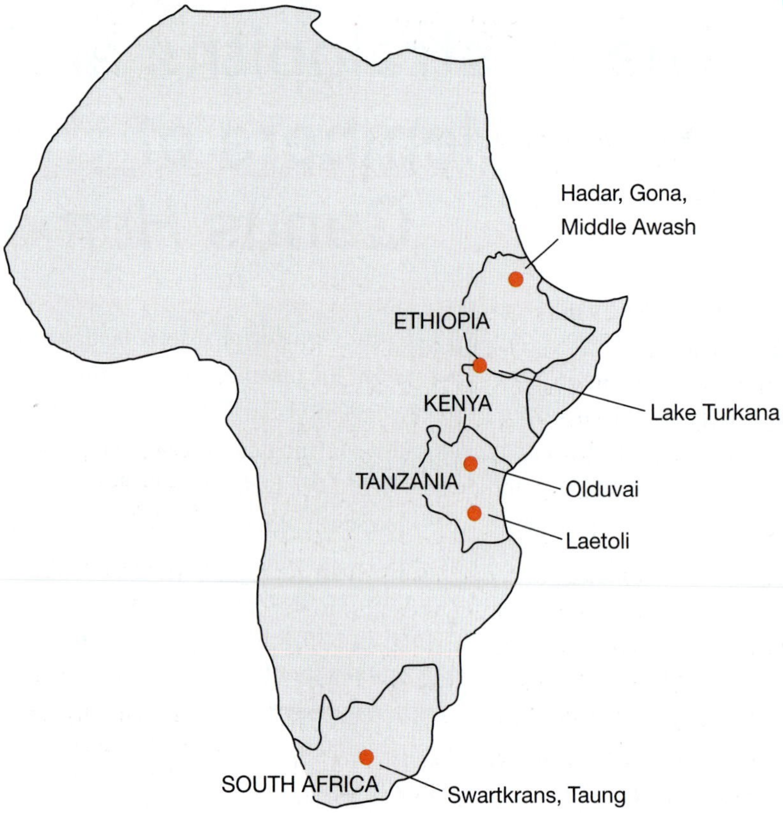

FIGURE 15.1 The Distribution of Australopiths and Early *Homo*
Australopiths (both gracile and robust forms) and early members of the *Homo* genus have been recovered from several major fossil sites in eastern and southern Africa.

teristics. The australopiths are a group of species that are linked by a few morphological features and are believed to be members of a shared evolutionary group. Depending on the approach to classification applied, this group may include as many as eleven species distributed across up to three genera: *Australopithecus*, *Paranthropus*, and *Kenyanthropus*. We have hundreds of australopith fossils, and the species vary mostly in size and robusticity. Many researchers argue that the differences between the early australopiths and the later robust australopiths are so great that the robust forms should be in their own genus, called *Paranthropus*, so we include both genus names (*Australopithecus* and *Paranthropus*) when referring to the robust species. We pay particular attention to the different types of australopiths in both eastern and southern Africa, as well as the significant differences that evolve over time in the later, more robust forms. We then introduce the earliest member of our own genus, *Homo*, and its defining characteristics. We conclude with a discussion of how the first *Homo* species differs from the australopiths and why some scholars think there may have been two early *Homo* species, instead of just one. Perhaps the most significant finding from fossil discoveries in recent years is that throughout the evolutionary history of our lineage, there were periods when several different human ancestors were alive at the same time. Since there are many evolutionary branches at different points in time, it makes it difficult to identify clear ancestor–descendant relationships for all the hominin species.

THE AUSTRALOPITHS (4 MYA–1 MYA)

The australopiths were a group of our ancestors that lived between about 4 and 1 mya (million years ago), during the early Pliocene to early Pleistocene, at numerous sites in eastern and southern Africa (FIGURE 15.1). All of these species were habitual bipeds, with a mixture of bipedal and arboreal adaptations. They varied mostly in size and robusticity: some species were smaller and more **gracile** (slender and light), and others were larger and more **robust** (thick and heavy). As a group, the australopiths generally had much smaller **cranial capacities** (space available for the brain) and body sizes than modern humans, and they had small canines, large premolars, and large molars. The later robust australopiths (sometimes placed in their own genus, *Paranthropus*) had notably larger faces, jaws, and teeth.

Australopithecus anamensis

The earliest australopith is *Australopithecus anamensis* (**FIGURE 15.2**). This species lived around 4 mya (early Pliocene) in eastern Africa. *Australopithecus anamensis* individuals had a number of generally apelike traits such as very large canines, parallel upper tooth rows, and asymmetrical lower premolars with outer cusps that were much larger than the inner cusps. Postcranial remains of this species indicate that it was a habitual biped with some adaptations for walking on two feet. There are enough similarities between *Au. anamensis* and earlier *Ardipithecus* specimens to suggest that they might be directly related in an ancestor–descendant relationship. In addition, the combination of ancestral, apelike traits and more derived, australopith-like traits seen in *Au. anamensis* has been interpreted as evidence that *Au. anamensis* was the first australopith and may have been ancestral to the later australopith species.

Australopithecus afarensis

Another early australopith is *Australopithecus afarensis*, which lived 3.6 to 3 mya (late Pliocene) in eastern Africa. Members of this species had cranial capacities (around 350–500 cubic centimeters, or cc) that were relatively small compared with ours today, but similar to those of living, nonhuman apes (**FIGURE 15.3**). In many other features, they appear to have been intermediate between a living chimpanzee and a living human. For example, their faces were more **prognathic** (protruding) than a human face but flatter than a chimpanzee face, and their canine teeth were larger than human canines but smaller than chimpanzee canines. *Australopithecus afarensis* has many similarities to *Au. anamensis*, suggesting that they share a direct ancestor–descendant relationship. In some features, *Au. afarensis* appears more human-like than does *Au. anamensis*. For example, the cusps of its lower premolars are relatively equal in size, and the upper tooth rows have an arched shape like that in humans, as opposed to the parallel rows seen in *Au. anamensis* and nonhuman apes. *Australopithecus afarensis* also seems to have had a broader diet than *Au. anamensis*, whose diet more closely resembles that of modern chimpanzees living in savanna environments. Researchers who conducted carbon isotope analysis that examines chemical traces in fossil teeth have found evidence that *Au. afarensis* had a very broad diet that probably incorporated a

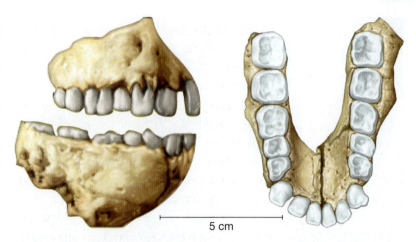

FIGURE 15.2 *Australopithecus anamensis*
Australopithecus anamensis had parallel tooth rows, large canines, and asymmetrical premolars, with outer cusps that were larger than the corresponding inner cusps.

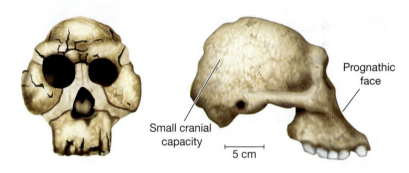

FIGURE 15.3 *Australopithecus afarensis*
Australopithecus afarensis had a smaller cranial capacity and a more prognathic face than humans today.

gracile having thin, light musculature and bone

robust having thick, dense, heavy musculature and bone

cranial capacity the amount of space available in the cranium for the brain

prognathic having a projecting or protruding face

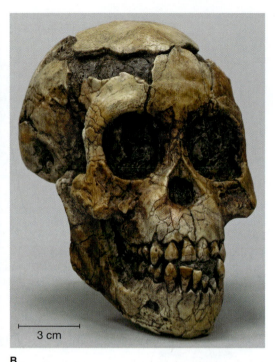

A   **B**

FIGURE 15.4 The Lucy Skeleton

(A) The *Australopithecus afarensis* specimen nicknamed Lucy provides valuable information about the postcrania of this species. For example, we can tell that the species had angled femurs and a somewhat short and broad pelvis. (B) From additional *Au. afarensis* individuals, such as the 3-year-old child nicknamed Selam, we can tell the species had shoulders suited for climbing.

(A) FOSSIL CREDIT: Housed in National Museum of Ethiopia, Addis Ababa. PHOTO CREDIT: © 1985 David L. Brill, www.humanoriginsphotos.com. (B) Bone Clones/boneclones.com

sexual dimorphism
the physical differences between adult males and adult females of a species

their postcranial traits. We know, for example, that these australopiths had angled femurs. They also had pelvises (or pelves) that were short and broad, although not as bowl-shaped as the pelvises of humans. In addition, the Laetoli footprints (discussed in Lab 14) that were left by members of this species indicate that *Au. afarensis* had slightly divergent big toes and arched feet. While these features of the *Au. afarensis* lower body suggest it was bipedal, some features of its upper body suggest it also had adaptations for arboreal locomotion. Lucy's fingers were similar in length to yours today, but they were more curved, like those of the earlier pre-australopith *Ardipithecus* species or a present-day nonhuman ape. This feature would have helped *Au. afarensis* to grasp and move more efficiently through trees. Similarly, Selam's well-preserved shoulder indicates that it was oriented like that of a nonhuman ape for more suspensory movement, and Selam's foot may have had more grasping ability than did those of adult *Au. afarensis*, suggesting that juveniles may have spent even more time climbing in trees than did adults.

Interestingly, Lucy is estimated to have been small (around 3.5 feet, or 1 m, tall), but other *Au. afarensis* fossils, particularly male individuals, are estimated to have been as much as 1.5 or 2 feet taller than Lucy. The level of **sexual dimorphism** found in many parts of the *Au. afarensis* skeleton is similar to that seen in living chimpanzees and gorillas. To some researchers, this suggests that *Au. afarensis* might have had a polygynous social structure. However, *Au. afarensis* had smaller canines, similar to those of pre-australopiths like *Ardipithecus*, suggesting that the species experienced less male–male competition than living apes with polygynous social structures. Because of such complex and potentially contradictory evidence, it is often difficult for researchers to determine the social organization of our extinct relatives.

wider range of plants than the diet of living chimpanzees or *Au. anamensis*. (For more information on how anthropologists use carbon isotope analysis, see Biological Anthropology in Practice on page 424.)

Australopithecus afarensis is the best-known australopith, represented by dozens of individuals. The most famous specimen of *Au. afarensis*, nicknamed Lucy, was introduced at the start of this lab (**FIGURE 15.4A**). More recently, in 2006, paleoanthropologists led by Zeresenay Alemseged announced the discovery of another remarkably complete fossilized *Au. afarensis* skeleton at the Dikika site in Ethiopia. The skeleton belonged to an approximately 3-year-old child that researchers have named Selam, meaning "peace" in the local Ethiopian language (**FIGURE 15.4B**). The remains of Lucy, Selam, and other *Au. afarensis* individuals tell us a lot about

Australopithecus africanus

Australopithecus africanus was first identified by Raymond Dart in the 1920s, making it the first australopith species discovered. Members of this species lived around 3 to 2 mya (late Pliocene to early Pleistocene) in southern Africa. Compared with the earlier *Au. afarensis* species, *Au. africanus* had a slightly larger cranial capacity (around 450–550 cc), slightly smaller incisors and canines, slightly larger premolars and molars, and a slightly flatter face (**FIGURE 15.5**). Despite these differences, however, carbon isotope evidence suggests that *Au. africanus* had a diverse diet similar to that of *Au. afarensis*. The postcranial traits of *Au. africanus* (such as a short, broad pelvis and long arms) show a mix of bipedal and arboreal adaptations similar to that seen in *Au. afarensis*. Furthermore, the two species seem to have had similar body sizes and degrees of sexual dimorphism.

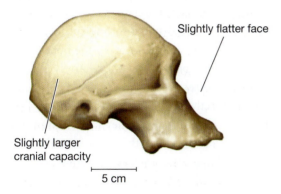

Slightly flatter face

Slightly larger cranial capacity

5 cm

FIGURE 15.5 *Australopithecus africanus*
Compared with *Australopithecus afarensis*, *Australopithecus africanus* had a slightly larger cranial capacity, slightly smaller front teeth, and a slightly flatter face.

Australopithecus garhi

Around the same time that *Au. africanus* was living in southern Africa 2.5 mya (at the end of the Pliocene), *Australopithecus garhi* was living in eastern Africa. Like the other australopiths, *Au. garhi* had a small cranial capacity (around 450 cc) and a prognathic face. It also had a small **sagittal crest** (a ridge of bone along the midline of the cranium) (**FIGURE 15.6**). In contrast to earlier australopiths, *Au. garhi* had larger canine, premolar, and molar teeth. Based on the evidence available, *Au. garhi* seems to have had longer legs than the earlier australopiths, potentially indicating a more bipedal lifestyle with

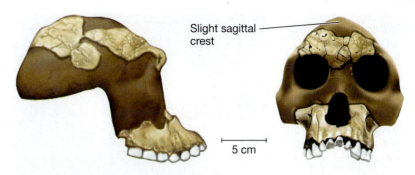

Slight sagittal crest

5 cm

FIGURE 15.6 *Australopithecus garhi*
Australopithecus garhi had a small cranial capacity, a slight sagittal crest, and a relatively prognathic face.
ARTIFACT CREDIT: Original in National Museum of Ethiopia, Addis Ababa. PHOTO CREDIT: © 1999 David L. Brill, humanoriginsphotos.com

less use of arboreal locomotion, but more postcranial evidence is needed before definitive interpretations can be made. The anatomical features seen in *Au. garhi* and its date of 2.5 mya have led some researchers to suggest that this species was ancestral to the early *Homo* species that followed.

The Earliest Stone Tools

Perhaps the most interesting feature of *Au. garhi* is its suggested tool-making behavior. Recent evidence from Ethiopia indicates that *Au. garhi* might have produced and used some of the first stone tools. Animal bones with cut marks have been found at an *Au. garhi* site in the Middle Awash region of Ethiopia (**FIGURE 15.7A**). These cut marks could only have been made by stone tools, and they suggest that *Au. garhi* was using stone tools to butcher animals. Stone tools recovered from another site in the Gona area of Ethiopia date to around 2.5 mya, the time when *Au. garhi* occupied the area. However, the tools were not found at the same site as the *Au. garhi* fossils, so it is difficult to say for certain that they were made by *Au. garhi*.

Additional stone tools and animal bones with cut marks have been found at even earlier sites in eastern Africa. Paleoanthropologists at the Lomekwi site in West Turkana, Kenya, unearthed numerous stone tools dating to 3.3 mya that could have been used to butcher and process animal meat and bone marrow for food (**FIGURE 15.7B**). And the Dikika site that was home to Selam has animal bones with possible cut

sagittal crest a ridge of bone along the midline of the cranium that allows for the attachment of extra-large chewing muscles

Oldowan technology the earliest stone tool technology, characterized by chopper and flake tools

chopper a large, heavy stone tool with a sharp edge where small pieces of rock have been removed

flake a small piece of rock that has been removed from a larger rock and can be used as is or further modified into a specialized tool

direct percussion a process of stone tool production where two rocks are hit directly together in order to break off flakes

zygomatic arch cheekbone area formed by numerous small bones, allowing a space for the jaw muscles that attach to the mandible below and the temporal bone above

A

B

Bifacial chopper

Discoid

Polyhedron

Hammer stone

Flake scraper

Flake

Heavy-duty (core) scraper

5 cm

C

FIGURE 15.7 Oldowan Tools
(A) Cut marks on animal bones from Gona, Ethiopia, dating around 2.5 mya, and (B) tools from Lomekwi, Kenya, dating to around 3.3 mya, indicate that australopiths were the first stone tool users. (C) Most Oldowan tools are flakes (the pieces of stone removed) or choppers (the stone that remains after flakes have been removed). Scale bar is for choppers on left only.

marks also dating to 3.3 mya. This mounting evidence suggests that even earlier australopith species may have been making and using stone tools as well.

These early stone tools are considered to be part of the **Oldowan technology** (FIGURE 15.7C). This technology was named after the Olduvai Gorge site in eastern Africa where stone tools like them were first found. Most Oldowan tools are either choppers or flakes. **Choppers** are large, heavy tools that have a sharp edge where smaller bits of rock have been broken off. The smaller bits of rock that are removed from choppers are called **flakes**. The size and weight of choppers make them well suited to chopping tasks, such as chopping up the long bones of animals to extract the marrow inside. In contrast, the smaller flakes have delicate, sharp surfaces that are well suited to fine cutting tasks, such as cutting animal meat off the bone. Producing these tools involves a relatively simple process of **direct percussion** (where two stones are hit directly together to break off flakes). The tools are generalized, so they can be used for a variety of tasks, and they vary considerably in size, shape, and raw material. However, if a small-brained australopith like *Au. garhi* made these tools, it suggests that tool use may not be as unique a behavior as was previously thought (see Lab 14 for more information about brain size, tool use, and the human lineage).

Australopithecus sediba

In 2010, researchers reported the discovery of a new australopith species called *Australopithecus sediba* (FIGURE 15.8). Found in southern Africa, this species dates to around 2 mya (middle Pleistocene). It had several features similar to those of *Au. africanus*, which lived in the same region from 3 to 2 mya and may have been its direct ancestor. For example, *Au. sediba* had a small cranial capacity (around 420 cc), a small overall body size, and long arms for arboreal locomotion. Interestingly, *Au. sediba* also shares several features with members of our own *Homo* genus. For example, *Au. sediba* had smaller teeth, mandibles, and **zygomatic arches** (cheekbones) than most australopiths. It

Photo by Brett Eloff, courtesy of Lee Berger and the University of Witwatersrand.

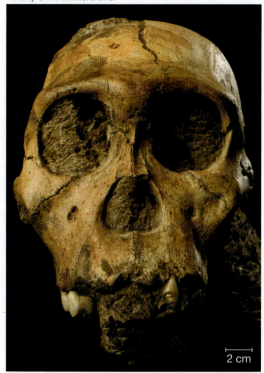

FIGURE 15.8 *Australopithecus sediba*
Australopithecus sediba was found in southern Africa. It is relatively gracile and has a combination of australopith-like traits and *Homo*-like traits.

also had a broad pelvis very similar to that seen in early members of the *Homo* genus. Because members of the *Homo* genus in eastern Africa pre-date *Au. sediba*, it is unlikely that the *Homo* genus originated from this lineage, but *Au. sediba* may have contributed to the diversity of the *Homo* genus that followed.

THE ROBUST AUSTRALOPITHS DIVERGE

Around 2.5 mya (early Pleistocene), the same time that *Au. africanus* was living in southern Africa and *Au. garhi* in eastern Africa, the earlier australopith lineage began to diversify, and a new branch of the australopith family tree emerged: the robust australopiths. These few species were noticeably different from the other, more gracile species that came before. They were more robust, with larger, denser facial and cranial features and larger back teeth (molars and

premolars). Interestingly, the front teeth (incisors and canines) of robust australopiths were actually smaller than those of earlier australopiths. Their size may have been reduced to allow enough space in the mouth for the larger back teeth. Along with enlarged chewing teeth, robust australopiths had larger mandibles, which would have needed larger jaw muscles to move. In turn, the larger jaw muscles needed larger zygomatic arches through which to pass on the way to their attachment points on the braincase. These jaw muscles were so large that they also needed extra bone, in the form of a sagittal crest, to attach to on the top of the head (**FIGURE 15.9**).

The combination of these robust cranial, facial, and dental features suggests that the robust australopiths may have been specially adapted for a diet that required more chewing, such as tougher vegetation. Because the differences between gracile and robust australopiths may be both physical (traits) and behavioral (diet), some paleoanthropologists consider the robust species to make up their own genus, called *Paranthropus*. Other experts disagree, and instead argue that the differences are not significant enough to warrant classification in a separate genus. They cite the general similarities across the species as well as recent carbon isotope analyses suggesting that most of the robust species had diets relatively similar to those of the gracile species. As such, these paleoanthropologists consider the robust species to be members of the genus *Australopithecus* alongside the gracile species.

Australopithecus (Paranthropus) aethiopicus

The earliest known robust australopith species is *Australopithecus aethiopicus*, which appeared in eastern Africa around 2.5 mya (at the start of the Pleistocene). While the cranial capacity (around 410 cc) of *Au. aethiopicus* was similar to that of the earlier australopiths, several of its cranial features were very different. *Australopithecus aethiopicus* shows the classic cranial and dental traits seen in robust australopiths. It had smaller front teeth, but larger premolars and molars, than gracile australopiths. It also had a

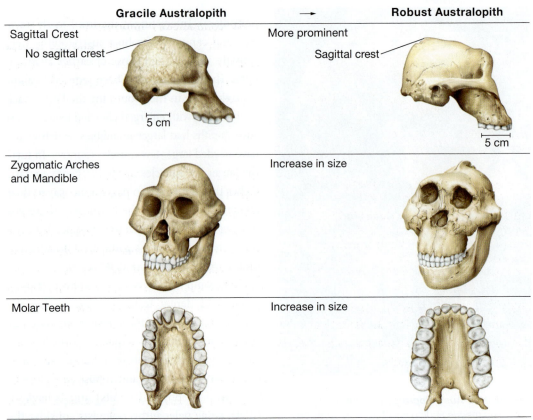

Gracile Australopith	→	Robust Australopith

Sagittal Crest
No sagittal crest

More prominent
Sagittal crest

5 cm

5 cm

Zygomatic Arches and Mandible

Increase in size

Molar Teeth

Increase in size

CENTER RIGHT AND LEFT: Adapted from Bone Clones, Inc. BOTTOM RIGHT: Adapted from photo by Walter Jahn. BOTTOM LEFT: Adapted from photo by Donald C. Johanson. Reprinted with permission.

FIGURE 15.9 Robust versus Gracile Australopiths
The robust australopiths (or paranthropines), such as *Australopithecus* (*Paranthropus*) *aethiopicus*, generally have larger, more robust features (particularly in their crania and teeth) than the gracile australopiths, such as *Australopithecus africanus*.

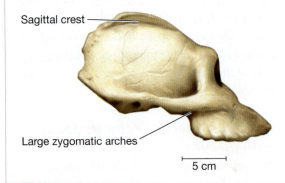

Sagittal crest

Large zygomatic arches

5 cm

FIGURE 15.10 *Australopithecus* (*Paranthropus*) *aethiopicus*
Australopithecus aethiopicus has the classic robust features seen in all robust australopiths: very large back teeth, very large facial features, and a sagittal crest.

large sagittal crest, a large mandible, and large zygomatic arches that made its face seem wide and flared (**FIGURE 15.10**). As with all robust australopiths, these enlarged features indicate that

Au. aethiopicus had a diet that required heavy chewing. However, it is not clear whether this early robust form evolved into the later robust *Australopithecus boisei* and *Australopithecus robustus* species.

Australopithecus (*Paranthropus*) *boisei*

Between 2.3 and 1.2 mya (Pleistocene), another robust australopith, named *Australopithecus boisei*, lived in eastern Africa. It had a slightly larger cranial capacity (around 510 cc) than *Au. aethiopicus*, and its cranial and dental features suggest a specialized diet that required heavy chewing (**FIGURE 15.11**). Among the robust australopiths, *Au. boisei* was the most robust and had the largest molars. It was long assumed that *Au. boisei* primarily ate small, hard foods, such as nuts and seeds, because its cranial and dental traits seemed well suited for grinding these

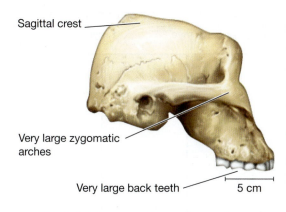

Sagittal crest

Very large zygomatic arches

Very large back teeth

5 cm

FIGURE 15.11 *Australopithecus (Paranthropus) boisei*
Australopithecus boisei was the most robust of the australopiths.

kinds of resources. However, recent carbon isotope analysis indicates that *Au. boisei* had a diet that emphasized tough vegetation, such as sedges and grasses, instead of nuts.

Australopithecus (Paranthropus) robustus

Named for its telltale robusticity, *Australopithecus robustus* lived in southern Africa around 2 to 1.5 mya (late Pleistocene) and was contemporaneous with *Au. boisei* in eastern Africa. It had a small cranial capacity of around 410–530 cc (**FIGURE 15.12**). Like the other robust australopiths, *Au. robustus* had traits adapted for heavy chewing, such as large molars, large zygomatic arches, and a large sagittal crest. However, carbon isotope analyses indicate that *Au. robustus* had a broader diet than *Au. boisei*. The poten-

tially contradictory information gained from the analysis of cranial traits and the isotope analyses suggests that diets and dietary adaptations were complex and variable in our ancient ancestors.

The Newest Australopith: *Australopithecus deyiremeda*

In 2015, researchers led by Yohannes Haile-Selassie announced the discovery of a new australopith that lived in eastern Africa at the same time as *Au. afarensis*, 3.5 to 3.3 mya. This new species is named *Australopithecus deyiremeda*. The species name *deyiremeda* means "close relative" in the local Afar language of Ethiopia, and it was chosen because *Au. deyiremeda* was probably a close relative of the contemporaneous *Au. afarensis* of the same region. *Australopithecus deyiremeda* is represented by several fossilized jaw fragments and teeth (**FIGURE 15.13**). Its back teeth are larger, and its front teeth smaller, than those of *Au. afarensis*. It also has larger jaws, indicating a greater emphasis on chewing and perhaps a diet slightly different from that of *Au. afarensis*. New finds such as *Au. deyiremeda* suggest that throughout hominin evolutionary history, multiple species existed side by side for extended periods of time. This now appears to be true for a range of contemporaneous early australopiths, for the late australopiths and early *Homo* species, and also for a range of contemporaneous late *Homo* species, as we will see in Lab 16.

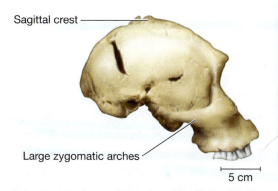

Sagittal crest

Large zygomatic arches

5 cm

FIGURE 15.12 *Australopithecus (Paranthropus) robustus*
Australopithecus robustus had the classic robust features seen in all the robust australopiths.

Laura Dempsey/Cleveland Natural History Museum

FIGURE 15.13 *Australopithecus deyiremeda*
Australopithecus deyiremeda was probably closely related to *Au. afarensis* and suggests that many species of australopiths existed at the same time.

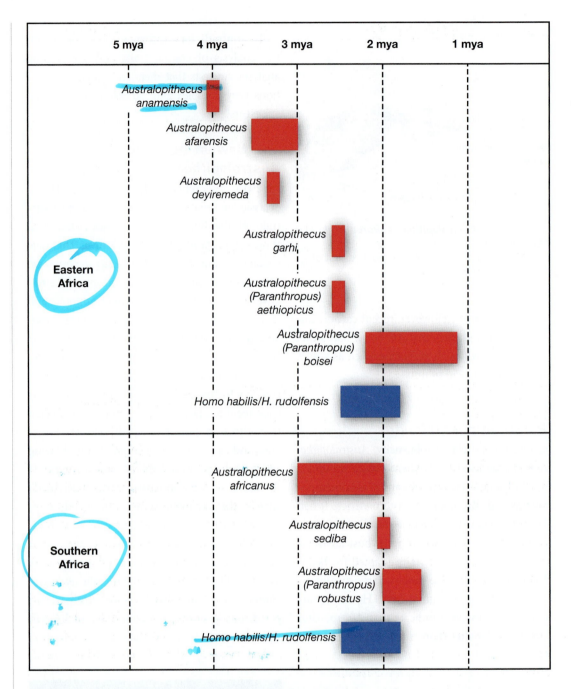

FIGURE 15.14 Time Line of *Australopithecus* and Early *Homo*
The fossil species discussed in this lab were distributed in eastern and southern Africa between 4 and 1 million years ago.

THE *HOMO* GENUS

From 2.5 to 1.8 mya (early Pleistocene), a very different type of species lived side by side with the robust australopiths in eastern and southern Africa **(FIGURE 15.14)**. This species, called *Homo habilis*, was the first member of our own genus. In contrast to the large teeth, jaws, and face characteristic of the robust australopiths, *H. habilis* had a much smaller chewing complex and a larger brain size **(FIGURE 15.15)**.

The name *Homo habilis*, meaning "handy man," is the result of the species' discovery with associated stone tools. At the time, tool use was

Late Australopith	→	Early *Homo*
Brain	Increase in size	
Face	Reduction in robusticity	
Teeth	Reduction in robusticity	

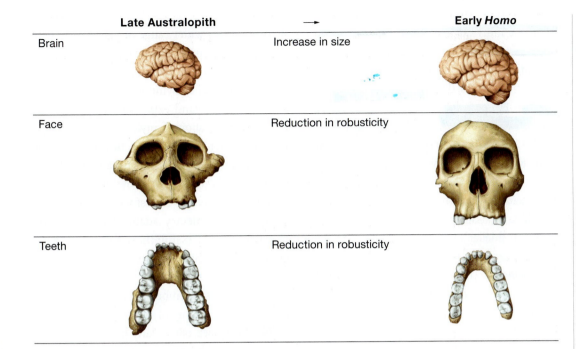

FIGURE 15.15 Robust Australopiths (Paranthropines) versus Early *Homo*
The robust australopiths and early members of the *Homo* genus coexisted in Africa but had very different traits.

believed to be limited to our genus, and *H. habilis* was thought to have been the first stone tool user. As we discussed above, recent discoveries of stone tools and animal bones with cut marks at multiple sites in eastern Africa from as early as 3.3 mya suggest that australopiths were the first tool users, not *H. habilis*.

Homo habilis

Like the australopiths, *H. habilis* was probably a habitual biped with short stature, relatively long arms, and hands suitable for climbing. However, some researchers question the limb proportion estimates for *H. habilis* and argue that it was an early obligate biped because it lacked an opposable hallux and had a longitudinal arch in its foot. More postcranial remains and analysis are needed before this debate can be settled. Compared with the australopiths, *H. habilis* had a slightly larger cranial capacity (averaging about 650 cc) and more gracile cranial and dental features (FIGURE 15.16). *Homo habilis* had smaller teeth, mandibles, and zygomatic arches, and it lacked the sagittal crests typical of robust australopiths. The recovered fossil material for early

Homo indicates that there was a fair amount of variation within this group. Some individuals had larger cranial capacities and slightly more robust cranial features and teeth. Other individuals had smaller cranial capacities (more similar to those of the australopiths) and more gracile cranial features and teeth. Some researchers believe this variation reflects minor differences due to sexual dimorphism (with the robust individuals being male and the more gracile individuals being female). These researchers classify

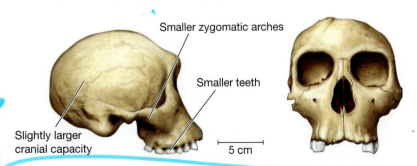

Smaller zygomatic arches

Smaller teeth

Slightly larger cranial capacity

5 cm

FIGURE 15.16 *Homo habilis*
Homo habilis had a slightly larger cranial capacity than the australopiths, and it had more gracile cranial features.

all of the individuals into the same single species, *Homo habilis*. Other researchers argue that the differences are more significant and warrant separation of the group into two distinct species—*Homo habilis* (the smaller individuals) and *Homo rudolfensis* (the larger individuals). In 2012, researchers reported fossil evidence from Koobi Fora, Kenya, that has further bolstered the latter view. These new Koobi Fora specimens are anatomically similar to the larger individuals classified as *H. rudolfensis*, but they are much smaller, indicating that large size alone is not responsible for the distinctive features of *H. rudolfensis*. This evidence suggests that there are two distinct clusters of early *Homo* fossils that reflect two distinct species.

The anatomical traits seen in *Homo habilis* suggest it had a diversified diet, particularly compared with the diet of the late australopiths. This dietary diversity is confirmed by carbon isotope analysis showing that early *Homo* individuals incorporated a wider range of plants into their diet than the more grass-focused *Au. boisei*. While robust forms like *Au. boisei* were very well adapted for chewing abrasive grassy diets during the grassland expansion across eastern Africa starting about 3 mya, early *Homo* were perhaps better adapted for a flexible diet that accommodated fluctuating climates and landscapes. While we do not know precisely what all our early human ancestors were eating, it is clear which dietary adaptations were ultimately more successful: those for a more generalized diet, which modern humans possess today.

These earliest members of our genus *Homo* mark the beginning of a shift toward more human-like traits, particularly bigger brains and smaller faces, and the use of stone tools. This shift becomes even more dramatic in the next species in the *Homo* lineage, *Homo erectus*, which is discussed in Lab 16.

CONCEPT REVIEW QUESTIONS

Name: _____   Section: _____

Course: _____   Date: _____

Answer the following questions in the space provided.

1. As a group, the australopiths lived around:

   A. 4 mya to 1 mya.
   B. 7 mya to 4.4 mya.
   C. 2.5 mya to 1 mya.
   D. 4 mya to 2.5 mya.

2. The fossil individual nicknamed Lucy was:

   A. a typical robust australopith.
   B. a habitual biped.
   C. unusually tall.
   D. alive around 2 mya.

3. Name *two* eastern African australopiths.

4. Name *two* southern African australopiths.

5. The oldest australopith is:

   A. *Australopithecus afarensis.*
   B. *Australopithecus garhi.*
   C. *Australopithecus africanus.*
   D. *Australopithecus anamensis.*

6. Describe the *two* primary tool types associated with the Oldowan technology.

7. Based on recent evidence from the eastern African sites of Lomekwi (Kenya), Dikika (Ethiopia), and Gona (Ethiopia), which of these species may be among the first stone tool users?

   A. *Homo habilis*
   B. *Australopithecus sediba*
   C. *Australopithecus garhi*
   D. *Australopithecus (Paranthropus) robustus*

8. Some researchers argue that the robust australopiths should be classified in a separate genus. What is that genus called?

9. I lived around 2.5 mya in eastern Africa. I had a small cranial capacity (around 410 cc), large molars, large zygomatic arches, and a sagittal crest. What species am I?

    A. *Australopithecus afarensis*

    B. *Australopithecus (Paranthropus) aethiopicus*

    C. *Homo habilis*

    D. *Australopithecus garhi*

10. Describe *one* feature that decreases in size between the australopiths and early members of the *Homo* genus.

LAB EXERCISES

Name: _____   Section: _____

Course: _____   Date: _____

EXERCISE 1 AUSTRALOPITH DENTITION

Work in a small group or alone to complete this exercise. In this lab, we learned that australopiths have larger premolars and molars than humans today. We also saw that within the australopith group, the robust species have even larger premolars and molars than their gracile counterparts. To determine these patterns, paleoanthropologists calculate the surface area (in square millimeters) for the last premolar, first molar, and second molar combined. Use the casts provided by your instructor (or the photos in the Lab 15 Exercise Image Library on p. 448) to calculate this information for the mystery fossil specimens.

STEP 1 Measure the length and width of each tooth in millimeters and enter the data into the chart provided. If working with casts, use sliding calipers to take the measurements.

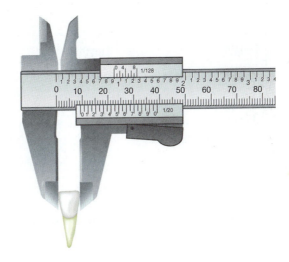

To use sliding calipers, begin with the jaws of the calipers closed. Then, open the jaws and place them around the tooth to be measured. Slowly and gently close the jaws until they are touching (but not damaging) both sides of the tooth. Look for the metric measurements on the fixed scale (the scale that does not move). It is usually indicated with an "mm" label. Check the position of the leftmost tick mark (0) on the sliding scale (the scale that moves). Read the numbers on the *fixed* scale where they align with the leftmost tick mark of the sliding scale. The bold numbers on the fixed scale are centimeters, and the smaller tick marks within are millimeters. For this exercise, you want the measurements in millimeters. (If your calipers provide only inches, multiply your measurements by 25.4 to generate measurements in millimeters.)

   Note: A ruler with millimeter notations may be used in place of sliding calipers.

STEP 2 Calculate the surface area for each tooth. Multiply the length by the width, and note the result in the space provided on the chart.

STEP 3 Calculate the surface area for all three teeth. For each mystery specimen, add the surface areas of all three teeth together and enter the result in the chart.

STEP 4 Interpret the data. Use your completed chart (and the general dentition patterns discussed in this lab) to answer the following questions.

Specimen	Last Premolar	First Molar	Second Molar	Total (all surface areas added together) in mm²
Specimen A	Length: Width: Surface area (length × width) in mm²:	Length: Width: Surface area (length × width) in mm²:	Length: Width: Surface area (length × width) in mm²:	
Specimen B	Length: Width: Surface area (length × width) in mm²:	Length: Width: Surface area (length × width) in mm²:	Length: Width: Surface area (length × width) in mm²:	
Specimen C	Length: Width: Surface area (length × width) in mm²:	Length: Width: Surface area (length × width) in mm²:	Length: Width: Surface area (length × width) in mm²:	

1. Which of the mystery specimens is a human? What evidence indicates this?

2. Which of the mystery specimens is a gracile australopith? What evidence indicates this?

3. Which of the mystery specimens is a robust australopith? What evidence indicates this?

EXERCISE 2   AUSTRALOPITH VARIATION

Work in a small group or alone to complete this exercise. Refer to the casts provided by your instructor (or the photos in the Lab 15 Exercise Image Library on p. 449) to answer the following questions.

1. Which of these mystery australopiths is a later, more robust form?

2. Describe *at least two* facial or cranial traits you used to make this determination. (Your instructor may request that you provide more traits.) Be sure to describe how each trait appears in the two fossils.

EXERCISE 3   AUSTRALOPITH BIPEDALISM

Work in a small group or alone to complete this exercise. Review the casts provided by your instructor (or the photos in the Lab 15 Exercise Image Library on p. 450) and answer the following questions.

1. Examine the Lucy (*Australopithecus afarensis*) skeleton. Describe *at least two* postcranial (below the head) traits that indicate that *Au. afarensis* was adapted for bipedalism.

2. Compare the Lucy (*Au. afarensis*) skeleton with the human (*Homo sapiens*) skeleton. Describe *at least two* postcranial traits that differ between these species.

3. What do your answers suggest about the kind of bipedalism practiced by *Au. afarensis*?

EXERCISE 4   *AUSTRALOPITHECUS SEDIBA*

Work in a small group or alone to complete this exercise. Review the casts provided by your instructor (or the photos in the Lab 15 Exercise Image Library on p. 451) and answer the following questions.

1. Examine the *Australopithecus sediba* skeleton. Describe *at least two* traits that *Au. sediba* shares with other australopiths (such as *Au. africanus* or *Au. afarensis*).

2. Describe *at least two* traits that *Au. sediba* shares with members of the *Homo* genus.

3. What do your answers suggest about the evolutionary relationship between these species?

4. *Au. sediba* lived in southern Africa around 2 mya. When did the first members of the *Homo* genus appear? And where?

5. Does your answer change your interpretation of the relationship between *Au. sediba* and the members of the *Homo* genus? Why or why not?

EXERCISE 5   AUSTRALOPITHS VERSUS THE GENUS *HOMO*

Work in a small group or alone to complete this exercise. Use the casts provided by your instructor (or the photos in the Lab 15 Exercise Image Library on p. 452) to answer the following questions.

1. Describe *at least two* traits that differ between these fossils. (Be sure to describe how each trait appears in the two fossils.)

2. Based on this information, which of these fossils is an australopith?

3. Based on this information, which of these fossils is a member of the *Homo* genus?

EXERCISE 6   THE EARLY MEMBERS OF THE GENUS *HOMO*

Work in a small group or alone to complete this exercise. Refer to the casts provided by your instructor (or the drawings in the Lab 15 Exercise Image Library on p. 453) to answer the following questions.

1. Describe *at least two* traits that differ between these fossils. (Be sure to describe how each trait appears in the two fossils.)

2. Do *you* believe these differences are the result of sexual dimorphism or of different adaptations? Why?

EXERCISE 7   STONE TOOL TECHNOLOGY

Work in a small group or alone to complete this exercise. Review the casts provided by your instructor (or the photo in the Lab 15 Exercise Image Library on p. 454) and answer the following questions.

1. What type of tool is this?

2. Describe the features of this tool that led you to identify it as this tool type.

3. What tool technology does this tool belong to?

4. Name *one* fossil species that may have made this stone tool.

CRITICAL THINKING QUESTIONS

On a separate sheet of paper, answer the following questions.

1. What do *you* think is the best way to classify the robust species of australopiths? Do you support the use of the genus *Paranthropus*? Why or why not? (Be sure to support your decision with specific evidence.)

2. The *Australopithecus sediba* finds demonstrate that evolution is mosaic, meaning that species often have a combination of ancestral and derived traits. How would this fossil material be interpreted if only the arm and hand bones were found? How would this fossil material be interpreted if only the pelvis were found? Based on this example, what problems do paleoanthropologists face when trying to interpret the fragmentary fossil record?

3. In this lab, we discussed the earliest known stone tools. Do you think those tools represent the first time our extinct relatives used tools? Why might older tools not be preserved in the fossil record? For comparison, describe three tools from your own life (for example, a cell phone, a pencil, and a plastic fork). Do you think these tools will be preserved 2.5 million years from today?

4. During a period of almost a million years, *Australopithecus boisei* and *Homo habilis* lived in the same region of eastern Africa. If these species shared a habitat, why didn't one of them outcompete the other? (*Hint*: Think about their possible ecologies and adaptations.)

5. Many of the traits we learned about in this lab have had a lasting effect on our lineage, and as a human, you still bear their consequences today. For example, humans are at high risk of knee injuries, such as tears in the ligaments that support the knee joint between the femur and tibia. What adaptation that traces back to australopiths, like Lucy, might put additional strain on your knee? Why would a trait with such negative consequences have evolved?

6. In this lab, we reviewed numerous fossil species and their defining characteristics. To help you make comparisons across these species and understand larger trends in our evolutionary history, complete the Australopith and Early *Homo* Chart on pp. 446–447.

7. Use your completed Australopith and Early *Homo* Chart to answer the following questions.

   A. In what geographic region(s) have numerous early hominin discoveries been made? How do those regions relate to the locations of the pre-australopith species that came before them?

   B. Review the behaviors listed on your chart and compare them with what you know about pre-australopiths. What behaviors are documented in australopiths and *Homo habilis* that are not seen in pre-australopiths? Why might these behaviors appear in the more recent species and not in the pre-australopith group?

   C. Choose one gracile australopith species and one robust australopith species, and list at least two traits that distinguish them. Also list at least two things they have in common. What do your answers suggest about their classification and relationship to each other?

   D. Choose any australopith species and compare it with *Homo habilis*. List at least two traits that distinguish these species. What do your answers suggest about their classification and relationship to each other? Which one are you more closely related to (with which do you have more in common)?

AUSTRALOPITH AND EARLY *HOMO* CHART

Fossil Species	Dates and Geographic Region	Cranial and Dental Traits	Postcranial Traits	Suggested Behavior
Australopithecus anamensis				
Australopithecus afarensis				
Australopithecus africanus				
Australopithecus garhi				
Australopithecus sediba				
Australopithecus (Paranthropus) aethiopicus				

AUSTRALOPITH AND EARLY *HOMO* CHART (*continued*)

Fossil Species	Dates and Geographic Region	Cranial and Dental Traits	Postcranial Traits	Suggested Behavior
Australopithecus (Paranthropus) boisei				
Australopithecus (Paranthropus) robustus				
Australopithecus deyiremeda				
Homo habilis (including H. rudolfensis)				

LAB 15 EXERCISE IMAGE LIBRARY
Students should use these images only if directed to by their instructor.

EXERCISE 1 AUSTRALOPITH DENTITION

All photos are shown at the same scale.

Photo by Paul Constantino

Bone Clones/boneclones.com

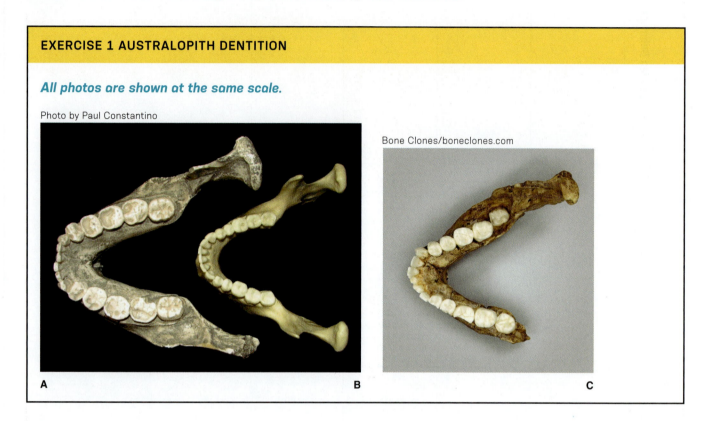

A   B   C

EXERCISE 2 AUSTRALOPITH VARIATION

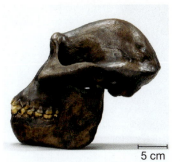

5 cm

5 cm

A

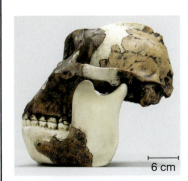

6 cm

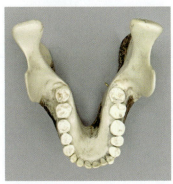

B

EXERCISE 3 AUSTRALOPITH BIPEDALISM

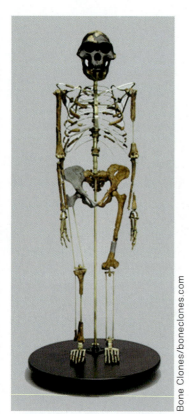

Reconstruction of articulated
Lucy remains (*Australopithecus
afarensis*, 3'7" feet, 1.09 meters)

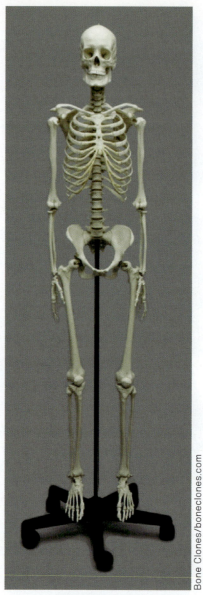

Modern human
(female, 5'6" feet, 1.68 meters)

Bone Clones/boneclones.com

Bone Clones/boneclones.com

EXERCISE 4 *AUSTRALOPITHECUS SEDIBA*

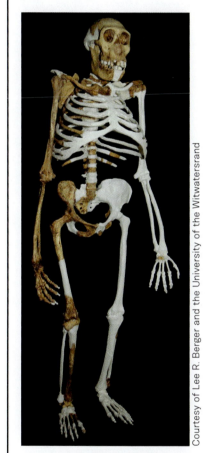

Courtesy of Lee R. Berger and the University of the Witwatersrand

Australopithecus sediba
(4'3" feet, 1.3 meters)

Bone Clones/boneclones.com

Australopithecus afarensis
(3'7" feet, 1.09 meters)

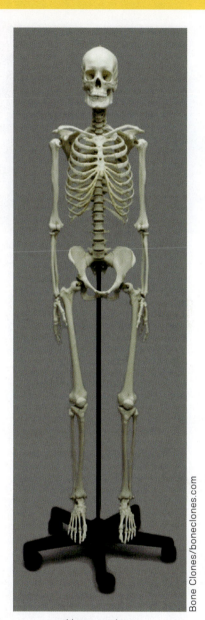

Bone Clones/boneclones.com

Homo sapiens
(5'6" feet, 1.68 meters)

EXERCISE 5 *AUSTRALOPITHS* VERSUS THE GENUS *HOMO*

Fossil A

Fossil B

EXERCISE 6 THE EARLY MEMBERS OF THE GENUS *HOMO*

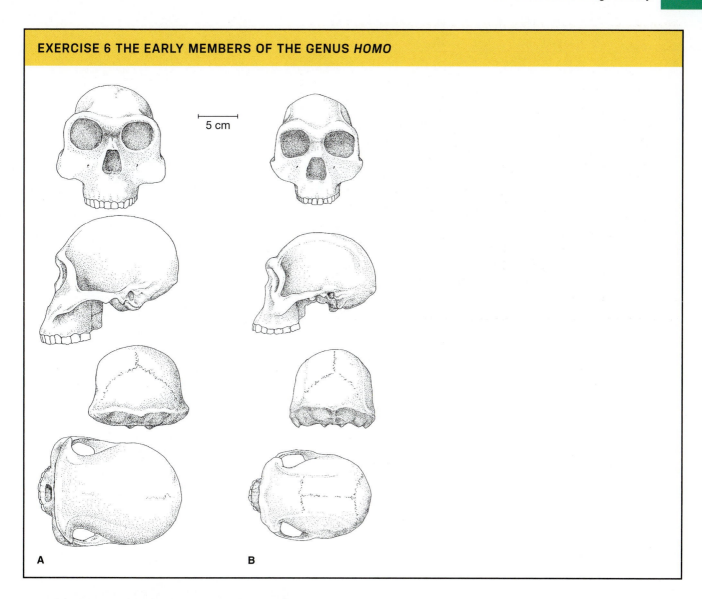

5 cm

A   B

EXERCISE 7 STONE TOOL TECHNOLOGY

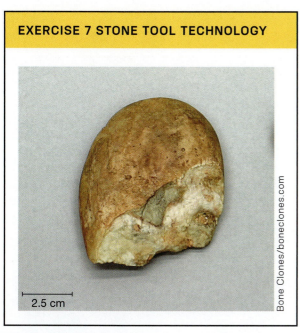

2.5 cm

Bone Clones/boneclones.com

David Lordkipanidze et al. 18 October 2013. A Complete Skull from Dmanisi, Georgia, and the Evolutionary Biology of Early *Homo. Science* 342 (6156): 236-331. Copyright © 2013 AAAS.

Excavations in Dmanisi have revealed unusual fossil specimens believed to be some of the first members of our lineage to live outside of Africa.

LAB 16

Lab Learning Objectives

By the end of this lab, students should be able to:

- describe the later species of our genus, including their distributions and defining characteristics.

- describe the variation seen in *Homo erectus* fossils, particularly the differences between specimens from Africa and from Asia.

- discuss what current evidence tells us about the relationship between humans and Neanderthals.

- compare and distinguish among the major stone tool technologies.

- describe the explanations for the origin and spread of humans.

- explain how unusual species, such as *Homo naledi* and *Homo floresiensis*, demonstrate the diversity of our recent evolutionary past.

Later Members of the Genus *Homo*

A round 1.75 mya (million years ago) in Eurasia, the world was changing. Fifty miles southwest of what is now the city of Tbilisi (the capital of the Republic of Georgia), the land held an array of environmental zones, including a river valley, meadows, and grasslands. This place (now called Dmanisi) was home to a variety of animals, such as deer, rodents, wild dogs, and rhinoceroses. It was also home to a group of our relatives called *Homo erectus*. Only 500,000 years after the species originated in Africa, it had expanded to another continent. How was *Homo erectus* able to make this extraordinary migration?

This Dmanisi population had an interesting mix of traits that reflected the transition from more ancestral, earlier *Homo* traits to more derived, later *Homo* traits. The small cranial capacity (600–775 cubic centimeters, or cc), small body size, and primitive shoulder anatomy of its members suggest that they were related to *Homo habilis* in Africa. However, the shapes of the mandible and cranium more closely resembled those of a newer species in Africa, called *Homo erectus*. They also had *H. erectus*–like lower limbs, with long, angled femurs, arched feet, and nondivergent big toes. Their legs were more specialized for bipedalism than those of the earlier *Homo habilis*, and their gait was more efficient. The Dmanisi

orthognathic having a flat face

brow ridge a bony ridge located above the eye orbits

population also used Oldowan tools. Although they did not travel great distances to acquire special rocks for their tools, they did select the best locally available materials. They produced choppers and flakes that helped them take better advantage of meat resources, which were probably obtained through intensive scavenging. This meat was part of a diverse diet that also included a range of plant and fruit resources.

The Dmanisi group is significant because their fossil remains show us an important transition in our evolutionary history. In addition to the physical changes that took place at this time, a remarkable cultural change occurred as well. For over 5 million years, our ancestors lived only in Africa, but around 1.8 mya, they began to move out and settle in other parts of the world. The Dmanisi population was among the first of our relatives to make this move out of Africa.

INTRODUCTION

In this lab, we conclude our exploration of our fossil relatives. We introduce the most important later *Homo* species and their defining physical

and cultural characteristics. We also consider the geographic distribution and coexistence of several of these species. We pay particular attention to the coexistence of humans and Neanderthals and what current evidence tells us about their relationship. In addition, we discuss the major explanations proposed for the origin and spread of our own species.

LATER MEMBERS OF THE GENUS *HOMO*

The later members of the genus *Homo* share some key traits that distinguish them from early species, such as *Homo habilis*. The later *Homo* species had larger cranial capacities, more **orthognathic** (or flatter) faces, and smaller teeth. Their postcrania were more similar to those of modern humans, and unlike our earlier relatives, these later *Homo* species were obligate bipeds. These species had wider geographic distributions than earlier species, and they lived in places outside of Africa (**FIGURE 16.1**). They also had more complicated cultures and technologies than earlier species.

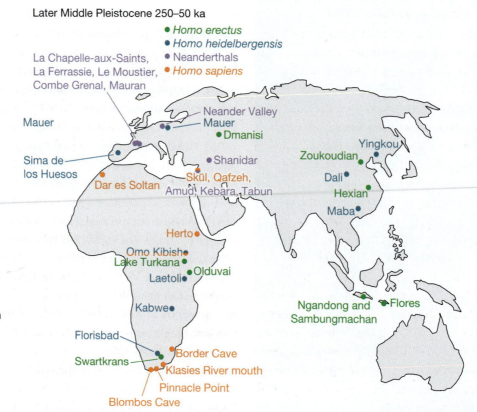

Later Middle Pleistocene 250–50 ka

- *Homo erectus*
- *Homo heidelbergensis*
- Neanderthals
- *Homo sapiens*

La Chapelle-aux-Saints, La Ferrassie, Le Moustier, Combe Grenal, Mauran

Mauer

Neander Valley
Mauer
Dmanisi
Yingkou
Zoukoudian
Sima de los Huesos
Shanidar
Dali
Skūl, Qafzeh, Amud, Kebara, Tabun
Hexian
Dar es Soltan
Maba
Herto
Omo Kibish
Lake Turkana
Olduvai
Laetoli
Kabwe
Ngandong and Sambungmachan
Flores
Florisbad
Swartkrans
Border Cave
Klasies River mouth
Pinnacle Point
Blombos Cave

FIGURE 16.1 The Distribution of Later *Homo*
Later members of the *Homo* genus have been recovered from fossil sites throughout Europe and Asia as well as in Africa.

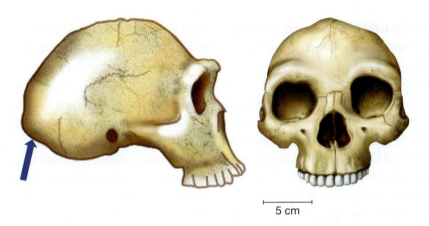

occipital torus a ridge of bone along the occipital bone that forms a small point when seen from the side

5 cm

FIGURE 16.2 *Homo erectus*
Homo erectus had a long, low cranium with a large cranial capacity. It had large brow ridges and an occipital torus (arrow). It also had small teeth.

Homo erectus

Homo erectus lived from about 1.8 mya to 300 kya (thousand years ago), during the late Pleistocene, in Africa and Asia, and from about 1.8 mya to 400 kya in Europe (if we include the early Dmanisi individuals discussed at the start of this lab). Members of this species had larger cranial capacities (averaging around 950 cc) than prior species (**FIGURE 16.2**). Some very early individuals, such as the Dmanisi group, had smaller cranial capacities (600 cc), and some later individuals, such as the Zhoukoudian group in modern-day China, had even larger cranial capacities (1,200 cc). *Homo erectus* crania were generally long and low, shaped like footballs when viewed from the side. These individuals also had pronounced **brow ridges**, relatively orthognathic faces, and an unusual projection at the back of the skull called an occipital torus. The **occipital torus** is a ridge of bone that runs along the occipital bone and forms a small point when seen from the side. In addition to these cranial traits, *H. erectus* mandibles and teeth, particularly their premolars and molars, were much smaller than those of earlier hominin species (such as the australopiths). These features may relate to a shift in diet. Whereas australopiths (especially robust species) relied on chewing, *Homo erectus* seems to have relied more on biting and tearing, so it did not require the larger chewing teeth seen in the australopiths.

One of the earliest and most famous *Homo erectus* specimens is nicknamed Nariokotome (or Turkana) Boy, after the site in eastern Africa where the specimen was recovered. Nariokotome Boy is a relatively complete skeleton from a single individual (**FIGURE 16.3**). It is believed to have belonged to a male who was around 8–10 years old when he died approximately 1.6 mya. This individual provides good evidence of *H. erectus* postcranial traits. He had long legs and shorter arms, which indicate that he did not practice the arboreal locomotion that was still part of the repertoire of our earlier ancestors. This conclusion is further supported by his barrel-shaped rib cage, which is more similar to ours than to that of arboreal nonhuman apes. Nariokotome Boy also had angled femurs and various other lower-limb traits that suggest he moved efficiently on two legs and could cover great distances with ease. Analysis of his skeleton also suggests that he would have been close to 6 feet (1.8 m) tall in adulthood. Together, these lines of evidence indicate that *H. erectus* individuals were efficient obligate bipeds with statures and limb proportions similar to those of modern humans today.

Evidence from fossilized dental remains and stone tools suggests that *Homo erectus* had a diverse diet that included more

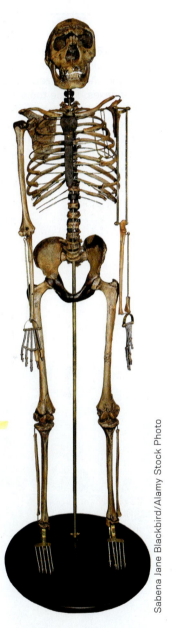

Sabena Jane Blackbird/Alamy Stock Photo

FIGURE 16.3 The Nariokotome Skeleton
The nearly complete *Homo erectus* specimen nicknamed Nariokotome Boy provides valuable information about the postcrania of this species. It shows that *H. erectus* was an efficient obligate biped with modern stature and limb proportions.

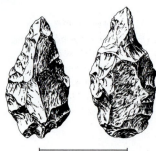

FIGURE 16.4 Acheulean Tools
The Acheulean tool technology is characterized by handaxes. These tools required a slightly more complicated production process than Oldowan tools, and they were more standardized than Oldowan tools.

meat than the diets of earlier species, but it is unclear whether this meat was scavenged or directly hunted. As for its social life, it was originally believed that *H. erectus* had less sexual dimorphism than earlier species. This would suggest a possible shift away from polygynous social structures. Recent evidence, however, suggests that *H. erectus* may have maintained the same degree of sexual dimorphism, and thus the polygynous social structures, of earlier fossil species. More evidence is needed to fully support one interpretation over the other, so *H. erectus* social structure remains an ongoing debate.

Early *Homo erectus* individuals used Oldowan tools (such as the choppers and flakes discussed in Lab 15), but around 1.5 mya, *Homo erectus* began to make and use new kinds of tools. These newer stone tools are considered to be part of the **Acheulean (Acheulian) technology** (FIGURE 16.4). This technology was named after a site in Saint Acheul, France, where

these tools were discovered in the mid-1800s, and it is characterized by tools called bifaces. A **biface** is a stone tool that has had flakes of stone removed from two sides. The most common biface in Acheulean sites is the handaxe. A **handaxe** is a biface that is shaped like a pear (or teardrop), with one end that is larger and rounded and another end that is more narrow and pointed. Most handaxes would fit neatly into the palm of your hand, and they were multipurpose tools that were probably used for butchering meat and/or digging up underground plant parts to be eaten. These versatile tools were useful in environments from Africa to Europe to western Asia, and they were effective enough that they remained largely unchanged for over a million years. Compared with the earlier Oldowan tools, Acheulean tools were manufactured through a slightly more complicated process that required more steps to produce the desired shape. In addition, the Acheulean tools were more standardized than Oldowan tools. An Oldowan chopper at one site can look very different from an Oldowan chopper at another site. However, Acheulean handaxes were the same shape and size from one place to another, across thousands of miles and hundreds of thousands of years.

One of the most significant aspects of *Homo erectus* is its geographic distribution. It was the first species of our genus to leave Africa, and within a few tens of thousands of years, *H. erectus* was found as far away from Africa as Southeast Asia (FIGURE 16.5). This migration into Eurasia between 1.8 mya and 800 kya (sometimes called **Out of Africa I**) was related to environmental shifts and changing food availability. Unlike many of the migrants in our recent history, *H. erectus* did not consciously set out to move to a new place. Instead, the species probably moved a little farther east with every generation. A group might settle in one region for a generation or two and take advantage of the wild animal herds and plant foods available in that area. As the environment changed and the animal herds moved farther east, the next generation of the *H. erectus* group might follow and settle in a new region for another generation

FIGURE 16.5 *Homo erectus* Migration
Homo erectus was the first member of our lineage to move out of Africa and settle in various areas of Europe and Asia. This migration was facilitated by the species' generalized anatomy and flexible technology.

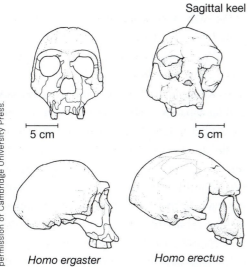

Sagittal keel

5 cm   5 cm

Homo ergaster   *Homo erectus*

FIGURE 16.6 *Homo erectus* **versus** *Homo ergaster*
Some researchers argue that *Homo erectus* fossils can be divided into two different species. Compared with typical African specimens (*Homo ergaster*), non-African specimens (*Homo erectus*) have a more pronounced occipital torus, a sagittal keel, and a longer and lower cranium.

or two. Over many generations, *H. erectus* was able to expand across Asia and up into Europe. Its ability to do this was probably facilitated by its generalized anatomy and flexible tool technology. Unlike highly specialized species (such as robust australopiths), *Homo erectus* had a diverse diet and a generalized anatomy that allowed it to do well in a wide range of habitats. Its more complicated but widely applicable stone tool technology may have helped it adapt to its varied surroundings as well.

As seen with the *Homo habilis* fossils discussed in Lab 15, there is significant variation within *Homo erectus* fossils, which suggests that the African and non-African individuals (particularly from Asia) may form two distinct groups. The non-African fossils show more exaggerated versions of the traits seen in the African fossils (**FIGURE 16.6**). Specifically, members of the non-African group had thicker cranial bones, an even longer and lower cranium, more pronounced brow ridges, a more pronounced occipital torus, and a unique cranial feature called a sagittal keel. The **sagittal keel** is a slight ridge of bone that runs along the midline of the cra-

nium. Although it is located in the same position as the sagittal crest of a gorilla or a robust australopith, it is much less pronounced and does not relate to large chewing muscle attachment. In addition to these cranial differences, the members of the non-African group were a little shorter and stockier than their African counterparts. Some researchers believe these differences are significant enough to warrant classifying the African and non-African fossils into two different species. These researchers argue that the more generalized African group should be called *Homo ergaster*, while the more exaggerated non-African group should be called *Homo erectus*.

Homo heidelbergensis

Around 600 kya (late Pleistocene), a new species, called *Homo heidelbergensis*, appeared in Africa and Europe (**FIGURE 16.7**). *Homo heidelbergensis* lived in these areas from around 600 to 130 kya and in Asia from around 200 to 130 kya. Members of this new group had several traits in common with *Homo erectus*. They had long and low crania and large brow ridges. Some of the individuals even had a small occipital torus. However, *Homo heidelbergensis* also had some unique traits. For example, it had a larger cranial capacity (around 1,200–1,300 cc)

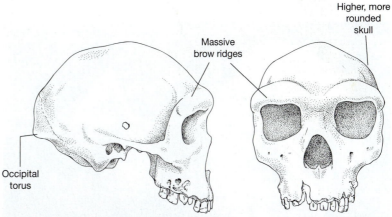

Higher, more rounded skull

Massive brow ridges

Occipital torus

By Kathryn Cruz-Uribe, reprinted with permission from *The Human Career: Human Biology and Cultural Origins*, 2nd edition, by R.G. Klein.

FIGURE 16.7 *Homo heidelbergensis*
Homo heidelbergensis had a long and low cranium, a large brow ridge, and a large cranial capacity. It also had small teeth, and its incisors often show extensive wear.

Mousterian technology a stone tool technology that used the Levallois technique to produce a variety of specialized flake tools

and smaller back teeth (premolars and molars) than *Homo erectus*. Some of the European individuals in particular also had tooth wear on their incisors. This wear indicates that they might have been using their teeth as tools. Perhaps they held animal hides or plant fibers in their teeth while using their hands to scrape the material with a stone tool.

As with the earlier members of the genus *Homo*, there is debate about how best to classify the *Homo heidelbergensis* fossils. A few researchers argue that these fossils share key features with modern humans, such as a very large cranial capacity. Based on this similarity, these researchers classify the *Homo heidelbergensis* fossils as members of our own species, *Homo sapiens*. Of course, these researchers acknowledge that these fossils are also different from us, especially in their cranial robusticity. To account for this robusticity, they consider the fossils to be *archaic* (or *early*) *Homo sapiens*, as opposed to *anatomically modern Homo sapiens* (humans of today). In contrast, other researchers emphasize the uniqueness of the fossil group. From their viewpoint, the robusticity seen in the fossils is significant enough to distinguish the specimens from our own species, so they classify the fossil group as a separate species, called *Homo heidelbergensis*. The large cranial capacity of *H. heidelbergensis* is believed to reflect a general trend toward larger cranial capacities that began with earlier members of the *Homo* genus, but these researchers do not consider it significant enough to warrant placing it in our species.

Homo heidelbergensis had a diverse diet that included meat from big game animals. It is often unclear whether our earlier ancestors hunted or scavenged the meat in their diet. However, tools and other evidence recovered from *H. heidelbergensis* sites suggest that they actively hunted large animals. Their hunting was probably facilitated by a shift in stone tool technology that occurred during this time. Early *Homo heidelbergensis* used Acheulean tools similar to those used by later *Homo erectus*, but later members of *Homo heidelbergensis* used a new tool technology, called the Mousterian technology.

The **Mousterian technology** is named after a site in France called Le Moustier, and it is very different from the earlier stone tool technologies (**FIGURE 16.8**). In both the Oldowan and the Acheulean technologies, emphasis was placed on core tools—the tools left when flakes had been removed. For a Mousterian toolmaker, the flakes themselves were the most important tools. These flakes were modified into a wide range of shapes that were each suitable for a specific task, such

A large stone of flint is chosen.

Small flakes are removed from the stone's perimeter using an antler or other tool.

One side of the stone has flakes removed from the entire surface, giving it the appearance of a tortoise shell.

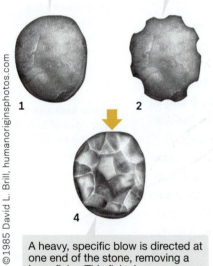

A heavy, specific blow is directed at one end of the stone, removing a large flake. This flake is convex on one side and flat on the other.

This flake can now be used for scraping or cutting. Further flake removal will produce a more specialized tool.

A

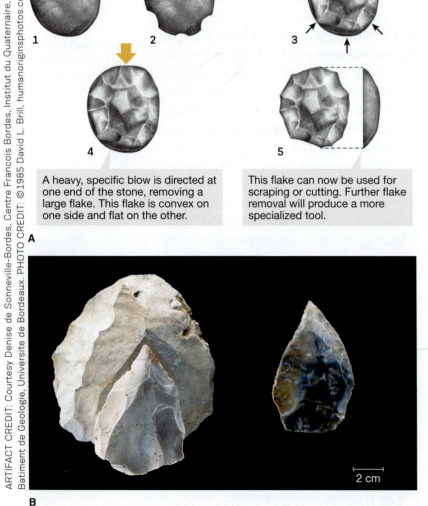

2 cm

B

FIGURE 16.8 Mousterian Tools
Using (A) the Levallois technique, Mousterian toolmakers produced (B) regular flakes that were then modified into different tools.

as scraping, drilling, or cutting. Whereas the Oldowan and Acheulean toolmakers used a few generalized tools to perform countless functions, the Mousterian toolmakers used a specific tool for each function. They even hafted (attached) stone points to wood shafts to make stone-tipped spears. To produce their specialized flake tools, Mousterian toolmakers used a much more complicated production process called the **Levallois technique**. The toolmaker first removed small flakes from around a core of rock, then created a platform at one end of the stone, and finally struck the platform to remove a precisely shaped flake. By repeating the process over and over, the toolmaker could produce numerous flakes, all of roughly the same shape and size, from a single core. After preparing these flakes, the toolmaker would then remove pieces of stone from the edge of each flake to form the specific tool desired. While the flake tools were shaped differently for different functions, these shapes were standardized across Mousterian sites. For example, a scraper tool in one area was very similar to a scraper tool in another area. While later *Homo heidelbergensis* did make Mousterian tools, the technology is most often associated with the Neanderthals; Mousterian tools are found at Neanderthal sites throughout Europe and western Asia.

Homo neanderthalensis

Homo neanderthalensis is perhaps the most famous of our extinct fossil relatives **(FIGURE 16.9)**. The Neanderthals lived around 130 to 30 kya (late Pleistocene) in Europe and western Asia. They shared several traits with the earlier *Homo heidelbergensis* fossils. For example, they had a long and low cranium and large brow ridges. They also had small back teeth (premolars and molars) and highly worn incisors, suggesting that they, too, may have used their front teeth as tools. In addition to these shared features, the Neanderthals had several unique traits. They had incredibly large cranial capacities (around 1,245–1,740 cc). In fact, the average Neanderthal cranial capacity (1,520 cc) was larger than the average human cranial capacity today (1,400 cc)! However, when we take into account estimates of Neanderthal body weight, their brain to body

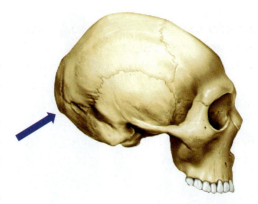

FIGURE 16.9 *Homo neanderthalensis*
Homo neanderthalensis had an incredibly large cranial capacity, large brow ridges, a large nasal opening, and an occipital bun (arrow).

ratio is lower than that of the average human today. The Neanderthals also had an unusual, round projection called an **occipital bun** located on the back of the skull. When you look at this feature on a Neanderthal cranium, it almost appears as if a dinner roll (or bun) is stuck on the back of the head.

Neanderthals also had several adaptations that helped them in their extreme environment. During the time of the Neanderthals, the planet was experiencing a massive Ice Age. During certain times, much of Europe was covered in glaciers, and temperatures were considerably colder than they are today. The unglaciated areas of southern Europe would have been bitterly cold habitats similar to what we find in Scandinavia, northern Russia, Alaska, or northern Canada today. Neanderthals in this extreme environment had large nasal openings that may have helped to warm the air when they inhaled. In addition, like Arctic human populations today, the Neanderthals had stocky bodies **(FIGURE 16.10)** that helped them to retain heat (see Lab 8 for more information about climate adaptations in humans). In addition to their physical adaptations, Neanderthals had cultural adaptations that helped them to survive in Ice Age Europe. They built fires, made use of caves as shelters, and probably had rudimentary clothing.

Like *Homo heidelbergensis*, Neanderthals had a diverse diet that emphasized big game animals. They hunted these animals using Mousterian tools, which required the Neanderthals

Levallois technique
a process used to produce regularly shaped flakes that can then be further modified into different tools

occipital bun a large, round projection located on the occipital bone

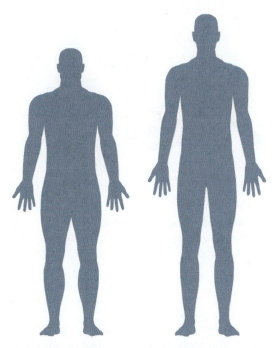

FIGURE 16.10 Neanderthal Body Size
Neanderthals (*left*) had stockier bodies than modern humans (*right*). This body form would have helped them to retain body heat in their Ice Age environment.

to spear their prey at close range. This risky hunting technique, along with other aspects of their lives, resulted in a lot of physical injuries. Despite being stocky and robust, many Nean-

Musee de l'Homme de Neandertal

FIGURE 16.11 A Neanderthal Burial
Evidence of purposefully arranged burials from numerous sites (such as this one from La Chapelle-aux-Saints) suggests that Neanderthals regularly buried their dead.

derthal fossils show evidence of traumatic injuries, such as broken bones. Interestingly, these injuries are often healed, suggesting that some individuals survived multiple injuries over a lifetime. In some cases, injured individuals would have been permanently disabled and may have required assistance from other members of the group to survive. In addition to possibly caring for their sick and injured, the Neanderthals regularly and intentionally buried their dead (**FIGURE 16.11**). These burials may reflect some sense of abstract thinking, such as a spirituality or consideration of an afterlife. Alternatively, the burials may reflect a more basic need to contain decomposition and avoid detection by predators and scavengers.

Neanderthals may have had aspects of culture and symbolic thought similar to those of modern humans. There is evidence that some Neanderthals made nonfunctional objects, such as decorated shells that may have been used as pendants or other personal ornaments. These types of artifacts are primarily associated with our own species, and the production of such things by Neanderthals supports the idea that they may have been symbolic thinkers. There is also some evidence (both from the fossil record and DNA analysis) that suggests Neanderthals may have had the ability to produce language. Although that language may not have directly resembled human language today, it may still have been possible for Neanderthals to engage in complex forms of communication. Additional evidence for Neanderthals' complex thinking is found in their dental calculus (or hardened plaque). Chemical analysis of Neanderthals' dental calculus indicates that they regularly incorporated a range of plants into their diet, including plants with little nutritional value that may have been consumed for medicinal purposes instead. This finding demonstrates that Neanderthals not only had sophisticated hunting technology, but also had knowledge about diverse plants in their environment. The abilities and thought processes of Neanderthals are hotly debated, with some researchers arguing that they had abilities similar to those of modern people and other researchers arguing that Neanderthals had far more limited abilities than humans.

The debate over Neanderthal culture and symbolic thought feeds into a larger debate about the relationship between Neanderthals and humans. Some researchers highlight the similarities between Neanderthals and humans and believe that the two groups are closely related. These researchers often classify *Homo neanderthalensis* as archaic *Homo sapiens* (along with *Homo heidelbergensis*). In the classification debates about most *Homo* species, we must turn to the fossil record for evidence. This limits us to differences in the size and shape of skeletal features, as in the case of *Homo heidelbergensis*. In the debate surrounding Neanderthal classification, however, we have another line of evidence available—ancient DNA.

As discussed in Lab 13, most fossils are mineralized remains that no longer contain organic materials and DNA. Some Neanderthals, however, have died recently enough that their skeletons have not fully fossilized. Therefore, in some cases, researchers have been able to extract trace amounts of Neanderthal DNA for analysis. Studies along these lines have examined both **mitochondrial DNA (mtDNA)** and **nuclear DNA**. The mtDNA evidence suggests that humans arose from a lineage in Africa that was separate from the Neanderthal populations living in Europe and western Asia. However, the nuclear DNA evidence suggests that when the humans arrived in those regions from Africa, they interbred with Neanderthals who already lived there. When combined, these results indicate that while humans and Neanderthals are related and share some genetic similarities because of ancient interbreeding, they probably originated as separate populations with unique evolutionary histories.

Homo sapiens

Our own species, *Homo sapiens*, first appeared in Africa around 200 kya, in western Asia around 100 kya, in Australia around 50 kya, in Europe around 35 kya, and in the Americas around 15 kya (late Pleistocene). In general, early *Homo sapiens* individuals were much more gracile than earlier *Homo* species, especially compared with their robust Neanderthal contemporaries. However, these early members of our species were still slightly more robust than humans today. They had small, orthognathic faces with small brow ridges (**FIGURE 16.12**). They also had small front and back teeth and a pronounced chin on the front of the mandible. The overall cranial shape was tall and rounded, giving *Homo sapiens* a distinct, vertical forehead. They also had large cranial capacities (averaging at least 1,350 cc) and a rounded occipital area (without specialized structures such as an occipital torus or bun). Their postcrania were relatively gracile, giving them a long and lean body type that was generalized and suitable for a range of environments.

From the beginning, *Homo sapiens* had diverse diets that included a wider range of prey than those of other *Homo* species. They hunted and ate medium-sized game animals, such as ancient deer species, as well as smaller game, such as birds and fish. They also had more complicated cultural and symbolic behavior than seen with earlier *Homo* species. Humans made complex

mitochondrial DNA (mtDNA) the DNA found in mitochondria, which is passed from mothers to offspring

nuclear DNA the DNA found in the nucleus of a cell

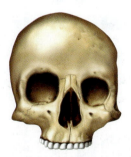
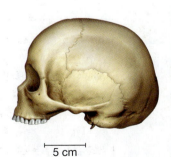
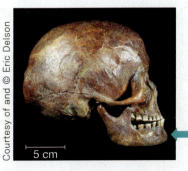

Courtesy of and © Eric Delson

5 cm   5 cm

FIGURE 16.12 *Homo sapiens*
Early *Homo sapiens* can be distinguished from other *Homo* species by its small brow ridges, tall cranium with a forehead, and pronounced chin (arrow).

clothing, using needles, and they used complex shelters that required building, rather than simply taking advantage of naturally formed caves. Humans also engaged in a wide range of behaviors that demonstrate their symbolic thinking. Their burials were more ritualistic than Nean-

derthal burials, and they regularly interred their dead with special tools, jewelry, and other grave goods. They also produced a variety of symbolic objects, such as carved figurines and cave paintings **(FIGURE 16.13)**. Although these symbolic creations are often referred to as "art," the actual

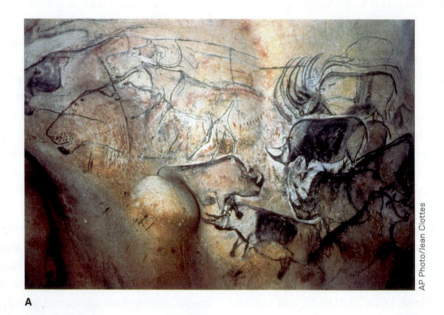

A

AP Photo/Jean Clottes

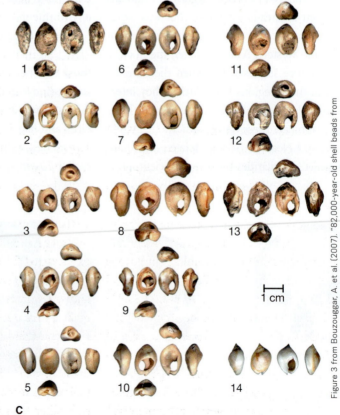

B

C

Heritage Image Partnership Ltd/Alamy Stock Photo

1 cm

Figure 3 from Bouzouggar, A. et al. (2007). "82,000-year-old shell beads from North Africa and implications for the origins of modern human behavior." PNAS 104:9964-9969. Copyright (2007) National Academy of Sciences, U.S.A.

FIGURE 16.13
Early "Art"

Homo sapiens produced a variety of symbolic objects, including (A) cave paintings, (B) carved figurines, and (C) personal ornaments (such as shell jewelry).

A

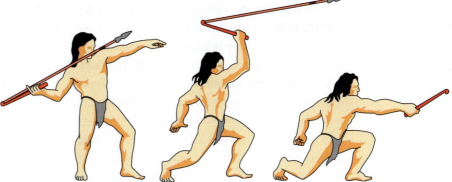

B

C

FIGURE 16.14 Upper Paleolithic Tools
(A) The Upper Paleolithic tools made by *Homo sapiens* required the production of elongated stone flakes called blades. A blade could then be modified into a point like the one shown here. (B) *Homo sapiens* also invented the atlatl, a notched stick that helped them to throw lightweight spears farther than before. (C) The Upper Paleolithic toolkit often included tools made from bone or antler, such as this barbed harpoon carved from antler and used to catch fish.

purpose behind their production is unclear. While the European examples are the most famous, similar evidence of symbolic thought was present in Africa and Asia before it appeared in Europe.

Homo sapiens used a new stone tool technology that was not seen in other species, referred to as the **Upper Paleolithic technology** in Europe (**FIGURE 16.14**). The Upper Paleolithic cultural period dates from about 40 to 10 kya. The term "Paleolithic" refers to the Stone Age, and the Upper Paleolithic is the most recent in a series of three Stone Age periods—the Lower, the Middle, and the Upper. The name "Upper Paleolithic" roughly translates as "Late Stone Age," and in Africa the corresponding cultural period

is referred to by this latter, alternate name. Similar technologies appeared in Africa, Asia, and elsewhere at around the same time and can be clustered together under this heading. Like the Mousterian technology, the Upper Paleolithic toolkit emphasized flake tools. However, Upper Paleolithic flakes had a special elongated form, at least twice as long as they were wide. These elongated flakes are called **blades**. Producing stone blades required a process even more lengthy and difficult than the Levallois technique, and raw blades still needed to be further modified to make specific tools. Like Mousterian tools, Upper Paleolithic blade tools were specialized for different functions and included scrapers, drills, knives, and stone arrow points. The forms of these tools were standardized within a region, so that, for example, multiple drills at a site had the same size and shape. However, the tool forms often varied from one region to the next, with each region having particular shape preferences and styles. Interestingly, Upper Paleolithic toolmakers were very selective about their raw materials, and these raw materials would be passed along long-distance trade networks across hundreds of miles. In addition, Upper Paleolithic toolmakers made a variety of objects from materials other than stone, such as harpoons made

Upper Paleolithic technology a complex stone tool technology characterized by tools made from special stone flakes called blades and also including tools made from antler and bone

blade a stone flake with a special elongated form

replacement model (Out of Africa II)
an explanation for the evolution of humans that argues the species evolved in Africa and then expanded to other regions, replacing related species as it went

assimilation model
an explanation for the evolution of humans that argues the species evolved in Africa and then expanded to other regions, interbreeding with related species as it went

from animal bones, beads and pendants made from shells, and tools made from antlers.

Interestingly, early *Homo sapiens* coexisted with other *Homo* species in various parts of the world. Most famously, humans coexisted with Neanderthals in western Asia for around 50,000 years and in Europe for around 5,000 years. It is unclear to what extent the two species interacted during these times. Based on the available evidence, it appears that the two groups did not engage in regular conflict on a large scale. Although Neanderthals were subject to frequent injury, these injuries cannot be clearly credited to attacks from the modern *Homo sapiens*. At the same time, the two groups may have engaged in more peaceful interactions. For example, some evidence suggests that Neanderthal technology may have been influenced either directly or indirectly by the more complicated techniques introduced by humans. Other evidence indicates that the two groups interacted more directly through interbreeding, as we will see below.

Today, humans occupy most of Earth's continents year-round (with the exception of Antarctica). Where did we come from, and how did we get to all of these places? Many researchers have attempted to answer these questions, proposing multiple explanations for the origin and dispersal of our species. One of the earliest explanations was called the **replacement model** or **Out of Africa II** (to differentiate it from the earlier migration of *Homo erectus*, called Out of Africa I). This model argues that modern humans originated in Africa recently **(FIGURE 16.15)**. From there, our ancestors spread into western Asia, Europe, eastern Asia, and beyond. On arriving in these regions, *Homo sapiens* replaced the earlier *Homo* species that occupied the territories, such as *Homo neanderthalensis* in Europe and *Homo erectus* in Asia. According to this model, all humans today have recent common ancestry in Africa, there was little to no interbreeding between humans and other *Homo* species, and any variation in people today is superficial and evolved recently.

Today, there is growing support for another explanation of human origins, called the **assim-**

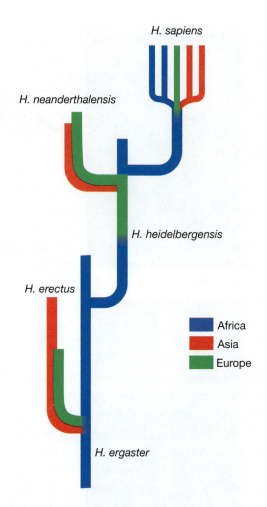

FIGURE 16.15 The Replacement Model
According to the replacement model, *Homo sapiens* evolved in Africa. From there, *Homo sapiens* spread to other regions and replaced the species (such as *Homo neanderthalensis*) that lived there previously.

ilation model (FIGURE 16.16). This more recent view builds on the African origin outlined in the replacement model while also accounting for the possibility of interbreeding across *Homo* populations. According to the assimilation model, *Homo sapiens* first evolved in Africa. From there, the species spread into other regions, such as western Asia and Europe. When settling in these regions, humans did not completely replace earlier *Homo* species. Rather, they interbred with local populations, such as Neanderthals in Europe.

Recall that the earliest *Homo sapiens* fossils appear in Africa around 200 kya. They then appear in western Asia around 100 kya, Australia around 50 kya, Europe around 35 kya, and the Americas around 15 kya. These fossil data suggest that we originated in Africa and then dispersed to the rest of the world. The genetic data also support this hypothesis. Researchers have studied mtDNA to track female lineages and **Y-chromosomal DNA** to track male lineages. These two forms of DNA do not recombine, so they accumulate changes slowly and can be used to estimate when groups split apart and began separate evolutionary tracks. Analyses of both types of DNA in living humans show that the greatest genetic diversity is found in Africa. This finding suggests that African populations have had the most time to accumulate mutations (variations) in their DNA. In addition, genetic variation is increasingly limited the farther one gets from Africa. This finding suggests that humans experienced multiple instances of the **founder effect** as they moved out of Africa, as each migration farther east carried only a subset of the existing variation. The observed pattern of decreasing variation suggests that people first migrated out of Africa along the South Asian coast. Subgroups then moved north and west into Eurasia. This genetic information matches nicely with the pattern of fossil data that shows East Asia and Australia being settled before Europe. Thus, both the fossil and genetic evidence support an African origin for *Homo sapiens*.

What about the possibility of interbreeding? DNA from partially fossilized Neanderthals is providing new insight into the possibility of interbreeding between humans and other *Homo* species. According to recent analyses of Neanderthal DNA, it appears that the last common ancestor of Neanderthals and humans lived as long ago as 800 kya. Meanwhile, the last common ancestor of all Neanderthals lived only 140 kya. This suggests that the Neanderthal and human lineages split long before the recent species evolved. Interestingly, Neanderthal DNA is more similar to the DNA of non-African humans than it is to that of African humans. For example, Neanderthals and modern European humans may share between 1% and 4% of

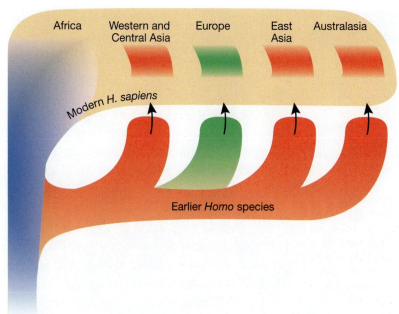

FIGURE 16.16 The Assimilation Model
According to the assimilation model, *Homo sapiens* evolved from a *Homo erectus* lineage in Africa. *Homo sapiens* then spread into other regions, where they interbred with the species already present (such as *Homo neanderthalensis* in Europe). The arrows in the diagram represent this interbreeding between earlier regional populations and incoming humans.

their nuclear DNA, but Neanderthals and modern humans from sub-Saharan Africa share 0% of their nuclear DNA. The similarity between the Neanderthal and non-African genomes suggests that humans interbred with Neanderthals after they left Africa. Thus, recent genetic analysis supports the interbreeding element of the assimilation model.

UNUSUAL MEMBERS OF THE *HOMO* GENUS

In recent years, new fossil discoveries have been demonstrating the complexity of the *Homo* genus. Researchers are learning that the transition to our current species may have been a more gradual transition that started earlier than expected. For example, fossils recovered from Jebel Irhoud in Morocco show a mix of *Homo heidelbergensis* and *Homo sapiens* traits as early as 300 kya. Although there is disagreement

Y-chromosomal DNA the DNA found in the Y chromosome that is passed from fathers to male offspring

founder effect a type of genetic drift that occurs when a subset of a larger population founds the next generation due to substantial population loss or population movement

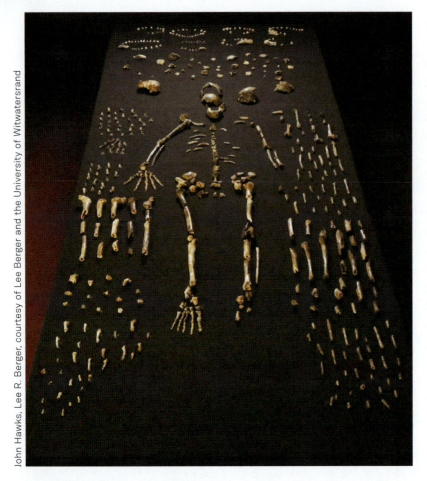

John Hawks, Lee R. Berger, courtesy of Lee Berger and the University of Witwatersrand

FIGURE 16.17 *Homo naledi*
Over 1,500 fossils, a sample seen here, were first discovered at the remote Rising Star Cave location in South Africa in 2013.

female crew whose small body sizes allowed them to make the narrow climb into the cave chamber. After careful excavation, the cave yielded the largest number of fossil remains from a single species found anywhere in Africa. Researchers have identified at least 15 individuals, using clues such as their distinct dental eruption and tooth wear patterns (see Biological Anthropology in Practice, p. 424). These specimens, assigned to the new species *Homo naledi*, had a few traits in common with earlier australopiths, such as small cranial capacities (around 465 to 560 cc) and shoulders suited for arboreal climbing (**FIGURE 16.17**). However, they had more in common with *Homo erectus*, such as a sagittal keel, large brow ridge, smaller teeth and mandible, and a human-like foot well suited to bipedalism. In 2017, the *Homo naledi* site was dated to just 335 to 236 kya, a time that overlaps with *Homo erectus*, *Homo heidelbergensis*, and perhaps the very beginnings of *Homo sapiens* in Africa. This date range suggests that the *Homo* genus included several contemporaneous species up until very recently.

Homo floresiensis

In 2003, researchers unearthed an unusual species, called *Homo floresiensis*, on the Indonesian island of Flores (**FIGURE 16.18**). Dated to around 100 to 60 kya, these individuals had small teeth and orthognathic faces, like other late *Homo* species, but they had somewhat more primitive locomotor adaptations, such as long arms and flat feet. They were sophisticated hunters that made and used flake tools. Most interestingly, *Homo floresiensis* individuals had remarkably short statures (around 3 to 3.5 feet, or 1 m) and small cranial capacities (around 400 cc). These unusual body proportions contributed to their nickname of "hobbits."

Researchers have hotly debated the reason behind *Homo floresiensis*'s unusual size, and most argue that it is the result of an evolutionary process, rather than a type of pathology. The *H. floresiensis* lineage appears to have been subject to a process known as **island** (or **endemic**) **dwarfism**. In this process, animal species that are large on the mainland often become smaller

island (endemic) dwarfism a process where animals that are large on the mainland evolve to be smaller on an island as an adaptation for the limited amount of available resources

about whether these fossils can be fully classified as *H. sapiens* because they lack the tall cranium characteristic of our species, they do have more human-like facial features. This suggests that the evolution of our human traits may have begun earlier than we thought and may have taken place all across the continent of Africa, rather than in only one region (eastern or southern Africa). In addition to these insights, anthropologists are uncovering distinct new *Homo* species that overlap with the previously known members of the *Homo* genus.

Homo naledi

After a tip from local spelunkers (cavers), paleoanthropologists uncovered a fossil site at Rising Star Cave in the Republic of South Africa in 2013. The site was incredibly difficult to access, and the excavation was completed by an all-

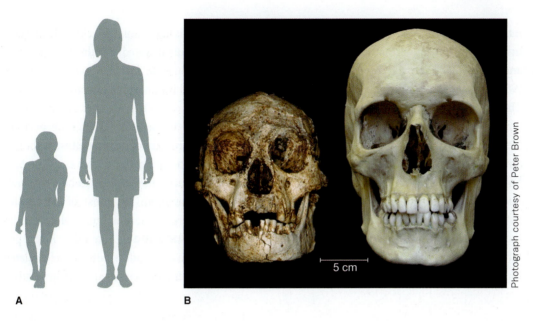

Photograph courtesy of Peter Brown

FIGURE 16.18 *Homo floresiensis*
Homo floresiensis (*left*) had a much smaller stature (A) and cranial capacity (B) than modern humans (*right*).

on islands, which is an adaptation in response to the limited amount of available resources. *Homo floresiensis* was probably a lineage of early *Homo erectus* that became a dwarf population after settling on the island of Flores. This hypothesis recently received additional supporting evidence when researchers found fossil specimens on Flores dated to 700 kya that also had unusually small bodies. These earlier specimens, currently classified as *H. floresiensis*, were probably descended from *H. erectus* and indicate that the transition to smaller stature began soon after the population moved to the island. Interestingly, the same process of island dwarfism that probably caused the unusual stature of *H. floresiensis* also produced other dwarf animal species on the island, such as dwarf elephants.

The Denisovans

In 2008, researchers working in a Siberian cave called Denisova discovered a fossilized hand phalanx fragment from a child. Because its archaeological context was dated to around 30–48 kya, the investigators hoped the fossil contained some organic material that had not fully fossilized,

and they submitted it for DNA analysis. They assumed that the analysis would indicate that the bone had belonged to either a Neanderthal or a human, both of which lived in the surrounding area at that time. The researchers were astounded when the results came back: the bone was identified as neither Neanderthal nor human, but something entirely different and previously unknown—a Denisovan. Since the initial discovery, two teeth and a foot bone have been recovered from the same cave. Given their anatomical and genetic characteristics, these remains also appear to belong to a Denisovan, rather than a Neanderthal or a human. Researchers believe the Denisovans are more closely related to Neanderthals than to humans, and that they diverged from the human lineage as long ago as 700 kya.

Like the Neanderthals, the Denisovans interbred with humans. Some modern humans from Southeast Asian islands and Australia may share as much as 6% of their genome with Denisovans, and modern Tibetans have a gene (*EPAS1*) that has also been found in Denisovan DNA. This gene helps Tibetans to live at extremely high altitudes, and it seems to have been inherited when ancient humans and Denisovans interbred an estimated 40 kya. Denisovans also interbred with Neanderthals, as seen in a 2018 analysis of DNA recovered from another, older (90,000-year-old) bone fragment from Siberia. The small piece of bone belonged to a female who researchers nicknamed Denny. Denny had mtDNA from a Neanderthal mother but a relatively equal amount of nuclear DNA from both Neanderthal and Denisovan lineages. This nuclear DNA pattern indicates that Denny inherited one set of chromosomes from a Neanderthal mother and the other set from a Denisovan father. Because the Denisovan data are still limited to a few finds, we are only scratching the surface on this fascinating species. Many questions remain unanswered, but there is hope that we will continue to learn more as additional fossil material is uncovered and analyzed.

Overall, the diversity of later *Homo* species mimics what we saw in earlier time periods, such as the diversity of australopiths. Although we are used to thinking of ourselves as the only humans on Earth, this appears to be a relatively recent phenomenon. For most of our evolutionary history, numerous human-like species coexisted (**FIGURE 16.19**). Like other living primates who share habitats with closely related species, different species of our human relatives

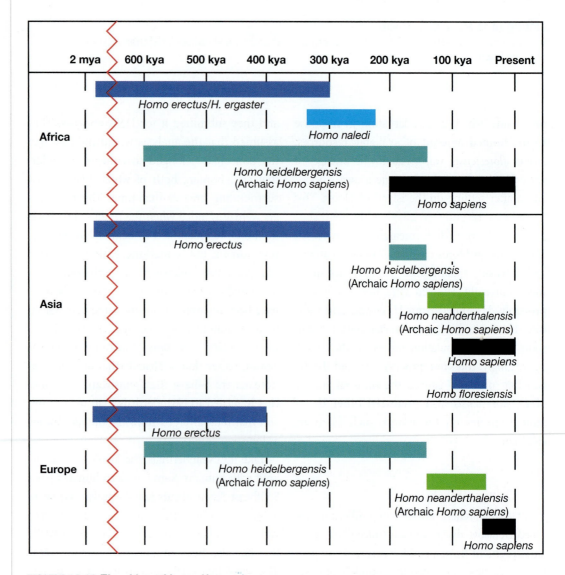

FIGURE 16.19 Time Line of Later *Homo*
The fossil *Homo* species discussed in this lab were distributed in Africa, Asia, and Europe within the last 1.8 million years.

probably lived side by side in the past, most likely because they did not focus on exactly the same resources. For example, while Neanderthals emphasized hunting big game, humans had tools that gave them the flexibility to pursue a wider range of foods. Based on the growing evidence of interbreeding among late *Homo* species, it is also possible that our ancestors used social behaviors, such as alliance building, to facilitate their coexistence. As paleoanthropology research continues, we hope to discover more about this pivotal time in our evolutionary history and how it has shaped the humans we are today.

CONCEPT REVIEW QUESTIONS

Name: _____   Section: _____

Course: _____   Date: _____

Answer the following questions in the space provided.

1. Which of the following species was the first to live outside of Africa?

   A. *Australopithecus garhi*
   B. *Homo erectus*
   C. *Homo sapiens*
   D. *Homo habilis*

2. Some researchers consider the African members of *Homo erectus* to be a separate species called:

   A. *Homo africanus.*
   B. *Homo sapiens.*
   C. *Homo heidelbergensis.*
   D. *Homo ergaster.*

3. Around 200 kya, I lived in Africa, Asia, and Europe. I had a long and low cranium, a large cranial capacity (around 1,300 cc), and a very small occipital torus. What fossil species am I?

   A. *Homo neanderthalensis*
   B. *Homo erectus*
   C. *Homo heidelbergensis*
   D. *Homo sapiens*

4. Describe *one* physical adaptation Neanderthals had for life in a cold climate.

5. Compared with Neanderthals, early humans had:

   A. a taller cranium and more vertical forehead.
   B. a more limited diet emphasizing big game animals.
   C. more physical adaptations for living in a cold climate.
   D. a larger average cranial capacity.

6. Why have we been able to recover ancient DNA from a few species, such as Neanderthals and Denisovans, but not from *all* the members of the *Homo* genus?

7. I lived on a small Indonesian island around 100 kya. I used stone tools to hunt animals, but I had a very small cranial capacity (around 400 cc) and a very small body. What fossil species am I?

   A. *Australopithecus afarensis*
   B. *Homo erectus*
   C. *Homo habilis*
   D. *Homo floresiensis*

For the remaining questions, match the tool technology on the left with the appropriate description on the right.

8. Acheulean _____

    A. This technology was used by *Homo sapiens* and is characterized by tools made from elongated blades of stone.

9. Mousterian _____

    B. This technology was used by *Homo erectus* and is characterized by bifacial handaxes.

10. Upper Paleolithic _____

    C. This technology was used by *Homo neanderthalensis* and is characterized by flakes made using the Levallois technique.

LAB EXERCISES

Name: _____   Section: _____

Course: _____   Date: _____

EXERCISE 1 EARLY VERSUS LATER MEMBERS OF THE GENUS *HOMO*

Work in a small group or alone to complete this exercise. Review the mystery fossils provided by your instructor (or depicted in the Lab 16 Exercise Image Library on p. 482) and answer the following questions.

1. Which of these mystery fossils is *Homo habilis*? *B*

2. Which of these mystery fossils is *Homo erectus*? *A*

3. Describe *at least two* traits you used to make these identifications. (Your instructor may request that you provide more traits.) Be sure to describe how each trait appears in the two fossils.

FOSSIL   A -
long, low   cranium   *(higher eyebrow ridges)*

~~smaller teeth~~   occiptal torus.

EXERCISE 2 THE EVOLUTION OF BIPEDALISM

Work in a small group or alone to complete this exercise. Use the *Australopithecus afarensis* and *Homo erectus* postcrania provided by your instructor (or depicted in the Lab 16 Exercise Image Library on p. 483) to answer the following questions.

1. Describe *at least two* postcranial traits that differ between these two species. (Your instructor may request that you provide more traits.) Be sure to describe how each trait appears in the two fossils.

2. What do these differences suggest about the two species' degrees of bipedalism?

habitual bipedalism

~~about~~ arbureal locomotion + bipedalism
lucy ↑

Work in a small group or alone to complete this exercise. Refer to the casts provided by your instructor (or the pictures in the Lab 16 Exercise Image Library on p. 484) to answer the following questions.

1. Describe *at least two* traits that differ between these fossils. (Your instructor may request that you provide more traits.) Be sure to describe how each trait appears in each of the fossils.

2. Why might these differences exist? (*Hint*: Consider factors such as date, environment, adaptation, and sexual dimorphism.)

3. Do you think these differences warrant the classification of these fossils as two distinct species (*Homo ergaster* and *Homo erectus*)? Why or why not?

Work in a small group or alone to complete this exercise. Refer to the *Homo heidelbergensis* and *Homo erectus* crania provided by your instructor (or depicted in the Lab 16 Exercise Image Library on p. 485) to answer the following questions.

1. Describe *at least one* trait that these two species have in common. (Your instructor may request that you provide more traits.)

2. Describe *at least one* trait that differs between the two species. (Your instructor may request that you provide more traits.) Be sure to describe how each trait appears in the two fossils.

EXERCISE 5 STONE TOOL TECHNOLOGY

Work in a small group or alone to complete this exercise. Examine the mystery stone tools provided by your instructor (or depicted in the Lab 16 Exercise Image Library on p. 486).

1. Which mystery tool is a handaxe?

2. Describe the features of this tool that led you to identify it as this tool type.

3. What tool technology does it belong to?

4. Name *one* fossil species that may have made this tool.

5. Which mystery tool is made from a Levallois flake?

6. Describe the features of this tool that led you to identify it as this tool type.

7. What tool technology does it belong to?

8. Name *one* fossil species that may have made this tool.

9. Which mystery tool is a blade?

10. Describe the features of this tool that led you to identify it as this tool type.

11. What tool technology does it belong to?

12. Name *one* fossil species that may have made this tool.

EXERCISE 6 *HOMO NEANDERTHALENSIS*

Work in a small group or alone to complete this exercise. Review the mystery fossils provided by your instructor (or depicted in the Lab 16 Exercise Image Library on p. 486) and answer the following questions.

1. Which of these mystery fossils is *Homo neanderthalensis*?

2. Which of these mystery fossils is *Homo sapiens*?

3. Describe *at least two* traits you used to make these identifications. (Your instructor may request that you provide more traits.) Be sure to describe how each trait appears in the two fossils.

EXERCISE 7 *HOMO FLORESIENSIS*

Work in a small group or alone to complete this exercise. Compare the mystery fossil crania provided by your instructor (or depicted in the Lab 16 Exercise Image Library on p. 487) and complete the chart below. Place an "X" in the appropriate column to indicate which mystery fossils have the traits listed. *Note*: A trait may be found in more than one mystery fossil.

	Mystery Fossil A	Mystery Fossil B	Mystery Fossil C
Large Cranial Capacity			
Low Cranium			
Presence of Chin			
Large Mandible			

1. Based on this information, which mystery fossil is *Homo floresiensis*?

2. Based on this information, which mystery fossil is *Homo sapiens*?

3. Based on this information, which mystery fossil is an australopith?

CRITICAL THINKING QUESTIONS

On a separate sheet of paper, answer the following questions.

1. Based on what we know of their physical *and* cultural traits, how were Neanderthals adapted for their life in Ice Age Europe? Did early humans in Europe have these same adaptations? How might these adaptations relate to the extinction of the Neanderthals and the continuation of humans? (*Hint*: Is it possible to be too specialized?)

2. Consider the stone tool technologies discussed in this lab and in Lab 15 (the Oldowan, Acheulean, Mousterian, and Upper Paleolithic). Describe the general trends in tool form, tool specialization, and tool production techniques across these technologies.

3. In this lab, we discussed two explanations for the origin and spread of humans. Which model do you think is the most accurate? Be sure to support your argument with evidence.

4. In this lab, we learned about the recently discovered species *Homo naledi*. Review the drawing of the Rising Star Cave below. Note the layout of the cave chambers and the location of the Dinaledi chamber, where the *Homo naledi* fossils were discovered.

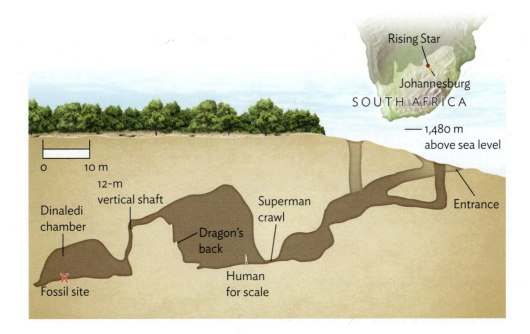

Current research suggests that there was no way for the remains to have accidentally fallen into the Dinaledi chamber, so it is possible that they were intentionally placed there. Which *Homo* species are known to have intentionally buried their dead? What does that suggest about their social behavior and intellectual capacity? If *Homo naledi* also intentionally disposed of their dead, what would this suggest about the relationship between brain size and complex thought?

5. In Exercise 7, you examined the unusual cranium of *Homo floresiensis*. Why do most researchers believe *Homo floresiensis* had such a small cranium?

6. Consider the diversity of the later *Homo* species discussed in this lab and how new DNA research is dramatically changing the way we interpret these species and their relationships. As we have seen, new research methods and lines of evidence have shed light on previously unknown aspects of our evolutionary history. But there are still unanswered questions. What specific question about recent human evolution do *you* think anthropologists should study next? (*Hint*: Consider topics such as physical adaptation, relationships and interbreeding, tool use, diet, social behavior, and symbolism.) What forms of evidence (data) should anthropologists collect to answer your question? Remember to account for preservation issues because they will limit the types of data available. Use resources from your classroom, credible online sources, or books to investigate whether research like this is under way. If so, who is conducting the research, and what are they finding? If not, why might this gap in the research exist?

7. Examine the list of general trends in human evolution below. Use your knowledge of our fossil ancestry to list these trends in order from oldest to most recent. Place a "1" next to the trend that occurred first (is the oldest) and number the remaining trends in order to the most recent ("5"). For each trend, note which fossil species is first associated with the change.

    _____ Increase in cranial capacity to an average of over 1,000 cc

    _____ Production and use of stone tools

    _____ Adaptations for bipedalism

    _____ Habitation (living) outside of Africa

    _____ Clear evidence of symbolic behavior ("art," elaborate and ritualized burial, etc.)

8. In this lab, we reviewed many different fossil species and their defining characteristics. To help you make comparisons across these species and understand larger trends in our evolutionary history, complete the following Later *Homo* Chart.

9. Use your completed Later *Homo* Chart to answer the following questions.

    A. In what geographic region(s) have numerous recent hominin discoveries been made? How do those regions compare with the locations of the australopith and early *Homo* species that came before them?

    B. Review the behaviors listed on your chart and compare them with what you know about australopiths and *Homo habilis*. What behaviors are documented in the later *Homo* species that are not seen in earlier species? Why might these behaviors appear in the more recent species?

    C. Compare *Homo erectus* and *Homo sapiens*, and list at least two traits that distinguish them. Also list at least two things they have in common. What does your answer suggest about their classification and relationship to each other?

    D. Choose any other late *Homo* species and compare it with *Homo sapiens*. List at least two physical traits that distinguish them and at least two traits they have in common. What does your answer suggest about their classification and relationship to each other?

LATER *HOMO* CHART

Fossil	Dates and Geographic Region	Cranial and Dental Traits	Postcranial Traits	Suggested Behavior
Homo erectus (*H. ergaster*)				
Homo heidelbergensis				
Homo neanderthalensis				
Homo sapiens				
Homo naledi				
Homo floresiensis				

LAB 16 EXERCISE IMAGE LIBRARY

Students should use these images only if directed to by their instructor.

EXERCISE 1 EARLY VERSUS LATER MEMBERS OF THE GENUS *HOMO*

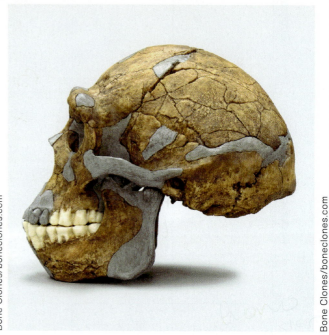

5 cm

Bone Clones/boneclones.com

Bone Clones/boneclones.com

A

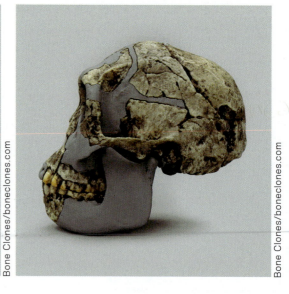

5 cm

Bone Clones/boneclones.com

Bone Clones/boneclones.com

B

EXERCISE 2 THE EVOLUTION OF BIPEDALISM

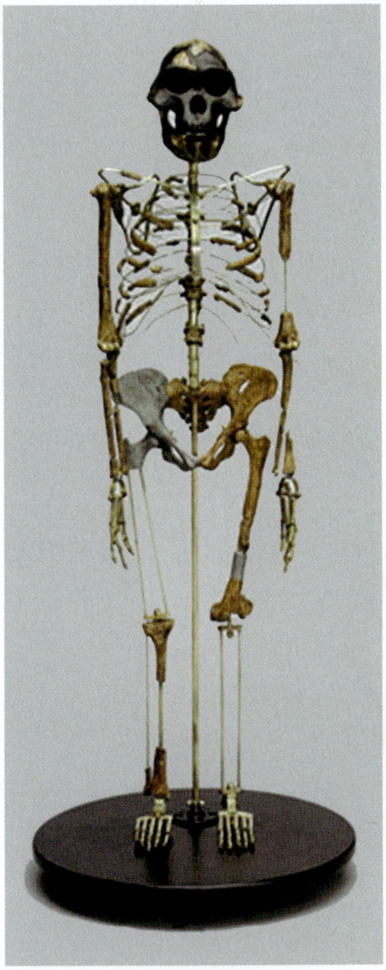

Bone Clones/boneclones.com

Reconstruction of articulated Lucy remains *Australopithecus afarensis*, 3'7" feet, 1.09 meters)

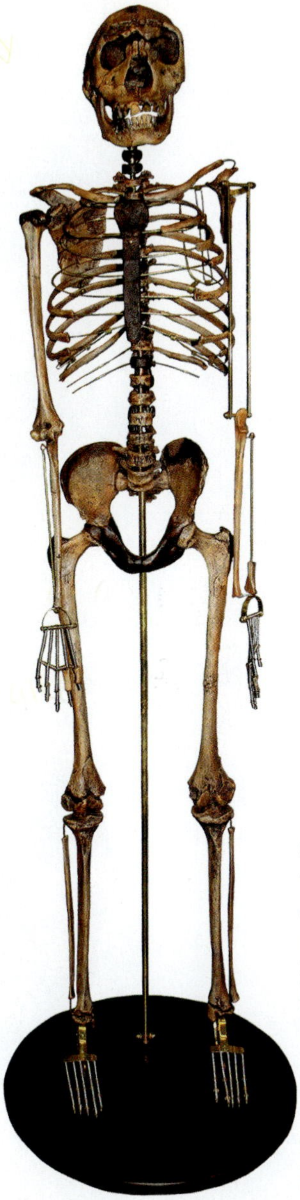

Sabena Jane Blackbird/Alamy Stock Photo

Nariokotome boy (*Homo erectus*, 5' feet, 1.52 meters)

habitual bipedalism

fairly regular

obligate bipedalism

EXERCISE 3 *HOMO ERECTUS* VARIATION

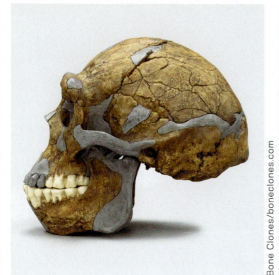

Shorter + stockier members of this species

homo erectus

5 cm

A

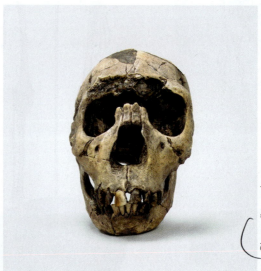

homo ergaster

(african)

5 cm

B

A.) non-african.
occipital torus
larger, lower cranium
sagittal keel

EXERCISE 4 *HOMO HEIDELBERGENSIS*

Bone Clones/boneclones.com

Bone Clones/boneclones.com

Homo heidelbergensis

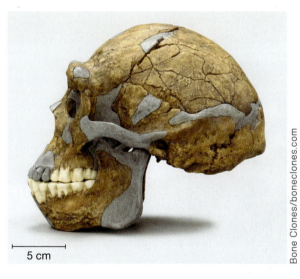

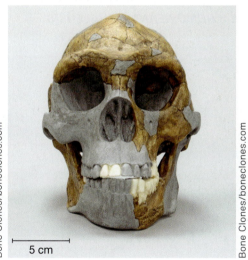

Bone Clones/boneclones.com

Bone Clones/boneclones.com

5 cm

5 cm

5 cm

5 cm

Homo erectus

EXERCISE 5 STONE TOOL TECHNOLOGY

1 cm

A

Pete Bostrum/Lithic Casting Lab

B

1 cm

Bone Clones/boneclones.com

C

Bone Clones/boneclones.com

EXERCISE 6 *HOMO NEANDERTHALENSIS*

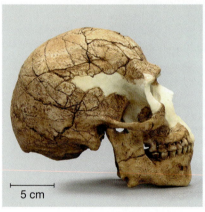

5 cm

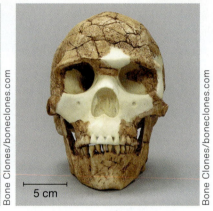

5 cm

Bone Clones/boneclones.com

A

5 cm

5 cm

Bone Clones/boneclones.com

B

EXERCISE 7 *HOMO FLORESIENSIS*

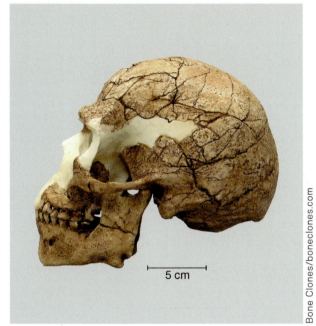

5 cm

A

5 cm

B

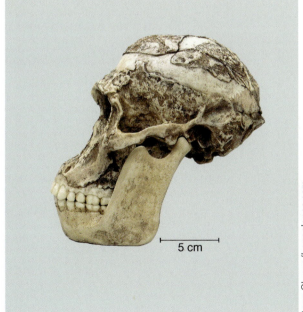

5 cm

C

GLOSSARY

A

absolute dating   any dating method that provides a numerical age estimate for the dated material; also called **chronometric dating**

acclimatization   a short-term, temporary adjustment the body makes to better suit its current environmental context

Acheulean (Acheulian) technology   the second and more widespread stone tool technology that was characterized by handaxes

adapiform   one of a group of early primates that lived between 56 and 34 mya

adaptation   a trait that has been favored by natural selection and helps a population be better suited to its environmental context

adenine   one of the nitrogen bases in DNA; its complement is thymine

adult   an individual that has reached physical maturity

affiliative behavior   behavior that is generally cooperative

affiliative communication   verbal or nonverbal communication that reinforces social relationships

aggressive behavior   behavior that challenges, threatens, or harms others

aging   the process of estimating an individual's age at death based on skeletal remains

alarm call   a vocalization that indicates a particular threat

allele   an alternative version of a gene

Allen's rule   the principle that, because equiaxed shapes have less surface area than elongated shapes, long limbs are well adapted for hot climates because they have relatively more surface to help vent excess body heat

analogy   a trait that is similar across organisms due to similar adaptations

ancestral trait   a trait that is shared by two organisms and inherited from a relatively distant common ancestor; also called a plesiomorphy

antemortem pathology   pathology that developed at any time prior to an individual's death

anterior   relative location toward the front of the body

anthropology   the study of people

anthropometry   the scientific study of the measurements and proportions of the human body

anthroposcopy   the observation of physical bodily characteristics by inspection as opposed to exact measurement

antibody   a protein that attacks antigens directly or marks them for attack by other parts of the immune system

anticodon   a triplet of bases in transfer RNA

antigen   (in ABO blood group system) the cell surface marker found on red blood cells that relates to an individual's ABO blood type and triggers antibody reactions to a foreign blood antigen

appendicular skeleton   the bones of the appendages (arms and legs)

arboreal   living in trees

arboreal quadrupedalism   a form of quadrupedalism that is practiced in the trees

archaeology   the study of the cultural life of past people as seen through their material remains, such as architecture, bones, and tools

argon–argon dating   a radiometric dating method that relies on the ratio of two argon isotopes and has a date range similar to that of potassium–argon dating

articulation   a place where bones meet in the body; a joint

assemblage   a collection of material (such as bones and/or artifacts) recovered from a forensic context or an archaeological or paleoanthropological site

assimilation model   an explanation for the evolution of humans that argues the species evolved in Africa and then expanded to other regions, interbreeding with related species as it went

atlas   the unusually shaped C1, a vertebra that works with the axis to allow for head movement and rotation

auditory ossicles   the three tiny bones that help form each middle ear

autosome   a chromosome other than one of the sex chromosomes

axial skeleton   the bones that lie along the midline (central axis) of the body

axis   the unusually shaped C2, a vertebra that works with the atlas to allow for head movement and rotation

B

bachelor group   an all-male social group where multiple adult males live together, without females or offspring

balanced polymorphism   a situation where multiple alleles for a trait are maintained in balance because natural selection favors the heterozygous condition

Bergmann's rule   the principle that, because volume increases more rapidly than surface area, a large, thick body is well adapted for cold climates because it has relatively less surface through which body heat can be lost

biface   a stone tool that has had flakes of stone removed from two sides

bilophodont molar   a molar with four cusps arranged in two parallel ridges (or lophs)

bioarchaeology   the study of skeletal remains from archaeological contexts

biocultural approach   a research approach that recognizes the close relationship between human biology and culture and attempts to study these two forces simultaneously

biological anthropology   the study of human evolution, including human biology, our close living and extinct relatives, and current similarities and differences within our species; also called physical anthropology

biological species concept   the principle that argues two organisms are from the same species if they can produce viable (fertile) offspring

bipedalism   a form of two-footed locomotion where movement occurs primarily through the use of the hind limbs

blade   a stone flake with a special elongated form

blunt force trauma   injury caused by contact with a blunt object, such as a club, which often creates depressions in the bone that are surrounded by small fractures

bone remodeling   the process of bone resorption and formation

brachiation   a form of suspensory locomotion where movement occurs through arm-over-arm swinging

brow ridge   a bony ridge located above the eye orbits

C

canal   a narrow tunnel or tubular channel in a bone

canine   a pointy tooth between the incisors and premolars

captive primate study   research conducted with primates in captivity (in laboratories or zoos)

carpal   one of the eight short bones of each wrist

cartilage   a type of flexible connective tissue found at the joints between bones and in the nose and ear

cartilaginous joint   a joint united by cartilage that allows some movement

cause of death   a medical determination of the physiological reason for an individual's death

centromere   the contracted area of a chromosome, whose position varies from one chromosome to the next and is therefore useful in distinguishing chromosomes

cervical vertebra   one of the seven vertebrae (C1–C7) that form the neck

cheek pouch   a pouch in the cheek and neck area that can expand to store food

chopper   a large, heavy stone tool with a sharp edge where small pieces of rock have been removed

chromatid   a single chromosome fiber that duplicates and occurs in pairs when a cell is about to divide

chromosome   a tightly coiled strand of DNA within the cell nucleus

chronometric dating   any dating method that provides a numerical age estimate for the dated material; also called **absolute dating**

cladistics   an approach to classification that emphasizes derived traits and de-emphasizes ancestral traits; also called phylogenetic systematics

cladogram   a diagram used to represent cladistic classifications, where lines are used to link organisms with different degrees of relationship to one another

class   the level of classification that includes multiple related orders

clavicle   a slightly curved bone that helps stabilize each shoulder; also called the collarbone

clinal distribution   a distribution of trait variations that has a continuous gradation across a geographic area

coalition   a group of primates that work together against other members of their social group

coccyx   a small bone that articulates with the inferior end of the sacrum; also called the tailbone

codominant   circumstance where multiple alleles are expressed in the phenotype, without one being clearly dominant over the other

codon   a triplet of bases in DNA (or messenger RNA)

color blindness   limited perception of certain colors, which may be the result of variation in the alleles for color vision

comparative approach   a research approach that emphasizes the importance of comparisons across cultures, times, places, species, and so forth

comparative stratigraphy   a relative dating method based on the assumption that things found in the same strata (or layers) will be from the same time interval because they were deposited together

connective tissue   body tissue made of cells, fibers (such as collagen fibers), and extracellular matrix

context   the time, space, environment, historical circumstances, and cultural practices within which a subject of anthropological investigation is situated

continental drift   the shifting of the continents that is caused by the movement of Earth's continental plates

cortical bone   the compact tissue that forms the outside surface of a lamellar bone

cranial capacity   the amount of space available in the cranium for the brain

cranial suture closure   the process of ossification where the cranial bones fuse together at the sutures, the extent of which can be used to age a skeleton

cranium   the skull without the jawbone

crossing-over   the stage in meiosis during which genetic information is exchanged between the two chromosomes in a homologous pair

cultural anthropology   the study of the cultural life of living people, including their cultural practices, beliefs, economics, politics, gender roles, and so forth; also called social anthropology

cusp   a rounded (or slightly pointed) projection on a tooth's chewing surface

cut mark   an indentation left on bone by a sharp instrument, such as a knife or stone tool

cytosine   one of the nitrogen bases in DNA; its complement is guanine

D

Darwin, Charles   often considered the father of evolutionary thinking, who devised the theory of natural selection to explain the process of evolution in the natural world

deciduous teeth   the first set of teeth, also called baby or milk teeth, that are later replaced by permanent teeth

dental caries   areas of the teeth that have undergone demineralization and decay due to acid exposure; also called cavities

dental comb   a tooth structure made of elongated and closely positioned lower incisors and canines that project out from the front of the face

dental enamel hypoplasia   a gap or horizontal line on a tooth that has less enamel than surrounding areas

dental eruption   the process whereby the deciduous teeth (and later the permanent teeth) grow into the mouth, the extent of which can be used to age juvenile skeletons

dental formula   a numerical count of the different tooth types in an animal

dental wear   the wearing down of tooth surfaces with continued use, the extent of which can be used to age adult skeletons

dentin   a calcified tissue found inside a tooth, beneath the enamel surface

dentition   the teeth

depression   a hollow or depressed area of a bone

derived trait   a trait that is a modification of an ancestral form; also called an apomorphy

diaphysis   the central area (shaft) of a long bone that forms separately from and fuses with the ends of the bone (epiphyses) during growth and development

direct percussion   a process of stone tool production where two rocks are hit directly together in order to break off flakes

dish-shaped face   a somewhat concave face formed by a sloping upper face and protruding lower face

distal   relative location farther away from the trunk of the body

diurnal   active primarily during the daylight hours

DNA (deoxyribonucleic acid)   the chemical that acts as the genetic blueprint for an organism

DNA replication   the process whereby DNA is copied

dominant   a dominant allele masks the effects of other alleles for a trait; may also be used in reference to dominant traits or dominant phenotypes

dorsal   relative location toward the back of the body

Down syndrome   a chromosomal condition that results from an extra chromosome 21

E

eburnation   the polishing of a bone surface caused by repeated direct contact between bones at a joint

enamel   the hard mineralized tissue on the exterior surface of a tooth

epiphyseal fusion   the process of ossification where the ends of a long bone fuse to its shaft, the extent of which can be used to age a juvenile skeleton

epiphysis (epiphyses, plural)   the area at the end of a long bone that forms separately from and fuses with the shaft of the bone during growth and development

estrus swelling   the swelling of the female genital region around the time of ovulation

ethmoid   the small, cube-shaped bone between the frontal and sphenoid bones in the cranium

eukaryote   organism (such as a plant or animal) that is made of many cells that have cell nuclei

evolution   change in allele frequency

evolutionary systematics   an approach to classification that emphasizes both derived traits and ancestral traits

F

family   the level of classification that includes multiple related genera

femur   the bone that forms the thigh of each leg

fibrous joint   a joint united by irregular, fibrous connective tissue that allows for little to no movement

fibula   the thinner and more lateral of the two bones in each lower leg

field primate study   research conducted with primates in their wild habitat

fission–fusion   a type of social organization that involves the fission of a large group into smaller groups to pursue sparsely distributed resources and the fusion of the smaller groups back into a large group at other times

flake   a small piece of rock that has been removed from a larger rock and can be used as is or further modified into a specialized tool

flat bone   a platelike bone consisting of a layer of trabecular bone sandwiched between two thin layers of flat cortical bone

focused observation   the observation of a single individual at a time

folivory   a diet that emphasizes leaves (foliage) and other plant parts

fontanelle   a soft spot on a baby's head where the space at a suture is particularly big

foramen (foramina, plural)   a hole in a bone

foramen magnum   the large hole at the base of the cranium that allows the brain to connect to the spinal cord

forelimb   the upper or front limb (commonly called the arm)

forensic anthropology   the application of knowledge and methods of skeletal analysis to assist in legal investigations

forward-facing eyes   eyes that are positioned at the front of the face and point directly ahead

fossa (fossae, plural)   a shallow depression in a bone

fossil   the traces or remains of an organism preserved in rock

fossilization   the process of fossil formation that occurs under certain conditions

founder effect   a type of genetic drift that occurs when a subset of a larger population founds the next generation due to substantial population loss or population movement

frontal bone   the most anterior bone of the cranium

frugivory   a diet that emphasizes fruit

G

gamete   a sex cell (in humans, sperm or egg)

gene   a section of DNA that codes for a particular trait

gene flow   the exchange of genes between previously isolated populations that begin to interbreed

genetic bottleneck   a substantial loss of genetic diversity (often through the founder effect)

genetic drift   changes in allele frequencies that occur randomly due to factors such as differential reproduction and sampling errors

genetic locus (loci, plural)   the location of a gene on a chromosome

genetic recombination   the mixing of genetic information into new combinations that occurs during meiosis

genotype   the specific alleles an organism has for a trait

genus (genera, plural)   the level of classification that includes multiple related species

gracile   having thin, light musculature and bone

grooming   the removal of foreign objects (such as insects or plant parts) from another primate's fur

groove   a furrow along the surface of a bone

group observation   the observation of many individuals simultaneously

guanine   one of the nitrogen bases in DNA; its complement is cytosine

gummivory   a diet that emphasizes tree gums (or sap)

gunshot wound   injury caused by bullets shot from various small arms (guns), which may create holes or nicks in bone, depending on where the bullet enters and exits the body; also called projectile trauma

H

habitual bipedalism   bipedal locomotion that is practiced regularly (or habitually)

half-life   the length of time it takes for one-half of an amount of a radioactive isotope to decay

hallux   the biggest and most medial of the toes on each foot

handaxe   a biface tool that is shaped like a pear or teardrop

Hardy–Weinberg equation   the equation ($p^2 + 2pq + q^2 = 1$) outlined by Godfrey Hardy and Wilhelm Weinberg to predict the probable genotype frequencies of a Mendelian trait in the next generation

heterozygous   an organism's genotype for a trait when it has one dominant allele and one recessive allele for the trait (such as *Rr*)

hind limb   the lower or back limb (commonly called the leg)

holistic approach   a research approach that emphasizes the importance of all aspects of the study subject and requires a consideration of context to gain an understanding of the broader picture

hominin   the classification group (tribe) containing humans and our extinct relatives since the split from other apes

homologous pair   a set of two matching chromosomes with similar types of genetic information, similar lengths, and similar centromere positions

homology   a trait that is similar across organisms because the organisms share common ancestry

homoplasy   the evolutionary development of similar traits in unrelated organisms

homozygous dominant   an organism's genotype for a trait when it has two dominant alleles for the trait (such as *RR*)

homozygous recessive   an organism's genotype for a trait when it has two recessive alleles for the trait (such as *rr*)

human biology   the study of human genetics, variation within our species, and how our species is affected by evolutionary processes

humerus   the upper bone in each arm

hyoid bone   the small, U-shaped bone suspended in the throat below the cranium

hypoxia   a condition where one cannot take in enough oxygen to meet the body's needs

I

ilium (ilia, plural)   the large, bladelike area of each os coxa (hip bone)

incisor   a spatula-shaped tooth at the front of the mouth

infanticide   the killing of infants or young members of the species

inferior   relative location lower on the body's axis

inferior nasal concha (conchae, plural)   one of a pair of scroll-like bones inside the nasal cavity

innominate bone   one of the paired bones that form the sides and front of the pelvis, resulting from the fusion of the ilium, ischium, and pubis; also called the **os coxa**

insectivory   a diet that emphasizes insects

intermembral index   a ratio of forelimb length to hind limb length that is often used to quantify locomotor adaptations

iron-deficiency anemia   a condition caused by a severe lack of iron in the body

irregular bone   a bone with a complex shape that is not easily classified as long, short, or flat

ischial callosity   a roughened patch of skin located in the ischial area (on the buttocks)

ischium   the bone that forms the underside (posteroinferior side) of an os coxa

island (endemic) dwarfism   a process where animals that are large on the mainland evolve to be smaller on an island as an adaptation for the limited amount of available resources

isotope   a variation of a chemical element that has a different number of neutrons in its nucleus than other variations of the same element

J

juvenile   a physically immature individual whose body is still growing and developing

K

karyotype   a picture of an individual's stained chromosomes, arranged in homologous pairs and laid out in order from largest to smallest

kingdom   the highest level of classification, which includes multiple related phyla

knife wound   an injury caused by a sharp, bladelike instrument, which often leaves telltale nicks or cut marks on bone

knuckle-walking   a form of terrestrial quadrupedalism that involves walking on the knuckles of the hands

K–Pg (Cretaceous–Paleogene) boundary (formerly known as the Cretaceous–Tertiary (K–T) boundary)   the temporal boundary between the Mesozoic and Cenozoic eras; marked by the large extinction event when many dinosaurs went extinct

L

lactase   an enzyme required in order to properly digest the lactose in milk

lactose   a sugar found in milk

lactose intolerance   a condition common to all mammals where adults cannot properly digest lactose

lactose tolerance   an unusual condition in some humans where adults can properly digest lactose

lamellar bone   a type of organized, mature bone

lateral   relative location farther from the midline of the body

law of independent assortment   law stating that the units (or genes) for different traits are sorted (and passed on) independently of one another

law of segregation   law stating that the units (or genes) for traits appear separately in the (sex cells of) parents and are then reunited in an offspring

law of superposition   a law stating that material from lower geological layers must be older than material from higher geological layers

Levallois technique   a process used to produce regularly shaped flakes that can then be further modified into different tools

linguistic anthropology   the study of how people make and use language

locomotion   an animal's form of movement in traveling from one place to another

long bone   a bone with an elongated middle shaft and distinct, slightly larger ends

lumbar vertebra   one of the five vertebrae (L1–L5) that form the lower back

M

mammary gland   a milk-producing gland in female mammals

mandible   the bone that holds the lower teeth and is primarily responsible for chewing; also called the jawbone

mandibular symphysis   the area where the two sides of an unfused mandible are attached by cartilage

manner of death   the circumstances surrounding death that may have contributed to death, such as traumatic injuries

mastoid process   the bony projection located posterior to the ear that allows for the attachment of neck muscles

maxilla (maxillae, plural)   one of the pair of bones that forms the face and holds the upper teeth

medial   relative location closer to the midline of the body

meiosis   the process of cell division that produces gametes

melanin   a pigment that helps to give skin its brownish color

Mendel, Gregor   a European monk who conducted tests on pea plants and identified two important principles of classification

Mendelian trait   a trait controlled by one gene (although there may be multiple alleles for that one gene)

messenger RNA (mRNA)   the RNA formed in the first stage of protein synthesis (transcription) that brings the genetic information from the cell nucleus to the ribosome

metacarpal   one of the five bones that form the palm of each hand

metatarsal   one of the five bones that form each foot

metric trait   a measurable osteometric trait of the skeleton

minimum number of individuals (MNI)   the smallest number of individuals that could be represented by the skeletal elements recovered

mitochondria (mitochondrion, singular)   cell organelles that produce energy for the cell and that contain their own DNA

mitochondrial DNA (mtDNA)   the DNA found in mitochondria, which is passed from mothers to offspring

mitosis   the process of cell division that occurs in somatic cells

molar   a large, multi-cusped tooth at the back of the mouth

monogamy   a form of social organization where one adult male, one adult female, and their offspring live together

Mousterian technology   a stone tool technology that used the Levallois technique to produce a variety of specialized flake tools

multimale polygyny   a form of social organization where multiple adult males, multiple adult females, and their offspring live together

mutation   a change in the genetic code that creates entirely new genetic material

N

nasal bone   one of a pair of small bones that forms the bridge of the nose

natural selection   the theory outlined by Charles Darwin to explain evolution; it argues that some traits are more suited to an organism's particular environmental context and are therefore passed on preferentially to the next generation, and these traits become more common in successive generations, resulting in evolutionary shifts in populations

New World   a name traditionally assigned to the American continents (North and South America)

nocturnal   active primarily during the night hours

nonhuman primate culture   group-specific, learned behavior in nonhuman primates

nonmetric trait   an anthroposcopic qualitative trait of the skeleton that cannot be measured, but instead is either present or absent

nonradiometric dating   any chronometric dating method that is not based on the principles of radioactive isotope decay

nuclear DNA   the DNA found in the nucleus of a cell

nucleotide   a set of linked phosphate, sugar, and nitrogen base molecules in DNA

nucleus   the area inside a eukaryotic cell that contains most of the cell's DNA

O

obligate bipedalism   bipedal locomotion that is practiced all the time

occasional bipedalism   bipedal locomotion that is practiced sometimes (or occasionally)

occipital bone   the bone that forms the back and base of the cranium

occipital bun   a large, round projection located on the occipital bone

occipital torus   a ridge of bone along the occipital bone that forms a small point when seen from the side

Oldowan technology   the earliest stone tool technology, characterized by chopper and flake tools

Old World   a name traditionally assigned to the majority of the non-American continents, specifically Africa, Asia, and Europe

omomyoid   one of a group of early primates that lived between 56 and 34 mya

opposable digit   a thumb or big toe capable of being positioned opposite the other digits (fingers or toes), which confers the ability to grasp objects

order   the level of classification that includes multiple related families

organelle   a type of cell part with its own function, like an organ of the body

orthognathic   having a flat face

os coxa (ossa coxae, plural)   one of the paired bones that forms the sides and front of the pelvis, resulting from the fusion of the ilium, ischium, and pubis; also known as the **innominate bone**

ossification   the process of bone mineralization and fusion that occurs as an individual develops into a physically mature adult

osteoarthritis   a condition where trauma or accumulated wear and tear on the joints results in loss of their cartilage lining

osteoblast   a bone cell responsible for forming bone

osteoclast   a bone cell responsible for removing bone

osteocyte   a bone cell responsible for bone maintenance

osteometric board   an instrument used to measure bones

osteometry   the study and measurement of the human or animal skeleton, especially in an anthropological context

osteophyte   a spicule of bone that often forms around the margin of a joint surface when the cartilage at the joint is worn down

Out of Africa I   the migration between 1.8 mya and 800 kya of *Homo erectus* out of Africa and into Asia and Europe

Out of Africa II   an explanation for the evolution of humans that argues the species evolved in Africa and then expanded to other regions, replacing related species as it went; also called the **replacement model**

P

palatine   one of the pair of bones that forms part of the hard palate in the mouth

paleoanthropology   the study of the anatomy and behavior of humans and our extinct relatives

paleomagnetic dating   a nonradiometric dating method based on changes in Earth's magnetic polarity

paleospecies   an extinct species that is known through fossil evidence

parietal bone   one of the paired bones posterior to the frontal bone that forms the top of the cranium

pastoralism   a lifestyle where raising domesticated herd animals is central to the diet and economy

patchy forest hypothesis   an explanation for the evolution of bipedalism that argues bipedalism was selectively favored because it was more energy efficient than quadrupedalism in the patchy forest environment of Africa

patella   the small, slightly triangular bone that helps form each knee joint; also called the kneecap

pathology   disease, or the changes that disease causes in the body

pedigree diagram   the method of diagramming inheritance that shows the phenotypes of individuals from multiple generations in a family

perimortem pathology   pathology and trauma that developed around the time of an individual's death and may have contributed to that death

permanent teeth   the second set of teeth, also called adult teeth, that replace the earlier deciduous teeth

phalanx (phalanges, plural)   one of the fourteen bones that form the fingers and toes on each hand or foot

phenotype   the physical expression of an organism's genotype for a trait

phylogram   a diagram used to represent evolutionary relationships that also accounts for the amount of change (and usually length of time) separating organisms

phylum (phyla, plural)   the level of classification that includes multiple related classes

plesiadapiform   one of a group of diverse primate-like mammals that lived over 56 mya and may be among the first primates

point mutation   a mutation that occurs at a single point (nitrogen base) in a DNA strand

polyandry   a form of social organization where one adult female, multiple adult males, and their offspring live together

polygenic trait   a trait controlled by alleles at multiple genetic loci

polygyny   a form of social organization where there are multiple adult females for each male

porotic hyperostosis   a form of bone destruction that usually presents in the cranial bones as porous and spongy bone surfaces

postcranial   relating to the bones below or behind the head

posterior   relative location toward the rear of the body

postmortem interval   the time that has elapsed since an individual died

postorbital bar   a bar of bone that sits lateral to the eye but does not fully enclose the eye in a bony pocket

postural feeding hypothesis   an explanation for the evolution of bipedalism that argues bipedalism was selectively favored as a way to more efficiently reach hanging fruit in small trees

potassium–argon dating   a radiometric dating method that relies on radioactive potassium isotopes with a half-life of about 1.3 billion years

prehensile tail   a tail with the ability to grasp objects and act like a fifth limb

premolar   a tooth with two cusps, between the canines and molars

primate ecology   the study of the relationship between primates and their environments

primatology   the study of living primates, particularly their similarities and differences and why those similarities and differences might exist

prognathic   having a projecting or protruding face

projection   an area of bone that protrudes from the main bone surface

prokaryote   organism (such as a bacterium) that has a cell without a nucleus and is often made of only a single cell

protein synthesis   the process of determining proteins from a DNA sequence

provisioning hypothesis   an explanation for the evolution of bipedalism that argues bipedalism was selectively favored because it helped males to provision females and improve reproductive success

proximal   relative location closer to the trunk of the body

pubis   the bone that forms the front (anterior) of an os coxa; also called the pubic bone

Punnett square   the method of diagramming inheritance where parental genotypes are used to estimate the probability of various genotypes in a potential offspring

Q

quadrupedalism   a form of locomotion that uses all four limbs

qualitative data   descriptive data about the qualities that are observed

quantitative data   focused and clearly measurable data

R

radiocarbon dating   a radiometric dating method that relies on carbon-14, an isotope with a half-life of 5,730 years

radiometric dating   any dating method that uses the principles of radioactive isotope decay to determine numerical age

radius   the more lateral of the two lower bones in each arm

recessive   a recessive allele is masked by a dominant allele for a trait; may also be used in reference to recessive traits or recessive phenotypes

relative dating any dating method that provides the age of something relative to the age of something else, rather than as a numerical age

replacement model an explanation for the evolution of humans that argues the species evolved in Africa and then expanded to other regions, replacing related species as it went; also called **Out of Africa II**

reproductive success the successful production of viable (fertile) offspring

rhinarium a damp pad at the end of the nose

rib bone one of the 12 long bones that form each side of the rib cage (or thoracic cage)

RNA (ribonucleic acid) a chemical that is similar to DNA, except it contains uracil instead of thymine; it plays vital roles in the process of protein synthesis

robust having thick, dense, heavy musculature and bone

S

sacrum the large, triangular bone at the base of the vertebral column and between the two hip bones

sagittal crest a ridge of bone along the midline of the cranium that allows for the attachment of extra-large chewing muscles

sagittal keel a very slight ridge of bone along the midline of the cranium

savanna environment open grassland interspersed with pockets of trees,

savanna hypothesis an explanation for the evolution of bipedalism that argues bipedalism was selectively favored as open grassland environments expanded throughout Africa in the past

scapula a large, flat bone that forms part of each shoulder joint; also called the shoulder blade

scientific method a cycle of scientific practices that helps scientists to gain knowledge and sparks further scientific inquiries

scientific theory a scientific explanation supported by substantial evidence

semibrachiation a form of suspensory locomotion where movement occurs through the use of the arms and a specially adapted prehensile tail, which can grasp tree branches

septum the soft tissue between the nostrils

sex chromosome one of the two different chromosomes (X and Y) involved in the determination of an organism's biological sex

sexing the process of estimating the likely sex of an individual based on skeletal remains

sex-linked trait a trait coded for by a gene on the X or Y chromosome (although typically used to refer to traits on the X chromosome)

sexual dimorphism the physical differences between adult males and adult females of a species

shared derived trait a modified trait that is shared by two or more organisms; also called a synapomorphy

short bone a bone with a cube-like shape, with similar width and length dimensions

sickle-cell anemia a disease that results from the sickle-cell allele

sickle-cell trait a variation of a gene that results from a point mutation and causes misshapen red blood cells

single-male polygyny a form of social organization where one adult male, multiple adult females, and their offspring live together

social hierarchy the assignment and distribution of different social status positions in a group

social science a discipline concerned with the study of human society, such as anthropology, psychology, or sociology

solitary spending most of one's time alone; refers to a form of social organization where adult females (and their offspring) occupy separate territories, and an adult male occupies a territory that overlaps with those of several females

somatic cell a non-sex cell that makes up different body parts; also called a body cell

species one of the most specific levels of classification uniting related organisms

sphenoid bone the butterfly-shaped bone between the cranial vault and the face bones

stature an individual's overall body height

sternum a bone formed by the fusion of three separate bones in the chest, also called the breastbone

strangulation the forcible choking of another individual, which often results in damage to the hyoid bone

stratigraphy the study of the deposition of geological and cultural layers (or strata)

Suchey–Brooks method a method of aging adult skeletons that relies on changes to the symphyseal surface of the pubic bone

superior relative location higher on the body's axis

suspensory locomotion a form of locomotion where the body is suspended (or hanging) below tree branches

suture an immovable fibrous joint between individual bones of the cranium

synovial joint a highly mobile joint held together by ligaments and by irregular connective tissue that forms a fluid-filled articular capsule

systematics the study of the relationships between organisms

T

tarsal one of the seven short bones that form each ankle

taxonomy the classification of organisms

temporal bone one of the pair of bones inferior to the parietal bone on each side of the cranium

terrestrial living on the ground

terrestrial quadrupedalism a form of quadrupedalism that is practiced on the ground

thermoregulation hypothesis an explanation for the evolution of bipedalism that argues bipedalism was selectively favored because it helped early hominins to stay cool during the hottest times of the day

thoracic vertebra one of the 12 vertebrae (T1–T12) that articulate with ribs in the chest area

threat display an action (such as flashing the teeth) that seeks to threaten others from a distance

threat yawn an opening of the mouth that displays the teeth in a threatening manner

thymine one of the nitrogen bases in DNA; its complement is adenine

tibia the larger and more medial of the two bones in each lower leg; also called the shinbone

trabecular bone the spongy (honeycomb-like) tissue that forms the inside of a lamellar bone

transcription the first step of protein synthesis where nuclear DNA is transcribed into messenger RNA that can leave the cell nucleus

transfer RNA (tRNA) a type of RNA that brings amino acids to a ribosome to form the amino acid chains in the second stage of protein synthesis (translation)

translation the second step of protein synthesis where messenger RNA is translated (or read) to form a sequence of amino acids that makes up a protein

Turner syndrome a chromosomal condition that results from having a single X chromosome without another sex chromosome

U

ulna the more medial of the two lower bones in each arm

unfused mandible a mandible (jawbone) made of two separate bones that are attached by cartilage along the midline

uniparous producing one offspring at a time

unique derived trait a modified trait that is unique to one group; also called an autapomorphy

Upper Paleolithic technology a complex stone tool technology characterized by tools made from special stone flakes called blades and also including tools made from antler and bone

V

vasoconstriction the constriction (narrowing) of the blood vessels near the surface of the body to help maintain heat in the body's core

vasodilation the expansion of the blood vessels near the surface of the body to help heat escape the body

ventral relative location toward the belly of the body

vertebra (vertebrae, plural) an irregularly shaped bone that is part of the vertebral column

vertebral column the row of bones that form the backbone

vertical clinging and leaping a form of locomotion where the body is oriented vertically and movement occurs by leaping from tree to tree

viable offspring offspring that are capable of reproduction

vitamin D–folate hypothesis one of the primary explanations for the evolution of human skin color, arguing that darker skin protects from folate loss in regions of high sun exposure and lighter skin fosters vitamin D production in regions of low sun exposure

vocalization a verbal communication

vomer a small, thin bone inside the nasal cavity

W

woven bone a type of bone tissue that is unorganized and primarily found in immature or healing bone

X

X chromosome the larger of the two sex chromosomes, having genetic information related to a wide range of traits

Y

Y-chromosomal DNA the DNA found in the Y chromosome that is passed from fathers to male offspring

Y chromosome the smaller of the two sex chromosomes, having genetic information that codes primarily for traits related to maleness

Y-5 molar a molar in the lower dentition that has five cusps positioned such that a pronounced Y-shaped groove forms between the cusps

Z

zygomatic arch cheekbone area formed by numerous small bones, allowing a space for the jaw muscles that attach to the mandible below and the temporal bone above

zygomatic bone one of the bones that forms the zygomatic arch

Agarwal, S. C., M. Dimitriu, and M. D. Grynpas. 2004. Medieval trabecular bone architecture: The influence of age, sex and lifestyle. *American Journal of Physical Anthropology* 124:33–44.

Alemseged, Z., F. Spoor, W. H. Kimbel, R. Bobe, D. Geraads, D. Reed, and J. G. Wynn. 2006. A juvenile early hominin skeleton from Dikika, Ethiopia. *Nature* 443:296–301.

American Association of Physical Anthropologists. 2003. Code of ethics. http://physanth.org/documents/3/ethics.pdf.

American Association of Physical Anthropologists. 2015. Statement on sexual harassment and assault. http://physanth.org/documents/66/AAPA_Statement_on_Sexual_Harassment_and_Assault.pdf.

Antón, S. C. and C. C. Swisher III. 2004. Early dispersals of *Homo* from Africa. *Annual Review of Anthropology* 33:271–296.

Arbib, M. A., K. Liebal, and S. Pika. 2008. Primate vocalization, gesture, and the evolution of human language. *Current Anthropology* 49:1053–1076.

Asfaw, B., T. White, O. Lovejoy, B. Latimer, S. Simpson, and G. Suwa. 1999. *Australopithecus garhi*: A new species of early hominid from Ethiopia. *Science* 284:629–635.

Balter, M. 2006. Radiocarbon dating's final frontier. *Science* 313:1560–1563.

Barsh, G. S. 2003. What controls variation in human skin color? *PLOS Biology* 1:19–22.

Bass, W. M. 1995. *Human Osteology: A Laboratory and Field Manual*, 4th edition. Columbia, MO: Missouri Archaeological Society.

Beall, C. M. 2001. Adaptations to altitude: A current assessment. *Annual Review of Anthropology* 30:423–456.

Beall, C. M. 2007. Two routes to functional adaptation: Tibetan and Andean high-altitude natives. Pp. 239–256 in J. C. Avise and F. J. Ayala, eds., *In the Light of Evolution*. Volume 1, *Adaptation and Complex Design*. Washington, DC: National Academies Press.

Beall, C. M. and A. T. Steegmann Jr. 2000. Human adaptation to climate: Temperature, ultraviolet radiation, and altitude. Pp. 163–224 in S. Stinson, B. Bogin, R. Huss-Ashmore, and D. O'Rourke, eds., *Human Biology: An Evolutionary and Biocultural Perspective*. New York: Wiley-Liss.

Beard, K. C. 2002. Basal anthropoids. Pp. 133–149 in W. C. Hartwig, ed., *The Primate Fossil Record*. Cambridge: Cambridge University Press.

Begun, D. R. 2002. European hominoids. Pp. 339–368 in W. C. Hartwig, ed., *The Primate Fossil Record*. Cambridge: Cambridge University Press.

Benefit, B. R. and M. L. McCrossin. 2002. The Victoriapithecidae, Cercopithecoidea. Pp. 241–253 in W. C. Hartwig, ed., *The Primate Fossil Record*. Cambridge: Cambridge University Press.

Berger, L. R. 2013. The mosaic nature of *Australopithecus sediba*. *Science* 340(6129):163–165.

Berger, L. R., S. J. de Ruiter, S. E. Churchill, P. Schmid, K. J. Carlson, P. H. G. M. Dirks, and J. M. Kibii. 2010. *Australopithecus sediba*: A new species of *Homo*-like australopith from South Africa. *Science* 328(5975):195–204.

Berger, L. R., J. Hawks, D. J. de Ruiter, S. E. Churchill, P. Schmid, L. K. Delezene, T. L. Kivell, H. M. Garvin, S. A. Williams, J. M. DeSilva, M. M. Skinner, C. M. Musiba, N. Cameron, T. W. Holliday, W. Harcourt-Smith, R. R. Ackermann, M. Bastir, B. Bogin, D. Bolter, J. Brophy, Z. D. Cofran, K. A. Congdon, A. S. Deane, M. Dembo, M. Drapeau, M. C. Elliott, E. M. Feuerriegel, D. Garcia-Martinez, D. J. Green, A. Gurtov, J. D. Irish, A. Kruger, M. F. Laird, D. Marchi, M. R. Meyer, M. Nalla, E. W. Negash, C. M. Orr, D. Racovcic, L. Schroeder, J. E. Scott, Z. Throckmorton, M. W. Tocheri, C. VanSickle, C. S. Walker, P. Wei, and B. Zipfel. 2015. *Homo naledi*, a new species of the genus *Homo* from the Dinaledi Chamber, South Africa. *eLife* 4:e09560. https://doi.org/10.7554/eLife.09560.

Berger, T. D. and E. Trinkaus. 1995. Patterns of trauma among the Neandertals. *Journal of Archaeological Science* 22:841–852.

Berra, T. M. 2008. *Charles Darwin: The Concise Story of an Extraordinary Man*. Baltimore: Johns Hopkins University Press.

Blau, S. and C. A. Briggs. 2011. The role of forensic anthropology in Disaster Victim Investigation (DVI). *Forensic Science International* 205:29–35.

Bloch, J. I., M. T. Silcox, D. M. Boyer, and E. J. Sargis. 2007. New Paleocene skeletons and the relationship of plesiadapiforms to crown-clade primates. *Proceedings of the National Academy of Sciences* 104:1159–1164.

Bolnick, D. A., D. Fullwiley, T. Duster, R. S. Cooper, J. H. Fujimura, J. Kahn, J. S. Kaufman, J. Marks, A. Morning, A. Nelson, P. Ossorio, J. Reardon, S. M. Reverby, and K. TallBear. 2007. The science and business of genetic ancestry testing. *Science* 318(5849):399–400.

Bolter, D. R., J. Hawks, B. Bogin, and N. Cameron. 2018. Palaeodemographics of individuals in Dinaledi Chamber using dental remains. *South African Journal of Science* 114(1/2):1–6.

Bond, M., M. F. Tejedor, K. E. Campbell Jr., L. Chornogubsky, N. Novo, and F. Goin. 2015. Eocene primates of South America and the African origins of New World monkeys. *Nature* 520:538–541. https://doi.org/10.1038/nature14120.

Bouzouggar, A., N. Barton, M. Vanhaeren, F. d'Errico, S. Collcutt, T. Higham, E. Hodge, S. Parfitt, E. Rhodes, J.-L. Schwenninger, C. Stringer, E. Turner, S. Ward, A. Moutmir, and A. Stambouli. 2007. 82,000-year-old beads from North Africa and implications for the origins of modern human behavior. *Proceedings of the National Academy of Sciences* 104:9964–9969. https://doi.org/10.1126/science.1150098.

Brace, C. L. 2002. The concept of race in physical anthropology. Pp. 239–253 in P. N. Peregrine, C. R. Ember, and M. Ember, eds., *Physical Anthropology: Original Readings in Method and Practice*. Upper Saddle River, NJ: Prentice Hall.

Brian, T. and F. Laczko, eds. 2014. *Fatal Journeys: Tracking Lives Lost during Migration*. Geneva, Switzerland: International Organization for Migration.

Brothwell, D. 1981 *Digging up Bones*, 3rd edition. Ithaca, NY: Cornell University Press.

Brown, P., T. Sutikna, M. J. Morwood, R. P. Soejono, Jatmiko, E. Wayhu Saptomo, and Rokus Awe Due. 2004. A new small-bodied hominin from the Late Pleistocene of Flores, Indonesia. *Nature* 431:1055–1061.

Brunet, M., F. Guy, D. Pilbeam, H. T. Mackaye, A. Likius, D. Ahounta, A. Beauvilain, C. Blondel, H. Bocherens, J.-R. Boisserie, L. De Bonis, Y. Coppens, J. Dejax, C. Denys, P. Duringer, V. Eisenmann, G. Fanone, P. Fronty, D. Geraads, T. Lehmann, F. Lihoreau, A. Louchart, A. Mahamat, G. Merceron, G. Mouchelin, O. Otero, P. P. Campomanes, M. P. De Leon, J.-C. Rage, M. Sapanet, M. Schuster, J. Sudre, P. Tassy, X. Valentin, P. Vignaud, L. Viriot, A. Zazzo, and C. Zollikofer. 2002. A new hominid from the Upper Miocene of Chad, Central Africa. *Nature* 418:145–151.

Buikstra, J. E. and D. H. Ubelaker, eds. 1994. *Standards for Data Collection from Human Skeletal Remains: Proceedings of a Seminar at the Field Museum of Natural History*. Arkansas Archaeological Survey Research Series, no. 44. Fayetteville, AR: Arkansas Archaeological Survey.

Byer, S. N. 2010. *Introduction to Forensic Anthropology*, 4th edition. Upper Saddle River, NJ: Prentice Hall.

Cain, M. L., C. K. Yoon, and A. Singh-Cundy. 2009. *Discover Biology*. New York: W. W. Norton & Company.

Cann, R. L., O. Rickards, and J. K. Lum. 1994. Mitochondrial DNA and human evolution: Our one lucky mother. Pp. 135–148 in M. H. Nitecki and D. V. Nitecki, eds., *Origins of Anatomically Modern Humans*. New York: Plenum.

Cann, R. L., M. Stoneking, and A. Wilson. 1987. Mitochondrial DNA and human evolution. *Nature* 325:31–36.

Caspari, R. 2003. From types to populations: A century of race, physical anthropology, and the American Anthropological Association. *American Anthropologist* 105:65–76.

Chaimanee, Y., C. Yamee, P. Tian, K. Khaowiset, B. Marandat, P. Tafforeau, C. Nemoz, and J.-J. Jaeger. 2006. *Khoratpithecus piriyai*, a late Miocene hominoid of Thailand. *American Journal of Physical Anthropology* 131:311–323.

Chaplin, G. and N. G. Jablonski. 2009. Vitamin D and the evolution of human depigmentation. *American Journal of Physical Anthropology* 139:451–461.

Churchill, S. E., T. W. Holliday, K. J. Carlson, T. Jashashvili, M. E. Macias, D. J. de Ruiter, and L. R. Berger. 2013. The upper limb of *Australopithecus sediba*. *Science* 340(6129):1233477. https://doi.org/10.1126/science.1233477.

Clancy, K. B. H., R. G. Nelson, J. N. Rutherford, and K. Hinde. 2014. Survey of Academic Field Experiences (SAFE): Trainees report harassment and assault. *PLOS One* 9(7):e102172. https://doi.org/10.1371/journal.pone.0102172.

Conroy, G. C. and H. Pontzer. 2012. *Reconstructing Human Origins: A Modern Synthesis*, 3rd edition. New York: W. W. Norton & Company.

Cooper, A. and C. B. Stringer. 2013. Did the Denisovans cross Wallace's line? *Science* 342(6156):321–323.

Covert, H. H. 2002. The earliest primates and the evolution of prosimians: Introduction. Pp. 13–20 in W. C. Hartwig, ed., *The Primate Fossil Record*. Cambridge: Cambridge University Press.

Cruciani, F., R. La Fratta, P. Santolamazza, D. Sellitto, R. Pascone, P. Moral, E. Watson, V. Guida, E. Beraud Colomb, B. Zaharova, J. Lavinha, G. Vona, R. Aman, F. Cali, N. Akar, M. Richards, A. Torroni, A. Novelletto, and R. Scozzari. 2004. Phylogenetic analysis of haplogroup E3b (E-M215) Y chromosomes reveals multiple migratory events within and out of Africa. *American Journal of Human Genetics* 74:1014–1022.

Dart, R. A. 1925. *Australopithecus africanus*: The man-ape of South Africa. *Nature* 115:195–199.

Deacon, T. W. 1997. What makes the human brain different? *Annual Review of Anthropology* 26:337–357.

Dean, M. C. and B. H. Smith. 2009. Growth and development in the Nariokotome youth, KNM-WT 15000: A dental perspective on the origins and early evolution of the genus *Homo*. Pp. 101–120 in F. E. Grine, J. G. Fleagle, and R. E. Leakey, eds., *The First Humans: Origins of the Genus Homo*. New York: Springer.

Deino, A. L., P. R. Renne, and C. C. Swisher III. 1998. ^{40}Ar/^{39}Ar dating in paleoanthropology and archeology. *Evolutionary Anthropology* 6:63–75.

DeSilva, J. M., C. M. Gill, T. C. Prang, M. A. Bredella, and Z. Alemseged. 2018. A nearly complete foot from Dikika, Ethiopia and its implications for the ontogeny and function of *Australopithecus afarensis*. *Science Advances* 4:eaar7723. https://doi.org/10.1126/sciadv.aar7723.

DeSilva, J. M., M. E. Morgan, J. C. Barry, and D. Pilbean. 2010. A hominoid distal tibia from the Miocene of Pakistan. *Journal of Human Evolution* 58:147–154.

Dirks, P. H. G. M., L. R. Berger, E. M. Roberts, J. D. Kramers, J. Hawks, P. S. Randolph-Quinney, M. Elliott, C. M. Musiba, S. E. Churchill, D. J. de Ruiter, P. Schmid, L. R. Backwell, G. A. Belyanin, P. Boshoff, K. L. Hunter, E. M. Feuerriegel, A. Gurtov, J. du G Harrison, R. Hunter, A. Kruger, H. Morris, T. V. Makhubela, B. Peixotto, and S. Tucker. 2015. Geological and taphonomic context for the new hominin species *Homo naledi* from the Dinaledi Chamber, South Africa. *eLife* 4:e09561. https://doi.org/10.7554/eLife.09561.

Dirks, P. H., E. M. Roberts, H. Hilbert-Wolf, J. D. Kramers, J. Hawks, A. Dosseto, M. Duval, M. Elliott, M. Evans, R. Grün, J. Hellstrom, A. I. Herries, R. Joannes-Boyau, T. V. Makhubela, C. J. Placzek, J. Robbins, C. Spandler, K. Wiersma, J. Woodhead, and L. R. Berger. 2017. The age of *Homo naledi* and associated sediments in the Rising Star Cave, South Africa. *eLife* 6:e24231. https://doi.org/10.7554/eLife.24231.

Donnelly, M. P., P. Paschou, E. Grigorenko, D. Gurwitz, C. Barta, R.-B. Lu, O. V. Zhukova, J.-J. Kim, M. Siniscalco, M. New, H. Li, S. L. B. Kajuna, V. G. Manolopoulos, W. C. Speed, A. J. Pakstis, J. R. Kidd, and K. K. Kidd. 2012. A global view of the *OCA2-HERC2* region and pigmentation. *Human Genetics* 131(5):683–696.

Dunsworth, H. and A. Walker. 2002. Early genus *Homo*. Pp. 419–435 in W. C. Hartwig, ed., *The Primate Fossil Record*. Cambridge: Cambridge University Press.

Estrada-Mena, B., F. J. Estrada, R. Ulloa-Arvizu, M. Guido, R. Méndez, R. Coral, T. Canto, J. Granados, R. Rubí-Castellanos, H. Rangel-Villalobos, and A. Garcia-Carrancá. 2010. Blood group O alleles in Native Americans: Implications in the peopling of the Americas. *American Journal of Physical Anthropology* 142:85–94.

Eunice Kennedy Shriver National Institute of Child Health and Human Development, NIH, DHHS. 1997. *Understanding Klinefelter Syndrome: A Guide for XXY Males and Their Families* (97-3202). Washington, DC: U.S. Government Printing Office.

Fan, P.-F., K. He, X. Chen, A. Ortiz, B. Zhang, C. Zhao, Y.-Q. Li, H.-B. Zhang, C. Kimock, W.-Z. Wang, C. Groves, S. T. Turvey, C. Roos, K. M. Helgen, and X.-L. Jiang. 2017. Description of a new species of *Hoolock* gibbon (Primates: Hylobatidae) based on integrative taxonomy. *American Journal of Primatology*. 79(5):e22631. https://doi.org/10.1002/ajp.22631.

Fleagle, J. G. 2013. *Primate Adaptation and Evolution*, 3rd edition. San Diego: Academic Press.

Fleagle, J. G. and M. F. Tejedor. 2002. Early platyrrhines of southern South America. Pp. 161–173 in W. C. Hartwig, ed., *The Primate Fossil Record*. Cambridge: Cambridge University Press.

Fleischman, J. M., A. E. Kendell, C. C. Eggers, and L. C. Fulginiti. 2017. Undocumented border crossing deaths in Arizona: Expanding intrastate collaborative efforts in identification. *Journal of Forensic Science* 62(4):840–849.

Fossey, D. 1983. *Gorillas in the Mist*. New York: Houghton Mifflin Company.

Fragaszy, D., P. Izar, E. Visalberghi, E. B. Ottoni, and M. G. De Oliveira. 2004. Wild capuchin monkeys (*Cebus libidinosus*) use anvils and stone pounding tools. *American Journal of Physical Anthropology* 64:359–366.

Franzen, J., P. D. Gingerich, J. Habersetzer, J. H. Hurum, W. von Koenigswald, and B. H. Smith. 2009. Complete primate skeleton from the middle Eocene of Messel in Germany: Morphology and paleobiology. *PLOS One* 4(5):e5723. https://doi.org/10.1371/journal.pone.0005723.

Galik, K., B. Senut, M. Pickford, D. Gommery, J. Treil, A. J. Kuperavage, and R. B. Eckhardt. 2004. External and internal morphology of the BAR 1002'00 *Orrorin tugenensis* femur. *Science* 305:1450–1453.

Gebo, D. L. 2010. Locomotor function across primates (including humans). Pp. 530–544 in C. S. Larsen, ed., *A Companion to Biological Anthropology*. Chichester, UK: Wiley-Blackwell.

Gebo, D. L. and K. D. Rose. 2002. Adapiformes: Phylogeny and adaptation. Pp. 21–43 in W. C. Hartwig, ed., *The Primate Fossil Record*. Cambridge: Cambridge University Press.

Gebo, D. L., M. Dagosto, K. C. Beard, T. Qi, and J. Wang. 2000. The oldest known anthropoid postcranial fossils and the early evolution of higher primates. *Nature* 404:276–278.

Gilbert, C. C., E. A. Goble, and A. Hill. 2010. Miocene Cercopithecoidea from the Tugen Hills, Kenya. *Journal of Human Evolution* 59:465–483.

Gravlee, C. C. 2009. How race becomes biology: Embodiment of social inequality. *American Journal of Physical Anthropology* 139: 47–57. https://doi.org/10.1002/ajpa.20983.

Gray, T. 1998. A brief history of animals in space. National Aeronautics and Space Administration. http://history.nasa.gov/animals.html.

Green, R. E., J. Krause, A. W. Briggs, T. Maricic, U. Stenzel, M. Kircher, N. Patterson, H. Li, W. Zhai, M. H.-Y. Fritz, N. F. Hansen, E. Y. Durand, A.-S. Malaspinas, J. D. Jensen, T. Marques-Bonet, C. Alkan, K. Prüfer, M. Meyer, H. A. Burbano, J. M. Good, R. Schultz, A. Aximu-Petri, A. Butthof, B. Höber, B. Höffner, M. Siegemund, A. Weihmann, C. Nusbaum, E. S. Lander, C. Russ, N. Novod, J. Affourtit, M. Egholm, C. Verna, P. Rudan, D. Brajkovic, Z. Kucan, I. Gušic, V. B. Doronichev, L. V. Golovanova, C. Lalueza-Fox, M. de la Rasilla, J. Fortea, A. Rosas, R. W. Schmitz, P. L. F. Johnson, E. E. Eichler, D. Falush, E. Birney, J. C. Mullikin, M. Slatkin, R. Nielsen, J. Kelso, M. Lachmann, D. Reich, and S. Pääbo. 2010. A draft sequence of the Neandertal genome. *Science* 328:710–722.

Goodall, J. 1986. *The Chimpanzees of Gombe: Patterns of Behavior*. Cambridge, MA: Harvard University Press.

Goodall, J. 1996. Foreword: Conserving great apes. Pp. xv–xx in W. C. McGrew, L. F. Marchant, and T. Nishida, eds., *Great Ape Societies*. Cambridge: Cambridge University Press.

Goodman, M., C. A. Porter, J. Czelusniak, S. L. Page, H. Schneider, J. Shoshani, G. Gunnell, and C. P Groves. 1998. Toward a phylogenetic classification of primates based on DNA evidence complemented by fossil evidence. *Molecular Phylogenetics and Evolution* 9:585–598.

Gunnell, G. F. 2002. Tarsiiformes: Evolutionary history and adaptation. Pp. 45–82 in W. C. Hartwig, ed., *The Primate Fossil Record*. Cambridge: Cambridge University Press.

Haile-Selassie, Y., L. Gibert, S. M. Melillo, T. M. Ryan, M. Alene, A. Deino, N. E. Levin, G. Scott, and B. Z. Saylor. 2015. New species from Ethiopia further expands Middle Pliocene hominin diversity. *Nature* 521:483–488.

Harcourt-Smith, W. E. H. 2007. The origins of bipedal locomotion. Pp. 1483–1518 in W. Henke and I. Tattersall, eds., *Handbook of Paleoanthropology*. New York: Springer.

Hardy, K., S. Buckley, M. J. Collins, A. Estalrrich, D. Brothwell, L. Copeland, A. García-Tabernero, S. García-Vargas, M. de la Rasilla, C. Lalueza-Fox, R. Huguet, M. Bastir, D. Santamaría, M. Madella,

J. Wilson, Á. Fernández Cortés, and A. Rosas. 2012. Neanderthal medics? Evidence for food, cooking, and medicinal plants entrapped in dental calculus. *Naturwissenschaften* 99: 617–626. https://doi.org/10.1007/s00114-012-0942-0.

Harmand, S., J. E. Lewis, C. S. Feibel, C. J. Lepre, S. Prat, A. Lenoble, X. Boës, R. K. Quinn, M. Brenet, A. Arroyo, N. Taylor, S. Clément, G. Daver, J.-P. Brugal, L. Leakey, R. A. Mortlock, J. D. Wright, S. Lokorodi, C. Kirwa, D. V. Kent, and H. Roche. 2015. 3.3-million-year-old stone tools from Lomekwi 3, West Turkana, Kenya. *Nature* 521:310–315.

Harmon, E. H. 2013. Age and sex differences in the locomotor skeleton of *Australopithecus*. Pp. 263–272 in K. E. Reed, J. G. Fleagle, and R. E. Leakey, eds., *The Paleobiology of Australopithecus*. Dordrecht: Springer.

Harrison, T. 2002. Late Oligocene to middle Miocene catarrhines from Afro-Arabia. Pp. 311–338 in W. C. Hartwig, ed., *The Primate Fossil Record*. Cambridge: Cambridge University Press.

Haslam, M., R. A. Hernandez-Aguilar, T. Proffitt, A. Arroyo, T. Falótico, D. Fragaszy, M. Gumert, J. W. K. Harris, M. A. Huffman, A. K. Kalan, S. Malaivijitnond, T. Matsuzawa, W. McGrew, E. B. Ottoni, A. Pascual-Garrido, A. Piel, J. Pruetz, C. Schuppli, F. Stewart, A. Tan, E. Visalberghi, and L. V. Luncz. 2017. Primate archaeology evolves. *Nature Ecology & Evolution* 1(10):1431–1437. https://doi.org/10.1038/s41559-017-0286-4.

Hay, R. L. and M. D. Leakey. 1982. The fossil footprints of Laetoli. *Scientific American* 246:50–57.

Hublin, J.-J., A. Ben-Ncer, S. E. Bailey, S. E Freidline, S. Neubauer, M. M. Skinner, I. Bergmann, A. Le Cabec, S. Benazzi, K. Harvait, and P. Gunz. 2017. New fossils from Jebel Irhoud, Morocco and the pan-African origin of *Homo sapiens*. *Nature* 546:289–292. https://doi.org/10.1038/nature22336.

Huerta-Sánchez, E., X. Jin, Asan, Z. Bianba, B. M. Peter, N. Vinckenbosch, Y. Liang, X. Yi, M. He, M. Somel, P. Ni, B. Wang, X. Ou, Huasang, J. Luosang, Z. X. Cuo, K. Li, G. Gao, Y. Yin, W. Wang, X. Zhang, X. Xu, H. Yang, Y. Li, J. Wang, J. Wang, and R. Nielsen. Altitude adaptation in Tibetans caused by introgression of Denisovan-like DNA. *Nature* 512:194–197. https://doi.org/10.1038/nature13.

Hunt, K. D. 1996. The postural feeding hypothesis: An ecological model for the evolution of bipedalism. *South African Journal of Science* 92:77–90.

Jablonski, N. G. 2002. Fossil Old World monkeys: The late Neogene radiation. Pp. 255–299 in W. C. Hartwig, ed., *The Primate Fossil Record*. Cambridge: Cambridge University Press.

Jablonski, N. G. and G. Chaplin. 1993. Origin of habitual terrestrial bipedalism in the ancestor of the Hominidae. *Journal of Human Evolution* 24:259–280.

Jablonski, N. G., M. G. Leakey, C. Kiarie, and M. Antón. 2002. A new skeleton of *Theropithecus brumpti* (Primates: Cercopithecidae) from Lomekwi, West Turkana, Kenya. *Journal of Human Evolution* 43:887–923.

Johanson, D. and M. Edey. 1981. *Lucy: The Beginnings of Humankind*. New York: Simon and Schuster.

Kay, R. F., J. G. Fleagle, T. R. T. Mitchell, M. Colbert, T. Bown, and D. W. Powers. 2008. The anatomy of *Dolichocebus gaimanensis*, a stem platyrrhine monkey from Argentina. *Journal of Human Evolution* 54:323–382.

Kay, R. F., C. Ross, and B. A. Williams. 1997. Anthropoid origins. *Science* 275:797–804.

Kelley, J. 2002. The hominoid radiation in Asia. Pp. 369–384 in W. C. Hartwig, ed., *The Primate Fossil Record*. Cambridge: Cambridge University Press.

Kimbel, W. H. and L. K. Delezene. 2009. "Lucy" redux: A review of research on *Australopithecus afarensis*. *Yearbook of Physical Anthropology* 52:2–48.

Krause, J., Q. Fu, J. M. Good, B. Viola, M. V. Shunkov, A. P. Derevianko, and S. Pääbo. 2010. The complete mitochondrial DNA genome of an unknown hominin from southern Siberia. *Nature* 464:894–897.

Larsen, C. S. 2014. *Our Origins: Discovering Physical Anthropology*, 3rd edition. New York: W. W. Norton & Company.

Leakey, M. G., C. S. Feibel, I. McDougall, and A. Walker. 1995. New four-million-year-old hominid species from Kanapoi and Allia Bay, Kenya. *Nature* 376:565–571.

Leakey, M. G., F. Spoor, M. C. Dean, C. S. Feibel, S. C. Antón, C. Kiarie, and L. N. Leakey. 2012. New fossils from Koobi Fora in northern Kenya confirm taxonomic diversity in early *Homo*. *Nature* 488:201–204.

Lewontin, R. C. 1972. The apportionment of human diversity. *Evolutionary Biology* 6:381–398.

Livingstone, F. B. 1958. Anthropological implications of sickle cell gene distribution in West Africa. *American Anthropologist* 60:533–562.

Livingstone, F. B. 1971. Malaria and human polymorphisms. *Annual Review of Genetics* 5:33–64.

Long, J. C., J. Li, and M. E. Healy. 2009. Human DNA sequences: More variation and less race. *American Journal of Physical Anthropology* 139:23–34.

Lordkipanidze, D., T. Jashashvili, A. Vekua, M. S. Ponce de León, C. P. E. Zollikofer, G. P. Rightmire, H. Pontzer, R. Ferring, O. Oms, M. Tappen, M. Bukhsianidze, J. Agusti, R. Kahlke, G. Kiladze, B. Martinez-Navarro, A. Mouskhelishvili, M. Nioradze, and L. Rook. 1997. Postcranial evidence from early *Homo* from Dmanisi, Georgia. *Nature* 449:305–310.

Lovejoy, C. O. 1981. The origins of man. *Science* 211:341–348.

Lovejoy, C. O. 2009. Reexamining human origins in light of *Ardipithecus ramidus*. *Science* 326:74e1–74e8.

Lovejoy, C. O., G. Suwa, L. Spurlock, B. Asfaw, and T. D. White. 2009. The pelvis and femur of *Ardipithecus ramidus*: The emergence of upright walking. *Science* 326:71e1–71e6.

Mangs, A. H. and B. J. Morris. 2007. The human pseudoautosomal region (PAR): Origin, function and future. *Current Genomics* 8:129–136.

McGraw, W. S. 2010. Primates defined. Pp. 222–242 in C. S. Larsen, ed., *A Companion to Biological Anthropology*. Chichester, UK: Wiley-Blackwell.

McGrew, W. C. 1998. Culture in nonhuman primates. *Annual Review of Anthropology* 27:301–328.

McHenry, H. M. 1984. Relative cheek-tooth size in *Australopithecus*. *American Journal of Physical Anthropology* 64:297–306. https://doi.org/10.1002/ajpa.1330640312.

McPherron, S. P., Z. Alemseged, C. W. Marean, J. G. Wynn, D. Reed, D. Geraads, R. Bobe, and H. A. Béarat. 2010. Evidence for stone-tool-assisted consumption of animal tissues before 3.39 million years ago at Dikika, Ethiopia. *Nature* 466:857–860.

Mintz, S. W. and C. B. Tan. 2001. Bean-curd consumption in Hong Kong. *Ethnology* 40(2):113–128.

Moura, A. C. A. and P. C. Lee. 2004. Capuchin stone tool use in Caatinga dry forest. *Science* 306:1909.

Naruto v. Slater. 2018. U.S. Court of Appeals for the Ninth Circuit, no. 16-15469.

Nater, A., M. P. Mattle-Greminger, A. Nurcahyo, M. G. Nowak, M. de Manuel, T. Desai, C. Groves, M. Pybus, T. B. Sonay, C. Roos, A. R. Lameira, S. A. Wich, J. Askew, M. Davila-Ross, G. Fredriksson, G. de Valles, F. Casals, J. Prado-Martinez, B. Goossens, E. J. Verschoor, K. S. Warren, I. Singleton, D. A. Marques, J. Pamungkas, D. Perwitasari-Farajallah, P. Rianti, A. Tuuga, I. G. Gut, M. Gut, P. Orozco-terWengel, C. P. van Schaik, J. Bertranpetit, M. Anisimova, A. Scally, T. Marques-Bonet, E. Meijaard, and M. Krützen. 2017. Morphometric, behavioral, and genomic evidence for a new orangutan species. *Current Biology* 27(22):3487–3498.

National Institute of Environmental Health Sciences. 2012. Dry Bones (or Skeleton Bones). http://kids.niehs.nih.gov/games/songs/childrens/dry_bonesmp3.htm.

Nelson, R. G., J. N. Rutherford, K. Hinde, and K. B. H. Clancy. 2017. Signaling safety: Characterizing fieldwork experiences and their implications for career trajectories. *American Anthropologist* 119(4):710–722. https://doi.org/10.1111/aman.12929.

Nengo, I., P. Tafforeau, C. C. Gilbert, J. G. Fleagle, E. R. Miller, C. Feibel, D. Fox, J. Feinberg, K. D. Pugh, C. Berruyer, S. Mana, Z. Engle, and F. Spoor. 2017. New infant cranium from the African Miocene sheds light on ape evolution. *Nature* 548:169–174. https://doi.org/10.1038/nature23456.

Nepomnaschy, P. A., K. Welch, D. McConnell, B. I. Strassmann, and B. G. England. 2004. Stress and female reproductive function: A study of daily variations in cortisol, gonadotrophins, and gonadal steroids in a rural Mayan population. *American Journal of Human Biology* 16:523–532.

Nishida, T. and K. Hosaka. 1996. Coalition strategies among adult male chimpanzees of the Mahale Mountains, Tanzania. Pp. 114–134 in W. C. McGrew, L. F. Marchant, and T. Nishida, eds., *Great Ape Societies*. Cambridge: Cambridge University Press.

Nystrom, P. and P. Ashmore. 2008. *The Life of Primates*. Upper Saddle River, NJ: Pearson Prentice Hall.

Pallante, M. A. 2017. From monkey selfies to open source: The essential interplay of creative culture, technology, Copyright Office practice, and the law. *Washington Journal of Law, Technology & Arts*, 12(2):123–124.

Peng, Y., H. Shi, X.-B. Qi, C.-J. Xiao, H. Zhong, R.-L. Z. Ma, and B. Su. 2010. The ADH1BArg47His polymorphism in East Asian populations and expansion of rice domestication in history. *BMC Evolutionary Biology* 10:15. https://doi.org/10.1186/1471-2148-10-15.

Proffitt, T., V. L. Luncz, S. Malaivijitnond, M. Gumert, M. S. Svensson, and M. Haslam. 2018. Analysis of wild macaque stone tools used to crack oil palm nuts. *Royal Society Open Science*. https://doi.org/10.1098/rsos.171904.

Pruetz, J. D. and P. Bertolani. 2007. Savannah chimpanzees, *Pan troglodytes verus*, hunt with tools. *Current Biology* 17:412–417.

Relethford, J. H. 2009. Race and global patterns of phenotypic variation. *American Journal of Physical Anthropology* 139:16–22.

Remis, M. J. 2000. Preliminary assessment of the impacts of human activities on gorillas *Gorilla gorilla gorilla* and other wildlife at Dzanga-Sangha Reserve, Central African Republic. *Oryx* 34:56–65.

Richmond, B. G. and W. L. Jungers. 2008. *Orrorin tugenensis* femoral morphology and the evolution of hominin bipedalism. *Science* 319:1662–1665.

Richter, D., R. Grün, R. Joannes-Boyau, T. E. Steele, F. Amani, M. Rué, P. Fernandes, J.-P. Raynal, D. Geraads, A. Ben-Ncer, J.-J. Hublin, and S. P. McPherron. 2017. The age of hominin fossils from Jebel Irhoud, Morocco, and the origins of the Middle Stone Age. *Nature* 546:293–296. https://doi.org/10.1038/nature22335.

Rightmire, G. P. 1998. Human evolution in the Middle Pleistocene: The role of *Homo heidelbergensis*. *Evolutionary Anthropology* 6:218–227.

Rodman, P. S. and H. M. McHenry. 1980. Bioenergetics and the origins of hominid bipedalism. *American Journal of Physical Anthropology* 52:103–106.

Rose, K. D. 2006. *The Beginning of the Age of Mammals*. Baltimore: Johns Hopkins University Press.

Ruvolo, M. 1997. Genetic diversity in hominoid primates. *Annual Review of Anthropology* 26:515–540.

Ruwende, C. and A. Hill. 1998. Glucose-6-phosphate dehydrogenase deficiency and malaria. *Journal of Molecular Medicine* 76(8):581–588.

Sapolsky, R. M. 2006. Social cultures among nonhuman primates. *Current Anthropology* 47:641–656.

Schneider, T. D. 2010. Placing refuge: Shell mounds and the archaeology of colonial encounters in the San Francisco Bay Area, California. Ph.D. dissertation, University of California, Berkeley.

Semaw, S. 2000. The world's oldest stone artefacts from Gona, Ethiopia: Their implications for understanding stone technology and patterns of human evolution between 2.6–1.5 million years ago. *Journal of Archaeological Science* 27:1197–1214.

Shoshani, J., C. P. Groves, E. L. Simons, and G. F. Gunnell. 1996. Primate phylogeny: Morphological vs. molecular results. *Molecular Phylogenetics and Evolution* 5:102–154.

Simons, E. L., E. R. Seiffert, T. M. Ryan, and Y. Attia. 2007. A remarkable female cranium of the early Oligocene anthropoid *Aegyptopithecus zeuxis* (Catarrhini, Propliopithecidae). *Proceedings of the National Academy of Sciences* 104:8731–8736.

Slon, V., F. Mafessoni, B. Vernot, C. de Filippo, S. Grote, B. Viola, M. Hajdinjak, S. Peyrégne, S. Nagel, S. Brown, K. Douka, T. Higham, M. B. Kozlikin, M. V. Shunkov, A. P. Derevianko, J. Kelso, M. Meyer, K. Prüfer, and S. Pääbo. 2018. The genome of the offspring of a Neanderthal mother and a Denisovan father. *Nature* 561:113–116. https://doi.org/10.1038/s41586-018-0455-x.

Smith, F. H. 2002. Migrations, radiations and continuity: Patterns in the evolution of Middle and Late Pleistocene humans. Pp. 437–456 in W. C. Hartwig, ed., *The Primate Fossil Record*. Cambridge: Cambridge University Press.

Smith, F. H. 2010. Species, populations, and assimilation in later human evolution. Pp. 357–378 in C. S. Larsen, ed., *A Companion to Biological Anthropology*. Chichester, UK: Wiley–Blackwell.

Soligo, C., O. A. Will, S. Tavarré, C. R. Marshall, and R. D. Martin. 2007. New light on the dates of primate origins and divergence. Pp. 29–49 in M. J. Ravosa and M. Dagosto, eds., *Primate Origins: Adaptations and Evolution*. New York: Springer.

Spencer, F. 1997. *History of Physical Anthropology: An Encyclopedia*. New York: Garland.

Sponheimer, M., Z. Alemseged, T. E. Cerling, F. R. Grine, W. H. Kimbel, M. G. Leakey, J. A. Lee-Thorp, F. K. Manthi, K. E. Reed, B. A. Wood, and J. G. Wynn. 2013. Isotopic evidence of early hominin diets. *Proceedings of the National Academy of Sciences* 110:10513–10518.

Stewart, T. D. 1979. *Essentials of Forensic Anthropology, Especially as Developed in the United States*. Springfield, IL: Charles C. Thomas.

Stoneking, M. and J. Krause. 2011. Learning about human population history from ancient and modern genomes. *Nature Reviews Genetics* 12:603–614.

Strait, D. S. 2010. The evolutionary history of the australopiths. *Evolution: Education and Outreach* 3:341–352.

Strier, K. B. 2010. *Primate Behavioral Ecology*, 4th edition. Upper Saddle River, NJ: Prentice Hall.

Strier, K. B. 2010. Primate behavior and sociality. Pp. 243–257 in C. S. Larsen, ed., *A Companion to Biological Anthropology*. Chichester, UK: Wiley-Blackwell.

Susman, R. L. 2005. *Oreopithecus*: Still apelike after all these years. *Journal of Human Evolution* 49:405–411.

Swallow, D. 2003. Genetics of lactase persistence and lactose tolerance. *Annual Review of Genetics* 37:197–219.

Takai, M., F. Anaya, N. Shigehara, and T. Setoguchi. 2000. New fossil materials of the earliest New World monkey, *Branisella boliviana*, and the problem of platyrrhine origins. *American Journal of Physical Anthropology* 111:263–281.

Tannen, D. 2003. Gender and family interaction. Pp. 179–201 in J. Holmes and M. Meyerhoff, eds., *Handbook on Language and Gender*. Oxford, UK, and Cambridge, MA: Blackwell.

Tejedor, M. F., A. A. Tauber, A. L. Rosenberger, C. C. Swisher, and M. E. Palacios. 2006. New primate genus from the Miocene of Argentina. *Proceedings of the National Academy of Sciences* 103: 5437–5441. https://doi.org/10.1073/pnas.0506126103.

Tishkoff, S. A., F. A. Reed, A. Ranciaro, B. F. Voight, C. C. Babbitt, J. S. Silverman, K. Powell, H. M. Mortensen, J. B. Hirbo, M. Osman, M. Ibrahim, S. A. Omar, G. Lema, T. B. Nyambo, J. Ghori, S. Bumpsted, J. K. Pritchard, T. B. Wray, and P. Deloukas. 2006. Convergent adaptation of human lactase persistence in Africa and Europe. *Nature Genetics* 39:31–40.

Trinkaus, E. 2005. Early modern humans. *Annual Review of Anthropology* 34:207–230.

Trinkaus, E. and P. Shipman. 1993. Neandertals: Images of ourselves. *Evolutionary Anthropology* 1:194–201.

Trotter, M. 1970. Estimation of stature from intact long limb bones. Pp. 71–84 in T. D. Stewart, ed., *Personal Identification in Mass Disasters*. Washington, DC: Smithsonian Institution, National Museum of Natural History.

Ubelaker, D. H. 1989. *Human Skeletal Remains: Excavation, Analysis, Interpretation*, 2nd edition. Washington, DC: Taraxacum.

United States Copyright Office. 2017. *Compendium of U.S. Copyright Office Practices § 101*, 3rd edition. https://www.copyright.gov/comp3/docs/compendium.pdf.

van den Bergh, G., Y. Kaifu, I. Kurniawan, R. T. Kono, A. Brumm, E. Setiyabudi, F. Aziz, and M. J. Morwood. 2016. *Homo floresiensis*-like fossils from the early Middle Pleistocene of Flores. *Nature* 534:245–248. https://doi.org/10.1038/nature17999.

van Schaik, C. P. and J. A. R. A. M. Van Hooff. 1996. Toward an understanding of the orangutan's social system. Pp. 3–15 in W. C. McGrew, L. F. Marchant, and T. Nishida, eds., *Great Ape Societies*. Cambridge: Cambridge University Press.

van Schaik, C. P., M. Ancrenaz, G. Borgen, B. Galdikas, C. D. Knott, I. Singleton, A. Suzuki, S. S. Utami, and M. Merrill. 2003. Orangutan cultures and the evolution of material culture. *Science* 299: 102–105.

Vekua, A., D. Lordkipanidze, G. P. Rightmire, J. Agusti, R. Ferring, G. Maisuradze, A. Mouskhelishvili, M. Nioradze, M. Ponce de León, M. Tappen, M. Tvalchrelidze, and C. Zollikofer. 2002. A new skull of early *Homo* from Dmanisi, Georgia. *Science* 297:85–89.

Walker, A. and R. Leakey. 1993. *The Nariokotome* Homo erectus *Skeleton*. Cambridge, MA: Harvard University Press.

Ward, C., M. Leakey, and A. Walker. 1999. The new hominid species *Australopithecus anamensis*. *Evolutionary Anthropology* 7:197–205.

Ward, S. C. and D. L. Duren. 2002. Middle and Late Miocene African hominoids. Pp. 385–397 in W. C. Hartwig, ed., *The Primate Fossil Record*. Cambridge: Cambridge University Press.

Watson, J. D. 1968. *The Double Helix: A Personal Account of the Discovery of the Structure of DNA*. New York: Atheneum.

Wheeler, P. E. 1991. The thermoregulatory advantages of hominid bipedalism in open equatorial environments: The contribution of increased convective heat loss and cutaneous evaporative cooling. *Journal of Human Evolution* 21(2):107–115.

White, T. D. 2002. Earliest hominids. Pp. 407–417 in W. C. Hartwig, ed., *The Primate Fossil Record*. Cambridge: Cambridge University Press.

White, T. D., B. Asfaw, Y. Beyene, Y. Haile-Selassie, C. O. Lovejoy, G. Suwa, and G. WoldeGabriel. 2009. *Ardipithecus ramidus* and the paleobiology of early hominids. *Science* 326(64):75–86.

White, T. D., M. T. Black, and P. A. Folkens. 2011. *Human Osteology*, 3rd edition. San Diego: Academic Press.

Whiten, A., J. Goodall, W. C. McGrew, T. Nishida, V. Reynolds, Y. Sugiyama, C. E. G. Tutin, R. W. Wrangham, and C. Boesch. 1999. Cultures in chimpanzees. *Nature* 399:682–685.

Williams, B. A., R. F. Kay, and E. C. Kirk. 2010. New perspectives on anthropoid origins. *Proceedings of the National Academy of Sciences* 107:4797–4804.

Wolpoff, M. H., A. G. Thorne, F. H. Smith, D. W. Frayer, and G. G. Pope. 1994. Multiregional evolution: A worldwide source for modern human populations. Pp. 175–199 in M. H. Nitecki and D. V. Nitecki, eds., *Origins of Anatomically Modern Humans*. New York: Plenum Press.

Wood, B. A. 2010. Systematics, taxonomy, and phylogenetics: Ordering life, past and present. Pp. 56–73 in C. S. Larsen, ed., *A Companion to Biological Anthropology*. Chichester, UK: Wiley-Blackwell.

Yuasa, I., K. Umetsu, S. Harihara, A. Kido, A. Miyoshi, N. Saitou, B. Dashnyam, F. Jin, G. Lucotte, P. K. Chattopadhyay, L. Henke, and J. Henke. 2006. Distribution of the F374 allele of the SLC45A2 (MATP) gene and founder-haplotype analysis. *Annals of Human Genetics* 70(6):802–811.

Zilhão, J., D. E. Angelucci, E. Badal-Garcia, F. d'Errico, F. Daniel, L. Dayet, K. Douka, T. F. G. Higham, M. J. Martínez-Sánchez, R. Montes-Bernárdez, S. Murcia-Mascarós, C. Pérez-Sirvent, C. Roldán-Garcia, M. Vanhaeren, V. Villaverde, R. Wood, and J. Zapata. 2010. Symbolic use of marine shells and mineral pigments by Iberian Neanderthals. *Proceedings of the National Academy of Sciences* 107: 1023–1028.

Zimmer, C. 2013. *The Tangled Bank: An Introduction to Evolution*, 2nd edition. Greenwood Village, CO: Roberts and Company.

FRONTMATTER

Photos: p. ix K. Elizabeth Soluri: Courtesy of Tsim Schneider; Sabrina C. Agarwal: Courtesy of Peter Pollard

PART ONE OPENER

Photos: p. 2 David Marchal/Science Source

LAB 1

Photos: p. 5 (left–right) Image BROKER/Superstock; HANDOUT/KRT/Newscom **Figure 1.1a–d** Bettmann/Corbis/Getty Image; Jeremy Fahringer/Living Tongues; John T. Fowler/Alamy Stock Photo; Horacio Villalobos/Corbis via Getty Images **Figure 1.2** LukaTDB/Shutterstock **Figure 1.3** Penelope Breese/Liaison/Getty Images **Figure 1.4** Des Bartlett/Science Source **Figure 1.6** Stu Porter/Alamy Stock Photo **p. 26** Courtesy of Julienne Rutherford.

LAB 2

Photos: p. 27 Jezper/Shutterstock **Figure 2.1a–b** Science Source; Omikron/Science Source **Figure 2.3** Biophoto Associates/Science Source **Figure 2.6** L. Willatt/Science Source

Drawn art: Figure 2.9b Adapted from OpenStax College. 2014. Concepts of biology. OpenStax CNX. cnx.org/contents/b3c1e1d2-839c-42b0-a314-e119a8aafbdd@8.49. Textbook content produced by OpenStax College is licensed under a Creative Commons Attribution License 3.0 License.

LAB 3

Photos: p. 55 (left–right) Courtesy of Teresa Soluri; Courtesy of Sabrina Agarwal **p. 62 (first row, both)** K. Elizabeth Soluri **p. 62 (second row)** Dean Clarke/Shutterstock; sirtravelalot/Shutterstock **p. 62 (third row)** UfaBizPhoto/Shutterstock; Simon Annable/Shutterstock **p. 62 (fourth row)** Tatjana Romanova/Shutterstock; NADA GIRL/Shutterstock **p. 62 (fifth row)** MRAORAOR/Shutterstock; OJO Images Ltd/Alamy Stock Photo **Figure 3.5** Monica Schroeder/Science Source **p. 80 (top row, left–right)** Anne Punch/Shutterstock; Phanie/Science Source; Vladimir Gjorgiev/Shutterstock; B. BOISSONNET/BSIP/agefotostock; CSP_victorO/agefotostock **p. 80 (bottom row, left–right)** CSP_bds/agefotostock; Zoonar/Sergieiev/agefotostock; Syda Productions/Shutterstock;

Berna Namoglu/Shutterstock; yurakrasil/Shutterstock **p. 80 (bottom)** szorny-stock/Alamy Stock Photo

Drawn art: Figure 3.1 "Seven Pairs of Contrasting Traits." © The Field Museum, Illustration by Greg Mercer. Reprinted with permission.

LAB 4

Photos: p. 81 Michael Nolan/Robert Harding World Imagery **Figure 4.1 (top–bottom)** Ryan M. Bolton/Shutterstock; Stubblefield Photography/Shutterstock **Figure 4.5** Duncan Walker/Getty Images/Stockphoto

PART TWO OPENER

Photos: p. 108 SIU/Visuals Unlimited, Inc.

LAB 5

Photos: p. 111 Image courtesy of Sabrina C. Agarwal **Figure 5.2** Image courtesy of Sabrina C. Agarwal **Figure 5.8** Courtesy of The Museum of Vertebrate Zoology, UC Berkeley. Photograph by Ashley Lipps **Figure 5.9** Courtesy of The Museum of Vertebrate Zoology, UC Berkeley. Photograph by Ashley Lipps **Figure 5.10** Courtesy of The Museum of Vertebrate Zoology, UC Berkeley. Photograph by Ashley Lipps **Figure 5.11** Courtesy of The Museum of Vertebrate Zoology, UC Berkeley. Photograph by Ashley Lipps **Figure 5.12** Courtesy of The Museum of Vertebrate Zoology, UC Berkeley. Photograph by Ashley Lipps **Figure 5.13** Courtesy of The Museum of Vertebrate Zoology, UC Berkeley. Photograph by Ashley Lipps **Figure 5.14** Courtesy of The Museum of Vertebrate Zoology, UC Berkeley. Photograph by Ashley Lipps **p. 131 (all)** Courtesy of The Museum of Vertebrate Zoology, UC Berkeley. Photograph by Ashley Lipps **p. 132 (all)** Courtesy of The Museum of Vertebrate Zoology, UC Berkeley. Photograph by Ashley Lipps

LAB 6

Photos: p. 133 MedicalRF.com/Visuals Unlimited, Inc. **Figure 6.2 (all)** Courtesy of The Museum of Vertebrate Zoology, UC Berkeley. Photograph by Ashley Lipps **Figure 6.4** Courtesy of The Museum of Vertebrate Zoology, UC Berkeley. Photograph by Ashley Lipps **Figure 6.5** Courtesy of The Museum of Ver-

tebrate Zoology, UC Berkeley. Photograph by Ashley Lipps **Figure 6.6 (both)** Courtesy of The Museum of Vertebrate Zoology, UC Berkeley. Photograph by Ashley Lipps **Figure 6.7** Bone Clones/boneclones.com **Figure 6.8 (both)** Courtesy of The Museum of Vertebrate Zoology, UC Berkeley. Photograph by Ashley Lipps **Figure 6.9** Courtesy of The Museum of Vertebrate Zoology, UC Berkeley. Photograph by Ashley Lipps **Figure 6.10 (both)** Courtesy of The Museum of Vertebrate Zoology, UC Berkeley. Photograph by Ashley Lipps **Figure 6.11** Courtesy of The Museum of Vertebrate Zoology, UC Berkeley. Photograph by Ashley Lipps **Figure 6.12** Courtesy of The Museum of Vertebrate Zoology, UC Berkeley. Photograph by Ashley Lipps **Figure 6.13** Courtesy of The Museum of Vertebrate Zoology, UC Berkeley. Photograph by Ashley Lipps **Figure 6.14** Courtesy of The Museum of Vertebrate Zoology, UC Berkeley. Photograph by Ashley Lipps **Figure 6.15 (both)** Courtesy of The Museum of Vertebrate Zoology, UC Berkeley. Photograph by Ashley Lipps **Figure 6.17a** Courtesy of The Museum of Vertebrate Zoology, UC Berkeley. Photograph by Ashley Lipps **Figure 6.18 (both)** Courtesy of The Museum of Vertebrate Zoology, UC Berkeley. Photograph by Ashley Lipps **Figure 6.20** Courtesy of The Museum of Vertebrate Zoology, UC Berkeley. Photograph by Ashley Lipps **Figure 6.21** Courtesy of The Museum of Vertebrate Zoology, UC Berkeley. Photograph by Ashley Lipps **Figure 6.22a–b** Courtesy of The Museum of Vertebrate Zoology, UC Berkeley. Photograph by Ashley Lipps **Figure 6.23 (both)** Courtesy of The Museum of Vertebrate Zoology, UC Berkeley. Photograph by Ashley Lipps **Figure 6.24 (both)** Courtesy of The Museum of Vertebrate Zoology, UC Berkeley. Photograph by Ashley Lipps **Figure 6.25 (all)** Courtesy of The Museum of Vertebrate Zoology, UC Berkeley. Photograph by Ashley Lipps **Figure 6.26** Courtesy of The Museum of Vertebrate Zoology, UC Berkeley. Photograph by Ashley Lipps **Figure 6.28** Courtesy of The Museum of Vertebrate Zoology, UC Berkeley. Photograph by Ashley Lipps **Figure 6.29** Courtesy of The Museum of Vertebrate Zoology, UC Berkeley. Photograph by Ashley Lipps **Figure 6.30** Courtesy of The Museum of Vertebrate Zoology, UC Berkeley.

Photograph by Ashley Lipps **Figure 6.31 (both)** Courtesy of The Museum of Vertebrate Zoology, UC Berkeley. Photograph by Ashley Lipps **Figure 6.32 (both)** Courtesy of The Museum of Vertebrate Zoology, UC Berkeley. Photograph by Ashley Lipps **Figure 6.33a–b** Courtesy of The Museum of Vertebrate Zoology, UC Berkeley. Photograph by Ashley Lipps **Figure 6.34 (both)** Courtesy of The Museum of Vertebrate Zoology, UC Berkeley. Photograph by Ashley Lipps **Figure 6.35 (both)** Courtesy of The Museum of Vertebrate Zoology, UC Berkeley. Photograph by Ashley Lipps **Figure 6.36a–b** Courtesy of The Museum of Vertebrate Zoology, UC Berkeley. Photograph by Ashley Lipps **Figure 6.36c** Bone Clones/boneclones.com; **Figure 6.37** Courtesy of The Museum of Vertebrate Zoology, UC Berkeley. Photograph by Ashley Lipps **Figure 6.38** Courtesy of The Museum of Vertebrate Zoology, UC Berkeley. Photograph by Ashley Lipps **Figure 6.39** Courtesy of The Museum of Vertebrate Zoology, UC Berkeley. Photograph by Ashley Lipps **Figure 6.40** Courtesy of The Museum of Vertebrate Zoology, UC Berkeley. Photograph by Ashley Lipps **Figure 6.41** Courtesy of The Museum of Vertebrate Zoology, UC Berkeley. Photograph by Ashley Lipps **Figure 6.42 (all)** Courtesy of The Museum of Vertebrate Zoology, UC Berkeley. Photograph by Ashley Lipps **Figure 6.43 (all)** Courtesy of The Museum of Vertebrate Zoology, UC Berkeley. Photograph by Ashley Lipps **Figure 6.44** Courtesy of The Museum of Vertebrate Zoology, UC Berkeley. Photograph by Ashley Lipps **Figure 6.45 (both)** Courtesy of The Museum of Vertebrate Zoology, UC Berkeley. Photograph by Ashley Lipps **Figure 6.46 (both)** Courtesy of The Museum of Vertebrate Zoology, UC Berkeley. Photograph by Ashley Lipps **Figure 6.47 (both)** Courtesy of The Museum of Vertebrate Zoology, UC Berkeley. Photograph by Ashley Lipps **Figure 6.48 (both)** Courtesy of The Museum of Vertebrate Zoology, UC Berkeley. Photograph by Ashley Lipps **Figure 6.49a** Courtesy of The Museum of Vertebrate Zoology, UC Berkeley. Photograph by Ashley Lipps **Figure 6.50** Courtesy of The Museum of Vertebrate Zoology, UC Berkeley. Photograph by Ashley Lipps **Figure 6.51** Courtesy of The Museum of Vertebrate Zoology, UC Berkeley. Photograph by Ashley Lipps **Figure 6.52** Courtesy of The Museum of Vertebrate Zoology, UC Berkeley. Photograph by Ashley Lipps **p. 172 (all)** Courtesy of The Museum of Vertebrate Zoology, UC Berkeley. Photograph by Ashley Lipps **p. 173 (all)** Courtesy of The Museum of Vertebrate Zoology, UC Berkeley. Photograph by Ashley Lipps **p. 175 (both)** Courtesy of The Museum of Vertebrate Zoology, UC Berkeley. Photograph by Ashley Lipps **p. 176 (both)** Courtesy of The Museum of Vertebrate Zoology, UC Berkeley. Photograph by Ashley Lipps **p. 177 (all)** Courtesy of The Museum of Vertebrate Zoology, UC Berkeley. Photograph by Ashley Lipps

Drawn art: Figure 6.22c Reprinted by permission from *Anatomy & Physiology* 7th Ed. © 2015 McGraw Hill. **Figure 6.49b** Figure reprinted from FootVitals.com by permission of Vincent C. Marino, DPM.

LAB 7

Photos: p. 179 Dr. Morley Read/Shutterstock **Figure 7.1** Photo courtesy of Melanie Miller **Figure 7.2 (both)** Courtesy of The Museum of Vertebrate Zoology, UC Berkeley. Photograph by Ashley Lipps **Figure 7.3a** Courtesy of The Museum of Vertebrate Zoology, UC Berkeley. Photograph by Ashley Lipps **Figure 7.3b** Bone Clones/boneclones.com **Figure 7.4 (both)** Courtesy of The Museum of Vertebrate Zoology, UC Berkeley. Photograph by Ashley Lipps **Figure 7.5 (both)** Courtesy of The Museum of Vertebrate Zoology, UC Berkeley. Photograph by Ashley Lipps **Figure 7.9** Gwen Robbins Schug, Appalachian State University **Figure 7.11 (all)** Courtesy of The Museum of Vertebrate Zoology, UC Berkeley. Photograph by Ashley Lipps **Figure 7.12** SPL/Science Source **Figure 7.16** Courtesy of The Museum of Vertebrate Zoology, UC Berkeley. Photograph by Ashley Lipps **Figure 7.17** Image courtesy of Sabrina Agarwal **Figure 7.18** Image courtesy of Sabrina Agarwal **Figure 7.19** Image courtesy of Sabrina Agarwal **Figure 7.20** Bone Clones/boneclones.com **Figure 7.21** Image courtesy of Sabrina Agarwal **Figure 7.22** Courtesy of Tiffiny Tung **Figure 7.23** Bone Clones/boneclones.com **p. 216 (left–right)** L. Bassett/Visuals Unlimited, Inc.; Andrey Simonenko/Alamy Stock Photo; Andrey Simonenko/Alamy Stock Photo **p. 217 (top, both)** Courtesy of The Museum of Vertebrate Zoology, UC Berkeley. Photograph by Ashley Lipps **p. 217 (bottom, both)** Bone Clones/boneclones.com **p. 218** Courtesy of The Museum of Vertebrate Zoology, UC Berkeley. Photograph by Ashley Lipps **p. 219 (all)** Bone Clones/boneclones.com **p. 220 (all)** Courtesy of Vertebrate Zoology, UC Berkeley. Photograph by Ashley Lipps **p. 221 (top, left)** Courtesy of The Museum of Vertebrate Zoology, UC Berkeley. Photograph by Ashley Lipps **p. 221 (top, right)** Ira Block/National Geographic Creative **p. 221 (bottom, left)** Courtesy of The Museum of Vertebrate Zoology, UC Berkeley. Photograph by Ashley Lipps **p. 221 (bottom, right)** Bone Clones/boneclones.com **p. 222 (top)** Courtesy of The Museum of Vertebrate Zoology, UC Berkeley. Photograph by Ashley Lipps **p. 222 (bottom)** Courtesy of Tiffiny Tung **p. 223** Bone Clones/boneclones.com **p. 224** Courtesy of The Museum of Vertebrate Zoology, UC Berkeley. Photograph by Ashley Lipps **p. 225** Courtesy of Kay Hinton, Emory University

Drawn art: Figure 7.8 Figure from *Forensic Anthropology Laboratory Manual* 4th Ed., by Steven N. Byers. Copyright © 2017 Steven N. Byers. Reproduced by permission of Taylor & Francis Books UK. **Figure 7.10** Figure from *Standards for Data Collection from Human Skeletal Remains: Proceedings of a Seminar at the Field Museum of Natural History* organized by Jonathan Haas, edited by Jane E. Buikstra and Douglas H. Ubelaker. (Arkansas Archeological Survey, 1994), reprinted with the permission of the Arkansas Archeological Survey.

LAB 8

Photos: p. 227 David Grossman/Alamy Stock Photo **Figure 8.1 (left–right)** Delbars/Shutterstock; John_Walker/Shutterstock; Lonathan Larsen/Diadem Images/Alamy **Figure 8.3** Courtesy of Cynthia Beall **Figure 8.8** Eye of Science/Science Source

Drawn art: Figure 8.2 & p. 243 (Lab Exercise 2) Map © George Chaplin. First published in *Skin: A Natural History* by Nina G. Jablonski, UCP 2013. Used with permission. **Figure 8.6** From *The Distribution of the Human Blood Groups and Other Polymorphisms* 2nd Edition, by Mourant et al (1976). Maps 1 and 2 and 3. Copyright © Oxford University Press, Inc. By permission of Oxford University Press. **p. 252 (Critical Thinking Question 7)** Figure from Donnelly, Michael P., et. al. "A global view of the OCA2-HERC2 region and pigmentation." *Human Genetics* 131(5): 683–696, May 2012, Copyright © 2011 The Authors. Reprinted by permission of Springer Nature Switzerland AG.

PART THREE OPENER

Photos: p. 256 LeonP/Shutterstock

LAB 9

Photos: p. 259 Rainbow/iStock/Getty Images Plus **Figure 9.2a–c** GlobalP/iStock/Getty Images Plus; DAVID MORRISON/Alamy Stock Photo; ChiccoDodiFC/Shutterstock **Figure 9.3a–b** Kevin Schafer/Getty Images; JYB/iStock **Figure 9.4a–b** Millard H. Sharp/Science Source; Chris Meier/doc-stock/Visuals Unlimited, Inc. **Figure 9.5 (both)** Courtesy of The Museum of Vertebrate Zoology, UC Berkeley. Photograph by Ashley Lipps **Figure 9.7 (left–right)** Arco Images GmbH/Alamy Stock Photo; John Warburton-Lee Photography/Alamy Stock Photo; Arco Images GmbH/Alamy Stock Photo **Figure 9.8 (left–right)** Arco Images GmbH/Alamy Stock Photo; John Warburton-Lee Photography/Alamy Stock Photo; Arco Images GmbH/Alamy Stock Photo **p. 276 a–b** Courtesy of The Museum of Vertebrate Zoology, UC Berkeley. Photograph by Ashley Lipps **p. 276 c–d** Chris Parsons/Getty Images; Sabena Jane Blackbird/Alamy Stock Photo

LAB 10

Photos: p. 277 NASA/MCT via Getty Images **Figure 10.6** Martin Harvey/Getty Images; **Figure 10.9a–b** Millard H. Sharp/Science Source; Nigel J. Dennis/Science Source **Figure 10.10** Robert Ross/Getty Images **Figure 10.11** Cheryl Ravelo/Reuters/Newscom **Figure 10.13 (left–right)** Ann Kakaliouras, Whittier College; Bill Coster/Alamy Stock Photo **Figure 10.14** Kevin Schafer/Getty Images **Figure 10.15** Dietmar Nill/naturepl.com **Figure 10.16** Ger Bosma/Alamy Stock Photo **Figure 10.17** Charles Krebs/Getty Images **Figure 10.18** © William K. Sacco **Figure 10.19** Courtesy of Joan Silk **Figure 10.20** Fredrik Stenström/Alamy Stock Photo **Figure 10.21** Kevin Schafer/Getty Images **Figure 10.22** Tom Brakefield/Getty Images **Figure 10.23** © William K. Sacco **Figure 10.24** McPhoto/Bernd Wasiolka/Alamy Stock Photo **Figure 10.25** Ralph Lee Hopkins/National Geographic Creative **Figure 10.26** Martin Harvey/Alamy Stock Photo **Figure 10.27** Roy Toft/National Geographic Image Collection/Getty Images **Figure 10.28** Michael Nichols/National Geographic Image Collection/Getty Images **p. 303 (both)** Courtesy of The Museum of Vertebrate Zoology, UC Berkeley. Photograph by Ashley Lipps **p. 304 (top, a)** Frederick Mark Sheridan-Johnson/Alamy Stock Photo **p. 304 (top, b)** DLILLC/Corbis/VCG/Getty Images **p. 304 (bottom, both)** Courtesy of The Museum of Vertebrate Zoology, UC Berkeley. Photograph by Ashley Lipps **p. 305 (top, a)** Harri Pekkinen/Alamy Stock Photo **p. 305 (top, b)** Bone Clones/boneclones.com **p. 305 (bottom, both)** Courtesy of The Museum of Vertebrate Zoology, UC Berkeley. Photograph by Ashley Lipps **p. 306 (bottom, a)** apple2499/Shutterstock **p. 306 (bottom, b)** raliand/Shutterstock **p. 307** Photo by James Luce

LAB 11

Photos: p. 309 (left–right) Sunset Boulevard/Corbis via Getty Images; Ignacio Palacios/Lonely Planet Images/Getty Images **Figure 11.1** Courtesy of Dawn Kitchen **Figure 11.2** Duncan McKay/Alamy Stock Photo **Figure 11.3** Norbert Rosing/National Geographic Creative **Figure 11.10** David Tipling/Getty Images **Figure 11.11** © the Jane Goodall Institute/By Bill Wallauer **Figure 11.12** Ian C. Gilby **p. 332** David Slater/Caters; **p. 334 (top–bottom)** Courtesy of Joan Silk; K. G. Preston-Mafham/Premaphotos Wildlife **p. 335 (top–bottom)** Ger Bosma/Alamy Stock Photo; Holger Ehlers/Alamy Stock Photo **p. 336 (top)** Reprinted from Current Biology, Vol. 17, Jill D. Pruetz, Paco Bertolani, Savanna Chimpanzees, Pan troglodytes verus, Hunt with Tools, pp. 412–17, © 2007, with permission from Elsevier **p. 336 (bottom)** Dr. Paco Bertolani

LAB 12

Photos: p. 337 (left–right) Robert Marien/Corbis; Ken Lucas/Visuals Unlimited, Inc. **Figure 12.5a** Anton Ivanov/Alamy Stock Photo **Figure 12.10** Juniors Bildarchiv GmbH/Alamy Stock Photo **Figure 12.12** Steffen Foerster/Shutterstock **p. 359 a–d** Panther Media GmbH/Alamy Stock Photo; Nop1/Shutterstock; Bubbers BB/Shutterstock; Michael Burrell/Alamy Stock Photo **p. 360 a** Bone Clones/boneclones.com **p. 360 b–d (all)** Courtesy of The Museum of Vertebrate Zoology, UC Berkeley. Photograph by Ashley Lipps **p. 361 (both)** Courtesy of The Museum of Vertebrate Zoology, UC Berkeley. Photograph by Ashley Lipps **p. 362** Courtesy of The Museum of Vertebrate Zoology, UC Berkeley. Photograph by Ashley Lipps **p. 363 (both)** Courtesy of The Museum of Vertebrate Zoology, UC Berkeley. Photograph by Ashley Lipps **p. 364 (both)** Courtesy of The Museum of Vertebrate Zoology, UC Berkeley. Photograph by Ashley Lipps **p. 365 (top left)** Ted Thai/The LIFE Picture Collection/Getty Images **p. 365 (top right)** Courtesy of The Museum of Vertebrate Zoology, UC Berkeley. Photograph by Ashley Lipps **p. 365 (bottom)** Bone Clones/boneclones.com

Drawn art: Figure 12.13 Figure adapted from photograph by Ashley Lipps. Courtesy of the Museum of Vertebrate Zoology, UC Berkely. **p. 396 top (Lab 13, Exercise 2)** Figure 3 from Kenneth D. Rose, "The Earliest Primates," *Evolutionary Anthropology*, Vol. 3, Issue 5 (1994): 159–173. Copyright © 1994 Wiley-Liss, Inc., A Wiley Company. Reprinted with permission of Wiley-Liss, Inc., a subsidiary of John Wiley & Sons, Inc.

PART FOUR OPENER

Photos: p. 366 Bettmann/Getty Images

LAB 13

Photos: p. 369 Christian Jegou/Publiphoto/Science Source **Figure 13.8** Takai et al. 1996. New specimens of the oldest fossil platyrrhine, Branisella boliviana, from Salla, Bolivia. American Journal of Physical Anthropology 99:301–314. Copyright © 1996, Wiley-Liss, Inc. **Figure 13.9** Drawing by Jorge Antonio Gonzalez **Figure 13.10** Courtesy of Southern Illinois University Carbondale **Figure 13.12 (both)** © Isaiah Nengo **Figure 13.13** © William K. Sacco **p. 387 (left–right)** Natural History Museum, Oslo, Norway; (right): Shaun Curry/AFP/Getty Images **p. 388** New primate genus from the Miocene of Argentina. Marcelo F. Tejedor, Adán A. Tauber, Alfred L. Rosenberger, Carl C. Swisher, María E. Palacios. Proceedings of the National Academy of Sciences Apr 2006, 103 (14) 5437–5441; DOI: 10.1073/pnas.0506126103 **p. 396 (right and left)** © David Pilbeam; **p. 396 (center)** The Natural History Museum/Alamy Stock Photo

LAB 14

Photos: p. 397 John Reader/Science Source **Figure 14.1** Gudkov Andrey/Shutterstock; **Figure 14.5** From Subjects: Three individual drawings, showing the angles of articulation for the knee, in lateral view: (1.) modern human; (2.) A. afarensis; (3.) ape. Original publication: Lucy: The Beginnings of Humankind, Johanson, Edey. © 1981 Luba Dmytryk Gudz/Brill Atlanta. Reprinted with permission **Figure 14.7** iStock/Getty Images **Figure 14.9** Nature-M.P.F.T./Getty Images **Figure 14.11** FOSSIL CREDIT: Housed in National Museum of Ethiopia, Addis Ababa. PHOTO CREDIT: © 2003 Tim D. White, humanoriginsphotos.com **Fig 14.12 (both)** FOSSIL CREDIT: Original fossils in National Museum of Ethiopia, Addis Ababa. DIGITAL RENDER CREDIT: © 2009 White, Suwa, et al., humanoriginsphotos.com **p. 419** J. Reader/Science Source **p. 421 (top, both)** Courtesy of The Museum of Vertebrate Zoology, UC Berkeley. Photograph by Ashley Lipps **p. 421 (bottom, both)** CLIPAREA/Custom media/Shutterstock **p. 422 (top, both)** Courtesy of The Museum of Vertebrate Zoology, UC Berkeley. Photograph by Ashley Lipps **p. 422 (bottom, left)** Courtesy of The Museum of Vertebrate Zoology, UC Berkeley. Photograph by Ashley Lipps **p. 422 (bottom, right)** Bone Clones/boneclones.com **p. 423 (top, both)** Courtesy of The Museum of Vertebrate Zoology, UC Berkeley. Photograph by Ashley Lipps **p. 423 (bottom)** FOSSIL CREDIT: Original in National Museum of Ethiopia, Addis Ababa. DIGITAL RENDER CREDIT: © 2009 White, Suwa, et al., humanoriginsphotos.com. **p. 424** Photo by Dr. Adrienne Zihlman, University of California, Santa Cruz

Drawn art: Figure 14.4b Bruce Latimer, Figure: Ape and human pelvis mechanics. Reprinted by permission of Bruce Latimer.

LAB 15

Photos: p. 425 (left) Bettmann/Getty Images **p. 425 (right)** FOSSIL CREDIT: Housed in National Museum of Ethiopia, Addis Ababa. PHOTO CREDIT: © 1985 David L. Brill, www.humanoriginsphotos.com **Figure 15.4a** FOSSIL CREDIT: Housed in National Museum of Ethiopia, Addis Ababa. PHOTO CREDIT: © 1985 David L. Brill, www.humanoriginsphotos.com **Figure 15.4b** Bone Clones/boneclones.com **Figure 15.6** ARTIFACT CREDIT: Orig-

inal in National Museum of Ethiopia, Addis Ababa. PHOTO CREDIT: © 1999 David L. Brill, humanoriginsphotos.com **Figure 15.7a** © 1999 Tim D. White, permitted by G. Richards and B. Plowman, humanoriginsphotos.com **Figure 15.7b** Polaris/Newscom **Figure 15.8** Photo by Brett Eloff, courtesy of Lee Berger and the University of Witwatersrand **Figure 15.13** The Cleveland Museum of Natural History **p. 448 a–b** Photo by Paul Constantino **p. 448c** Bone Clones/boneclones.com **p. 449 (all)** Bone Clones/boneclones.com **p. 450 (both)** Bone Clones/boneclones.com **p. 451 (left)** Courtesy of Lee R. Berger and The University of The Witwatersrand **p. 451 (center–right)** Bone Clones/boneclones.com **p. 452 (both)** Bone Clones/boneclones.com **p. 453** Bone Clones/boneclones.com

Drawn art: Figure 15.9 Center figures adapted from Bone Clones, Inc.; Bottom right adapted from photo by Walter Jahn; Bottom left adapted from photo by Donald C. Johanson. Reprinted with permission.

LAB 16

Photos: p. 455 David Lordkipanidze et al. 18 October 2013. A Complete skull from Dmanisi, Georgia, and the Evolutionary Biology of Early Homo. Science 342 (6156): 236–331. Copyright © 2013 AAAS **Figure 16.3** Sabena Jane Blackbird/Alamy Stock Photo **Figure 16.8b** ARTIFACT CREDIT: courtesy Denise de Sonneville-Bordes, Centre Francois Bordes, Institut du Quaternaire, Batiment de Geologie, Universite de Bordeaux. PHOTO CREDIT: © 1985 David L. Brill, humanoriginsphotos.com **Figure 16.11** Musee de l'Homme de Neandertall **Figure 16.12 (right)** Courtesy of and © Eric Delson **Figure 16.13a–c** AP Photo/Jean Clottes; Heritage Image Partner-

ship Ltd/Alamy Stock Photo; Figure 3 from Bouzouggar, A. et al. (2007). "82,000-year-old shell beads from North Africa and implications for the origins of modern human behavior." PNAS 104:9964–9969. Copyright (2007) National Academy of Sciences, U.S.A. **Figure 16.14a** ARTIFACT CREDIT: Musee National de Prehistoire, Les Eyzies de Tayac. PHOTO CREDIT: © 1985 David L. Brill, humanoriginsphotos.com **Figure 16.14c** ARTIFACT CREDIT: Courtesy R. Deffarge, Institut du Quaternaire, Batiment de Geologies, Universite de Bordeaux. PHOTO CREDIT: © 1985 David L. Brill, www.humanoriginsphotos.com **Figure 16.17** John Hawks, Lee R. Berger courtesy of Lee Berger and the University of Witwatersrand **Figure 16.18b** Photograph courtesy of Peter Brown **p. 482 (all)** Bone Clones/boneclones.com **p. 483 (left–right)** Bone Clones/boneclones.com; Sabena Jane Blackbird/Alamy Stock Photo **p. 484 (all)** Bone Clones/boneclones.com **p. 485 (all)** Bone Clones/boneclones.com **p. 486 (top a, c)** Bone Clones/boneclones.com **p. 486 (top b)** Pete Bostrum/Lithic Casting Lab **p. 486 (bottom, all)** Bone Clones/boneclones.com **p. 487 (all)** Bone Clones/boneclones.com

Drawn art: Figure 16.6 Figure from *The Cambridge Encyclopedia of Human Evolution*, edited by Stephen Jones, Robert D. Martin, and David R. Pilbeam, p. 244. Copyright © 1992 Cambridge University Press. Reprinted with the permission of Cambridge University Press. **Figure 16.7** Figure by Kathryn Cruz-Uribe reprinted with permission from *The Human Career: Human Biological and Cultural Origins*, 2nd Ed. by R.G. Klein. **Figure 16.14b** Drawing from Bones, Boats, and Bison, 1999: 153, University of New Mexico Press. Reprinted by permission of E. James Dixon.

INDEX

Homo E. 1.8 mya to 300 kya.
              Africa & Asia
                   to 400 ky a
                        Europe.

Stone tools
          Acheulean tools.
            Acheulean